Social Fairness and Econo

This volume brings together papers inspired by the work of Duncan Foley, an extraordinarily productive economist who has made seminal contributions to a wide variety of areas. Foley's work cannot be easily classified, but one thread that runs through it is a critical examination (along both ethical and analytical lines) of conventional neoclassical economic theory, particularly involving general equilibrium theories of value and money. Foley was a pioneer of complexity economics as well, which adopts approaches to these questions drawn from natural sciences, so the collection therefore has an interdisciplinary quality that will interest a wide variety of readers.

Some of the chapters are intellectual biographies that contextualize and identify Foley's contributions to Keynesian macroeconomics, Marxian value theory, and complexity theory in economics. The topics covered include the economics of complexity; the ethics of general equilibrium theory; the economics of climate change; applications of Keynesian, Marxian and Ricardian political economy; and money and financial crises.

The collection should be useful to scholars who work in various economic traditions critical of the currently dominant free-market approach, but it also speaks to scholars of critical theory in various disciplines beyond economics, such as the mathematicians, physicists, and other natural scientists who are interested in understanding the complexity of social processes using their analytical frameworks. This book should also appeal to graduate students in economics who are working in these traditions, as well as scholars (including current graduate students in orthodox programs) who are dissatisfied with the current state of economic theory and would like to satisfy their intellectual curiosity by sampling the contributions of critical theorists.

Lance Taylor is Arnhold Professor Emeritus of International Cooperation and Development at the New School University, New York, USA.

Armon Rezai is Assistant Professor in Environmental Economics at the Vienna University of Economics and Business, Austria.

Thomas Michl is Professor of Economics at Colgate University, Hamilton, USA.

Routledge frontiers of political economy

Social Fairness and Economics

Economic essays in the spirit
of Duncan Foley

**Edited by Lance Taylor, Armon Rezai
and Thomas Michl**

LONDON AND NEW YORK

First published 2013
By Routledge
2 Park Square, Milton Park, Abingdon, Oxfordshire OX14 4RN

Simultaneously published in the USA and Canada
By Routledge
711 Third Avenue, New York, NY 10017

First issued in paperback 2014

*Routledge is an imprint of the Taylor and Francis Group,
an informa business*

British Library Cataloguing in Publication Data
A catalogue record for this book is available from the British Library

Library of Congress Cataloging in Publication Data
Social fairness and economics : economic essays in the spirit of Duncan
Foley / edited by Lance Taylor, Armon Rezai, and Thomas Michl.
    p. cm.
Includes bibliographical references and index.
1. Economics–Moral and ethical aspects. 2. Equilibrium (Economics)
3. Foley, Duncan K. I. Taylor, Lance, 1940– II. Rezai, Armon.
III. Michl, Thomas R.
HB72.S583 2012
330.15–dc23   2012026892

ISBN 978-0-415-53819-0 (hbk)
ISBN 978-1-138-90225-1 (pbk)
ISBN 978-0-203-10950-2 (ebk)

Typeset in Times New Roman
by Cenveo Publisher Services

Contents

Figures

Tables

Contributors

Martín Abeles, United Nations Economic Commission for Latin America and the Caribbean.

Samuel Bowles, Research Professor and Director of the Behavioral Sciences Program, Santa Fe Institute; Professor of Economics, University of Siena.

Graciela Chichilnisky, Professor of Economics and Mathematical Statistics and Director of Columbia Consortium for Risk Management, Columbia University; Sir Louis Matheson Distinguished Professor, Monash University.

Leila Davis, PhD student, Department of Economics, University of Massachusetts.

Gérard Duménil, Economist and Director of Research at the National Centre for Scientific Research (CNRS).

Amitava Krishna Dutt, Professor of Economics and Political Science, Department of Political Science, University of Notre Dame.

Peter Flaschel, Professor of Theoretical Economics, Department of Economics, University of Bielefeld.

Nils Fröhlich, Assistant Professor, Department of Economics, Technical University Chemnitz.

A. J. Julius, Assistant Professor, Department of Philosophy, UCLA.

Heinz D. Kurz, Professor of Economics and Director of the Graz Schumpeter Centre, University of Graz.

Dominique Lévy, Associate Researcher at the Paris School of Economics, Ecole Normale Superieure.

Joseph L. McCauley, Professor, Department of Physics, University of Houston.

Perry Mehrling, Professor of Economics, Barnard College, Columbia University.

Thomas Michl, Professor of Economics, Colgate University.

Philip Mirowski, Professor of Economics, Department of Economics and Policy, University of Notre Dame.

Simon Mohun, Professor of Political Economy, School of Business and Management, Queen Mary, University of London.

Michael J. Piore, David W. Skinner Professor of Political Economy, Department of Economics, MIT.

J. Barkley Rosser, Jr., Professor of Economics, Department of Economics, James Madison University.

Neri Salvadori, Professor of Economics, University of Pisa.

Rajiv Sethi, Professor of Economics, Barnard College, Columbia University; External Professor, Santa Fe Institute.

Anwar Shaikh, Professor, Department of Economics, New School for Social Research.

Peter Skott, Professor, Department of Economics, University of Massachusetts – Amherst.

K. Vela Velupillai, Professor of Economics, University of Trento.

Roberto Veneziani, Senior Lecturer, School of Economics and Finance, Queen Mary, University of London.

Edward N. Wolff, Professor of Economics, Department of Economics, New York University.

Victor M. Yakovenko, Professor, Department of Physics, University of Maryland.

Introduction

Lance Taylor, Armon Rezai and Thomas Michl

In his magisterial *History of Economic Analysis* (1954), Joseph Schumpeter, argues that in economics any "... analytic effort is of necessity preceded by a preanalytic cognitive act that supplies the raw material for the analytic effort. In this book, this preanalytic cognitive act will be called Vision" (p. 41). Schumpeter goes on to illustrate his point by discussing the close linkages between Keynes's macroeconomics in his *Economic Consequences of the Peace* (1920) and the *General Theory* (1936).

This book is devoted to exploring aspects of Duncan K. Foley's extremely wide economic Vision. As the papers herein demonstrate, his ideas range over many areas of economics. There are two themes that recur. One is analytical, taking the form of deep insight into the inner logic of economic models – many examples are presented below. The other is passion for social justice or fairness. As Foley (2006) observes, capitalism imposes "antagonistic, impersonal, and self-regarding social relations" (p. 2) and much of economic orthodoxy seeks to demonstrate that such selfish behavior is actually to the benefit of our fellow human beings. If one abandons the confined realm in which this assertion is true, basic questions of how to be a good person and live a good and moral life – questions about social justice – become a central concern.

Socio-economic ideology and methodology

The first Part of this book, on "Socio-economic ideology and methodology," addresses both aspects of Foley's thought. For people outside the economics profession (and to those few inside who have not been sheltered from a full range of debate), the quotation above is easy to comprehend. **Michael Piore**'s chapter provides a good introduction to its implications. The paper, a combination of academic memoire and essay on the nature of economics, provides an insightful account of the historical and intellectual currents that influenced Piore's own and Foley's personal trajectories. He recounts the profession's transition away from institutionalist economics toward hard-core neoclassical theory, the contradictions that befell efforts to synthesize neoclassical and Keynesian economics, and the rise of Marxism as a potential rival during the tumultuous 1960s. From the narrative one gains an appreciation of the Kuhnian paradigm conflicts that lie behind the schisms, as well as insight into the source of Duncan Foley's widely recognized methodological pluralism – his ability to make fundamental contributions in multiple theoretical frameworks ranging from Marxism to general equilibrium theory to applied neoclassical welfare analysis. Piore identifies an interest in the role of money and the quest to understand the social and economic aspects of the world we live in as the threads that connect the various phases of Foley's intellectual career.

The multiple interactions among social and economic factors are analyzed in the contribution by **Samuel Bowles**. He develops a framework to investigate the adverse effects that market-oriented, self-regarding behavior, usually attributed to the rational agent, has on well-being in different areas of social life. He takes up Foley and his "Adam's fallacy" which is "the idea that it is possible to separate an economic sphere of life, in which the pursuit of self-interest is guided by objective laws to a socially beneficent outcome, from the rest of social life, in which the pursuit of self-interest is morally problematic" Foley (2006, p. xii). Bowles includes the state of moral virtues which are crowded out by market interaction. Since the market does not include the external cost of its extent on moral well-being, Adam's invisible hand does not bring about a first best world. Culture and institutions which enable the working of the capitalist system are corrupted by the system's own thriving. A legislator can correct the externality by constricting market activity to a level below baseline and increase economic output by lowering transaction costs. Bowles illustrates the point by using the Coasean concept of the firm because he wants to show that a form of "cultural–institutional market failure" arises even within conventional liberal economic models once the external effects of markets on culture are included.

Social institutions such as markets interact in multiple ways; they also change over time. Such evolution can be characterized by nonlinear dynamics, abrupt changes, and complex behavior. **J. Barkley Rosser, Jr.**, describes the evolution of complexity economics and the evolution of Duncan Foley as a complexity economist. Foley's intellectual career interestingly parallels the emergence of the complexity concept in economics. His shifting views had significance for debates about complexity's meaning and usefulness. Foley's thought arguably can be divided into three phases: one in which he was essentially a conventional general equilibrium (GE) theorist, one in which he focused on a Marxian perspective on GE theory, and one in which he moved more in the direction of physics-based models of economics and how they relate to GE.

The transition from the first to second stage was substantially driven by a search to solve certain loose ends in GE theory, particularly regarding the role of money. This was both an impetus toward Marxist analysis (discussed below) and an initial recognition of complexity issues. The second shift can be viewed as more fully embracing complexity. However, he has been involved in at least two different lines of inquiry in that regard. In his Introduction to a book by the late Peter Albin (1998), he was more in line with the computational complexity view that Albin advocated for economics. In his later more econophysical work he has arguably been more open to the competing dynamic complexity perspective. Rosser argues that Foley's combination of the computational and dynamic approaches into the four-level hierarchy developed by Chomsky (1959) and Wolfram (1986) was an ingenious intellectual achievement.

In another major contribution, Foley (1994) proposed a statistical general equilibrium theory of markets, in which there is a probability distribution of trades at different prices, and market clearing is achieved only statistically. This approach helps elucidate the complexities and spontaneous order that the trades create. It falls naturally into the domain of econophysics, with general equilibrium being obtained at an entropy-maximizing distribution of prices. The nature of the equilibrium will of course depend on the underlying distribution of trades. In his contribution, **Victor Yakovenko** reviews statistical models for the probability distributions of money, wealth, and income developed in the econophysics literature since the late 1990s. In line with Foley, economic transactions in the models take the form of random transfers of money between the agents in payment for goods and services subject to the restriction that trades are mutually advantageous. Starting from the initially equal distribution of money, the system spontaneously develops a highly unequal distribution analogous to the Boltzmann–Gibbs distribution of energy in physics. Analysis of the empirical data on income distribution in the USA reveals a two-class society characterized by an exponential distribution for the lower class and a power law for the upper class. Yakovenko further shows that energy consumption per capita around the world follows an exponential distribution as well.

Neoclassical economics: dispersed and decentralized exchange

The First and Second Welfare Theorems, which rest on Walrasian general equilibrium, are the focal points for discussion of social justice in current economic debate. Foley's emphasis on fairness takes a radically different perspective. These issues are addressed in Part II on "Neoclassical economics: dispersed and decentralized exchange."

Walrasian theory builds on the idea that every market participant at given prices will choose from among all feasible consumption and production plans those that are weakly preferred. The prices which support such exchange processes materialize, making the actions of agents consistent. Duncan Foley has been critical of this view of exchange processes throughout his academic career. In his thesis, Foley (1967, 1970) adapted the methods of general equilibrium theory to the problem of public goods. Recently, he has challenged the Welfare Theorems on the basis of their reliance on equilibrium prices (Foley, 1994, 2010; Foley and Smith, 2008). The process of exchange through which equilibrium prices are discovered has distributional effects that need to be considered in order to achieve a deep understanding of the Welfare Theorems.

In his contribution, **A. J. Julius** plays a variation on this theme by asking "When people set out to exchange goods and labor with one another, each so as to improve their own consumption prospects, where will their exchanges take the economy as a whole?" Julius puts forward a model in which capitalists and workers engage in production, and discusses different mechanisms of price formation. He rejects the standard auctioneer assumption which implies that social institutions other than the market have no role in market exchange. Social policy, collective bargaining and shopfloor conflict as well as norms of deference, solidarity, or justice all play a limited role. Julius uses a model of catallactic exchange (according to the Archbishop of Dublin Richard Whately, "catallaxy" refers to friendly exchange (von Mises, 1949); Friedrich Hayek (1976) uses the term to describe a market equilibrium process of mutually beneficial exchange among a population of traders) to study the disequilibrium processes which lead to equilibrium prices and what the properties of these prices are. As Foley (2010) has argued previously, such allocations are not necessarily efficient. Julius emphasizes the role of social institutions in molding the exchange process and elaborates on Foley's argument that the income distribution is path-dependent.

The understanding that externalities are pervasive is one of the thicker threads running through the body of Foley's work, starting with his dissertation. Climate change is arguably the largest market failure in history, a point raised in Rezai, Foley, and Taylor (2012) where the adverse welfare implications of staying on a climatic Business-As-Usual trajectory are made clear. **Leila Davis** and **Peter Skott** take this analysis as their launching pad and introduce an additional externality stemming from consumption. They show that policy implications vary depending whether an environmental externality is present or not. Most of the economic analysis of global warming is conducted using models based on optimal growth theory. Davis and Skott show that by ignoring direct consumption externalities, integrated assessment models overestimate the social return to conventional investment and underestimate the optimal amount of investment in mitigation. Thereby, consumption externalities worsen the environmental externality. Empirical evidence about the influence of relative consumption on utility suggests that the bias could be quantitatively significant, and the results from a simple survey by Davis and Skott support this conclusion.

Market objectives can conflict with sustainable economic goals. Financial innovation and short-term risk management can cause widespread uncertainty, volatility, and default. **Graciela Chichilnisky** explores how to benefit from short sales and financial innovation while avoiding the runaway volatility and widespread defaults that they can cause. She identifies the axioms for risk management introduced by von Neumann and Morgenstern (1953) as behind the conflict between individual gain and sustainable markets. This conflict can be resolved by the introduction of "sustainable markets" which differ from Arrow–Debreu markets in that traders have sustainable preferences that are sensitive to both frequent and also rare catastrophic events. In sustainable markets prices take on a new role: they reflect both the value of instantaneous consumption managing frequent risks, and the value of preventing rare events or "Black Swans" that lead to widespread volatility and default.

Setting out a review of misleading ideas of equilibrium together with their social origins, the econophysicist **Joseph McCauley** argues that misconceptions in economics originate from such confusions. For McCauley, an appropriate definition of equilibrium is the one used in physics and dynamical systems theory. Economists often mix up stationarity of a time series with stationary increments of a nonstationary series. His key points are that unregulated, efficient markets are described by nonstationary processes with uncorrelated, nonstationary increments, while an equilibrium market as seen by economists is stationary. The two sorts of processes are mutually exclusive, that is, stability and absence of market regulation are mutually exclusive.

In his contribution, **K. Vela Vellupillai** critically discusses another feature of general equilibrium – its computability or lack thereof. The standard existence proofs of equilibrium are nonconstructive, and do not provide a means by which the equilibrium can be computed. To Vellupillai, such algorithmic indeterminacies are intrinsic to the foundations of orthodox economic theory in the mathematical mode. He uses Foley's brilliant and pioneering Yale doctoral dissertation (1967) and the mathematical themes within it as a specimen, and views them as a Computable Economist would.

In a personal preamble to his paper, Vellupillai reviews his own exposure to the work of Duncan Foley. He identifies fairness as its leitmotif, the prime motivation for Foley's numerous, many-faceted, and outstanding contributions to macroeconomics, microeconomics, general equilibrium theory, the theory of taxation, history of economic thought, the magnificent dynamics of classical economics, classical value theory, Bayesian statistics, formal dynamics, and, most recently, fascinating forays into an interpretation of economic evolution from a variety of complexity theoretic viewpoints.

Classical political economy: growth and distribution

Several of these lines of thought come together in Part III on "Classical political economy: growth and distribution." Fairness remains the ostinato theme, now repeating in terms of class conflict and unemployment.

As part of his effort to understand the role of money in the economy, Foley ventured into Marxian theory. Several of his contributions are viewed as major advances. One was a novel formulation of Marx's transformation problem, presented in *Understanding Capital* (1986), building upon earlier work by Foley (1982) and Gérard Duménil (1980). Duménil and Foley (2008) basically argue that there really is no transformation problem because through the introduction of the Monetary Equivalent of Labor Time "[t]here is only one economy, one system, not two. There is no 'underlying,' hidden economy, which operates in 'values' where the distributional realities that structure the functioning of capitalism could be determined."

In practice, in the aggregate, hours of productive labor are equivalent to nominal value-added times the value of money. This definition has been applied widely, but begs the question of how to define "productive labor." In part paralleling work by the late New School economist David Gordon (1996), **Simon Mohun** presents a class-based analysis of data for the USA in which he shifts income accruing to circulation and supervisory workers from "labor" to "capital" to estimate a "class rate of profit." It turns out to be a good predictor of economic crises, and is used by Mohun to analyze the political economy of institutional change in the US economy over the past nine decades.

In their contribution, **Peter Flaschel**, **Nils Fröhlich**, and **Roberto Veneziani** build on the Foley–Duménil "New Interpretation" to analyze the Marxian theory of profits. They study the relationship between the aggregate value rate of profit and the aggregate price rate of profit, and show that the two rates coincide up to negligible and unsystematic deviations by using flow as well as stock matrix data for the German economy (1991–2000). Flaschel et al. argue that movements in the actual aggregate rate of profit should be understood by focusing on the main determinants of the value rate, namely absolute and relative surplus value, as well as technical progress affecting the value of the aggregate capital stock.

Heinz Kurz and **Neri Salvadori** take a different tack on the question of the transformation problem. They discuss Karl Marx's concept of the "average commodity" and its relationship with David Ricardo's concept of the "medium [commodity] between the extremes," on the one hand, and Piero Sraffa's "Standard commodity," on the other. These authors developed their concepts in an attempt to formulate a consistent theory of value and distribution starting from the classical surplus approach. Kurz and Salvadori argue that Marx's and Ricardo's concepts, while pointing in the right direction, failed to accomplish the task. To them, it was Sraffa who finally managed to solve the problem via a series of steps in which he scrutinized critically the contributions of Ricardo and Marx, and elaborated on those ideas of the two authors that he considered to be fertile.

In Volume II of *Capital*, Marx addressed issues of reproduction, effective demand, and realization in a growing capitalist economy. Foley (1983a) proposed a unifying concept for Marx's schemes in the form of a *circuit of capital*. The circuit is a stock-flow consistent representation of the capitalist system as an ever-expanding circular flow of commodities and money. In his chapter **Martín Abeles** introduces economic transactions with the rest of the world into Foley's original model, and re-examines the capitalist limits to growth and realization when the current and capital accounts of the balance of payments are taken into account. The fact that imports and exports are not assumed to balance in the long run allows for the analysis of persistent net international debtor or creditor positions, and hence the examination of different accumulation regimes. In another paper, Foley (2003) proposed a useful taxonomy (inspired by Hyman Minsky's classification of financial portfolios) for the characterization of different accumulation-cum-financial paths. Abeles applies this framework to analyze configurations of the circuits of capital in the international context.

Anwar Shaikh develops the somewhat neglected correspondence between the classical forms of circulation and modern national accounts. He shows that the difference between initiated and completed production explains the finding that the orthodox measure of value added overstates the classical measure by the amount of the increase in the wage bill. Nonetheless, as long as all labor is assumed to be production labor, conventional national accounts arrive at exactly the same definition of gross profit on production (Gross Operating Surplus) as do classical accounts (the money form of Gross Surplus Value). Finally, investment in circulating capital plays a central role in classical analysis and Shaikh demonstrates that it is directly available in conventional accounts as the sum of the changes in inventories of materials and work-in-process.

While there have been recent advances in the modeling of endogenous technological change in neoclassical (including "endogenous") growth models, analysis in Classical–Marxian models seems to have lagged behind. However, there are exceptions, including contributions by Duncan Foley. **Amitava Dutt** reviews, and makes additions to, the literature by incorporating a number of alternative approaches. He shows that, although this task is relatively easy, to get a comprehensive view of the interaction between growth, distribution and technological change, Classical–Marxian models have to endogenize a number of parameters, including the labor share and capital productivity, and introduce additional features not analyzed in the basic model, such as the role of high-skilled workers.

The chapter by **Gérard Duménil** and **Dominique Lévy** summarizes their extensive work on the vexing question of the proper relationship between Marx and Keynes. Again, this is an area to which Duncan Foley has devoted considerable attention. For example, Foley (1985) compares Marx's rejection of Say's Law, based on the view that capital as self-expanding value systematically lengthens its turnover time (the time it takes to traverse the circuit of capital), to Keynes's rejection of the Law, based on speculative behavior in securities markets. Duménil and Lévy offer a typology of macroeconomic theories that situates the Keynesian preoccupation with demand in the domain of short-run, high-frequency fluctuations in the "dimension" of the economy that permits them to express themselves in variable rates of capacity utilization, while Classical–Marxian theory is concerned with lower frequency fluctuations in productive capacity itself. They also propose that the historical trend of capitalist economies has been toward greater instability in dimension, requiring the development of central banking and fiscal policy to contain the resulting crisis tendencies, and they view recurrent crises such as the Great Depression and the current turbulence through this lens.

The dichotomy between a short run dominated by Keynesian dynamics and a long run characterized by a tendency for capitalism to achieve normal utilization of capacity is the basis for **Thomas Michl**'s chapter on monetary and fiscal policy. He offers one possible mechanism by which the economy tends to gravitate around normal levels of utilization at low frequencies – the interest-rate policies of a central bank devoted to managing the inflation process (inflation-targeting). In a macroeconomic model with a class structure of accumulation, public debt has (Keynesian) stimulative effects in the short run, but (Classical–Marxian) growth-reducing effects in the long run because it creates a rentier element in the capitalist class that consumes out of interest income, requiring an offsetting increase in interest rates to suppress inflationary demand effects.

Nonetheless, it is possible for debt reduction policies to achieve employment objectives, provided that they are combined with a sufficiently stimulative monetary policy.

The chapter by **Edward Wolff** examines the evidence that downsizing by manufacturing enterprises has been associated with improvements in productivity, profitability, share prices, or other measures of performance. This work intersects with Duncan Foley's ongoing interest in the empirical implementation of classical, Marxian, and Keynesian economic theory, such as his recent work with Deepankar Basu (Basu and Foley, 2011) on the changing nature of Okun's and Verdoorn's Laws. Wolff shows that downsizing is an enduring feature of the neoliberal era – measured by the number of workers, the average manufacturing establishment has declined substantially in size since 1967, by 23–37 percent (depending on the metric). Despite the surfeit of economic conjectures, theories, and hypotheses, both popular and theory-based, downsizing does not seem to be associated in any clear or robust way with performance. Instead, the one empirical regularity that stands out is the strong positive association between unionization and worker compensation, and its negative association with profitability and share prices, which supports the view that de-unionization has played a pivotal role in the distributional dynamics of neoliberal capitalism. There does not seem to be any way to evade the central place that class conflict occupies in economic life.

Complexity: barriers and bounds to rationality

The final Part of this book contains three essays on "Complexity: barriers and bounds to rationality." The first, by **Rajiv Sethi** takes off from an influential book on *Monetary and Fiscal Policy in a Growing Economy* which Foley co-authored in 1971 with the late Miguel Sidrauski. They proposed a stock-flow consistent model, incorporating markets for money, bonds, and capital assets, as well as flows of labor, investment, and consumption goods. They did not, however, provide an account of expectation formation, and therefore left unfilled one of the major gaps in the *General Theory*.

Sethi examines how expectation formation may be modeled. Today's canonical models are based on equilibrium analysis, typically within a representative agent framework featuring intertemporal optimization and coordinated expectations. While such models can replicate co-movements in economic magnitudes under normal conditions, they have little to say about severe economic disruptions and financial crises. A serious analysis of disequilibrium dynamics is an essential and missing ingredient of the theory, and theories of learning and evolutionary selection can provide the foundations for such an analysis. Evolutionary models are particularly promising in finance, where they can be used to examine changes in the composition of trading strategies and the effects of such changes on market stability. The dynamics of learning in response to inconsistent plans by heterogeneous agents may provide a basis for a robust theory of economic fluctuations. Sethi contextualizes these arguments in an application to the financial crisis.

The financial crisis and its origins are also the subject of **Philip Mirowski's** contribution. He argues that, while discussions of the crisis that began in 2008 have mostly traveled along well-worn paths, they miss certain salient aspects of the current contraction that have exhibited unprecedented characteristics. In particular, the microstructure of financial markets has changed in distinct ways. Mirowski explores a theme dear to Duncan Foley's heart, the idea that incidents like the flash crash of 2010 and the contraction of 2008 might be framed as crises of market complexity. While many explanations situate the roots of the crisis in human weaknesses (irrationality, criminal fraud, hedonistic consumerism), Mirowski argues that financial markets themselves and the instruments used in them have evolved to a point where the inherent complexity necessarily leads to instability.

The chapter by **Perry Mehrling** also elaborates on the hierarchical nature of money and credit in today's financial markets. Foley (1983b) questioned Marx's decision to ground his monetary theory on a commodity-money or gold standard, arguing instead that grounding money on credit or trust stands a better chance of making sense of the modern fiat monetary system that has severed all but the slenderest attachments to gold. Mehrling's lucid treatment suggests that the Schumpeterian distinction (monetary theory of credit vs. credit theory of money) needs to be transcended by a hierarchical conception that recognizes both sides of the Schumpeterian coin as simultaneously valid. From this vantage point, many of the historical debates (such as between monetarists and Keynesians or the Currency and Banking Schools) or the modern debate over endogenous versus exogenous money can be fruitfully reconceptualized, since both sides have addressed aspects of money and credit that are always present.

Missing section(s)

As noted above, K. Vela Velupillai in his chapter observes that Foley has contributed to many fields of study. Some not represented in this book (for a variety of reasons) include agent-based modeling, theory of taxation, history of economic thought, information theory and Bayesian statistics, and control of circadian oscillations of physiology and behavior. Both the topics we have managed to include and those that we could not, make up an enormous volume of thought. The editors and authors of this volume all hope it pays back a small portion of the intellectual debts that we owe to Duncan Foley.

References

Albin, Peter S. (1998) *Barriers and Bounds to Rationality: Essays on Economic Complexity and Dynamics in Interactive Systems*, edited and with an introduction by Duncan K. Foley, Princeton: Princeton University Press.

Basu, Deepankar, and Duncan K. Foley (2011) 'Dynamics of Output and Employment in the U.S. Economy in the Neoliberal Era', *Political Economy Research Institute Working Paper No. 248.*

Chomsky, Noam (1959) 'On Certain Properties of Grammars', *Information and Control*, 2:137–167.

Duménil, Gérard (1980) *De la Valeur aux Price de Production*, Paris: Economica.

Duménil, Gérard, and Foley, Duncan K. (2008) 'The Marxian Transformation Problem', in Steven N. Durlauf and Lawrence E. Blume (Eds.), *The New Palgrave Dictionary of Economics*, London, Basingstoke: Palgrave Macmillan.

Foley, Duncan K. (1967) 'Resource Allocation and the Public Sector', *Yale Economic Essays*, 7:43–98.

Foley, Duncan K. (1970) 'Lindahl's Solution and the Core of an Economy with Public Goods', *Econometrica*, 8:66–72.

Foley, Duncan K. (1982) 'The Value of Money, the Value of Labor Power and the Marxian Transformation Problem', *Review of Radical Political Economy*, 14:37–47.

Foley, Duncan K. (1983a) 'Money and effective demand in Marx's scheme of expanded reproduction', in *Marxism, Central Planning, and the Soviet Economy: Essays in Honor of Alexander Erlich*, P. Desai (Ed.), Cambridge MA: MIT Press.

Foley, Duncan K. (1983b) 'On Marx's Theory of Money', *Social Concept*, 1:5–19.

Foley, Duncan K. (1985) 'Say's Law in Marx and Keynes', *Cahiers d'Economie Politique*, 10:183–94.

Foley, Duncan. K. (1994) 'A Statistical Equilibrium Theory of Markets', *Journal of Economic Theory*, 62:321–345.

Foley, Duncan K. (2003) 'Financial fragility in developing economies', in Amitava Dutt and Jaime Ros (Eds.), *Development Economics and Structuralist Macroeconomics: Essays in Honor of Lance Taylor*, Cheltenham: Edward Elgar.

Foley, Duncan K. (2006) *Adam's Fallacy: A Guide to Economic Theology*, Cambridge MA: Harvard University Press.

Foley, Duncan K. (2010) 'What's Wrong with the Fundamental Existence and Welfare Theorems?', *Journal of Economic Behavior & Organization*, 75:115–131.

Foley, Duncan K., and Thomas R. Michl (1999) *Growth and Distribution*, Cambridge MA: Harvard University Press.

Foley, Duncan K., and Miguel Sidrauski (1971) *Monetary and Fiscal Policy in a Growing Economy*, New York: Macmillan.

Foley, Duncan K., and Eric Smith (2008) 'Classical Thermodynamics and Economic General Equilibrium Theory', *Journal of Economic Dynamics and Control*, 32:7–65.

Gordon, David M. (1996) *Fat and Mean: The Corporate Squeeze of Working Americans and the Myth of Managerial 'Downsizing'*, New York: The Free Press.

Hayek, Friedrich A. (1976) *Law, Legislation, and Liberty*, volume 2, Chicago: University of Chicago Press.

Keynes, John Maynard (1920) *The Economic Consequences of the Peace*, New York: Harcourt, Brace and Howe.

Keynes, John Maynard (1936) *The General Theory of Employment, Interest, and Money*, New York: Harcourt, Brace.

Rezai, Armon, Duncan K. Foley, and Lance Taylor (2012) 'Global Warming and Economic Externalities', *Economic Theory*, 49:329–351.

Schumpeter, Joseph (1954) *History of Economic Analysis*, New York: Oxford University Press.

Von Mises, Ludwig (1949) *Human Action*, New Haven: Yale University Press.

Von Neumann, John, and Oskar Morgenstern (1953) [1944] *Theory of Games and Economic Behavior*, Princeton: Princeton University Press.

Wolfram, Stephan (Ed.) (1986) *Theory and Applications of Cellular Automata*, Singapore: World Scientific.

Personal remarks

Festschrift conference April 21, 2012

*Transcribed by Brandt Weathers and
edited by Duncan K. Foley**

Yesterday we talked about C. P. Cavafy's poem *Ithaca*, which recounts Odysseus's travels on his return home and the wonderful things that he saw and experienced. Cavafy imagines himself addressing Odysseus when he gets to Ithaca, saying "Ithaca may seem like a relatively poor place, compared to the splendors you have seen on your way back to it, but you should be grateful to Ithaca because it has given you," he says in Greek, "τ'ωραῖο ταξεῖδι," "the beautiful journey." This has indeed been a very beautiful journey for me, especially this last day and a half. I hope it has been for you, too, because it gave you all a chance to see my life, or my world. This has been a kind of a sample, a slice of my world. I really like my world ... [laughter] I think it's a lot of fun and it keeps me going and I enjoy it very much.

There are many things in these wonderful papers and talks to discuss, but actually what I thought I'd do is talk about myself [laughter], which I don't do all that often. But it seemed that this was one time that I might do that. Maybe to begin talking about myself I might take up the, sort of, portrait, to some degree, that people have painted of me. Especially about this thing of, "oh he's worked on so many different topics and he keeps coming back to the same ones." You could read that in a slightly different way, which is, "this is a guy that gets bored very easily [laughter] and never can finish working out a particular problem." There's certainly some truth in that side of it.

I think to understand me you have to begin with my mother [laughter]. Maybe a few people here, maybe even Herb [Scarf], have met my mother. There are many, many wonderful things about my mother who died 16 years ago. But I wanted to just tell you about two of them that are important for some of the issues that have come up over the past day and a half about me.

One is a little is about my mother's politics and values. My mother was the daughter of a quite prosperous Columbus, Ohio businessman. But she had a

*This is an edited version of impromptu remarks I made at the New School for Social Research Festschrift Conference in my honor, April 22, 2012. As is often the case the unedited transcription is sometimes very difficult to follow. I've edited this for clarity, but sought to retain the basic flavor of the occasion. I'd like to thank Brandt Weathers and Jon Cogliano for recording and transcribing the talk.

very instinctive dislike of inequality and of the harsh side of American life. In the 1930s, before I was born, for example, she had traveled to Harlan County, Kentucky in the midst of the coal wars that were going on there – the union wars – to do social outreach work. She told stories when I was growing up of sitting on furniture during the depression because Ohio law had a provision that you couldn't remove furniture when you were evicting people if somebody was sitting on it. So they would have parties to try to get one step ahead of the sheriff.

My mother was also an anti-anti-communist. People sometimes call themselves "red diaper babies." That is not true for me. My mother was not a communist, in the sense of a being a very committed left-wing activist, but she was instinctively very impatient with anti-communism. I remember during the McCarthy period my father bought one of the very first television sets, a Zenith model with a screen about that big [holds up hands about the size of a postcard] that weighed about 150 pounds [laughter]. I remember my mother looking at the McCarthy hearings on this tiny black-and-white TV, and how little use she had for the anti-communism of that era.

My mother's politics and values had a big influence on me. Another big influence she had on me is that, somewhere along in early child development before or just at the time I was beginning to be conscious, my mother conveyed to me an unusual sense of, if not a self-confidence, a centeredness, as a human being. This has had some important consequences for my life. One is that I don't feel as much existential insecurity as I know many other people do. I think this centeredness has also made me less sensitive to both support and criticism. It has insulated me from other people's opinions both positive and negative in a way. This insulation might even be characterized somewhere on the autistic spectrum [laughter] if you wanted to look at it that way.

In this connection, I want to tell a story about myself. Barkley [Rosser] is authorized to repeat this story [laughter]. You're getting it from the horse's mouth. In 1948, Thomas E. Dewey ran for the second time for president on the Republican ticket against Harry Truman and there were several other candidates: Strom Thurmond and, on the left, the Socialist candidate Norman Thomas [a few say "and Henry Wallace"] and Henry Wallace also, so there were five. I was six years old, and during that campaign somebody gave me a Dewey button. This Dewey button had a little gadgety feature so that you could pull a string and a flap flipped Dewey's picture up to reveal a panel saying "vote GOP" or something like that. I *loved* that [laughter] because of this gadgety string thing that you could pull. I think my parents voted for Norman Thomas in that election, but I was wearing a Dewey pin. A few days after the election, which, as you know if you look it up, Truman won [laughter], my mother got a call from a parent of one of my classmates in first grade. This mother said, "could you please tell Duncan that Truman won the election." And my mother said, "well everybody knows Truman won the election." And this woman said, "Yes, but my son doesn't believe that Truman won the election, because he says, 'Duncan Foley said Dewey won the election [laughter] and Duncan Foley is never wrong [burst of loud laughter and clapping].'"

Well there's a couple of very good things for people in this room to learn from this story [laughter] not the least of which that Duncan Foley is sometimes wrong [laughter]. Let me fast forward to economics. Mike Piore said that I cared a lot about economics. I think, at a certain level, that's true. But it is also true that it was very hard to get me into economics. When I was a senior at Swarthmore College, the only clear career goal that I had was *not* to be a college professor ... that was about it. In fact what I was really interested in doing was something like being in the foreign service. I even went so far as to take the foreign service examination and got up to the oral examination in the spring of 1964.

One of the main subjects of that foreign service interview was the fact that I was a Quaker. My family had started to go to Quaker meeting when I was about nine years old. Quaker meeting made a tremendous impression on me in several ways that are still relevant. One of them was the Quaker Peace Testimony. You might wonder why a Quaker pacifist might want to be a foreign service officer for the United States [laughter] and in fact that was the subject of the foreign service interview [louder laughter]. And I think that they finally decided that if I could defend myself on that ground they would want me out there defending US policies, if I could see my way clear to doing that.

But during that time, I was courting a Greek woman, which is how I know a little bit of modern Greek. There was a rule that you couldn't be in the foreign service if your wife was not an American citizen, and although they could make that happen a little faster, it couldn't happen right away. So under the circumstances I decided to attend Yale, where I'd been admitted to the Economics Ph.D. program, with the idea of taking a year of economics, which I thought would help in the foreign service. During the summer before I came to Yale, the romantic relationship collapsed, for which I feel no regrets in retrospect. But I turned up in New Haven with no particular reason for being there [laughter]. I got into Herb's mathematical economics course, which I have written about [in Arnold Heertje's *Makers of Modern Economics*, vol. IV], as he said, and it made a tremendous impression on me.

Some people have noted the fact that I graduated from Yale in two years, with the implication that that reflects well on me. I sometimes, however, think of it as a kind of misprocessing, a quality control error [laughter]. If I had stayed at Yale longer and really understood what I was getting into in economics, I think I might have had some second thoughts. But as it was, this was 1966 when I graduated and there were jobs and I zoomed off to MIT, where Mike Piore picked up that part of the story.

Mike correctly remarks that there was something uncomfortable for me about MIT, and he wondered whether I would have had the kind of intellectual development that I have if I had stayed at MIT, or for that matter at Stanford, where I went from MIT. Looking back, I would say that I could not have developed intellectually in the directions I did in those contexts. To my mind, that's a rather serious and important flaw in elite American educational and scholarly life in my lifetime. There was something about those very high-powered places that, despite the presence of many brilliant colleagues and many wonderful students, made me feel uncomfortable and constricted and made it difficult for me to do the work that I wanted to do. Tracy [Mott] is nodding away here; he remembers the Stanford of the 1970s. There's a picture that I hang in my office, one of Brueghel's pictures of Hell, which I sometimes say I keep to remind me of my Stanford days [laughter] ... it was difficult.

Mike is exactly right, and this has come up several times in the talks about my work, including Rajiv Sethi's, that the immediate issue that was bothering me intellectually at the time that I moved from MIT to Stanford had to do with the integration of Monetary Theory and General Equilibrium Theory. There were, however, some other things that were bothering me a lot about economics. Some of those things had to do with my father who was, what you might call a "real scientist." He was an industrial physicist and he was used to building instruments and making measurements on real systems. Coming from that background, I was very unhappy with the way that economics treated data and with the relation between models and verification or falsification, however you want to think of it, in economics. I was also, at a very early stage, concerned with the problem of whether to think of prices as single scalars or dispersed distributions. It seemed to me that statistical elements had to come into the way the foundations of economic theory were formulated.

I came to Stanford with probably half of an intention to drop out of economics. Dropping out because, I was – well – I was getting bored. I was getting bored with the mainstream work and there were other things I thought I wanted to do with my life. Politics or something like that. Now if you look at dropping out from a certain point of view – I'm going to use a very strong word here but I'm trying to use it in a narrow technical way – it's a *kind* of suicide. It's a way of eliminating yourself , not from the planet altogether, but as a factor in a certain milieu, in a certain community. I hasten to say that, partly because of what I mentioned before about my centered sense of myself, I've never actually been prone to the kinds of depression and existential worries about life that I know many other people grapple with. That just has not been my problem. But as far as economics goes, this idea that I might commit scientific suicide was definitely on the table.

What saved that situation or changed that situation was that I got interested in something, namely Marxist political economy, due to a wonderful, vigorous group of graduate students including Tracy [Mott], and some faculty such as Jack Gurley (not in his [John G.] Gurley and [Edward] Shaw guise, but as the Maoist in the Stanford economics department), Donald Harris, and Bridget O'Laughlin. So I got interested in economics again.

Well, that turned out to be the wrong thing [laughing] from the point of view of my job at Stanford. I think the Stanford economics department would have been much happier if I hadn't gotten interested in economics again. I had gone to Stanford without tenure, but as an associate professor with the assurance, "don't worry we'll promote you very soon." When I came around to the Chair's office to say, "well you talked about promoting me soon, how about doing that – or giving me tenure," he said, "well we're just now in a financial freeze and there's only necessary tenure ..." [Lance Taylor says "sounds like the New

School" – laughter results.] Yes. I said, "what's necessary?" And he said, "well you'd have to have an outside offer and be threatening to leave if you didn't get it," which I didn't particularly want to do.

The situation started to unfold as a "case" in the usual semi-comedy of academic departmental life, but I think behind that comedy there were more serious issues. In fact, as my "case" developed, it became a question of: was I or was I not a Marxist economist? Now that question has come up also in other contexts, and I've found it very difficult to convince people that I either am or am not. I'll just say a couple of things about that. One is that, as the Dewey story shows, I have a conservative temperamental [laughter] and intellectual streak. I mean, have you ever seen a picture of Thomas E. Dewey? Only a certain kind of six-year-old [loud laughter] is going to go for that. Just to put that on the record, I did write a column for the Ripon Forum in the 1960s. Somebody might want to look at some of those columns. The idea of the Ripon Society was to strengthen moderate Republicanism, and to try to prevent Ronald Reagan from becoming President of the United States. We know how that came out.

So they were unable to resolve at Stanford whether I was a Marxist economist or not. As a result I felt I had to leave Stanford and that was the closest I have come to being depressed. I'm not sure what it was about that experience that was so depressing to me. Certainly there was the sense that I was depressed about what it told me about the economics profession and the Stanford economics department – but maybe more importantly the economics profession, because I didn't really think the Stanford economics department was anything more than a kind of random sample of the economics profession. Maybe what it told me about was American society and my relation to the economics profession. All of those things prompted a lot of rethinking on my part.

An experience like my time at Stanford does leave one bruised. There's a traumatic quality to that experience of rejection. One of the things that one has to deal with in that kind of rejection is anger. Now, the Quakers have a lot trouble with anger [laughter]. In fact, if you go to Quaker meeting there are frequent messages about people's difficulties managing anger or, maybe even more often, expressing anger in a constructive way. Anger is a very important part of human life, but it can be very corrosive, when someone turns his anger back on himself.

I thought about anger quite a bit during that period in my life. I chose, as a personal strategy for dealing with the situation, what's often called sublimation. In my case the sublimation strategy was to shift the anger away from my colleagues at Stanford or myself to a resolution that I would be angry at orthodox or mainstream economics.

The form that anger took was a resolution to do something so that the particular neoclassical way of talking about the social world and teaching economics would be changed. Even at that time it was pretty clear that this was a pretty Don-Quixote-like vision. Or at least – and this was a more reasonable ambition – to try to do what I could to make sure that, first of all, some different ideas were around for people who wanted to look at the world in a different way. And second, that insofar as I was an educator and a teacher, to foster a stream of students of a younger generation who would have some knowledge of other ways of looking at world and would be maximally annoying [laughter] to orthodox economists.

So I urge you to put some of the very lovely things people have said about me over this day and a half in that context [laughter]. I had my own agenda, and one of the satisfactions I have from this day and a half is precisely feeling that I've made some progress [loud laughter] on some of those areas. That's a matter of great, great personal satisfaction.

Many people in our world are very concerned about things like who is a professor in the Stanford University economics department. And you wonder exactly why that's such a highly motivating, incentivizing question. Partly because of this centered personality that I got from my mother, I was probably less prone or less vulnerable to that kind of pressure than many people would be. But I have learned some important things from my experience with the economics profession through the Stanford episode.

First of all, I don't think that I suffered materially in any respect. But there is a sidelight to that, which is that this was probably due to the open texture of American society and American academic life and to its competitive structure. If I had been working in Soviet Russia, the material (and personal) consequences could have been very different.

But the material issues are perhaps not really so important. The other dimension that you might think could be threatened by being sidled out of orthodox economics and out of places like the Stanford economics department was that there could be some impoverishment of the quality of my intellectual life and community. I would like to say that that has not happened *in the slightest*; if anything it's been the other way around [people murmur in agreement]. The wealth of ideas and intensity and beauty of interaction with people as colleagues and students in the time since I left Stanford has been *wonderful* for me. I just don't see why people think that the Stanford economics department or the MIT economics department have any monopoly on a vigorous and fertile intellectual life.

Partly because of Quakerism, partly because of the radicalism of the 1960s, I also became wary of and rather averse to, the larger world that's the media, TV, journalism, public debate – what at The New School people often call being a "public intellectual." One of the things I like about academic life is that it's intensely personal. It has a lot to do with immediate interactions with people. That's one of the things I like very much about this last day and a half, that this conference is at a scale that is extremely agreeable to me. It's amazing to me to look out and see all of you sitting here in this room representing many different parts of my life, different parts of my "ταξεῖδι," my journey.

There are, as I said last night, three people I would like to mention who are *not* here who have been very important to me. One is Miguel Sidrauski, who had a huge influence on me when I was at MIT, both personally and intellectually. A second is Peter Albin. I was very delighted to find so much echo of Peter Albin's ideas in the talks here. Phil [Mirowski] said he got some of his ideas from *me* [Duncan]. But, Phil, in many ways I'm channeling Peter Albin in the areas you spoke about: it was Peter who thought of many of the things you were picking up on. I was just trying to make those ideas more available. A third is Suzanne de Brunhoff, who is in Paris and can't come due to her health situation, but also was a person who opened up a whole world to me through her work on money and Marx.

I am a very privileged person. I started to realize this when I was maybe about six or eight years old. I would wake up at night and say to myself, "you know there's a lot of people in the world who aren't living in a nice, cozy, semi-suburban Philadelphia house the way I am; for whom life is a lot less secure and a lot harder." As I have grown older I have come to understand that I'm privileged not just in that world, class perspective, but in many other ways, for example by being male, by being white in a racist society. But I feel very privileged in other dimensions, too. That privilege is something I think people like me have to come to terms with. What do you do with this privilege? There are many different things one can do with it, but I think it's necessary to think about doing something with it.

I feel particularly privileged to have had the experience of teaching and research and collegial interaction with students and faculty at Barnard and at The New School and at Columbia. I particularly would like to thank the organizers, Lance [Taylor], and Armon [Rezai], and Tom Michl for putting this "ωραίο ταξείδι" in place for me in this last day and a half.

People said very nice things last night about me, and I think that's OK once in a lifetime. I think if you got it too often it would probably be somewhat disequilibrating [laughter], but they were really, *really* nice things to hear, and I liked hearing them a lot.

But, you know, look at it the other way, look at it from my point of view. I'm sitting there in my office and all these interesting people are coming in and telling me their ideas and their experiences and their findings – I'm learning a huge amount. I've learned an enormous amount about all kinds of things from theses that I've advised and other work with students and they're keeping me from *being bored*, to go back to that theme.

As I said, this conference was a way for you to look into my world. But in a larger sense, and certainly in a statistical sampling sense, you *are* my world. If you look at each other I hope you see as in a mirror why my life is fun and why I like it so much.

[applause]

[Lance Taylor asks, "encore?" Loud laughter. Duncan says, "No, no" and smiles.]

Part I
Socio-economic ideology and methodology

1 Keynes and Marx, Duncan and me

Michael J. Piore

It is always a question in writing for a festschrift as to whether to present a piece of one's own research – presumably inspired by the person being honored – or to write specifically about that person himself. In this case, there is not a real choice. Duncan and I come from very different traditions in economics. Indeed, I am not sure whether Duncan recognizes me as an economist at all, so the direct overlap of our work is limited. Yet, Duncan has represented a critical reference point in my own thinking and intellectual development. In part, this is because he comes out of what is now the mainstream of the discipline, and hence speaks with a voice to which I have always felt compelled to listen and where possible to respond. But it is also because he has been one of the few critical voices speaking from that perspective, and hence always seemed to promise to help us understand not only the limits of mainstream economics that are apparent from the outside but also its internal weaknesses as well. But, perhaps most fundamentally, I have always felt that we were wrestling with the same questions about the role of economics in the world, however different our perspectives and our answers. In this, the way in which Duncan has exercised his influence on me is a puzzle, and it is some of the pieces of that puzzle which I am going to try to lay out here and draw together.

I know Duncan because we both came to the Economics Department at MIT as assistant professors in the same year, 1966; had we not met in this way, we probably would never have met at all. We began our graduate studies at about the same time as well, in the early 1960s. We came, as I have already suggested, from very different places. Duncan represented the "flower" of the new brand of theoretical economics. I was essentially hired by the industrial relations faculty, which represented an older approach to economics, and had the year before I arrived actually moved out of the Economics Department to the Sloan School of Business (although my own appointment was in the Economics Department, in which, it was made quite clear to me when I was hired, I had to make my career). But, despite these differences, a major part of the attraction of economics for each of us was that it was a moral science which spoke to the problems of the world and promised, if not to resolve those problems, then at least to ameliorate them (this is the theme of Duncan's most recent book (Foley, 2006)). We were both active politically, although again in different ways (which it turned out mirrored the differences in our approach to economics). Duncan was active in the Ripon Society, a libertarian Republican organization. I was a New Deal Democrat, committed to the labor movement. For both of us, however, these political commitments were an extension of our scientific work and an expression of the moral dimensions of the discipline.

The attractions of economics

As a moral science, which spoke to political concerns, economics was then at its apogee, surrounded by a missionary aura, and MIT's Economics Department was at the forefront of the discipline, the acknowledged leader of the forces which created and sustained its scientific and moral authority. These forces were basically twofold. One was Keynesian economics, the way in which it spoke to the central policy concerns of prosperity, growth and full employment, and the predominance which it achieved in policy deliberations under the Kennedy – and then Johnson – Administrations. Kennedy's Council of Economic Advisors (CEA) was staffed from the very beginning by leading Keynesian economists: Bob Solow from MIT was Chief of Staff; James Tobin, one of Duncan's mentors at Yale, was a member of the Council itself; Paul Samuelson was an advisor. I was a summer intern at the Council in the first two years of the Kennedy Administration, and Samuelson was regularly seen seated in the halls of the Executive Office Building at a makeshift desk typing memos and preparing Congressional testimony. The ultimate triumph of the CEA's brand of Keynesian economics was President Kennedy's speech at Yale in 1962, in which he explicitly endorsed the economics of his advisors and preached its lessons. Walter Heller, the Chairman of Kennedy's Council, successfully negotiated the transition to the Johnson Administration after Kennedy's assassination, and the new president espoused Keynesian lessons as well.

The second component of the missionary aura that surrounded economics was the sense that it had come into its own as a genuine science, whose understanding of the world was capable of rigorous mathematical formulation and systematic empirical investigation. The leading expositors of this approach were Paul Samuelson and the faculty who collected around him at MIT. But it was an approach that was of course also practiced at other leading graduate schools, including Yale where Duncan studied. When Duncan came to MIT, he was one of the most promising members of the new generation trained in this tradition. The victory of the approach was, however, more recent at MIT than the school's reputation in the outside world suggested. The Department has been built around labor economics and industrial relations; the endowment of the industrial relations program had been drawn down to attract a new generation of professors. In economics, industrial relations drew heavily upon the German historical school and the Wisconsin institutional school, which the new theoretical school explicitly saw as its protagonists; and, as I already noted, its final victory only occurred the year before our arrival with the withdrawal of the remaining industrial relations faculty to the business school.

The neoclassical synthesis and its contradictions

While the intersection of the new Keynesian economics and the technical turn in theoretical analysis was, I think, responsible for the enormous attraction that economics exercised, its sense of mission, and its vocation as a moral science (the term "moral," I should note, was not used at the time, no doubt out of deference to the discipline's scientific aspirations), the two developments did not sit easily with each other. Technical economics was concerned with what has come to be called neoclassical economics, an understanding of the economy built around the assumption of rational, self-interested individuals organized into a larger social organization through a competitive market, and the price signals which the interaction of those individuals generated. Keynesian macroeconomics was difficult to formulate in this way, and essentially assumed that prices, through which the system was coordinated in the competitive model, were too rigid to perform this function. The marriage of Keynesian macroeconomics and neoclassical microeconomics – the neoclassical synthesis – was thus built around a fundamental contradiction. There was a contradiction as well between the new technical achievements of the field and the newly achieved relevance to public policy. Those contradictions were overshadowed, and in a sense justified, at least for the generation which preceded us, by the moral relevance which the discipline had achieved in figuring out how to speak to the problems of the Great Depression and to sustain full employment in the post-World-War-II period. For our generation of economists, who did not experience the Depression directly, and for whom a full employment economy seemed less problematic, the resolution of the contradictions became the leading intellectual challenge of the discipline (Sethi, 2010).

Resolving the contradiction

The logic of the problem suggested that there were two alternative ways in which the contradictions could have been resolved. One was to reformulate microeconomics using a set of assumptions about human motivation and about the efficacy of market clearing mechanisms consistent with Keynesian economics. The other was to reformulate macroeconomics with a set of assumptions consistent with neoclassical economics. Coming to economics out of industrial relations, I was attracted to the first of these approaches and much of my early work was motivated, albeit rather indirectly, in this way. Duncan in fact used to maintain that the reason I survived at MIT was that the neoclassical synthesis was maintained there – in a way in which for example it never survived in Chicago – by pushing all of the contradictions into the labor market, and accepting a theory of the labor market completely at odds with other markets in the economy. In the end, the discipline itself adopted the second approach, seeking to reformate macroeconomics (and labor market theory as well) so as to make it consistent with neoclassical assumptions. Duncan, who was attracted to neoclassical theory in part because of its libertarian moral implications, would have been a natural exponent of the Chicago approach. But in the reinterpretation of Keynes which has accompanied the current crisis I have come to see Duncan's early work as representing a third approach, that of incorporating money into the neoclassical model (a point to which I will return) (Foley and Sidrauski, 1971).

The revolutionary impact of the late 1960s and early 1970s

How this contradiction would have played out if economics had retained the moral authority which initially attracted Duncan and I to the discipline is difficult to say. The promise that economics offered in the early 1960s when we went into the field was progressively undermined in the course of the decade and the one that followed. The social order was shaken by the civil rights movement, by Johnson's war on poverty, by the Vietnam War and the reaction against it, and by the student movement. The issues at stake here could not be addressed through the economic growth which Keynesian economics promised, or by the economic efficiency promised by the market-based models of neoclassical economics. They involved the distribution of income (not simply its level) and, even more, they involved power, respect, and social status, things which could not be reduced to material resources. Indeed, the student rebellion ultimately called into question the value of material resources altogether. The problems of the period could not be addressed through the economic models in which we had put our faith. Events seemed to undermine and betray the claims of economics as a moral science.

The Marxist alternative

Marxian economics was the obvious alternative. It made claims of moral relevance, scientific objectivity, and technical prowess comparable to those of conventional economics, but at the same time seemed to speak to the issues raised in the politics of the period and link them to the operation of the economy in a way that conventional theory could not.

It is a little hard in retrospect to recapture what Marxist economics represented for mainstream economics at the time. Basically, I think that in the education of our generation (of Duncan's and mine), it was irrelevant. At Harvard (where I was a graduate student), at least, it had not totally disappeared from the curriculum; it was presented in theory courses and in courses on the Soviet Union, but exclusively in terms of the labor theory of value. As students, we thought of it as a foil, basically as a pedagogical device to develop the ideas of marginal utility, relative scarcity, and general equilibrium. It was obviously not viewed in that way by our professors, who devoted whole lectures to criticizing it, presenting their critiques with a passion that was otherwise reserved for fundamental theoretical accomplishments. But in the Cold War atmosphere in which we had been brought up, this was not particularly remarkable in a subject so closely connected to communism and the Soviet Union. At any rate, those parts of Marx that spoke to the issues that emerged in the 1960s and 1970s – alienation, class conflict, ideological hegemony – were never touched upon; one would never have known they existed. For me, as a student in labor economics and industrial relations, Marx ironically played even less of a role than it did in my economic theory courses; his theories of history and class conflict were simply not mentioned. I later came to believe that the whole field of industrial relations was invented to provide an alternative framework for thinking about the labor conflicts and collective actions that plagued American society in the 1930s and the immediate post-World-War-II period. Economics itself provided no way of thinking about these problems at all, except maybe to suppress them in the way one might repeal a tariff or break up a monopoly, an approach to public policy in labor relations which had disastrous social consequences. Marx provided a definite alternative, but one embedded in a much broader social critique. And industrial relations was an alternative to the Marxist vocabulary, a way of thinking about unions, strikes and industrial unrest without the revolutionary overtones that the Marxist vocabulary brought with it (Piore, 2011, p. 25).

Duncan and I were of course not the only members of our generation who turned to what came to be called radical economics. Indeed, for a period of time, it seemed to preoccupy the whole of the profession, and when some of what the MIT and Harvard Economics Departments viewed as their "best and brightest" began to turn in this direction, it was clear that a good deal more was at stake here than the labor theory of value. I remember seminars sponsored by the graduate economics club at MIT, attended by virtually the whole of the department, faculty, and students, at which radical papers were presented, on several occasions by graduates of the Department itself. The reaction of our senior colleagues was apoplectic – it is hard to think of another word. They were so angry and upset that they could not seem to compose a coherent response to the radical critique. In retrospect, I do not even remember what that the papers were actually about; I remember only the theater of the events and virtually nothing at all about the substance. The way in which dissent was treated in these seminars seemed to support what might be termed a vulgar Marxian view of how ideological alternatives to theories celebrating capitalism are suppressed.

But an emphasis on these grand confrontations gives a misleading impression of what it meant to turn away from mainstream economics and hence the way in which the mainstream exercised its ideological hegemony, especially over those for whom so much of the attraction of the field was its theoretical rigor, coherence, and sophistication. Since this was not the way the attraction of the discipline was constituted for me personally, I see this primarily through the eyes of the students who were my advisees. It is captured by three vignettes that over the years continue to reverberate in my mind.

One is of a student reporting an interview with a colleague of mine and Duncan's about the student's aspirations to be a theorist (he was already a champion swimmer). He was told, he felt rather brutally – although I am sure knowing my colleague that the brutality was unintended – that he had come to economics too late, that like an Olympic swimmer, you had to begin training (presumably in math) when you were very young.

The second story that sticks in my mind is a student who decided in the middle of his first year that he wanted to quit the program in order to study forestry at Yale (in the days before the environmental movement made such a choice fashionable), but who came under such intense pressure from his colleagues, his fellow students in the program, that he decided he could not leave (although later he did in fact leave for the Yale forestry program). I am not sure exactly why that particular story seems so relevant here. I think what it reflected is the way the students submitted themselves to the rigors of the training in formal theory that the program entailed and the way, having done so, they were committed to hold to the theory in their later work as researchers and policy advisors.

For me, the most telling of these stories emerged in an "exit" interview I had with a visiting French student, actually a post doc, as he was about to leave at the end of his postdoctoral year to return home. This guy had been, by common consensus in France, the most promising Marxist doctoral student (a student of Robert Boyer who was the leader of the French Regulationist school). He was an "Olympian": He had been training, as it were, in math throughout his formal education in a way that I think only the French can train. When we talked, as he was leaving MIT, he was in despair. He found the intellectual give and take among the theorists the most intense and exciting intellectual experience he had ever had (or ever imagined having). But it all took place within the set of theoretical assumptions of neoclassical economics, and carried strong ideological implications that he found abhorrent. He wondered whether one could keep up with these theoretical developments working alone, alone outside of MIT. And he was quite sure that you could not produce a critique of comparable rigor from outside, let alone a model reflecting an alternative ideological perspective.

Duncan left MIT in 1973 to go to Stanford for family reasons, and I wonder if he would have turned toward Marxism in quite the way he did if he had stayed. He is certainly the only member of the faculty who did so. The number of faculty members was of course much larger at Harvard, and there were MIT graduates on the faculty of Harvard who did turn toward Marxism; these were the seminar speakers who provoked the strong reaction when they came back to talk to the Graduate Economics Forum. But the interactions among the faculty – and between faculty and students – at Harvard never had the intensity of those among the younger faculty at MIT, and in those days, theory was taught by people who came to Harvard late in their careers.

The attractions of Marxism

Those of us who did turn toward Marx found a variety of different things. An important part of the attraction, which I think most of us shared – certainly Duncan and I – was, as I have already suggested, that it recognized the forces which seemed to be moving American society in the late 1960s and 1970s, in much the same way that Keynesian economics recognized the forces moving society in the Depression and the earlier postwar decades, and incorporated them into an analytical framework which recognized the economy as well; indeed, which made the economy the central focus and showed how it impacted other human concerns and values. It offered, moreover, a moral vision, and it made claims as a science in much the same way that conventional economics did. In other words, it promised essentially the same analytical rigor and moral relevance that the neoclassical synthesis offered to our professors who had lived through the Great Depression and was promised to us when we were initially attracted to economics, but it spoke in a way that conventional economics could not to the dominant moral concerns of the time.

But beyond this, Duncan and I were attracted to very different aspects of Marxism. For me, Marx offered something which economics theory did not: a theory of history and of social conflict. It appealed to that side of me which came out of labor economics and industrial relations, but it provided a way of problematizing the theory in which I had in effect been raised, and a bridge into a whole realm of social science theory which not only was not part of my education, but of which my education had left me completely unaware. Indeed, it was through Marx that I really discovered the roots of industrial relations in institutional economics and the Wisconsin School. That these were intellectual traditions which linked the concerns of industrial relations directly and intimately to high economic theory was an added bonus – a major bonus I would add – but not what attracted me in the first place.

The limits of Marxism

But while Marxism opened for me a whole domain of intellectual inquiry and social theory, Marxism itself ultimately proved limiting. The evolution of society has not followed the path that Marx predicted. The social conflicts that have dominated American society from the 1960s onward have not been about class in the economic sense of the term but about race, sex, and other identities which Marx and his followers barely recognized; technology has evolved in a very different direction as well. Thus, while Marx is an important referent in my intellectual development, my sense of how economics, and of how social theory more broadly, need to develop, derives as much from a critique of Marx as from Marxian theory itself, in fact it probably derives even more from a critique of the critique which Marxian theory offers to conventional economics.

I have no warrant to speak for Duncan, but I think that what he found attractive in Marx were a very different set of insights – a set of insights that basically have to do with the role of money in the economy. The role of money has been at the center of Duncan's research from the very beginning. His initial ambition was to insert money into the heart of conventional economic theory, building it into a general equilibrium model. The notion of the "core" is in that sense a metaphor for his theoretical preoccupation. But in a deeper sense, this ambition is in conflict with the whole enterprise of conventional theory. That theory starts from a definition of economics as a discipline that is rooted in a tension between limited resources and unlimited desire. That tension is conceived of as a reflection of nature itself; it is about "real things." In this sense, money can facilitate the operation of the economy, but a view that it will fundamentally change economic relations, and the analysis of the ways in which it might do so, is alien to the spirit of the enterprise. In conventional economics, money almost has to be viewed as a veil on the operation of the real world, which theory can legitimately abstract from in order to focus on the fundamental forces.

Marx on the other hand starts from the proposition that the very nature of capitalism is the separation of the economy from the real goods and services it produces and distributes, i.e., the separation of use value and exchange value. (I say in deference to my graduate theory professors that use value and utility are not quite the same thing but in this context they might as well be.) In pre-capitalism – as in standard economics – people think in terms of real things, commodities not in the abstract, but as very specific goods and services. They convert those things into money so as to facilitate the process of production. But basically they are interested in obtaining more real goods and services: $C > M > C'$. But capitalism inverts this relationship: people become interested in money and in goods and services not in themselves but for what they represent as money. The direction of causality is reversed, and the economy is motivated by $M > C > M'$. This is a completely different way of looking at the operation of the system; indeed, it is a completely different system. And while Marx himself may have had relatively little to say about it, it leads into a different intellectual territory.

This insight of Marx, unlike his insights into social class or the technological trajectory of the system, has not, I think, been overtaken by history. In fact, in a certain sense, the financial crisis and its aftermath have brought these issues back to the fore. The sense in which this is true is clear, and the continuity in Duncan's own intellectual trajectory is evident, in his 2009 Barnard Lecture (Foley, 2009).

This is of course not apparent in public discourse. What is being proclaimed is not a Marxian renaissance but a Keynesian one. What is striking, however, is how little the economics of the current crisis resembles the economics that attracted us to the discipline in the 1960s when Keynesian economics was at its prime. It is not just that the immense self-confidence and optimism of the earlier period, the sense that we had mastered our environment, has been lost (even as the crisis has pushed the issues which sapped that self-confidence in the late 1960s and 1970s to the very margins of political debate), but more importantly, the intellectual unity and coherence which the discipline then seemed to have is gone. It is as if we face not one crisis but three, each engendering its own discussion and debate.

The first of these crises was of course the financial crisis, which reached its pinnacle in the fall of 2008. The second is the crisis in the real economy which ensued, with its high and persistent rates of unemployment (not simply of labor but, significantly, of all productive resources). The third is the recovery which has yet to be achieved. Keynes had a lot to say about all three crises. He wrote extensively about the finance and the financial crises of the post-World-War-I period which fed into the Great Depression; it is these writings that have recently attracted the most attention and this is what the rediscovery of Keynes is mostly about. But the Keynesian economics of our graduate education in the 1960s, of Kennedy's Council of Economic Advisors, and of his 1962 Yale address had virtually nothing to do with this part of Keynes. It focused on government fiscal policy as an instrument for managing the economy, and its lessons for the present time are about how to meet the crisis of persistent unemployment in the real economy through an expansion of Federal expenditures – in short the stimulus package. In retrospect, however, this is more a lesson about welfare policy than the economy, and certainly not of mainstream economics. As I have just noted, mainstream economics defines itself by scarcity (limited resources and unlimited desires), but the unemployed resources of the Great Depression and of the current period are free – if they are not employed by government they will go to waste. In other they are not scarce. And, Keynes was quite explicit about this, some other logic is required. But that logic, whatever it is, will not bring about a recovery. The government expenditures which draw the unemployed resources into production will have a multiplier effect on private expenditures, on consumption and investment and thus bring about an expansion. But, as soon as they are withdrawn the multipliers will operate in reverse and the economy will fall back into recession (what Keynes called a lower level equilibrium trap). On how to produce a genuine recovery, Keynesian economics, it is apparent at least in retrospect, has very little to offer. And actually on my own reading, Keynes himself offered very little either. What is called for is an integrated understanding of all these crises, or, rather what one would say if one had such an understanding, the crisis in all three of its phases.

This is exactly what Duncan offered in his 2009 Barnard Lecture (Foley, 2009). The lecture seems particularly prescient because it predicts at that relatively early time the inability of the stimulus package to produce an economic recovery. But its intellectual interest is in the way in which it works from Marx's insight about capitalism to develop an integrated framework for an understanding of the crisis. I have to say that the social critique and sense of history which are so central to a Marxian approach are not so well integrated into the analysis; they crop up largely at the edges. But the paper is definitely a sign of the consistency of Duncan's research program and of its power. And in the current climate of pessimism about economics as a discipline and the economy as a human enterprise, it is a shining light, one which I think might attract students to the discipline in the present decade in the way that we were attracted by the ideas spawned by the Great Depression.

References

Foley, Duncan K. (2006) *Adam's Fallacy: A Guide to Economic Theology*. Cambridge, Mass: Belknap Press of Harvard University Press.

Foley, Duncan K. (2009) "The Anatomy of Financial and Economic Crisis," Paper prepared for Gildersleeve Lecture delivered at Barnard College, April 17.

Foley, Duncan K., and Miguel Sidrauski (1971) *Monetary and Fiscal Policy in a Growing Economy*. New York: Macmillan.

Piore, Michael J. (2011) "Whither Industrial Relations: Does It Have a Future in Post-Industrial Society," *British Journal of Industrial Relations*, 49(4), 792–801.

Sethi, Rajiv (2010) "Foley, Sidrauski, and the Microfoundations Project," *Rajiv Sethi: thoughts on economics, finance, crime and identity*, Blog, November 19, 2010, http://rajivsethi.blogspot.com/2010/11/foley-sidrauski-and-microfoundations.html.

2 The sophisticated Legislator meets Adam's fallacy

A cultural–institutional market failure

Samuel Bowles

Adam's fallacy

Adam's fallacy, according to Duncan Foley (2006: xii), is "the idea that it is possible to separate an economic sphere of life, in which the pursuit of self interest is guided by objective laws to a socially beneficent outcome, from the rest of social life, in which the pursuit of self-interest is morally problematic." He thus challenges "the foundation of political economy and economics as an intellectual discipline," which, he writes, is based on the "separation of an economic sphere ... from the much messier, less determinate and morally more problematic issues of politics, social conflict and values." Here I propose to correct Adam's fallacy by integrating the "economic sphere" with the world of "politics, social conflict, and values."

Once Adam's fallacy is corrected, I find that even a perfectly competitive economy falls short of what Smith's invisible hand promised. The reason is that in addition to producing goods and services, the economy produces people – favoring some preferences and identities over others. And the amoral self interest that would proliferate in the idealized economy for which the invisible hand would do its wonders (should such an economy ever exist) would not provide the cultural underpinnings of a well working system of exchange.

The idea that incentives that appeal to the material interests may reduce the salience of ethical motives, on which the functioning of markets and other institutions depend, is hardly new. Peter Berkowitz writes "liberalism depends on virtues that it does not readily summon and which it may even stunt or stifle" (1999: xiii). A similar view was famously advanced by Daniel Bell (1976) in his *Cultural Contradictions of Capitalism* and earlier works (Bell, 1973: 48) "The historic justifications of bourgeois society – in the realms of religion and character – are gone ... The lack of a rooted moral belief system is the cultural contradiction of the society." Prominent exponents of related themes include Edmund Burke, Alexis de Tocqueville, Joseph Schumpeter, Frederick Hayek, and Jurgen Habermas.[1]

These writers advanced the idea that liberal society is dynamically unstable and hence prone to cultural–institutional collapse. I have dubbed this the thesis that liberalism is a parasite on tradition. But the parasite thesis is unconvincing (Bowles, 2011). In very brief: while recognizing the possibly deleterious cultural effects of markets, advocates of the parasite thesis have overlooked the ways in which other attributes of liberal societies – notably the rule of law and a reduction in barriers to occupational and spatial mobility – have supported a flourishing civic culture (at least by comparison with many traditional societies). But the effects of markets on culture stressed by the advocates of the parasite thesis are the basis of a quite different (static rather than dynamic) critique of markets and the one that I will advance here: namely, that the nexus of culture and institutions characteristic of a market-based society results in an inefficient allocation of economic resources.

I call this outcome a cultural–institutional market failure because it results from the effects of markets and other institutions on the cultural transmission of preferences and beliefs, and the corresponding effects of the distribution of preferences and beliefs (culture) on the kinds of contracts, forms of economic organization, and other economic institutions that economic actors will be motivated to adopt. The main conceptual challenge is thus to model the joint dynamics of individual preferences and beliefs and population-level institutions, one in which both institutions and people are endogenous. Students of the interaction of culture and institutions – advocates of the parasite thesis and others – have not used either formal modeling or sophisticated empirical methods in their work. But advances in evolutionary game theory and its application to cultural dynamics, as well as recent experiential results from behavioral economics, now allow an empirically grounded formal model of the causal processes underlying the interaction of cultures and economic institutions.

A cultural–institutional equilibrium

An adequate model must illuminate the way in which institutions affect the evolution of culture and the way culture affects the evolution of institutions. With respect to the first, the idea that institutions affect culture is commonly illustrated by the role of families and religious and educational organizations in the socialization process; but it extends to institutions less transparently associated with the evolution of norms, tastes and the like (Bowles, 1998). Supporting evidence comes from studies of parents' child-rearing values: for example, parents value obedience more in their children and independence less if at work they take rather than give orders (Kohn, Naoi, Schoenbach, and Schooler, 1990). Using behavioral experiments, my co-authors and I have also documented the influence of cooperative production (hunting large animals, for example, or the cooperative provision of local public goods) on values supporting cooperation in other settings (Gintis, Bowles, Boyd, and Fehr, 2005). There is also extensive evidence that the explicit economic incentives on which markets rely either reduce the psychological salience or inhibit the learning of social preference such as fairmindedness, altruism, reciprocity, and intrinsic motivation to contribute to the public good (Bowles and Polania-Reyes, 2012; Bowles, 2008).

Guido Tabellini (2008) provides evidence of a quite different sort: generalized (rather than familial) trust appears to thrive in countries with a long history of liberal political institutions. Tabellini shows that the reverse relationship also holds: the quality of public institutions is associated statistically with more generalized trust. The effect of culture on institutions arises because the kinds of preferences and beliefs that are prevalent in a population will influence the comparative advantage of particular institutions. By institutions I mean formal and informal rules governing social interactions, from the organization of families and firms to the structure of government. The extent to which economic activity is governed by markets as opposed to states, firms, communities, families, or other institutions differs across societies and over time, and it is subject to deliberate alteration both by states and by individual economic actors (Coase, 1937; Ben-Porath, 1980; Ostrom, 1990; Belloc and Bowles, 2012 and 2013). These choices will depend on the distribution of individual preferences and beliefs in a population – that is, on its culture.

The dependence of culture on institutions and the reverse leads one to expect a limited set of compatible matches between the two. Recently developed models of the coevolution of cultures and institutions (Bowles, 2004; Bowles and Gintis, 2011) allow a precise formalization of this thesis. I simplify by representing institutions by a measure of the extent to which markets (as opposed to other institutions) allocate resources (m), while representing preferences by a single-valued measure of civic virtue (v), where the latter represents the prevalence of norms that contribute in essential ways to the functioning of the institutions of a liberal market economy, including such things as truth telling, adherence to socially valuable norms, a strong work ethic, and generosity toward others, even strangers. To make the model concrete, in a population in which there are some people who are amoral and self interested and others who act on the basis of the social preferences just mentioned, then v could be the fraction of the population who are the latter type. In the same population there might be two allocation mechanisms – markets and collective allocation – and the extent of the market, m, could then be the fraction of an individual's livelihood acquired through the former. The objective of the model is to represent the mutual determination of m and v so as to characterize the pair or pairs $\{m, v\}$, such that both are stationary – that is, subject to change only due to exogenous events. These stationary pairs – the compatible matches between cultures and institutions – are termed cultural–institutional equilibria.

Modeling cultural–institutional dynamics

The structure of the model captures three key ideas.

The first is that what I have just called civic virtues improve institutional functioning by reducing the transaction costs of exchange and cooperation. "No social system can work ... in which everyone is ... guided by nothing except his own ... utilitarian ends" wrote Joseph Schumpeter (1950: 448). Kenneth Arrow (1971: 22) added:

> In the absence of trust ... opportunities for mutually beneficial cooperation would have to be foregone ... norms of social behavior, including ethical

and moral codes (may be) ... reactions of society to compensate for market failures.

In the major markets of a modern economy – the markets for labor, credit, and knowledge – complete contracts are the exception, and as a result the market failures to which Arrow refers are ubiquitous. These markets as well as other economic institutions function as well as they do because social norms and other-regarding motives foster a positive work ethic, an obligation to tell the truth about the qualities of a project or a piece of information, and a commitment to keep promises.

The second key idea is that virtue is crowded out by markets. The experimental evidence for this proposition has already been mentioned. Sandra Polonia-Reyes, Sung-Ha Hwang, and I have recently explored the causal mechanisms accounting for crowding out. A possible mechanism is that markets frame action settings providing clues that the situation is one in which the pursuit of self interest is morally acceptable (Hwang and Bowles, 2012a). Another is that markets (as well as market-like incentives used by public bodies) reward self-interest and penalize those with other-regarding or ethical values, or that markets reduce the scope for or visibility of generous actions, or in other ways provide environments inimical to the learning of civic values (Hwang and Bowles, 2012b). In the second set of mechanisms, preferences are endogenous (rather than simply state dependent), and that is the case I consider here. (These processes are summarized in non-technical language and related evidence provided in Bowles and Polania-Reyes (2012).)

The experimental evidence suggests that crowding out of virtue occurs in markets to a greater extent than in plausible alternative non-market allocation mechanisms. Thus there is a stationary level of virtue expressed by the function $v = v(m)$ where $v(m)$ is termed a cultural equilibrium conditional on the given value of m. What this means is that if $v > v(m)$ there are more "virtuous" people in the population than is consistent with the economy's market structure, so that some of them will abandon their pro-social preferences; and conversely, if $v < v(m)$. Thus when $v = v(m)$ the process of cultural updating is such that the level of virtue in the population does not change (i.e. is stationary, unless m changes). Thus the $v(m)$ function is given by the values of m and v for which $dv/dt = \alpha(m, v) = 0$ where the function $\alpha(m, v)$ is derived from a process of cultural transmission in which an individual's values are periodically updated taking account of the relative payoffs of bearers of different values and the frequency of types in the population, given the extent of the market (as modeled in Bowles (2004)). For example if v is substantial it may nonetheless be stationary if, for the given value of m, the payoff disadvantage of acting on one's pro-social preferences is exactly compensated by one's conformist desire to behave like most others do. The crowding out function $v(m)$ is illustrated in panel A of Figure 2.1; the arrows indicate the direction of adjustment from out-of-equilibrium states (that is the values of dv/dt for values of $v \neq \alpha(m, v)$).

The basic point embodied by the $v(m)$ function is expressed in its downward slope; a greater extent of the market is associated with fewer virtuous citizens

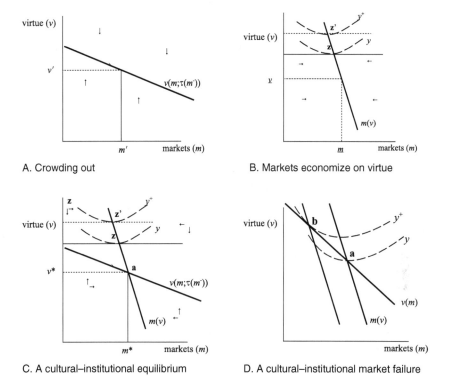

Figure 2.1 A cultural–institutional equilibrium. Arrows indicate the direction of adjustment. Panel A: the effect of the extent of markets on virtue. Panel B: The effect of virtue on the extent of markets. Panel C: A temporary cultural–institutional equilibrium Panel D. Point a is the cultural–institutional equilibrium, while point b is a Pareto-superior cultural–institutional configuration induced by an exogenous limitation of the market (the leftward shift of the $m(v)$ function.)

in cultural equilibrium. This is an empirical statement, and it is not always true: in a few experiments market-like incentives appear to crowd *in* pro-social preferences (Galbiati and Vertova, 2010; Bowles and Polania-Reyes, 2012). An upward sloping $v(m)$ function would capture the reasoning of the exponents of *"doux commerce,"* including Voltaire and Smith, who held that "where there is commerce the ways of men are gentle," as Montesquieu (1961: 81) put it (Hirschman, 1977).

The third key proposition is that markets economize on virtue. "Market-like arrangements," according to Schultze (1977: 18), "reduce the need for compassion, patriotism, brotherly love, and cultural solidarity." This is important in what follows, because the extent of the market in allocating resources is determined in a decentralized way by the choices of countless economic agents, and it will vary with the cost advantages of markets relative to other institutions that may accomplish the same ends. For example, whether firms produce or purchase a particular component of the product they produce – the problem analyzed by Coase (1937) – depends on the supervision and other costs of the direct command relations that distinguish firms from markets (and that are entailed by production of the component), relative to the costs of search, bargaining over prices, and other costs of using the market. These costs will depend on the ethical, self-interested, and other motives of those involved. Marianna Belloc and I provide a model of this process, showing that where values such as reciprocity and fairness are prevalent, organizations based on partnerships may thrive, while in highly self-interested populations production may be carried out in organizations with close and punitive supervision (Belloc and Bowles, 2012 and 2013).

As a result, the level of values will influence the extent of the market; and because of the comparative advantage in governing interactions among entirely self-interested individuals enjoyed by markets (relative to bureaucracies, families, and other institutions), the relationship is inverse: higher levels of values being associated with a reduced extent of the market. The function $m(v)$ gives the stationary values of m for given values of v based on individuals structuring their interactions with others (choosing among, say, contractual or friendship, or familial ways of interacting in some particular activity) based on the relative payoffs of these various structures. Thus for any given level of virtue (say, v) there is an equilibrium extent of the market (m) that is stationary, in the sense that no actor with the capacity to alter the extent of the market may benefit from doing so. I call $m(v)$ an institutional equilibrium for the given level of civic values.

Thus, paralleling the case of the "markets crowd out virtue," function, the $m(v)$ function gives the values of v and m for which $dm/dt = \beta(m, v) = 0$. The function $\beta(m, v)$ is derived from a process in which individuals periodically alter or reaffirm the contractual or other means by which they govern their economic interactions with others in light of the benefits and costs of the alternatives (market and non-market), given the distribution of types in the population as modeled in Belloc and Bowles (2012 and 2013). This "markets economize on virtue" function is shown in panel B of Figure 2.1, where, as in panel A, the arrows give the out-of-equilibrium adjustment process – the extent of markets shrinking when it exceeds the level indicated by the function, and expanding when the reverse is true. The downward slope of the function captures the idea that the larger is the virtuous fraction of the population, the lesser will be the extent of the market.

It will be important in what follows to say a bit more about the construction of the "markets economize on virtue" function. In the figure, the loci labeled y and y^+ are output isoquants, namely loci of pairs of m and v that yield a total income (of the society in question) of y and y^+, respectively, with $y < y^+$. The position of the isoquants indicates that virtue contributes to the productivity of the society (its total income). Suppose, for illustration, that (as Coase hypothesized) the extent of the market is determined by an implicit transaction-cost-minimizing process that maximizes income net of these costs for a given level of values. Then the $m(v)$ function is the locus of all points for which m is the solution to the problem: maximize $y(v, m)$ for the given level of v, which will be found where the isoquant is tangent to the horizontal dotted line indicating the given level of v.

The given value of m is stationary because, conditional on the level of v, it maximizes the society's income *ex hypothesi* because of the Coasean process underlying the determination of the extent of markets. (The maximization is implicit in the Coasean assumptions, rather than the deliberate choice of any individual, each of whom is seeking to minimize the transactions costs of the transactions in which they are engaged.) The idea that entirely decentralized contracting and other interactions would implement an efficient set of institutions in the Coasean sense is of course unrealistic; the key point is that markets will be used more were virtue is less. I adopt the Coasean framework simply because it makes clear that the cultural–institutional market failure thesis does not require any departures from conventional liberal economic models – other than the fact that markets have cultural consequences.

Because we want to know the conditions under which both culture and institutions will be stationary, we are interested in a state that is common to both functions, namely the intersection of the two lines representing relationships labeled "markets crowd out virtue" and "markets economize on virtue." The joint influence of these two relationships, shown in Panel C of Figure 2.1, gives us the equilibrium values of the level of virtue and extent of the market $\{v^*, m^*\}$, termed a cultural–institutional equilibrium. In Bowles (2011) I present a related model that differs in two ways: I take account of the long-term effects of markets on traditional institutions, such as lineage-based family structures and religious organizations, and show that there may be more than one stable cultural–institutional equilibrium. This is the case because all that we know about the $m(v)$ and $v(m)$ functions is that they slope downward, so were they non-linear (unlike here) they could intersect any number of times. Where there is more than a single stable equilibrium it may be that two identical societies differing only in their recent history may differ dramatically in their culture and institutions – one with extensive use of markets and limited virtue, and the other with the converse – with the possibility of precipitous transitions between the two. But to study cultural–institutional market failures – my topic here – a single stable equilibrium is sufficient, and much simpler.

The sophisticated Legislator corrects a cultural–institutional market failure

Let's now introduce a social planner recently graduated from the New School. Having studied *Adam's fallacy*, she had been motivated to venture beyond the confines of economics and had read: "Legislators make the citizen good by inculcating habits in them," in Aristotle's *Ethics*, "It is in this that a good constitution differs from a bad one." (Aristotle, 1962: 103). Could the sophisticated Legislator – that's what we'll call her – improve on the Coasean "income maximizing" institutional arrangements in the cultural–institutional equilibrium, namely point **a** in panel C of Figure 2.1?

A tall order, but she knows where to go: room 1123, 6 East 16th Street at the New School. She draws panel C of the figure on the whiteboard and explains to her former teacher how it works. Intrigued, he suggests that she consider educational programs that might enhance the level of citizen virtue, shifting up the $v(m)$ function (in panel C of the figure) and supporting a higher level of income in the new, more virtuous and less market oriented, cultural–institutional equilibrium. But the Legislator demurs, reminding Foley that public policies designed to change preferences would be regarded as paternalistic and in violation of the basic liberal precept that the state ought not to favor any particular conception of the good (or the good life; Goodin and Reeve (1989), Barry (1996)).

"What about the other function," she asks? Already at the whiteboard, Foley writes

$$\max_m = y(m, v) \text{ subject to } v = v(m) \text{ or } \max_m = y(m, v(m))$$

but he then recalls that the Legislator was never much of a whiz in math, and it had been a few years since she had seen something like this. "Because of your liberal biases," Foley patiently explains, "we have to take the $v(m)$ function as inviolate, so we're going to find the level of m along the $v(m)$ function that maximizes income." "And ..?", she wonders where this is going. "And then find some policies that will shift the $m(v)$ function so that the income-maximizing m is part of a cultural–institutional equilibrium." It's all coming back to her now: "OK, we find the point on the $v(m)$ function that is tangent to one of the isoquant things, right?" Foley writes

$$v'(m) = -y_m/y_v$$

"Or, the ..." he begins. She takes over, jumping to the whiteboard, tapping her finger on point **b** "... the marginal rate of transformation of markets into (degraded) values must be equal to the marginal rate of substitution of markets and values as influences on income." "Brava!", and Foley returns to his desk:

"How you implement this is your department; you're the Legislator." "No problem," she's happy to be back on more familiar ground, "there is no shortage of ways to make market transactions more expensive. The Tobin tax, named after one of your former teachers, is just an example."

She opens her computer without looking at Foley: "Sorry, but let me get this down" and starts typing:

From the Coasean *allegedly* income maximizing cultural–institutional equi-librium **a** [she smiles when she adds the italics], there must exist an exogenous restriction of market extent that would displace the market extent function to the left (given by the dashed line) and therefore shift the cultural institutional equilibrium to point **b**, resulting in a larger aggregate income. The income-maximizing level of restricted market use balances the income losses entailed by the use of non-market institutions (in cases for which, conditional on a given v, markets would do better) against the cultural benefits made possible by attenuating the deleterious market effects on culture. This cultural–institutional market failure arises because pro-social values facilitate exchange by reducing transaction costs, and in adopting contractual and other institutional choices, economic actors do not take account of the endogenous nature of preferences and hence do not internalize the negative externalities associated with market incentives.

She smiles again and looks up from her keyboard.

"Let me see" Foley says. She pushes her PC to the other side of the desk.

After a minute or two, beaming, he says "Bravissima!"

Acknowledgments

This chapter aims to celebrate the life and work (so far) of Duncan Foley. Thanks to the Behavioral Sciences Program of the Santa Fe Institute for support of this research. The model presented here draws on Bowles and Polania-Reyes (2012), Hwang and Bowles (2012 and 2013), Belloc and Bowles (2012 and 2013), and Bowles and Hwang (2008), and will be extended in Bowles (2013). I thank my just-mentioned co-authors as well as Lance Taylor, Elisabeth Wood, and two anonymous referees for their contributions.

Note

1 Burke (1791: 64); Burke (1890[1790]: 4–86); Tocqueville (1945: I 12; II 208, 334–337, 339); Hayek (1948); Polanyi (1957: 76–77, 177); Habermas (1975: 77,79); Hirsch (1976: 117–118); Schumpeter (1950). Some of the relevant passages appear in the appendix to Bowles (2011) that is available on my web page: http://www.santafe.edu/~bowles

References

Aristotle (1962) *Nicomachean ethics*. Indianapolis: Bobbs-Merrill.

Arrow, Kenneth J. (1971) 'Political and economic evaluation of social effects and externalities,' in *Frontiers of quantitative economics*. M. D. Intriligator (Ed.). Amsterdam: North Holland, pp. 3–23.

Barry, Brian (1996) *Justice as Impartiality*. Oxford: Clarendon Press.

Bell, Daniel (1973) *The coming of post-industrial society: a venture in social forecasting*. New York: Basic Books, Inc.

Bell, Daniel (1976) *The cultural contradictions of capitalism*. New York: Basic Books.

Belloc, Marianna, and Samuel Bowles (2012) 'International trade and the persistence of cultural–institutional diversity.' *Santa Fe Institute Working Paper 09-03-005*.

Belloc, Marianna, and Samuel Bowles (2013) 'The persistence of inferior cultural-institutional persistence conventions.' *American Economic Association, Papers and Proceedings*.

Ben-Porath, Yoram (1980) 'The F-connection: families, friends, and firms and the organization of exchange.' *Population and Development Review*, 6:1, 1–30.

Berkowitz, Peter (1999) *Virtue and the making of modern liberalism*. Princeton: Princeton University Press.

Bowles, Samuel (1998) 'Endogenous preferences: the cultural consequences of markets and other economic institutions.' *Journal of Economic Literature*, 36:1, 75–111.

Bowles, Samuel (2004) *Microeconomics: behavior, institutions, and evolution*. Princeton: Princeton University Press.

Bowles, Samuel (2008) 'Policies designed for self interested citizens may undermine "the moral sentiments:" evidence from experiments.' *Science*, 320:5883 (June 20).

Bowles, Samuel (2011) 'Is liberal society a parasite on tradition?' *Philosophy and Public Affairs*, 39:1, 47–81.

Bowles, Samuel (2013) *Machiavelli's mistake: why good laws are no substitute for good citizens*. New Haven: Yale University Press (forthcoming).

Bowles, Samuel, and Herbert Gintis (2011) *A cooperative species: human reciprocity and its evolution*. Princeton: Princeton University Press.

Bowles, Samuel, and Sung-Ha Hwang (2008) 'Social preferences and public economics: mechanism design when preferences depend on incentives.' *Journal of Public Economics*, 92:8–9, 1811–1820.

Bowles, Samuel, and Sandra Polania-Reyes (2012) 'Economic incentives and social preferences: substitutes or complements?' *Journal of Economic Literature*, 50:2, 368–425.

Burke, Edmund (1791) *A letter from Mr. Burke to a member of the National Assembly in answer to some objections to his book on French affairs*. London: Dodsley, Pall-Mall.

Burke, Edmund (1890)[1790] *Reflections on the revolution in France*. New York: Macmillian.

Coase, R. H. (1937) 'The nature of the firm.' *Economica*, 4, 386–405.

Foley, Duncan (2006) *Adam's fallacy: a guide to economic theology*. Cambridge, MA: Harvard University Press.

Galbiati, Roberto, and Pietro Vertova (2010) 'How laws affect behaviour: obligations, incentives and cooperative behavior.' Universita Bocconi.

Gintis, Herbert, Samuel Bowles, Robert Boyd, and Ernst Fehr (Eds.) (2005) *Moral sentiments and material interests: the foundations of cooperation in economic life*. Cambridge, MA: MIT Press.

Goodin, Robert E., and Andrew Reeve (Eds.) (1989) *Liberal Neutrality*. London: Routledge.

Habermas, Jurgen (1975) *Legitimation crisis*. Boston: Beacon Press.

Hayek, Friedrich (1948) *Individualism and economic order*. Chicago: University of Chicago Press.

Hirsch, Fred (1976) *Social limits to growth*. Cambridge, MA: Harvard University Press.

Hirschman, Albert O (1977) *The passions and the interests: political arguments for capitalism before its triumph*. Princeton: Princeton University Press.

Hwang, Sung Ha, and Samuel Bowles (2012a) 'Optimal incentives with state-dependent preferences.' *Journal of Public Economic Theory*, in press.

Hwang, Sung-Ha, and Samuel Bowles (2012b) 'The sophisticated planner's dilemma: optimal incentives with endogenous preferences.' Santa Fe Institute.

Kohn, Melvin, Atsushi Naoi, Carrie Schoenbach, Carmi Schooler, et al. (1990) 'Position in the class structure and psychological functioning in the U.S., Japan, and Poland.' *American Journal of Sociology*, 95:4, 964–1008.

Montesquieu, Charles de Secondat (1961) *L'esprit des lois*. Paris: Garnier.

Ostrom, Elinor (1990) *Governing the commons: the evolution of institutions for collective action*. Cambridge, UK: Cambridge University Press.

Polanyi, Karl (1957) *The great transformation: the political and economic origins of our time*. Beacon Hill: Beacon Press.

Schultze, Charles L. (1977) *The public use of private interest*. Washington, D.C: Brookings Institution.

Schumpeter, Joseph (1950) 'The march into socialism.' *American Economic Review*, 40:2, 446–456.

Tabellini, Guido (2008) 'Institutions and culture.' *Journal of the European Economic Association*, 6:2, 255–294.

Tocqueville, Alexis de (1945) *Democracy in America*. New York: Vintage.

3 The complex evolution of Duncan K. Foley as a complexity economist

J. Barkley Rosser, Jr.

Introduction

Duncan K. Foley has always dealt with the larger and deeper questions of economics since the day he walked into Herbert Scarf's class on mathematical economics at Yale University in the 1960s, with Scarf becoming his major professor. Scarf (1960, 1973) was the leading figure in the study of how to compute general equilibria and the problems of their uniqueness and stability, problems that Foley (2010a) has pursued to the present day in the form of the related issues of convergence to general equilibria from non-equilibrium states. The pursuit of these issues would lead him to the problem of microfoundations of macroeconomics, which he saw as involving money and which he studied with the late Miguel Sidrauski (Foley and Sidrauski, 1971). Considering the problem of money would lead him to pursue the study of Marxian economics as possibly resolving this problem (Foley, 1982), a pursuit that would lead to his experiencing professional problems in the 1970s. But, he has continued to pursue the broader issue of the role of money in the economy, even while feeling some frustration along the way at trying to fill this "one of the big lacunae of economic theory."[1]

While these topics as discussed so far are not obviously parts of what is called complexity economics, the pursuit of these matters would indeed lead him to pursue various forms of complexity economics. The initial link would be his reviving the model of Goodwin (1951) in a paper on the role of liquidity in business cycles, looking at the endogenous appearance of limit cycles, although these are at most on the edge of complexity models (Foley, 1986). This laid the groundwork for him to pursue ideas and approaches regarding statistical mechanics he had been previously interested in, and also the role of the computer in economic decision-making and a more algorithmic and engineering approach to economics.[2] Meeting the late Peter Albin in the late 1980s would lead to collaboration with him (Albin and Foley, 1992; Albin with Foley, 1998) in which he pursued a more computational approach to complexity, albeit with some discussion of dynamic issues as well. During the same period he also took up the problem of applying statistical mechanics to general equilibrium theory (Foley, 1994), following on the work of Föllmer (1974), leading to a more specifically econophysics approach that linked more fully to considerations of the law of entropy (Foley and Smith, 2008), as he became associated with the Santa Fe Institute and moved more clearly to pursue the complexity approach to modeling economics.

The rest of this essay honoring Duncan will focus on how his work in this area of complexity economics has related to ongoing controversies regarding the nature of complexity, and particularly which approach is most useful for economics. In particular, there has been an ongoing debate between those who focus more on computational complexity (Velupillai, 2009), and those who concentrate on dynamic complexity (Rosser, 2009). It can be broadly said that, while Foley has tended to pursue and advocate more the computational complexity approach based on his work with Albin, he has also studied and articulated views about the dynamic approach, and has suggested possible ways that the two approaches can be reconciled.

A brief overview of competing approaches to complexity

What complexity is, is a topic that has been beaten more or less to death in the existing literature, so we shall keep our discussion short here. Over a decade ago, Seth Lloyd of MIT famously gathered 45 definitions of complexity (Horgan, 1997, Chap. 11), with this not being a comprehensive list. The list can be viewed as comprising *meta-complexity*, the full set of definitions of complexity. Many of these 45 can be aggregated into sub-categories, with the sub-categories arguably containing more of these definitions than any other computational complexity, or variants thereof. Many of these definitions are variations on a theme of the minimum length of a computer program required to solve a problem, but there are many variations on this. Furthermore, a hardline group argues that the only truly computationally complex systems are those that are undecidable due to halting problems in their programs (Blum, Cucker, Shub, and Smale, 1998). In any case, an argument made by those advocating the superiority of the computational approach to complexity is that it may be more precisely measurable, assuming one can agree on what is the appropriate measure, with well-defined hierarchies involved; although the hierarchy favored by Foley is not necessarily the same as that emphasized by some others.

Among economists, almost certainly the main rival is dynamic complexity, defined by Rosser (1999), following Day (1994) as being systems that do not endogenously move to a point, a limit cycle, or a smooth implosion or smooth explosion.[3] Such systems inevitably involve either nonlinear dynamics or coupled linear systems that can be reduced to nonlinear systems (Goodwin, 1947). There are sub-categories of this form of complexity, with the "4 C's" described by Horgan (1997) being the main ones: cybernetics, catastrophe theory, chaos theory, and heterogeneous agent complexity. This latter has increasingly become what many mean by the term "complexity" in economics, with Arthur, Durlauf, and Lane (1997) laying out crucial characteristics of this approach, favored at the Santa Fe Institute, and often involving computer simulations. Given the interest of Foley in models using computer simulations of the sorts used at the Santa Fe Institute, such as cellular automata, it is not surprising that he is interested in these forms of complexity, although often emphasizing more the computability side of their use over the dynamics side of their use. As laid out by Arthur, Durlauf, and Lane (1997), this approach is very much an antithesis of a general equilibrium perspective, with agents interacting locally with each other without ever necessarily being in any overall or general equilibrium, and not ever necessarily arriving at one. Many econophysics models arguably follow this pattern, although it can be debated whether or not Foley's own forays into econophysics fully fit this model.

Foley on computational complexity

Foley's most important direct work on questions related to computational complexity arose from his collaborations with the late Peter Albin. Most significantly, when Albin fell ill while working on a book covering his approach to this, Foley stepped in and edited a volume consisting mostly of previously published papers by Albin (Albin with Foley, 1998). As part of this, he wrote a substantial introductory chapter (pp. 3–72) in which he laid out his own perspective on such matters as nonlinear dynamical systems, the nature of complexity, various approaches to computational complexity, and other related issues. As the introductory chapter to a book mostly by Albin, it very much followed Albin's views, although it would seem that at least at that time, Foley's views were fairly much in synch with those of Albin. This becomes important in that Albin was arguably the first economist to study computational complexity as it relates to economic systems (Albin, 1982, reprinted as Chap. 2 of Albin with Foley, 1998), although the subject of computational complexity in general had long been studied by many others in addition to those mentioned in the following paragraphs.

In particular, Albin emphasized computability problems associated with the halting problem, and the limits (or "barriers and bounds") this imposed on full rationality by economic agents. Drawing on the literature deriving from Gödel's Incompleteness Theorem as connected to computer science by Alan Turing (1936–37), he emphasized especially the role of self-referencing in bringing about these failures to halt, or infinite do-loops in programs. Such self-referencing can lead to such problems as the Cretan Liar paradox, "Is a Cretan who says 'All Cretans are liars' telling the truth?" Such questions can lead to an endless going back and forth between "yes" and "no," becoming undecidable as the program fails to halt at a solution. Albin argued that economies are full of such self-referencing, which implies such non-decidabilities from a computability perspective, a swarm of unstoppable infinite regresses, and Foley agreed.[4]

Albin was strongly influenced by the ideas of Stephen Wolfram (1986), who in turn has been strongly influenced by those of Noam Chomsky (1959). In his discussion of complexity in the introductory chapter of Albin with Foley (1998), Foley follows through on these lines, discussing in succession computational complexity, linguistic complexity, and machine complexity. His initial discussion of computational complexity makes it clear that he is going to embed it within the four-level hierarchy developed by Chomsky, and show how undecidability is a form of computational complexity that undermines full rationality. This is followed by a discussion of how computational complexity and dynamic complexity relate, which in turn is followed by a more detailed discussion of cellular automata and the forms of complexity in them.

Central to this entire discussion is the four-level hierarchy of languages, initially due to Chomsky (1959). Chomsky defines a formal language as consisting of finite sets of an alphabet of T terminal symbols (words), intermediate variables V, and a distinguished variable S that serves to initiate productions in the language. These take the form of $P \rightarrow Q$, where P is a string composed of one or more variables with zero or more terminals and Q is a string composed of any combination of variables and terminals.

The lowest of these is the category of *regular languages*, generated by grammars that take the form $P \rightarrow T$ or $P \rightarrow TQ$, where P and Q are variables and T is a string of terminal symbols that make up the regular language. At the next level up are the *context-free languages*, which include the regular languages. The grammars generating these take the form of $P \rightarrow Q$, where P is a string of variables and Q a string composed of terminal symbols and variables, without contextual restrictions. Above this is the level of *context-sensitive languages* that are generated by grammars such that $P \rightarrow Q$ have the length of Q at least as long as the length of P, this group likewise contains another one lower down. For these, if Q is a non-empty string and $P_1PP_2 \rightarrow P_1QP_2$, then Q and P can be substituted for each other in the context of P_1 and P_2, but not necessarily in other contexts. The highest level of these grammars generates *unrestricted languages*, which only need to follow the most general rules described above and will include the most complex formal languages. Each of the higher levels contains within it the level below it in an embedded or nested form.

This hierarchy is then seen to translate directly to a four-level hierarchy of machine complexity. At the lowest level is the finite automaton that that has a finite set of states and reads simple inputs off a tape to generate simple outputs, with a pocket calculator as an example. This corresponds to the regular languages. By adding an unbounded pushdown stack on which the automaton can store and retrieve symbols on a first-in and last-out basis, one can recognize context-free languages. Having two bounded pushdowns moves one to the context-sensitive level. Having two unbounded pushdowns generates the level of unrestricted languages and becomes equivalent to an abstract Turing machine. Foley interprets all of these as representing informational and computational problems for economic decision-makers.[5]

Foley then pulls what is the neat trick of applying all this to the analysis of dynamic complexity, which he sees as also having such a hierarchy, although in this he follows Wolfram. The dynamic equivalent of regular languages and finite automata are simple linear dynamical systems that converge on point attractors. The next stage up, equivalent to context-free languages and one pushdown automaton, consists of nonlinear systems that endogenously generate periodic cycles as their attractors.

Context-sensitive languages and the two-bounded pushdown automata are equivalent to nonlinear dynamical systems that can go to a chaotic attractor. The break between this level and the previous one is equivalent to the line between the non-dynamically complex and the dynamically complex systems according to the Day–Rosser definition. Foley notes that at this level there can be long-period relations, such as a parenthesis that opens and is closed much later. He identifies this with such economic phenomena as a loan being made that must then be paid back at some later time. He also notes that for this level, computing costs may rise so sharply that it may become impractical to actually solve problems, even if they are decidable in principle. This is somewhat equivalent to the break between *P* and *NP* systems more generally in the computational complexity literature, although it remains unproven that these really are distinct levels.

Finally, the equivalent of the unrestricted languages and two-unbounded pushdown automata are equivalent to Turing machines and may be undecidable. Monotonicities holding at the other levels break down at this level.

Foley then discusses Wolfram's more specific adaptation of these categories to cellular automata. Type 1 evolve to uniform states. Type 2 evolve to periodic patterns from arbitrary initial conditions. Type 3 evolve to irregular patterns. And Type 4 generate a much broader range of possibilities, including non-monotonic ones in which a simple outcome may be the result of an enormously complicated set of generated structures. Foley links this to "edge of chaos" ideas of self-organizing systems, and sees this level as that level where new structures can emerge. In Albin's discussion of this, he ties it to the original von Neumann (1966) formulation for cellular automata that can self-reproduce, with von Neumann likening the jump from one level to another as being marked by complexity thresholds.

This is a stunning way of integrating the supposedly competing approaches to complexity, and I find it impressive. However, I also question whether this fully captures all the dynamic phenomena one observes in dynamically complex systems. In particular, there is the matter of emergence, argued by many to be at the very heart of dynamic complexity in systems ranging from evolution to urban development (Rosser, 2011). Two responses to this are that it may be captured by the highest level of Chomsky–Wolfram complexity. Another is to say that the supposed inability of computational systems to deal with this is a sign that such emergence is really not a proper complexity concept, with computational systems that provide genuine novelty (Moore, 1990) being the more useful concept.[6]

The dynamic complexity of Foley's econophysics

In the wake of his work with Peter Albin, Duncan Foley was also moving in another direction, into the world of complexity economics, of reconsidering the role of statistical mechanics as a foundation for general equilibrium theory, or more accurately, an alternative version of that theory. Mirowski (1989) has documented that the seminal developer of statistical mechanics theory, J. Willard

Gibbs (1902),[7] had a profound influence on efforts in the US to mathematize neoclassical economic theory, both through Irving Fisher and later through Paul Samuelson (1947), who always looked to Gibbs as a source and inspiration, thanks to the direct influence of Gibbs's student, Edwin Bidwell Wilson at the University of Chicago. However, after this time the ideas of Gibbs were progressively less directly influential on economists. In any case, Samuelson was more influenced by other parts of Gibbs's work than by that on statistical mechanics.

The idea that an equilibrium might not be just a vector of prices (an idea certainly consistent with Gibbsian vector analysis), but a probability distribution of prices was the idea that Foley would pursue.[8] His important paper of 1994 in the *Journal of Economic Theory* would do just that, and would fit in with the emerging new confluence of economics and physics ideas that was happening at the Santa Fe Institute with which he would become affiliated, and which would take form as *econophysics* shortly thereafter, with H. Eugene Stanley coining this term in 1995, a year after Foley's article appeared (Rosser, 2008).

Central to Foley's approach was the idea that an equilibrium state should be associated with a maximization of entropy, a deeply Gibbsian idea, as Gibbs was also a founder of chemical thermodynamics. This was an aspect that Samuelson did not approve of so much. He made this clear at a symposium honoring Gibbs (Samuelson, 1990, p. 263):

> I have come over the years to have some impatience and boredom to find those who try to find an analogue of the entropy of Clausius or Boltzman or Shannon[9] to put into economic theory. It is the *mathematical* structure of *classical* (phenomenological, macroscopic, nonstochastic) *thermodynamics* that has isomorphisms with *theoretical economics*.

Not for Samuelson would there be stochastic processes or probability distributions of price outcomes. His Gibbs was the "nonstochastic" Gibbs.

Foley followed the later Gibbs of statistical mechanics, the student of the foundation of temperature in the stochastic processes of molecular dynamics. It was in this nonlinear world that phase transitions became important in studying such phenomena as the freezing, melting, boiling, or condensation of water at critical temperatures. Foley's interest in nonlinear dynamics had long been more along the lines of understanding bifurcations of dynamical systems than in the precise natures of erratic trajectories, chaotic or not. Statistical mechanics offered an approach to understanding such bifurcations within the purview of his old topic of study, general equilibrium theory.

In any case, he pursued the idea of a thermodynamic equilibrium in which entropy is maximized.[10] A difference between this sort of equilibrium and the more standard Walrasian one is that this statistical mechanics equilibrium lacks the welfare economics implications that the Walrasian equilibrium has. There would be no Pareto optimality for such a stochastic equilibrium, an equilibrium in which a good is being exchanged for many different prices across a set of heterogeneous traders in discrete bilateral transactions, with the set of those prices conforming to the distribution given by the maximization of entropy, this is occurring across all goods and services.

One limit of the traditional Gibbsian model is that it is a conservative system, which usually means, for a model of economic exchange, that one is dealing with a pure exchange model. While much of general equilibrium theory has been developed using such an assumption, Foley was able to expand this to include both production and exchange. The key strong assumption he made was that all possible transactions in the economy have an equal probability. A curious outcome of this model is the possibility of negative prices coinciding with positive ones for the same good. While conventional theory rejects such ideas, and indeed even the idea of a negative price for something at all,[11] such outcomes have been observed in real life, as in the Babylonian bride markets as reported by Herodotus, wherein the most beautiful brides command positive prices, while the ugliest command negative ones, even in the same auction. This phenomenon is coming to be known as the "Herodotus paradox," (Baye, Kovenock, and de Vries, 2012), and it is to Foley's credit that he allows for such outcomes, in contrast with long traditions of general equilibrium theory that insist on strictly non-negative prices for equilibrium solutions.

In his model there are m commodities, n agents of r types, k with offer set A^k. The proportion of agents of type k who achieve a particular transaction x out of mn possible ones is given by $h^k[x]$. The *multiplicity* of an assignment is the number of ways n agents can be assigned to S actions, with n_s being the number of agents assigned to action s, which is given by

$$\mathbf{W}[\{n_s\}] = n!/(n_1!\ldots n_s!\ldots n_S!). \tag{1}$$

A measure of this multiplicity is the informational entropy of the distribution, which is given by

$$\boldsymbol{H}\{h^k[x]\} = -\Sigma_{k=1}{}^r \mathbf{W}^k \Sigma_{x=1}{}^{mn} h^k[x] \ln h^k[x]. \tag{2}$$

This is then maximized subject to a pair of feasibility constraints given by

$$\Sigma_{x\varepsilon Ak} h^k[x] = 1, \tag{3}$$

$$\Sigma_{k=1}{}^r \mathbf{W}^k \Sigma_{x\varepsilon Ak} h^k[x]x = 0, \tag{4}$$

resulting in a unique solution if the feasibility set is non-empty of the canonical Gibbs form given by

$$h^k[x] = \exp[-\pi x]/\Sigma_x \exp[-\pi x], \tag{5}$$

where the vectors $\pi \varepsilon R^m$ are the entropy shadow prices.

Foley has continued to follow this line of inquiry (Foley and Smith, 2008), which is more in line with developments in econophysics from this time forward. Foley has not pursued the issue of whether or not these distributions will obey power laws, a major concern of econophysicists, although he does accept their argument that financial market returns do tend to follow such laws. He has expressed the view that these newer ideas from physics can help move economics into a broader social science perspective along more realistic lines than has been seen in the past (Colander, Holt, and Rosser, 2004: p. 212):

> The study of economic data surely has a future, but the question is whether it will be recognizable as economics in today's terms and whether it will exhibit any unity of subject matter and method.

Conclusion

Duncan Foley's intellectual career has emphasized fundamental issues of economic theory, particularly general equilibrium theory. This initially concerned the loose ends of uniqueness and stability and how the role of money might allow for a proper microfoundation for macroeconomics. However, as he pursued these questions through various approaches and over time, he eventually moved towards the two leading strands of complexity within economics, the computational and the dynamic. He became involved in the former through his collaboration with the late Peter Albin, the first economist to seriously deal with problems of computational complexity. They followed the route of using the four-hierarchy-level model of Chomsky as adumbrated by Wolfram. A particular emphasis of their interests were in the problems of non-decidability that can arise in such systems, and how this limits full rationality by agents.

He would also move towards the sorts of dynamics associated with the econophysics movement by using the statistical mechanics methods developed initially by J. Willard Gibbs, although as applied to information theory by such figures as Shannon and Jaynes. This allowed him to establish a maximum entropy equilibrium of a distribution of price outcomes that could allow for both positive and negative prices for specific goods, and that also lacked any welfare implications.

A particular outcome of his earlier work was a possible integration of the computational and dynamic approaches. This involved classifying patterns of dynamic paths arising from nonlinear economic systems into the four-level hierarchy developed by Chomsky and Wolfram. One may not agree that this is the best way to reconcile these mostly competing approaches to economic complexity. However, it must be granted that this is an ingenious intellectual achievement, and not the only one that Duncan Foley has achieved in his distinguished intellectual career.

Notes

1 Colander, Holt, and Rosser (2004, 196). This is from an interview with Foley in this book, and in connection with that remark he compared studying money to an odyssey like that of Ulysses trying to reach his home in Ithaca, finally confessing when asked, "So, you haven't reached Ithaca yet?" that "No, and I probably never will" (ibid.).

2 He worked as a computer programmer in an instrument and control company for three summers when young (Colander, Holt, and Rosser, 2004, 186).

3 Ironically, this definition is not among the 45 that Lloyd listed earlier in the 1990s, although a few of those he listed have some similarities to it.

4 Velupillai (2000) has emphasized the distinction between "computable economics" and "computational economics," with the former more concerned with these matters of whether or not a program halts or not, as Albin and Foley see it, whereas more conventional computational economics is more concerned with such issues as trying to figure out the most efficient way to program a system or problem or class of problem (Tesfatsion and Judd, 2006). Curiously enough, the issue of computational complexity is involved with the concerns of computational economics, as the most efficient program may also be the shortest in length, which is tied to many of the more widely used measures of computational complexity.

5 Mirowski (2007) uses this four-level hierarchy to extend this analysis directly to markets, arguing that they are fundamentally algorithms, and that market forms themselves evolve in a manner consistent with natural selection, with the equivalent of finite automata being spot markets, with futures markets the next level up, options markets above and embedding both of them, and so forth.

6 Foley (2010b) has continued to deal with problems of computational complexity at a theoretical level.

7 Gibbs also invented vector analysis independently of Oliver Heaviside.

8 Hans Föllmer (1974) would pursue this idea, only to have no one until Foley follow up on it with a more general approach.

9 It was Shannon (1951) who initially linked entropy with information theory. A major influence on Foley's thinking came through this link as discussed by Jaynes (1957).

10 While not doing so along the lines of Foley, others who have applied the entropy concept to either economics or spatial dynamics have included Wilson (1970), Georgescu-Roegen (1971), Stutzer (1994), and Weidlich (2000). Julius Davidson (1919) posed the law of entropy as the ultimate foundation for the law of diminishing returns.

11 As long as the price for something is strictly negative, then one can turn it into a positive price for removing that something. We pay for water being supplied when it is scarce, but pay for it to be removed when there are floods.

References

Albin, P.S. (1982) 'The metalogic of economic predictions, calculations, and propositions', *Mathematical Social Sciences*, 3: 329–358.

Albin, P.S., and Foley, D.K. (1992) 'Decentralized, dispersed exchange without an auctioneer: A simulation study', *Journal of Economic Behavior and Organization*, 18: 27–51.

Albin, P.S., with Foley, D.K. (1998) *Barriers and Bounds to Rationality: Essays on Economic Complexity and Dynamics in Interactive Systems*, Princeton: Princeton University Press.

Arthur, W.B., Durlauf, S.N., and Lane, D.A. (1997) 'Introduction', in Arthur, W.B., Durlauf, S.N., and Lane, D.A. (eds.) *The Economy as an Evolving Complex System II*, Reading: Addison-Wesley.

Baye, M.A., Kovenock, D., and de Vries, C. (2012) 'The Herodotus paradox', *Games and Economic Behavior*, 74: 399–406.

Blum, L., Cucker, F., Shub, M., and Smale, S. (1998) *Complexity and Real Computation*, New York: Springer.

Chomsky, N. (1959) 'On certain properties of grammars', *Information and Control*, 2: 137–167.

Colander, D., Holt, R.P.F., and Rosser, J.B., Jr. (2004) *The Changing Face of Economics: Conversations with Cutting Edge Economists*, Ann Arbor: University of Michigan Press.

Davidson, J. (1919) 'One of the physical foundations of economics', *Quarterly Journal of Economics*, 33: 717–724.

Day, R.H. (1994) *Complex Economic Dynamics: An Introduction to Dynamical Systems and Market Mechanisms, Volume I*, Cambridge, MA: MIT Press.

Foley, D.K. (1982) 'Realization and accumulation in a Marxian model of the circuit of capital'. *Journal of Economic Theory* 28: 300–319.

Foley, D.K. (1986) 'Liquidity–profit rate cycles in a capitalist economy', *Journal of Economic Behavior and Organization*, 8: 363–376.

Foley, D.K. (1994) 'A statistical equilibrium theory of markets', *Journal of Economic Theory*, 62: 321–345.

Foley, D.K. (2010a) 'What's wrong with the fundamental existence and welfare theorems?', *Journal of Economic Behavior and Organization*,75: 115–131.

Foley, D.K. (2010b) 'Model description length priors in the urn problem', in Zambelli, S. (ed.) *Computable, Constructive and Behavioural Economic Dynamics: Essays in Honour of Kumaraswamy (Vela) Velupillai*, Milton Park: Routledge.

Foley, D.K., and Sidrauski, M. (1971) *Monetary and Fiscal Policy in a Growing Economy*, New York: Macmillan.

Foley, D.K., and Smith, E. (2008) 'Classical thermodynamics and general equilibrium theory', *Journal of Economic Dynamics and Control*, 32: 7–65.

Föllmer, H. (1974) 'Random economies with many interacting agents', *Journal of Mathematical Economics*, 1: 51–62.

Georgescu-Roegen, N. (1971) *The Entropy Law and the Economic Process*, Cambridge: Harvard University Press.

Gibbs, J.W. (1902) *Elementary Principles of Statistical Mechanics*, New Haven: Yale University Press.

Goodwin, R.M. (1947) 'Dynamical coupling with especial reference to markets having production lags', *Econometrica*, 15: 181–204.

Goodwin, R.M. (1951) 'The nonlinear accelerator and the persistence of business cycles', *Econometrica*, 19: 1–17.

Horgan, J. (1997) *The End of Science: Facing the Limits of Knowledge in the Twilight of the Scientific Age*, New York: Broadway Books.

Jaynes, E.T. (1957) 'Information theory and statistical mechanics', *Physical Review*, 106: 620–638; 108: 171–190.

Mirowski, P. (1989) *More Heat than Light: Economics as Social Physics, Physics as Nature's Economics*, Cambridge, UK: Cambridge University Press.

Mirowski, P. (2007) 'Markets come to bits: Evolution, computation, and makomata in economic science', *Journal of Economic Behavior and Organization*, 63: 209–242.

Moore, C. (1990) 'Undecidability and unpredictability in dynamical systems', *Physical Review Letters*, 64: 2354–2357.

Rosser, J.B., Jr. (1999) 'On the complexities of complex economic dynamics', *Journal of Economic Perspectives*, 13: 169–192.

Rosser, J.B., Jr. (2008) 'Debating the role of econophysics', *Nonlinear Dynamics, Psychology, and Life Sciences*, 12: 311–323.

Rosser, J.B., Jr. (2009) 'Computational and dynamic complexity in economics', in Rosser, J.B., Jr. (ed.) *Handbook of Complexity Research*, Cheltenham: Edward Elgar.

Rosser, J.B., Jr. (2011) *Complex Evolutionary Dynamics in Urban-Regional and Ecologic-Economic Systems*, New York: Springer.

Samuelson, P.A. (1947) *The Foundations of Economic Analysis*, Cambridge, MA: Harvard University Press.

Samuelson, P.A. (1990) 'Gibbs in economics', in Caldi, G., and Mostow, G.D. (eds.) *Proceedings of the Gibbs Symposium*, Providence: American Mathematical Society.

Scarf, H.E. (1960) 'Some examples of global instability of competitive equilibrium', *International Economic Review*, 1: 157–172.

Scarf, H.E. (1973) *The Computation of Economic Equilibria*, New Haven: Yale University Press.

Shannon, C.E. (1951) 'Prediction and entropy of printed English', *The Bell System Technical Journal*, 30: 50–64.

Stutzer, M.J. (1994) 'The statistical mechanics of asset prices', in Elworthy, K.D., Everitt, W.N., and Lee, E.B. (eds.) *Differential Equations, Dynamical Systems, and Control Science: A Festschrift in Honor of Leonard Markus*, New York: Marcel Dekker.

Tesfatsion, L., and Judd, K.L. (eds.) (2006) *Handbook of Computational Economics, Volume 2: Agent-Based Computational Economics*, Amsterdam: Elsevier.

Turing, A.M. (1936–37) 'On computable numbers with an application to the *Entscheidungsproblem*', *Proceedings of the London Mathematical Society, Series 2*, 43: 544–546.

Velupillai, K.V. (2000) *Computable Economics*, Oxford: Oxford University Press.

Velupillai, K.V. (2009) 'A computable economist's perspective on computational complexity', in Rosser, J.B., Jr. (ed.) *Handbook of Complexity Research*, Cheltenham: Edward Elgar.

von Neumann, J., completed by Burks, A.W. (1966) *Theory of Self Reproducing Automata*, Urbana: University of Illinois Press.

Weidlich, W. (2000) *Sociodynamics: A Systematic Approach to Mathematical Modelling in the Social Sciences*, Amsterdam: Harwood.

Wilson, A.G. (1970) *Entropy in Urban and Regional Modelling*, London: Pion.

Wolfram, S. (ed.) (1986) *Theory and Applications of Cellular Automata*, Singapore: World Scientific.

4 Applications of statistical mechanics to economics

Entropic origin of the probability distributions of money, income, and energy consumption

Victor M. Yakovenko

"Money, it's a gas." Pink Floyd, Dark Side of the Moon

How I met Duncan Foley

Although I am a theoretical physicist, I have been always interested in economics and, in particular, in applications of statistical physics to economics. These ideas first occurred to me when I was an undergraduate student at the Moscow Physical-Technical Institute in Russia and studied statistical physics for the first time. However, it was not until 2000 when I published my first paper on this subject (Drăgulescu and Yakovenko, 2000), joining the emerging movement of econophysics (Farmer, Shubik, and Smith, 2005; Hogan, 2005; Shea, 2005). At that time, I started looking for economists who might be interested in a statistical approach to economics. I attended a seminar by Eric Slud, a professor of mathematics at the University of Maryland, who independently explored similar ideas and eventually published them in Silver, Slud, and Takamoto (2002). In this paper, I saw a reference to a paper by Foley (1994). So, I contacted Duncan in January 2001 and invited him to give a talk at the University of Maryland, which he did in March. Since then, our paths have crossed many times. I visited the New School for Social Research in New York several times, and we also met and had discussions at the Santa Fe Institute, where I was spending a part of my sabbatical in January–February 2009, hosted by Doyne Farmer. During these visits, I also met other innovative economists at the New School, professors Anwar Shaikh and Willi Semler, as well as Duncan's Ph.D. student at that time Mishael Milaković, who is now a professor of economics at the University of Bamberg in Germany.

As is explained on the first page of Foley (1994), Duncan learned statistical physics by taking a course on statistical thermodynamics at Dartmouth College. For me, the papers by Foley (1994, 1996, 1999) conjure an image of people who meet on a bridge trying to reach the same ideas by approaching from the opposite banks, physics and economics. Over time, I learned about other papers where economists utilize statistical and entropic ideas, e.g. Aoki and Yoshikawa (2006); Golan (1994); Molico (2006), but I also realized how exceedingly rare a statistical approach is among mainstream economists. Duncan is one of the very few innovative economists who has studied statistical physics deeply and attempted to make use of it in economics.

One puzzling social problem is persistent economic inequality among the population in any society. In statistical physics, it is well known that identical ("equal") molecules in a gas spontaneously develop a widely unequal distribution of energies as a result of random energy transfers in molecular collisions. By analogy, very unequal probability distributions can spontaneously develop in an economic system as a result of random interactions between economic agents. This is the main idea of the material presented in this chapter.

First, I will briefly review the basics of statistical physics and then discuss and compare the applications of these ideas to economics in Foley (1994, 1996, 1999) and in my papers, from the first paper (Drăgulescu and Yakovenko, 2000) to the most recent review papers (Banerjee and Yakovenko, 2010; Yakovenko and Rosser, 2009) and books (Cockshott, Cottrell, Michaelson, Wright, and Yakovenko, 2009; Yakovenko, 2011). As we shall see, statistical and entropic ideas have a multitude of applications to the probability distributions of money, income, and global energy consumption. The latter topic has relevance to the ongoing debate about the economics of global warming (Rezai, Foley, and Taylor, 2012). Duncan Foley and Eric Smith of the Santa Fe Institute have also published a profound study of the connection between phenomenological thermodynamics in physics and the utility formalism in economics (Smith and Foley, 2008). This paper will not be reviewed here because of limited space. Unfortunately, there is still no complete understanding of a connection between statistical mechanics and phenomenological thermodynamics as applied to economics. These issues remain open for future study. I will only focus on statistical mechanics in this chapter.

Entropy and the Boltzmann–Gibbs distribution of energy in physics

In this section, I briefly review the basics of statistical physics, starting from a discrete model of a quantum paramagnet. Let us consider a collection of N atoms and label the individual atoms with the integer index $j = 1, 2, \ldots, N$. It is convenient to visualize the atoms as sitting on a lattice, as shown in Figure 4.1. Each atom has an internal quantum degree of freedom called the spin s and can be in one of the q discrete states. These states are labeled using the index $k = 1, 2, \ldots, q$. The system is placed in an external magnetic field, so each discrete state has a different energy ε_k. Then, the state of an atom j can be characterized by the energy ε_j that this atom has. (Throughout the chapter, I use the indices i and j to label individual atoms or agents, and the index k to label possible states of the atoms or agents.) A simple case with $q = 2$ is illustrated in Figure 4.1, where each atom can be in one of the two possible states $k = 1 =\uparrow$ or $k = 2 =\downarrow$, which are depicted as the spin-up and spin-down states. Alternatively, one can interpret each atom as a bit of computer memory with two possible states 0 and 1. For $q = 8$, each atom would correspond to a byte with 8 possible values. The atoms can be also interpreted as economic agents, where the index k indicates an internal state of each agent.

Figure 4.1 A quantum paramagnet, where each atom has the spin $s = 1/2$ and is in one of the two possible states ($q = 2$): $k = 1 = \uparrow$ or $k = 2 = \downarrow$. The atoms are labeled consecutively using the integer index $j = 1, 2, \ldots, N$.

For a given configuration of atoms, let us count how many atoms are in each state k and denote these numbers as N_k, so that $\sum_{k=1}^{q} N_k = N$. Let us introduce the multiplicity Ω, which is the number of different atomic configurations that have the same set of the numbers N_k. Calculating Ω, we treat the atoms as distinguishable, because they are localized on distinguishable lattice sites labeled by the index j in Figure 4.1. For example, let us consider the case of $N = 2$ and $q = 2$, i.e. two atoms with two possible states. The set $N_1 = 1$ and $N_2 = 1$ can be realized in two possible ways, so $\Omega = 2$. In one configuration, the first atom $j = 1$ is in the state $k = 1 = \uparrow$ with the energy $\varepsilon_1 = \varepsilon_\uparrow$, whereas the second atom $j = 2$ is in the state $k = 2 = \downarrow$ with the energy $\varepsilon_2 = \varepsilon_\downarrow$. In another configuration, the states of the atoms are reversed. On the other hand, the set $N_1 = 2$ and $N_2 = 0$ can be realized in only one way, where both atoms are in the state $k = 1 = \uparrow$ with the energies $\varepsilon_1 = \varepsilon_2 = \varepsilon_\uparrow$, so $\Omega = 1$. In general, the multiplicity Ω can be calculated combinatorially as the number of different placements of N atoms into q boxes with the fixed occupations N_k of each box:

$$\Omega = \frac{N!}{N_1! N_2! N_3! \ldots N_q!}. \tag{1}$$

The logarithm of multiplicity is called the entropy $S = \ln \Omega$. Using the Stirling approximation for the factorials in the limit of large numbers N_k, we obtain

$$S = N \ln N - \sum_{k=1}^{q} N_k \ln N_k = - \sum_{k=1}^{q} N_k \ln \left(\frac{N_k}{N} \right). \tag{2}$$

In the absence of further information, we assume that all microscopic configurations of atoms are equally probable. Then, the probability of observing a certain set of the numbers N_k is proportional to the number of possible microscopic realizations of this set, i.e. to the multiplicity Ω. So, the most probable set of the numbers N_k is the one that maximizes Ω or S subject to certain constraints. The typical constraints for a closed system are that the total number of atoms N and the total energy E are fixed:

$$N = \sum_{k=1}^{q} N_k, \qquad E = \sum_{k=1}^{q} \varepsilon_k N_k = \sum_{j=1}^{N} \varepsilon_j. \tag{3}$$

To implement the constraints, we introduce the Lagrange multipliers α and β and construct the modified entropy

$$\tilde{S} = S + \alpha \sum_{k=1}^{q} N_k - \beta \sum_{k=1}^{q} \varepsilon_k N_k. \tag{4}$$

Maximization of S is achieved by setting the derivatives $\partial\tilde{S}/\partial N_k$ to zero for each N_k. Substituting equation (2) into equation (4) and taking the derivatives, we find that the occupation numbers $P(\varepsilon_k) = N_k/N$ for the states k depend exponentially on the energies of these states ε_k

$$P(\varepsilon_k) = \frac{N_k}{N} = e^{\alpha - \beta \varepsilon_k} = e^{-(\varepsilon_k - \mu)/T}. \tag{5}$$

Here the parameters $T = 1/\beta$ and $\mu = \alpha T$ are called the temperature and the chemical potential. The values of α and β are determined by substituting equation (5) into equation (3) and satisfying the constraints for given N and E. The temperature T is equal to the average energy per particle $T \sim \langle \varepsilon \rangle = E/N$, up to a numerical coefficient of the order of one. The interpretation of equation (5) is that the probability for an atom to occupy a state with the energy ε depends exponentially on the energy: $P(\varepsilon) \propto \exp(-\varepsilon/T)$.

This consideration can be generalized to the case where the label k becomes a continuous variable. In this case, the sums in equations (2), (3), and (4) are replaced by integrals with an appropriate measure of integration. The typical physical example is a gas of atoms moving inside a large box. In this case, the atoms have closely spaced quantized energy levels, and the number of quantum states within a momentum interval Δp and a space interval Δx is $\Delta p \, \Delta x/h$, where h is the Planck constant. Then, the measure of integration in equations (2), (3), and (4) becomes the element of volume of the phase space $dp \, dx/h$ in the one-dimensional case and $d^3p \, d^3r/h^3$ in the three-dimensional case. The energy in equation (5) becomes the kinetic energy of an atom $\varepsilon = p^2/2m$, which is bounded from below $\varepsilon \geq 0$.

Equation (5) is the fundamental law of equilibrium statistical physics (Wannier, 1987), known as the Boltzmann–Gibbs distribution. However, one can see that the above derivation is really an exercise in theory of probabilities and, as such, is not specific to physics. Thus, it can be applied to statistical ensembles of different natures, subject to constraints similar to equation (3). Interpreting the discrete states of the atoms as bits of information, one arrives at the Shannon entropy in the theory of information. Entropy concepts have been applied to such disparate fields as ecology (Banavar, Maritan, and Volkov, 2010; Kelly, Blundell, Bowler, Fox, Harvey, Lomas, and Woodward, 2011) and neuroscience (Varshney, Sjöström, and Chklovskii, 2006; Wen, Stepanyants, Elston, Grosberg, and Chklovskii, 2009).

The economy is also a big statistical system consisting of a large number of economic agents. Thus, it is tempting to apply the formalism presented above to the economy as well. However, there are different ways of implementing such an analogy. In the next section, I briefly summarize an analogy developed in Foley (1994, 1996, 1999).

Statistical equilibrium theory of markets by Duncan Foley

In Foley (1994), Duncan proposed a statistical equilibrium theory of markets. This theory is an alternative to the conventional competitive equilibrium theory originated by Walras and by Marshall. In the conventional theory, an auctioneer collects orders from buyers and sellers and determines an equilibrium price that clears the market, subject to budget constraints and utility preferences of the agents. In this theory, all transactions take place at the same price, but it is not quite clear how the real markets would actually converge to this price. In contrast, Duncan proposed a theory where there is a probability distribution of trades at different prices, and market clearing is achieved only statistically.

Foley (1994) studied an ensemble of N economic agents who trade n types of different commodities. The state of each agent $j = 1, 2, 3, \ldots, N$ is characterized by the n-component vector $x_j = (x_j^{(1)}, x_j^{(2)}, x_j^{(3)}, \ldots, x_j^{(n)})$. Each component of this vector represents a possible trade that the agent j is willing to perform with a given commodity. Positive, negative, and zero values of x_j represent an increase, a decrease, and no change in the stock of a given commodity for the agent j. All trades in the system are subject to the global constraint

$$\sum_j x_j = 0, \tag{6}$$

which represents conservation of commodities in the process of trading, i.e. commodities are only transferred between the agents. An increase $x_i > 0$ of a commodity stock for an agent i must be compensated by a decrease $x_j < 0$ for another agent j, so that the algebraic sum (6) of all trades is zero. However, equation (6) does not require bilateral balance of transactions between pairs of agents, and allows for multilateral trades.

The vector x_j can be considered as an n-dimensional generalization of the variable ε_j introduced in the previous section to characterize the state of each atom. Different kinds of trades x_k are labeled by the index k, and the number of agents doing the trade x_k is denoted as N_k. Then the constraint (6) can be rewritten as

$$\sum_k x_k N_k = 0. \tag{7}$$

For a given set of N_k, the multiplicity (1) gives the number of different assignments of individual agents to the trades x_k, such that the numbers N_k are fixed. Maximizing the entropy (2) subject to the constraints (7), we arrive to an analog of equation (5), which now has the form

$$P(x_k) = \frac{N_k}{N} = c e^{-\pi \cdot x_k}. \tag{8}$$

Here c is a normalization constant, and π is the n-component vector of Lagrange multipliers introduced to satisfy the constraints (7). Foley (1994) interpreted π as the vector of entropic prices. The probability for an agent to perform the set of trades x depends exponentially on the volume of the trades: $P(x) \propto \exp(-\pi \cdot x)$.

In Foley (1996), the general theory (Foley, 1994) was applied to a simple labor market. In this model, there are two classes of agents: employers (firms) and employees (workers). They trade in two commodities $(n = 2)$: $x^{(1)} = w$ is wage, supplied by the firms and taken by the workers, and $x^{(2)} = l$ is labor, supplied by the workers and taken by the firms. For each worker, the offer set includes the line $x = (w > w_0, -1)$, where -1 is the fixed offer of labor in exchange for any wage w greater than a minimum wage w_0. The offer set also includes the point $x = (0, 0)$, which offers no labor and no wage, i.e. the state of unemployment. For each firm, the offer set is the line $x = (-K, l > l_0)$, where $-K$ is the fixed amount of capital spent on paying wages in exchange for the amount of labor l greater than a minimum value l_0.

A mathematically similar model was also developed in Foley (1999) as a result of conversations with Perry Mehrling. This model also has two commodities $(n = 2)$, one of which is interpreted as money and another as a financial asset, such as a bond or a treasury bill.

Let us focus on the labor market model of Foley (1996). According to equation (8), the model predicts the exponential probability distributions for the wages w received by the workers and for the labor l employed by the firms. Let us try to compare these predictions with empirical data for the real economy. The probability distribution of wages can be compared with income distribution, for which a lot of data is available and which will be discussed in the section Empirical Data. On the other hand, the distribution of labor employed by the firms can be related to the distribution of firm sizes, as measured by the number of employees. However, Foley (1996) makes an artificial simplifying assumption that each firm spends the same amount of capital K on labor. This is a clearly unrealistic assumption because of the great variation in the amount of capital among the firms, including the capital spent on labor. Thus, let us focus only on the probability distribution of wages, unconditional on the distribution of labor. To obtain this distribution, we take a sum in equation (8) over the values of $x^{(2)}$, while keeping a fixed value for $x^{(1)}$. In physics jargon, we "integrate out" the degree of freedom $x^{(2)} = l$ and thus obtain the unconditional probability distribution of the remaining degree of freedom $x^{(1)} = w$, which is still exponential

$$P(w) = c\, e^{-w/T_w}. \tag{9}$$

Here c is a normalization constant, and $T_w = 1/\pi^{(1)}$ is the wage temperature.

Now let us discuss how the constraint (7) is satisfied with respect to wages. The model has N_f firms, which supply the total capital for wages $W = KN_f$, which enters as a negative term into the sum (7). Since only the total amount matters in the constraint, we can take W as an input parameter of the model.

Given that the unemployed workers have zero wage $w = 0$, the constraint (7) can be rewritten as

$$\sum_{w_k > w_0} w_k N_k = W, \tag{10}$$

where the sum is taken over the employed workers, whose total number we denote as N_e. The average wage per employed worker is $\langle w \rangle = W/N_e$. Using equation (9) and replacing summation over k by integration over w in equation (10), we relate $\langle w \rangle$ and T_w

$$\langle w \rangle = \frac{W}{N_e} = \frac{\int_{w_0}^{\infty} w P(w) \, dw}{\int_{w_0}^{\infty} P(w) \, dw}, \quad T_w = \langle w \rangle - w_0. \tag{11}$$

So, the wage temperature T_w is a difference of the average wage per employed worker and the minimal wage.

The model of Foley (1996) also has unemployed workers, whose number N_u depends on the measure of statistical weight assigned to the state with $w = 0$. Because this measure is an input parameter of the model, one might as well take N_u as an input parameter. I will not discuss the number of unemployed further, and will focus on the distribution of wages among the employed workers. It will be shown in the section Empirical Data that the exponential distribution of wages (9) indeed agrees with the actual empirical data on income distribution for the majority of population.

Statistical mechanics of money

The theory presented in the previous section focused on market transactions and identified the states of the agents with the possible vectors of transactions x_j. However, an analogy with the Boltzmann–Gibbs formalism can be also developed in a different way, as proposed by Drăgulescu and Yakovenko (2000). In this paper, the states of the agents were identified with the amounts of a commodity they hold, i.e. with stocks of a commodity, rather than with fluxes of a commodity. This analogy is closer to the original physical picture presented in the second section, where the states of the atoms were identified with the amounts of energy ε_j held by the atoms (i.e. the stocks of energy), rather than with the amounts of energy transfer in collisions between the atoms (i.e. the fluxes of energy). In this section, I summarize the theory developed by Drăgulescu and Yakovenko (2000).

Similarly to the previous section, let us consider an ensemble of N economic agents and characterize their states by the amounts (stocks) of commodities they hold. Let us introduce one special commodity called money, whereas all other commodities are assumed to be physically consumable, such as food, consumer goods, and services. Money is fundamentally different from consumable goods, because it is an artificially created, non-consumable object. I will not dwell on the historical origins and various physical implementations of money, but will proceed straight to the modern fiat money. Fundamentally, money is bits of information (digital balances) assigned to each agent, so money represents an informational layer of the economy, as opposed to the physical layer consisting of various manufactured and consumable goods. Although money is not physically consumable, and the well-being of the economic agents is ultimately determined by the physical layer, nevertheless money plays an extremely important role in the modern economy. Many economic crises were caused by monetary problems, not by physical problems. In the economy, the monetary subsystem interacts with the physical subsystem, but the two layers cannot transform into each other because of their different nature. For this reason, an increase in material production does not result in an automatic increase in money supply.

Let us denote money balances of the agents $j = 1, 2, \ldots, N$ by m_j. Ordinary economic agents can only receive money from and give money to other agents, and are not permitted to "manufacture" money, e.g. to print dollar bills. The agents can grow apples on trees, but cannot grow money on trees. Let us consider an economic transaction between the agents i and j. When the agent i pays money Δm to the agent j for some goods or services, the money balances of the agents change as

$$m_i \rightarrow m_i' = m_i - \Delta m,$$
$$m_j \rightarrow m_j' = m_j + \Delta m. \tag{12}$$

The total amount of money of the two agents before and after the transaction remains the same

$$m_i + m_j = m_i' + m_j', \tag{13}$$

i.e. there is a local conservation law for money. The transfer of money (12) is analogous to the transfer of energy in molecular collisions, and equation (13) is analogous to conservation of energy. Conservative models of this kind are also studied in some economic literature (Kiyotaki and Wright, 1993; Molico, 2006).

Enforcement of the local conservation law (13) is crucial for successful functioning of money. If the agents were permitted to "manufacture" money, they would be printing money and buying all goods for nothing, which would be a disaster. In a barter economy, one consumable good is exchanged for another (e.g. apples for oranges), so the physical contributions of both agents are obvious. However, this becomes less obvious in a monetary economy, where goods are exchanged for money, and money for goods. The purpose of the conservation law (12) is to ensure that an agent can buy goods from society only if he or she has contributed something useful to society and received monetary payment for these contributions. Money is an accounting device, and, indeed, all accounting rules are based on the conservation law (12).

Unlike ordinary economic agents, a central bank or a central government, who issued the fiat money in the first place, can inject money into the economy, thus changing the total amount of money in the system. This process is analogous to an influx of energy into a system from external sources. As long as the rate of money influx is slow compared with the relaxation rate in the economy, the system remains in a quasi-stationary statistical equilibrium with slowly changing parameters. This situation is analogous to slow heating of a kettle, where the kettle has a well defined, but slowly increasing, temperature at any moment of time. Following the long-standing tradition in the economic literature, this section studies the economy in equilibrium, even though the real-world economy may be totally out of whack. An economic equilibrium implies a monetary equilibrium too, so, for these idealized purposes, we consider a model where the central authorities do not inject additional money, so the total amount of money M held by all ordinary agents in the system is fixed. In this situation, the local conservation law (13) becomes the global conservation law for money

$$\sum_j m_j = M. \tag{14}$$

It is important, however, that we study the system in a statistical equilibrium, as opposed to a mechanistic equilibrium envisioned by Walras and Marshall. For this reason, the global constraint (14) is actually not as crucial for the final results, as it might seem. In physics, we usually start with the idealization of a closed system, where the total energy E in equation (3) is fixed. Then, after deriving the Boltzmann–Gibbs distribution (5) and the concept of temperature, we generalize the consideration to an open system in contact with a thermal reservoir at a given temperature. Even though the total energy of the open system is no longer conserved, the atoms still have the same Boltzmann–Gibbs distribution (5). Similarly, routine daily operations of the central bank (as opposed to outstanding interventions, such as the recent quantitative easing by the Federal Reserve Bank) do not necessarily spoil the equilibrium distribution of money obtained for a closed system.

Another potential problem with conservation of money is debt, which will be discussed in more detail in the next section. To simplify initial consideration, we do not allow agents to have debt in this section. Thus, by construction, money balances of the agents cannot drop below zero, i.e. $m_i \geq 0$ for all i. Transaction (12) takes place only when an agent has enough money to pay the price, i.e. $m_i \geq \Delta m$. An agent with $m_i = 0$ cannot buy goods from other agents, but can receive money for delivering goods or services to them. Most econophysics models, see reviews by Chakraborti, Tokea, Patriarca, and Abergel (2011a,b); Yakovenko and Rosser (2009), and some economic models (Kiyotaki and Wright, 1993; Molico, 2006) do not consider debt, so it is not an uncommon simplifying assumption. In this approach, the agents are liquidity-constrained. As the recent economic crisis brutally reminded us, liquidity constraint rules the economy, even though some players tend to forget about it during debt binges in economic bubbles.

The transfer of money in equation (12) from one agent to another represents payment for delivered goods and services, i.e. there is an implied counterflow of goods for each monetary transaction. However, keeping track explicitly of the stocks and fluxes of consumable goods would be a very complicated task. One reason is that many goods, e.g. food and other supplies, and most services, e.g. getting a haircut or going to a movie, are not tangible and disappear after consumption. Because they are not conserved, and also because they are measured in many different physical units, it is not practical to keep track of them. In contrast, money is measured in the same unit (within a given country with a single currency) and is conserved in local transactions (13), so it is straightforward to keep track of money.

Thus, I choose to keep track only of the money balances of the agents m_j, but not of the other commodities in the system. This situation can be visualized as follows. Suppose money accounts of all agents are kept on a central computer server. A computer operator observes the multitude of money transfers (12) between the accounts, but he or she does not have information about the reasons for these transfers and does not know what consumable goods were transferred in exchange. Although purposeful and rational for individual agents, these transactions look effectively random for the operator. (Similarly, in statistical physics, each atom follows deterministic equations of motion, but, nevertheless, the whole system is effectively random.) Out of curiosity, the computer operator records a snapshot of the money balances m_j of all agents at a given time. Then the operator counts the numbers of agents N_k who have money balances in the intervals between m_k and $m_k + m_*$, where m_* is a reasonably small money window, and the index k labels the money interval. The operator wonders what the general statistical principle is that governs the relative occupation numbers $P(m_k) = N_k/N$. In the absence of additional information, it is reasonable to derive these numbers by maximizing the multiplicity Ω and the entropy S of the money distribution in equations (1) and (2), subject to the constraint $\sum_k m_k N_k = M$ in equation (14). The result is given by the Boltzmann–Gibbs distribution for money

$$P(m) = c\, e^{-m/T_m}, \tag{15}$$

where c is a normalizing constant, and T_m is the money temperature. Similarly to equation (11), the temperature is obtained from the constraint (14) and is equal to the average amount of money per agent: $T_m = \langle m \rangle = M/N$.

The statistical approach not only predicts the equilibrium distribution of money (15), but also allows us to study how the probability distribution of money $P(m, t)$ evolves in time t toward the equilibrium. Drăgulescu and Yakovenko (2000) performed computer simulations of money transfers between the agents in different models. Initially all agents were given the same amount of money, say, \$1000. Then, a pair of agents (i, j) was randomly selected, the amount Δm was transferred from one agent to another, and the process was repeated many times. The time evolution of the probability distribution of money $P(m, t)$ is shown in computer animation videos by Chen and Yakovenko (2007); and Wright (2007). After a transitional period, money distribution converges to the stationary form shown in Figure 4.2. As expected, the distribution is fitted well by the exponential function (15).

In the simplest model considered by Drăgulescu and Yakovenko (2000), the transferred amount $\Delta m = \$1$ was constant. Computer animation (Chen and

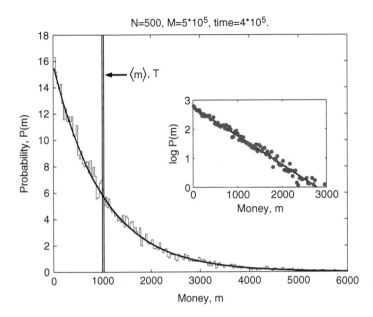

Figure 4.2 Histogram and points: The stationary probability distribution of money $P(m)$ obtained in computer simulations of the random transfer models (Drăgulescu and Yakovenko, 2000). *Solid curves:* Fits to the exponential distribution (15). *Vertical line:* The initial distribution of money.

Yakovenko, 2007) shows that the initial distribution of money first broadens to a symmetric Gaussian curve, typical for a diffusion process. Then, the distribution starts to pile up around the $m = 0$ state, which acts as the impenetrable boundary, because of the imposed condition $m \geq 0$. As a result, $P(m)$ becomes skewed (asymmetric) and eventually reaches the stationary exponential shape, as shown in Figure 4.2. The boundary at $m = 0$ is analogous to the ground-state energy in physics, i.e. the lowest possible energy of a physical system. Without this boundary condition, the probability distribution of money would not reach a stationary shape. Computer animations (Chen and Yakovenko, 2007; Wright, 2007) also show how the entropy (2) of the money distribution, defined as $S/N = - \sum_k P(m_k) \ln P(m_k)$, grows from the initial value $S = 0$, where all agents have the same money, to the maximal value at the statistical equilibrium.

Drăgulescu and Yakovenko (2000) performed simulations of several models with different rules for money transfers Δm. As long as the rules satisfy the time-reversal symmetry (Drăgulescu and Yakovenko, 2000), the stationary distribution is always the exponential one (15), irrespective of initial conditions and details of transfer rules. However, this symmetry is violated by the multiplicative rules of transfer, such as the proportional rule $\Delta m = \gamma m_i$ (Angle, 1986; Ispolatov, Krapivsky, and Redner, 1998), the saving propensity (Chakraborti and Chakrabarti, 2000), and negotiable prices (Molico, 2006). These models produce

Gamma-like distributions, as well as a power-law tail for a random distribution of saving propensities (Chatterjee and Chakrabarti, 2007). Despite some mathematical differences, all these models demonstrate spontaneous development of a highly unequal probability distribution of money as a result of random money transfers between the agents (Chakraborti, Tokea, Patriarca, and Abergel, 2011a,b). The money transfer models can be also formulated in the language of commodity trading between the agents optimizing their utility functions (Chakrabarti and Chakrabarti, 2009), which is closer to the traditional language of the economic literature. More involved agent-based simulations were developed by Wright (2005, 2009) and demonstrated emergence of a two-classes society from the initially equal agents. This work was further developed in a book by Cockshott, Cottrell, Michaelson, Wright, and Yakovenko (2009), integrating economics, computer science, and physics. Empirical data on income distribution discussed in the next section show direct evidence for the two-class society.

Let us compare the results of this and the previous section. In the previous section, the Boltzmann–Gibbs formalism is applied to the fluxes of commodities, and the distribution of wages (9) is predicted to be exponential. In this section, the Boltzmann–Gibbs formalism is applied to the stocks of commodities, and the distribution of money balances (15) is predicted to be exponential. There is no contradiction between these two approaches, and both fluxes and stocks may have exponential distributions simultaneously, although this is not necessarily required. These papers were motivated by different questions. The papers by Foley (1994, 1996, 1999) were motivated by the long-standing question about how markets determine prices between different commodities in a decentralized manner. The paper by Drăgulescu and Yakovenko (2000) was motivated by another long-standing question about how inequality spontaneously develops among equal agents with equal initial endowments of money. In neoclassical thinking, equal agents with equal initial endowments should forever stay equal, which contradicts everyday experience. The statistical approach argues that the state of equality is fundamentally unstable, because it has a very low entropy. The law of probabilities (Farjoun and Machover, 1983) leads to the exponential distribution, which is highly unequal, but stable, because it maximizes the entropy. Some papers in the economic literature have modeled the distributions of both prices and money balances within a common statistical framework (Molico, 2006).

It would be very interesting to compare the theoretical prediction (15) with empirical data on money distribution. Unfortunately, it is very difficult to obtain such data. The distribution of balances on deposit accounts in a big enough bank would be a reasonable approximation for the distribution of money among the population. However, such data are not publicly available. In contrast, plenty of data on income distribution are available from the tax agencies and population surveys. These data will be compared with the theoretical prediction (9) in the section Empirical Data. However, before that, I will discuss in the next section how the results of this section would change when the agents are permitted to have debt.

Models of debt

From the standpoint of individual economic agents, debt may be considered as negative money. When an agent borrows money from a bank, the cash balance of the agent (positive money) increases, but the agent also acquires an equal debt obligation (negative money), so the total balance (net worth) of the agent remains the same. Thus, the act of money borrowing still satisfies a generalized conservation law of the total money (net worth), which is now defined as the algebraic sum of positive (cash M) and negative (debt D) contributions: $M - D = M_b$, where M_b is the original amount of money in the system, the monetary base (McConnell and Brue, 1996). When an agent needs to buy a product at a price Δm exceeding his money balance m_i, the agent is now permitted to borrow the difference from a bank. After the transaction, the new balance of the agent becomes negative: $m_i' = m_i - \Delta m < 0$. The local conservation law (12) and (13) is still satisfied, but now it involves negative values of m. Thus, the consequence of debt is not a violation of the conservation law, but a modification of the boundary condition by permitting negative balances $m_i < 0$, so $m = 0$ is not the ground state any more.

If the computer simulation with $\Delta m = \$1$, described in the previous section, is repeated without any restrictions on the debt of the agents, the probability distribution of money $P(m, t)$ never stabilizes, and the system never reaches a stationary state. As time goes on, $P(m, t)$ keeps spreading in a Gaussian manner unlimitedly toward $m = +\infty$ and $m = -\infty$. Because of the generalized conservation law, the first moment of the algebraically defined money m remains constant $\langle m \rangle = M_b/N$. It means that some agents become richer with positive balances $m > 0$ at the expense of other agents going further into debt with negative balances $m < 0$.

Common sense, as well as the current financial crisis, indicate that an economic system cannot be stable if unlimited debt is permitted. In this case, the agents can buy goods without producing anything in exchange by simply going into unlimited debt. equation (15) is not applicable in this case for the following mathematical reason. The normalizing coefficient in equation (15) is $c = 1/Z$, where Z is the partition function

$$Z = \sum_k e^{-m_k/T_m}, \tag{16}$$

and the sum is taken over all permitted states k of the agents. When debt is not permitted, and money balances are limited to non-negative values $m_k \geq 0$, the sum in equation (16) converges, if the temperature is selected to be positive $T_m > 0$. This is the case in physics, where kinetic energy takes non-negative values $\varepsilon \geq 0$, and there is a ground state with the lowest possible energy, i.e. energy is bounded from below. In contrast, when debt is permitted and is not limited by any constraints, the sum in the partition function (16) over both positive and negative values of m_k diverges for any sign of the temperature T_m.

It is clear that some sort of a modified boundary condition has to be imposed in order to prevent unlimited growth of debt and to ensure overall stability and

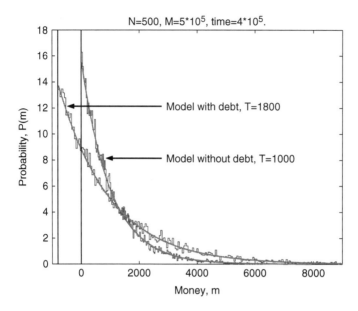

Figure 4.3 Histograms: Stationary distributions of money with and without debt (Drăgulescu and Yakovenko, 2000). The debt is limited to $m_d = 800$. *Solid curves:* Fits to the exponential distributions with the money temperatures $T_m = 1800$ and $T_m = 1000$.

equilibrium in the system. Drăgulescu and Yakovenko (2000) considered a simple model where the maximal debt of each agent is limited to m_d. In this model, $P(m)$ again has the exponential shape, but with the new boundary condition at $m = -m_d$ and the higher money temperature $T_d = m_d + M_b/N$, as shown in Figure 4.3. This result is analogous to equation (11) with the substitution $w_0 \rightarrow -m_d$. By allowing the agents to go into debt up to m_d, we effectively increase the amount of money available to each agent by m_d.

Xi, Ding, and Wang (2005) considered a more realistic boundary condition, where a constraint is imposed on the total debt of all agents in the system, rather than on individual debt of each agent. This is accomplished via the required reserve ratio R (McConnell and Brue, 1996). Banks are required by law to set aside a fraction R of the money deposited into bank accounts, whereas the remaining fraction $1 - R$ can be lent to the agents. If the initial amount of money in the system (the money base) is M_b, then, with repeated lending and borrowing, the total amount of positive money available to the agents increases up to $M = M_b/R$, where the factor $1/R$ is called the money multiplier (McConnell and Brue, 1996). This is how "banks create money." This extra money comes from the increase in the total debt $D = M_b/R - M_b$ of the agents. Now we have two constraints: on the positive money M and on the maximal debt D. Applying the principle of maximal entropy, we find two exponential distributions, for positive and negative

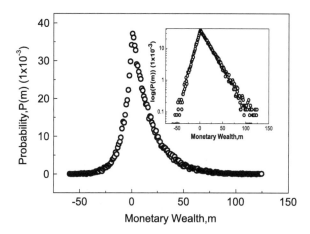

Figure 4.4 The stationary distribution of money for the required reserve ratio $R = 0.8$ (Xi, Ding, and Wang, 2005). The distribution is exponential for both positive and negative money with different temperatures T_+ and T_-, as shown in the inset on log-linear scale.

money, characterized by two different temperatures, $T_+ = M_b/RN$ and $T_- = M_b(1 - R)/RN$. This result was confirmed in computer simulations by Xi, Ding, and Wang (2005), as shown in Figure 4.4.

However, in the real economy, the reserve requirement is not effective in stabilizing debt in the system, because it applies only to retail banks insured by FDIC, but not to investment banks. Moreover, there are alternative instruments of debt, including derivatives, credit default swaps, and various other unregulated "financial innovations." As a result, the total debt is not limited in practice and can reach catastrophic proportions. Drăgulescu and Yakovenko (2000) studied a model with different interest rates for deposits into and loans from a bank, but without an explicit limit on the total debt. Computer simulations by Drăgulescu and Yakovenko (2000) show that, depending on the choice of parameters, the total amount of money in circulation either increases or decreases in time, but never stabilizes. The interest amplifies the destabilizing effect of debt, because positive balances become even more positive and negative balances even more negative. Arguably, the current financial crisis was caused by the enormous debt accumulation, triggered by subprime mortgages and financial derivatives based on them. The lack of restrictions was justified by a misguided notion that markets will always arrive at an equilibrium, as long as government does not interfere with them. However, an equilibrium is possible only when the proper boundary conditions are imposed. Debt does not stabilize by itself without enforcement of boundary conditions.

Bankruptcy is a mechanism for debt stabilization. Interest rates are meaning-less without a mechanism for triggering bankruptcy. Bankruptcy erases the debt of an agent (the negative money) and resets the balance to zero. However, somebody else (a bank or a lender) counted this debt as a positive asset, which also becomes erased. In the language of physics, creation of debt is analogous to particle–antiparticle generation (creation of positive and negative money), whereas cancellation of debt corresponds to particle–antiparticle annihilation (annihilation of positive and negative money). The former and the latter dominate during booms and busts and correspond to monetary expansion and contraction.

Besides fiat money created by central governments, numerous attempts have been made to create alternative community money from scratch (Kichiji and Nishibe, 2007). In such a system, when an agent provides goods or services to another agent, their accounts are credited with positive and negative tokens, as in equation (12). Because the initial money base $M_b = 0$ is zero in this case, the probability distribution of money $P(m)$ is symmetric with respect to positive and negative m, i.e. "all money is credit." Unless boundary conditions are imposed, the money distribution $P(m, t)$ would never stabilize in this system. Some agents would try to accumulate unlimited negative balances by consuming goods and services and not contributing anything in return, thus undermining the system.

Empirical data on income distribution

In this section, the theoretical prediction (9) for the probability distribution of wages will be compared with the empirical data on income distribution in the USA. The data from the US Census Bureau and the Internal Revenue Service (IRS) were analyzed by Drăgulescu and Yakovenko (2001a). One plot from this paper is shown in Figure 4.5. The data agree very well with the exponential distribution, and the wage temperature $T_w = 20.3$ kUS$/year for 1996 is obtained from the fit. Equation (9) also has the parameter w_0, which represents the minimal wage. Although the data deviate from the exponential distribution in Figure 4.5 for incomes below 5 kUS$/year, the probability density at $w = 0$ is still non-zero, $P(0) \neq 0$. One would expect difficulties in collecting reliable data for very low incomes. Given limited accuracy of the data in this range and the fact that the deviation occurs well below the average income T_w, we can set $w_0 = 0$ for the practical purposes of fitting the data. Although there is a legal requirement for a minimum hourly wage, there is no such requirement for an annual wage, which depends on the number of hours worked.

The upper limit of the income data analyzed by Drăgulescu and Yakovenko (2001a) was about 120 kUS$/year. Subsequently, Drăgulescu and Yakovenko (2001b, 2003) analyzed income data up to 1 MUS$/year and found that the upper tail of the distribution follows a power law. Thus, income distribution in the USA has a two-class structure, as shown in Figure 4.6. This figure shows the cumulative distribution function $C(r) = \int_r^{\infty} P(r') dr'$, where $P(r)$ is the probability density, and the variable r denotes income. When $P(r)$ is an exponential or a power-law function, $C(r)$ is also an exponential or a power-law function. The straight line

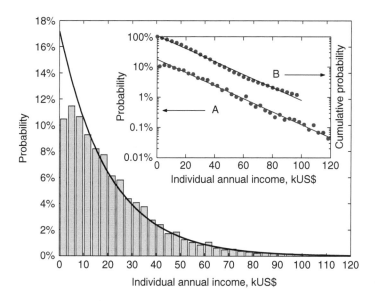

Figure 4.5 Histogram: Probability distribution of individual income from the US Census Bureau data for 1996 (Drăgulescu and Yakovenko, 2001a). *Solid line:* Fit to the exponential law. *Inset plot A:* The same with the logarithmic vertical scale. *Inset plot B:* Cumulative probability distribution of individual income from the PSID data for 1992.

on the log-linear scale in the inset of Figure 4.6 demonstrates the exponential Boltzmann–Gibbs law for the lower class, and the straight line on the log–log scale in the main panel illustrates the Pareto power law for the upper class. The intersection point between the exponential and power-law fits in Figure 4.6 defines the boundary between the lower and upper classes. For 1997, the annual income separating the two classes was about 120 kUS$. About 3% of the population belonged to the upper class, and 97% belonged to the lower class. Although the existence of social classes has been known since Karl Marx, it is interesting that they can be straightforwardly identified by fitting the empirical data with simple mathematical functions. The exponential distribution (9) applies only to the wages of workers in the lower class, whereas the upper tail represents capital gains and other profits of the firms' owners.

Silva and Yakovenko (2005) studied the historical evolution of income distribution in the USA during 1983–2001 using the IRS data. The structure of income distribution was found to be qualitatively similar for all years, as shown in Figure 4.7. The average income in nominal dollars has approximately doubled during this time interval. So, the horizontal axis in Figure 4.7 shows the normalized income r/T_r, where the income temperature T_r was obtained by fitting the exponential part of the distribution for each year. The values of T_r are shown

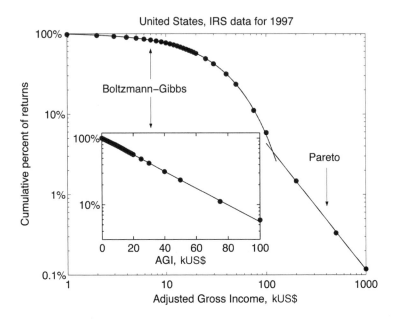

Figure 4.6 Cumulative probability distribution of tax returns for USA in 1997 shown on log-log (main panel) and log-linear (inset) scales (Drăgulescu and Yakovenko, 2003). Points represent the IRS data, and solid lines are fits to the exponential and power-law functions.

in Figure 4.7. The plots for the 1980s and 1990s are shifted vertically for clarity. We observe that the data points for the lower class collapse on the same exponential curve for all years. This demonstrates that the relative income distribution for the lower class is extremely stable and does not change with time, despite a gradual increase in the average income in nominal dollars. This observation confirms that the lower class is in a statistical "thermal" equilibrium.

On the other hand, Figure 4.7 also shows that the income distribution of the upper class does not rescale and significantly changes in time. Banerjee and Yakovenko (2010) found that the exponent α of the power law $C(r) \propto 1/r^{\alpha}$ has decreased from 1.8 in 1983 to 1.3 in 2007, as shown in panel (b) of Figure 4.8. This means that the upper tail has become "fatter." Another informative parameter is the fraction f of the total income in the system going to the upper class (Banerjee and Yakovenko, 2010; Silva and Yakovenko, 2005):

$$f = \frac{\langle r \rangle - T_r}{\langle r \rangle}. \tag{17}$$

Here $\langle r \rangle$ is the average income of the whole population, and the temperature T_r is the average income in the exponential part of the distribution. Equation (17) gives a well-defined measure of the deviation of the actual income distribution

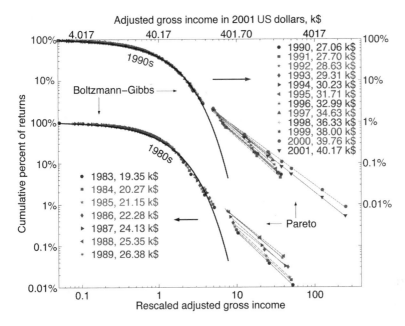

Figure 4.7 Cumulative probability distributions of tax returns for 1983–2001 plotted on a log–log scale versus r/T_r (the annual income r normalized by the average income T_r in the exponential part of the distribution) (Silva and Yakovenko, 2005). The columns of numbers give the values of T_r for the corresponding years.

from the exponential one and, thus, of the fatness of the upper tail. Panel (c) in Figure 4.8 shows the historical evolution of the parameters $\langle r \rangle$, T_r, and f (Banerjee and Yakovenko, 2010). We observe that T_r has been increasing approximately linearly in time (this increase mostly represents inflation). In contrast, $\langle r \rangle$ had sharp peaks in 2000 and 2007 coinciding with the heights of speculative bubbles in financial markets. The fraction f has been increasing for the last 20 years and reached maxima exceeding 20% in the years 2000 and 2007, followed by sharp drops. We conclude that speculative bubbles greatly increase overall income inequality by increasing the fraction of income going to the upper class. When bubbles collapse, income inequality decreases. Similar results were found for Japan by Aoyama, Souma, and Fujiwara (2003); Fujiwara, Souma, Aoyama, Kaizoji, and Aoki (2003).

Income inequality can be also characterized by the Lorenz curve and the Gini coefficient (Kakwani, 1980). The Lorenz curve is defined in terms of the two coordinates $x(r)$ and $y(r)$ depending on a parameter r:

$$x(r) = \int_0^r P(r')\,dr', \quad y(r) = \frac{\int_0^r r'P(r')\,dr'}{\int_0^\infty r'P(r')\,dr'}. \tag{18}$$

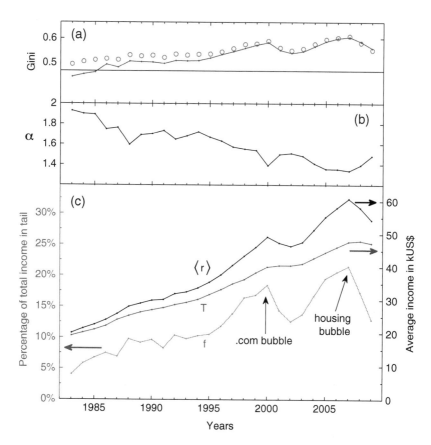

Figure 4.8 (a) The Gini coefficient G for income distribution in the USA in 1983–2009 (connected line), compared with the theoretical formula $G = (1+f)/2$ (open circles). (b) The exponent α of the power-law tail of income distribution. (c) The average income $\langle r \rangle$ in the whole system, the average income T_r in the lower class (the temperature of the exponential part), and the fraction of income f, equation (17), going to the upper tail (Banerjee and Yakovenko, 2010).

The horizontal coordinate $x(r)$ is the fraction of the population with income below r, and the vertical coordinate $y(r)$ is the fraction of the total income this population accounts for. As r changes from 0 to ∞, x and y change from 0 to 1 and parametrically define a curve in the (x, y) plane. For an exponential distribution $P(r) = c\exp(-r/T_r)$, the Lorenz curve is (Drăgulescu and Yakovenko, 2001a)

$$y = x + (1-x)\ln(1-x). \tag{19}$$

Figure 4.9 shows the Lorenz curves for 1983 and 2000 computed from the IRS data (Silva and Yakovenko, 2005). The data points for 1983 (squares) agree reasonably

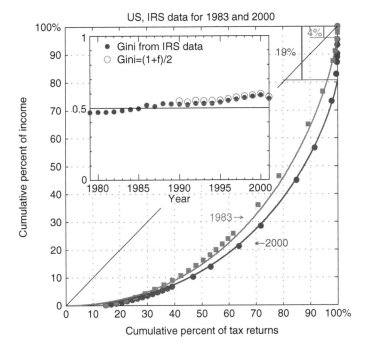

Figure 4.9 Main panel: Lorenz plots for income distribution in 1983 and 2000 (Silva and Yakovenko, 2005). The data points are from the IRS, and the theoretical curves represent equation (20) with the parameter f deduced from equation (17). *Inset:* The closed circles are the IRS data for the Gini coefficient G, and the open circles show the theoretical formula $G = (1+f)/2$.

well with equation (19) for the exponential distribution, which is shown by the upper curve. In contrast, the fraction f of income in the upper tail becomes so large in 2000 that equation (19) has to be modified as follows (Drăgulescu and Yakovenko, 2003; Silva and Yakovenko, 2005)

$$y = (1-f)[x+(1-x)\ln(1-x)] + f\,\Theta(x-1). \tag{20}$$

The last term in equation (20) represents the vertical jump of the Lorenz curve at $x = 1$, where a small percentage of the population in the upper class accounts for a substantial fraction f of the total income. The lower curve in Figure 4.9 shows that equation (20) fits the data points for 2000 (circles) very well.

The deviation of the Lorenz curve from the straight diagonal line in Figure 4.9 is a measure of income inequality. Indeed, if everybody had the same income, the Lorenz curve would be the diagonal line, because the fraction of income would be proportional to the fraction of the population. The standard measure of income inequality is the Gini coefficient $0 \le G \le 1$, which is defined as the area between the Lorenz curve and the diagonal line, divided by the area of the triangle beneath

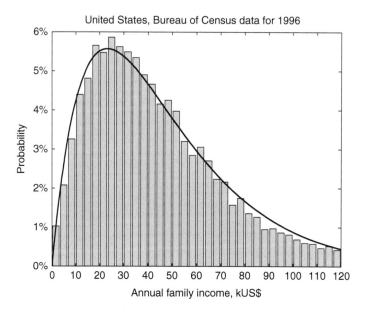

Figure 4.10 Histogram: Probability distribution of family income for families with two adults, US Census Bureau data (Drăgulescu and Yakovenko, 2001a). *Solid line:* Fit to equation (21).

the diagonal line (Kakwani, 1980). It was shown by Drăgulescu and Yakovenko (2001a) that the Gini coefficient is $G = 1/2$ for a purely exponential distribution. Historical evolution of the empirical Gini coefficient is shown in the inset of Figure 4.9 and in panel (a) of Figure 4.8. In the first approximation, the values of G are close to the theoretical value $1/2$. However, if we take into account the upper tail using equation (20), the formula for the Gini coefficient becomes $G = (1+f)/2$ (Silva and Yakovenko, 2005). The inset in Figure 4.9 and panel (a) in Figure 4.8 show that this formula gives a very good fit of the IRS data starting from 1995 using the values of f deduced from equation (17). The values $G < 1/2$ in the 1980s cannot be captured by this formula, because the Lorenz data points for 1983 lie slightly above the theoretical curve in Figure 4.9. We conclude that the increase of income inequality after 1995 originates completely from the growth of the upper-class income, whereas income inequality within the lower class remains constant.

So far, we have discussed the distribution of individual income. An interesting related question is the distribution $P_2(r)$ of family income $r = r_1 + r_2$, where r_1 and r_2 are the incomes of spouses. If individual incomes are distributed exponentially $P(r) \propto \exp(-r/T_r)$, then

$$P_2(r) = \int_0^r dr' P(r')P(r - r') = c\,r \exp(-r/T_r), \tag{21}$$

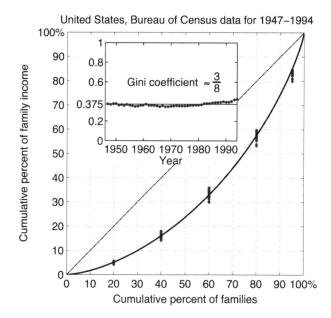

Figure 4.11 Main panel: Lorenz plot for family income, calculated from equation (21) and compared with the US Census Bureau data points for 1947–1994 (Drăgulescu and Yakovenko, 2001a). *Inset:* Data points from the US Census Bureau for the Gini coefficient for families, compared with the theoretical value $3/8 = 37.5\%$.

where c is a normalization constant. Figure 4.10 shows that equation (21) is in good agreement with the family income distribution data from the US Census Bureau (Drăgulescu and Yakovenko, 2001a). It is assumed in equation (21) that incomes of spouses are uncorrelated. This simple approximation is indeed supported by the scatter plot of incomes of spouses shown in Drăgulescu and Yakovenko (2003). The Gini coefficient for the family income distribution (21) was analytically calculated by Drăgulescu and Yakovenko (2001a) as $G = 3/8 = 37.5\%$. Figure 4.11 shows the Lorenz quintiles and the Gini coefficient for 1947–1994 plotted from the US Census Bureau data (Drăgulescu and Yakovenko, 2001a). The solid line, representing the Lorenz curve calculated from equation (21), is in good agreement with the data. The Gini coefficient, shown in the inset of Figure 4.11, is close to the calculated value of 37.5%. Stability of income distribution until the late 1980s was pointed out by Levy (1987), but a very different explanation of this stability was proposed.

The exponential distribution of wages (9) was derived assuming random realizations of all possible configurations in the absence of specific regulations of the labor market. As such, it can be taken as an idealized limiting case for comparison with actual distributions in different countries. If specific measures are implemented for income redistribution, then the distribution may deviate from the exponential one. An example of such a redistribution was studied by Banerjee, Yakovenko, and Di Matteo (2006) for Australia, where $P(r)$ has a sharp peak at a certain income stipulated by government policies. This is in contrast to the data presented in this section, which indicate that income distribution in the USA is close to the idealized one for a labor market without regulation. Numerous income distribution studies for other countries are cited in the review paper by Yakovenko and Rosser (2009).

Probability distribution of energy consumption

So far, we have discussed how monetary inequality develops for statistical reasons. Now let us discuss physical aspects of the economy. Since the beginning of the industrial revolution, the rapid technological development of human society has been based on consumption of fossil fuel, such as coal, oil, and gas, accumulated in the Earth for billions of years. As a result, physical standards of living in modern society are primarily determined by the level of energy consumption per capita. Now, it is exceedingly clear that fossil fuel will be exhausted in the not-too-distant future. Moreover, consumption of fossil fuel releases CO_2 into the atmosphere and affects global climate. These pressing global problems pose great technological and social challenges (Rezai, Foley, and Taylor, 2012).

Energy consumption per capita varies widely around the globe. This heterogeneity is a challenge and a complication for reaching a global consensus on how to deal with the energy problems. Thus, it is important to understand the origin of the global inequality in energy consumption and characterize it quantitatively. Here I approach this problem using the method of maximal entropy.

Let us consider an ensemble of economic agents and characterize each agent j by the energy consumption ϵ_j per unit time. Notice that here ϵ_j denotes not energy, but power, which is measured in kiloWatts (kW). Similarly to the second section, let us introduce the probability density $P(\epsilon)$, so that $P(\epsilon)d\epsilon$ gives the probability to have energy consumption in the interval from ϵ to $\epsilon + d\epsilon$. Energy production, based on extraction of fossil fuel from the Earth, is a physically limited resource, which is divided for consumption among the global population. It would be very improbable to divide this resource equally. Much more likely, this resource would be divided according to the entropy maximization principle, subject to the global energy production constraint. Following the same procedure as in the second section, we arrive at the conclusion that $P(\epsilon)$ should follow the exponential law analogous to equation (5)

$$P(\epsilon) = c e^{-\epsilon/T_\epsilon}. \tag{22}$$

Here c is a normalization constant, and the temperature $T_\epsilon = \langle \epsilon \rangle$ is the average energy consumption per capita.

Using data from the World Resources Institute, Banerjee and Yakovenko (2010) constructed the probability distribution of energy consumption per capita around the world, and found that it approximately follows the exponential law, as shown

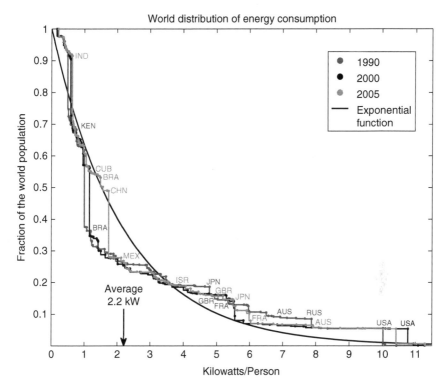

Figure 4.12 Cumulative distribution functions $C(\epsilon)$ for the energy consumption per capita around the world for 1990, 2000, and 2005. The solid curve is the exponential function (22) with the parameter $T_\epsilon = \langle \epsilon \rangle = 2.2$ kW.

in Figure 4.12. The world average energy consumption per capita is $\langle \epsilon \rangle = 2.2$ kW, compared with 10 kW in the USA and 0.6 kW in India (Banerjee and Yakovenko, 2010). However, if India and other developing countries were to adopt the same energy consumption level per capita as in the USA, there would not be enough energy resources in the world to do that. One can argue that the global energy consumption inequality results from the constraint on energy resources, and the global monetary inequality adjusts accordingly to implement this constraint. Since energy is purchased with money, a fraction of the world population ends up being poor, so that their energy consumption stays limited.

Figure 4.13 shows the Lorenz curves for the global energy consumption per capita in 1990, 2000, and 2005 from Banerjee and Yakovenko (2010). The black solid line is the theoretical Lorenz curve (19) for the exponential distribution (22). In the first approximation, the empirical curves are reasonably close to the theoretical curve, but some deviations are clearly visible. On the Lorenz curve for 1990, there is a kink or a knee indicated by the arrow, where the slope of the curve changes appreciably. This point separates developed and developing countries.

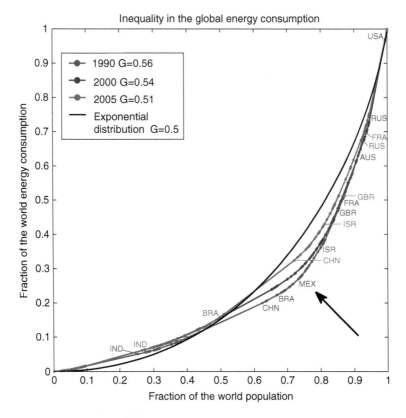

Figure 4.13 Lorenz curves for the energy consumption per capita around the world in 1990, 2000, and 2005, compared with the Lorenz curve (19) for the exponential distribution.

Mexico, Brazil, China, and India are below this point, whereas Britain, France, Japan, Australia, Russia, and the USA are above it. The slope change of the Lorenz curve represents a gap in the energy consumption per capita between these two groups of countries. Thus, the physical difference between developed and developing countries lies in the level of energy consumption and utilization, rather than in more ephemeral monetary measures, such as dollar income per capita. However, the Lorenz curve for 2005 is closer to the exponential curve, and the kink is less pronounced. It means that the energy consumption inequality and the gap between developed and developing countries have decreased, as also confirmed by the decrease in the Gini coefficient G given in Figure 4.13. This result can be attributed to the rapid globalization and stronger mixing of the world economy in the last 20 years. However, the energy consumption distribution in a well-mixed globalized world economy approaches the exponential one, rather than an equal distribution.

The inherent inequality of global energy consumption makes it difficult for the countries at the opposite ends of the distribution to agree on consistent measures to address energy and climate challenges. While not offering any immediate solutions, I would like to point out that renewable energy has different characteristics from fossil fuel. Because solar and wind energy is typically generated and consumed locally and not transported on the global scale, it is not subject to the entropy-maximizing redistribution. Thus, a transition from fossil fuel to renewable energy gives hope for achieving a more equal global society.

Conclusions

The statistical approach and entropy maximization are very general and powerful methods for studying big ensembles of various natures, be they physical, biological, economical, or social. Duncan Foley is one of the pioneers of applying these methods in economics (Foley, 1994, 1996, 1999). The exponential distribution of wages, predicted by the statistical equilibrium theory of a labor market (Foley, 1996), is supported by empirical data on income distribution in the USA for the majority of population. In contrast, the upper tail of income distribution follows a power law and expands dramatically during financial bubbles, which results in a significant increase of the overall income inequality. The two-class structure of American society is apparent in the plots of income distribution, where the lower and upper classes are described by the exponential and power-law distributions. The entropy maximization method also demonstrates how a highly unequal exponential probability distribution of money among the initially equal agents is generated as a result of stochastic monetary transactions between the agents. These ideas also apply to the global inequality of energy consumption per capita around the world. The empirical data show convergence to the predicted exponential distribution in the process of globalization. Global monetary inequality may be a consequence of the constraint on global energy resources, because it limits energy consumption per capita for a large fraction of the world population.

Notes

1 In quantum mechanics, s takes integer or half-integer values, and $q = 2s + 1$, but this is not important here.
2 Note that $N = \sum_k N_k$ in equation (2) should also be differentiated with respect to N_k.
3 In physics, the elementary particles are indistinguishable and obey Fermi–Dirac or Bose–Einstein statistics, rather than Boltzmann statistics. In contrast, the economic agents are distinguishable because of their human identity. Thus, Boltzmann statistics for distinguishable objects are appropriate in this case.
4 To simplify consideration, I use only one monetary instrument, commonly known to everybody as "money."
5 Here we treat the bank as being outside of the system consisting of ordinary agents, because we are interested in money distribution among these agents. The debt of the agents is an asset for the bank, and deposits of cash into the bank are liabilities of the bank (McConnell and Brue, 1996).

6 When the energy spectrum ε_k is bounded both from above and below, the physical temperature T may take either positive or negative values. For a quantum paramagnet discussed earlier, the negative temperature T corresponds to the inverse population, where the higher energy levels ε_k have higher population N_k than the lower energy levels.

References

Angle, J. (1986) "The surplus theory of social stratification and the size distribution of personal wealth," *Social Forces*, 65: 293–326.

Aoki, M., and Yoshikawa, H. (2006) *Reconstructing Macroeconomics: A Perspective from Statistical Physics and Combinatorial Stochastic Processes*, Cambridge: Cambridge University Press.

Aoyama, H., Souma, W., and Fujiwara, Y. (2003) "Growth and fluctuations of personal and company's income," *Physica A*, 324: 352–358.

Banavar, J.R., Maritan, A., and Volkov, I. (2010) "Applications of the principle of maximum entropy: from physics to ecology," *Journal of Physics Condensed Matter*, 22: 063101.

Banerjee, A., and Yakovenko, V.M. (2010) "Universal patterns of inequality," *New Journal of Physics*, 12: 075032.

Banerjee, A., Yakovenko, V.M., and Di Matteo, T. (2006) "A study of the personal income distribution in Australia," *Physica A*, 370: 54–59.

Chakrabarti, A.S., and Chakrabarti, B.K. (2009) "Microeconomics of the ideal gas like market models," *Physica A*, 388: 4151–4158.

Chakraborti, A., and Chakrabarti, B.K. (2000) "Statistical mechanics of money: how saving propensity affects its distribution," *The European Physical Journal B*, 17: 167–170.

Chakraborti, A., Tokea, I.M., Patriarca, M., and Abergel, F. (2011a) "Econophysics review: I. Empirical facts," *Quantitative Finance*, 11: 991–1012.

Chakraborti, A., Tokea, I.M., Patriarca, M., and Abergel, F. (2011b) "Econophysics review: II. Agent-based models," *Quantitative Finance*, 11: 1013-1041.

Chatterjee, A., and Chakrabarti, B.K. (2007) "Kinetic exchange models for income and wealth distributions," *The European Physical Journal B*, 60: 135–149.

Chen, J., and Yakovenko, V.M. (2007) Computer animation videos of money-transfer models, http://www2.physics.umd.edu/~yakovenk/econophysics/animation.html.

Cockshott, W.P., Cottrell, A.F., Michaelson, G.J., Wright, I.P., and Yakovenko, V.M. (2009) *Classical Econophysics*, Oxford: Routledge.

Drăgulescu, A.A., and Yakovenko, V.M. (2000) "Statistical mechanics of money," *The European Physical Journal B*, 17: 723–729.

Drăgulescu, A.A., and Yakovenko, V.M. (2001a) "Evidence for the exponential distribution of income in the USA," *The European Physical Journal B*, 20: 585–589.

Drăgulescu, A.A., and Yakovenko, V.M. (2001b) "Exponential and power-law probability distributions of wealth and income in the United Kingdom and the United States," *Physica A*, 299: 213–221.

Drăgulescu, A.A., and Yakovenko, V.M. (2003) "Statistical mechanics of money, income, and wealth: a short survey," in *Modeling of Complex Systems: Seventh Granada Lectures*, edited by P.L. Garrido and J. Marro, American Institute of Physics (AIP) Conference Proceedings 661: 180–183.

Farjoun, E., and Machover, M. (1983) *Laws of Chaos: A Probabilistic Approach to Political Economy*, London: Verso.

Farmer, J.D., Shubik, M., and Smith, E. (2005) "Is economics the next physical science?" *Physics Today*, 58(9): 37–42.

Foley, D.K. (1994) "A statistical equilibrium theory of markets," *Journal of Economic Theory*, 62: 321–345.

Foley, D.K. (1996) "Statistical equilibrium in a simple labor market," *Metroeconomica*, 47: 125–47.

Foley, D.K. (1999) "Statistical equilibrium in economics: method, interpretation, and an example," Notes for the ISER Summer School in Siena, 4–11 July 1999, http://homepage. newschool.edu/~foleyd/stateqnotes.pdf.

Fujiwara, Y., Souma, W., Aoyama, H., Kaizoji, T., and Aoki, M. (2003) "Growth and fluctuations of personal income," *Physica A*, 321: 598–604.

Golan, A. (1994) "A multivariable stochastic theory of size distribution of firms with empirical evidence," *Advances in Econometrics*, 10: 1–46.

Hogan, J. (2005) "Why it is hard to share the wealth," *New Scientist*, issue 2490, 12 March: 6.

Ispolatov, S., Krapivsky, P.L., and Redner, S. (1998) "Wealth distributions in asset exchange models," *The European Physical Journal B*, 2: 267–276.

Kakwani, N. (1980) *Income Inequality and Poverty*, Oxford: Oxford University Press.

Kelly, C.K., Blundell, S.J., Bowler, M.G., Fox, G.A., Harvey, P.H., Lomas, M.R., and Woodward, F.I. (2011) "The statistical mechanics of community assembly and species distribution," *New Phytologist*, 191: 819–827.

Kichiji, N., and Nishibe, M. (2007) "Network analyses of the circulation flow of community currency," *Evolutionary and Institutional Economics Review*, 4: 267–300.

Kiyotaki, N., and Wright, R. (1993) "A search-theoretic approach to monetary economics," *The American Economic Review*, 83: 63–77.

Levy, F. (1987) "Changes in the distribution of American family incomes, 1947 to 1984," *Science*, 236: 923–927.

McConnell, C.R., and Brue, S.L. (1996) *Economics: Principles, Problems, and Policies*, New York: McGraw-Hill.

Molico, M. (2006) "The distribution of money and prices in search equilibrium," *International Economic Review*, 47: 701–722.

Rezai, A., Foley, D.K., and Taylor, L. (2012) "Global warming and economic externalities," *Economic Theory*, 49: 329–351.

Shea, C. (2005) "Econophysics," *New York Times Magazine*, 11 December: 67.

Silva, A.C., and Yakovenko, V.M. (2005) "Temporal evolution of the 'thermal' and 'superthermal' income classes in the USA during 1983–2001," *Europhysics Letters*, 69: 304–310.

Silver, J., Slud, E., and Takamoto, T. (2002) "Statistical equilibrium wealth distributions in an exchange economy with stochastic preferences," *Journal of Economic Theory*, 106: 417–435.

Smith, E., and Foley, D.K. (2008) "Classical thermodynamics and economic general equilibrium theory," *Journal of Economic Dynamics and Control*, 32: 7–65.

Varshney, L.R., Sjöström, P.J., and Chklovskii, D.B. (2006) "Optimal information storage in noisy synapses under resource constraints," *Neuron*, 52: 409–423.

Wannier, G.H. (1987) *Statistical Physics*, New York: Dover.

Wen, Q., Stepanyants, A., Elston, G.N., Grosberg, A.Y., and Chklovskii, D.B. (2009) "Maximization of the connectivity repertoire as a statistical principle governing the shapes of dendritic arbors," *Proceedings of the National Academy of Sciences of the USA*, 106: 12536–12541.

Wright, I. (2005) "The social architecture of capitalism," *Physica A*, 346: 589–620.

Wright, I. (2007) Computer simulations of statistical mechanics of money in Mathematica, http://demonstrations.wolfram.com/StatisticalMechanicsOfMoney/.

Wright, I. (2009) "Implicit microfoundations for macroeconomics," *Economics*, 3(2009–19), http://dx.doi.org/10.5018/economics-ejournal.ja.2009-19.

Xi, N., Ding, N., and Wang, Y. (2005) "How required reserve ratio affects distribution and velocity of money," *Physica A* 357: 543–555.

Yakovenko V.M., and Rosser, J.B. Jr. (2009) "Colloquium: Statistical mechanics of money, wealth, and income," *Reviews of Modern Physics*, 81: 1703–1725.

Yakovenko, V.M. (2011) "Statistical mechanics approach to the probability distribution of money," in *New Approaches to Monetary Theory: Interdisciplinary Perspectives,* edited by Heiner Ganssmann, Oxford: Routledge.

Part II
Neoclassical economics
Dispersed and decentralized exchange

5 Class in catallaxy

A. J. Julius

A degree of freedom

A capitalist economy is capable of an uncountable infinity of distributions of income between the capitalists who own its nonlabor inputs and the workers who turn those inputs into outputs. The resolution of this indeterminacy falls to the customary or contested institutions and practices that organize competition and bargaining among and between capitalists and workers.

I will argue here for a version of this indeterminacy thesis. The thesis is often raised in opposition to a Walrasian picture of economic life. My argument for it will begin at the starting point of most Walrasian economic explanations and predictions. Describing a population of persons in terms of their consumption preferences, their initial holdings of goods, and their access to technologies for producing new goods, I will suppose that these persons come together to exchange their goods or labor, each acting to improve her or his own consumption prospects, and I will ask where such exchanges take the economy as a whole. "Pretty much anywhere; depends on the institutions" is the answer that I'll defend.

Two classes

Consider a population of $M + N$ persons falling into two classes, capitalists indexed by $c = 1, 2, \ldots, M$ and workers indexed by $w = M+1, M+2, \ldots, M+N$.

Before production or exchange the cth capitalist owns a collection of previously produced quantities of n kinds of goods, indicated by a nonnegative n-vector $\boldsymbol{\omega}_c$.[1] She consumes quantities of the n goods at two dates, separated by a period of production. A continuous increasing concave function u_c represents her preferences over consumption sequences described by pairs of nonnegative n-vectors $(\mathbf{y}_c, \bar{\mathbf{y}}_c)$. Every capitalist has access to the same Leontief production technology characterized by a productive, indecomposable $n \times n$ matrix of material input requirements $\mathbf{A}$ and a nonnegative n-vector of labor requirements $\mathbf{l}$. For any nonnegative n-vector $\mathbf{x}_c$, a capitalist who employs $\mathbf{l}\mathbf{x}_c$ units of labor on $\mathbf{A}\mathbf{x}_c$ units of nonlabor inputs acquires $[\mathbf{I} - \mathbf{A}]\mathbf{x}_c$ as a net output of the n goods.

Each worker has a unit of labor power, a capacity to work throughout the production period. She owns no other resources. She consumes goods only at the start of the period. The wth worker's preferences are represented by a continuous increasing concave $u_w(\mathbf{y}_w, h_w)$ on her consumption $\mathbf{y}_w$ and on the fraction of the period h_w transforms after she works outside the home.

Let me emphasize that I am simply assuming that the capitalists own produced goods and no labor, that the workers own labor and no produced goods, that the capitalists have access to a technology that is closed off to the workers, and that the capitalists face a decision about how to allocate their consumption over time while the workers consume their wage goods right away. I adopt these assumptions because they underwrite an especially simple characterization of class income distributions in the exchange equilibria of a production economy where production takes time.[2]

The question of exchange

The capitalists would like to spread their consumption into the future. They can do this only if some worker will work up some capitalist's input stocks into goods available at the end of the period. For their part the workers would also like to consume something. But they will eat only if previously produced goods now owned by the capitalists come into the workers' possession.

Suppose that workers try to sell their labor power to capitalists for consumption goods to be delivered before production. Suppose that every capitalist, while trying to buy labor from the workers, also seeks to buy and sell previously and prospectively produced goods that yield a better profile of consumption. What is going to happen? Which exchanges will take place, bringing about which division of labor and which distribution of income?

Price-taking equilibrium

A Walrasian economist tries to answer these questions by imposing a special structure on the exchange of goods and labor. She describes a set of *perfectly competitive markets* where labor, previously produced goods, and prospectively produced goods are traded all at once and each at a uniform price. Every participant in these markets, believing that she can carry out any transaction she can afford at the given prices, opts for a transaction, production, and consumption plan that promises a final bundle of goods that she weakly prefers to all other affordable and productively attainable bundles. The Walrasian economist then looks for a system of uniform prices that directs these traders toward mutually consistent plans.

Continuing the earlier example, we can suppose that the capitalists contract for pre- and post-production deliveries of material goods and that workers commit fractions of their labor time to capitalists' production projects while purchasing consumption goods to be delivered at the start of the period. Faced with a wage rate v, an n-vector $\mathbf{p}$ of prices for goods delivered before production, and an $\mathbf{n}$-vector $\bar{\mathbf{p}}$ of prices for goods delivered after production, a capitalist chooses a production plan $\mathbf{x}_c$ and a consumption plan $\mathbf{y}_c, \bar{\mathbf{y}}_c$ that maximize $u_c(\mathbf{y}_c, \bar{\mathbf{y}}_c)$ subject to the budget

$$\mathbf{p}\mathbf{y}_c + \bar{\mathbf{p}}\bar{\mathbf{y}}_c + \mathbf{p}\mathbf{A}\mathbf{x}_c + \upsilon \mathbf{l}\mathbf{x} \leq \mathbf{p}\omega_c + \bar{\mathbf{p}}\mathbf{x}_c \qquad (1)$$

A worker chooses a nonnegative $\mathbf{y}_w$ and a h_w in $[0,1]$ to maximize her own $u_w(\mathbf{y}_w, h_w)$ subject to

$$\mathbf{p}\mathbf{y}_w \leq \upsilon(1 - h_w) \qquad (2)$$

So everyone makes a plan that she likes no less than any other plan she can afford at the prices she takes as given.

A *price-taking equilibrium* is a list of prices $(\mathbf{p}^*, \bar{\mathbf{p}}^*, \upsilon^*)$ and a complex of consumption and production plans $(\mathbf{y}_c^*, \bar{\mathbf{y}}_c^*, \mathbf{x}_c^*)_{c=1,2,\ldots,M}$ and consumption and labor plans $(\mathbf{y}_w^*, h_w^*)_{w=M+1,M+2,\ldots,M+N}$ that solve these constrained-maximization problems for those prices and that together satisfy

$$\sum_{c=1}^{M} \mathbf{y}_c^* + \sum_{w=M+1}^{M+N} \mathbf{y}_w^* + \mathbf{A}\sum_{c=1}^{M} \mathbf{x}_c^* \leq \sum_{c=1}^{M} \omega_c \qquad (3)$$

$$\sum_{c=1}^{M} \bar{\mathbf{y}}_c^* \leq \sum_{c=1}^{M} \mathbf{x}_c^* \qquad (4)$$

$$\sum_{c=1}^{M} \mathbf{x}_c^* \mathbf{1} \leq N - \sum_{w=M+1}^{M+N} h_w^* \qquad (5)$$

Under the guidance of these prices people apparently plan to consume or employ in aggregate no more of each commodity than they're collectively holding or planning to produce.

Although it is billed as a model of exchange, this idealization prescinds from any direct representation of transactions between traders. The omission is said to be explained by the focus on equilibrium. So long as everyone trades at the same prices, and so long as those prices call up consistent plans, it makes no difference who trades what with whom. Everyone puts in what she plans to put in and takes out what she plans to take out. What everyone plans to do adds up to something that they can all do.

Interest, profit, and wage

Suppose that as part of her initial endowment a capitalist owns a unit of the ith good. Starting from a plan that meets her budget constraint with strict equality, she decides to postpone her consumption of that unit to the end of the production period. If she sells the unit for immediate delivery, she can afford to purchase $p_i^*/\bar{p}_i^*$ units of the good for her later consumption. In effect she makes a loan of this good to someone who consumes it or uses it in production, and the "own rate of interest" defined in

$$1 + \rho_i^* \equiv \frac{p_i^*}{\bar{p}_i^*} \tag{6}$$

measures her return on this commodity loan. At a constrained utility maximum

$$\frac{\partial u_c/\partial y_i}{\partial u_c/\partial \bar{y}_i} = \frac{p_i}{\bar{p}_i} \tag{7}$$

and so in equilibrium

$$\frac{\partial u_c/\partial y_i}{\partial u_c/\partial \bar{y}_i} = 1 + \rho_i^*;$$

this interest rate also reports the capitalists' marginal rate of substitution between earlier and later consumption of the good.

Unless the input prices $\mathbf{p}$ are proportional to the output prices $\bar{\mathbf{p}}$, these own-interest rates will vary from commodity to commodity. But by turning to production we can find a kind of equalization of return.

Equilibrium prices must satisfy

$$\bar{\mathbf{p}}^* \le \mathbf{p}^* \mathbf{A} + \upsilon^* \mathbf{l} \tag{8}$$

If this inequality were not met for some good, then, by producing greater and greater quantities of that good, a household could afford larger and larger consumption bundles delivering ever greater utility, and no constrained maximum would exist. For any good i that's to be produced it must be that

$$\bar{p}_i^* = \mathbf{p}^* \mathbf{a}_i + \upsilon^* l_i \tag{9}$$

so that all operated activities make the maximum profit of zero.

With a commodity bundle $\mathbf{d}$ serving as numéraire, an undiscounted profit rate on the production activity $\mathbf{a}_i, l$ may be defined as in

$$1 + r_i^{\mathbf{d}} \equiv \frac{\bar{p}_i}{\mathbf{p}^* \mathbf{a}_i + \upsilon^* l_i} \frac{\mathbf{pd}}{\overline{\mathbf{pd}}} \tag{10}$$

This measures a capitalist household's return on the material goods and wage payments tied up during the production period, using the undiscounted prices corresponding to the numéraire. Since every operated activity satisfies (9), the first ratio on the right-hand side equals 1, and in fact

$$1 + r_i^{\mathbf{d}} = \frac{\mathbf{p}^* \mathbf{d}}{\bar{\mathbf{p}}^* \mathbf{d}} \equiv 1 + \rho_{\mathbf{d}}. \tag{11}$$

Profit rates on operated activities, measured in the undiscounted prices associated with a numéraire of $\mathbf{d}$, are equalized at the own-rate of interest of that composite commodity.[3]

Taking the cth capitalist's budget constraint (1) to be satisfied with equality and substituting from the zero-profit condition, you may write the value of her consumption of the newly produced goods $\bar{\mathbf{y}}_c$ as

$$\bar{\mathbf{p}}^*\bar{\mathbf{y}}_c = \mathbf{p}^*\left[\omega_c - \mathbf{y}_c\right]. \tag{12}$$

These magnitudes can in turn be expressed in $\mathbf{d}$-units by dividing through by $\bar{\mathbf{p}}^*\mathbf{d}$ and substituting from (11) to arrive at

$$\frac{\bar{\mathbf{p}}^*\bar{\mathbf{y}}_c}{\bar{\mathbf{p}}^*\mathbf{d}} = (1 + \rho_\mathbf{d})\frac{\mathbf{p}^*\left[\omega_c - \mathbf{y}_c\right]}{\mathbf{p}^*\mathbf{d}}. \tag{13}$$

The value in $\mathbf{d}$-units of the capitalist's consumption of the produced good equals the value in $\mathbf{d}$-units of the inputs she's contributed to production, marked up by the own-rate interest of the composite commodity $\mathbf{d}$.

For a given numéraire $\mathbf{d}$, then, the real wage $\upsilon_\mathbf{d}^* \equiv \upsilon^*/\mathbf{p}^*\mathbf{d}$ and the composite own rate $\rho_\mathbf{d}^*$ make a low-dimensional representation of the distribution of income between capital and labor inhering in the equilibrium prices.

Distribution by tastes, technology, and endowment

Suppose it were true that, for each possible technology, allocation of endowments, and specification of preferences, there's a unique equilibrium configuration of prices and plans. As we've just seen, the equilibrium prices include a price for labor and a profile of ratios between the input and output prices of the produced goods – a wage rate and a structure of interest rates. The Walrasian economist explains this distribution of income between labor and capital as an incident of the unique socially consistent configuration of price-taking market interaction motivated and constrained by the given endowments, tastes, and technology.

To offer this explanation is to propose a strong division of explanatory labor between the market and other social institutions or practices. Public taxation and spending; the legal recognition and enforcement of property; the organization of family life; material culture; collective bargaining and shopfloor conflict; norms of deference, solidarity, or justice: any of these might help to explain the prevailing distribution, but their roles are necessarily limited. They can help to cause or to constitute the endowments, tastes, and technology that the market maps to a price-taking equilibrium. Or they can serve to *re*distribute commodities and income away from that equilibrium. They do not directly interact with or compose the market's own exchange and production processes that decide which distribution results from the market's data of endowments, tastes, and technology. These institutions are kept to the background, their influence felt only in the prehistory or the aftermath of market exchange.

Exogenous distribution

A *classical* economist asks which system of temporally invariant goods prices, profit rates, and wage rates supports a sustainable pattern of production by equalizing rates of profit across the activities operated in that pattern. Applied to the Leontief technology and numéraire defined earlier, these conditions are

$$\mathbf{p} = (1+r)(\mathbf{p}\mathbf{A} + \upsilon\mathbf{l}) \tag{14}$$

$$\mathbf{p}\mathbf{d} = 1 \tag{15}$$

The classical economist finds this equal-profit-rate condition met at each of a continuum of price systems. She notices that the profit rate and the real wage vary inversely across that continuum. And she argues that extramarket institutions resolve this indeterminacy by imposing a boundary condition on distribution that selects a (price, profit, wage) system from the continuum of possibilities. She has in mind that custom, policy, bargaining, or class struggle can dictate a particular value for the real wage, for example, and that commodity prices form to equalize profit rates at that wage. In this way the classical economist reaches her own version of the indeterminacy thesis that I set out in the first section.[4]

The price system (14, 15) is sometimes promoted as a rival to the Walrasian intertemporal equilibrium described in earlier sections. I've never been sure what that rivalry amounts to or how we should go about picking a winner. The Walrasian model, like the classical one, calls for an equalization of profit rates. The crucial differentia of (14, 15) are apparently twofold. First, those equations presuppose that inputs and outputs are sold at constant relative prices. And, second, they accommodate this restriction on prices by abstracting away any requirement that demand not exceed an aggregate supply that is limited by the endowments of labor and produced goods. Why should we suppose that prices are constant? Why should we ignore an endowment-constrained balance of supply and demand? Then again, why not?[5]

Sidestepping these questions about the classical assumptions, I want now to point out that the Walrasian assumptions give rise to two grave internal problems. We can solve those problems, I will claim next, if we relax the Walrasian's special restrictions on exchange in favor of a more general characterization of genuinely decentralized market interaction. This *catallactic* conception will turn out to sponsor a version of the indeterminacy thesis championed by the classical economist.

Why these prices?

The Walrasian economist says that equilibrium prices organize the exchange and production decisions of individual actors into a consistent macroscopic pattern. A closer look shows this to be false. To bring out the deepest difficulties I will go on supposing that only one equilibrium exists. The question to ask first is whether people will come to trade at the equilibrium prices that correspond to their tastes, technology, and endowments.

Suppose that everyone believes that prices will form such that everyone can carry out a constrained-best price-taking plan at those prices. And suppose that everyone knows the endowments, preferences, and technology that characterize the rest of the economy. And suppose that everyone can compute the corresponding unique equilibrium. Then everyone will infer that others will trade at that equilibrium's prices, and she will set out to trade at them herself.

But this is silly. Not only does it require universal economic sophistication, universal computational prowess, and universal knowledge of the economy's structure. It also attributes to every trader the belief that all traders will converge on price expectations that allow for mutually consistent price-taking behavior economywide. What would warrant that belief? Since the argument now underway is meant to *show* that trade will take place at the equilibrium prices, it should in any case not *assume* that this belief is warranted.

A second possibility is that people will arrive at the equilibrium as the asymptotically stable rest point of some exchange process through which people trade their goods and labor at initially non-equilibrium prices. It's an awkward proposal. By the definition of equilibrium the price-taking transaction behavior given in the section Price-taking Equilibrium cannot be universalized outside equilibrium. We'll need a different characterization of transactions. Any such characterization must feature some market actors whose actions help to determine the prices at which goods are traded. And it must limit a person's transactions to those that particular trading partners are willing to carry out. The disequilibrium process is thus bound to show a qualitative discontinuity with the price-taking exchange behavior of the section Price-taking Equilibrium, whose outstanding features are that no person can affect prices and that a person's transactions are limited only by her own budget constraint in those prices.[6]

Suppose that these perplexities are somehow overcome. Suppose that, starting from the initial endowments, people follow a disequilibrium trading process until it converges to an equilibrium price system and allocation. On their way to equilibrium people will have traded goods at non-equilibrium prices. The "endowments" that define their equilibrium destination are not the actual holdings of goods with which they began. The supposed convergence of this disequilibrium process to a price-taking equilibrium fails to imply that, starting from their actual endowments, people will reach the equilibrium prices that the Walrasian theory assigns to that starting point.[7]

Why these quantities?

A second problem strikes me as even more serious. Put aside the doubts just aired. Suppose that people come to believe that trade will take place at the equilibrium prices corresponding to their original endowments. What will they do then? The Walrasian answers that they will arrange to trade and produce goods in a socially consistent pattern. But this answer is also unsupported.

In equilibrium every operated activity earns zero profits. Every capitalist is indifferent between all intensities of operation of any mixture of those activities. She is happy to produce nothing. She is happy to produce on a vast scale whose input requirements dwarf the economy's aggregate endowment. And she is equally content with all intermediate possibilities.

When the Walrasian economist observes that at the equilibrium prices capitalists are willing to produce in a pattern that clears the markets for goods and labor, she forgets to add that they're also willing to produce in any of an uncountable infinity of non-market-clearing patterns. Prices do not live up to their reputation for organizing a socially consistent program of production by the many producers.[8]

Starting over

I conclude that we should not hold onto the Walrasian's special structure for exchange. Throwing it off, we are free to return to a less restricted version of the question of exchange with which I started. When people set out to exchange goods and labor with one another, each so as to improve her or his own consumption prospects, where will her or his exchanges take the economy as a whole?

Catallactic exchange

I'll now assume that persons meet to consider possible contracts arranging for deliveries of goods before or after the production period or for labor during it.[9] Let the vectors z_{jk}, $\bar{z}_{jk}$ describe the deliveries called for under any contracts extant between the jth and the kth actors. A positive (negative) ith component in z_{jk} indicates that the kth (jth) person is to deliver to the jth (kth) a quantity of the ith good equal in magnitude to that component. Let the number e_{cw} describe the fraction of the wth worker's labor time that she's contracted to spend on the cth capitalist's production. Let

$$e_c \equiv \sum_{w=M+1}^{M+N} e_{cw}, e_w \equiv \sum_{c=1}^{M} e_{cw}, z_j \equiv \sum_{k=1}^{M+N} z_{jk}, \bar{z}_c \equiv \sum_{k=1}^{M} \bar{z}_{ck}. \tag{16}$$

And let a vector z concatenate all the z_{jk}, $\bar{z}_{jk}$, e_{cw}, e_{wc} representing the capitalists' and workers' contractually obligated deliveries.

The cth capitalist chooses a production and consumption plan to maximize her utility, given that she will give or take the goods or labor that she's contracted for:

$$max_{x_c \geq 0, y_c \geq 0, \bar{y}_c \geq 0} \, u_c(y_c, \bar{y}_c) \text{ subject to} \tag{17}$$

$$y_c + Ax_c \leqq \omega_c + z_c \tag{18}$$

$$\bar{\mathbf{y}}_c \leqq \mathbf{x}_c + \bar{\mathbf{z}}_c \tag{19}$$

$$\mathbf{l}\mathbf{x}_c \leq e_c. \tag{20}$$

Let the function $v_c(\mathbf{z})$ report the solution value of this problem.[10] For her part the wth worker is represented by a

$$v_w(\mathbf{z}) \equiv max_{\mathbf{y}_w \geq 0, 0 \leq h_w \leq 1} u(\mathbf{y}_w, h_w) \text{ subject to} \tag{21}$$

$$\mathbf{y}_w \leq \mathbf{z}_w \tag{22}$$

$$h_w \leq 1 - e_w \tag{23}$$

I'll collect all persons' value functions as $\mathbf{v}(\mathbf{z})$.

Let Z be the set of possible states $\mathbf{z}$ such that for all w $0 \leq e_w \leq 1$ and such that for all c the constraints (18, 19, 20) are met for some nonnegative production plan $\mathbf{x}_c$. For any $\mathbf{z}$ in Z, then, everyone can deliver the goods or labor she's obligated to provide under the contracts in that $\mathbf{z}$. Because labor power and the nonlabor inputs are in fixed supply, Z is bounded.

A negotiation process unfolding over rounds $t = 1, 2, 3, \ldots$ determines for each $\mathbf{z}_t$ the new state $\mathbf{z}_{t+1}$ of contracts that results from agreements reached during the tth round. I'll assume that any one such process can be represented by some continuous $\phi : Z \to Z$ such that a solution of

$$\mathbf{z}_{t+1} = \phi(\mathbf{z}_t) \tag{24}$$

for an initial $\mathbf{z}_0$ with all components equal to zero represents a path of contracts negotiated under the process.

I'll assume throughout that

$$\mathbf{v}(\phi(\mathbf{z})) \geqq \mathbf{v}(\mathbf{z}): \tag{25}$$

no change to the contracts makes a person worse off. I will assume throughout that

$$\phi(\mathbf{z}) \neq \mathbf{z} \to \mathbf{v}(\phi(\mathbf{z})) \geq \mathbf{v}(\mathbf{z}): \tag{26}$$

any change in the contracts makes someone strictly better off. Finally, I will assume in the next five sections that

$$\phi(\mathbf{z}) = \mathbf{z} \to \nexists \mathbf{z}' \in Z, \mathbf{v}\left(\mathbf{z}'\right) \geq \mathbf{v}(\mathbf{z}): \tag{27}$$

contracts go unchanged only if no feasible change would make someone better off while making no one worse off.

Catallactic equilibrium

A state that satisfies the consequent of (27) I'll call a *catallactic equilibrium*. I'll now show that, for any continuous $\phi : Z \rightarrow Z$ satisfying (25, 26, 27), every negotiation path $\mathbf{z}_t$ solving (24) converges to such an equilibrium.

Because $\mathbf{z}_t$ is confined to the bounded set Z, there is an infinite subsequence $\{t_\tau\}$ for which the limit

$$lim_{\tau \rightarrow \infty} \mathbf{z}_{t_\tau} = \mathbf{z}^* \tag{28}$$

exists. Let $\mathbf{z}_t^*$ be the negotiation path that solves (24) given the limit point $\mathbf{z}^*$ as its initial position. Solutions of (24) are continuous with respect to their initial positions, so

$$\text{for all } t, \ \mathbf{z}_t^* = \phi^t \left(lim_{\tau \rightarrow \infty} \mathbf{z}_{t_\tau} \right) = lim_{\tau \rightarrow \infty} \mathbf{z}_{t+t_\tau} \tag{29}$$

where ϕ^t is the tth iterate of the function ϕ. Now consider the sum of the households' values

$$V(\mathbf{z}) \equiv \sum_{j=1}^{M+N} v_j(\mathbf{z}) \tag{30}$$

This function is bounded and – by (25) – nondecreasing on any solution path, and there exists the limit

$$lim_{t \rightarrow \infty} V(\mathbf{z}_t) = V^* \tag{31}$$

The sum of value functions is continuous, and so

$$\text{for all } t, \ V\left(\mathbf{z}_t^*\right) = V\left(lim_{\tau \rightarrow \infty} \mathbf{z}_{t+t_\tau}\right) = lim_{\tau \rightarrow \infty} V\left(\mathbf{z}_{t+t_\tau}\right) = V^* \tag{32}$$

So V is in fact constant on the path $\mathbf{z}_t^*$. But V can be constant only if

$$\text{for all } t, \ \mathbf{z}_t^* = \mathbf{z}^* \tag{33}$$

since by (26) any change in some contract would yield a strictly greater value of V. So by (27) any such limit point is an equilibrium.[11]

The question of exchange reconsidered

My question was "What will happen when capitalists and workers set out to trade so as to improve their consumption prospects?" My new answer is that they'll converge to a catallactic equilibrium where no one is worse off than before trade. The set of such equilibria forms a continuum, and a series of individually advantageous exchanges will convey the economy to some point on that continuum.[12]

This answer marks a twofold improvement over the Walrasian one. First, the equilibria it mentions are the asymptotically stable rest points of dynamical systems representing the decentralized market interactions that it describes. There is no mystery as to how people find their way to these equilibria.

Second, people reach equilibrium intending to produce goods in a socially consistent pattern. Everyone has contracted to receive or supply particular quantities of labor and produced inputs, and they have contracted to deliver particular outputs. Bound by their contracts, people are planning to produce as much of each good altogether as they're altogether planning to consume. A web of informationally decentralized, contractually specified individual *quantity* constraints secures the coordination of production that centrally broadcast uniform prices fail to achieve.

Power-dependent distribution

Every negotiation path ends up somewhere in the equilibrium set. But it depends for its particular destination on the institutions of bargaining and on the balances of power that shape them.

For one very crude illustration of that dependence, suppose that at every round of negotiation a worker is grouped with one or several capitalists to consider changes to their contracts. Agreed changes maximize a weighted sum of the parties' value functions, subject to their existing contracts with outsiders and to the further condition that no one be made worse off.

If in every such meeting the worker's value function carries no weight in the sum to be maximized, contracts converge to an equilibrium in which for every worker

$$v_w\left(\mathbf{z}_t^*\right) = u_w\left(\mathbf{0}, 1\right) \tag{34}$$

and the capitalists claim all gains to trade realized along the way. If instead the capitalists' value functions take zero weight, then in equilibrium

$$v_c\left(\mathbf{z}_t^*\right) = u_c\left(\omega_c, \mathbf{0}\right) \tag{35}$$

and all benefit redounds to the workers.

Intermediate weightings presumably split the cooperative surplus in ways that are harder to analyze at this level of abstraction. But the comparison between these extremes is already enough to show that the distribution generated from a particular constellation of tastes, technology, and endowment can favor workers or capitalists according as the institutional configuration of bargaining tilts toward one or the other class.

Shadow prices in equilibrium

Let $(\mathbf{p}_c, \bar{\mathbf{p}}_c, \upsilon_c)$ be the Lagrange multipliers or shadow prices corresponding to the jth capitalist's optimal program at the equilibrium contracts. Every capitalist's prices are, in equilibrium, proportional to some $(\mathbf{p}^*, \bar{\mathbf{p}}^*, \upsilon^*)$, and the shadow prices $(\mathbf{p}_w, \upsilon_w)$ supporting a worker's program are also proportional to $(\mathbf{p}^*, \upsilon^*)$.

Suppose that were false. It would follow that some pattern $\triangle \mathbf{z}$ of feasible small deviations from the economy's equilibrium contract state would satisfy

$$\text{for all } j \text{ and } k, \ \mathbf{p}_j \triangle \mathbf{z}_{jk} + \bar{\mathbf{p}}_j \triangle \bar{\mathbf{z}}_{jk} + \upsilon_j \triangle e_{jk} \geq 0 \tag{36}$$

and

$$\text{for some } j \text{ and } k, \ \mathbf{p}_j \triangle \mathbf{z}_{jk} + \bar{\mathbf{p}}_j \triangle \bar{\mathbf{z}}_{jk} + \upsilon_j \triangle e_{jk} > 0 \tag{37}$$

Since by an envelope theorem the vector of an actor's shadow prices coincides with the gradient of her value function, these small changes would help the jth actor and hurt no one, contradicting the definition of equilibrium.

Let's go ahead and normalize the capitalists' shadow prices in equilibrium to $(\mathbf{p}^*, \bar{\mathbf{p}}^*, \upsilon^*)$ and the workers' multipliers to $(\mathbf{p}^*, \upsilon^*)$. These have a familiar structure. The Kuhn–Tucker conditions for a solution of each capitalist's maximization problem include that

$$\bar{\mathbf{p}}^* \leq \mathbf{p}^* \mathbf{A} + \upsilon^* \mathbf{l} \tag{38}$$

with

$$\bar{p}_i^* = \mathbf{p}^* \mathbf{a}_i + \upsilon^* l_i \tag{39}$$

for any good that's produced. Equilibrium shadow prices equalize discounted shadow profits at zero.

Path-dependent distribution

A person's final consumption is decided, not by these shadow prices, but by the history of the exchange and labor agreements she's reached on the way to equilibrium. Most of those arranged for transfers of goods or labor at ratios different from the equilibrium prices. It follows that, while shadow prices in catallactic equilibrium mimic Walrasian market prices by annihilating discounted profits, my earlier Walrasian analysis of capitalists' *income* in terms of those prices does not carry over to catallaxy. Let me explain.

The Kuhn–Tucker conditions for a constrained maximum of the cth capitalist's utility include the equalities

$$\mathbf{p} \mathbf{y}_c + \mathbf{p} \mathbf{A} \mathbf{x}_c = \mathbf{p} \omega_c + \mathbf{p} \mathbf{z}_c \tag{40}$$

$$\bar{\mathbf{p}} \bar{\mathbf{y}}_c = \bar{\mathbf{p}} \mathbf{x}_c + \bar{\mathbf{p}} \bar{\mathbf{z}}_c \tag{41}$$

and

$$\bar{\mathbf{p}} \mathbf{x}_c = \mathbf{p} \mathbf{A} \mathbf{x}_c + \upsilon \mathbf{l} \mathbf{x}_c \tag{42}$$

A rearrangement gives

$$\bar{\mathbf{p}}\bar{\mathbf{y}}_c = \mathbf{p}\left[\omega_c - \bar{\mathbf{y}}_c\right] + \mathbf{p}\mathbf{z}_c + \bar{\mathbf{p}}\bar{\mathbf{z}}_c + \upsilon \mathbf{l}\mathbf{x}_c \tag{43}$$

Because workers don't participate in the market for prospectively produced goods, it turns out that

$$\sum_{c=1}^{M} \bar{\mathbf{z}}_c = \mathbf{0} \tag{44}$$

and so that

$$\sum_{c=1}^{M} \bar{\mathbf{p}}^* \bar{\mathbf{y}}_c = \sum_{c=1}^{M} \mathbf{p}^* \left[\omega_c - \mathbf{y}_c\right] + \sum_{c=1}^{M} \mathbf{p}\mathbf{z}_c + \sum_{c=1}^{M} \upsilon^* \mathbf{l}\mathbf{x}_c \tag{45}$$

The capitalists' aggregate consumption of produced goods, as valued in the equilibrium shadow prices, equals the aggregate value of the material inputs they've invested plus a further term

$$\sum_{c=1}^{M} \mathbf{p}\mathbf{z}_c + \sum_{c=1}^{M} \upsilon^* \mathbf{l}\mathbf{x}_c \tag{46}$$

that subtracts the shadow value of the wage goods they collectively deliver to the workers from the shadow value of the workers' labor. This number might be negative or positive. It won't be zero except by fluke.

In the corresponding price-taking equilibrium, on the other hand, capitalist consumption satisfies

$$\bar{\mathbf{p}}^* \bar{\mathbf{y}}_c = \mathbf{p}^* \left[\omega_c - \mathbf{y}_c\right]$$

The value of capitalists' consumption in catallaxy is greater or less than in this price-taking equilibrium according to how the negotiation of wage agreements outside equilibrium made for a positive or negative value of (46).

The section **Interest and Profit** also pointed out that in the price-taking equilibrium

$$\frac{\bar{\mathbf{p}}^* \bar{\mathbf{y}}_c}{\bar{\mathbf{p}}^* \mathbf{d}} = (1 + \rho_\mathbf{d}) \frac{\mathbf{p}^* \left[\omega_c - \mathbf{y}_c\right]}{\mathbf{p}^* \mathbf{d}}:$$

a capitalist's real consumption in **d** units equals her investment marked up by the own rate of interest of the numéraire commodity, which relates the marginal utilities of earlier and later consumption. In catallaxy, by contrast, the right-hand side of this expression bears the further term

$$\frac{1}{\bar{\mathbf{p}}^* \mathbf{d}} \left[\mathbf{p}^* \mathbf{z}_c + \upsilon^* \mathbf{l}\mathbf{x}_c\right] \tag{47}$$

Again this may be positive or negative. It will take different values for different capitalists. And its values will depend on the particular institutionally determined negotiation path by which the equilibrium was approached. There's no hope of equating the value of capitalists' consumption with the value of their investments marked up by a uniform rate of return, defined from the equilibrium prices and expressing the capitalists' substitution between immediate and deferred consumption.

An exogenous real wage

Consider a negotiation process that, in place of (27), obeys, for some $\hat{v}$ and $\mathbf{d}$,

$$\left[\mathbf{z}' = \phi(\mathbf{z}) \text{ for some } \mathbf{z} \text{ in } Z \text{ and } e'_{cw} > 0 \right] \rightarrow \frac{\mathbf{z}'_{wc}}{e'_{cw}} = \hat{v}\mathbf{d} \tag{48}$$

and

$$\phi(\mathbf{z}) = \mathbf{z} \rightarrow \nexists \mathbf{z}' \in Z : \left[\mathbf{v}\left(\mathbf{z}'\right) \geq \mathbf{v}(\mathbf{z}) \text{ and } e'_{cw} > 0 \rightarrow \frac{\mathbf{z}'_{wc}}{e'_{cw}} = \hat{v}\mathbf{d} \right] \tag{49}$$

and that also satisfies my original assumptions (25) and (26). This process requires that labor be paid in units of the numéraire bundle $\mathbf{d}$ at the given real wage $\hat{v}$. And it allows a contract state to persist only if no change consistent with this real-wage condition improves some person's situation while worsening no one's.

It's easy to show that every path of a continuous process ϕ that obeys (25, 26, 48, 49) converges to a state that satisfies the consequent of (49).[13] For any $\hat{v}$ that's not too large, this equilibrium supports production projects that pay a real wage of $\hat{v}$ to every worker they employ.

This result makes another interesting contrast with the Walrasian outlook on class. To impose an exogenous real wage on the Walrasian system is to force an excess supply (or demand) in its market for labor. By the accounting identity known as Walras' Law this calls for an offsetting excess demand (or supply) in some other market. Price-taking equilibrium has no room for a politically concerted or culturally conventional real wage.

The catallactic conception is more permissive. It allows that where tradition or politics dictates a particular value for the real wage, a series of individually advantageous decentralized agreements will reconcile individual production and consumption plans to that distributive boundary condition. It gives another glimpse of social possibilities that were not dreamt of in the Walrasian philosophy.[14]

Notes

1. I'll reserve boldfaced symbols for vectors or vector-valued functions. I'll write the scalar product of vectors $\mathbf{x}$ and $\mathbf{y}$ as $\mathbf{xy}$. That $\mathbf{x} \geq \mathbf{y}$ is that no component of $\mathbf{x}$ is less than the corresponding component of $\mathbf{y}$. That $\mathbf{x} \geq \mathbf{y}$ is that $\mathbf{x} \geq \mathbf{y}$ and $\mathbf{x} \neq \mathbf{y}$. I'll use the subscript i for an arbitrary good and j or k for an arbitrary actor of either class.

2. Roemer (1982) stages a variety of capitalist class structures in Walrasian general equilibrium.

3. This conception of profit rates in the undiscounted price system of an intertemporal general equilibrium is due to Malinvaud (1972: ch. 10). See also Duménil and Lévy (1985).

4. Sraffa (1960) gives the authoritative modern statement of this classical idea. My way of contrasting the explanatory structures of Walrasian and classical price theory follows Marglin (1984). Mandler (1999a) and Mandler (1999b: ch. 2) also ascribe an indeterminacy thesis to Sraffa.

5. Hahn (1982a) presses these points.

6. This discontinuity between equilibrium and disequilibrium was pointed out by Arrow (1959).

7. Fisher (1983) emphasizes that, if equilibrium is reached by disequilibrium trade, the initial endowments fail to play their expected role in determining the final prices and allocation.

8. Linearity is not crucial for this conclusion. Any constant-returns technology, for example, would require a zero-profit equilibrium price system that leaves the scale of individual production undetermined.

9. This conception of genuinely decentralized exchange, which can be traced back at least to Edgeworth (1881), was most recently retrieved by Axtell (2005) and by Foley (2010).

10. I'm writing this value function as a function of the entire contract state z for convenience's sake. A person's solution depends only on her own contracts.

11. This convergence proof closely follows the argument of Uzawa (1962). For other discussions of the stability of catallactic processes see Smale (1976), Hahn (1982b), Axtell (2005), and Foley (2010).

12. To confirm that it's a continuum, notice that for any convex combination of the individual value functions, a contract state z that maximizes that combination subject to the constraint that every person be able to fulfill her contracts given her endowments, is a catallactic equilibrium. Thanks to the continuity of the value functions, the solutions of these problems are continuous in the weights assigned to the value functions. By setting all but one weight to zero, you ensure that only the person receiving positive weight is strictly better off in the associated solution, so there must be several distinct solutions corresponding to different weightings. So the equilibrium set must include an uncountable infinity of distinct contract states.

13. Take another look at the argument of the section Catallactic Equilibrium. Before its final sentence, that argument appeals only to the properties (25) and (26). Since the exogenous-wage process has those properties as well, the argument shows that every solution of this process has some limit point z^* such that $z^* = \phi(z^*)$. In light of (49) it must be that this z^* satisfies the consequent of that conditional.

14. I learned the catallactic conception of exchange from Duncan Foley, and this chapter runs variations on themes from Foley (2010). To my fellow students in his microeconomic theory course at the New School this chapter will also read as a poor fascimile of his lecture notes for that magnificent class. I thank Foley along with Rajiv Sethi, Gil Skillman, Peter Skott, Roberto Veneziani, Luca Zamparelli, and two anonymous readers of an earlier draft.

References

Arrow, K. J. (1959) "Toward a theory of price adjustment," in Abramovitz, M. (ed.) *The Allocation of Economic Resources*, Palo Alto, CA: Stanford University Press.

Axtell, R. (2005) "The complexity of exchange," *Economic Journal*, 115: 193–210.

Duménil, G. and Lévy, D. (1985) "The classicals and the neoclassicals: a rejoinder to Hahn," *Cambridge Journal of Economics*, 9(4): 327–345.

Edgeworth, F. Y. (1881) *Mathematical Psychics*, London: Kegan Paul.

Fisher, F. (1983) *Disequilibrium Foundations of Equilibrium Economics*, Cambridge, UK: Cambridge University Press.

Foley, D. K. (2010) "What's wrong with the fundamental existence and welfare theorems?" *Journal of Economic Behavior and Organization*, 75(2): 115–131.

Hahn, F. (1982a) "The neo-Ricardians," *Cambridge Journal of Economics*, 6: 353–374.

Hahn, F. (1982b) "Stability," in Arrow, K. and Intriligator, M. (eds) *Handbook of Mathematical Economics*, vol. 2, Amsterdam: Elsevier.

Malinvaud, E. (1972) *Lectures on Microeconomic Theory*, Amsterdam: North-Holland.

Mandler, M. (1999a) "Sraffian indeterminacy in general equilibrium," *Review of Economic Studies*, 66: 693–711.

Mandler, M. (1999b) *Dilemmas in Economic Theory*, Oxford: Oxford University Press.

Marglin, S. (1984) *Growth, Distribution, and Prices*, Cambridge, MA: Harvard University Press.

Roemer, J. (1982) *A General Theory of Exploitation and Class*, Cambridge, MA: Harvard University Press.

Smale, S. (1976) "Exchange processes with price adjustment," *Journal of Mathematical Economics*, 3: 211–226.

Sraffa, P. (1960) *Production of Commodities by Means of Commodities*. Cambridge, UK: Cambridge University Press.

Uzawa, H. (1962) "On the stability of Edgeworth's barter process," *International Economic Review*, 3: 218–232.

6 Positional goods, climate change and the social returns to investment

Leila Davis and Peter Skott

Introduction

Climate change affects countries differently, and within regions the impact varies across groups. The time dimension introduces other distributional elements: the costs of global warming are borne (mainly) by future generations while the investment in mitigation may impose costs on the current generation.

The uneven distribution of costs and benefits is not unique to climate change and environmental policy. Policy generally benefits some people while others are hurt, and Pareto rankings of the outcomes are typically not available. Instead, decisions have to be based on social welfare evaluations that make (implicit or explicit) interpersonal comparisons, weighing up costs and benefits so as to arrive at a net result. The standard approach in the economic literature on climate change has been to use the utility function of "the representative agent" as a social welfare function.

The approach is in line with trends within macroeconomics where models based on an optimizing representative agent are ubiquitous. The models are seen as "micro-founded," even though well-behaved preferences at the agent level fail to imply that aggregate outcomes behave as if they were generated by an optimizing representative agent, a result that has been well-known since the work of Debreu (1974), Mantel (1976) and Sonnenschein (1972). Abstracting from these existence problems, moreover, a welfare analysis based on the preferences of the representative agent can lead to systematic biases. In this chapter we focus on the intertemporal dimension and the biases that arise when consumption has a positional component. To simplify the analysis and highlight these particular effects, we disregard problems associated with intra-generational distribution and assume that all agents are identical with respect to both preferences and endowments; Skott and Davis (2012) examine biases that derive from intra-generational inequality.

The chapter is in five sections. The next section considers representative agents and the role of the rates of return. The third section introduces positional goods and sets up a small model to analyze how they affect the optimal amount of investment in mitigation. The fourth section relates the formal model to procedures used in climate models to evaluate the costs and benefits of mitigation, and presents the results of a small survey to evaluate the importance of the biases identified by the model. The final section summarizes the results and offers a few concluding remarks.

Representative agents and rates of return

Consider a market economy and assume that the trajectories of aggregate consumption, investment and output can be described as if determined by an intertemporally optimizing representative agent. Given this highly restrictive assumption, it may seem reasonable to use the utility function of the representative agent as the social welfare function. Woodford (2003), for instance, suggests that the utility function of the representative agent "provides a *natural objective* in terms of which alternative policies should be evaluated" (12; emphasis added), while, according to Blanchard (2008), contemporary macro models with formal optimization enable one "to derive optimal policy based on the *correct* (within the model) welfare criterion" (9; emphasis added). Most tellingly, perhaps, the evaluation of outcomes based on the stipulated utility function of the representative agent is usually presented without any argument or caveat.[1]

Using this "descriptive" representative-agent approach, the social welfare function has to be calibrated to fit empirical observations.[2] An optimizing representative agent in a standard discounted-utility model chooses a consumption path that satisfies the Euler equation

$$\hat{c} = \frac{1}{\theta}(r - \rho) \tag{1}$$

where c is consumption and a hat over a variable denotes a growth rate ($\hat{c} = \frac{dc}{dt}/c$); ρ is the pure rate of time preference, θ the intertemporal elasticity of substitution and r the real rate of return on saving. We have observations for r and $\hat{c}$, and the choices of the representative agent should match these observations. It follows that although the social welfare function has two parameters, θ and ρ, there is only one degree of freedom.

Most economic analyses of climate change have followed the descriptive approach. The Stern Review (Stern 2007) is an exception. Stern adopted a "prescriptive" approach to social welfare and argued that on ethical grounds the pure discount rate should be close to zero. He combined the low discount rate with a logarithmic specification of the instantaneous utility function ($\theta = 1$), and this combination of parameters fuels the strong recommendations of the Stern Review.

Not surprisingly, Stern's assumptions have been challenged. Nordhaus (2008) rejects Stern's "lofty vantage point of the social planner" as being "misleading in the context of global warming and particularly as it informs the negotiations of policies among sovereign states" (174). Advocating a descriptive approach, Nordhaus wants to base the analysis on the revealed preferences of the representative agent. This approach, he argues, does not assume "the social desirability of the distribution of incomes over space or time under existing conditions." Instead,

> The calculations of changes in world welfare arising from efficient climate-change policies examine potential improvements within the context of the existing distribution of income and investments across space and time.
>
> (Nordhaus 2008: 174–175)

There is an internal tension in Nordhaus's defense of the descriptive approach. He also argues that

> The individual rates of time preference, risk preference, and utility functions do not, in principle at least, enter into the discussion or arguments at all. An individual may have high time preference, or perhaps double hyperbolic discounting, or negative discounting, but this has no necessary connection with how social decisions weight different generations. Similar cautions apply to the consumption elasticity.
>
> (172)

It seems inconsistent, however, to argue that there is "no necessary connection" between individual choice and the appropriate criteria for social decisions and, at the same time, insist on a descriptive representative-agent approach to social valuation. The rationale behind the descriptive approach is precisely that the representative agent describes the average behavior of the individuals; why insist on the descriptive approach if individual choices are irrelevant?

Leaving aside this inconsistency, Stern's combination of a logarithmic utility function and a near-zero discount rate fails to meet the descriptive test if the annual real rate of return is taken to fall in a range that matches the observed return on private capital.[3] More importantly, whatever one may think about ethics and the pure rate of discount, there is a tradeoff, Nordhaus argues, between investment in mitigation and investment in other areas including traditional capital, R&D, education, etc. If r measures the social rate of return to these conventional investment projects, investment in emissions reduction must get a similar return:

> In choosing among alternative trajectories for emissions reductions, the key economic variable is the real return on capital, r, which measures the net yield on investments in capital, education, and technology. In principle, this is observable in the marketplace. ... The return on capital is the discount rate that enters into the determination of the efficient balance between the cost of emissions reductions today and the benefit of reduced climate damages in the future. A high return on capital tilts the balance toward emissions reductions in the future, while a low return tilts reductions toward the present.
>
> (Nordhaus 2008: 59)

According to Nordhaus, the Stern Review with its low discount rate for investment in abatement would misallocate investment to such an extent that an attempt to maintain the welfare of current generations "would leave the future absolutely worse off; it would be Pareto-deteriorating. The Stern Review's approach is inefficient because it invests too much in low-yield abatement strategies too early" (180). Looking at this from another angle, the Stern parameters have implications for the optimal levels of conventional investment. Using these parameters and the observed values of the return to capital, the optimal global saving rate would be about twice the current level, an implication that does not, Nordhaus suggests, seem "ethically compelling" if global per capita consumption is expected to grow from around US$6,600 today to around US$87,000 in two centuries measured in constant 2005 dollars (Nordhaus 2008: 179).

This general argument has considerable appeal.[4] But it relies on the implicit assumption that socially optimal trajectories require an expected rate of return to mitigation that is (approximately) equal to the observed private rate of return on capital. This assumption may be invalid. As pointed out by Weitzman (2007, 2009), the returns to mitigation may be high in bad states of the world, and this can dramatically reduce the appropriate discount rate for investment in abatement. Michl (2010) also comments on the use of the rate of return on private capital as the basis for discounting mitigation. He notes in particular the implications of the capital controversy for the identification of the rate of return on capital with a "marginal product of capital." Hoel and Sterner (2007) consider the effects of changes in the relative price of environmental goods; an increasing relative price effectively reducing the discount rate. Like these contributions, our argument in this chapter focuses on the appropriate discount rate for investment in mitigation and, like Weitzman and Hoel and Sterner, we argue that it can be much lower than the private real rate of return. But the mechanism is different.[5]

Environmental externalities are not the only externalities. Utility derives not just, or even primarily, from absolute consumption, once a certain level has been reached. The level of consumption relative to other people and relative to own past consumption may be at least as important. A substantial literature has emphasized these effects,[6] and the argument has empirical support. Recent empirical studies have shown a high correlation between relative income and reported well-being; prominent examples include Blanchflower and Oswald (2004) who examine data for the US and the UK, Luttmer (2005) with US data, and Fafchamps and Shilpi (2008) with data for Nepal. The use in these studies of reported "well-being" or "happiness" as a measure of utility raises many issues, but it would be hard to reject the influence of relative income and status on utility, and "happiness" studies are not the only source of empirical support.[7] Johansson-Stenman, Carlson and Daruvala (2002) analyze experimental choices between hypothetical societies and find a strong concern for relative income. Evidence from the experimental and behavioral literature also suggest that "social preferences" shape the behavior of many people (Fehr and Schmidt 2003).

The relevance of status and relative income effects for economic policy has been examined by, among others Ng and Wang (1995) and Howarth (2000), but to our knowledge there have been no attempts to analyze the implications for climate change and the appropriate discount rate for investment in abatement.

A model

Consider a simple two-period model. There are two goods, a standard good and an environmental good. The standard good (y) is a private good, but the consumption of this good involves a positional element, and increased consumption imposes a negative externality on other agents. We disregard the uneven distribution of the effects of climate change and treat the environmental good as a pure public good.

All agents are identical, and the preferences of an agent can be described by the following utility function

$$U = u(c_0^k, c_0, x_0) + \frac{1}{1+\rho} u(c_1^k, c_1, x_1): \quad u_1 > 0, u_2 < 0, u_3 > 0 \tag{2}$$

where $u(., ., .)$ is the per-period utility function; c is the consumption of the standard good and x the environmental good; superscripts k indicate agent and subscripts on a variable (0 or 1) indicate period; c−variables without a superscript refer to average consumption across all agents; by definition the consumption of the public environmental good x is uniform across agents.[8]

The standard good can be used for either consumption, conventional investment (i) or investment in abatement (m), and we assume

$$c_1^k = F(i_0^k); \quad F' > 0 \tag{3}$$

$$x_1 = G(i_0, m_0); \quad G_1 < 0, G_2 > 0 \tag{4}$$

$$y_0^k = c_0^k + i_0^k + m_0^k \tag{5}$$

$$c_0^k \geq 0, i_0^k \geq 0, m_0^k \geq 0 \tag{6}$$

Note that agent k's consumption of the standard good in period 1 depends on the agent's own investment while the consumption of the environmental good is determined by aggregate conventional and abatement investment.[9] The amounts y_0 and x_0 of the standard and environmental good that are available in period 0 are taken as exogenous, and all agents have the same initial endowment of the standard good ($y_0^k = y_0$).

We now consider four different scenarios:

A: **Business as usual**

Without policy intervention, agents maximize (2) subject to (3), (5), and (6). It is readily seen that the solution has $m_0^k = 0$ and that it satisfies a standard Euler equation

$$u_1(c_0^k, c_0, x_0) = u_1(c_1^k, c_1, x_1) \frac{F'(i_0^k)}{1+\rho} \tag{7}$$

where subscripts on a function indicate partial derivatives (e.g. $u_1 = \partial u(c_0^k, c_0, x_0)/ \partial c_0^k$). In equilibrium, $c_j^k = c_j$ and $i_0^k = i_0$, and we have

$$u_1(c_0, c_0, x_0) = u_1(c_1, c_1, x_1) \frac{F'(i_0)}{1+\rho} \tag{8}$$

B: Addressing the environmental externality

A benevolent social planner should take into account both the environmental externalities (equation (4)) and the positional-good externality ($u_2 \le 0$). But consider first the case in which the social planner overlooks the positional-good externality; that is, she mistakenly believes that $u_2 = 0$.

Social welfare is given by

$$U = u(c_0, c_0, x_0) + \frac{1}{1+\rho} u(c_1, c_1, x_1): \quad u_1 > 0, u_2 \le 0, u_3 > 0 \tag{9}$$

Maximizing (9) subject to (3)–(6) and the symmetry condition ($c_j^k = c_j, i_j^k = i_j, m_j^k = m_j$), and setting $u_2 = 0$, we get the following first-order conditions:

$$u_1(c_0, c_0, x_0) = \frac{u_1(c_1, c_1, x_1)F'(i_0) + u_3(c_1, c_1, x_1)G_1(i_0, m_0)}{1+\rho} \tag{10}$$

$$u_1(c_0, c_0, x_0) = \frac{u_3(c_1, c_1, x_1)G_2(i_0, m_0)}{1+\rho} \tag{11}$$

C: Addressing the positional-good externality

In this case, the social planner overlooks the environmental externality. Equation (4) is ignored and the values of both x_0 and x_1 are treated as exogenous. The planner therefore sets $m_0 = 0$ and chooses i_0, c_0 to maximize (9) subject to (3), (5)–(6) and the symmetry condition.

The first-order condition in this case becomes

$$u_1(c_0, c_0, x_0) + u_2(c_0, c_0, x_0) = \left[u_1(c_1, c_1, x_1) + u_2(c_1, c_1, x_1)\right] \frac{F'(i_0^k)}{1+\rho} \tag{12}$$

D: Addressing both environmental and positional-good externalities

The first-order conditions now take the following form:

$$u_1(c_0, c_0, x_0) + u_2(c_0, c_0, x_0) = \frac{\left[u_1(c_1, c_1, x_1) + u_2(c_1, c_1, x_1)\right]F'(i_0)}{1+\rho}$$
$$+ \frac{u_3(c_1, c_1, x_1)G_1(i_0, m_0)}{1+\rho} \tag{13}$$

$$u_1(c_0, c_0, x_0) + u_2(c_0, c_0, x_0) = \frac{u_3(c_1, c_1, x_1)G_2(i_0, m_0)}{1+\rho} \tag{14}$$

Comparing scenarios A and B, the climate externality tends to reduce the optimal amount of conventional investment (use equations (9) and (10) and note the negative impact of i_0 on x_1 via G_1 in the numerator on the right-hand side of (10)), and equation (11) implies positive amounts of investment in mitigation if $u_3 G_2$ is sufficiently high at $m_0 = 0$. These are standard results.

The positional-good externality in scenario C may influence the optimal rate of investment, but in benchmark cases – including when u is CES – the optimal solution is identical to the one in the A scenario.[10] The intuition behind this seemingly paradoxical result is that although the benefits from future increases in consumption are reduced by the externalities, so are the costs from the required reduction in consumption, and these cost and benefit effects offset each other.

Comparing cases B and D, however, it is apparent that the consumption externalities become important for optimal investment when environmental externalities are present too. Formally, this follows from the fact that the coefficients on G_1 are the same on the right hand side of (10) and (13). Intuitively, the consumption externalities do not reduce the negative impact of current investment on future consumption of the environmental good and this reduces the optimal value of i_0. The optimal investment in mitigation, on the other hand, is boosted by the reduction in the social cost of a reduction in the period-0 consumption of the standard good (equations (11) and (14) have the same right hand side but the left hand side has been reduced in (14)).

A special case
Consider a special case in which the standard and environmental goods are perfect substitutes. Thus, let

$$u(c^k, c, x) = v(z) \tag{15}$$

where

$$z = c^k - \gamma c + x \tag{16}$$

is the amount of "generalized consumption" and where it is assumed that v takes the standard CIES form.[11]

Using these specifications the first-order conditions – taking into account both consumption and environmental externalities – can be written

$$v'(z_0)(1 - \gamma) = \frac{v'(z_1)}{1 + \rho}((1 - \gamma)F' + G_1) \tag{17}$$

$$v'(z_0)(1 - \gamma) = \frac{v'(z_1)}{1 + \rho}G_2 \tag{18}$$

Hence, optimality requires that

$$G_2 = (1 - \gamma)F' + G_1 \tag{19}$$

Equation (19) states the required equality between the social rates of return to the two types of investment. $G_2 = \partial z_1 / \partial m_0$ is the return to investment in mitigation. The gross private return to conventional investment is given by $\partial z_1^k / \partial i_0^k = F'$; including the environmental externality the social return is reduced to $F' + G_1$, and consumption externalities introduce an additional wedge: the social benefits of an increase in the consumption of the standard good is reduced by the factor $1 - \gamma$.

Any mapping of this stylized two-period model into real-world decision problems raises problems, but equation (19) can be used to derive a quick back-of-the-envelope estimate of the magnitude of the positional-good effect. Thus, consider a period length of 50 years, let the annual private return to conventional investment be six per cent, and assume that this return is reduced to five per cent when the environmental externality is included (i.e. $F' = \exp(rT) = \exp(0.06 \times 50)$, $F' + G_1 = \exp(0.05 \times 50)$). If $\gamma = 0.5$, equation (19) implies that the required annual return to environmental investment is 1.5 per cent,[12] a value that is virtually identical to the one used by the Stern Review.[13]

The special case has wider relevance. Consider a more general specification of "generalized" consumption. Formally, let

$$u(c^k, c, x) = v(z) \tag{20}$$

$$z = H(c^k, c, x) \tag{21}$$

In terms of generalized consumption goods, the private return to conventional investment now is given by $H_1 F'$; taking into account the environmental externality, the return in terms of generalized consumption goods is $H_1 F' + H_3 G_1$, and when both externalities are included the return falls to $(H_1 + H_2)F' + H_3 G_1$. Optimality requires that this expression equal the return to investment in abatement, which, in terms of the generalized good, is now $H_3 G_2$.[14] Formally, using (13)–(14) and (20)–(21), the first-order conditions imply

$$H_3 G_2 = [H_1 + H_2]F' + H_3 G_1 \tag{22}$$

This optimality condition can be rewritten

$$H_3 G_2 = \left[1 + \frac{H_2}{H_1}\right] H_1 F' + H_3 G_1 \tag{23}$$

Equation (23) differs from (19) in two ways. The expressions for the returns in terms of generalized consumption, first, are slightly more complicated ($H_3 G_1$, $H_3 G_2, H_1 F'$ instead of G_1, G_2, F'); this difference is of no significance. The ratio $-H_2/H_1$, secondly, takes the place of the constant γ. In equilibrium, however, we have $c^k = c$ and the ratio will be constant if H takes a standard CES form: if $H(c^k, c, x) = [\alpha_1 (c^k)^\delta - \alpha_2 c^\delta + \beta x^\delta]^{1/\delta}$ we have

$$-H_2/H_1 = \frac{\alpha_2 (c^k)^{\delta-1}}{\alpha_1 c^{\delta-1}} = \frac{\alpha_2}{\alpha_1} = \gamma \tag{24}$$

The benchmark case with $\gamma = 0.5$ is in line with the evidence. The empirical studies by Blanchflower and Oswald (2004), Luttmer (2005), and Fafchamps and Shilpi (2008) estimated a Cobb–Douglas utility function (a special case of the CES function),

$$H(c^k, c, x) = (c^k)^\alpha c^{-\gamma} x^\beta \tag{25}$$

Blanchflower and Oswald (2004) obtained estimates for $-H_2/H_1$ of about 0.4 while Luttmer (2005) and Fafchamps and Shilpi (2008) found values of about 0.75 or higher. The experimental approach in Johansson-Stenman et al. (2002) gave estimates of about 0.35.

Our analysis of positional goods, it could be argued, does not necessarily invalidate a representative-agent approach. In fact, our model has been cast in terms of identical agents. But a representative-agent analysis easily goes wrong. Thus, assume for the sake of the argument that the model in this section gives an accurate picture of the economy. In equilibrium $c^k = c$ and the welfare of the representative-agent can be written as a reduced-form function of conventional and environmental consumption,

$$W = w(c_0, x_0) + \frac{1}{1+\rho} w(c_1, x_1) \tag{26}$$

Using the descriptive approach and the general specification (26), it is required that the properties of the correct welfare function W match the observed behavior, that is, it is assumed that observed consumption patterns can be derived from maximizing W subject to the relevant constraints. This assumption is invalid. The patterns of actual consumption in the business-as-usual regime are the same no matter how strong is the consumption externality (the value of γ in the special case above), and this observational equivalence implies that the correct parameters in the welfare function cannot – as a matter of principle – be decided on the basis of the macroeconomic evidence. In this sense the "descriptive approach" is intrinsically flawed. Moreover, if (26) is fitted to the macroeconomic evidence, the positional externalities fail to be incorporated and the welfare conclusions will be systematically biased. Putting it differently, in equilibrium the correct representation of the social welfare may take the form (26) whether or not there are consumption externalities. But the calibration of (26) to the evidence is only legitimate in the absence of consumption externalities.

A survey

Climate change influences the production of some market goods – agricultural output is the obvious example – but many of its effects concern non-market "goods" like climate-related diseases. In order to incorporate environmental externalities into existing economic models, monetary values have to be determined for the non-market effects. These values are assigned by estimating either individuals' willingness to pay for the environmental goods or their willingness to accept compensation for damages.

The estimates are based on either stated preference or revealed preference techniques. Revealed preference techniques use market information associated with the effect being evaluated to infer a monetary value – i.e. "surrogate markets" are used to value non-market environmental goods (Intergovernmental Panel on Climate Change (IPCC) 1996: 184). Hedonic wage studies, for example, use market information on wage differentials to derive estimates for the value of a statistical life. These market-based revealed preference techniques are limited in scope, as it is often difficult to find relevant market information with which to infer a monetary value for the non-market good or service in question. As such, costs and benefits are often estimated using the contingent valuation method, whereby monetary values are assigned according to individuals' stated willingness to pay or willingness to accept compensation. Thus, the values depend on what individuals' behavior would have been if markets for the environmental goods and services had existed – through what the IPCC terms "hypothetical markets" (184). Hypothetical markets reflect individuals' responses to questions regarding their personal willingness to pay, and "monetary estimates are thus able to cover both market and nonmarket impacts" (183).

The procedure requires a delineation of the target population, i.e. those individuals must be identified that are affected by the environmental effect. Willingness to pay is estimated using surveys that directly ask respondents how much they are willing to pay, and these individual responses are aggregated to determine total willingness to pay, from which monetary values are inferred. The resulting evaluations can be questioned (see, for example, Venkatachalam 2004; Ackerman and Heinzerling 2004). Willingness to pay fundamentally reflects ability to pay, and the preferences and values of the rich are thus inherently overrepresented relative to those of the poor. At a more technical level, contingent valuation surveys suffer from potential biases arising from incentives to misrepresent preferences or from implied cues within the survey design that prompt certain responses (Mitchell and Carson 1989).[15]

The positional character of consumption can impart an additional bias: a higher willingness to pay can be expected if it is clarified that the reduction in consumption will be imposed on everyone.[16] We carried out a simple survey to preliminarily investigate this hypothesis. The survey considers a particular environmental change. The subjects are informed that global warming and other environmental changes threaten the survival of some animal species and that, according to some estimates, as many as 25 per cent of all species will be extinct before 2100 under current trends. Policy intervention, it is added, may change the scenario and ensure the survival of these endangered species. The extinction of species was chosen as a simple and concrete example of a pure public good threatened by global warming.[17]

The presentation of the environmental problem – the extinction of the species – was followed by a willingness-to-pay question. We used three different versions of the question. In a first version, respondents were asked how large a proportion of their stream of current and future income they would be willing to give up in order to ensure that no existing species become extinct. A second version asked how large a proportion of current and future incomes should be given up to ensure that no existing species become extinct, now supposing that the costs of intervention are shared such that all incomes are reduced by the same percentage. These two questions highlight the difference between a single individual's willingness to pay for environmental protection, and the willingness to pay for environmental protection when there is no relative loss in income. The purpose of the survey is not to value environmental goods or damages, but to investigate the role of positional effects in individuals' willingness to pay. As such, what is important is not the exact loss that respondents are willing to accept to protect the environment, but any systematic differences between willingness to pay when costs are individual and when costs are shared.

The positional effect can be seen as an example of the role of reference points in the evaluation of outcomes. Other people's consumption represents one such reference point; own past consumption is another reference point. Consumption is valued not just relative to other people's consumption, but also in relation to own past consumption. The behavioral economics literature has documented the existence of loss aversion: people tend to place more value on avoiding losses than on acquiring gains (Tversky and Kahneman 1991). Loss aversion – while distinct from the positional effects that have been the focus of the previous three sections – has implications for the measurement of willingness to pay.

The first two versions of the willingness-to-pay question are framed in terms of levels, and it is possible that respondents interpreted the questions to require an absolute decline relative to their current income. If the cost of environmental protection is understood to require a level reduction in take-home pay, concerns regarding ability to meet other financial commitments such as mortgage payments or car payments may decrease willingness to pay. On the other hand, if the question is defined in terms of a lower future growth rate of income – implying smaller future income gains instead of a future income loss – loss aversion may not be expected to play a significant role, and we would expect an increased willingness to pay. A third version of the question therefore defined the issue in terms of reductions in the future growth rate of income. As in the second question, the losses are to be shared – everyone will experience the same reduction in future income growth – and the question is constructed such that the intervals describing reductions in the future growth rate of income roughly correspond to the intervals describing reductions in the level of the current and future income stream. Exact correspondence between levels and growth rates depends on the discount rate, the growth rate and the time horizon. Table 6.1 in the Appendix shows the growth reductions consistent with various parameters.[18]

The survey was carried out in March 2011. It was answered by a total of 496 students, 142 of whom received question one, 192 of whom received question two and 162 of whom received question three. The participants were University of Massachusetts students in large introductory classes on microeconomics and macroeconomics; teaching assistants administered the survey, and each discussion

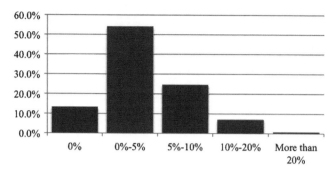

Figure 6.1 Responses to question 1.

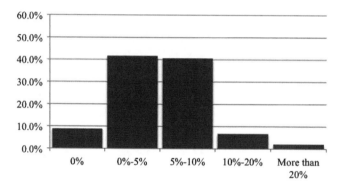

Figure 6.2 Responses to question 2.

section was randomly assigned one of the questions (all students in a section received the same question). The questions are reproduced in the Appendix.

The first issue is whether individuals are more willing to give up income in order to protect the environment if the costs are shared and their relative position is maintained (the positional effect). To consider this issue, the relevant comparison is between the results of question 1 and question 2. As expected, the survey indicates that sharing increases the willingness to pay. When the loss is individual, approximately 54 per cent of respondents said that they would be willing to give up zero to five per cent of their current and future stream of income in order to prevent the extinction, while 25 per cent of respondents would be willing to give up five to ten per cent of their current and future income stream (see Figure 6.1). When the payment is to be shared, on the other hand, the percentage of respondents who were willing to give up five to ten per cent of current and future incomes increases to 41 per cent (see Figure 6.2). Thus, the standard estimates of willingness to pay for environmental goods used in climate change analysis may be skewed downwards.

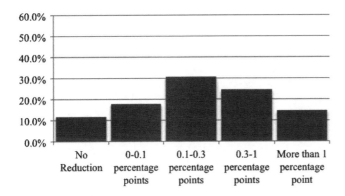

Figure 6.3 Responses to question 3.

The results may support the existence of positional externalities in consumption. The outcome may also, however, be interpreted to indicate other effects including, importantly, concerns about fairness.[19] The distinction between positionality and fairness concerns will be important for some purposes, but the implications for the valuation of environmental goods is similar: there will be a higher willingness to pay when costs are shared.

Figure 6.3 shows the responses to the third version of the question (effects of loss aversion). Only 18 per cent of respondents said that 0 to 0.1 percentage points of income growth should be given up to ensure the survival of species endangered by climate change (corresponding to a zero to five per cent reduction in future levels of income) – a rate considerably lower than with either of the two previous questions. In contrast, 31 per cent of respondents would be willing to accept a 0.1 to 0.3 percentage point reduction in future income growth (corresponding to a five to ten per cent reduction in future levels of income), and 25 per cent of respondents would be willing to accept a 0.3 to one percentage point reduction in future income growth (corresponding to a 10 to 20 per cent reduction in future levels of income). To investigate whether the results indicate loss aversion, we can then compare these results from question 3 with those of question 2. In the second question (in which the costs are to be shared and the question is asked in terms of levels), while 41 per cent of respondents thought we should give up five to ten per cent of future income growth to prevent the extinction, only seven per cent of respondents were willing to give up 10 to 20 per cent of future income. Finally, while approximately two per cent of respondents were willing to give up more than 20 per cent of future incomes to prevent the environmental damage, 15 per cent of respondents were willing to make the corresponding payment when the question was defined in terms of growth rates. The responses to questions 2 and 3, therefore, suggest that consumption externalities operate through loss aversion (and, thus, through taking ones own income as a reference point) in addition to through positional effects relative to others.

As the objective of the survey is not to determine a monetary value for the species that potentially face extinction as a consequence of climate change, the exact intervals in the questions are unimportant. The important point is that the results indicate a significantly higher willingness to pay for environmental protection when the costs are to be shared equally among the population and thus entail no relative loss in income; and, furthermore, that this higher willingness to pay is even more substantial when the costs take the form of slower future growth rather than a level reduction in current and future incomes. The mean and median responses to question 3 are more than double those to question 1.[20]

Conclusion

It is sometimes suggested that the science behind climate change may be weak, but that the economics in the integrated assessment models is well-established and sound. We are not in position to evaluate the science but well-established as it may be, the economics is questionable. Weitzman (2009) has emphasized the treatment of catastrophic risk, and Rezai, Foley and Taylor (2012) and Ackerman, Stanton and Bueno (2010) find that changes in some of the specifications give results that are dramatically different from those of Tol and Nordhaus.

This chapter has raised a different concern. Consumption externalities associated with positional goods and status concerns are well-documented. Using a simple two-period model we have shown that the interaction between these consumption externalities and environmental externalities has implications for the appropriate discount rate: the required return on investment in mitigation is lower than the private return to conventional investment. The magnitude of the difference depends on the weight of positional consumption in utility. An empirical literature has examined this question, and using estimates from this literature, the effect on the appropriate discount rate is quantitatively highly significant. This conclusion finds support in our survey of willingness to pay. Subjects show a much greater willingness to pay when the costs are shared and when the costs are expressed in terms of lower future growth, rather than in reductions in the level of income. Overall, the results suggest that incorporation of consumption externalities into climate change analysis may have important implications for the calculation of the social costs and benefits of mitigation. By ignoring consumption externalities, the existing integrated assessment models produce an inflated estimate of the optimal level of greenhouse gas emissions today.

The argument has been cast within a standard optimal-growth framework. It is not obvious, however, that this framework should dominate the discussion. The appropriateness of a utilitarian approach in general and the specific version used by the integrated assessment models can be challenged.[21] The issues are beyond the scope of this chapter, and we do not pretend to have answers. It can be a problem, however, if an influential discipline makes strong recommendations based on a questionable but seemingly "objective" set of ethical principles. The problem is compounded if the recommendations are couched in a mathematical formalism that makes it hard for outsiders to follow the analysis.

Acknowledgments

An earlier version of this chapter was presented at the Analytical Political Economy Workshop, Queen Mary University of London, May 2011, and at the Adam Smith Seminar, University of Hamburg. We thank the participants and Frank Ackerman, Jim Boyce, Alex Coram, Liz Stanton and Roberto Veneziani for helpful comments and suggestions. We are grateful also to two anonymous referees whose constructive comments led to significant improvements in this version of the chapter.

Notes

1 Nordhaus (2008, 39) simply comments that

> policies are chosen to maximize a social welfare function that is the discounted sum of the population-weighted utility of per capita consumption. Equation (A.1) is the mathematical statement of the objective function. This representation is a standard one in modern theories of optimal economic growth.

2 The "prescriptive"/"descriptive" terminology is used by Arrow et al. (IPCC, 1996).
3 This is the range used by Nordhaus (2008); see e.g. p. 57.
4 The argument appears to be in line with Rezai et al. (2012). The pure discount rate and the tradeoff between current and future generations are not nearly as important as is commonly believed, they argue. The real question is whether the composition of investment should be changed, and starting from a business-as-usual case in which all investment is guided by private profit, the answer is yes: addressing the climate externality can lead to Pareto improvements if some investment is re-directed from conventional areas to mitigation.
5 The discount rate is not the only variable that matters for optimal mitigation. The specification of the damage function can produce dramatic effects on optimal mitigation. Thus, Rezai et al. (2012) use a version in which the proportional effect on output of an increase in atmospheric CO_2 goes to infinity as the CO_2 concentration approaches a finite level (which is set at just over twice the current level in their simulations). This assumption, which is quite different from the specifications in DICE (the Dynamic Integrated model of Climate and the Economy developed by Nordhaus), contributes to the contrast between their findings and those of Nordhaus. As pointed out by Weitzman (2009: 16) the damages at high CO_2 concentrations are typically found by extrapolation using a functional form that is largely arbitrary, and there is little justification for the standard versions.
  Ackerman et al. (2010) modify the standard Nordhaus-type assumptions in another direction by respecifying the costs of abatement, using estimates from a study by McKinsey & Co.
6 The contributions include Veblen (1899), Duesenberry (1949), Hirsch (1977), Easterlin (1974, 2001), Sen (1983) and Frank (1985, 2005).
7 Frey and Stutzer (2002) survey the behavioral literature on "happiness."

8 Veblen effects are commonly represented by a utility function of the form

$$V = V\left(c_i, \frac{c}{c_i}, x\right)$$

Without restrictions on the partial derivatives, this alternative representation is equivalent to the specification in (2). The standard Veblen assumptions – $V_1 > 0$, $V_2 < 0$ – imply that $U_1 = V_1 - V_2 \frac{c}{c_i^2} > 0$ and $U_2 = V_2 \frac{1}{c_i} < 0$.

9 Climate change need not enter purely as a public good. It also affects the production of some conventional goods; agricultural goods, for instance. In terms of the model, these effects could be captured by including the state of the environment as an argument in the production function for the private good:

$$c_1^k = \tilde{F}(i_0^k, x_1)$$

This extension of the model would complicate some of the expressions but leave the qualitative results unchanged.

10 The conditions (8) and (12) are equivalent if there is a constant λ such that

$$u_2(c, c, x) = \lambda u_1(c, c, x)$$

for all c, x. This condition is met for the CES specification of u,

$$u = [\alpha_1 (c^k)^\delta - \alpha_2 c^\delta + \beta x^\delta]^{1/\delta}$$

11 The unit coefficient on c^i and x can be obtained by an appropriate choice of units. Thus, there is no loss of generality in using (16) rather than $z = \alpha c^i - \gamma c + \beta x$.

12 Solve the equation

$$\exp(r_m \times 50) = (1 - \gamma)F' + G_1$$

13 Stern's benchmark assumptions are $\rho = 0.1\%, \theta = 1$ and $\hat{c} = 1.3\%$, with an implied r-value of 1.4.

   Note, however, that according to the positional-goods argument, abatement benefits that take the form of increased production of positional goods should not be discounted at the low rate.

14 Strictly speaking, these expressions give the returns in terms of generalized consumption to the investment of one unit of the standard good. The return to the investment of one unit of the generalized good can be obtained by adjusting the expressions using the common factor $(\partial z_0 / \partial c)^{-1}$.

15 The IPCC notes that, "although controversial, these approaches are well established in the literature" (184). Similarly, Nordhaus's estimates of the impacts of climate change rely on a willingness to pay approach (Nordhaus and Boyer 2000: 71). While Nordhaus writes that valuation techniques with "an objective behavioral component, whether in market prices or individual actions" are generally preferable since "Valuation techniques that are largely subjective – such as contingent valuation – are difficult to validate," he also notes that techniques like contingent valuation are "needed in some areas" (Nordhaus 2006a: 151). Impacts – which are calculated by sector – are estimated through an impact index that represents "the fraction of annual output that subregion j

would be willing to pay to avoid the consequences on sector i of a temperature increase of $T°C$" (73). These impacts are then used to estimate the damage functions, which indicate the per cent loss in output at different levels of global temperature increase. Thus, while many impacts are measured using surrogate markets, hypothetical markets and contingent valuation remain a commonly used method by which to evaluate and incorporate non-market costs of climate change into analysis.

16 Evidence based on actual behavior – e.g. wage premia for risky jobs as an indicator of the value of life – also suffers from this bias. It reflects individual behavior which (by definition) does not internalize the externalities associated with positional goods.

17 While some respondents commented that they did not have a high willingness to pay because some threatened species are likely to be entirely irrelevant to their own future wellbeing, use of a more dramatic example (that may enter more directly into respondents' utility functions) is likely to detract from and complicate the interpretation of the results. We wanted a climate effect that is well-defined and that has a clear public-good character.

18 The upper limits in the growth formulation are somewhat higher than in the level formulation for most reasonable parameters. This choice was deliberate. Since we expect higher willingness to pay in the case of growth reductions, responses to the third question that are concentrated in the upper intervals are consistent with an even greater willingness to pay for environmental protection in the context of growth rather than level reductions – i.e. the bias incorporated in the intervals would further support the hypothesis.

19 These results may also indicate other effects including, for example, a "small number effect" if respondents feel that a 0–0.1 percentage points decline in income growth is small relative to the equivalent loss in income levels.

20 Assuming a uniform distribution within each interval and setting $\rho - g = 3\%$, the means are 4.46, 5.7 and 10.8, respectively, for questions 1, 2 and 3.

21 Economists are aware that there are alternative ethical principles. Nordhaus (2006b: 8) for instance, points out that "it should be clear that alternative ethical perspectives are possible. Moreover, as I suggest below, alternative perspectives provide vastly different prescriptions about desirable climate change policies." The actual analysis and recommendations, however, are almost invariably based on welfare functions associated with representative-agent models. Sen (1982) is an exception. He suggests that future generations have a right to a non-degraded environment and rejects the "welfarism" of the standard analysis.

References

Ackerman, F. and Heinzerling, L. (2004) *Priceless: On Knowing the Price of Everything and the Value of Nothing*. The New Press, New York.

Ackerman, F., Stanton, E., and Bueno, R. (2010) "CRED: A new model of climate and development". DESA Working Paper No. 96, United Nations Department of Economic and Social Affairs.

Blanchard, O. (2008) "The state of macro". NBER working paper 14259, http://www.nber.org/papers/w14259.

Blanchflower, D., and Oswald, A. (2004) "Well-being over time in Britain and the USA". *Journal of Public Economics*, 88(7–8): 1359–1386.

Debreu, G. (1974) "Excess demand functions". *Journal of Mathematical Economics*, 1(1): 15–21.

Duesenberry, J. (1949) *Income, Saving and the Theory of Consumer Behavior*. Harvard University Press, Cambridge.

Easterlin, R. (1974) "Does economic growth improve the human lot? Some empirical evidence". In *Nations and Households in Economic Growth: Essays in Honor of Moses Abramovitz*, R. David and M. Reder (eds.). Academic Press, New York, pp. 89–125.

Easterlin, R. (2001) "Income and happiness, towards a unified theory". *The Economic Journal*, 111(473): 465–484.

Fafchamps, M., and Shilpi, F. (2008) "Subjective welfare, isolation, and relative consumption". *Journal of Development Economics*, 86(1): 43–60.

Fehr, E., and Schmidt, K. (2003) "Theories of Fairness and Reciprocity – Evidence and Economic Applications". In M. Dewatripont, L. Hansen and St. Turnovsky (eds.), *Advances in Economics and Econometrics – 8th World Congress*, Econometric Society Monographs, Cambridge, Cambridge University Press.

Frank, R. (1985) "The demand for unobservable and other nonpositional goods". *American Economic Review*, 75(1): 101–16.

Frank, R. (2005) "Positional externalities cause large and preventable welfare losses". *American Economic Review*, 95(2): 137–141.

Frey, B., and Stutzer, A. (2002) "What can economists learn from happiness research?". *Journal of Economic Literature*, 40(2): 402–435.

Hirsch, F. (1977) *Social Limits to Growth*. Routledge and Kegan Paul Ltd., London.

Hoel, M., and Sterner, T. (2007) "Discounting and relative prices". *Climatic Change*, 84: 265–280.

Howarth, R. (2000) "Climate change and the representative agent". *Environmental and Resource Economics*, 15(2): 135–148.

Intergovernmental Panel on Climate Change (1996) "Climate Change 1995: Economic and Social Dimensions of Climate Change". Contribution of Working Group III to the Second Assessment Report of the Intergovernmental Panel on Climate Change.

Johansson-Stenman, O., Carlson, F., and Daruvala, D. (2002) "Measuring future grandparents' preferences for equality and relative standing". *Economic Journal*, 112(479): 362–383.

Luttmer, E. (2005) "Neighbors as negatives: relative earnings and well-being". *The Quarterly Journal of Economics*, 120(3): 963–1002.

Mantel, R. (1976) "Homothetic preferences and community excess demand functions". *Journal of Economic Theory*, 12(2): 197–201.

Michl, T. (2010) "Discounting Nordhaus". *Review of Political Economy*, 22(4): 535–549.

Mitchell, R., and Carson, R. (1989) *Using Surveys to Value Public Goods: The Contingent Valuation Method*. Resources for the Future, Washington D.C.

Ng, Y., and Wang, J. (1995) "A case for cardinal utility and non-arbitrary choice of commodity units". *Social Choice and Welfare*, 12(3): 255–266.

Nordhaus, W.D. (2006a) "Principles of National Accounting for Nonmarket Accounts". In *A New Architecture for the U.S. National Accounts*, D. Jorgenson, J. Landefeld and W.D. Nordhaus, eds., University of Chicago Press, Chicago.

Nordhaus, W.D. (2006b) "The ' Stern Review' on the economics of climate change". NBER Working Paper 12741, http://www.nber.org/papers/w12741

Nordhaus, W.D. (2008) *A Question of Balance: Weighing the Options on Global Warming*. Yale University Press, New Haven.

Nordhaus, W.D., and Boyer, J. (2000) *Warming the World: Economic Models of Global Warming*. MIT Press, Cambridge.

Rezai, A., Foley, D., and Taylor, L. (2011) "Global Warming and Economic Externalities". *Economic Theory*, 49(2): 329–351.

Sen, A. (1982) "Approaches to the choice of discount rates for social benefit-cost analysis". In *Discounting for Time and Risk in Energy Policy*, R.C. Lind et al., eds., pp. 325–353, Resources for the Future, Washington D.C.

Sen, A. (1983) "Poor, relatively speaking". *Oxford Economic Papers*, 35(2): 153–169.

Skott, P., and Davis, L. (2012) "Distributional biases in the evaluation of climate change". *Ecological Economics*, doi:10.1016/j.ecolecon.2012.06.014.

Sonnenschein, H. (1972) "Market excess demand functions". *Econometrica*, 40(3): 549–563.

Stern, N. (2007) *The Economics of Climate Change: The Stern Review*. Cambridge University Press, Cambridge. Online at http://www.hm-treasury.gov.uk/independent_reviews/stern_review_climate_change/sternreview_index.cfm.

Tversky, A., and Kahneman, D. (1991) "Loss aversion in riskless choice: a reference-dependent model". *The Quarterly Journal of Economics*, 106(4): 1039–1061.

Veblen, T. (1899) *The Theory of the Leisure Class: An Economic Study of Institutions*. The Macmillan Company, New York.

Venkatachalam, L. (2004) "The contingent valuation method: a review". *Environmental Impact Assessment Review*, 24(1): 89–124.

Weitzman, M.L. (2007) "A review of 'The Stern Review on the Economics of Climate Change'". *Journal of Economic Literature*, 45(3): 703–724.

Weitzman, M.L. (2009) "On modeling and interpreting the economics of catastrophic climate Change". *Review of Economics and Statistics*, 91(1): 1–19.

Woodford, M. (2003) *Interest and Prices: Foundations of a Theory of Monetary Policy*. Princeton University Press, Princeton.

Appendix: survey questions and results

QUESTION 1:

Global warming and other environmental changes threaten the survival of some animal species. According to some studies as many as 25 per cent of all species may become extinct before 2100 under current trends. Policy intervention may change this scenario and ensure the survival of the endangered species.

How large a proportion of your stream of current and future income would you be willing to give up in order to ensure that no existing species become extinct?

_____ 0–5%

_____ 5–10%

_____10–20%

_____ more than 20%

QUESTION 2:

Global warming and other environmental changes threaten the survival of some animal species. According to some studies as many as 25 per cent of all species may become extinct before 2100 under current trends. Policy intervention may change this scenario and ensure the survival of the endangered species.

Suppose that the costs of the intervention are shared and that all incomes are reduced by the same percentage. In your view, how large a proportion of current and future incomes should we be willing to give up in order to ensure that no existing species become extinct?

_____ 0–5%

_____ 5–10%

_____10–20%

_____ more than 20%

QUESTION 3:

Global warming and other environmental changes threaten the survival of some animal species. According to some studies as many as 25 per cent of all species may become extinct before 2100 under current trends. Policy intervention may change this scenario and ensure the survival of the endangered species.

Suppose that the intervention is financed by reducing the growth rate of the average income and that this reduction is the same for everyone. As an example, if the intervention requires reducing the growth rate of average income from 2% a year to 1.5%, then everyone will experience income growth that is 0.5 percentage points lower than without intervention. In your view, how large a reduction of the growth rate of future incomes should we be willing to accept to ensure that no existing species become extinct?

_____0 percentage points

_____0–0.1 percentage points

_____0.1–0.3 percentage points

_____0.3–1 percentage points

_____ more than 1 percentage point

Table 6.1 Survey results

	0%	0–5%	5–10%	10–20%	More than 20%
	0 percentage points	*0–0.1 percentage points*	*0.1–0.3 percentage points*	*0.3–1 percentage points*	*More than 1 percentage point*
Question 1	13.4%	54.2%	24.6%	7.0%	0.7%
Question 2	8.9%	41.7%	40.6%	6.8%	2.1%
Question 3	11.7%	17.8%	30.7%	24.5%	14.7%

Table 6.2 Growth reductions consistent with intervals of level reductions for various g and ρ; $(T = \infty)$

Level reductions	$g - \rho = -1\%$	$g - \rho = -2\%$	$g - \rho = -3\%$	$g - \rho = -4\%$
0%	0% growth reduction	0% growth reduction	0% growth reduction	0% growth reduction
0–5%	0–0.05% growth reduction	0–0.11% growth reduction	0–0.16% growth reduction	0–0.21% growth reduction
5–10%	0.05–0.11% growth reduction	0.11–0.22% growth reduction	0.16–0.33% growth reduction	0–0.44% growth reduction
10–20%	0.11–0.25% growth reduction	0.22–0.5% growth reduction	0.33–0.75% growth reduction	0.44–1% growth reduction
More than 20%	more than 0.25% growth reduction	more than 0.5% growth reduction	more than 0.75% growth reduction	more than 1% growth reduction

7 Markets with Black Swans

Graciela Chichilnisky

Introduction: Markets with Black Swans

Black Swans are rare but catastrophic events. They are famously difficult to assess using standard measures of risk (Posner, 2004), and arise from financial innovation that causes widespread volatility and default (Chichilnisky and Wu, 2006). It is well known that market behavior focuses on short term and immediate risks, and seldom considers system-wide risks that are infrequent but potentially catastrophic. These are Black Swans and impact the economy as a whole. An ongoing puzzle is whether it is possible to benefit from market trading and innovation without the risk of Black Swans.

This chapter shows how a classic method to measure and manage risks introduced in the first part of the last century by Von Neumann and Morgenstern, and subsequently adopted by all major economists since the 1950 to price securities such as stocks and bonds, makes the economy insensitive to catastrophic events. An axiom introduced by Von Neumann and Morgenstern led to the use of *expected utility* optimization, a criterion that typically ignores rare events (Chichilnisky, 1996, 2000, 2009a, 2011). This was followed by similar axioms of decision theory – all of them equivalent – introduced by Arrow (1971), who called it "Monotone Continuity"; Hernstein and Milnor (1953), who called it "Continuity"; and DeGroot (2004), who called it A-4. In its various forms the axiom became a standard feature in the theory of markets under uncertainty, leading to the criterion of "expected utility optimization." In its simplest form, as we show in this article, Von Neumann–Morgenstern's axiom creates a systematic bias against, or insensitive behavior towards, events that are rare but potentially catastrophic (Chichilnisky, 1996a,b, 2000, 2002). The problem is quite general, and it appears in all sorts of markets, with either bounded or unbounded state spaces, and includes markets with infinitely many states of nature, described for example by real numbers, where the existence of market equilibrium reflects expected utility optimization that neglects, as shown in Chichilnisky (2000), catastrophic events or Black Swans.[1]

It is unquestionable that the global economy is vulnerable to catastrophic risks. Black Swans are rare but catastrophic events that are modifying our views. Rezai, Foley, and Taylor (2012) study a growing economy with climate change, which is a potentially catastrophic risk. A global carbon market created to deal with the risk of climate change as part of the United Nations Kyoto Protocol, is now international law and trading US$200 Bn/year (Chichilnisky and Sheeran, 2009). The Great Depression is another type of Black Swan. Another is the global financial crisis that started in 2007 after a period of intense financial innovation as predicted in Chichilnisky and Wu (2006). In 2009, at the height of the global financial crisis, a newly created global institution, the G-20, broadcast a Leaders' Statement about the need for "sustainable development" alerting the world about potential *catastrophic risks*.[2]

This chapter establishes the economic foundations for markets with Black Swans, how to successfully manage risks and attain efficient market solutions when facing rare but potentially catastrophic events. The results are new in several ways. First, we define a new concept of a market with Black Swans, a significant extension of Arrow–Debreu markets to encompass rare but catastrophic events that are beyond the standard theory of markets, Chichilnisky (1996a,b,c,d, 1998, 1999, 2000, 2002, 2006, 2009a,b,c, 2010a,b, 2011, 2012). Secondly, we show how standard decision theory based on Von Neumann Morgenstern axioms fails in these markets, and how to improve upon this situation by defining a new type of preference – *sustainable preferences* – that are sensitive to rare as well as to frequent events. These preferences represent more realistically the way traders perceive Black Swans and how to manage risks in situations involving catastrophic events, and were introduced in Chichilnisky (2000, 2009c, 2012). Finally we show the interconnection of traders's decisions and the consistency of our definitions by providing a single condition – *limited arbitrage* – and showing that it is necessary and sufficient for the existence of an efficient market equilibrium in markets with Black Swans.

Sustainability

As defined by the G-20 (see note 1) *sustainability* means that the economy must live within its means – both financial and ecological – and can continue into the future avoiding catastrophes.[3] A natural question is whether unchecked profit making in a market economy conspires against sustainability or, reciprocally, whether a society that is committed to sustainability must in some way restrain or even discard markets. This would be a major challenge, since markets are today a widespread form of organization. This chapter argues that it is possible to reconcile markets and sustainability, but it requires markets to be sensitive to rare events. Equivalently, it requires that traders have "sustainable preferences" as introduced in Chichilnisky (1996a,b, 2000, 2002). These new preferences lead to new ways to evaluate financial assets such as shares and bonds. Since markets follow the traders' priorities, when traders have sustainable preferences markets become sustainable: sustainable decisions are made and financial instruments are priced accordingly. Financial innovation is possible under certain conditions. Limited diversity of the traders restrains their willingness to inflict widespread risks of default on the economy as a whole, because it checks the size of the trades they are willing to entertain. This self-limiting process is the essence of the *limited arbitrage* condition introduced in Chichilnisky (1991, 1994a,b 1996e,f, 1997) and, in a nutshell, explains the existence results of the chapter. Whether markets clash with sustainability hinges therefore on whether traders have *sustainable preferences*, and on whether the economy as a whole has *limited arbitrage*.

Sustainable preferences are based on new axioms for decision theory that require equal treatment of the frequent and rare events such as Black Swans, see Chichilnisky (1996a,b). They reflect an increasing body of empirical evidence about how humans value widespread risks (Chichilnisky, 1996a,b). Based on the concept of sustainable preferences, this chapter defines markets with Black Swans, which differ from standard Arrow–Debreu markets, in two ways: (i) traders have *sustainable preferences* and (ii) traders engage in short trades. Markets with sustainable preferences overcome rare but realistic risks of widespread volatility and default because they are neither focused on frequent nor on rare events; they are in fact sensitive to both, as required for sustainable development. Market prices take a new role: they represent the value of consumption under current uncertainty as well as the value of consumption in a Black Swan event. This approach resolves the conflict between a market's short-term objectives and the goals of sustainability, without eliminating market organization. We show also that these markets exhibit a suitable ambiguity – as would be expected in an economy with rare events – which we show in our last section to be connected with the "uncertainty principle" and the "incompleteness" results of Godel.

We establish the existence of equilibrium by showing that, when traders have sustainable preferences, a single condition – *limited arbitrage* (Chichilnisky, 1991, 1993, 1994a,b, 1996e,f) – is necessary and sufficient for the existence of Pareto efficient market equilibrium, without requiring bounds on short sales. To achieve this, we have to overcome three interlinked technical issues that require a careful use of topology and continuity: (i) continuity of preferences and prices, (ii) compactness of trading sets and efficient allocations, both of which (i and ii) are used to prove existence of solutions, and (iii) appropriate supporting prices for efficient allocations.[4] We adopt the "sup norm" topology that allows a uniform treatment among all generations, a topology that was already used for the same purpose in T. Koopmans's classic work (Koopmans, 1960, 1972).

Sustainable markets

This section defines *sustainable markets*, see Chichilnisky (1996g, 1997a,b, 2012a,b).

Definitions

A competitive market has $H \geq 2$ traders and $N \geq 2$ commodities that are traded over various states of nature $t \in R_+$. The consumption of commodities yields utility $u(x(t))$ at each state t, where $x(t) \in R^N$, and $u(x) : R^N \to R_+$ is a concave increasing real valued function that represents instantaneous utility in state t. Following the classic work of Debreu (1953), and Chichilnisky (1996a,b, 2009a,b), one can view consumption over states of nature $(x(t)_{t \in R+})$ as elements of $L_\infty(R^N)$, with a standard Lebesgue measure μ. Similarly, utility defined over various states of nature $f(t) = u(x(t))$ are elements of the linear space $L_\infty(R)$, where L_∞ is the space of all essentially bounded measurable real valued functions on R with the sup norm $\| f \| = ess \sup_{t \in R} | f(t) |$. In this context a *preference over uncertainty* $U : L_\infty \to R$ is a real valued *linear* function ranking utility paths $u(x(t))$, while $U : L_\infty (R^N) \to R$ denotes the ranking of consumption paths $(x(t))$, which is based on a concave instantaneous utility $u : R^N \to R$, and is generally *non-linear*. We say that the preference over uncertainty U is *insensitive to rare events* when it disregards utility in events of small enough probability, namely $U(f) > U(g) \Leftrightarrow U(f') > U(g')$ for any a.e. (almost anywhere) modification of f and g that occurs on sets of small measure, namely when $f'(t) = f(t)$ and $g'(t) = g(t)$ for all $t \notin S$, where $\mu(S) < \varepsilon$. Similarly a ranking is insensitive to frequent events when it disregards utility modifications on sets of large measure, formally, for any two paths f, g, there exists an $N(f, g) \in R : U(f) > U(g) \Leftrightarrow U(f') > U(g')$ for any a.e. modification of f, g that occurs on sets of measure at least $N(f,g)$, namely whenever $f'(t) = f(t)$ and $g'(t) = g(t)$ for all $t \in S$ with $\mu(S) > N(f,g)$. The logical negation of these two insensitivity properties defines *sensitivity* to rare and frequent events, respectively. In the former case we say that preference is sensitive to Black Swans.

Axioms for sustainable preferences

A *sustainable preference* U is an increasing ranking that (as a state dependent preference) satisfies three axioms.[5]

Axiom 1. $U : L_\infty \to R$ is continuous and linear[6]
Axiom 2. $U : L_\infty \to R$ is sensitive to frequent events
Axiom 3. $U : L_\infty \to R$ is sensitive to Black Swans

These axioms were introduced in Chichilnisky (1996a,b). The first two are consistent with Von Neumann's classic axioms of choice over uncertainty and are satisfied by expected utility, for example

$$U(f) = U(x(t)) = \int_{R+} u(x(t))e^{-\delta t} d\mu, \qquad \delta > 1$$

where $f \in L_\infty$ represents a time path $u(x(t))$, δ is an uncertainty "discount factor." Observe that the expected utility $U(f)$ defined above is linear on utility paths $u(t)$, and thus satisfies Axiom 1, but it may not be linear in consumption x. Sustainable preferences that satisfy Axioms 1, 2, and 3 are also linear on utility paths but may not be linear on consumption. The third axiom, however, is not satisfied by expected utilities (Chichilnisky, 1996a,b). All *sustainable preferences* have been characterized in a representation theorem established in Chichilnisky (1996a,b, 2009a,b, 2010a,b) to be of the form

$$U(f) = \lambda U_1(f) + (1 - \lambda)U_2(f) \tag{1}$$

where $U_1(.)$ is a function in L_1 and $U_2(.)$ is in $L_\infty^* - L_1$, $0 < \lambda < 1$, both $U_1(f)$ and $U_2(f)$ are increasing and non-zero, and specifically:

$$U(f) = U(x(t)) = \lambda \int_{R^+} u(x)\phi(x)d\mu + (1 - \lambda)\chi(u(x))$$

where $U_1(f) = \lambda \int_{R_+} u(x)\phi(x)dt$, $U_2(f) = (1 - \lambda)\chi(u(x)$, $0 < \lambda < 1$, $\phi \in L_1$, e.g. $\phi(t) = e^{-\delta t}$, and $\chi \in L_\infty^* - L_1$ is a purely finitely additive measure on R that gives measure to "Black Swan" events (for a proof, see Chichilnisky (1996a,b, 2009a,b, 2010a,b)).

Markets with Black Swans

Definition: A market with Black Swans is an Arrow–Debreu market without bounds on short sales, and where traders have sustainable preferences that are sensitive to rare events

A sustainable market economy can be represented as $E = \{X, \Omega_h, U_h : X \to R, h = 1, \ldots H\}$. It has $H \geq 2$ traders indexed by $h = 1, 2, \ldots, H$, $N \geq 2$ commodities that are traded over uncertainty $t \in R_+$; the *consumption space* or *trading space* is the Banach space $X = L_\infty$ with the sup norm $\| . \|_{\sup}$ (Debreu, 1953), Chichilnisky (1996a,b, 2009a,b); this assumption implies no bounds on short sales. $\Omega_h \in X$ represents trader $h's$ property rights, $\Omega = \sum_h \Omega_h$ represents society's total resources over time; and traders' preferences over uncertainty $U_h : L_\infty \to R_+$ are based as above on concave instantaneous utility $u_h : R^N \to R_+$ and define sustainable preferences over uncertainty.

Traders may have zero endowments of some goods, and endowments could be negative or positive; since the trading space is $X = L_\infty$, short selling is allowed. We consider general preferences where the normalized gradients to indifference surfaces define either an open or a closed map on every indifference surface, namely (i) indifference surfaces contain no half-lines, for example strictly convex preferences, or (ii) the normalized gradients to any closed set of indifferent vectors define a closed set, for example linear preferences. In this chapter for simplicity we identify case (ii) with linear preferences. The assumptions and the results of the chapter are ordinal, and $U_h(0) = 0$ and $\sup_{x \in X} U_h(x) = \infty$. Preferences are increasing so that $U_h(x(t)) > U_h(y(t))$ when for all t, $x(t) \geq y(t)$ and for a set of positive Lebesgue measure, $x(t) > y(t)$. In addition, we assume the traders' preferences are uniformly non-satiated, which means that they can be represented by a utility U with a bounded rate of increase: for smooth preferences, which are Frechet differentiable, $\exists \varepsilon, K > 0 : \forall x \in X$, $K > \| DU(x) \| > \varepsilon$. If a utility function is uniformly non-satiated, its indifference surfaces are within a uniform distance from each other: $\forall r, s \in R, \exists N(r,s) \in R$ such that $f \in U^{-1}(r) \Rightarrow \exists y \in U^{-1}(s)$ with $\| f - g \| \leq N(r,s)$, see Chichilnisky and Heal (1998a,b).

Assumption 1: Each trader has a sustainable preference that is represented by an increasing, uniformly non-satiated function of consumption over uncertainty $U : L_\infty \to R^+$ **based on a concave instantaneous utility** $u : R^N \to R$ **such that** $U(0) = 0$ **and** $\sup_{f \in X} U(f) = \infty$.

Prices are real valued linear functions on X that are continuous with the sup norm (Debreu, 1953). The space of *feasible allocations* over uncertainty is $\{(f_1(t), \ldots, f_H(t)) \in X^H : \sum_{h=1}^H f_h(t) = \sum_{h=1}^H \Omega_h = \Omega\}$. To simplify notation when it is clear we obviate the state variable t. A utility vector $U = (U_1(f_1) \ldots U_H(f_H))$ is *feasible* if the allocation $(f_1, \ldots, f_H)$ is feasible.

The set of *individually rational feasible allocations* is the set of utility allocations $\{U_1(f_1) \ldots U_H(f_H)\}$ that are feasible and preferred to the initial endowments, $\forall h, U_h(f_h) \geq U_h(\Omega_h)$. A utility vector $U = (U_1(f_1), \ldots, U_H(f_H))$ – which need not be feasible – is *efficient or undominated* if there is no allocation $G = (g_1, \ldots, g_H)$ such that $\forall h, U_h(g_h) \geq U_h(f_h)$ and $U_k(g_k) > U_k(f_k)$ for some k, and there exists a sequence of feasible allocations $(f_1^j, \ldots, f_H^j)_{j=1,2,\ldots}$ such that $G = \lim_{j \to \infty} (f_1^j, \ldots, f_H^j)_{j=1,2,\ldots}$. A *feasible efficient allocation* is a feasible allocation that is also efficient.

The *Pareto frontier* $P(E) \subset R_+^H$ is the set of individually rational and efficient feasible utility vectors. A *competitive equilibrium of the economy* E consists of a price vector $p^* \in X_+^*$ and an allocation $(f_1^*, \ldots, f_H^*) \in X^H$ such that f_h^* optimizes U_h over the budget set $B_h(p^*) = \{f \in X : \langle p^*, f \rangle = \langle p^*, \Omega_h \rangle\}$ and clears the markets $\sum_{h=1}^H f_h^* - \Omega_h = 0$. A feasible allocation $(f_1, \ldots, f_H)$ is a *quasi-equilibrium* when there is a price $p \neq 0$ with $\forall h, \langle p, \Omega_h \rangle = \langle p, f_h \rangle$, and $\langle p, g \rangle \geq \langle p, f_h \rangle$ for any g implies $U_h(g) \geq U_h(f_h)$. A quasi-equilibrium is a *competitive equilibrium* when $U_h(g) > U_h(f_h) \Rightarrow \langle p, g \rangle > \langle p, f_h \rangle$.

The following concept of a *global cone* contains global information about a trader since, in ordinal terms, the sequences in this cone achieve utility values that eventually exceed those of all trades. The global cone was introduced in Chichilnisky (1991, 1993, 1994a,b, 1996e,f), see also Chichilnisky and Heal (1998a,b).

Definition: The cone A_h consists of all sequences of net trades $\{f^j\}$ in X along which the hth trader's utility increases and exceeds that of any other vector in the space; it can be based on rays of directions in X along which the hth trader's utility exceeds eventually all utility values:

$$A_h(\Omega_h) = \left\{ \{f^j\} : \forall g \in X, \exists j : U_h(f^j) > U_h(g) \right\}$$

Definition: The *global cone* $G_h(\Omega_h)$ is the set of all sequences of net trades in X along which the hth trader's utility never ceases to increase; it can be based on rays of directions with ever increasing utility:

$$G_h(\Omega_h) = \left\{ \{f^j\} :\sim \exists Max_j U_h(f^j) \right\}.$$

We assume that $G_h(\Omega_h)$ has a simple structure, which was established in different forms in Chichilnisky (1991, 1994b, 1998), Chichilnisky and Heal (1998): when preferences have no half-lines in their indifferences, case (i), then $G_h(\Omega_h)$ is the closure of $A_h(\Omega_h)$, and in case (ii) when preferences have half-lines in their indifference surfaces, for example linear preferences, then $G_h(\Omega_h) = A_h(\Omega_h)$.

Definition The *market cone* $D_h(\Omega_h)$ is

$$D_h(\Omega_h) = \left\{ p \in X : \forall \{g\} \in G_h(\Omega_h), \exists i : \langle g^j, p \rangle > 0 \text{ for } j > i \right\}$$

This is the set of all prices assigning eventually strictly positive value to net trades in the global cone. We assume the results of the following proposition, which was established in different forms in Chichilnisky (1991, 1994a,b, 1995, 1996c,d, 1998), Chichilnisky and Heal (1998), and is used in proving the connection between limited arbitrage and the existence of a sustainable market equilibrium:

Proposition 1: If a utility $U : X \to R$ is uniformly non-satiated, then

(A) $A(\Omega) \neq \emptyset$, and the cones $G(\Omega)$ and $D(\Omega)$, are all convex and uniform across vectors Ω in X.[7] For general preferences $G(\Omega)$ and $D(\Omega)$ may not be uniform, Chichilnisky (1998), Chichilnisky and Heal (1998)
(B)   In case (i), preferences have no half-lines in their indifferences, $G_h = \overline{A_h}$; with linear preferences case (ii) $G_h = A_h$.

Limited arbitrage and gains from trade with Black Swans

This section defines limited arbitrage and provides an intuitive interpretation in terms of gains from trade in markets with Black Swans. The following definitions and results are used in establishing the existence of a competitive equilibrium and extend Chichilnisky (1991, 1994a, 1996c,d, 1998), Chichilnisky and Heal (1998), and Chichilnisky (2011, 2012a) to markets with Black Swans.

Definition: *Gains from trade* are defined as

$$\mathcal{G}(E) = \sup \left\{ \sum_{h=1}^{H} (U_h(f_h) - U_h(\Omega_h)) \right\} \text{ where } \forall h,\ f_h = (f_h^j) \text{ satisfies}$$

$$\sum_{h=1}^{H} (f_h - \Omega_h) = 0 \text{ and } U_h(f_h^{j+1}) > U_h(f_h^j) > U_h(\Omega_h) \geq 0.$$

Definition: The economy E satisfies *limited arbitrage* when

$$\bigcap_{h=1}^{H} D_h \neq \emptyset \tag{2}$$

Geometrically, *limited arbitrage* (2) bounds arbitrage opportunities in the economy by limiting the utility that can be achieved by the traders when trading with each other. Under the assumptions, Proposition 2 below applies in case (i) and (ii): either indifference surfaces contain no half-lines (e.g. strictly convex preferences) of (ii) linear preferences.

Proposition 2: In markets with Black Swans limited arbitrage implies bounded gains from trade, namely $\mathcal{G}(E) < \infty$.

Proof: The proof relies on limited arbitrage, and follows the proofs of similar propositions in Chichilnisky (1991, 1998) and Chichilnisky and Heal (1998) adapted to markets with sustainable preferences. Along the way we also highlight properties of sustainable preferences that are useful for understanding the structure of sustainable preferences, and the existence of a competitive equilibrium in sustainable markets.

Assume E has limited arbitrage and without loss of generality that $\forall h$, $\Omega_h = 0$. For every h, let $U_h = U_{1h} + U_{2h}$, where U_{1h} and U_{2h} are the two (non-zero) parts of the sustainable preference U_h that exist according to the representation of sustainable preferences provided in (1) above, see Chichilnisky (1996a,b). If gains from trade $\mathcal{G}(E)$ were not bounded there would be a sequence of feasible, individually rational allocations of increasing utility $\{g^j\} = \{g_1^j, \ldots, g_H^j\}_{j=1,2\ldots}$ satisfying (i) $\forall j$, $\sum_{h=1}^{H} g_h^j = 0$, (ii) $\forall h,j$ $U_h(g_h^{j+1}) > U_h(g_h^j)$ and (iii) for some k, $\lim_{j\to\infty}(U_k(g_k^j)) = \infty$, which implies that $\lim_{j\to\infty} \| g_k^j \|_\infty = \infty$. Define the set of traders K by $k \in K \iff \lim_{j\to\infty} U_k(g_k^j) = \infty$ so that in particular $\lim_j \| g_k^j \| = \infty$; then by assumption $K \neq \emptyset$. We show that limited arbitrage contradicts (i); (ii) and (iii) so that gains from trade $\mathcal{G}(E)$ cannot be unbounded with limited arbitrage. By definition of limited arbitrage (2) for $j > j_0$ there exists a p and a j_0 such that $\sum_{h\in K} \langle p, g_h^j \rangle > 0$ for $j > j_0$, because (ii), (iii) imply that $\forall h$, $\{g_h^j\}$ is in $G_h(0)$. However, by (i) $\forall j$, $\sum_{h=1}^{H} g_h^j = 0$ so that $\forall p > 0$, $\sum_{h\in J} \langle p, g_h^j \rangle = 0$, a contradiction. The contraction arises from assuming that $\mathcal{G}(E)$ is not bounded. Therefore, limited arbitrage implies bounded gains from trade, as we wanted to show.

Next, we derive properties of general sustainable preferences, as stated above. Observe that, under limited arbitrage, when the sequence of purely finitely additive utilities $\{U_{2h}(g_h^j)\}$ in (2) grows without bound as $j \to \infty$, so does the countably additive sequence $\{U_{1h}(g_h^j)\}_{j\to\infty}$ in (2). Assume, to the contrary, that $\{U_{2h}(g_h^j)\}$ grows without bound but $\{U_{1h}(g_h^j)\}$ is bounded. Since as we saw above gains from trade $\sum_h U_h(g_h^j)$ are bounded under limited arbitrage, for each h, $\{U_h(g_h^j)\}_j$ is bounded. However, for each j, $U_{2h}^j = U_h^j - U_{1h}^j$ and the right-hand side is bounded by assumption, because U_h^j is bounded and we just assumed U_{1h}^j to be bounded as well. Therefore, the sequence $\{U_{2h}(g_h^j)\}_j$ must be bounded, which is a contradiction. Therefore, under the conditions, when the sequence of purely finitely additive utilities $\{U_{2h}(g_h^j)\}_{j\to\infty}$ grows without bound so does the countably additive sequence of utilities $\{U_{1h}(g_h^j)\}$. For each h consider the sequence of normalized vectors $(g_h^j/\|\,g_h^j\,\|)$, denoted also $\{g_h^j\}$. We now show that the sequence of normalized vectors $\{g_h^j\}$ has a weak* limit, and that its weak* limit is not zero. First observe that the normalized sequence $\{g_h^j\}$ is contained in the unit sphere of L_∞, which is weak* compact by Alaoglu's theorem. Consider a subsequence with a weak* limit; we show that this weak* limit is not zero. Since $X = L_\infty$ and utilities are continuous and sustainable, the preferred sets have non-empty interiors and by the properties of sustainable preferences presented above there exist two non-zero prices $p_1 \in L_1$ and $p_2 \in L_\infty^* - L_1$,[8] such that p_1 supports the preferred set of U_{1h} at $\{0\}$, denoted U_{1h}^0, and p_2 supports the preferred set of U_{2h} at $\{0\}$ denoted U_{2h}^0, so that $p = p_1 + p_2$ supports the preferred set of U_h at $\{0\}$, U_h^0. We saw that, under limited arbitrage and with sustainable preferences, for any h, $\lim_j U_{2h}(g_h^j) = \infty$ implies that $\lim_{j\to\infty} U_{1h}(g_h^j) = \infty$, namely when purely finitely additive utility values grow without bound, the corresponding countably additive parts do too. This implies in turn that $\forall h$, when the limiting utility values $\lim_j U_h(g_h^j) = \lim_j(U_{1h}(g_h^j) + U_{2h}(g_h^j)) = \infty$, then $\lim_{j\to\infty} U_{1h}(g_h^j) = \infty$, since $\lim_j U_h(g_h^j) = \infty$ and $U_h^j(g_h^j) = U_{1h}(g_h^j) + U_{2h}(g_h^j)$ implies that either $\lim_{j\to\infty} U_{1h}(g_h^j) = \infty$ as we wish to prove, or else $\lim_{j\to\infty} U_{2h}(g_h^j) = \infty$, which in turn implies that $\lim_{j\to\infty} U_{1h}(g_h^j) = \infty$ as seen above. Thus in all cases $\lim_j U_h(g_h^j) \to \infty$ implies $\lim_{j\to\infty} U_{1h}(g_h^j) = \infty$ as we wished to prove. Next observe that for all h there exist a subsequence denoted also $\{g_h^j\}$, j_0 and $r > 0$, such that $\langle p_1, g_h^j \rangle \geq r$ when $j > j_0$. Otherwise, $\lim_j \langle p_1, g_h^j \rangle = 0$ and in particular for any $t > 0$, and $\varepsilon > 0$, $\exists j : U_{1h}(g_h^j) > t$ and $(p_1, g_h^j) < \varepsilon$. But $\forall y$ satisfying $\langle p_1, y \rangle < 0$, $U_{1h}(y) < U_{1h}^0$ because p_1 supports U_{1h}^0. Therefore by continuity $\lim_j U_{1h}(g_h^j) \leq 0$, a contradiction since we showed that $\lim_{j\to\infty} U_{1h}(g_h^j) = \infty$. Therefore

$$\forall j > j_0, \quad \langle p_1, g_h^j \rangle \geq r > 0, \tag{3}$$

which implies that the sequence $\{g_h^j\}$ is weak* bounded away from zero, by definition, since $p_1 \in L_1$. Therefore we have shown that the weak* compact sequence $\{g_h^j\}$ contains a subsequence, denoted also $\{g_h^j\}$, with a weak* limit denoted g_h, which is not zero because of (3). Consider now the cone C defined by all strictly positive convex combinations of the vectors g_h for all h. Either C is strictly contained in a half-space, or it defines a subspace of X. Since by construction $\sum_{h=1}^{H} g_h = 0$, C cannot be strictly contained in a half-space. Therefore

C defines a subspace. In particular there is $H' \subset H$, k, and $\forall h \in H'$, $\lambda_h > 0$, such

that $(*) -g_k = \sum_{h=1}^{H'} \lambda_h g_h$. ∎

Corollary 1: Limited arbitrage is necessary and sufficient for bounded gains from trade in case (ii).

Proof: Consider preferences in case (ii), which include linear preferences. Since $G_h = A_h$ in this case as shown in Proposition 1, the set of traders K defined by $k \in K \iff \lim_{j \to \infty} U_k(g_k^j) = \infty$ equals H. In this case bounded gains from trade imply there can be no sequence $\{g_h^j\}$ satisfying (i), (ii), and (iii) in Proposition 2, so the reciprocal of the statement of this proposition is immediate. Thus limited arbitrage is necessary and sufficient for bounded gains from trade when preferences are in case (ii). ∎

Market equilibrium with Black Swans

This section establishes the existence of an equilibrium in markets with Black Swans. The markets considered in this article allow unbounded short sales, namely the trading domain X is the entire space. This section shows that under the *limited arbitrage* condition traders only wish to engage in bounded trades with each other, and this implies that the set of efficient trades is compact:

Theorem 1: Limited arbitrage is necessary and sufficient for the compactness of a non-empty Pareto frontier $P(E)$ in markets with Black Swans.

Proof: The result is new and is based on Propositions 1 and 2 above. It extends the results of Chichilnisky (2011) to markets with uncertainty and Black Swans. Assume limited arbitrage is satisfied. Observe that the Pareto frontier is in euclidean space $P(E) \subset R_+^H$. Proposition 2 showed that with limited arbitrage, $P(E)$ is always bounded. To show compactness it suffices to show that $P(E)$ is closed with limited arbitrage. Without loss of generality, consider a sequence of allocations $\{g_h^j\}_{j=1,2,\dots}$ satisfying $\forall j$, $\sum_{h=1}^H g_h^j = 0$, so that $\lim_{j \to \infty} \sum_{h=1}^H g_h^j = 0$, and the corresponding utility values $U_1(g_1^j), \dots, U_H(g_H^j) \in R_+^H$. Assume that the utility values converge either to ∞ or to a utility allocation $V = (V_1, \dots, V_H) \in R_+^H$ that is undominated by the utility allocation of any other feasible allocation; V may or may not be a utility allocation corresponding to a feasible allocation. When limited arbitrage is satisfied, we show that V is the utility allocation corresponding to a feasible allocation. It suffices to consider the case where the sequence of feasible utility allocations $\{U_1(g_1^j), \dots, U_H(g_H^j)\}$, and therefore the corresponding allocations $\{g_h^j\}_{j=1,2,\dots}$, $h = 1, \dots, H$ are unbounded. Observe that, as shown in the proof of Proposition 2, the countably additive parts of the utilities $\{U_{11}(g_1^j), \dots, U_{1H}(g_H^j)\}_{j \to \infty}$ are also unbounded in this case; the the normalized sequence $\{g_h^j/\| g_h^j \|\}_j = 1, 2, \ldots$, denoted also $\{g_h^j\}_{j=1,2,\ldots}$ is weak* precompact by Alaoglu's theorem, and as shown in the proof of Proposition 2 it has a weak* convergent subsequence, denoted also $\{g_h^j\}_{j=1,2,\ldots}$ with a non-zero weak* limit $g_h = \lim_{j \to \infty} \{g_h^j\}_{j=1,2,\ldots}$. If $\forall h, g_h^j \notin G_h$ then eventually the utility values of the traders attain their limit for all h, the utility vector V is achieved by a feasible allocation and the proof is complete. The case when for some trader k, $g_k^j \in G_k$ remains to be considered; without loss assume that $\forall h, g_k^j \in G_k$ remains to be considered. As in Proposition 2, consider the open convex cone C of strictly positive linear combinations of the (non-zero) vectors $g_h, h = 1, 2, \ldots, H$, $C = \{w = \sum_h \mu_h g_h \text{ where } \forall h, \mu_h > 0\}$. Either (a) C is contained strictly in a half-space of X or else (b) C is a subspace of X. By construction $\forall j, \sum_h g_h^j = 0$, which eliminates case (a). Therefore case (b) must hold, in particular, there exists $k, g_k \in K$ and $\forall h, \lambda_h \geq 0$ satisfying

$$-g_k = \sum_{h=1}^{H} \lambda_h g_h$$

However, limited arbitrage implies that $\exists p \in \cap_h D_h$ so that $\forall h, \langle p, g_h \rangle \geq 0$, which contradicts $-g_k = \sum_{h=1}^{H} \lambda_h g_h$. The contradiction arises from assuming that the Pareto frontier is not closed under limited arbitrage, therefore $P(E)$ must be closed. Limited arbitrage implies therefore a closed non-empty Pareto frontier $P(E) \subset R^H$ which, from Proposition 2, is also bounded and hence compact. This establishes sufficiency. The reciprocal is established as follows. Failure of limited arbitrage means, as seen above, that for any $(U_1(g_1), \ldots, U(g_H)) \in P(E)$, there exists $(v_1, \ldots, v_H)$ satisfying $\forall h, \sum_{h=1}^{H} v_h = 0$ and $U_h(g_h + v_h) > U_h(g_h)$, a contradiction. Therefore limited arbitrage is necessary for a compact non-empty $P(E)$.   ∎

Corollary 2: Limited arbitrage implies that the Pareto frontier $P(E)$ is homeomorphic to a simplex.

This follows from Theorem 1, and the convexity of preferences, Arrow and Hahn (1971), Lemma 3, Chapter 5, p. 81.   ∎

Theorem 2: Consider a market with Black Swans $E = \{X, U_h, \Omega_h, h = 1, \ldots, H\}$ where $H \geq 2$, $X = L_\infty$, and $\forall h$, trader h has a sustainable preference U_h. Then the economy E has a market equilibrium if and only if it satisfies limited arbitrage, and a market equilibrium is Pareto efficient.

Proof: Necessity first. Without loss assume that $\forall h, \Omega_h = 0 \in X$. Let p^* be a price equilibrium and let $f^* = (f_1^*, \ldots f_H^*)$ be the corresponding equilibrium allocation. If limited arbitrage fails, $\exists h$ and $\{g^j\} \in G_h$ such that $\langle p^*, g^j \rangle \leq 0$ for some $j > j_0$ namely g^j is affordable at prices p^*. Recall that G_h is the same for every allocation by Proposition 1. It follows that $\exists j_0 > 0$ such that for $j > j_0$, $U_h(f_h^* + g^j) > U_h(f_h^*)$ which, together with the affordability of g^j, contradicts the fact that f^* is an equilibrium allocation. Limited arbitrage is therefore necessary for existence of an equilibrium.

For sufficiency, Theorem 1 established that the Pareto frontier is homeomorphic to a simplex when limited arbitrage is satisfied. The standard Negishi fixed point argument on the Pareto frontier $P(E)$ in utility space R^H establishes therefore the existence of a pseudo-equilibrium, see Negishi (1960) and Chichilnisky and Heal (1984). To complete the proof, observe that $\forall h = 1, 2, \ldots H$, there exists always an allocation in X of strictly lower value than the pseudo-equilibrium f_h^* at the price p^*. Therefore by Lemma 3, Chapter 4, p. 81 of Arrow and Hahn (1971) the quasi-equilibrium $\langle p^*, g^* \rangle$ is also a competitive equilibrium, completing the proof of existence. Pareto efficiency follows from the fact that the equilibrium is in the Pareto frontier $P(E)$. ∎

Market value and the uncertainty principle

The existence of an equilibrium ensures the logical consistency of the concept of markets with Black Swans. The main condition required for existence is limited arbitrage, a condition that has been used to prove existence in the literature (Chichilnisky, 1991, 1994a,b, 1996c,d,e,f, 1998, 2011, 2012a; Chichilnisky and Heal, 1998a), and is extended in this case to markets with Black Swans, where traders have sustainable preferences. The results extend Chichilnisky (2011), which does not include markets with uncertainty.

The notion of an equilibrium price in a market with Black Swans requires further discussion. An equilibrium price is defined here – as is usual – as a continuous linear function on commodities or trades, and this price establishes the economic value of commodities at a market equilibrium. The space of prices is here L_∞^*, the dual of the space of commodities L_∞ that has been characterized (see the Appendix) as consisting of the linear sum of two subspaces, one subspace consisting of prices in L_1 that have a ready interpretation, and the second subspace consisting of finitely additive measures on R that require further explanation. Since preferences are sustainable, a price equilibrium will have the same form as a sustainable preference as characterized above and in Chichilnisky (1996a,b), namely a convex combination of a path of prices through time that is an element of L_1 and of a purely finitely additive measure; for example, a measure that focuses its weight on rare events. In this context, therefore, a market price may assign two types of economic values: (i) a value to commodities in the various (frequent) states of nature, and in addition (ii) a value to commodities in rare and catastrophic states. The second term (ii) may seem unusual in standard markets, but it seems entirely appropriate for a market equilibrium in economies with Black Swans. It modifies the conventional notion of prices just as is needed to value rare events that are potentially catastrophic, as seems required for markets with Black Swans.

A finitely additive part of the price that assigns value to rare events establishes a connection between sustainable markets and the "Uncertainty Principle" through the "Axiom of Choice" in the foundation of mathematics, which postulates that there exists a universal and consistent fashion to select an element from every set; see Dunford and Schwartz (1958), Yosida (1974), Yosida and Hewitt (1952), Chichilnisky and Heal (1997), Kadane and O'Hagan (1995), Purves and Sudderth (1976), Dubins (1975), and Dubins and Savage (1965). This principle establishes the existence of propositions that cannot be proven to be true or false, the "incompleteness of mathematics." The Axiom of Choice has been proven by Godel (1940) to be independent from the rest of mathematics, so that statements that require this axiom are neither true nor false by themselves, but their validity depends on the axiomatic foundation that one chooses.

It is possible to illustrate – but not in general construct – a purely finitely additive measure on R, or on any finite open interval (a, b) of R, see examples in Chichilnisky (2010a,b). This issue of constructibility is not unique to markets with Black Swans: it is an issue shared by the proof of the second fundamental theorem of welfare economics, see Debreu (1953), which requires the Hahn–Banach theorem and therefore the Axiom of Choice. The proof of existence of such purely finitely additive functions can be achieved in various ways, but each requires the Axiom of Choice or a related result. To illustrate the problem, consider the function $\phi(g(t)) = \lim_{t \to \infty} g(t)$ that is defined only on a closed strict subspace L'_∞ of L_∞ consisting of functions that have a limit at infinity. This function is continuous and linear on L'_∞. One can use Hahn–Banach's theorem to extend this function ϕ from the closed subspace $L'_\infty \subset L_\infty$ to the entire space L_∞ preserving the norm. Since the extension is not in L_1 it defines a purely finitely additive measure, as shown in the Appendix. However, in a general form Hahn–Banach's theorem requires the Axiom of Choice, which has been shown to be independent from the rest of the axioms of mathematics (Godel, 1940). Alternatively, one can extend the notion of a *limit* to encompass all functions in L_∞ including those with no standard limit. This can be achieved by defining convergence along a *free ultrafilter* arising from Stone–Cech compactification of the real line R as in Chichilnisky and Heal (1997). However, the existence of a *free ultrafilter* requires once again the Axiom of Choice (Godel, 1940). This illustrates why the actual construction of a *purely finitely additive measure* requires the Axiom of Choice. Since sustainable markets have prices that include purely finitely additive measures, this provides a connection between the Axiom of Choice and sustainable markets. It appears that the consideration of rare events that could be catastrophic conjures up the Axiom of Choice that is independent from the rest of mathematics (Godel, 1940).

Appendix

Example: A preference that is sensitive to Black Swans but insensitive to frequent risks

Consider $W(f) = \liminf_{x \in R}(f(x))$. This utility is insensitive to the frequent risks and therefore does not satisfy Axiom 2. In addition this map is not linear, failing Axiom 3.

The dual space L_∞^*:   countably additive and purely finitely additive measures

See Yosida (1974), Yosida and Hewitt (1952), Dunford and Schwartz (1958). A measure η is called *finitely additive* when for any family of pairwise disjoint measurable sets $\{A_i\}_{i=1,\dots N}$ $\eta(\bigcup_{i=1}^N A_i) = \sum_{i=1}^N \eta(A_i)$. The measure η is called *countably additive* when for any countable family of pairwise disjoint measurable sets $\{A_i\}_{i=1,\dots\infty}$ $\eta(\bigcup_{i=1}^\infty A_i) = \sum_{i=1}^\infty \eta(A_i)$. The space of continuous linear functions on L_∞ is the "dual" of L_∞, and is denoted L_∞^*. This space has been characterized, e.g. in Yosida (1974) and Yosida and Hewitt (1952). $L_\infty^* = L_1 + (L_\infty^1 - L_1)$: it consists of L_1 functions g that define countably additive measures v on R by the rule $v(A) = \int_A g(x)dx$ where $\int_R |g(x)| \, dx < \infty$ so that v is *absolutely continuous* with respect to the Lebesgue measure, plus measures that are not countably additive, also called purely finitely additive measures, forming a subspace denoted $L_\infty^1 - L_1$. While a countable measure can be identified with an L_1 function, namely its so called "density," purely finitely additive measures cannot be identified by such functions.

Acknowledgments

This research was conducted at the Columbia Consortium for Risk Management (CCRM) directed by the author at Columbia University in New York, and its Program on Information and Resources (PIR). We acknowledge support from Grant No 5222-72 of the US Air Force Office of Research (AFOSR). The initial results on sustainable preferences were presented as an invited address at Stanford University's 1993 Seminar on Reconsideration of Values, organized by Kenneth Arrow, in 2000 at the Fields Institute for Mathematical Sciences in Toronto Canada, at the 2005 NBER Conference *Mathematical Economics: The Legacy of Gerard Debreu* at UC Berkeley, at the Department of Economics of the University of Kansas National Bureau of Economic Research General Equilibrium Conference, September 2006, the Department of Statistics of the University of Oslo, Norway, Fall 2007, the Department of Statistics of Columbia University, Fall 2007, the AFOSR in Arlington VA, January 2009, Dayton Ohio 201, and Arlington VA January 2011, and the Colloqium at the Mathematics Department and the Institute for Behavioral Sciences of the University of California at Irvine, May 18, 2011. We thank the above institutions and individuals for supporting the research as well as Eduardo Jose Chichilnisky, Salk Institute, La Jolla, California, Lance Taylor and two anonymous reviewers, for valuable comments and suggestions.

Notes

1 Within economies with infinitely many states of nature, for example, the "cone condition" introduced by Chichilnisky and Kalman (1980), also known as "properness," and frequently to prove existence of market equilibrium with infinitely many states of nature

(cf. Yannelis and Zame, 1986; Chichilnisky, 1993), a form of averaging of risks is required that once again underestimates Black Swan events, Chichilnisky (2000, 2002). Chichilnisky (1993) showed that the original "cone condition" is the same as the later condition named "properness." This condition as shown below in this chapter implies optimizing utility functions which – as in the case of expected utility – are insensitive to rare but catastrophic events.

2 The G-20 Meeting took place in Pittsburgh, USA, 24–25 September 2009. The G-20 Leaders' Statement can be found at http://www.pittsburghsummit.gov/mediacenter/ 129639.htm. Here are relevant quotes from the Leaders' Statement: "As we commit to implement a new, sustainable growth model, we should encourage work on measurement methods so as to better take into account the social and environmental dimensions of economic development." and "Modernizing the international financial institutions and global development architecture is essential to our efforts to promote global financial stability, foster sustainable development, and lift the lives of the poorest." These statements substantiate the extent to which sustainable development has become a mainstream international priority.

3 The link between sustainability, poverty, and development is deep and critical. The subject exceeds the scope of this chapter and the reader is referred for example to Chichilnisky and Sheeran (2009) and Chichilnisky (1994).

4 With infinitely many states of nature, compactness requires weaker topologies that can imply insensitivity towards rare events (Yannelis and Zame, 1986). Furthermore, supporting prices that are continuous with the "sup norm" can lead to paradoxical results (Chichilnisky and Kalman, 1980). To resolve this continuity–compactness dilemma and avoid paradoxes we rely on the properties of sustainable preferences that are sensitive to the present and the future, and use the notion of "limited arbitrage" introduced in Chichilnisky (1991, 1994a, 1996c, 1998). Taken together, sustainable preferences and the notion of limited arbitrage, overcome the problems of insensitivity to rare events and unlimited short sales by limiting somewhat the diversity of the traders (Chichilnisky, 1994b), bounding the "gains from trade" that they can achieve trading with each other, while creating sensitivity to frequent and rare events and ensuring existence of solutions. In Proposition 2, we show that limited arbitrage is equivalent to bounded gains from trade, and it ensures the compactness of Pareto utility allocations, as needed for the existence of solutions, based on earlier results of Chichilnisky (1991, 1998) and Chichilnisky and Heal (1984, 1998). To complete the existence result, Theorem 1 proves that, in a sustainable market, limited arbitrage is equivalent to the compactness of the set of Pareto efficient allocations, and Theorem 2 establishes that it is necessary and sufficient for the existence of sustainable as well as efficient competitive market equilibrium. The next section discusses the role of prices in a sustainable market economy. These assign economic value both to instantaneous and long-run consumption, providing a connection with the axiom of choice that is at the foundation of mathematics. It ought to be clarified that a sustainable market equilibrium is shown to exist, but it is a somewhat different concept than what is normally defined as a market equilibrium, since in sustainable markets, market prices take a new role: they represent the value of consumption with frequent risks as well as the value of consumption in Black Swans risks – a concept that differs from currently used market equilibrium prices. Indeed, when sustainable constraints are taken into consideration, new concepts and features of economics arise as demonstrated throughout this entire special volume on the economics of the global environment, see Asheim, Mitra, and Tungodden (2011), Burniaux and Martins (2011), Chipman and Tian (2011), Dutta and Radner (2011), Figuieres and Tidball (2011), Karp and Zhang (2011), Lauwers (2011), Lecocq and Hourcade (2011), and Rezai, Foley, and Taylor (2011).

5 The axioms for sustainable preferences were introduced in Chichilnisky (1996a,b), and similar axioms were introduced for the foundations of preferences under uncertainty, for

non-parametric econometrics (Chichilnisky, 2009a,b), for relative likelihoods and the foundations of probability and statistics (Chichilnisky, 2010a,b).

6 The time preference U ranks paths over time $u(t) \in L_\infty$ and Axiom 1 requires U to be continuous and linear. Observe that since the instantaneous utility function $u : R^N \to R$ is concave and need not be linear, the ranking of consumption paths need not be linear as a function of consumption, $x(t)$.

7 The cones $C(\Omega) = \{\{f\} \subset X : \lim_{j \to \infty} f^j = U(j^{j_0})$ for some $j_0\}$ are also convex and uniform across vectors Ω.

8 This follows from the initial results of Chichilnisky (1996a,b). $L_\infty^* - L_1$ denotes the complement of L_1 in L_∞^*, namely the space of purely finitely additive measures, see also the Appendix.

References

Arrow, K. (1971) *Essays in the Theory of Risk Bearing,* Markham Publishing Co., Chicago.

Arrow, K. J., and Hahn, F. (1971) *General Competitive Analysis.* Holden-Day, San Francisco.

Asheim, G., Mitra, T., and Tungodden, B. (2011) Sustainable Resources: Social Welfare Functions, *Economic Theory* Special Issue on the Global Environment.

Burniaux, J.-M., and Martins, J.O. (2011) Carbon Leakages: A General Equilibrium View, *Economic Theory* Special Issue on the Global Environment.

Chichilnisky, G. (1991) Limited Arbitrage is Necessary and Sufficient for the Existence of Competitive Equilibrium With or Without Short Sales, Discussion Paper No. 650, Columbia University Department of Economics, December 1991. Also in *Economic Theory* 95, 79–108, 1995.

Chichilnisky, G. (1993) The Cone Condition, Properness and Extremely Desirable Commodities, *Economic Theory* 3, 177–182.

Chichilnisky, G. (1994a) Arbitrage and Gains from Trade: A United Perspective on Resource Allocation, *American Economic Review* 84, 427–434.

Chichilnisky, G. (1994b) Limited Arbitrage is Necessary and Sufficient for the Existence of a Competitive Equilibrium and the Core, and it Limits Voting Cycles *Economics letters* 46, 321–331.

Chichilnisky, G. (1996a) An Axiomatic Approach to Sustainable Development, *Social Choice and Welfare* 13, 231–257.

Chichilnisky, G. (1996b) What is Sustainable Development?, *Resource Energy Economics* 73, 467–491.

Chichilnisky, G. (1996c) Markets with Endogenous Uncertainty: Theory and Policy, *Theory and Decision* 41, pp. 99–131.

Chichilnisky, G. (1996d) Updating Von Neumann Morgenstern Axioms for Choice under Catastrophic Risks, Invited Presentation, Proceedings of a Workshop on Catastrophic Environmental Risks, The Fields Institute for Mathematical Sciences, University of Toronto, Canada, June 9–11.

Chichilnisky, G. (1996e) Markets and Games: A Simple Equivalence Among the Core, Equilibrium and Limited Arbitrage *Metroeconomica* 47, 266–280.

Chichilnisky, G. (1996f) Limited Arbitrage is Necessary and Sufficient for the Non-emptiness of the Core *Economics letters* 52, 177–180.

Chichilnisky, G. (1996g) Financial Innovation in Property Catastrophe Reinsurance: The Convergence of Insurance and Capital Markets *Risk Financing Newsletter* 13(2), June.

Chichilnisky, G (1997a) What Is Sustainable Development, *Land Economics* 73, 467–491.

Chichilnisky, G. (1997b) Property Cat Woes Have Financial Solutions, *World Reinsurance Report* September 1, s-20–s-24.

Chichilnisky, G. (1998) A Unified Perspective on Resource Allocation: Limited Arbitrage is Necessary and Sufficient for the Existence of a Competitive Equilibrium, the Core and Social

Choice, in G. Chichilnisky (Ed.), *Topology and Markets*, Fields Institute for Research in Mathematical Sciences and the American Mathematical Society, Toronto, Canada.

Chichilnisky, G. (1999) Catastrophe Futures: Financial Markets for Unknown Risks, in G. Chichilnisky (Ed.) *Markets, Information, and Uncertainty*, Cambridge University Press, pp. 120–140 (with G. Heal).

Chichilnisky, G. (2000) An Axiomatic Approach to Choice Under Uncertainty with Catastrophic Risks, *Resource & Energy Economics* 22, 221–231.

Chichilnisky, G. (2002) Catastrophic Risk, in AH. ElShaarawi and WW. Piegorsch (Eds.) *Encyclopedia of Environmetrics* Volume 1, John Wiley & Sons, Ltd, Chichester, pp. 274–279.

Chichilnisky, G. (2006) Catastrophic Risks: The Need for New Tools, Financial Instruments and Institutions, in *Privatization of Risk*, Social Science Research Council, June.

Chichilnisky, G. (2009a) The Limits of Econometrics: Non Parametric Estimation in Hilbert Spaces, *Econometric Theory* 25, 1070–1086.

Chichilnisky, G. (2009b) The Topology of Fear, *Journal of Mathematical Economics* 45, 807–816.

Chichilnisky, G. (2009c) Catastrophic Risks, *International Journal of Green Economics* 3, 130–141.

Chichilnisky, G. (2009d) Avoiding Extinction: Equal Treatment of the Present and the Future, *Economics: The Open-Access*, Open-Assessment E-Journal 3, 200932, 1–25.

Chichilnisky, G. (2010a) The Foundations of Statistics with Black Swans, *Mathematical Social Sciences* 59, 184–192.

Chichilnisky, G. (2010b) The Foundations of Probability with Black Swans, *Journal of Probability and Statistics*, Article ID 838240.

Chichilnisky, G. (2011) Catastrophic Risks with Finite of Infinite States, *International Journal of Ecological Economics & Statistics* 23, 3–18.

Chichilnisky, G. (2012a) Sustainable Markets with Short Sales, *Journal of Economic Theory* 49(2), 293–308.

Chichilnisky, G. (2012b) Economic Theory and the Global Environment, *Journal of Economic Theory* 49(2) 217–226.

Chichilnisky, G., and Chanel, O. (2009a) The Influence of Fear in Decisions: Experimental Evidence, *Journal of Risk and Uncertainty* 39(3), 271–298.

Chichilnisky, G., and Chanel, O. (2012) Valuing Life: Experimental Evidence Using Sensitivity to Rare Events, *Ecological Economics*, March S.

Chichilnisky, G., and Heal, G.M. (1984) Existence of a Competitive Equiibrium in Sobolev Spaces without Bounds on Short Sales, *Journal of Economic Theory* 59, 364–384. Initially circulated as Chichilnisky, G., and Heal, G.M., Existence of a Competitive Equilibrium in Lp and Sobolev Spaces, IMA Preprint series #79, Institute for Mathematics and its Applications, University of Minnessota, Minneapolis, Minnesota, June 1984.

Chichilnisky, G., and Heal, G.M. (1997) Social choice with infinite populations, *Social Choice and Welfare* 14, 303–319.

Chichilnisky, G., and Heal, G.M. (1998a) A Unified Treatment of Finite and Infinite Economies: Limited Arbitrage is Necessary and Sufficient for the Existence of Equilibrium and the Core, *Economic Theory* 12, 163–176.

Chichilnisky, G., and Heal, G.H. (1998b) Global Environmental Risks, in G. Chichilnisky, G.M. Heal, and A. Vercelli (Eds.), *Sustainability: Dynamics and Uncertainty*, Kluwer Academic Publishers, The Netherlands, pp. 23–46.

Chichilnisky, G., and Heal G.M. (1998c) Managing Unknown Risks: The Future of Global Reinsurance, *The Journal of Portfolio Management* 24, 85–91.

Chichilnisky, G., and Kalman, P. (1980) An Application of Functional Analysis to Models of Efficient Allocation of Economic Resources, *Journal of Optimization Theory and Applications* 30, 19–32.

Chichilnisky, G., and Sheeran, K. (2009) *Saving Kyoto*. New Holland Publishers, London.

Chichilnisky, G., and Wu, H.-M. (2006) General Equilibrium with Endogenous Uncertainty and Default, *Journal of Mathematical Economics*, 42.

Chipman, J., and Tian, G. (2011) Detrimental Externalities Pollution Rights and the "Coase Theorem", *Economic Theory* Special Issue on the Global Environment.

Debreu, G. (1953) Valuation Equilibrium and Pareto Optimum, *Proceedings of the National Academy of Sciences* 40, 588–592.

DeGroot, M. (2004) *Optimal Statistical Decisions*. Wiley-Interscience, New York.

Dubins, L. (1975) Finitely Additive Conditional Probabilities, Conglomerability and Disintegration, *The Annals of Probability* 3, 89–99.

Dubins, L., and Savage, L. (1965) *Inequalities for Stochastic Processes: How to Gamble if You Must*, McGraw Hill, New York.

Dunford, N., and Schwartz, J.T. (1958) *Linear Operators, Part I*, Interscience, New York.

Dutta, P., and Radner, R. (2011) Capital Growth in a Global Warming Model, *Economic Theory* Special Issue on the Global Environment.

Figuieres, C., and Tidball, M. (2011) Sustainable Exploitation of a Natural Resource: a Satisfying Use of Chichilnisky's Criterion, *Economic Theory* Special Issue on the Global Environment.

Godel, K. (1940) *The Consistency of the Continuum Hypothesis. Annals of Mathematical Studies 3*, Princeton University Press, Princeton.

Hernstein, I.N., and Milnor, J. (1953) An Axiomatic Approach to Measurable Utility, *Econometrica* 1, 291–297.

Kadane, J.B., and O'Hagan, A. (1995) Using Finitely Additive Probability: Uniform Distributions of the Natural Numbers, *Journal of the American Statistical Association* 90, 525–631.

Karp, L., and Zhang, J. (2011) Taxes v. Quantities for a Stock Pollutant with Endogenous Abatement Costs and Asymetric Information, *Economic Theory* Special Issue on the Global Environment.

Koopmans, T.C. (1960) Stationary Ordinal Utility and Impatience, *Econometrica* 28, 287–309.

Koopmans, T.C. (1972) Representation of Preferences Orderings Over Time, in B. McGuire and R. Radner (Eds.), *Decision and Organization*, North Holland Amsterdam.

Lauwers, L. (1993) Infinite Chichilnisky Rules, *Economics Letters* 4, 349–352.

Lauwers, L. (2011) Intergenerational Equity, Efficiency and Constructability, *Economic Theory* Special Issue on the Global Environment.

Lecocq, F., and Hourcade, J.C. (2011) Unspoken Ethical Issues in the Climate Affair: Insights from a Theoretical Analysis of the Negotiations, *Economic Theory* Special Issue on the Global Environment.

Negishi, T. (1960) Welfare Economics and Existence of an Equilibrium for a Competitive Economy, *Metroeconomica* 12, 92–97.

Ostrom, E. (2011) Nested Externalities and Polycentric Institutions: Must We Wait for Global Solutions to Climate Change before Taking Actions at Other Scales?, *Economic Theory* Special Issue on the Global Environment.

Posner, R. (2004) *Catastrophes: Risk and Response,* Oxford University Press, Oxford.

Purves, R.W., and Sudderth, W.D. (1976) Some Finitely Additive Probability, *The Annals of Probability* 4, 259–276.

Rezai, A., Foley, D., and Taylor, L. (2011) Global Warming and Economic Externalities, *Economic Theory* Special Issue on the Global Environment.

The World Bank, *State and Trends of the Carbon Market*, Carbon Finance at the World Bank, Annual Publication 2005–2012.

Yannelis, N., and Zame, W. (1986) Equilibria in Banach Lattices without Ordered Preferences, *Journal of Mathematical Economics* 15, 85–110.

Yosida, K. (1974) *Functional Analysis*, 4th edition, Springer Verlag, New York and Heidelberg.

Yosida, K., and Hewitt, E. (1952) Finitely Level Independent Measures, *Transactions of the American Mathematical Society* 72, 46–66.

8   Equilibrium vs. market efficiency

Joseph L. McCauley

Introduction

Rational expectations (Sargent, 1987) confuses stationary markets with efficient markets. We will explain why efficient markets and equilibrium markets are mutually contradictory, why if you have "efficiency" then you cannot have equilibrium (McCauley, 2009). An efficient market admits no equilibrium, so it exhibits no stationary price. In stark contrast, a stationary market would necessarily fluctuate about an equilibrium price, a stationary price. Rational expectations includes contradictory ideas because equilibrium is contradictorily defined in economics (McCauley, 2009). Strange as it seems, assumptions of equilibrium in economics are marked by lack of attention to the precise definition of equilibrium in dynamical systems theory, physics, and the theory of stochastic processes. There's an historic reason for this.

Origins of rational expectations

From an historical standpoint, rational expectations can be seen as the successful attempt to introduce randomness without contradicting the neo-classical economic model (McCann, 1994). Muth (1961: 315) introduced randomness into prices by assuming a fluctuating *ad hoc* excess demand. He then set the excess demand equal to zero and derived a fluctuating price, which he mis-identified as equilibrium. Prices are stationary in equilibrium, and vanishing excess demand can only imply a stationary price. Muth's *ad hoc* definition of excess demand was incorrect, it was not derived from empirical analysis.

In equilibrium, correctly defined, all one-point averages are constant, and all pair correlations depend only on the lag time T, not the time t at which observations begin (McCauley, 2009). Real markets are nonstationary, with very different behavior of one-point averages and pair correlations, as we'll show below. Muth and his successors did not look carefully enough at their assumptions: we'll also show that it's quite easy to devise a very simple trading strategy to suck money systematically out of a hypothetical equilibrium market. That cannot be done in an efficient market.

A Markov process has no memory. The conditional probability density depends only on the present state and the last observed state. In particular, the drift and diffusion coefficients may depend only on the present state and on no state from the past.

An example of a martingale is a drift-free Markov process. More generally, the conditional expectation of the random variable $x(t)$ in a martingale is the last observed state $x(t - T)$, $\langle x(t) \rangle = x(t - T)$. This means that the pair correlations obey

$$\langle x(t)x(t - T) \rangle = \langle x^2(t - T) \rangle = \sigma^2(t - T)$$

where $\sigma^2(t)$ is the variance at time t. We will refer to Markov processes and martingales in what follows.

"Value" in real markets

Following Kolmogorov, a stochastic process can be defined in principle by specifying the corresponding infinite hierarchy of n-point densities. To identify a class of process we need at least the two-point density, or the pair correlations. In practice, one generally cannot measure densities (unless scaling holds) but one can sometimes measure pair correlations. We will depend on the latter.

Let $(x_1, \ldots, x_n)$ represent observed points in a time series at times $(t_1, \ldots, t_n)$ where $t_k < t_{k+1}$. Finance markets generate time series that reflect a certain class of stochastic process, as we will explain below. As we have stated above, a stochastic process $x(t)$ would be *precisely* specified/defined by the infinite hierarchy of n-point densities (Gnedenko, 1967; Stratonovich, 1963)

$$f_{n-1}\left(x_1, t_1; \ldots; x_{k-1}, t_{k-1}; x_{k+1}, t_{k+1}; \ldots; x_n, t_n\right) = \int dx_k f_n\left(x_1, t_1; \ldots; x_n, t_n\right)$$

$$(1)$$

so that, e.g.,

$$f_1(x, t) = \int dy f_2(y, s; x, t) \tag{2}$$

and

$$f_n(x_n, t_n; \ldots; x_1, t_1)$$
$$= p_n(x_n, t_n \mid x_{n-1}, t_{n-1}; \ldots; x_1, t_1) f_{n-1}(x_{n-1}, t_{n-1}; \ldots; x_1, t_1)$$
$$= p_n(x_n, t_n \mid x_{n-1}, t_{n-1}; \ldots x_1, t_1) \ldots p_2(x_2, t_2 \mid x_1, t_1) f_1(x_1, t_1) \tag{3}$$

where p_n is the transition density depending on n points. In finance, $x(t) = \ln S(t)/S_c(t)$ is the log return where $S(t)$ is the price of the underlying asset (stock, bond, or foreign exchange) at time t. The price $S_c(t)$ locates the peak of the one-point returns density $f_1(x, t)$ at time t and so is consensus value, or just "value." "Value" is simply the price that the largest fraction of agents agree on at any given point of time, the most probable price. There is no assumption of market clearing or equilibrium, this definition of value is not restricted to equilibrium. In particular, it applies to both nonstationary and hypothetical stationary markets (McCauley, 2009).

Could value be known, then we could distinguish undervalued from overvalued. Radio engineers knew in the 1930s that one-point densities cannot be measured, there's too much scatter in the data. However, certain averages can be reliably measured (Bassler, McCauley, and Gunaratne, 2007: 17297; Bassler, Gunaratne, and McCauley, 2008: 769; McCauley, 2008a: 5188). We know in principle what we mean by the notion of "value" but we cannot expect to be able to measure it. What do we need in order to pin down an underlying class of stochastic dynamics generating the market? Value is therefore of no practical use in trading, whatever traders may believe.

The one-point density defines value, but a one-point density cannot pin down an underlying stochastic process; completely different classes of process can exhibit the same one-point density (Hänggi and Thomas, 1977; McCauley, 2010). Pair correlations provide the lowest level of description of a class of stochastic processes, so we need at least the two-point density f_2 or the two-point conditional density p_2 in order to have any hope of understanding the underlying dynamics. In practice, the two-point density cannot be extracted from data due to scatter, so we need to measure the pair correlations $\langle x(t+T)x(t)\rangle$ from time series analysis.

Hypothetical stationarity markets

Muth (1961) introduced and Lucas (1972) propagated the contradictory formulation of rational expectations. Ignoring those historic misleading notions, we can formulate the idea of a hypothetical equilibrium market correctly.

A stationary random process reflects the generalization of equilibrium to a stochastic process. Here, prices fluctuate about an equilibrium price that we can identify as "value." Value in such a market is time-invariant because the one-point density is time-independent. That is, "value" would be fixed once and for all in a stationary market. We could distinguish over- from under-valued if we could find an equilibrium market and then measure the one-point density.

Adhering to precise definitions in mathematics and physics, the correct definition of equilibrium in a stochastic process is: all averages are time-invariant. So in a stationary process, all densities f_n and all transition densities p_n of all orders n must be time translationally invariant (McCauley, 2009; Gnedenko, 1967; Stratonovich, 1963):

$$f_n(x_1, t_1 + T; \ldots; x_n, t_n + T) = f_n(x_1, t_1; \ldots; x_n, t_n) \qquad (4)$$

and

$$p_2(x_n, t_n \,|\, x_{n-1}, t_{n-1}) = p_2(x_n, T \,|\, x_{n-1}, 0)$$

as well.

It follows that the *normalizable* one-point density $f_1(x)$ is t-independent, so that the mean $\langle x(t) \rangle$, variance $\sigma^2 = \langle x^2(t) \rangle - \langle x(t) \rangle^2$, and all one-point averages are constants.

The one-point density describes fluctuations about statistical equilibrium. A warning: stationary processes may be Markovian, but *time translationally invariant Markov processes are generally not stationary*. In a time translationally invariant Markov process a *normalizable* t-independent one-point density generally doesn't exist (McCauley, 2009). The Wiener process (known in economics as "white noise") is the simplest example of a nonequilibrium Markov process.

Under stationarity, time translational invariance of the transition density $p_2(x_n, t + T \,|\, x_{n-1}, 0)$ implies pair correlations

$$\langle x(t + T)x(t) \rangle = \langle x(T)x(0) \rangle \tag{5}$$

depending on lag time T alone, independent of starting time t. With no drift this yields if $x(0) = 0$. In practice, constant mean and variance and a pair correlation depending on time lag alone are the empirical signatures of statistical equilibrium. However, an equilibrium market could not clear pointwise due to fluctuations: only a small fraction of agents (those with prices near the peak of the one-point density) agree on price. In the neo-classical straightjacket every agent agrees on price in equilibrium. Sociologically seen, trying to enforce this notion is the reason for Muth's historic mistake.

How to vacuum money out of an equilibrium market

The title of this section refers to the explanation by Merton and Scholes to a trader of what they were trying to do with the Black–Scholes option pricing model, suck nickels out of finance markets as with a vacuum cleaner (The Trillion Dollar Bet, no date). They, too, believed in a contradictory notion of market equilibrium, and failed catastrophically (Dunbar, 2000) because markets do *not* "return to historic values" in the long run. Recurrence would hold in an equilibrium market, but not in a nonstationary one.

Recurrence is the generalization to nonperiodic systems of the notion of simple periodicity. A system is periodic if an initial state repeats precisely after a definite amount of time τ, which is called the period. Generally, there is no period but there may be recurrence. A state is said to recur if after a finite amount of time the trajectory passes within a specified finite distance of the initial state. The amount of time required increases as you reduce the distance from the initial state and the nearby state, and there is no period. Stationary processes are generally recurrent.

It's trivial to devise a trading strategy that allows you to beat an equilibrium market (McCauley, 2009). Under stationarity, one knows that the prices will repeatedly fluctuate about equilibrium. When the price drops a standard deviation from value, for example, then buy. Hold until the price hits value plus one standard deviation and then sell. Such fluctuations are systematically guaranteed, you can even calculate the *recurrence time* (McCauley, 2010) by using Ito's lemma along with the construction of a suitable martingale. With recurrence guaranteed, a trader could suck money out of an equilibrium market systematically with little or no risk. The trader need only have enough cash to survive without having to sell before the expected price increase appears (bet/cash should always be small). Because you're only trading on equilibrium fluctuations, the buy/sell strategy can be repeated *ad infinitum*. It's clear that an equilibrium market can't be efficient, if by efficient we mean a market that's hard or impossible to beat (Mandelbrot, 1966).

Finance markets are nonstationary. Equilibrium is not found either in the historically best-known model (Gaussian returns; Osborne, 1964; Black and Scholes, 1973) or in real data (Bassler *et al.*, 2007, 2008; McCauley, 2008b). What class of model characterizes a finance market?

Real markets, efficient markets, martingale markets

Here and in all that follows we assume a normal liquid market, a market where the "noise traders" (Black, 1986) trade frequently enough that bid/ask spreads are very small relative to price (McCauley, 2009). A crash is not a normal liquid market. In a crash liquidity dries up. To zeroth order, there are many limit orders to sell with few or no buyers in a market crash. A market crash is certainly not a fluctuation described by fat tails in a one-point returns distribution, a market crash is instead a liquidity drought. That's what happened to LTCM in 1998, and housing-based financial instruments in September 2007 and in 2008 (McCauley, 2009).

Due to the sparseness of data it's impossible to model a crash falsifiably. But there are nonmathematical signs that a bubble is about to burst. These signs take the form of unusually risky behavior, as described in McKay (1980) and Kindelberger (1996). Before the stock market crash of 2000 ordinary people quit their jobs, mortgaged their houses a second time and used the cash in "day trading." Leading up to the derivatives crash of 2007–8, some agents bought houses for the short term to resell for a profit, houses were bought and resold as if they were hot stocks. The market crash of 1929 led to a liquidity crisis. The reason that crashes between 1960 and 2000 did not lead to a liquidity crisis, but the 2007–8 crash did, is described elsewhere (McCauley, 2009).

By the efficient market hypothesis (EMH), we mean a detrended *normal liquid market* that is in principle impossible to beat systematically. This means that there are no *readily available* correlations or patterns that can be exploited for profit. A Markovian market would be unbeatable in this sense, because a detrended Markov market has no memory to exploit. A detrended Markov process is very generally nonstationary without time translational invariance, and recurrence of prices cannot be predicted or expected. More generally, a detrended Markov process is a martingale, but the reverse is not necessarily true. Martingales behave Markovian at the level of pair correlations even if the entire process has nonMarkov features, like memory of an initial condition in the distant past (Hänggi and Thomas, 1977; McCauley, 2010). However, that sort of trivial memory cannot be exploited for financial advantage.

To formulate the dynamics of hard-to-beat markets, we assume that the increment autocorrelations vanish, where by increments we mean differences in levels $x(t, T) = x(t + T) - x(t)$, $x(t, -T) = x(t) - x(t - T)$. The statement that trading during an earlier time interval provides no signals for traders in a later nonoverlapping time interval *at the level of pair correlations* is simply that

$$\langle (x(t_1) - x(t_1 - T_1))(x(t_2 + T_2) - x(t_2)) \rangle = 0 \tag{6}$$

if there is no time interval overlap, $[t_1 - T_1, t_1] \cap [t_2, t_2 + T_2] = \emptyset$, where $\emptyset$ denotes the empty set on the line. This is a very different condition than assuming that the increments are statistically independent, and is much weaker than assuming that the market is Markovian.

Consider any stochastic process $x(t)$ where the differences are uncorrelated, meaning that (6) holds. From this condition we obtain the autocorrelation function for levels (returns). Let $t > s$, then

$$\langle x(t)x(s) \rangle = \langle (x(t) - x(s))x(s) \rangle + \langle x^2(s) \rangle = \langle x^2(s) \rangle > 0 \tag{7}$$

since $x(s) - x(t_0) = x(s)$, so that $\langle x(t + T)x(t) \rangle$ is simply the variance in levels $x(t)$ at the earlier time t. *This condition is equivalent to a martingale process:*

$$\int dy\, y\, p_2(y, t + T \,|\, x, t) = x \tag{8}$$

$$\langle x(t + T)x(t) \rangle = \iint dx\, dy\, xy\, p_2(y, t + T; x, t)f_1(x, t)$$

$$= \int xf_1(x, t)dx \int y dy\, p_2(y, t + T; x, t) = \int x^2 f_1(x, t)dx \tag{9}$$

At the level of pair correlations, a martingale cannot be distinguished from a drift-free Markov process. Note also that (6) can be interpreted as asserting that earlier returns have no correlation with future gains. This condition can't be assumed, it must be deduced via data analysis.

Next, we emphasize the key point for data analysis and modeling. Combining

$$\langle (x(t + T) - x(t))^2 \rangle = \langle (x^2(t + T) \rangle + \langle x^2(t) \rangle - 2\langle x(t + T)x(t) \rangle \tag{10}$$

with (10) we get

$$\left\langle (x(t+T) - x(t))^2 \right\rangle = \left\langle x^2(t+T) \right\rangle - \left\langle x^2(t) \right\rangle \tag{11}$$

which depends on both t and T, excepting the rare case where $\langle x^2 \rangle$ is linear in t. *Uncorrelated differences are generally nonstationary* (this is bad news for cointegration[1]).

It's easy to show that, with one rare exception, time-translationally invariant martingales are nonstationary processes. The daily and weekly behavior of this mean square fluctuation has been described in (Bassler *et al.*, 2007: 17297; Bassler *et al.*, 2008: 769) for foreign exchange (FX) markets.

The difference correlations of a stationary process do not vanish,

$$\left\langle x(t, T)x(t, -T) \right\rangle = \left\langle x(2T)x(0) \right\rangle - \sigma^2 \tag{12}$$

reflecting pair correlations that can be traded on for profit. Price recurrence is the basis for a successful trading strategy in a hypothetical stationary market. Real markets are martingales, nonstationary processes with nonstationary differences.

A successful mathematics-based trading strategy should carry with it the prediction of the first passage time, which is related to the idea of recurrence. For a martingale without time translational invariance the standard procedure for calculating the first passage time fails. The question of how to formulate the first passage time for a general nonstationary process is hard to answer.

Recurrence in financial markets

A first passage time is a relaxation of the condition of recurrence, albeit it is related in spirit. Given the present price of a stock, what is the average waiting time for the stock to hit an entirely different price? Clearly, formulating this problem requires as a first step that we know the dynamical model that generates the stock prices. All that we know is that we have the martingale class, with the first difference $x(t, T) = x(t + T) - x(t)$ given as (Bassler *et al.*, 2007)

$$\left\langle x^2(t, T) \right\rangle \approx T \int D(x, t) f_1(x, t) dx \tag{13}$$

for $T \ll t$ but we cannot say *which* martingale. Martingales are diffusive processes but the diffusion coefficient $D(x, t)$ is constant or t-dependent only for the Wiener process or for transformations on Wiener processes. A constant diffusion coefficient would imply Gaussian returns, but the observed returns are not Gaussian. The observed returns can be fit by an exponential density during a certain time interval of day (McCauley, 2009). Qualitatively, a variable diffusion coefficient (one dependent on both returns and time) describes systematic nonuniformities in traders' behavior. This is discussed in Seemann, McCauley, and Gunaratne (2011) for the exponential density, e.g.

$$f_1(x,t) \propto t^{-1/2} e^{-x/|t|^{1/2}} \tag{14}$$

the diffusion coefficient is

$$D(x,t) \propto 1 + |x| / |t|^{1/2} \tag{15}$$

The t-dependence of (13) has been measured for FX markets (McCauley, 2009; Bassler *et al.*, 2007, 2008; Seeman *et al.*, 2011) but far more data would be required (a 30 years long time series would not be enough) to extract the diffusion coefficient $D(x,t)$.

The exponential model (14,15) with a different Hurst exponent H ($H = 1/2$ in (14,15)) can be used to fit FX returns over a certain time interval during daily trading. FX returns over longer time intervals do not scale. Scaling with $0 < H < 1$ is described, with $u = |x| / |t|^H$, by

$$f_1(x,t) = |t|^{-H} F(u) \tag{16}$$

and

$$D(x,t) = |t|^{2H-1} D(u)$$

The financial martingale describes a nonstationary process where the variance grows linearly with the time, so is not approximable by stationarity. But back to the question of recurrence.

By construction, this martingale is nonstationary with nonstationary differences. If we could formulate and solve the problem of first passage time for a martingale without time translational invariance then we could address the question of a profitable trading strategy quantitatively. We might also be able to analyze the following problem: if two stocks appear to be significantly relatively mispriced, then how long should we expect to wait to see the discrepancy disappear? Here's the fundamental difficulty with trying to formulate and solve all such questions.

The standard method for formulating a first passage time assumes a time-translationally invariant stochastic process, a process where $D(x,t) = D(x)$. In that case the first passage time problem can be reduced to the solution of an ordinary differential equation. If the diffusion coefficient depends inseparably on both x and t, then that method cannot be used. In a word, we do not even understand how to formulate the problem. There is therefore no reliable mathematical prediction to tell us that we should bet on a return to parity of two stocks that are (subjectively) judged to be relatively mispriced. This degree of ignorance does not prevent trading houses from promoting short and long trades based on the idea of mispricing. LTCM's experience of the Gamblers' Ruin in October 1997 was based on a misplaced belief in recurrence, that was shown to be wrong when liquidity dried up for Russian bonds (Dunbar, 2007). This chapter does not provide much that's of interest for banks and traders, except advice on how not to go broke, and on how to avoid causing financial crises.

Acknowledgment

This contribution is dedicated to the festschrift for my good friend Duncan Foley. Duncan has long been interested in equilibrium vs. nonequilibrium in economics, and in fundamental ideas in economics. I hope that he will enjoy my small contribution to the celebration of his life and teaching. This chapter reflects work done with Gemunu Gunaratne, Kevin Bassler, and Lars Seemann. I'm grateful to Duncan for a very nice endorsement of my 2009 book (McCauley, 2009), and for many interesting and very helpful email exchanges on various aspects of economics and finance. The background required to understand this chapter in depth is developed in my book, which was written for both students and experts.

Note

1 Cointegration is a method for describing how two entirely different time series, like FX rates, and relative price levels in two countries, should behave. The method assumes stationary increments except in special cases, but differences between different financial time series are not stationary (McCauley, 2009).

References

Bassler, K.E., McCauley, J.L., and Gunaratne, G.H. (2007) Nonstationary Increments, Scaling Distributions, and Variable Diffusion Processes in Financial Markets, *PNAS* 104, 17297.

Bassler, K.E., Gunaratne, G.H., and McCauley, J.L. (2008) Empirically Based Modeling in Finance and Beyond and Spurious Stylized Facts, *Int. Rev. Fin. An.* 17, 769.

Black, F. (1986) Noise, *J. of Finance* 3, 529.

Black, F., and Scholes, M. (1973) The Pricing of Options and Corporate Liabilities, *J. Political Economy* 81, 637.

Dunbar, N. (2000) *Inventing Money, Long-Term Capital Management and the Search for Risk-Free Profits*, New York: Wiley.

Gnedenko, B.V. (1967) *The Theory of Probability*, tr. by B.D. Seckler, New York: Chelsea.

Hänggi, P., and Thomas, H. (1977) Time Evolution, Correlations and Linear Response of Non-Markov Processes, *Zeitschr. für Physik* B26, 85.

Lucas, R.E. (1972) Expectations and the Neutrality of Money, *J. Economic Theory* 4, 103.

Mandelbrot, B. (1966) Forecasts of Future Prices, Unbiased Markets and Martingale Models, *J. Business* 39, 242.

Kindleberger, C.P. (1996) *Manias, Panics, and Crashes, A History of Financial Crises*, New York: Wiley.

McCann, Jr., C.R. (1994) *Probability Foundations of Economic Theory*, London: Routledge.

McCauley, J.L. (2008a) Time vs. Ensemble Averages for Nonstationary Time Series, *Physica* A387, 5188.

McCauley, J.L. (2008b) Nonstationarity of Efficient Financial Markets: FX Market Evolution from Stability to Instability, *Int. Rev. Fin. An.* 17, 820.

McCauley, J.L. (2009) *Dynamics of Markets: The New Financial Economics*, Cambridge: Cambridge University Press.

McCauley, J.L. (2010) NonMarkov Ito processes with 1-state memory, *Physics Procedia* 3, 1659.

McKay, C. (1980) *Extraordinary Popular Delusions and the Madness of Crowds*, New York: Harmony Books.

Muth, J.F. (1961) Rational Expectations and the Theory of Price Movements, *Econometrica* 29, 315.

Osborne, M.F.M. (1964) Brownian motion in the stock market, in: *The Random Character of Stock Market Prices*, P. Cootner (ed.), Cambridge MA: MIT Press.

Sargent, T.J. (1987) *Macroeconomic Theory*, New York: Academic Press.

Seemann, L., McCauley, J.L., and Gunaratne, G.H. (2011) Intraday Volatility and Scaling in High Frequency Foreign Exchange Markets, *Int. Rev. Fin. An.* 20, 121.

Stratonovich, R.L. (1963) *Topics in the Theory of Random Noise,* tr. by R. A. Silverman, New York: Gordon & Breach.

The Trillion Dollar Bet (no date), http://www.pbs.org/wgbh/nova/stockmarket/.

9 Foley's Thesis[1], Negishi's method, existence proofs and computation

K. Vela Velupillai

Duncan Foley's many-faceted and outstanding contributions to macroeconomics, microeconomics, general equilibrium theory, the theory of taxation, history of economic thought, the *magnificent dynamics* of classical economics, classical value theory, Bayesian statistics, formal dynamics and, most recently, fascinating forays into an interpretation of economic evolution from a variety of complexity theoretic viewpoints have all left – and continue to leave – significant marks in the development and structure of economic theory. He belongs to the grand tradition of visionaries who theorize with imaginative audacity on the dynamics, evolution and contradictions of capitalist economies – a tradition that, perhaps, begins with Marx and Mill, continues with Keynes and Schumpeter, reaching new heights with the iconoclastic brilliancies of a Tsuru and a Goodwin, a Chakravarty and a Nelson, and to which Duncan Foley adds a lustre of much value.

In this contribution I return to mathematical themes broached in Foley's brilliant and pioneering Yale doctoral dissertation (Foley, 1967) and attempt to view them as a *Computable Economist*[2] would. The intention is to suggest that algorithmic indeterminacies are intrinsic to the foundations of economic theory in the mathematical mode.

Introduction

> Consider a two-agent, two-good exchange economy with given initial allocation of goods over the agents.
> a). Explain *Negishi's strategy for proving the existence of a Walrasian equilibrium*. Illustrate his procedure in an Edgeworth box diagram.
> Duncan Foley's *Advanced Microeconomics Examination in Class*, New School University, May 10, 2005, *Second Question*; italics added

In an interview held on November 30, 2001, at his apartment in New York City, reported in Colander *et al.*, (2004), Foley, in answering the interviewers' specific question to "tell [them] about [his] thesis," made the interesting and important observation that:

> My thesis adapted the methods of general equilibrium theory to the problem of public goods. It has some results that I still think are neat. I proposed an analog of competitive equilibrium for public goods ... and *proved* that it was Pareto efficient .... *[T]he method was exactly the same as Koopmans's proof* [in Koopmans (1957)] of the Pareto efficiency of price equilibria. ... In proving this theorem I independently discovered *Negishi's method* for proving the existence of Walrasian competitive equilibrium, which is based on *moving along the Pareto efficient surface* by changing household weights in a social welfare function rather than using a Tâtonnement argument on prices.
>
> Foley, 2004, p. 186; italics added

I have known Duncan Foley, personally, for over a decade and have, in that period, communicated with him intensively (via the ubiquitous channel provided by e-mail) on many topics – both professional and personal, with a clear dominance of the former. No subject has occurred with more frequency or intensity than the problems posed by consideration of computability of Walrasian equilibria in their Arrow–Debreu versions, and their existence proofs underpinned by non-constructive methods. In the ten years – or so – that we have exchanged correspondence on these issues – and the couple of times we were able to meet personally and talk about them – it was clear that some "convergence" towards mutually agreed (and agreeable) positions had been achieved, albeit from vastly different starting positions. I believe Foley came around to understand my conviction – based on absolutely rigorous and completely documented (in the form of fairly respectable mathematical publications, e.g. Velupillai (2006) and Velupillai (2009a) – about the uncomputability of Arrow–Debreu equilibria, and also the appeal made, in almost all orthodox mathematical economics when generating existence proofs, to non-constructive methods of proof.

For example in an e-mail to me as recently as October 11, 2010, with the subject line "Computability of Walrasian equilibrium," Foley wrote (italics added):

> I take your position to be that Walrasian equilibrium is *uncomputable* in the price simplex due to the *non-constructivity* of the Bolzano–Weierstrass theorem, *a conclusion with which I agree*.[3]

In earlier correspondence, on January 26, 2010, this time with the subject referred to as: "Constructibility of exchange equilibrium," Foley wrote (again, italics added):

> I take your point that conventional ("ordinary") economic theory operates uncritically in the domain of real analysis, and that if the problem of exchange equilibrium [that is, a point in or near the contract set] is posed

in this fashion finding a point in the exchange equilibrium (Pareto set) is non-constructive.

To this e-mail, Foley appended an earlier interchange between us on related issues, where he had written (italics added):

> My conjecture is that there is a *constructive algorithmic* (and even economic) *method* to find exchange equilibrium (not necessarily Walrasian equilibrium) allocations by allowing agents to find and make mutually advantageous trades. I'm not sure you and I ever reached a meeting of minds on this question, but I'd like to pursue it further.

My response to this important *conjecture* was (italics in the original):

> Unfortunately, I am unable to agree with your 'conjecture'. To 'find [an] exchange equilibrium', with a "constructive algorithmic method' (by the way, *if* 'constructive' *then* 'algorithmic'!), means you must first define the domain and range of the agents' decision space 'constructively'. Once you do this, the whole problem of an algorithm becomes trivial. 'Allowing agents to make mutually advantageous trades', means – in algorithmic mathematics – that these 'trades' are in terms of constructive or computable numbers, which they are not in any kind of ordinary economic theory.

It has only gradually dawned on me that Foley has always had in mind – or, perhaps, only in the deep recesses of his fertile mind – "*Negishi's method* for proving the existence of Walrasian competitive equilibrium," which he had "independently discovered" over 35 years ago, and for which discovery the orthodox mathematical economists have never given him adequate – indeed, *any* – credit. Not even usually sympathetic doctrine historians, specializing in the development of mathematical economics, have – to the best of my knowledge – acknowledged Foley's pioneering contribution, from this point of view, in his remarkably original thesis. From my personal point of view, it is a matter of lasting regret that the thesis was never published as a book, which could have been used as a text in any serious graduate course in mathematical economics in which refreshing economics was coupled to innovative mathematics. Above all, it could have provided a broader social and political scientific basis for one strand of computable general equilibrium theory.

In this chapter I take up the thread, with which I have been weaving a tale, of computability and constructivity in mathematical and computational economics, mostly via "conversations" with Duncan Foley in e-mail interchanges, and try to make explicit my standpoint on *Negishi's method*. This is the subject matter of the section Negishi's method, below, preceded by a section where I outline my more professional indebtedness – one that is common to my own generation of theoretically minded, mathematically literate and (I hope!) socially and politically enlightened economists – to the vast and fascinating canvasses on which Duncan

Foley has been fashioning a vision of economics that is far richer than any kind of orthodoxy has been able to devise. The concluding section is a reflection on the lessons that one might be able to extract for a kind of economic theory that is formalized in terms of an empirically useful mathematics.

A personal preamble

> If the society as a whole has the *complexity level of a general-purpose computer* [or Turing Machine], it will be *impossible* for any other general-purpose computer to work out its evolution except by direct simulation. To carry out the program of rational explanation of behavior in this context would require positing that each individual agent in society had some way of simulating the potential evolution of a system of interlinked Turing machines. At this point the rational explanation program runs into deep paradoxes of self-reference.
>
> Foley, 1998, p. 40

This pithy characterization of the conundrums of the "rational explanation [research] program" in economics is typical of the way Duncan Foley has been able to locate one or another of the lacunae in orthodox economic theory, whether mathematically underpinned or not. Essentially, Foley has invoked the celebrated *halting problem for Turing machines* to point out where the "rational explanation of behavior" must fall foul of formal possibilities of evolutionary predictability. As a matter of fact, it is not even necessary – for this failure to manifest itself – to posit "that each individual agent ... had some way of simulating the potential evolution of interlinked Turing machines"; it is sufficient to posit that "society as a whole has the complexity of [one single Turing machine]." Moreover, even if the "individual agent had some way of simulating the potential evolution of [one single] Turing machine," it will not be possible to circumvent the consequences of the *halting problem for Turing machines.*

I was a graduate student of economics at the University of Lund in the very early 1970s. At that time in Lund, the writings of the great past economic pioneers of that university were still being assigned to graduate students almost routinely (*in the original languages*: Swedish, Norwegian, and German). Even standard graduate courses in macroeconomics, growth theory, and capital theory had, in their required reading lists, texts by Wicksell and Lindahl, Lundberg and Ohlin, and Palander and Landgren. So, it was not surprising that the graduate course in public finance was heavily influenced by the Swedish tradition in public finance and taxation – i.e., the tradition emanating from the doctoral dissertations of Wicksell and Lindhal (but also influenced by Leif Johansen's contemporary work at Oslo). We were genuinely fortunate graduate students at Lund.

Thus, in the early 1970s, I was already introduced to Duncan Foley's pioneering work on "Lindahl prices." Both his doctoral dissertation (as published in *Yale Economic Essays*, Foley, 1967) and his *Econometrica* paper of 1970 (Foley, 1970) were part of the required reading, together with parts of Wicksell's

Finanzthoretische Untersuchungen[4] (Wicksell, 1896) and more substantial parts of Lindahl's *Die Gerechtigkeit der Besteurung*[5] (Lindahl, 1919). Foley was placed in the grand tradition of Swedish public finance, as he was entitled to be.

However, two important caveats should be added to this legitimate claim to a Swedish lineage for Foley's early work on public finance in the general equilibrium tradition. Firstly, the internal debate in Sweden, particularly between Myrdal (1930) and Lindahl (1959) somehow did not get reflected in the details of Foley's thesis, nor in his later Marxist oriented stance on public finance. I state this only because Myrdal's sustained critique of the Wicksell–Lindahl tradition in public finance (ibid., particularly chapter 7), would, I am sure, have been handsomely endorsed by the later Foley (1978).[6]

Secondly, Foley's lifelong work on macroeconomic theory has not reflected the possible link one can discern between the public finance of the Swedes – particularly in how it determined a very special vision of national income accounting and balance-sheet constructions, as stressed by Hicks in his beautiful *Lindahl festschrift* contribution (Hicks, 1956) – and the macroeconomic dynamics they developed, largely prior to and independently of Keynes of the *General Theory*. I have tried, over the years, to stress this connection, as a way of suggesting a foundation for macroeconomics in the Swedish tradition in public finance (Velupillai, 1991).

In any case, being a graduate student at Lund was my path towards an introduction to Duncan Foley's pioneering work. Since then, from time to time, my own visions have been broadened and deepened by Duncan Foley's sustained original contributions, in a wide and interesting variety of ways, to various frontiers in economic theory – latterly mostly in macroeconomics, a field that has always remained central in my research agenda and teaching activities.

By the time I went to Cambridge in 1973 and my own interest in macroeconomics was being fostered by the great Cambridge pioneers of that field (particularly Nicky Kaldor and Richard Goodwin, my PhD supervisors at Cambridge), the *Foley–Sidrauski book* (Foley & Sidrauski, 1971) had also become standard reading for us. Growth theory, capital theory and distribution theory were the exciting topics being discussed at Cambridge at that time, and once again I had a Foley work assigned as required reading (the Foley–Sidrauski book).

I teach advanced macroeconomics at the graduate level in Trento. Last year I began using the finely crafted *Foley–Michl book* on *Growth and Distribution* (Foley & Michl, 1999) as the main supplementary textbook for this course, where growth theory is emphasized.[7] The Foley–Michl book is refreshingly modern, but is so by showing and grounding the evolution of modern theories of growth in the works of our great classical masters.

I mention it in this way to show a remarkable consistency in the way Foley's masterly contributions to economic theory proceed – at least in the way I have learned from his writings. They are always grounded in the works of our classical and neoclassical pioneers. Unlike much modern work, where it is either a Whig interpretation or, worse, ahistorical stories, Foley's work reminds us that we stand on the shoulders of giants, mostly past masters but often also contemporaries.[8]

These aspects are beautifully developed and evident in his *Schumpeter Lectures* (Foley, 2003). His mastery of the classical economists for their broad insights, for their magnanimity and, above all, for their visions of what Baumol called "magnificent dynamics," is unsurpassed in modern economic scholarship, especially – but not only – because of Foley's remarkable mastery of a wide variety of mathematical techniques, in addition to a deep understanding of mathematical philosophy.

Mentioning Baumol in the above paragraph recalls to my mind the way I finally resolved a perplexity regarding Foley's intellectual work. I had wondered why his work on Lindahl prices did not continue and how the macroeconomic work got done, almost in a parallel fashion, and how they both, then, led to his political economy outlook on public expenditure, on the one hand, and, on the other, how the monetary-fiscal framework of the work with Sidrauski – still relevant at some frontiers of macroeconomic theory – moved on to issues of growth, distribution and capital theories, often in the Cambridge (UK) tradition. By chance, my interest in the theory of public finance was reignited in the late 1980s and I had occasion to read Baumol's book of that period on *Superfairness* (Baumol,1986). There, on p. 72, I read as follows:

> All of [the work on fairness theory] appears to have its roots in Foley's writings. … Foley reports that he was led to think of the [fairness] criterion after seeing a movie in which Bob Dylan graphically emphasized the importance of fairness issues.

I think I understood then how there was a unified thread in Foley's work in public finance in the framework of general equilibrium theory, macrodynamics, history of economic thought, and the evolution of capitalist institutions: it was a passionate concern for *fairness* in all its dimensions and ramifications. This is also why I think Duncan is such a fine and knowledgeable all-round economist, with a wonderful mastery of so many aspects of economic theory. Again, his mathematical competence makes it easy for him to master many frontiers of economic theory and keep abreast of developments.

My own work in the last two decades or so has been in that exciting interface between dynamical systems theory, and computability and computational complexity theory. In addition to this I have also been concentrating on the relevance of constructive mathematics for formalizing economic theory – particularly microeconomics and economic dynamics. There are few economists I'd rather talk to, converse with, have my works read by for critical comments, than Duncan Foley.[9]

Duncan Foley's long Introduction to the collected essays of Peter Albin (Foley, 1998), is a masterly piece, linking dynamics and computability theory, via the formalism of Formal Languages Theory. It contains one of the most pedagogical expositions of the Chomsky hierarchy for economists. I have never failed, in the last decade or so, to have it in my various reading lists for almost any course of lectures I give. In that Introduction – but not only in that – Duncan's expository skills, backed by vast and deep mathematical knowledge and competence, underpinned by a thorough understanding of economic theory, come to the surface in a most felicitous way.

Foley has, in recent years, been focusing on interpreting economic phenomena from the point of view of varieties of complexity theories. He has also begun to wonder about thermodynamic interpretations of economic processes. They are not new issues to his fertile mind; but he seems to be taking a new turn, underpinned by new visions. I expect these new directions will bear fruit in the same way his thoughts have led to innovative works, right from the beginning, with those classics on classics: Lindahl prices, motivated by issues of fairness.

Thus, it must be the case that fairness is one motif in the humane tapestry Duncan Foley has made available to many of us, when we consider ourselves economists in the humanistic mode. Perhaps I am also on the right track when I believe his recent work and interest in non-linear dynamics and complexity are motivated by his incessant search for the first principles of what Karl Polanyi felicitously called *The Great Transformation* – the transformation that was brought about by industrialization of the advanced economic societies.

Somehow, despite these many faceted interests and contributions, and the central motif of fairness, I have always felt that mathematical rigour and computation have played an important part in the way Foley has theorized, even when no explicit formulas, equations, or other mathematical hieroglyphics appear in his imaginative writings. In my own decade-long "conversations" with Duncan Foley these two aspects have been the dominant themes. Perhaps that is why the subject matter of this contribution, to pay homage to Foley, is underpinned by the conundrums of *proof* and *computation*.

Negishi's method, fundamental theorems of welfare economics, equilibrium existence proofs and computation

> In proving the existence theorem I independently discovered *Negishi's method for proving the existence of Walrasian competitive equilibrium*, which is based on *moving along the Pareto efficient surface* by changing household weights in a social welfare function rather than using a tâtonnement argument on prices.
>
> Foley, 2004, p. 186; italics added

Negishi himself, reflecting on his youthful masterpiece[10] more than three decades later (Negishi, 1994, p. xiv; italics added), remarked:

> The *method of proof* used in this essay [i.e., in Negishi (1960)] has been found useful also for such problems as equilibrium in infinite dimensional space and computation of equilibria.

What exactly was Negishi's *method of proof* and how did it contribute to the *computation of equilibria*?

Duncan Foley's pithy characterization of the difference between the standard approach to *proving the existence* of an Arrow–Debreu *equilibrium*, and its *computation*, by a tâtonnement procedure – i.e., algorithm – of a mapping from the price simplex to itself, and the alternative *Negishi method* of iterating the weights assigned to individual utility functions that go into the definition of a social welfare function, which is maximized to determine – i.e., compute – the equilibrium, captures the key innovative aspect of the latter approach. Essentially, therefore, the difference between the standard approach to the proof of existence of equilibrium Arrow–Debreu prices, and their computation, and the Negishi approach boils down to the following:

- The standard approach proves the existence of Arrow–Debreu equilibrium prices by an appeal to a fixed point theorem and computes them – the equilibrium prices – by invoking the *Uzawa equivalence theorem* (Uzawa, 1962)[11] and devising an algorithm for the excess demand functions that map a price simplex into itself to determine the fixed point (Scarf, 1973).
- The Negishi approach *proves*, given initial endowments, *the existence* of individual welfare weights defining a social welfare function, whose *maximization* (subject to the usual constraints) *determines* the identical Arrow–Debreu *equilibrium*. The standard mapping of excess demand functions, mapping a price simplex into itself to determine a fixed point, is replaced by a mapping from the space of utility weights into itself, appealing to the same kind of fixed point theorem (in this case, the Kakutani fixed point theorem) to prove the existence of equilibrium prices.
- In other words, the method of proof of existence of equilibrium prices in the one approach is replaced by the *proof of existence* of "equilibrium utility weights," both appealing to traditional *fixed point theorems* (Brouwer, 1910; von Neumann, 1937 (1945–6); Kakutani, 1941[12]).
- In both cases (the computation of equilibrium prices on the one hand and, on the other, the computation of equilibrium weights) algorithms are devised that are *claimed* to determine (even if only *approximately*) the same fixed points.

Before proceeding any further, I should add that I am in the happy position of being able to refer the interested reader to a scholarly survey of Negishi's work. Takashi Negishi's outstanding "contributions to economic analysis" are brilliantly and comprehensively surveyed by Warren Young in his recent paper (Young, 2008). Young's paper provides a particularly appropriate background – together with at least a nodding acquaintance with § II & § III of Foley's Thesis (Foley, 1967, pp. 64–76) – to the issues I tackle in this section. It – Young's paper – is especially relevant also because his elegant summary of Negishi's "contribution to economic analysis" identifies Negishi (1960) as one of the two crucial pillars[13] on which to tell a coherent and persuasive story of what he calls the Negishi "research program" (ibid., p. 162; second set of italics, added):[14]

> To sum up, a number of major research programs can be identified, therefore, as emanating from Negishi's now *classic* papers, that of (1960) [Negishi, 1960] and 1961 [Negishi, 1961], respectively. Negishi's 1960 paper forms the basis for both 'theoretical' and 'applied' research programs in general equilibrium analysis, and his 1961 paper ... has been *almost as influential* in demarcating ongoing research up to the present in the field of imperfect competition and non-tatonnement processes. These papers ... attest to Negishi's considerable influence on the development of modern economic theory and analysis.

However, no one – to the best of my knowledge – has studied Negishi's *method of proof* from the point of view of *constructivity* and *computability*, the issues that were at the center of my dialog with Duncan Foley. Young's perceptive – and, in my opinion, entirely correct – identification of the crucial role played by Negishi (1960) in "both 'theoretical' and 'applied' research program in general equilibrium analysis" is, in fact, about *methods of existence proofs* and *computable general equilibrium* (CGE), and its offshoots, in the form of *applied computable general equilibrium analysis* (ACGE) – even leading up to current frontiers in computational issues in DSGE models (cf., Judd, 2005, pp. 52–7, for example).

Before I turn to these issues of the constructivity and computability of Negishi's method of existence proofs and the underpinning of some aspects computation in CGE and ACGE models in Negishi's approach (rather than, for example, in the standard approach pioneered by Scarf, 1973), there is one important economic theoretic *confusion* that needs to be sorted out. This is the question of the role played by the fundamental theorems of welfare economics in Negishi's method of the proof of the existence of a general (Walrasian) equilibrium.

It is generally agreed – and especially by Foley – that the *Negishi method of existence proof* is an applications of fixed point theorems on the *utility simplex*, in contrast to the "standard" way of applying such theorems to the *price simplex* (cf., Cheng, 1991, p. 138, and above). This fact has generated a remarkable confusion about the question of which fundamental theorem of welfare economics underpins the Negishi method! For a method that has been around for over half a century, it is somewhat disheartening to note that frontier research and researchers seem still to be confused on which of the two fundamental theorems of welfare economics is relevant in Negishi's method. Thus, we find Judd, as recently as only a few years ago (op.cit., pp. 52–3) claiming, unreservedly, that (italics added):

> The Negishi method exploits the first theorem of welfare economics, which states that any competitive equilibrium of an Arrow–Debreu model is Pareto efficient.

On the other hand, we find Warren Young (op.cit., p. 152; italics added) equally confidently stating that:

> In his pioneering 1960 paper, Negishi provided a completely new way of proving the existence of equilibrium, *via the Second Welfare Theorem.* He established equivalence between the equilibrium problem set out by Arrow–Debreu and what has been called 'mathematical programming', thereby developing a 'method' that has been used with much success by later economists working in both theoretical and applied general equilibrium modelling .... .

Fortunately, Negishi himself returned to a discussion of the "Negishi method, or Negishi approach" more recently (Negishi, 2008, p. 168) and may have helped sort out this conundrum (ibid., p. 167; italics added):

> The so-called Negishi method, or Negishi approach, has often been used in studies of dynamic infinite-dimensional general equilibrium theory, and the numerical computation of such equilibria .... . This method is an application of the Negishi theorem (Negishi 1960), which demonstrates the existence of a general equilibrium *using the first theorem of welfare economics*, which states that any competitive equilibrium of an Arrow–Debreu model is Pareto efficient. In other words, a general equilibrium of a competitive economy is considered as the maximization of a kind of social welfare function (i.e., the properly weighted sum of individual utilities, where the weights are inversely proportional to the marginal utility of income.

Negishi is one of those rare economists who is both a scholar of the history of economic theory and one of the most competent general equilibrium theorists and – even if he had not been the originator of the Negishi method – therefore one may feel forced to reject Warren Young's claim[15]!

As a matter of fact, from my *computable economics* – i.e., from a constructivist and recursion theoretic – point of view, this conundrum is a non-problem for several reasons. First of all, both fundamental theorems of welfare economics are proved non-constructively and lead to uncomputable equilibria. Secondly, all – to the best of my knowledge – of the current algorithms utilized in CGE, ACGE, and DSGE modelling appeal to undecidable disjunctions and are effectively meaningless from a computability point of view. Thirdly, and most importantly, *Negishi's theorem*[16] is, itself, *proved* non-constructively. Finally, at the risk of challenging the mature reflections of one of the great and masterly contributors to general equilibrium theory, I would like to point out that there is no meaning that can be attached to Negishi's method if applied to "*dynamic infinite*-dimensional general equilibrium theory" – even if such a thing can be defined (or, indeed, has been defined, except in the utterly fictional and non-rigorous world of newclassical claims of dynamic stochastic general equilibrium modelling – i.e., so-called DSGE modelling).

There are two theorems in Negishi (1960). I shall concentrate on *Theorem 2* (ibid., p. 5), which (I think) is the more important one and the one that came to play the important role justly attributed to it via the *Negishi research program* outlined by Young (op.cit.).[17]

Proposition 1: *The proof of the existence of maximizing welfare weights in the Negishi theorem is non-constructive*

Proof: (Sketch) Negishi's proof relies on satisfying the Slater (Complementary) Slackness Conditions (Slater, 1950[18]). Slater's proof[19] of these conditions invokes the Kakutani fixed point theorem (Theorem 1 in Kakutani, 1941), and Kakutani's Min–Max Theorem (Theorem 3, ibid.). These two theorems, in turn, invoke Theorem 2 and the Corollary (ibid., p. 458), which are based on Theorem 1 (ibid., p. 457). This latter theorem is itself based on the validity of the Brouwer fixed point theorem, which is not just non-constructive, but also non-constructifiable (cf., Brouwer, 1952).   ∎

Proposition 2: *The vector of maximizing welfare weights, derived in the Negishi theorem, is uncomputable*

Proof: A straightforward implication of Claim 1   ∎

Discovering the exact nature and source of appeals to non-constructive modes of reasoning, appeals to undecidable disjunctions and reliance on non-constructive mathematical entities in the formulation of a theorem is a tortuous exercise. The nature of the pervasive presence of these three elements – i.e., non-constructive modes of reasoning, primarily the reliance on *tertium non datur*, undecidable disjunctions and non-constructive mathematical entities – in any standard theorem and its proof, and the difficulties of discovering them, is elegantly outlined by Fred Richman (1990, p. 125; italics added):

> Even those who like algorithms have remarkably little appreciation of the thoroughgoing algorithmic thinking that is required for a constructive proof. This is illustrated by the nonconstructive nature of many proofs in books on numerical analysis, the theoretical study of practical numerical algorithms. I would guess that most realist mathematicians are unable even to recognize when a proof is constructive in the intuitionist's sense.
>
> *It is a lot harder than one might think to recognize when a theorem depends on a nonconstructive argument. One reason is that proofs are rarely self-contained, but depend on other theorems whose proofs depend on still other theorems. These other theorems have often been internalized to such an extent that we are not aware whether or not nonconstructive arguments have been used, or must be used, in their proofs.* Another reason is that the law of excluded middle [LEM] is so ingrained in our thinking that we do not distinguish between different formulations of a theorem that are trivially equivalent given LEM, although one formulation may have a constructive proof and the other not.

Finally, it is easy to demonstrate that Foley's theorems in section III of his pioneering thesis (Foley, 1967) are proved non-constructively. For example, this is straightforward in the case of the theorem in paragraph 3.29 (see p. 72, where Brouwer's fixed point theorem is invoked). It is less straightforward to demonstrate the upper-semicontinuity of the mapping on the simplex K (pp. 69–70). The theorem of paragraph 3.22 is, on the other hand, easily shown to be nonconstructive due to its appeal to the Bolzano–Weierstrass theorem (p. 69). Similar considerations apply to the theorems of section II (but there, separating hyperplane theorems are invoked, rather than fixed point theorems – although the former are no more constructive or effective than the latter, unless defined on very specially structured normed spaces).

These are further reasons to pay close attention to Richman's carefully spelled out constructive thoughts. For, a supreme economic theorist like Duncan Foley, who also happens to be mathematically able, could use words like "construct" (for example, bottom p. 60) in an otherwise wholly non-constructive setting and not suspect that

> proofs are rarely self-contained, but depend on other theorems whose proofs depend on still other theorems. These other theorems have often been internalized to such an extent that we are not aware whether or not constructive arguments have been used, or must be used, in their proofs.

In any case, Foley's candid "confession," in his interview of November, 2001 (Foley, 2004), quoted in the opening lines of this chapter, should have made all this obvious. This is because he acknowledges that the method he used *"was exactly the same as Koopmans's proof* [in Koopmans (1957)] of the Pareto efficiency of price equilibria." This, I believe is a reference to the pedagogically excellent, although mathematically deceptively simple, exposition in chapter 2 of Koopmans (1957). The methods used by Koopmans, a combination of fixed point theorems and separating and supporting hyperplane theorems, are intrinsically non-constructive and uncomputable. Moreover, the whole method adopted by Koopmans in this beautiful exposition rules out Diophantine considerations – to which I now turn, in conclusion.

Diophantine conclusions

> I have argued here as forcibly as I can that it is a serious error to indict mathematical thinking or the use of mathematics per se as the source of these [specific] flaws [in macroeconomics and finance]. *What economics needs is not more or less mathematics and statistics, but mathematics and statistics better adapted to its problems and its limitations.* In the long run the discipline of economics will be shaped as much by its sociology and the philosophy of science and scientific interchange that commands its consensus as by particular methods or theoretical approaches.
>
> Foley, 2010, p. 16; italics added

As always, Foley's thoughts on formalization in economics are both perceptive and prescient. To understand the intrinsic problems and limitations of economics, without first transmogrifying them into a stunted mathematical formalism, is the art of good theorizing. The great classical economists, some of the later neoclassicals, almost all the Austrians – even including Schumpeter among them – did not need any mathematical formalism at all to theorize imaginatively and derive momentous policy conclusions. Surely, this is true of Keynes, the immediate post-Wicksellian Swedes – I have in mind, in particular, Lindahl, Myrdal, Hammarskjöld, and Lundberg – and the first generation Chicago economists, too. That a master mathematical economist expresses such an enlightened, almost visionary attitude to the place of mathematics in economics should be taken seriously by the modern economic theorist with his or her penchant for mathematising everything in sight indiscriminately.

I find this particular vision that Foley enunciates intellectually most congenial and fully coherent with my own research program in economics. I have argued for over 20 years that the kind of mathematics we should use should be dictated by, and adapted to, the "problems and limitations" of the natural domain of economic data, the nature and constraints of economic decision making, and the social and political constraints on them that make the search for determined and determinate solutions to constructively provable intractable problems a vain and chimerical pursuit.

However, like Foley, I do not associate such a vision with any less a need for mathematics – but with a need for a different kind of mathematics and, in my case, I have tried to make a sustained case for what may now be called *Diophantine economics*. Mathematical formalisms of economic entities – data structures, institutions, behavior, etc., – must respect the Diophantine nature of their domains of definition. I have discussed these issues in some detail in Velupillai (2005). This constraint, when respected, leads to the natural algorithmic indeterminacies of *Diophantine decision problems*.[20] Constructive and computable mathematics are a natural framework within which to frame Diophantine problems. The constructive and computable indeterminacies discussed in the previous section are elements in the research program on Diophantine economics I am trying to develop (cf., Velupillai, 2011).

In this connection I may ask the following question. Lindahl's *Thesis* is a book of a little over 200 pages. It has exactly two diagrams (on p. 89 and on p. 159). The only mathematical symbolism in the book is confined to the contents of exactly one footnote (pp. 90–2). How, then, can we assume that Lindahl's intense and deep economic theoretical reasoning, backed by impeccable doctrine-historical scholarship and wide empirical knowledge of public finances and taxation, underpinned by ethical arguments and constitutional constraints imposed by one kind of democratic arrangement, can be formalized by one kind of mathematics? It is here that I think Foley's wise precept to seek out "mathematics and statistics better adapted to [the problems of economics] and its limitations" becomes highly relevant.

The dichotomy between *proof* and *computation* that is characteristic of orthodox mathematical economics has led to the many unwarranted claims and propositions of applied general equilibrium theory – not to mention policies underpinned by the fundamental theorems of welfare economics. Mathematical economics of almost any variety is intrinsically non-algorithmic and, *a fortiori*, non-Diophantine. One unfortunate reason for this is the enforced dichotomy between proof and computation. Orthodox mathematical economics is seriously deficient in the epistemology of computation and the philosophy of mathematics, also partly due to this unnatural dichotomy.

In Diophantine economics there is no such dichotomy.

Mathematical political science and social choice theory did not consider the Arrow Impossibility Theorem a shackle on mathematical theorizing. There is no need for the economic theorist to consider the natural indeterminacies, undecidabilities and uncomputabilites of Diophantine decision problems any less constraining on mathematical theorizing in economics.

One of the most stunted uses of the notion of a *social equilibrium* is the one by that doyen of mathematical economics, Debreu (1952). I have rarely seen a better, more enlightened, more imaginative use of the phrase social equilibrium than that by the young Foley, in his extraordinary doctoral dissertation's concluding pages (Foley, 1967, pp. 92–3; italics added):

> The study of societies at the present time is a study of *social equilibrium*. This important concept can be defined only *vaguely*, as a state where the interaction of the millions of individuals in a society produces certain relatively constant aggregate features. ... Economic and political equilibria are special aspects of general social equilibrium, which includes the relative constancy of religion, law, family, and all the features of existence without which we could not recognize social life at all.

As economists struggle to encapsulate moral and ethical constraints in their formulation of behavioral and institutional hypotheses, mediated and humbled by the vicissitudes of history and its contours, the kind of social equilibrium Foley, with characteristic imagination, conceived almost half a century ago, becomes relevant almost with a vengeance.

Notes

1 This refers, of course, to Duncan Foley's remarkably original and brilliant – and unfortunately little acknowledged – Yale doctoral dissertation of 1967 (Foley, 1967). In the by now vast orthodox literature on computable general equilibrium theory, and its applied offshoots, I have not been able to detect a single reference to what I may call *Foley's method* (ibid., pp. 64–73), which could provide – as legitimately as *Negishi's method* – an alternative to the orthodox approach to "computing" Walrasian (Arrow–Debreu) equilibrium prices, using, for example, variants of *Scarf's method* (Scarf, 1973).

2 I coined the description *computable economics* at the end of the 1980s to characterize the formalization of economic theory and its various closures in terms of the mathematics of computability theory and constructive analysis. More recently I have to adopt the slightly more general description *algorithmic economic theory* (cf. Velupillai, 2011).

3 My "position" is more "radical," as could be discerned from the results reported in Velupillai (2006, 2009a). The uncomputability of Walrasian equilibria is *not only* due to the intrinsic *undecidable disjunctions* in the Bolzano–Weierstrass theorem, but also due to the *methods of proof* used in the Brouwer (or Kakutani) fixed point theorem – and other constructive and computability issues, all of which are discussed in the above two cited papers.

4 My copy of this book once belonged to Östen Unden, Sweden's acting Prime Minister in the transition regime between Per Albin Hansson's death and the eventually long tenure of Tage Erlander. Unden served also as the Social Democrats' Foreign Minister for a long period under Erlander, but also for a brief period in the mid-1920s. My copy of this Wicksellian classic is dated "Mars 1907" by Unden, i.e., when he was still only 20 years old!

5 I am in the happy and privileged position of owning the author's presentation copy to Wicksell's personal friend, Gustaf Steffen!

6 My first encounter with this line of research by Foley was in late 1977, during my tenure as a Research Fellow at CORE in Louvain-La-Neuve, during the academic year 1977/8. In the autumn of 1977 I obtained, quite accidentally, a copy of Foley's draft paper on *Marxist Theories of the Fiscal Process*, prepared for an International Seminar in Public Economics, at Namur, in Belgium, in November, 1976. I still own an almost tattered copy of the paper (Foley, 1976)!

7 The main assigned textbook was Lance Taylor's *Reconstructing Macroeconomics* (Taylor, 2004), one of the most refreshingly original alternatives to the orthodoxies of the New classicals and the New Keynesians.

8 Lindahl was not long dead when Foley's work on Lindahl prices first appeared; I should like to add that when I myself went to Cambridge for my PhD and was interviewed by Nicky Kaldor his only question to me was: "Why do you want to come here when you have Lindahl in Sweden?" – this in 1973 and Lindahl had been dead just over ten years! His spirit, like those of the other contemporary and past Swedes, was very much alive in Cambridge at that time.

9 With the obvious exception of my friend and colleague, Stefano Zambelli.

10 Foley was not quite 30 years old when "proving the existence theorem" and Negishi still only 27. In both cases their contributions were among the first few formal publications in two outstanding academic careers, each path-breaking in its own way. These facts alone place in perspective Clower's mature reflection (Clower, 1984, pp. 263–4):

> Economics is less obviously a young man's game than mathematics, but I doubt that many economists have had a really new idea after the age of thirty-five. I must confess that, one way or another, everything I have done in the second half of my life reminds me (at least retrospectively) of something I did or thought about earlier.

This is, of course, an echo of Schumpeter's view, expressed most clearly in his 1914 (when he was himself 31 years of age) obituary of Böhm-Bawerk (cited in an English translation in Allen, 1991, p. 51; italics added):

> The generalization has been often surmised, and has been more and more firmly established by biographical research … that the roots of important original achievements can almost always be found *in the third decade in the lives of scholars, that sacred decade of fertility.*

This "sacred decade" for Keynes, is discussed with a particular felicitous example by Schumpeter in his monumental *History of Economic Analysis* (Schumpeter, 1954, pp. 41–2). This is the obverse side of the view expressed by Keynes in the closing passage of the *General Theory* that (Keynes, 1936, pp. 383–4; italics added):

> [I]n the field of economic and political philosophy there are not many who are influenced by new theories *after they are twenty-five or thirty years of age* … .

11 The essential content of the theorem is the mathematical equivalence between a precise statement of Walras' existence theorem (WET) and Brouwer's (or any other relevant) Fix-Point theorem. The Uzawa equivalence theorem is the fulcrum around which the *theory* of *Computable General Equilibrium* modelling revolves. This key theorem provides the theoretical justification for relying on the use of the algorithms that have been devised for determining general economic equilibria as fix points using essentially non-constructive topological arguments. To the best of my knowledge, none of the standard advanced textbooks in mathematical economics, microeconomics, or general equilibrium theory (Kreps, Varian, etc.), except the two by Cornwall (1994) and Starr (1977), even refer to Uzawa's theorem. See also Velupillai (2006) for an extensive technical discussion of Uzawa's equivalence theorem.

12 There is a curious – albeit inessential – "typo" in Negishi's reference to Kakutani's classic as having been published in 1948. The "typo" is not corrected even in the reprinted version of Negishi (1960) in Negishi (1994).

13 The other one being Negishi (1961). I am in full agreement with Young's important observation that it is Negishi (1960) that is more important, which is why I have added italics to the phrase "almost as influential," in the above quote.

14 Even Young's comprehensive list of references – 108, in all, in an article that distills the essence of the Negishi "research program" in only 12 pages – manages to forget to refer to Foley (1967).

15 The puzzle here is that the Young and Negishi articles appear "back-to-back," in the same issue of the *International Journal of Economic Theory* and the two distinguished authors thank each other handsomely in their respective acknowledgments!

16 *Negishi's theorem* is one thing; *Negishi's method* is quite a different thing. The latter *should* refer to the "method of proof," but the vast literature on the issue – admirably documented in Young (2008) – is *not* free of confusion on this point. Essentially, the "method" refers to the fact that a mapping is defined, not on the price simplex, but on the "utility simplex" (as mentioned above with a reference to Cheng, 1991).

17 To demonstrate the *non-constructive* elements of Theorem 1 (ibid., p. 5), I would need to include almost a tutorial on constructive mathematics to make clear the notion of *compactness* that is *legitimate in constructive analysis*. For reasons of "readability" and "deeper" reasons of aesthetics and mathematical philosophy, I shall refer to my two main results as "Claims" and their plausible validity as "Remarks," and not as "Theorems" and "Proofs," respectively.

18 Slater (1950) must easily qualify for inclusion in the class of pioneering articles that remained forever in the *samizdat* status of a *Discussion Paper*!

19 I should add that the applied general equilibrium theorists who use Negishi's method to 'compute' (uncomputable) equilibria do not seem to be fully aware of the implications of some of the key assumptions in Slater's complementary slackness conditions. That Negishi (1960) is aware of them is clear from his *Assumption 2* and *Lemma 1*.

20 In Diophantine economics, orthodox optimization paradigms are replaced by the more general framework of Diophantine decision problems, where emphasis is placed on problem solving, finding methods to solve problems and classifying the algorithmic difficulties of such methods. It is squarely within what I have come to call *classical behavioral economics*, that which was pioneered by Herbert Simon, underpinned by a

model of computation (in Simon's case, even if mostly implicitly, it is the *Turing model of computation*). Some of the formal definitions of the above concepts can be found in Velupillai (2009b, 2010).

References

Allen, Robert Loring (1991) *Opening Doors: The Life & Work of Joseph Schumpeter, Volume 1: Europe,* Transaction Publishers, New Brunswick, New Jersey.

Arrow, Kenneth J., and Frank. H. Hahn (1971) *General Competitive Analysis,* Oliver & Boyd, Edinburgh, Scotland.

Baumol, William J. (1986) *Superfairness,* The MIT Press, Cambridge, Massachusetts.

Brouwer, Luitzen E.J. (1910) Über eineindeutige, stetige Transformationen von Flächen in sich, *Mathematische Annalen,* 69, 176–180.

Brouwer, L.E.J. (1952) An Intuitionist Correction of the Fixed-Point Theorem on the Sphere, *Proceedings of the Royal Society,* Series A, 213, 1–2.

Cheng, Harrison H.C. (1991) Asset Market Equilibrium in Infinite Dimensional Complete Markets, *Journal of Mathematical Economics,* 20, 137–152.

Clower, Robert W. (1984) *Money and Markets: Essays by Robert W. Clower,* Donald A. Walker (Ed.), Cambridge University Press, Cambridge, UK.

Colander, David, Richard P.F. Colt and J. Barkley Rosser, Jr (Eds.) (2004) *The Changing Face of Economics: Conversations with Cutting Edge Economists,* University of Michigan Press, Ann Arbor, Michigan.

Cornwall, Richard R. (1984) *Introduction to the Use of General Equilibrium Analysis,* North-Holland, Amsterdam.

Debreu, Gerard (1952) A Social Equilibrium Existence Theorem, *Proceedings of the National Academy of Sciences,* 38(10), 886–893.

Foley, Duncan K. (1967) Resource Allocation and the Public Sector, *Yale Economic Essays,* 7, 43–98.

Foley, Duncan K. (1970) Lindahl's Solution and the Core of an Economy with Public Goods, *Econometrica,* 8(1), 66–72.

Foley, Duncan K. (1976) Marxist Theories of the Fiscal Process, Draft of a paper prepared "for use" at the *International Seminar in Public Economics,* Namur, Belgium, November 25–.

Foley, Duncan K. (1978) State Expenditure from a Marxist Perspective, *Journal of Public Economics,* 9(2), 221–238.

Foley, Duncan K. (1998) Introduction, Chapter 1, pp. 3–72, in: *Barriers and Bound to Rationality: Essays on Economic Complexity and Dynamics in Interactive Systems,* by Peter S. Albin, Edited with an Introduction by Duncan K. Foley, Princeton University Press, Princeton, New Jersey.

Foley, Duncan K. (2000) Complexity and Economic Education, Chapter 10, pp. 167–173, in: *The Complexity Vision and the Teaching of Economics,* David Colander (Ed.), Edward Elgar, Cheltenham, UK.

Foley, Duncan K. (2003) *Unholy Trinity: Labor, Capital and Land in the New Economy* (The Graz Schumpeter Lectures), Routledge, London.

Foley, Duncan K. (2004) *Interview, November 30, 2001,* Chapter 7, pp. 183–213, in: Colander et al. (2004).

Foley, Duncan K. (2010) Mathematical Formalism and Political Economic Content, Paper presented at the *Conference of the Institute of New Economic Thinking,* Cambridge, UK, April, 8–10.

Foley, Duncan K., and Thomas R. Michl (1999) *Growth and Distribution*, Harvard University Press, Cambridge, Massachusetts.

Foley, Duncan K., and Miguel Sidrauski (1971) *Monetary and Fiscal Policy in a Growing Economy*, Macmillan, New York.

Hicks, John R. (1956) Methods of Dynamic Analysis, pp. 130–151, in: *25 Economic Essays in English, German and Scandinavian Languages in Honour of Erik Lindahl*, Ekonomisk Tidskrift, Stockholm.

Judd, Kenneth L. (2005) Solving Dynamic Stochastic Competitive General Equilibrium Models, Chapter 3, Part Two, pp. 45–66, in: *Frontiers in Applied General Equilibrium Modelling: In Honour of Herbert Scarf*, Timothy J. Kehoe, T.N. Srinivasan and John Whalley (eds.), Cambridge University Press, Cambridge, UK.

Kakutani, Shizuo (1941) A Generalization of Brouwer's Fixed Point Theorem, *Duke Mathematical Journal*, 8, 457–459.

Keynes, John Maynard (1936) *The General Theory of Employment, Interest and Money*, Macmillan & Co., London.

Koopmans, Tjalling C. (1957) *Three Essays on The State of Economic Science*, McGraw-Hill Book Company, New York & London.

Lindahl, Erik (1919) *Die Gerechtigkeit Der Besteuerung: Eine Analyse Der Steuerprincipien Auf Grundlage Der Grenznutzentheorie*, Gleerupska Universitets-Bokhandeln, Lund.

Lindahl, Erik (1959) Om Skatteprincipier Och Skattepolitik, pp. 151–171, in: *Ekonomi, Politik, Samhälle: En Bok Tillägnad Bertil Ohlin På Sextio-Årsdagen*, John Bergvall, Erik Dahmén, Olle Dahlén, Gunnar Gerdner and Birger Lundström (Eds.), Bokförlaget Folk och Samhälle, Stockholm.

Myrdal, Gunnar (1930) *Vetenskap Och Politik I Nationalekonomien*, P. A. Norstedt & Söners Förlag, Stockholm.

Negishi, Takashi (1960) Welfare Economics and Existence of Equilibrium for a Competitive Economy, *Metroeconomica*, XII, 92–97; reprinted as Chapter 1, pp. 3–8, in Negishi (1994).

Negishi, Takashi (1961) Monopolistic Competition and General Equilibrium, *Review of Economic Studies*, 28, 196–201.

Negishi, Takashi (1994) *General Equilibrium Theory – The Collected Essays of Takashi Negishi, Volume 1*, Edward Elgar, Aldershot, Hants., UK.

Negishi, Takashi (2008) Unnoticed Predecessors of the Early Negishi Theorems, *International Journal of Economic Theory*, 4, 167–173.

Richman, Fred (1990) Intuitionism as Generalization, *Philosophia Mathematica*, 5, 124–128.

Scarf, Herbert (1973) *The Computation of Economic Equilibria* (with the collaboration of Terje Hansen), Yale University Press, New Haven.

Schumpeter, Joseph A. (1954) *History of Economic Analysis*, Edited from manuscript by Elizabeth Boody Schumpeter, George Allen & Unwin Ltd., London.

Slater, Morton (1950) Lagrange Multipliers Revisited, *Cowles Commission Discussion Paper*, Mathematics # 403, November 7.

Starr, Ross M. (1977) *General Equilibrium Theory: An Introduction*, Cambridge University Press, Cambridge, UK.

Taylor, Lance (2004) *Reconstructing Macroeconomics: Structuralist Proposals and Critiques of the Mainstream*, Harvard University Press, Cambridge, Massachusetts.

Uzawa, Hirofumi (1962) Walras' Existence Theorem and Brouwer's Fixed Point Theorem, *The Economic Studies Quarterly*, 8, 59–62.

Velupillai, Kumaraswamy (1991) The Political Arithmetics of the Stockholm School, chapter 13, pp. 333–345, in: *The Stockholm School of Economics Revisited*, Lars Jonung (Ed.), Cambridge University Press, Cambridge, UK.

Velupillai, K. Vela (2005) The Unreasonable Ineffectiveness of Mathematics in Economics, *Cambridge Journal of Economics*, 29, 849–872.

Velupillai, K. Vela (2006) Algorithmic Foundations of *Computable* General Equilibrium Theory, *Applied Mathematics and Computation*, 179, 360–369.

Velupillai, K. Vela (2009a) Uncomputability and Undecidability in Economic Theory, *Applied Mathematics and Computation*, 215, 15.

Velupillai, K. Vela (2009b) A Computable Economist's Perspective on Computational Complexity, chapter 4, pp. 36–83, in: *The Handbook of Complexity Research*, J. Barkley Rosser, Jr. (Ed.), Edward Elgar Publishing Ltd.

Velupillai, K. Vela (2010) Foundations of Boundedly Rational Choice and Satisficing Decisions, *Advances in Decision Sciences*, April.

Velupillai, K. Vela (2011) Towards an Algorithmic Revolution in Economic Theory, *Journal of Economic Surveys*, 25, 401–430.

von Neumann, John (1937, [1945–6]) A Model of General Economic Equilibrium, *The Review of Economic Studies*, 13, 1–9.

Wicksell, Knut (1896) *Finanztheoretische Untersuchungen nebst Darstellung und Kritik der Steuerwesens Schwedens*, Verlag von Gustav Fischer, Jena.

Young, Warren (2008) Negishi's Contributions to the Development of Economic Analysis: Research Programs and Outcomes, *International Journal of Economic Theory*, 4, 151–165.

Part III

Classical political economy

Growth and distribution

10 Rate of profit and crisis in the US economy

A class perspective

Simon Mohun

Introduction

In *Understanding Capital* (Foley, 1986), Duncan Foley proposed a way of thinking about Marx's categories that developed the approach of his earlier article (Foley, 1982; see also Duménil, 1983; Mohun, 1994). Marx had built his analysis in *Capital* Volume 1 on the basis of the labour theory of value, which postulated that the price of each commodity p_i was its labour value λ_i divided by the value of the money commodity λ_{mc}. For (the typical) commodity i at unit level,

$$p_i = \frac{\lambda_i}{\lambda_{mc}} \tag{1}$$

His subsequent Volume 3 analysis showed that such value-price relations could not in general hold because of the different compositions of capital (ratios of labour to non-labour input) involved in the production of commodities. Competition tendentially equalized the rate of profit, and entailed price-value deviations for individual commodities. Notwithstanding individual price-value deviations, Marx tried to show that the labour theory of value continued to hold at an aggregate level. Subsequent commentary on and evaluation of Marx's demonstration has become known as "the transformation problem", and a huge literature has established positions along a spectrum varying from praise of Marx's complete success to condemnation of his complete failure.

Foley's approach sidestepped this debate, by proposing that Marx be interpreted as saying that, in the aggregate, hours of productive labour (H_p) and money value added (Y) are essentially the same thing; the one is always equal to the other, with the value of money λ_m relating the different dimensions.[1] That is, whatever the individual price-value deviations,

$$Y = \frac{H_p}{\lambda_m} \tag{2}$$

Money is no longer a commodity such as gold, but is a composite whose value is defined by equation (2). Further, while labour-power is commodified under capitalist relations of production, it is not a produced commodity. With neither composition of capital nor profit to consider, the tendential equalization of profit rates through competition has no relevance, so that at this level of abstraction, the relation between the value of labour-power and its price is unaffected by price-value deviations. Therefore equation (1) applies and the price of labour-power per hour of productive labour hired (the hourly wage rate w_p) is simply its value per hour of labour hired (λ_z) divided by the value of money, or

$$w_p = \frac{\lambda_z}{\lambda_m} \tag{3}$$

Equations (2) and (3) obviously hold in a world in which equation (1) holds for all commodities. But Foley's proposal that equations (2) and (3) also hold in a world of unequal or non-equivalent exchange (in which equation (1) does not generally hold) provided a powerful way of using the labour theory of value empirically. For, since total value added in hours (H_p), is the sum of variable capital (V) and surplus value (S), and since total money value added is the sum of total wages (W_p) and surplus value in money terms (MSV), then it is easy to show that

$$W_p = \frac{V}{\lambda_m} \tag{4}$$

$$\lambda_z = \frac{W_p}{Y} \tag{5}$$

and

$$MSV = \frac{S}{\lambda_m} \tag{6}$$

In particular, surplus-value in money terms remains proportional to surplus-value in (socially necessary) labour hours, and therefore unequal exchange makes no difference to the fundamentals of the analysis of exploitation and profit. In the course of his argument, Foley made reference to the applicability of the categories to the US economy, using real (rounded) numbers (Foley, 1986, pp. 14–15, 46, 122–124). While his purpose was to illustrate the theoretical concepts and provide plausible orders of magnitude, his approach raised the possibility of a more sustained empirical analysis on this value-theoretic basis.

This chapter investigates data for the US economy within this framework. It begins by relating the 1982 Foley approach to the forces and relations of production in order to develop a focus on capital productivity (the ratio of money value added to the fixed capital stock) as encapsulating the forces of production, and the money surplus value share as encapsulating the relations of production. Combining the two generates the overall rate of profit for the economy as a whole, whose long run development is then explored.

There are a number of substantial and influential analyses which have proposed a long run Marxist analysis of the US economy. Representative analyses include Brenner (1998, 2002), Duménil and Lévy (1993, 2004, 2011), Gillman (1957),

Moseley (1991), Shaikh (1999, 2010), Shaikh and Tonak (1994) and Weisskopf (1979). This chapter proposes that the profit share and consequently the rate of profit have not been sufficiently well-specified in the Marxist literature. Profits are by definition the residual from money value added once wages have been paid. But little attention has been given to how to measure wages.[2] Generally wages are taken to be employee compensation (possibly together with some estimate of the wage component of self-employed income). But in class terms this includes both working-class labour income and non-working-class labour income. Conventionally defined wages and profits are not class categories, and if class is to be the primary category of analysis, this makes a substantial difference to how the data have to be constructed. This recognition problematizes the conventionally defined rate of profit as the key indicator of the development of capitalism. Constructing a "class rate of profit" requires that the labour income accruing to those who are not members of the working class be explicitly considered, and this in turn requires both a specification of how the non-working-class might be empirically identified, and a specification of how to measure their labour income.[3]

In short, class matters. This chapter therefore focuses particularly on the relations of production. Using annual data beginning in 1909, it finds that a class-defined rate of profit (with a numerator comprising profits plus the labour income that does not accrue to the working class) is generally rising through time; that is, there is a marked long run tendency of this class rate of profit to rise. That rise is punctuated by short run stagnation of profitability that precedes serious crises in 1913, 1929, 1979 and 2007–8. Resolutions of the crises which these short run downturns precede more than overcome the preceding stagnation. But processes of crisis resolution require régime change.[4] In 1913, that change was relatively minor (the formation of a national banking system, whose roots lay in response to the crisis of October 1907). In the second two cases, the changes were major (to a weak form of social democracy after 1929, and to neoliberal finance after 1979). As of 2012, resolution of the crisis of 2007–8 is uncertain and continuing.

Forces and relations of production

Classical Marxism

The forces of production are "material productive forces" (Marx, 1987 [1859], p. 263) and concern the appropriation of the natural world to human ends. They describe the knowledge of science and technology, and how this is put to practical effect in the organization of production. For most of human history, such knowledge has increased only slowly, but after about 1500 this began to change. In the modern era (from about 1770 onwards) the forces of production have evolved rapidly, posing potentialities of great change.

The relations of production are concerned with how the surplus product is produced by the immediate producers, and how it is then appropriated. These issues are generally determined by ownership of and control over the means of production, that is, by property relations. They therefore depend upon both the physical force and the ideologies that maintain those property relations. Following the development of settled agriculture, and the possibilities of storage of a surplus and consequent acquisition of wealth, these relations revolved around the ownership and control over land and the means to cultivate it. More recently, they have been concerned with how surplus labour is extracted in industrial production processes and realized in trade, surplus product appearing as profit.

Considering both forces and relations of production together, in Marx's phrase, the relations of production are "appropriate to a given stage in the development of their material forces of production" (ibid). So the forces of production determine what relations of production are possible at any time. At the same time, the forces of production are only applied under particular relations of production, so that the relations of production determine how the forces of production are developed. In contrast to the dynamism of the forces of production, changes in property relations are severely constrained by the prevailing pattern of asset ownership and the material interests to which that pattern gives rise. Prevailing relations of production can thereby limit potentialities, to such an extent that

> the material productive forces of society come into conflict with the existing relations of production, or – this merely expresses the same thing in legal terms – with the property relations within the framework of which they have operated hitherto. From forms of development of the productive forces these relations turn into their fetters. Then begins an era of social revolution.
>
> Marx, 1987 [1859], p. 263

But as well as determining transformations of one mode of production into another, this opposition between forces and relations of production also determines transformations within modes of production. A number of possible political, legal and ideological forms are compatible with a given pattern of property relations, and as long as that basic pattern is maintained, varieties of regime change involving significant institutional and political change within modes of production are possible.

Capitalist forces of production

In capitalism, the forces of production are developed through innovation in products and processes, with the motor force being competition between competing capitals. An innovating capitalist can undercut rivals, taking market share and extra profit. Rivals must copy and similarly innovate, or ultimately they will fail.

Innovation enables a reduction in unit costs via productivity increases. This is typically achieved by adding to the non-labour inputs (means of production) with which labour works. Such investment depends upon the relation between the cost of the extra means of production per worker-hour and the benefit of the productivity increase to which it leads. The use-value equivalent of this value criterion concerns the question of how much productivity increase a given increase in capital intensity yields. Define the constant price productive fixed capital stock

(k_p) as the nominal fixed capital stock worked by productive labour (K_p) deflated by the net value added deflator (p_Y),

$$k_p = \frac{K_p}{p_Y} \tag{7}$$

and similarly define constant price money value added y as

$$y = \frac{Y}{p_Y} \tag{8}$$

Then labour productivity is y/H_p and capital intensity is k_p/H_p. The development of the forces of production might mean that the rate of growth of labour productivity exceeds the rate of growth of capital intensity, so that y/k_p is rising. Periods in which smaller increases in capital intensity lead to larger increases in productivity are characteristic of periods of innovation with very widespread application across all sorts of products and processes (for example, the development and use of electric power, or the development of semiconductor industries).

Conversely, the rate of growth of capital intensity might exceed the rate of growth of labour productivity, so that y/k_p is falling. Periods in which increases in capital intensity lead to rather smaller increases in productivity are characteristic of periods of innovation in which it is increasingly difficult to extract increases in labour productivity; new technologies are not widely generalizable and are much more product and process-specific. This can be equivalently characterized by noting that y/k_p is the inverse of the ratio of "dead" to living labour. Then if capital intensity is rising faster then labour productivity, the ratio of dead to living labour is rising, so that technical change is capital-using and labour-saving. This particular relationship between changes in capital intensity and changes in labour productivity is typical of much of capitalism's history (Marquetti, 2003).[5] But it is evidently not the only possible relationship.

Multiplying the ratio y/k_p (or equivalently Y/K_p) by the proportion of the capital stock that is productive (K_p/K) yields the ratio Y/K, called "capital productivity".[6] So capital productivity expresses first, the relation between capital intensity and the labour productivity it generates; and second, what proportion of the capital stock is worked by productive labour. But there is no automaticity in the direction of change in either of these expressions. For example, increases in labour productivity have to be extracted, and precisely how this is done depends not only upon technological development but also upon the balance of class power in the workplace. So the forces of production are developed under capitalist relations of production, and are expressed by capital productivity and its movements through time.

The forces of production in US capitalism

Capital productivity in the US economy for the period 1890 to 2010 is depicted in Figure 10.1, along with its trend.[7]

Figure 10.1 Capital productivity and trend, USA, 1890–2010.

In broad trend terms, capital productivity was falling from 1890 to 1916. It then rose for half a century to the mid-1960s, with two short interruptions, one due to the 1929 crash and its immediate consequences, and the other due to the post-1945 transition to a peacetime economy after the exceptional mobilization of resources for World War II. After the mid-1960s, there was a substantial fall until 1982, in turn almost completely reversed by a rise until 2000, when a further sharp fall began. Two features are worth emphasizing. First, the whole period after World War II had higher *levels* of capital productivity than the whole period before. Second, sustained periods of broadly falling capital productivity were confined to just three periods: 1890–1916, 1966–82 and 2000–9, so that only about a third of the whole period 1890–2010 was characterized by Marx-biased technical progress in which capital intensity rose faster than the labour productivity it induced. The step-change from the early-1930s to the early-1940s, the first half of the 1960s and the two decades after 1980 were all periods in which labour productivity rose faster than capital intensity.

Capitalist relations of production

Capitalism requires the existence of a property-less class whose members are forced into the market to sell the only asset they possess (their capacity to work). Movements in the value of labour-power therefore provide an indication of the state of class relations, or, equivalently, how much surplus-value in money terms accrues to those who employ the working class. For, expanding equation (5) and using equation (8),

$$\lambda_z = \frac{w_p H_p}{Y} = \left(\frac{w_p}{p_Y}\right) \div \left(\frac{y}{H_p}\right) \tag{9}$$

so that the value of labour-power depends upon the ratio of the real product wage rate (of productive labour) to labour productivity. Consequently, the value of labour-power will fall (rise) if the real product wage rate is rising less fast (faster) than productivity.

A falling value of labour-power entails a rising rate of surplus value, a rising share of money surplus value in money value added and growing class inequalities. For a given level of employment, there is a growing quantity of surplus-value, which must be invested if it is to be accumulated as capital. If it is not, then it is either hoarded as idle balances, or is used for speculation as money attempts to create more money without the intermediation of production. This possibility might be summarized as "underconsumption" (wages are too low to support the demand that accumulation requires). The other possibility is that the value of labour-power is not falling, so that the total quantity of surplus value, the rate of surplus value, and the share of money surplus value in money value added are all non-increasing. From the perspective of capital, this involves an undesirable strength of the working class, with "too little" surplus value being produced relative to the amount of capital invested, and hence an "overproduction" of capital relative to surplus value.

Since money surplus-value is net money value added less the wages paid to productive labour, then in terms of share

$$\frac{MSV}{Y} = 1 - \frac{W_p}{Y} = 1 - \lambda_z \tag{10}$$

The money surplus value share is hence an index of capitalist relations of production, but it is not independent of the forces of production. This is because of the latter's role in determining first, the technological possibilities for productivity increases which impact upon the value of labour-power; second, the technologies of circulation which speed up turnover (such as the evolution of "just-in-case" into "just-in-time" methods of distribution and inventory control); and third, the technologies of supervision and surveillance.

The conventionally measured US profit share

Subtracting the unproductive wage share W_u/Y from both sides of the first part of equation (10), and noting that $MSV = Y - W_p$ and $W = W_p + W_u$,

$$\frac{MSV - W_u}{Y} = \frac{Y - W_p - W_u}{Y} = 1 - \frac{W}{Y} = \frac{\Pi}{Y} \tag{11}$$

so that the profit share is the money surplus value share less the unproductive wage share. Figure 10.2 shows the profit share for the US economy from 1890 to 2010.

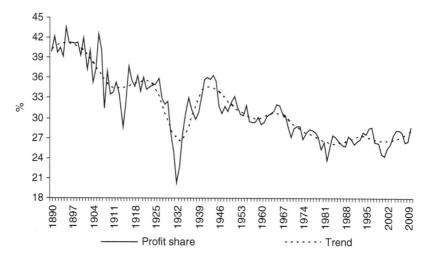

Figure 10.2 The profit share and trend, USA, 1890–2010.

In long run terms, the profit share fell. While there were a number of episodes of small rise, and a violent fluctuation from 1926 to 1941, nevertheless the whole period was broadly characterized by a falling share to 1982, and thereafter a barely rising share.

In terms of the money surplus value share, Figure 10.2 is not very informative, because there is no separate information about the unproductive wage share.[8] Yet the profit share is commonly taken as an index of the relations of production, since "wages" are paid to labour and "profits" to capital. A generally falling profit share is taken as an indicator of the rising strength of labour, a sustained shift from capital to labour indicating increasing working class strength relative to capital (only marginally reversed in the era after 1980). In this manner, the profit share is interpreted as a class category.

But this is a muddle. The profit share is what remains of money value added after subtracting the wage share, and wages include the labour income of top echelons of management in the same way as they include the labour income of the workers who clean the offices of top management: both receive "employee compensation". Saez (2012, Table A7) reports the composition of income within the top decile of the income distribution of household tax units. In 2007, for example, over the bottom half of the top decile, wages on average accounted for 88.6% of total income; for percentiles 95 to 99, 80.1%, and for the top percentile 54.3%. Even in the top one hundredth of the top decile, wages were 38.1% of income, averaging $7.35 millions (in 2010 prices). Wages measured by employee compensation are too inclusive a category to be of use as a class category, so that profits substantially underestimate non-working-class income. This problematizes both the conventionally defined profits share and the conventionally defined profit rate, if they are to be of any use in constructing an interpretation of US economic development in terms of class and class conflict. The latter require in the first instance a more nuanced understanding of "wages".

Wages and profits in a class analysis

Marx famously wrote,

> ... individuals are dealt with here only in so far as they are the personifications of economic categories, the bearers of particular class-relations and interests.
>
> Marx *Capital I,* 1976 [1867], p. 92

Personifying the capital relation is impossible in the National Income and Product Accounts (NIPA), because it is impossible to distinguish just who are the bearers of the economic category of capital. And yet within the labour process it is obvious to both blue-collar and white-collar workers who bears that relation: employment is typically participation in a structured hierarchical and authoritarian network of relationships, and the work performed and compensation received are very different in different parts of that hierarchy. Following Marglin (1974), this suggests distinguishing class categories in the labour force by the criterion of control over the work of others.[9] Defining those who are so controlled as "working class", those who do the controlling are then "supervisors". Most of the latter will not be directly capitalists in the sense of having sufficient resource to avoid the compulsion of selling their labour-power, although some will be. But regardless of that, all supervisors are structurally the *de facto* bearers of the capital relation because they supervise the labour of the working class.

Pursuing this, first note that unproductive wages comprise the wages of circulation workers (W_u^c) and the wages of those who supervise and control both productive labour and circulation labour (W_u^s). Hence the wage term in equation (11) can be expanded so that

$$\frac{\Pi}{Y} = \frac{MSV - W_u}{Y} = \frac{MSV - W_u^c - W_u^s}{Y} \tag{12}$$

Equation (12) can then be transformed into one denoting class shares by adding the supervisory wage share to both sides, so that

$$\left(\frac{\Pi + W_u^s}{Y}\right) = \frac{MSV - W_u^c}{Y} = \frac{Y - W_p - W_u^c}{Y} = 1 - \left(\frac{W_p + W_u^c}{Y}\right) \tag{13}$$

Hence, the working class share is the total production worker wage share $(W_p + W_u^c/Y)$, and the non-working-class share is the sum of the profit share and the supervisory wage share $(\Pi + W_u^s/Y)$. This latter will henceforth be called the "supervisory plus capitalist class share" in a binary class model there is no other possibility.[10]

Shares are constructed by combining NIPA data with data from the Employment, Hours and Earnings Survey of the Bureau of Labor Statistics (BLS), which has (non-farm) data on employment, hours and earnings, disaggregated according to whether supervisory functions above shop-floor level are a part of the job. So define "production workers" as production workers in mining and manufacturing, construction workers in construction, and non-supervisory workers in service-producing industries; "supervisory workers" are then the remainder.

Production workers comprised 88.6% of all in employment in 1948; this figure fell slowly to 82.1% by 1970, and remained around that level thereafter (a mean of 81.0% and standard deviation of 0.68 percentage points between 1970 and 2010). More significant, however, than their numerical strength is how much they were paid. From 1948 to 1973, production workers' employment share fell by 6.2 percentage points, and their wage share of money value added fell by 5.4 percentage points. From 1973 to 2007, while their employment share remained roughly constant, their wage share of money value added fell by 10.4 percentage points. This large change throws some light on the effects of class struggle. Table 10.1 shows the shares in value added in 1948 (the beginning of the "golden age"), 1966 (the year of peak profitability post-1945), 1979 (the year ending in the Volcker interest rate rise) and 2007 (the year beginning the Great Recession).

In both the "golden age" years to 1966 and the years after 1979, what share of value added production workers lost, supervisory workers gained. But in the 15 years after 1966, the supervisory wage share rose almost entirely at the expense of the profit share. As is often remarked, these were the years of "profit squeeze", but it is less often remarked that the squeeze was by supervisory workers, not production workers: supervisory workers were taking more money surplus value as labour income, squeezing profits in the process.

Table 10.2 displays another way of looking at the growth of inequality, showing average labour income as a proportion of the average income of a production worker, for supervisory workers (in italics) and at various percentiles of the wage distribution reported by Saez (2012).[11]

Table 10.1 Shares in current price value added, levels and percentage points changes, USA, selected years

Levels	1948	1966	1979	2007
Production wage share	53.5	46.8	47.3	37.6
Supervisory wage share	14.9	21.3	25.6	34.5
Profit share	31.7	31.9	27.1	27.8
Δ% (percentage points)		1948–66	1966–79	1979–2007
Production wage share		−6.6	0.5	−9.6
Supervisory wage share		6.4	4.3	8.9
Profit share		0.2	−4.8	0.7

Table 10.2 Average labour income relative to the average labour income of a production worker, USA, selected dates and percentiles

Percentiles	1948	1979	2007	Δ% p.a. 1948–79	Δ% p.a. 1979–2007
P0–90	1.0	1.0	1.1	−0.1	0.5
Supervisory	2.2	2.3	4.2	0.3	2.8
P90–100	3.0	3.4	5.6	0.4	2.4
P90–95	2.1	2.5	3.3	0.6	1.1
P95–99	3.0	3.4	5.1	0.4	1.8
P99–100	7.4	7.6	19.2	0.1	5.5

Interpreting Table 10.2, the average income of a supervisory worker was 2.2 times that of a production worker in 1948, 2.3 times in 1979, and 4.2 times in 2007. From 1948 to 1979, average supervisory worker income, relative to that of a production worker, grew by an average of 0.27% p.a., and from 1979 to 2007 at more than 10 times that rate, by an average of 2.8% p.a. Broadly, 1979 was very little different from 1948, but 2007 was very different from 1979, particularly the higher the percentile of the income distribution considered. Thus, trends in how much supervisory workers were paid were similar to what happened at the top percentiles of income distribution.[12]

Deriving a longer run picture is more speculative, because of the paucity of data, and its construction from 1947 back to 1909 requires some strong assumptions (sketched in the Appendix). Figure 10.3 depicts the results, showing the various shares of money value added and their long run trends: the working class share (northwest quadrant), the supervisory wage share (northeast quadrant), the profit share (southeast quadrant) and the non-working-class income share, (southwest quadrant).

The scales in each quadrant are dimensionally the same for comparability. Since the working class wage share, the supervisory wage share and the profit share sum to unity, the working class wage share and the non-working-class income share in the left-hand quadrants are the mirror images of each other.

The proximate reason for the rise in working class wage share from 1922 to a peak in 1949, and its sustained fall after 1949, is determined by equation (9), written in terms of production workers. Table 10.3 shows these proximate underlying determinants.[13] From 1922 to 1949, the annual average rate of growth of the real annual wage of a production worker substantially exceeded productivity growth, whereas after 1949 this relationship was reversed, annual average real wage growth halving and annual productivity growth increasing by 50%. Hence prior to 1949 the non-working-class income share fell, whereas after 1949 it saw a substantial increase.

In Figure 10.3, the left-hand quadrants display periods when class shares were relatively flat. From 1926 to 1931 the working class wage share increased by just 1.85 percentage points, whereas the supervisory wage share rose by 9 percentage

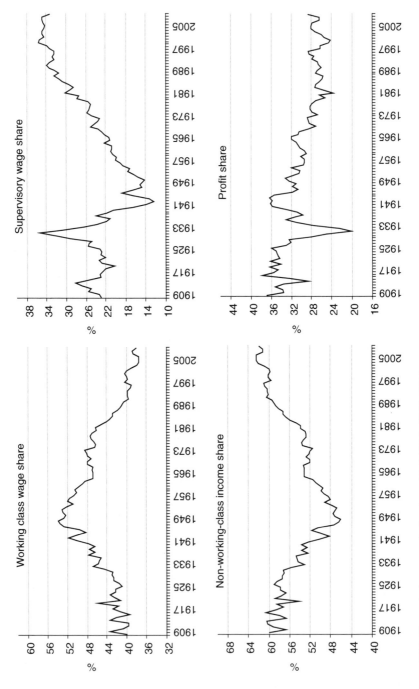

Figure 10.3 Shares in (current price) value added, USA, 1909–2010.

Table 10.3 Labour productivity and the real wage, USA, selected dates and annual average rates of change; US$2005

	1922	1949	2007	Δ% p.a. 1922–49	Δ% p.a. 1949–2007
Production worker wage	6,927	15,295	35,291	4.5	2.3
Labour productivity	16,371	28,424	93,781	2.7	4.0

points and the profit share fell by 10.8 percentage points. The flat period in shares from 1966 to 1979 is clearly visible, whereas the right-hand quadrants display a falling profit share and a rising supervisory wage share, and thus a profit squeeze by supervisory workers, as already illustrated in Table 10.1 above. A third episode of flat class shares occurred over the decade after 1992, when movements in the profit share were roughly balanced by opposite movements in the supervisory wage share so that in particular the years of the dot.com boom and bust were also characterized by supervisory wages squeezing profits. In terms of share of aggregate value added, it was as if capitalists *qua* supervisory workers first struggled over what they paid their workers, and then looked at what was left. When they had the power to do so, this determined how much labour income they could take for themselves, leaving the residual as profits. Sometimes that power was so pronounced that the supervisory wage share increased directly at the expense of the working class wage share, as in the years 1979 to 1992.

But they did not always have that power. From 1932 to 1940, class shares were relatively flat, but the supervisory wage share collapsed by 15.1 percentage points as the profit share recovered from its nadir of 1932. And from 1940 to 1944, the supervisory wage share fell by a further 6.9 percentage points as the profit share rose further in the war time economy. Over the two decades after World War II, it might appear that the supervisory wage share rose at the expense of the working class wage share. But this is misleading. Suppose there had been constant proportions of class in total employment (rather than the fall in production workers' employment share by 6.2 percentage points from 1948 to 1973). What would have happened to the non-working-class income share if the production workers' employment share had remained constant at its 1948 level, but everything else had changed as it in fact did? After constructing counterfactual production worker wages, and subtracting from total wages to determine counterfactual supervisory wages, adding the actual profits share gives the counterfactual non-working-class income share. From 1948 to 1960, this counterfactual share averaged 46.7%, with a standard deviation of 0.54 (compared with the actual figures of 48% and 1.2, respectively.) The low standard deviation for the counterfactual share indicates an approximate relative constancy of non-working-class income share from 1948 to 1960. Thereafter, through to 1966, both hypothetical and actual non-working-class income share rose by more than 3 percentage points because of a rising profit share.

All of this suggests that the changes posited by the New Deal were institutionalized and consolidated by the wartime economy into a (weak) form of social democracy, producing a flatlining of the non-working-class income share (assuming constant proportions of class in total employment) which was both unlike the pre-war experience and unlike the post-1979 experience. Since proportions of class in total employment *were* roughly constant after 1973, Figure 10.3 sharply indicates the striking changes in class share after 1979, to such an extent that the actual non-working-class income share under neoliberalism surpassed its 1929 level in 1988 and its peak 1916 level in 2003. Three years into the crisis that began in 2007, the non-working-class income share remained higher than its 1916 level.

In terms of theory, it should be noted that the non-working-class income share is not the money surplus value share. For the non-working-class income share is given by equation (13):

$$\left(\frac{\Pi + W_u^s}{Y}\right) = \frac{MSV - W_u^c}{Y} = 1 - \left(\frac{W_p + W_u^c}{Y}\right)$$

whereas the money surplus value share is evidently

$$\frac{MSV}{Y} = \left(\frac{\Pi + W_u^s}{Y}\right) + \frac{W_u^c}{Y} = 1 - \frac{W_p}{Y} \tag{14}$$

An analysis based on class and a strict value analysis are not the same, because production workers located in circulation activities are members of the working class but produce no value. Data to measure their wage share is only available from 1964, and, from 1964 to 2010, it averaged 12.8%, with a standard deviation of 0.335. This (surprising) constancy of the wage share of production workers in circulation activities implies that that the money surplus value share, while different in level from the non-working-class income share, is almost identical to it in terms of time path. A scatter of the money surplus value share against the non-working-class income share yields an R^2 of 0.99; that of the money surplus value share against the profit share yields an R^2 of 0.14 (and with the wrong sign). Hence the non-working-class income share is an excellent proxy for the money surplus value share (at least for the 46 years to 2010).

The rate of profit

The forces of production and the relations of production together are reflected in movements in capital intensity, the real product wage rate, labour productivity and the division of the employed labour force (and hence the capital stock) into productive and unproductive components. Development of the forces of production is summarized in movements of capital productivity, and the relations of production in movements of the relevant income share. Combining forces and relations of production into one single index generates the (macroeconomic) rate of profit as the key summary statistic for evaluating trends in capitalism. But this is dependent on what is taken as the relevant income share, the profit share or the non-working-class income share.

The conventionally measured rate of profit

Conventionally, the relevant income share is taken as the profit share, so that the macroeconomic rate of profit *r* is determined as

$$r = \frac{\Pi}{Y}\frac{Y}{K} \tag{15}$$

Its timepath and trend from 1890 to 2010 are depicted in Figure 10.4.

In trend terms, the rate of profit was fluctuating. From 1890 to around 1916, the trend was falling, followed by a decade of rising trend. There was then a collapse into the Great Depression, and a strong recovery through to 1944. After a small fluctuation this peak (in trend terms) was revisited in the mid-1960s. Thereafter, the trend was falling until the early 1980s, and it then rose modestly to the end of the century. These movements are broadly the same as the movements in capital productivity in Figure 10.1. Moreover, since the profit share was generally falling, its downward trend amplified the effects of downward movements in capital productivity on the rate of profit, and dampened the effect of upward movements.

Since profits (after tax) are partly distributed and partly retained, with retained earnings plus borrowings financing investment, and since investment determines capital accumulation, then it seems obvious to try to relate trends in profitability to patterns of accumulation. High levels of profitability would be associated with high rates of growth, and declining profitability with increasing difficulties in accumulation. Indeed, much Marxist theory goes further, and insists on a focus on downward movements in the rate of profit as the cause of crisis (even if theory is undeveloped on the precise mechanisms whereby falling profitability results in crisis).

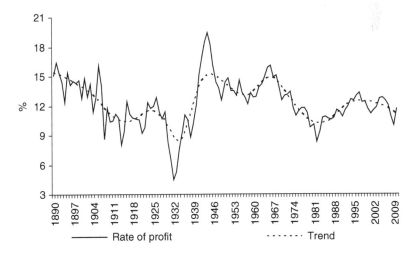

Figure 10.4 The rate of profit, USA, 1890–2010.

There are two difficulties with this. First, the time-frame of analysis requires better specification. The declining profitability of 1926–29 and 2004–7 were short-run processes, in each case at the end of a longer period of substantial rise. The decline of 1966–79 was a much longer run process. Hence a unified empirical explanation, covering all three periods of declining profitability preceding crisis, is challenging. Second, if the rate of profit is to summarize forces and relations of production in a class-divided society, then the rate of profit as determined in equation (15) is not an adequate statistic, because the profit share as a class income share is incorrectly specified.

The class rate of profit

If the relevant income share is taken to be the non-working-class income share, then the "maximal class rate of profit" $\left(r_{class}^{max}\right)$ is determined as the product of this non-working-class income share, and capital productivity.[14]

$$r_{class}^{max} = \frac{(\Pi + W_u^s)}{Y}\frac{Y}{K} \tag{16}$$

Its timepath is shown in Figure 10.5.

In contrast to the understanding informed by the rate of profit in Figure 10.4, a sharp focus on class indicates that the history of US capitalism is one of fluctuations in the maximal class rate of profit along a rising path. Until 1949, the non-working-class income share was falling. Over this period, falling capital productivity had an amplified effect on the maximal class rate of profit, and rising capital productivity a dampening effect. After 1949, this was reversed: the non-working-class income share was generally rising, amplifying the effects of rising capital productivity on the maximal class rate of profit, and dampening the effects

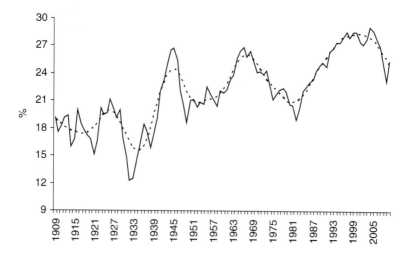

Figure 10.5 The maximal class rate of profit, USA, 1909–2010.

of its downward movements. Nevertheless, compared with the rate of profit in Figure 10.4, while the trend is quite different, the maximal class rate of profit fluctuated in a similar manner, with the same peaks and troughs. So it is worth investigating further whether movements in the conventional and maximal class rates of profit are similarly associated with subsequent crisis.

The maximal class rate of profit and crisis

"Crisis" is a notoriously overused word. Of medical origin, its precise meaning encapsulates an event (or set of events) following which there is a decisive change for better or for worse. Inspection of Figure 10.5 shows six significant downturns (more than a 3 percentage points fall) in the maximal class rate of profit between 1910 and 2010: 1913–14, 1916–21, 1926–32, 1945–49, 1966–82 and 2004–9. Two of these episodes were characterized by demobilization and the transition to a peacetime economy (1916–21, 1945–49); that of 1913–14 was prompted by a decline in railway profits, fears of credit restrictions on the establishment of the Federal Reserve System, and the cutting off of export markets to Europe (Flamant and Singer-Kérel, 1970); and the remaining three saw major crises erupt in the autumn of 1929, the autumn of 1979, and the late summer of 2007. Is there then an empirical regularity: do short run falls in the maximal class rate of profit precede crisis, and is this different from falls in the conventional rate of profit?

Short run quantitative regularities

Consider the trough to peak years of US business cycles.[15] Profitability ought to be rising in an upturn, implying increasing difficulties if it is not. Table 10.4 ranks cycle upturns according to the rate of growth in the two rates of profit, conventionally defined and class defined. It omits the war-affected upturns of 1914–18, 1918–19, 1938–44 and 1945–48 on the grounds that economies mobilized for military production create conditions of abnormal profitability (and

Table 10.4 Ranking of NBER cycles (peak to peak) by percentage fall in the rate of profit

Rank	Cycle upturn	Conventional r	Cycle upturn	Maximal class r	Rank
1	**1974–79**	**−3.7**	**1974–79**	**−2.6**	1
2	**1927–29**	**0.0**	**2001–7**	**−1.8**	2
3	1990–2000	2.6	**1927–29**	**−0.5**	3
4	1958–60	5.7	1970–73	0.8	4
5	1970–73	7.3	**1911–12**	**4.7**	5
6	**1911–12**	**7.3**	1958–60	7.2	6
7	**2001–7**	**7.8**	1949–53	11.7	7
8	1949–53	8.3	1990–2000	13.6	8
9	1960–69	8.3	1960–69	15.6	9
10	1921–23	33.2	1982–90	32.8	10
11	1982–90	37.0	1921–23	33.7	11
12	1932–37	136.7	1932–37	43.9	12

demobilization years, the reverse) which are untypical of "normal" capitalist development.

Table 10.4 provides some evidence of the causal efficacy of rates of profit in predicting crisis. For, consider movements in the maximal class rate of profit. A falling rate preceded major crisis in each of the peacetime cyclical upturns immediately prior to the crises of 1929, 1979 and 2007, and there was no other peacetime cyclical upturn with a falling maximal class rate of profit. These falls, being percentage falls rather than percentage points falls, were small. It would be therefore be more appropriate to say that *stagnation of the maximal class rate of profit during a peacetime cyclical upturn invariably preceded a major crisis*. The 1970–73 upturn marking the end of the "golden age" must then be considered. There had certainly been intimations of crisis, as the war in Vietnam was lost amidst domestic political turmoil, and international instability, as the dollar's link to gold was broken and the Bretton Woods system of fixed exchange rates collapsed. But the end of the "golden age" produced political stasis rather than crisis and crisis resolution; while stagnation of the maximal class rate of profit in the 1970–73 upturn was part of the run-up to the crisis of 1979, that crisis itself took a further six years to break. Finally, the upturn of 1911–12 can similarly be incorporated into a stagnationist thesis. Hence there is indeed an empirical regularity: peacetime cyclical upturns in which the maximal class rate of profit increased by less than 5% culminated in crisis, and no crisis occurred in the absence of such stagnation. In terms of movements of the conventional rate of profit during cyclical upturns, those of 1974–79 and 1927–29 might imply a similar stagnationist thesis. But this is not true for either the upturn of 1911–12 or that of 2001–7. In particular, the 2007 crisis is inexplicable in terms of movements in conventional profitability. A stagnationist thesis for the conventional rate of profit cannot therefore be empirically defended.

This is, however, a weak result. It is restricted to cyclical upturns as defined *ex post* by the NBER. If *every* three year change in profitability is calculated and ranked, no such pattern as displayed in Table 10.4 emerges. Similarly for the ranking of every two year change in profitability. There is therefore no general sense in which a short run falling rate of profit (however defined) empirically results in crisis.

Short run qualitative regularities

In what effects does stagnation in the maximal class rate of profit manifest itself? Crises are sufficiently infrequent as to provide only a very small sample for study, and generalization is therefore hazardous. But some features are clear. In both the crisis of 1929 and the crisis of 2007–8, a background of increasing international imbalances was an important feature. So too was speculation fueled by credit and bubbles in asset markets. The two were closely related, as international surpluses financed the credit which fuelled speculation.

Of course there were major differences. In the 1920s, imbalances were created by the way in which reparation payments (US loans enabled Germany to pay its reparations to the war victors, who used the proceeds to repay their wartime loans from the US) interacted with a structure of gold standard fixed exchange rates in which some currencies (such as sterling) were overvalued, and others (such as the French franc) undervalued. The crisis of 1929 broke out in the stockmarket, where speculation had been fuelled by credit as brokers' loans financed clients' purchases on margin. Loans at call could be called at no notice, and once foreign loans to the US market were called in October 1929, credit rationing to preserve the profitable market in brokers' loans created severe difficulties in goods markets that depended on easy credit, such as autos, whose production had peaked in March 1929. Credit restrictions also impacted quickly on commodities' prices, because most inter- and intra-country trade depended on very short term bank credit to finance the transport and storage of finished goods prior to their sale. As trade credit was reduced, sellers who could neither store goods nor divert them elsewhere were forced to cut prices, often dramatically. Hence bankruptcies were spread, both in the US and internationally, first in commerce, then in production and finally in banks (Kindleberger, 1984, Temin, 1989).

In the "noughties", some countries (oil exporting, Germany and especially China) had accumulated large current account surpluses, and others (the US and the UK) large current account deficits. Because the Chinese exchange rate was highly managed, Chinese surpluses were accumulated as central bank reserves, and invested mostly in US Treasuries. The consequence was a fall in real risk-free medium- and long-term rates of interest to historically low levels (roughly halving in the 15 years after 1990). This had three effects (Turner, 2009). First, there was a rapid growth in credit, much of which found its way into the housing market, fuelling a housing price bubble. Second, on the demand side, investors were eager in an era of historically low returns to purchase any financial asset that appeared to yield more return, especially if that return could be gained apparently without assuming extra risk. And third, on the supply side, financial institutions invented, packaged, and traded a variety of securitized credit instruments claiming to disperse risk, which were eagerly purchased. These instruments were increasingly complex, allowing both the hedging of underlying credit exposures, and the creation of synthetic credit exposures which could then be further hedged. But the complexity of these instruments concentrated rather than dispersed risk. The crisis of 2007–8 broke out in wholesale money markets, as lenders were increasingly reluctant to accept securitized bonds as collateral, because of uncertainty as to the extent of their contamination by securitized subprime mortgage derivative bonds after the burst in the bubble in house prices the previous year.[16] The uncertainty then spread to the market in commercial paper, in which borrowers seek to finance their short-term activities (such as payroll), and, once funds dried up, deleveraging was forced, and crises of liquidity and solvency were inevitable.

As well as involving international imbalances and leveraged speculation, the crises of 1929 and 2007–8 erupted in situations in which inequalities had been growing. Production worker wages were too low to support the levels of demand that would warrant the levels of investment that could increase the rate of accumulation. In the late 1920s, leverage was used to finance stock market speculation. In the "noughties", while inadequate wages were boosted by the expansion of consumer debt, accumulation remained "jobless", and leverage was used by finance, through securitization, to speculate in increasingly opaque financial derivatives resting on house price appreciation. Once the crisis broke, credit restrictions quickly impacted on the real economy, and in each case aggregate demand fell sharply. The short run fall in class profitability was thereby exacerbated.

However, the crisis of 1979 was different. It was not precipitated by a confidence-shattering market collapse (as in 1929 and 2007–8). It was rather precipitated in October 1979 by a major change in US interest rate policy, as the Federal Reserve Board under Volcker tried to squeeze inflation out of the system with a high real interest rate policy. While the transition from the fixed exchange rate world of Bretton Woods to an era of floating exchange rates had created difficulties in the 1970s, relative capital immobility (compared with the 1920s and the "noughties") precluded serious speculative excess. The economy was too regulated to allow of a market resolution, so that the crisis mechanism was essentially political and not economic.

Longer run regularities

While short run stagnation in the maximal class rate of profit is a harbinger of crisis, there are also long run features of crisis. For the market-based crisis of 1929 and the politically induced crisis of 1979 proved similar in one crucial respect: resolution of the crisis in each case led to régime change. After 1929, this took some considerable time, as the framework laid down by the New Deal was then overlaid by the transition to a wartime regulated economy. Many of the elements of this regulated framework were carried forward into the post-war years. Currency, credit and financial institutions remained heavily regulated, both nationally and, under US tutelage, internationally. While private ownership remained fundamental, the era was characterized by guarantees of full employment (sometimes implicit, sometimes explicit), the development of state-sponsored social protection mechanisms, active state interventions in industry, an (often grudging) acceptance of the legitimacy of labour unions and collective bargaining, and generally rising living standards. There was also a very substantial reduction in inequalities to a level that was maintained for the 20 years to the early 1970s. In this manner, the free market era dominated by finance up to 1929 was succeeded by a (more or less) social democratic era dominated by "managerialism", a culture of actively managing capitalism through constraints on the operation of market forces.

But as the "golden age" came to an end, the regulatory structures that had underpinned it were increasingly questioned. Beginning in the late 1960s, and with gathering momentum through the 1970s, there was a recognition of the end of an era, but considerable confusion as to what might replace it, and no resolution of what had come to be seen as its fundamental problems. Labour unions were increasingly seen as too powerful as they attempted to maintain real wages;

at the same time oligopolistic firms attempted to maintain profitability. Demand management policies were problematic; managerial interests wanted buoyant demand, and hence the monetary accommodation of inflationary pressures, whereas financial interests wanted monetary contraction via higher interest rates. This stalemate played out as "stagflation", but increasingly the view took hold that the regulatory state had to be rolled back. There was no inevitability about this. But those who wanted to defend the old order were often members of defensive institutions (such as labour unions) who were dismissed as the anachronistic defenders of sectional interests, relics from an era no longer relevant. Following the credit tightening of October 1979, inflation peaked in the spring of 1980, and in November 1980 Reagan was elected President. By 1982, the deregulation movement was proceeding apace, with state-sponsored and successful attacks on labour union resistance, and the dismantling of what were seen as excessive regulatory structures particularly in banking and finance. Increasingly, the market was celebrated as the only legitimate arena of social activity, and money as its the only measure. In this manner, finance restored its prerogatives of the pre-1929 era over the managerialism of the "golden age".

The crisis of October 1979 thus initiated régime change, and with a much faster transition than after 1929. After 1929 the transition to the "golden age" took a long time because there was no clear manifesto driving the transition. People knew what they did not want, and the structures eventually put in place were reactive in this manner, as well as shaped by the changed international conditions during and following World War II. By contrast, the transition to what became called "neoliberalism" was rapid once the crisis was initiated. Its agents knew exactly what they wanted, whereas the defenders of social democracy were increasingly compromised by their defence of the structures of a "golden age" that had in fact ended 10 years before. Globalization and financialization accordingly swept away the era of social democracy, restoring the hegemon of finance. And history then rhymed, as 2007–8 recalled 1929.[17]

Conclusion

This chapter has proposed that in order to comprehend the development of US capitalism, class categories must be constructed that can be used empirically. Proceeding on the basis of a particular interpretation of the labour theory of value, it finds that, for the US economy, the maximal class rate of profit has a marked long run tendency to rise, in contrast with the conventionally defined rate of profit. The difference between the two is determined by the addition of supervisory wages to the numerator. In a binary class model, there is little else one can do. An obvious direction for further research is to render the underlying model richer, by empirically distinguishing capitalist class wages from non-capitalist supervisory wages. Then three wage shares could be measured: the working class wage share, the capitalist class wage share and the non-capitalist supervisory wage share, the last being loosely a managerial wage share. That would enable some escape from the awkward neologisms of "non-working-class income share" and "maximal class rate of profit", through a direct identification of the capitalist class share and the corresponding class rate of profit. The time trend of this class rate of profit will lie somewhere between the conventional rate of profit, in which capitalists have no labour income, and the maximal class rate of profit, in which all supervisory wages are treated as capitalist labour income.

While that is for future research, the binary class model developed here has shown a dynamic capitalism structured around the increasing extraction of money surplus value, with rare but dramatic interruptions by crisis. These crises follow short run stagnation in the maximal class rate of profit from trough to peak of the (peacetime) business cycle. Market-based crises (1929, 2007–8) are initiated by a speculative crash. "Too much" surplus value is produced relative to demand, and, since wages are too low because of rising inequality, surplus value is channelled into speculation rather than investment. In a regulated economy, by contrast, crisis has to be politically induced (1979), which requires a permissive ideological context and a willingness to exert the prerogatives of class power. Either way, resolution of crisis requires régime change.

US capitalism has seen a number of régime changes. The formation of a national banking system was a successful systemic response to falling capital productivity. Free markets in an unregulated environment were eventually regulated into a form of social democracy, which harnessed and consolidated rising capital productivity until the mid-1960s. The subsequent 15 years of falling capital productivity were successfully reversed by the transition to neoliberal finance and deregulation at the end of the 1970s. Falling capital productivity in the early twenty-first century appears to require some further change in capitalist relations of production.

From 2010 onwards, the crisis that began in August 2007 became a sovereign debt crisis. While history suggests the necessity of régime change, it also suggests that the transition will be protracted and unstable, because there is little consensus as to the direction of travel. For the revivalism of free markets has served greatly to weaken the progressive forces of the labour movement, both materially and ideologically, and it seems likely that the capital relation will be preserved. Then the transition in the coming years is likely to revolve around how far financial and managerial interests within capital are inseparably fused, versus how far they can be separated in such a way that managerialism sees its interests as best served by some accommodation with the mass of working people.

Appendix: Data sources and construction

The data are derived from the National Income and Product Accounts (August 2011) and the Fixed Asset tables (August 2011), published by the Bureau of Economic Analysis at <http://www.bea.gov>; the Employment, Hours and Earnings data, published by the Bureau of Labour Statistics (BLS) at <http://www.bls.gov>; Kendrick (1961); Lebergott (1964); Bureau of the Census (1949, 1966, 1975, 2006), and Carter *et al.* (2006); and the Internal Revenue Service, as reported by Saez (2012). Following Shaikh and Tonak (1994), BLS categories are mapped on to NIPA data in the manner described by Mohun (2005, 2006).

Value added in money terms

National accounts provide measures of value added, but these are typically a hybrid combination of use-value and value. They not only measure everything (legal) that goes through the market; they also measure activities for which there is no market price. Activities that are not marketed are not (Marxian) value-creating. The two most important examples are the output of general government (which is accounted for by general government employee compensation), and a variety of activities, which, because they do not take measurable monetary form, are given an imputed monetary value.

These imputations are substantial, amounting in the US to 14.9% of GDP in 2007. The largest imputation (45.4% of all imputations) was the rental value imputed to owner-occupied housing, followed by employment related imputations (27%, the vast majority being employer contributions for health and life insurance), then consumption of general government fixed capital (11.6%), and then financial services furnished without payment (11.5%).[18] In general, from a Marxist perspective of the production of value and surplus value that can be accumulated as further capital, these imputations should be excluded, because they are not market transactions. But some imputations are different, in that they are not invented, but redirected, so that their consumption is attributed to the recipient rather than the payer. Employer contributions for health and life insurance fall into this category, and in principle comprise part of employee compensation and so part of the value of labour-power.

Hence value added in money terms requires subtracting all imputations except employer contributions for health and life insurance, and subtracting general government employee compensation (net of imputations). The aggregate from which these are subtracted is net domestic product (NDP) rather than gross domestic product (GDP), because the focus is on new value created, whereas the consumption of fixed capital is a charge to replace the depreciated portion of the fixed capital stock. So value added in money terms is NDP less general government employee compensation (both net of all imputations except employer contributions for health and life insurance).[19]

Profits

Conceptually, profits comprise everything that is not wages, the residual after the subtraction of wages from Y. Pre-tax profits include both taxes on production and imports less subsidies, and taxes on corporate income. Profits also include interest and rent, specifically net interest and miscellaneous payments, business current transfer payments, and rental income of persons. Finally, they include the profits component of proprietors' income (estimated as all such income that is not a labour income, where the latter is proxied by the average labour income in each relevant industry or industry group). Hence, the notion of profits is a very inclusive one (but remains less than surplus value in money terms because it does not include unproductive wages).

The capital stock

The fixed capital stock is taken to be non-residential equipment, software and structures (at replacement prices), together with inventories. Since in principle any investment made in order to make money should be cumulated into a measure of the capital stock, tenant-occupied residential structures are also included. But owner-occupied residential structures are excluded, as is general government fixed capital. Fixed capital stock data are end-of-year figures, and so the rate of profit in year t is computed as profits in year t divided by the sum of inventories in year t and fixed capital in year $t - 1$.

Trends

The trends in Figures 10.1, 10.2, 10.3, 10.4 and 10.5 are determined by a nearest neighbour loess fit, using a polynomial of degree 2, and a bandwidth of 0.2. Choice of these two parameters determines the trend, and there is always a compromise between smoothness and capturing the peaks and troughs (Cleveland, 1993, ch. 3). The higher the bandwidth, the smoother the trend.

Production workers and supervisory workers: numbers

In calculating numbers of workers, an important caveat affects goods-producing industries. Whereas in all other (private-service-providing) industries, non-production workers are executive, managerial and supervisory workers, this is not true in mining, in which the category "production workers" not only excludes executive, managerial and supervisory workers, but also excludes those working in finance (including accounting, collection and credit), trade (purchasing, sales and advertising), personnel, cafeterias, and professional or technical positions (including legal and medical). Neither is it true in construction, which in addition excludes those working in clerical positions; and manufacturing, which, as well as all categories excluded in mining and construction, also excludes those working in product installation or servicing, recordkeeping not related to production, delivery as well as sales, and force account construction[20] (Bureau of Labor Statistics, 2009, Ch. 2, Concepts, and Appendix). This entails that "supervisory workers" in mining, manufacturing and construction include employees who do not perform supervisory functions. Since these three industries comprised 40.3% of employment in non-farm private industries in 1973, a proportion that had halved by 2007, the numbers of supervisory workers are overestimated, and by an indeterminate amount, although decreasing with the declining employment weight of mining, manufacturing and construction through time.

Data prior to 1948 are constructed on the basis of manufacturing data. The construction assumes that the ratio of production workers to total employment tracks the time path of that ratio for manufacturing.

Production workers and supervisory workers: wages

The overestimation of the numbers of supervisory workers (in mining, manufacturing and construction) is likely to have the following effects. First, the effect on average production worker labour income will be small, because the categories of worker "wrongly" categorized as supervisory workers are likely to be paid similar wages on average as production workers. The denominators underlying the ratios displayed in Table 10.2 will not therefore be altered very much if more accurate measurements were possible. Secondly, it exaggerates the level of the supervisory worker wage share at the expense of the production worker wage share, for the latter will rise if there are more production workers. Thirdly, because trends in supervisory labour income are dominated by what happens at the top of the income distribution, the trend of the wage share in value added of supervisory workers is unlikely to be significantly altered. And fourthly, the average labour income (and the hourly wage rate) of a supervisory worker will be increased if lower waged numbers in mining, manufacturing and construction could be reclassified to "production worker" status. The numbers in the Supervisory row in Table 10.2 must therefore be considered very much as lower bounds at best.

Pre-1948 wages for each sector j are constructed on the basis of the manufacturing weekly wage, weighted by the NIPA ratio of average employee compensation for sector j to average employee compensation in manufacturing.

Acknowledgements

I am grateful to participants at the annual Analytical Political Economy Seminar (held at Queen Mary), and the London Seminar on Contemporary Marxist Theory for helpful comments. The usual disclaimer applies.

Notes

1 The subscript p denotes "productive" throughout. Not all capitalist wage-labour produces value and surplus-value. That which does is called "productive", whereas "unproductive labour" consumes rather than produces surplus-value. See for example Foley (1986, pp. 116–22).
2 Moseley (1991) and Shaikh and Tonak (1994) are partial exceptions, but their concern was primarily to measure Marxian variables, and then to relate their measures to the conventionally defined rate of profit. Hence their focus was directed to productive and unproductive labour, and not to class.
3 This approach was first broached in Mohun (2006).
4 While this thesis is most prominent in the work of Duménil and Lévy (2004, 2011), the supportive evidence presented here is differently constructed and has a different emphasis. See also Foley (2010) and Michl (2011).

5 Because it was the case on which Marx focused, it is sometimes called "Marx-biased technical change".

6 This account is simplified. More properly, the deflator in equation (7) should be one appropriate to fixed capital, in which case Y/K is complicated by a ratio of deflators. But it is not necessary to pursue this here.

7 Data sources for all figures are given in the Appendix. The trend is a ("loess") locally weighted least squares regression. See the Appendix for more detail.

8 The unproductive wage share has been investigated by Moseley (1991), Shaikh and Tonak (1994) and Mohun (2005, 2006).

9 Discussion of the separation of control from ownership has of course a long twentieth-century pedigree.

10 I return to this in the Conclusion section.

11 Salary distribution percentiles are measured in terms of household tax units. This is a completely different basis of measurement from that of individual production and supervisory worker income. It is therefore remarkable how close the average labour income of the bottom nine deciles of the labour income distribution of tax units is to the average individual production worker wage.

12 Note that the 1948 and 1979 figures in Tables 10.1 and 10.2 are not incompatible. Table 10.1 concerns wage shares, while Table 10.2 concerns relative incomes. The changes in wage share are driven by changing wages *and* by a falling percentage of total full-time equivalents of production workers through to 1966, but relative incomes barely changed.

13 This is a little loose. See the discussion following equation (14).

14 Because the supervisory plus capitalist class share is a good proxy for the money surplus value share (at least since 1964), the maximal class rate of profit is a similarly good proxy for a "Marxian rate of profit" (the ratio of money surplus value to the capital stock).

15 As dated by the National Bureau of Economic Research (NBER). Because the data of this paper are annual and NBER cycle turning points are by month, if the turning point is in January, February or March of year t, the turning point year is taken as year $t-1$. Also, the cycle defined by the peaks of 1980 and 1981 is absorbed into the cycle beginning in 1979.

16 This was manifested as a run in the repo market as ever-increasing haircuts were demanded on collateral by lenders, until the market froze completely in August 2007. Over the following year, deleveraging effectively wiped out the shadow banking sector. See Gorton (2010).

17 The reference is to an aphorism attributed to Mark Twain: "History does not repeat itself, but it does rhyme".

18 The remaining 4.6% comprise the rental value of non-residential fixed assets owned and used by non-profit institutions serving households, premium supplements for property and casualty insurance, farm products consumed on farms, and margins on owner-built housing.

19 The flow of money to pay services such as those supplied by the servants discussed by Adam Smith should also be excluded, but in a developed capitalist economy these flows are very small (and are taken for the US to be represented by the category "private households"). All other money flows are attributable to the production of value.

20 Construction work performed by an establishment, engaged primarily in some business other than construction, for its own account and for use by its employees.

References

Brenner, R. (1998) "The Economics of Global Turbulence". *New Left Review* 229: 1–264.

Brenner, R. (2002) *The Boom and the Bubble*. London and New York: Verso.

Bureau of the Census (1949) *Historical Statistics of the United States 1789–1945*. Washington DC: US Government Printing Office.

Bureau of the Census (1966) *Long Term Economic Growth 1860–1965*. Washington DC: US Government Printing Office.

Bureau of the Census (1975) *Historical Statistics of the United States*, Colonial Times to 1970, Bicentennial Edition. Washington DC: US Government Printing Office.

Bureau of Labor Statistics (2009) *Handbook of Methods*. Washington DC: US Government Printing Office. Available at http://www.bls.gov/opub/hom/homch2_b.htm

Carter, S. B., S. S. Gartner, M. R. Haines, A. L. Olmstead, R. Sutch and G. Wright (eds) (2006) *Historical Statistics of the United States, Earliest Times to the Present: Millennial Edition*. New York and Cambridge: Cambridge University Press.

Cleveland, W. S. (1993) *Visualizing Data*. Summit NJ: Hobart Press.

Duménil, G. (1983) "Beyond the Transformation Riddle: A Labor Theory of Value". *Science & Society* 47: 427–450.

Duménil, G., and D. Lévy (1993) *The Economics of the Profit Rate*. Aldershot UK and Vermont USA: Edward Elgar.

Duménil, G., and D. Lévy (2004) *Capital Resurgent*. Cambridge Mass. and London: Harvard University Press.

Duménil, D., and D. Lévy (2011) *The Crisis of the Early 21st Century: A Critical Review of Alternative Interpretations*. Paris: EconomiX, PSE.

Flamant, M., and Singer-Kérel (1970) *Modern Economic Crises*. London: Barrie & Jenkins.

Foley, D. K. (1982) "The Value of Money, the Value of Labour Power, and the Marxian Transformation Problem". *Review of Radical Political Economics* 14: 37–47.

Foley, D. K. (1986) *Understanding Capital*. Cambridge, Mass: Harvard University Press.

Foley, D. K. (2010) "The Political Economy of Post-crisis Global Capitalism". Available at http://homepage.newschool.edu/~foleyd/FoleyPolEconGlobalCap.pdf

Gillman, J. M. (1957) *The Falling Rate of Profit*. London: Dennis Dobson.

Gorton, G. B. (2010) *Slapped by the Invisible Hand*. New York: Oxford University Press.

Kendrick, J. W. (1961) *Productivity Trends in the United States*. National Bureau for Economic Research.

Kindleberger, C. P. (1984) *A Financial History of Western Europe*. London: George Allen & Unwin.

Lebergott, S. (1964) *Manpower in Economic Growth*. New York: McGraw-Hill.

Marglin, S. A. (1974) "What Do Bosses Do? The Origins and Functions of Hierarchy in Capitalist Production. Part 1". *Review of Radical Political Economics* 6: 60–112.

Marquetti, A. A. (2003) "Analyzing Historical and Regional Patterns of Technical Change from a Classical-Marxian Perspective". *Journal of Economic Behavior & Organization* 52: 191–200.

Marx, K. (1976b [1867]) *Capital I*. Harmondsworth: Penguin.

Marx, K. (1981 [1894]) *Capital III*. Harmondsworth: Penguin.

Marx, K. (1987 [1859]) A Contribution to the Critique of Political Economy. In Karl Marx and Frederick Engels, *Collected Works*, Vol. 29. Moscow: Progress Publishers, and London: Lawrence & Wishart.

Michl, T. (2011) "Finance as a Class?". *New Left Review* 70: 117–125.

Mohun, S. (1994) "A Re(in)statement of the Labor Theory of Value". *Cambridge Journal of Economics* 18: 391–412.

Mohun, S. (2005) "On Measuring the Wealth of Nations: the U.S. Economy, 1964–2001". *Cambridge Journal of Economics* 29: 799–815.

Mohun, S. (2006) "Distributive Shares in the U.S. Economy, 1964-2001". *Cambridge Journal of Economics* 30: 347–370.

Moseley, F. (1991) *The Falling Rate of Profit in the Postwar United States Economy*. New York, St. Martin's Press.

Saez, E. (2012) *Tables and Figures Updated to 2010*. Available at http://elsa.berkeley. edu/~saez/

Shaikh, A. M. (1999) "Explaining the Global Economic Crisis". *Historical Materialism* 5: 103–44.

Shaikh, A. M. (2010) "The First Great Depression of the 21st Century". In L. Panitch, G. Albo and V. Chibber (eds.), *The Crisis This Time. Socialist Register 2011*. London: Merlin Press and New York: Monthly Review Press.

Shaikh, A. M., and E. A. Tonak (1994) *Measuring the Wealth of Nations*. Cambridge: Cambridge University Press.

Temin, P. (1989) *Lessons from the Great Depression*. Cambridge Mass. and London: The MIT Press.

Turner, A. (2009) "*The Turner Review. A Regulatory Response to the Global Banking Crisis*". London: Financial Services Authority.

Weisskopf, T. E. (1979) "Marxian Crisis Theory and the Rate of Profit in the US Economy". *Cambridge Journal of Economics* 3: 341–378.

11 The sources of profitability

*Peter Flaschel, Nils Fröhlich and
Roberto Veneziani*

Introduction

One of the key contributions of the so-called "New Interpretation" formulated by
Duménil (1980) and Foley (1982) is the idea that there really is no "transformation
problem" to be solved in Marx's Labor Theory of Value (LTV).[1] The attempt
to "transform" labor values into production prices is theoretically dubious and
empirically meaningless. In the New Interpretation, the focus of the LTV is on
aggregate relationships, on the essential *monetary* dimension of the economy, and
on the relation between *actual* money magnitudes and their labor counterparts.
One of the key assumptions of the New Interpretation is that the value of labor
power was measured by the actual wage share, and not by the labor embodied in
some bundles of goods consumed by, or affordable to workers.

Although the New Interpretation provides a rigorous and consistent macro
framework to interpret the economy from a Marxian perspective, its emphasis
on monetary magnitudes obscures the role of labor values. Indeed, according to
critics, in the New Interpretation, monetary accounts are all that is required to
analyze capitalist economies and it is unclear whether labor accounts are of any
theoretical relevance.

This chapter aims to show that, even if one adopts the key assumptions of
the New Interpretation, a system of labor accounts can be developed, which
is independent from money accounts and which provides theoretically and
empirically relevant insights on observed phenomena in capitalist economies.
To be precise, we would argue that Marx's LTV is dual in nature, in the same
way as a System of National Accounts (SNA) expressed in real magnitudes forms
a dual structure with respect to prices and quantities. A real SNA is designed to
promote an understanding of the key processes driving the motion of nominal
magnitudes. Analogously, Marx's labor value aggregates were designed as the
essential elements of an understanding of what happens underneath the surface of
the process of capital accumulation.

In a recent paper, Flaschel *et al.* (2011) have shown that the standard measures
of labor content used in the Input-Output (IO) literature, the classic Marxian labor
values, represent the only sound labor productivity indices. Further, by using the
standard Marxian labor values, they have provided a general proof of the Law of

Decreasing Labor Content (LDLC) – arguably one of the key laws of capitalist accumulation – by demonstrating that capital-using labor-saving technical change tends to decrease the labor content of commodities.

In this chapter, we argue that standard labor values provide important insights into one of the most important issues in Marxian economics, namely the determinants of the general rate of profit. And Marx had a clear interest in demonstrating that his LTV explained the key variables determining profitability. This is far from trivial: following the approach pioneered by Foley (1982), it is possible to obtain an equality between aggregate surplus value and aggregate profit. But, as concerns the denominator of the profit rate, things are less clear-cut, for

> [i]t is necessary to remember this modified significance of the cost-price, and to bear in mind that there is always the possibility of an error if the cost-price of a commodity in any particular sphere is identified with the value of the means of production consumed by it.
>
> Marx, 1954: 165

Yet, this chapter shows that such a logical error in the comparison of value and price magnitudes is empirically irrelevant and the key insights of the Marxian theory of exploitation are valid.

In the next section, we set out the key features of a standard IO model and define labor values and the aggregate price rate of profit. It is important to note at the outset that no assumption of uniform profitability across sectors is made in this chapter: in our view there is no uniform, single principle at work in the dynamic price formation processes of agriculture, manufacturing, services and banking, and significant intersectoral differences in market forms, entry and exit conditions, turn-over times, scope and size effects, etc. make any assumptions of uniform profitability rather dubious.[2] Therefore our theoretical and empirical analysis focuses on actual prices, rather than production prices.

In the following section, we define the value rate of profit and derive an analytical expression for the deviation between the price and value profit rates. We identify the key determinants of the value rate of profit, which are three central Marxian categories: the total labor time performed in the process of production in a certain year, the value of labor power, and the labor value of the total capital stock. Differences in the two rates instead are explained by deviations in the valuation of the total capital stock in price and in value terms.

The next two sections present our empirical findings concerning trends in profitability in the German economy, 1991–2000. We adopt a fairly general definition of labor values which includes the treatment of heterogeneous labor, fixed capital and open economy issues, and we show that deviations between the price and value rates of profit are indeed negligible (always below 3% and around 1% in more than half of the sample). Although we do not address the issue of causality in this chapter, we interpret this finding as strongly supportive of the idea that the actual (market) price rate of profit is determined by the three key value magnitudes of Marx's theory of exploitation: total labor time performed, the value of labor power, and the labor value of the total capital stock. All other means for changing the general rate of profit are unsystematic in nature and quantitatively negligible. Marx's value rate of profit, and its above decomposition, therefore explains the basic reasons by which the capitalist class as a whole can increase profitability, but – as Marx (1954: 167–8) notes – not necessarily in a uniform way for all the members of this class.

This analysis confirms the irrelevance of the Marxian transformation problem: the central sources of, or restrictions for overall profitability are provided in Marx's *Capital*, Vol. I, even though there is no one-to-one correspondence at the micro-level between labor value expressions determined within production and prices determined in the sphere of circulation (a fact stressed by Marx on many occasions). The success of capitalists as a class, however, depends on the creation of absolute and relative surplus value as defined in Marx's *Capital*, and on the decrease in the labor time needed to reproduce the capital stock.

Value and price

We consider the standard IO model, which includes an n-sectoral intermediate consumption of goods and labor input–output system A, l with a capital stock matrix K, a capital depreciation matrix K_δ, a vector of gross outputs x and a vector of final demands $y = x - Ax - K_\delta x$. Let I denote the identity matrix. For the sake of simplicity, we assume that the aggregate consumption matrix $A + K_\delta$ is productive and the vector of labor inputs l is strictly positive.

If wages w, a scalar, are paid ex post, we can define the Leontief-type production price equations[3]

$$p = p(A + K_\delta) + wl + rpK, \quad py = lx. \tag{1}$$

The uniform rate of profit r is calculated on capital advanced,[4] not on capital consumed. It is well known that equation (1) can be uniquely solved for any $w \in [0, 1]$, giving a positive price vector p and a positive rate of profit r, except for $w = 1$, where profits are zero and prices equal labor values v. Formally:

$$p = wl(I - (A + K_\delta) - rK)^{-1} = wl \sum_{n=0}^{\infty} (A + K_\delta + rK)^n. \tag{2}$$

Given the normalization $py = lx$, the following wage–profit curve can be derived from equation (1):

$$w = \frac{lx}{l(I - (A + K_\delta) - rK)^{-1} y} = \frac{lx}{l \sum_{n=0}^{\infty} (A + K_\delta + rK)^n y}, \tag{3}$$

which is strictly decreasing in r. These matrix operations are common in Sraffian economics (though fixed capital is treated as a joint product there), yet they are not really necessary to analyze nominal and real IO data, where sectoral profit rates are significantly different and the dynamics of the average (aggregate) rate of profit can be better understood by using Marxian labor values instead of prices of production as we shall show in this chapter.

Solving equation (1) for $w = 1$ ($r = 0$) defines IO oriented labor values as in Bródy (1970):

$$v = v(A + K_\delta) + l = l(I - A - K_\delta)^{-1} = l \sum_{n=0}^{n=\infty} (A + K_\delta)^n, \tag{4}$$

which satisfy by definition the equation $vy = lx$. These are the labor values around which the transformation problem of values into prices of production is often debated (see e.g. Bródy, 1970; Foley, 1982). Yet, following Foley (1982), we are not interested here in showing how vectors of labor values are transformed into prices of production, because this is just an academic or exegetical exercise with little or no empirical relevance. Furthermore, we aim to show that labor values can contribute to the theoretical and empirical investigation of actual price and profit rate dynamics, while prices of production as in Sraffa (1960) are an abstract theoretical construct with limited relevance for the understanding of the actual evolution of prices and quantities of an economy.

In contrast, Flaschel (2010) and Flaschel et al. (2011) have shown that labor values have a clear role as part of an SNA in that they (and only they) measure labor productivity. Indeed, labor values were also used as productivity indicators in the original formulation of the UN's SNA by Richard Stone (United Nations, 1968), albeit without acknowledging the intimate relationship of the UN measures of labor productivity with Marx's concept of embodied labor. We here study how these measures of labor content (and, in reciprocal form, of labor productivity) can contribute to the analysis of actual prices and profitability, without using prices of production as an intermediate step, a procedure rightly criticized by Farjoun and Machover (1983) as overly restrictive, redundant and not justifiable by real observations.

Indeed, the aggregate equalities derived above do not hold only if production prices p are considered. The equation $py = lx$ is just a normalization and can be extended to *any* nominal prices p_n and nominal wages w_n. Therefore, in what follows we shall set $p := \frac{lx}{p_n y} p_n$, so that $py = lx$ and $w = \frac{lx}{p_n y} w_n$. Similarly, if the actual wage share $w \in (0, 1)$ is interpreted as Marx's "value of labor power" as argued by Foley (1982), then the following aggregate equality also holds for *any* normalized price vector p, w:

$$py - wlx = vy - wlx, \tag{5}$$

i.e., profits must equal (or are a redistribution of) surplus values. Therefore, if the rate of surplus value e is defined by $e := (1 - w)/w$, a third aggregate relationship relating labor values to *actual* (market) prices immediately follows from equation (5)

$$r_p = \frac{(1-w)lx}{pKx} = \frac{1-w}{w}\frac{wlx}{pKx} = e\frac{V}{C},$$ (6)

where r_p is the *average* (market) price rate of profit, C denotes aggregated constant capital, and V is aggregated variable capital.[5] Foley's (1982) approach emphasizes *macro* relations and is not linked to any specific theory of price, or labor value, determination. Thus the above aggregate relationships also hold in our approach to labor values as the SNA-oriented full labor costs schedule behind the surface of actual price and quantity dynamics.

Aggregate labor value ratios: the systematic components in their price expressions

As mentioned above, we view labor values as a theoretical skeleton behind the surface of price-quantity dynamics, i.e. as part of an SNA – such as the UN's (United Nations, 1968) – which is designed to define measurable categories to understand the capitalist process of economic and social reproduction.[6] From this viewpoint, there is nothing to "transform". Rather, one should show how labor values can be used to detect the laws of motion of capitalism. From a Marxian perspective, the first and most important step is to understand the determinants of the average (not a uniform) price rate of profit or – put differently – to what extent the generation of absolute and relative surplus value (measured in labor values), and technical progress drive profitability.

Let w be the value of labor power as in Foley (1982). The average value rate of profit can be defined as follows:

$$r_v = \frac{v(I - A - K_\delta)x - wlx}{vKx} = (1-w)\frac{lx}{vKx}.$$ (7)

The average value rate of profit depends on three fundamental magnitudes: the wage share w in national income $py = lx$, the amount of hours worked, and the labor value of the total capital stock.[7] The wage share relates the Marxian theory of exploitation to Goodwin's (1967) distributive cycle, and thus to the reserve army mechanism, and is related to what Marx called the generation of relative surplus value. The hours actually worked by the workforce have to do with the generation of absolute surplus value, and can be increased if monthly hours worked are increased, if absenteeism is forced down, if holidays are reduced and if (not covered by the model) work intensity is increased.

The labor value of the total capital stock is affected by accumulation and technical change. As formally proved by Flaschel *et al.* (2011) in a general n-sectoral IO model, under mild assumptions any profitable (cost reducing) capital-using labor-saving technical change yields a decrease in labor values v. Noting that capital-using labor-saving (i.e. Marxian) technical progress has characterized most phases of capitalist development (see Marquetti, 2003), this underpins the

LDLC originally formulated by Farjoun and Machover (1983).[8] If the LDLC is sufficiently strong, it can outweigh the physical increases in the capital stock matrix K and lead to an increase in the value rate of profit. The tension between increases in the capital stock and decreases in labor values may be considered as a fundamental contradiction in the capitalist process of technical change, and is related to Marx's discussion of changes in the technical composition of capital (vKx/lx). Whether the LDLC is sufficiently strong to reduce the technical composition of capital is an empirical issue, which we consider in the section Three sources of profitability, below.

To summarize: basic forces driving an increase in the value rate of profit would be a decrease in the wage share and an increase in the hours performed by workers. Further, Marxian technical change might increase the value rate of profit, provided it leads to a significant change in the labor content of commodities that outweighs the increase in K.

Having identified the determinants of the value rate of profit, the question is whether this can help us to understand movements in the actual price rate of profit. For it is price, not value magnitudes, that is relevant for economic agents and their decisions. By equation (6) and (7), the deviation of the actual price rate of profit from the value rate of profit is:

$$\frac{r_p}{r_v} = \frac{(v-p)Kx}{pKx} + 1 \quad \text{or} \quad \frac{r_v}{r_p} = \frac{(p-v)Kx}{vKx} + 1. \tag{8}$$

If the total labor costs of the commodities produced explain the bulk of costs mirrored by actual prices, then r_v and r_p will be close. However, the two rates of profit will also be very similar if price and values differ in sectors with relatively low capital intensity, or if sectoral differences cancel out in the aggregate. In these cases, the theoretical value rate of profit and the actual price rate of profit would differ only by unsystematic, historically determined price-value deviations. Any factors influencing the value rate of profit will also affect the price rate of profit in the same direction. The theoretical and empirical relation between the actual price rate of profit r_p and the value rate r_v, in our view, represents the fundamental topic to be addressed in order to analyze Marx's value theory of profit. We investigate this empirical issue in the next section. By focusing on the labor values, or productivity indexes v, as measured by IO analysts, we attempt to test whether the production-based rate r_v provides a proxy for the average price rate of profit r_p, or at least whether a robust correlation exists between them. The aim is to understand whether the forces underlying the evolution of r_v would then drive changes in r_p. In this case, the Marxian theory of exploitation would provide the foundation for the analysis of profitability in capitalism: the three factors discussed above which determine the motion of r_v would be the essential forces driving r_p.

A general approach to the measurement of Marxian labor values

The data for our empirical investigation of the model $A, K, K_\delta, l, I, x, y$, are taken from Kalmbach *et al.* (2005) and concern the German economy for the years 1991–2000.[9] Kalmbach *et al.* group the 71 original sectors into seven macro-sectors. The industrial sector is divided into agriculture, manufacturing, and construction. Within manufacturing itself, Kalmbach *et al.* further distinguish more traditional industries from the so-called "*export core*" (a crucial subsector in an export-oriented country like Germany), which comprises the four single production sectors with the highest exports: chemical, pharmaceutical, machinery, and motor vehicles. They also distinguish between three main types of services: business-related services, consumer services, and social services. For their aggregation, Kalmbach *et al.* (2005) adopt a broad definition of business-related services by including wholesale trade, communications, finance, leasing, computer and related services, research and development services, in addition to business-related services *in a narrow sense*. Consumer services instead include: retail trade, repair, transport, insurance, real estate services, and personal services. Table 11.1 summarizes the seven (macro) sectors thus obtained and the sectoral output shares (in percentages, for the year 2000).

The double-deflated technological coefficients of the seven-sectoral aggregation are reported in Table 11.2, which shows the intermediate IO matrix A of the German economy for the year 1995 per million Euro of output value. There are also (not shown) a depreciation matrix, K_δ, based on a fixed capital matrix, K, and a vector of labor coefficients, l.

We have constructed the price vector p from data on nominal output levels x_n and real output levels x, the latter based on constant prices of the year 1995. Three more characteristics of the data should be noted here. First, in the definition of labor values, we are using the depreciation matrix K_δ, and therefore we can ignore physical joint production. Second, the average nominal wage level is defined in Kalmbach *et al.* (2005) by dividing the sum of all wage incomes $\sum_{tj} w_{n_{tj}} l_{tj}$ by total employment lx, where t is the type of worker working in sector j. This implies that wage differentials are used to homogenize labor inputs when defining labor values, consistently with our theoretical focus on the aggregate wage level w_n and

Table 11.1 The seven-sectoral structure of the economy

S1:	Agriculture	1.33
S2:	Manufacturing, the export core	12.37
S3:	Other manufacturing	22.55
S4:	Construction	6.29
S5:	Business-related services	21.36
S6:	Consumer services	23.35
S7:	Social services	12.75

Source: Kalmbach *et al.* (2005)

Table 11.2 Technological coefficients of the seven-sectoral aggregation (Germany, 1995)

	S1	S2	S3	S4	S5	S6	S7
S1	0.030	0.000	0.047	0.000	0.000	0.002	0.002
S2	0.081	0.241	0.050	0.021	0.003	0.008	0.014
S3	0.159	0.226	0.338	0.286	0.030	0.060	0.065
S4	0.010	0.005	0.009	0.020	0.007	0.034	0.020
S5	0.137	0.107	0.126	0.088	0.291	0.118	0.080
S6	0.032	0.044	0.045	0.100	0.071	0.139	0.044
S7	0.034	0.008	0.013	0.007	0.009	0.014	0.025

Source: Kalmbach *et al.* (2005)

on the wage share w. It should also be noted that employment is measured in terms of workers and not in terms of hours worked.

Third, the matrix A is constructed in Kalmbach *et al.* (2005) using data on the industrial consumption of domestic and imported commodities. It thus provides the technological matrix of intermediate inputs irrespective of their origin. This implies that labor values are measured on the basis of the domestic technology and independently of the conditions under which the imported commodities were actually produced. This, in our view, is a more appropriate way of dealing with international labor values than Steedman's (2003) approach, where terms of trade enter the definition of labor values. To measure labor values as if foreign commodities were domestically produced makes our approach (which is very similar to the approach pioneered by Gupta and Steedman, 1971) much simpler than Steedman's (2003). Furthermore, our approach is adequate if one wants to study the economy not only from the viewpoint of labor productivity, but also from a reproduction perspective where the flow relationships of actual inputs to outputs are the focus of interest, independently of whether the inputs are produced domestically or internationally. The role of terms of trade for calculating and comparing value and price rates of profit concerns the issue of international exploitation, which must be left here for future research.[10]

The notion of labor values employed in this chapter is therefore very general, but also very specific in its treatment of international trade (where domestic techniques matter, but not the origin of inputs), of heterogeneous labor (where wage differentials are used to compare different skills), and of fixed capital. On the basis of this broad definition of labor values, in the next section we consider the deviation between the value and the price rate of profit. We find that the Marxian theory of the determinants of profitability remains valid, even though the central relevance of living and embodied labor, and the conflict about income distribution is not immediately clear to economic agents.

Three sources of profitability

This section provides an empirical illustration of the previous analysis, based on the IO data set constructed by Kalmbach *et al.* (2005). Let $\langle x \rangle$ denote the diagonal matrix formed by the column vector of real outputs x. Let x_n be the column vector of nominal production levels and let u be a row vector of 1's. Based on Foley (1982), our empirical results are obtained by applying the following definitions:

$$p_n := x_n^T \langle x \rangle^{-1} \quad \text{(price vector)}, \tag{9}$$

$$\gamma := \frac{lx}{p_n y} \quad \text{(value of money)},^{11} \tag{10}$$

$$p := \gamma p_n \quad \text{(normalized price vector)}, \tag{11}$$

$$w := \gamma w_n \quad \text{(value of labor power)}. \tag{12}$$

Recalling and transforming the deviations from r_p to r_v given in equation (8) we get:

$$\frac{r_v}{r_p} = \frac{(p-v)Kx}{vKx} + 1 = \frac{\left(p\langle v \rangle^{-1} - u\right)\langle v \rangle Kx}{vKx} + 1. \tag{13}$$

Table 11.3 shows the value and the price rate of profit, and their deviation. Clearly, the price rate of profit mirrors the value rate of profit up to a deviation of negligible degree. Interestingly, the value rate of profit is always larger than its price analogue, a phenomenon for which there is no obvious explanation.

These figures are only an empirical illustration of what might be called the "fuzzy connection" between the average price and value rate of profit. The relationship between actual prices and labor values is in general sufficiently close to make their deviation irrelevant at the aggregate level.[12] Labor magnitudes, based on the standard IO measure of the labor contents of commodities, are the theoretical construct behind actual (average) money magnitudes, and have been designed by Marx to understand the laws of motion of capitalism. Labor values represent the substance of human interrelationships, namely the abstract type of labor that agents are providing for and interchanging with their fellow countrymen.

Table 11.3 Price rate of profit (r_p) and value rate of profit (r_v) (percentage)

Year	r_p	r_v	r_v/r_p
1991	14.71	15.05	1.023
1992	13.33	13.70	1.028
1993	12.15	12.39	1.020
1994	12.80	13.10	1.024
1995	12.79	12.95	1.013
1996	12.76	12.84	1.006
1997	13.48	13.61	1.010
1998	13.37	13.41	1.003
1999	13.03	13.06	1.002
2000	12.82	13.02	1.016

We can consider an economy from the viewpoint of the physical flow of commodities, or from the viewpoint of nominal (price) flow magnitudes, but also from the viewpoint of abstract labor flows, understood as the SNA labor time skeleton underlying monetary flows. Relating this labor-time oriented SNA to the flow of actually observed magnitudes is not a "transformation problem", but it rather provides a representation of the economy from a different angle, as convincingly argued by Stahmer (2000).

By definition, the value of the net product is equal to the total labor time performed and total profits are equal to total surplus value. Instead, only an approximate relationship, or connection, holds between the average rate of profit and the average value rate of profit, as shown in Table 11.3. This relationship is, however, so strong as to suggest that the Marxian concepts of absolute and relative surplus value and his measure of the technical composition of capital suffice to explain the determinants of the average price rate of profit.

Table 11.4 analyzes price-value deviations,[13] and it forcefully shows that prices and values (though normalized in the same way) differ substantially in some of the seven sectors. In Marxian terms, this suggests that distinct processes may regulate the generation and the distribution of profits. At the aggregate level, profitability can be increased solely by Marxian mechanisms: an increase in absolute surplus value ($lx \uparrow$) or in relative surplus value ($w \downarrow$), and a decrease in the labor value of the capital stock, through capital-using labor-saving technical change which raises labor productivity (lowering labor values) to a sufficient degree.[14] The latter phenomenon seems, however, absent in the German economy (1991–2000), as shown in Table 11.5: although labor productivity, $1/v_j, j = 1, \ldots, 7$, increased (see Appendix), the aggregate value of the capital stock did not unambiguously decrease.

Table 11.3 shows that the average price rate of profit has fallen in 1991–1993, 1994–1996, and again in 1998–2000. Table 11.5 suggests that this can be related to tendencies in the technical composition of capital as well as in the value of labor power w to rise.

Table 11.4 Price-value ratios

Year	S1	S2	S3	S4	S5	S6	S7
1991	0.5580	1.127	1.0171	0.9700	1.179	1.025	0.8942
1992	0.5835	1.099	1.0041	0.9975	1.172	1.027	0.9062
1993	0.5882	1.054	0.9896	0.9996	1.190	1.037	0.9168
1994	0.6071	1.078	0.9905	1.0000	1.181	1.039	0.9097
1995	0.6236	1.124	0.9812	0.9705	1.149	1.045	0.9095
1996	0.6749	1.112	0.9923	0.9555	1.127	1.056	0.9046
1997	0.6815	1.137	1.0122	0.9487	1.110	1.057	0.8934
1998	0.6583	1.136	1.0001	0.9415	1.107	1.051	0.8981
1999	0.6530	1.105	1.0083	0.9447	1.112	1.052	0.9026
2000	0.6650	1.154	1.0565	0.9412	1.081	1.034	0.8916

Table 11.5 Wage share, employment, labor value of capital stock, price value of capital stock, and technical composition

Year	w	lx^a	vKx^a	pKx^a	$(vKx)/(lx)$
1991	0.698	38.5	77.1	78.9	2.01
1992	0.717	37.9	78.3	80.5	2.07
1993	0.728	37.4	82.2	83.8	2.20
1994	0.715	37.3	81.2	83.1	2.18
1995	0.714	37.4	82.5	83.5	2.21
1996	0.713	37.3	83.4	83.9	2.24
1997	0.699	37.2	82.3	83.2	2.21
1998	0.700	37.6	84.3	84.5	2.24
1999	0.706	38.1	85.6	85.8	2.25
2000	0.710	38.8	86.5	87.8	2.23

[a]Measured in million persons

Conclusions

This chapter shows how the central value aggregates of Marx's theory of exploitation provide the essential determinants of the general (average) price rate of profit of a capitalist economy. Systematic changes in profitability can be analyzed by focusing on labor value magnitudes which are more informative than the corresponding price expressions, due to the "chaotic" nature of interacting processes of commodity exchange in space and time. When suitably aggregated, the evolution of labor values (or total labor costs) captures the essential and the inertial laws of motion behind profitability in capitalist economies. Corresponding actual market price averages, though based on significantly varying price formation schemes, may also lose their theoretical arbitrariness when deviations between economy-wide price and value aggregates are compared, in particular concerning the building blocks in the formation of average rates of profit.

In a capitalist society, labor power is the only commodity that is not produced by firms and where no profits accrue in the course of its reproduction (in contrast to slavery). Moreover, labor is indispensable for social reproduction, while all other commodities can be substituted for each other in one way or another. Reducing the value of labor power – through either a lengthening of the work-day, or a reduction in workers' hourly wages and consumption – is therefore one of the central mechanisms by which the average rate of profit of an actual capitalist economy can be increased. Labor-productivity that increases technical change can also reduce the reproduction value of the capital stock of the economy, and thus contribute to an increase in its general rate of profit, but only if the quantity increase in the capital stock is smaller than its falling labor content.

Summarizing, the flow of direct and indirect labor through the economy and the appropriation of part of it by capitalists, and average market exchange ratios may deviate to some degree. But this deviation is characterized only by a small amount of fuzziness at the aggregate level, and the correlation between the value and the price rate of profit, in particular, is robust. The main factors analyzed by Marx in *Capital*, Vol. I, in his theory of exploitation and technical change, determine profitability both in the sphere of production and in the sphere of exchange. Marx's general law of capitalist accumulation regulates the value of labor power w in the conflict about income distribution, whereas the conflict between capital and labor within production drives the technical composition of capital $(vKx)/(lx)$. These two conflicts determine the central variable for capital as a whole, namely the average rate of profit.

The analysis in this chapter leaves open the issue of a theory of market prices. However, our results show that there is no need to transform labor values into hypothetical prices of production in order to demonstrate their usefulness for an analysis of the process of capital accumulation and the formation of the general rate of profit. Here, labor values can be considered as part of Richard Stone's System of National Accounts, as forcefully suggested by Flaschel (2010). Viewed in this way, they can then be used to study the actually observed price-quantity dynamics of capitalist economies.

Acknowledgments

We thank Angelo Reati, Ian Wright and two anonymous referees for detailed comments and suggestions on an earlier version of the paper. The usual caveats apply.

Notes

1 See also Mohun (1994), Duménil and Foley (2008), and Duménil *et al.* (2009).
2 A thorough empirical and discussion of persistent intersectoral differences in profitability is in Flaschel *et al.* (2011a). See also Reati (1986).
3 The normalization $py = lx$ implies that the value of money is equal to one. As noted by an anonymous referee, this "makes it irrelevant whether equations are expressed in terms of hours or money, and this in turn loses something important about the distinction between values and prices". However, no result in the chapter (theoretical or empirical) depends upon this normalization, which is imposed only for convenience.
4 Note that the production of all commodities requires some inventories, and therefore there is a corresponding entry in the matrix of capital advancements.
5 The normalization obviously does not change the price rate of profit.
6 See also Pasinetti (1981), in particular VII.4, for a similar interpretation of the Marxian LTV.
7 In other words, intermediate and capital consumption do not matter for the value of labor power as defined by Foley (1982).
8 Details can be found in Farjoun and Machover (1983), chapters 4 and 7.
9 We thank Reiner Franke for supplying us with the data needed for the present chapter.
10 It may be worth noting in passing that our approach may also be relevant for the analysis of international exploitation, by comparing such labor values for different countries. In the context of this chapter, however, since terms of trade influence the actual prices of domestically produced commodities, this may increase the deviations of our measure of labor value aggregates and their price expressions.

11 This expression is the reciprocal of the Monetary Expression of Labor Time (MELT).
12 See Fröhlich (2010) for a more detailed empirical study. Shaikh (1984) is one of the first studies that found out that there is a strong positive correlation between prices and values on a sectoral level.
13 The time series of labor values and normalized prices are shown in the Appendix.
14 Innovations similar to Harrod-neutral technical change would be an example of such a situation.

References

Bródy, A. (1970) *Proportions, Prices and Planning*, Amsterdam: North Holland.

Duménil, G. (1980) *De la Valeur aux Prix de Production*, Paris: Economica.

Duménil, G., and Foley, D.K. (2008) 'The Marxian Transformation Problem', in S.N. Durlauf and L.B. Blume (eds.) *The New Palgrave: A Dictionary of Economics*, Basingstoke: Palgrave Macmillan.

Duménil, G., Foley, D.K., and Lévy, D. (2009) 'A Note on the Formal Treatment of Exploitation in a Model with Heterogeneous Labor', *Metroeconomica*, 60: 560–567.

Farjoun, E., and Machover, M. (1983) *Laws of Chaos*, London: Verso Edition and NLB.

Flaschel, P. (2010) *Topics in Classical Micro- and Macroeconomics*, Heidelberg: Springer.

Flaschel, P., Franke, R., and Veneziani, R. (2012) 'The Measurement of Prices of Production: An Alternative Approach', *Review of Political Economy*, 24: 417–435.

Flaschel, P., Franke, R., and Veneziani, R. (2011) 'Labor Productivity and the Law of Decreasing Labor Content', Bielefeld University: Working paper.

Foley, D.K. (1982) 'The Value of Money the Value of Labor Power and the Marxian Transformation Problem', *Review of Radical Political Economy*, 14: 37–47.

Fröhlich, N. (2010) 'Labour Values, Prices of Production and the Missing Equalization of Profit Rates: Evidence from the German Economy', Chemnitz University of Technology: Working paper.

Goodwin, R. (1967) 'A Growth Cycle', in C.H. Feinstein (ed.) *Socialism, Capitalism and Economic Growth*, Cambridge (UK): Cambridge University Press, 54–58.

Gupta, S., and Steedman, I. (1971) 'An Input-Output Study of Labour Productivity in the British Economy', *Oxford Bulletin of Economics and Statistics*, 33: 21–34.

Kalmbach, P., Franke, R. , Knottenbauer, K., and Krämer, H. (2005) *Die Interdependenz von Industrie und Dienstleistungen – Zur Dynamik eines komplexen Beziehungsgeflechts*, Berlin: Edition Sigma.

Marquetti, A. (2003) 'Analyzing Historical and Regional Patterns of Technical Change from a Classical-Marxian Perspective', *Journal of Economic Behavior and Organization*, 52: 191–200.

Marx, K. (1954) *Capital. A Critique of Political Economy, Vol. I.* London: Lawrence & Wishart.

Mohun, S. (1994) 'A Re(in)statement of the Labour Theory of Value', *Cambridge Journal of Economics*, 18: 391–412.

Pasinetti, L.L. (1981) *Structural Change and Economic Growth. A Theoretical Essay on the Dynamics of the Wealth of Nations*. Cambridge, Mass.: Cambridge University Press.

Reati, A. (1986) 'The Deviation of Prices from Labor Values: An Extension to the Non-Competitive Case', *Cambridge Journal of Economics*, 10: 35–42.

Shaikh, A. (1984) 'The Transformation from Marx to Sraffa', in E. Mandel and A. Freeman (eds.) *Ricardo, Marx, Sraffa: The Langston Memorial Volume*, London: Verso, 43–84.

Sraffa, P. (1960) *Production of Commodities by Means of Commodities*, Cambridge (UK): Cambridge University Press.

Stahmer, C. (2000) 'The Magic Triangle of Input-Output Tables', in S. Simon and J. Proops (eds.) *Greening the Accounts*, Cheltenham: Edward Elgar, 155–180.

Steedman, I. (2003) 'Marx after Sraffa and the Open Economy', Manchester Metropolitan University: Discussion Papers in Economics.

United Nations (1968) *A System of National Accounts*, New York: Studies in Methods, Series F, No. 2, Rev. 3.

Appendix: Additional data

Table 11.6 Labor values (persons per million Euros of output value)

Year	S1	S2	S3	S4	S5	S6	S7
1991	54.68	26.53	30.23	28.53	24.45	27.22	30.69
1992	47.44	25.82	28.78	27.40	23.82	26.67	29.88
1993	45.24	26.55	28.55	27.77	23.62	26.95	30.04
1994	44.65	25.09	27.48	27.12	23.40	26.32	29.63
1995	42.95	23.83	27.30	27.60	23.32	25.64	29.45
1996	38.76	23.87	26.46	27.65	23.06	25.29	29.45
1997	37.81	22.98	25.62	27.02	22.83	25.02	29.11
1998	37.42	22.94	25.63	26.92	22.39	25.02	28.92
1999	36.46	23.46	24.89	26.65	21.82	24.93	28.86
2000	35.90	22.39	23.79	26.14	22.03	24.99	28.63

Table 11.7 Normalized price vector (persons per million Euros of output value)

Year	S1	S2	S3	S4	S5	S6	S7
1991	30.51	29.89	30.75	27.67	28.82	27.91	27.44
1992	27.68	28.37	28.89	27.33	27.92	27.38	27.08
1993	26.61	27.99	28.25	27.76	28.12	27.94	27.54
1994	27.11	27.05	27.22	27.12	27.63	27.34	26.95
1995	26.78	26.78	26.78	26.78	26.78	26.78	26.78
1996	26.16	26.54	26.26	26.42	25.99	26.70	26.64
1997	25.77	26.13	25.94	25.64	25.34	26.45	26.01
1998	24.64	26.07	25.63	25.34	24.79	26.30	25.98
1999	23.81	25.93	25.10	25.17	24.26	26.22	26.05
2000	23.88	25.84	25.13	24.60	23.82	25.84	25.52

12 On the *"vexata questio* of value"

Ricardo, Marx and Sraffa

Heinz D. Kurz and Neri Salvadori

Introduction

A considerable part of Duncan Foley's work is devoted to the theory of value and income distribution in Karl Marx and in the classical authors from Adam Smith to David Ricardo; see, especially, Foley (1982, 1986, 2000, 2006) and Duménil and Foley (2010). Foley has expressed a fair amount of sympathy for Marx's achievements in this regard, and has also responded to the criticism of labour-value-based reasoning in the aftermath of the publication of Piero Sraffa's *Production of Commodities by Means of Commodities* (Sraffa, 1960). As we interpret Duncan's contribution, he was not totally convinced by Sraffa's reformulation and rectification of the classical approach to the theory of value and distribution, and defended Marx's theory against the criticism of labour-value-based reasoning that derived from it (see especially Steedman, 1977). We comment on Duncan's point of view briefly towards the end of the third section.

In this short chapter we deal with the similarities and the differences between the approaches of Ricardo, Marx and Sraffa. Our focus of attention will be Ricardo's famous search for an "invariable measure of value", for which Marx showed so little understanding and respect, but which assumed a role in Sraffa's contribution concerning what he called the "Standard commodity". Apparently Marx missed the deeper meaning of Ricardo's following statement in the *Principles*:

> It is ... of considerable use towards attaining a correct theory, to ascertain what the essential qualities of a standard are, that we may know the causes of the variation in the relative value of commodities, and that we may be enabled to calculate the degree in which they are likely to operate.
>
> Ricardo, 1951–1973, *Works* I: 17 n. 3

Or as Sraffa put it in the introduction to the Ricardo edition: Ricardo in some of his statements "came close to identifying the problem of a measure of value with that of the law of value" (Sraffa, 1951: xli). Attention will focus exclusively on the value theoretic problem of the dependence of relative normal prices on the distribution of income, given the system of production in use, and not on interspatial and intertemporal comparisons relating to different systems of production. The latter concern played an important and initially exclusive role in Ricardo's thinking. It was only in the third edition of his *Principles* (1821) that he also raised the problem, which is our exclusive concern in this chapter.

The composition of the chapter is as follows. The next section deals with how Marx received Ricardo's search for an invariable measure of value. Since Marx was convinced he had succeeded in elaborating a correct theory of value, based on the supposition that the source and only source of value is (abstract) labour, an idea he felt was present in Ricardo, the latter's concern struck him as a regression. The following section briefly summarizes Ricardo's various attempts at specifying the properties of an invariable standard of value, and how these attempts gradually brought him closer to a "correct theory" of value. The fourth section reviews Sraffa's resumption and solution of that part of Ricardo's problem that has a solution, and is followed by our Conclusions.

This chapter is closely related to two other papers by us and could be read together with them, these are: our contribution to the Festschrift in honour of Luigi Pasinetti (Kurz and Salvadori, 1993) and one of our contributions to the Festschrift in honour of Ian Steedman (2010). Apparently, the "*vexata questio* of value*", as Ricardo's friend McCulloch called it (Ricardo, 1951–1973, *Works* IX: 369), still intrigues economists, including Duncan Foley.

Marx: the commodity with an "average composition of capital"

In volume 2 of his *Theories of Surplus Value*, Marx (1968) deals at great length with Ricardo's chapter "On Value" in the *Principles*. He actually dissects sections I–V and VII of the chapter almost word by word, and expounds his agreements and disagreements with Ricardo's point of view in painstaking detail. This is in marked contrast to his treatment of section VI, "On an Invariable Measure of Value", which is said to deal with "the 'measure of value' but contains nothing important". Marx adds: "The connection between value, its immanent measure – i.e., labour time – and the necessity for an external measure of the values of commodities is not understood or even raised as a problem" (Marx, 1968: 202). Marx goes on to say that "The very opening of this section shows the superficial manner in which it is handled" (202). In short, to Marx the section came as a disappointment and was of no value whatsoever.

What is the reason for this? Marx credited Ricardo with having determined value by labour time and with having thus unravelled the source, and only source, of value. He chastised Ricardo for not having seen that the "law of value" also governs deviations of "prices of production" from labour values in conditions of free competition, due to different proportions of constant and variable capital employed in the production of different commodities, different proportions of fixed and circulating capital, different degrees of durability of the fixed capital items, etc. Closely related to this criticism is the objection that Ricardo did not explain the general rate of profit as the ratio between the sum total of surplus value generated in the system and the sum total of the constant and variable capitals employed in it:

> Instead of *postulating* this *general rate of profit*, Ricardo should rather have examined in how far its existence is in fact consistent with the determination of value by labour-time, and he would have found that instead of being consistent with it, *prima facie*, it *contradicts* it, and that its existence would therefore have to be explained through a number of intermediary stages, a procedure which is very different from merely including it under the law of value. He would then have gained an altogether different insight into the nature of profit ...
>
> Marx, 1968: 174

(Unless otherwise stated, all emphases in quotations are in the original.)

Marx credits himself with having accomplished, "through a number of intermediary stages", what in his view is missing in Ricardo, and why Ricardo therefore could only "smuggle in the *presupposition of a general rate of profit*" (Marx, 1968: 190).

The "procedure" Marx speaks of is, of course, the one in volume III of *Capital*, which leads to the famous problem of the "transformation" of values into prices of production (Marx, 1959: Part II). The upshot of Marx's argument is the contention that the aggregate of surplus values equals the aggregate of profits and the aggregate of values equals the aggregate of production prices. In this context Marx speaks also of the "average commodity" ("Durchschnittsware").[1]

Seen from this perspective, Ricardo's search for an invariable measure of value, conceived of as a single commodity, must indeed have looked strange to Marx. As he argues in volume III of *Capital*, the composition of capital of the economy as a whole has the sought average composition between constant and variable capital, etc., and would therefore be an ideal standard of value in Ricardo's sense. Supposedly this is so because, for the economy as a whole, aggregate surplus value (alias profits) and aggregate variable capital (alias wages) add up to a given magnitude, that is, a magnitude that is independent of it being shared out between workers and capitalists in terms of wages and profits: if one of the two rises (falls), the other one has to fall (rise) by the same amount. The price of the social product therefore need not change, when distribution changes, whereas the prices of single commodities whose production does not exhibit the same average composition of capital *en miniature*, will have to change.

Hence in Marx's view Ricardo was chasing a will-o'-the wisp. If one was interested in studying the dependence of relative prices on the distribution of the product amongst the different claimants, workers and capitalists, this could be done in terms of studying the behaviour of the price of single commodities relative to that of the social product as a whole. The price of the social product is *ex definitione* fixed and equal to its value, whereas the price of the commodity reflects the need to bring about a uniform rate of profit in conditions of free competition.

Marx discusses the dependence of relative prices on income distribution in chapter XI, "Effects of General Wage Fluctuations on Prices of Production", of volume III of *Capital* (Marx, 1959).

To stress again, what has already been said. Marx on the one hand credits Ricardo with having discerned the "law of value":

> Hence the great theoretical satisfaction afforded by these first two chapters [of the *Principles*; the reference is to the chapters "On Value" and "On Rent"]; for they provide with concise brevity a critique of the old, diffuse and meandering political economy, present the whole bourgeois system of economy as subject to *one fundamental law*, and extract the quintessence out of the divergency and diversity of the various phenomena.
>
> Marx, 1968: 169, emphasis added

On the other hand he criticises Ricardo for not having made full and consistent use of the "one fundamental law", the "law of value", with respect to all phenomena that *prima facie* seem to contradict it, but in fact do not. In Marx's words:

> But this theoretical satisfaction afforded by these first two chapters because of their originality, *unity of fundamental approach*, simplicity, concentration, depth, novelty and comprehensiveness, is of necessity lost as the work proceeds.
>
> Marx, 1968: 169, emphasis added

Most importantly, Marx takes issue with Ricardo's view that prices of commodities are not only regulated by the labour-time necessary for their production, but also by some "*other reasons*" (Marx, 1968: 202). This is said to show conclusively that Ricardo had not fully understood the "one fundamental law" whose discovery Marx ascribes to Ricardo and which gives rise to Marx's "great theoretical satisfaction".

Marx's discussion of the dependence of relative normal prices on income distribution in terms of the composite product of the system as a whole is motivated as follows. First, Marx was convinced that he was possessed of a correct theory of the general rate of profit and relative prices based on the "law of value". The systematic deviations of relative prices from relative labour values were thus best analysed in terms of a commodity exhibiting the average composition of capital, that is, the composition of capital of the economy as a whole. But there was a second argument in favour of this approach. Hypothetically changing the distribution of income from a situation, in which (surplus) wages are zero (and profits are at their maximum value), to a situation, in which they exhaust the entire product (and profits vanish), implies that in the second case workers would hypothetically have access not only to what Marx called "wage goods", but also to "luxuries" and investment goods, i.e. commodities they typically cannot afford and which are consumed by the richer strata of society or used to extend the scale of production. Hence, from this vantage point the entire product of the system has, in principle, to be taken as the relevant commodity bundle defining the measure under consideration.

The questions to which we now have to turn are: First, is Marx's confidence in the correctness of his own theory of the general rate of profit and of relative normal prices warranted? Second, is his interpretation of Ricardo faithful to what Ricardo had written? The debate after the publication of volume III of *Capital* has shown that Marx's theory cannot generally be sustained. We may therefore immediately turn to the second question and postpone some remarks on the first one to the section "Sraffa: a tool for the analysis", below. In order to form a judgement on Marx's interpretation of Ricardo, we have to have a closer look at Ricardo's theory and the role the "invariable measure of value" played in it.

Ricardo: "a medium between the extremes"

Since we have discussed in some detail the role of Ricardo's search for an invariable measure of value in his attempt to elaborate "a correct theory" of value and distribution elsewhere (see Kurz and Salvadori, 1993), we can be brief here.

Originally, Ricardo was concerned exclusively with a standard of value which would measure the value of commodities at different times and places, that is, he was interested in intertemporal and interspatial comparisons. In the first two editions of the *Principles*, published in 1817 and 1819, respectively, he maintained that in order to be invariable in value a commodity should require "at all times, and under all circumstances, precisely the same quantity of labour to obtain it" (Ricardo, 1951–1973, *Works* I: 27 n.). Value measured in the invariable standard he called "absolute value".

While already in the first two editions Ricardo showed he was well aware of the fact that the labour embodied rule did not strictly apply as a theory of relative prices, he did not think that this rendered obsolete his original definition of the invariable measure of value. However, in the third edition, published in 1821, he admitted that the same difficulties encountered in determining relative prices carried over to his definition of the essential properties of a correct standard (see Ricardo, 1951–1973, *Works* I: 44–5). Henceforth, he superimposed the problem of measurement with respect to *different* technical environments and the altogether different problem of measurement with respect to the *same* technical environment, but a changing distribution of income.

As Ricardo's attempts at tackling the latter problem shows, his search was essentially a search for the "circumstances which determine the value of commodities" (Ricardo, 1951–1973, *Works* IX: 358), where the term "value" is not used in Marx's sense of labour value, but in the sense of exchange value or "natural price". Ricardo now advocated the view that there are *two circumstances* affecting relative value at any point in time instead of only one: (1) the technical conditions of production, which are reflected in quantities of labour embodied in the different commodities, and (2) the division of the product between wages and profits. Ricardo assured himself of the second circumstance in terms of some simple numerical examples, where he hypothetically varied the wage rate, given the technical conditions of production, and showed that the rate of profits has to vary in the opposite direction, and relative prices typically will change (see, in particular, Ricardo, 1951–1973, *Works* IV: 373–8). He arrived at the following specification of the standard of value he was seeking:

> It is not like Mr. Malthus's measure one of the extremes it is not a commodity produced by labour alone which he proposes, not a commodity whose value consists of profits alone, but one which may fairly be considered as the *medium between these two extremes*, and as agreeing more nearly with the circumstances under which the greater number of commodities are produced than any other which can be proposed.
>
> Ricardo, 1951–1973, *Works* IV: 372, emphasis added

Ricardo was thus concerned with rendering as precise as possible the "medium" under consideration, by analysing carefully what he called "the variety of circumstances under which commodities are actually produced" (Ricardo, 1951–1973, *Works* IV: 368). The upshot of his efforts is reflected in his specification of the production of the various commodities in terms of different proportions of fixed capital (machinery, tools, etc.) and circulating capital, where the latter includes not only raw materials, etc., but also the wages of labour (means of subsistence), different durabilities of fixed capital and different durabilities of circulating capital (see also Sraffa, 1951: xlii). He expressed the differences also in more compact formulas, such as the "proportions in which immediate labour and accumulated labour enter into the different commodities" (Ricardo, 1951–1973, *Works* IV: 379), or the proportions in which "labour and capital" are employed in production. However, he insisted that what matters are the "different set[s] of commodities" of which capital consists in different lines of production (Ricardo, 1951–1973, *Works* IV: 393), and that a scalar representation of any such set involves assessing the various capital goods in terms of their normal prices.

At an earlier time Ricardo had made use of the Smithian concept of the reduction of prices to dated quantities of labour, and had come close to what Paul Samuelson called the "time-phased model of production". In fact, Ricardo had stated in a letter to McCulloch of 13 June 1920 that relative prices will necessarily deviate from relative quantities of labour embodied in the different commodities because of the role of time: "All the exceptions to the general rule [i.e. the labour embodied rule] come under this one of time", and that "there are such a variety of cases in which the time of completing a commodity may differ" (Ricardo, 1951–1973, *Works* VII: 193). This idea reappears in the manuscript on "Absolute Value and Exchangeable Value" of 1823 in the following form: "In this then consists the difficulty of the subject that the circumstances of time for which advances are made are so various" (Ricardo, 1951–1973, *Works* IV: 370). Vladimir K. Dmitriev's conceptualization of Ricardo's idea in terms of price equations of the following type are close:

$$p_i = (1+r)wl_{0i} + (1+r)^2 wl_{1i} + (1+r)^3 wl_{2i} + \ldots (i = 1, 2, \ldots, n),$$

where p_i is the price of the commodity, r the rate of profits, w the wage rate (in terms of the "invariable standard of value"), and l_{ji} are the amounts of labour expended in the production of one unit of the commodity i in period j before the completion of the product at the end of period 0 (see Dmitriev, 1974).

Let us summarize Ricardo's search for a measure of value that is invariant with regard to changes in income distribution (setting aside his different concern with intertemporal and interspatial comparisons). First, as Sraffa stressed, Ricardo's search came indeed close to elaborating a correct theory of value and distribution. Second, Ricardo felt that the measure he was looking for had to be a real "object in nature", that is, a particular commodity that served the purpose under consideration. However, he became increasingly aware of the fact that a single commodity would probably not exhibit the requested properties, and therefore, third, also tinkered with the idea of having a measure composed of several commodities. Yet he did not advocate the idea that the sum total of commodities produced in the system as a whole could serve the purpose. In other words, he did not advocate a measuring device that is similar to the one Marx proposed.

Marx had no access to Ricardo's correspondence in this regard, nor to his unpublished works, especially the draft and unfinished later version of Ricardo's paper "Absolute and Exchangeable Value", composed shortly before Ricardo passed away in late 1823. His reading was confined to the third edition of the *Principles*. Therefore, he could not know the various steps Ricardo took in order to grope towards a correct theory of value and the role the standard of value played in this. Seen against the background of Ricardo's entire writings on the issue at hand, Marx's comments look somewhat one-sided and devoid of a deeper understanding of Ricardo's problem.

Before we turn to Sraffa's contribution, a comment is apposite on some Marxists' preoccupation with the labour theory of value as an allegedly indispensable element of Marxist economics. Duncan Foley is perhaps the most important theorist of our time who has made an attempt to salvage the labour theory of value in terms of a sophisticated re-interpretation of it. Originally, we did not have the intention to enter into a discussion of this vexed issue, but since the editors of this Festschrift have explicitly asked us to comment on it, we do so in all brevity. We are afraid to have to say that we dissent from the view of our friend Duncan, but we are confident that this will not in the least affect our mutual friendship.

Duncan Foley reinterpreted Marx's approach to the problem of the general rate of profit in terms of the so-called "law of value" in such a way that the labour theory of value emerged unscathed; see, in particular, Foley (1982) and Duménil and Foley (2010). This necessitated reformulating some of Marx's concepts and abandoning his distinction between the sphere of values and that of prices. The result was the so-called "new interpretation" or "single system labour theory of value". In our view this new interpretation is difficult to sustain. Whether or not it is a faithful representation of what Marx wrote need not concern us here. Our main difficulty with the "new interpretation" is that it wrongly conveys the impression that the surplus-based approach to the theory of value and distribution of (the classical economists and) Marx stands or falls with the labour theory of value. However, this is not the case. As we have argued above, the labour theory of value had been endorsed by Ricardo as a useful device to ascertain, as best as he could, the general rate of profits in the absence of a consistent theory of value and distribution. And Marx was convinced that he was already possessed of such a theory, centred around the "law of value". He was wrong. Had he been right, all attempts by Marxists to salvage his labour-value-based approach would have been unnecessary and futile.

Those who insist on the importance and in fact indispensability of the labour theory of value typically contend that it is needed in order to demonstrate the "exploitative" nature of profits. We wonder why they are not satisfied with pointing towards the fact that workers do not get the whole net product. What is gained by employing the labour theory of value? As we see it, the crux of the matter *today* is this: when Marx was writing, that is, before marginal productivity theory began to filter into the academic and public discourse, one might still have been content with the observation that positive profits presuppose a positive surplus value (or surplus labour). But once marginalist theorists had argued that profits do not express exploitation but rather the productivity enhancing effects of the employment of capital, an entirely new situation emerged. What if marginal productivity theory happened to be correct? As Paul Samuelson's concept of the "surrogate production function" shows, marginal productivity theory and the labour theory of value are not incompatible with one another, the contrary is true (Samuelson, 1962). Therefore, some modern Marxists' preoccupation with the labour theory of value appears to us to be misguided. What is needed is a demonstration that marginal productivity theory in its various forms cannot be sustained.

In this context it is perhaps useful to draw the attention to the fact that, in a note written as early as 16 January 1946, Sraffa had anticipated *ante litteram* the flaw in Samuelson's argument and also in that of several Marxists, who cling to the labour theory of value:

> The Irony of it is, that if the "Labour Theory of Value" applied exactly throughout, then, and only then, would the "marginal product of capital" theory work!
> It would require that all products had the same org.[anic] comp.[osition]; and that at each value of *r*[rate of interest or profits] each comm.[odity] had an "alternative method", and that the relations within each pair should be the same (i.e. that marg.[inal] prod[uct]s. should be the same; + also the elasticities should be the same); so that, even when the System is switched, and another Org. Comp. came into being, it should be the same for all products. Obviously this would be equivalent to having only one means-product (wheat).
> Then, commodities would always be exchanged at their Values; and their relative Values would not change, even when productivity of labor [sic] increased.[2]

Hence defining profits as surplus value and the net product as value added cannot, by itself, support the claim that profits are based on exploitation: marginal productivity theory has to be refuted.

This was clear to Sraffa, to whose view on the matter we now turn, but it does not seem to be clear to some Marxist economists.

Sraffa: a tool for the analysis

With regard to the Standard commodity, we have to consider three separate issues. There is first the role the Standard commodity plays in *Production of Commodities by Means of Commodities* (Sraffa, 1960) and the echoes of the Ricardian search for an invariable measure of value in it; this was analysed by us a while ago (cf. Kurz and Salvadori, 1993) and only a few remarks are needed here. Second, there is the path Sraffa followed to arrive at such a concept. While we have also dealt with this issue previously (Kurz and Salvadori, 2010), we did not consider the implications of our historical reconstruction for economic analysis. Third, there are the interpretations and speculations concerning the nature and meaning of the Standard commodity published after the publication of Sraffa's book, and how Sraffa responded to some of them.

In *Production of Commodities* Sraffa considers the Standard commodity first and foremost an analytical tool capable of simplifying the study of price changes as income distribution changes. However, a few sections in Part I of *Production of Commodities* would not be necessary for the general argument; no doubt Sraffa included them to pay tribute to Ricardo's search for an "invariable measure of value": we know now when this problem is solvable and when it is not, and what the solution is when there is one. However, it is clear that Sraffa (1960) refers exclusively to that aspect of Ricardo's search which is concerned with the impact of changes in distribution on relative prices, *given the technological environment*.

To be more precise, we have to compare Chapters III and VI of *Production of Commodities*. In Chapter III Sraffa provides a "preliminary survey" on movements of prices connected with movements in income distribution. It is a preliminary survey, since it is the analysis of these movements that can be performed without using the Standard commodity. In Chapter VI, on the other hand, we find the complete analysis. It uses the Standard commodity, which is introduced in Chapter IV and fully analysed in Chapters IV and V. In fact, the results presented in Chapter VI could not have been contained in the "preliminary survey". This is so because it was first necessary to show that

(i) the rate of profits, r, reaches a finite and unique maximum, R, when the wage rate, w, equals zero and the corresponding prices of basic commodities are positive (§§ 39–41);

(ii) R is the lowest positive real number such that the price equations are satisfied with $w = 0$ (§ 42);

(iii) for $0 \leq r \leq R$ the prices of basic commodities in general vary with r but remain positive and finite (§ 39);

(iv) in each system of production there exists a (composite) commodity such that if it is chosen as numéraire, then the wage rate w is a linear function of the profit rate with the form

$$w = \frac{R - r}{R} \ (\S \ 43).$$

In order to demonstrate the above statements Sraffa introduces the *Standard commodity*, the *Standard system* and the *Standard national income* (§ 26 and, in general terms, §§ 33–34). Then he shows that within the Standard system

$$r = R(1 - w) \tag{1}$$

where R is the *Standard ratio*, which coincides with the Maximum rate of profits (§§ 27–30). This relation is then shown to be valid also in the "actual economic system" if the Standard commodity is chosen as numéraire (§ 31). Clearly, the role of the Standard commodity is that of a special numéraire. The theorist chooses the numéraire; it neither depends on "observed facts" nor can it alter the "mathematical properties" of the system under consideration. Finally, it is shown that non-basic products play no role in the construction of the Standard system (§ 35) and that there exists a Standard commodity on the assumption that there is at least one basic commodity (§ 37), and the former is unique (§ 41).

It deserves to be mentioned that these results can also be obtained by using the Perron–Frobenius Theorem (see Kurz and Salvadori, 1995). In fact, Sraffa's demonstration of the existence and uniqueness of the Standard commodity can be considered a (not fully complete) proof of this theorem. Yet Sraffa does even better by simultaneously providing an economic rationale of the analytical tools he uses. It should be clear now that in *Production of Commodities* the Standard commodity is first and foremost an analytical tool that is useful in the study of price changes as income distribution changes (see Kurz and Salvadori, 1987, 1993).

How did Sraffa arrive at this analysis? The Standard commodity's characteristic feature was foreshadowed in several earlier notes and papers, some already written in the first of the periods into which his activity can be divided, and which extended from 1927 to 1931, after which he had to leave the matter in order to focus his attention on editing the works and correspondence of David Ricardo. For example, in a paper he had begun to write in February 1931, he contemplated the case in which "the value of total capital in terms of total goods produced cannot vary [as income distribution changes], since the goods are composed exactly in the same proportions as the capitals which have produced them" (Sraffa Papers, D3/12/7: 157(3)). He was sure that in any real economy this condition was never actually met, but that it might perhaps be approximately true. Some 12 years later, in a note composed a few weeks before the discovery of the Standard commodity, he clarified that his earlier proposition was based on the "statistical compensation of large numbers" (D3/12/35: 28). Thereafter, he called the assumption that the value of social capital relative to the social product does not change with a change in distribution "My Hypothesis" or simply "Hypothesis".

He had encountered a similar hypothesis in Ricardo, and then in Marx at the beginning of the 1940s, if not earlier, who had characterized a given system of production in terms of a given "organic composition of capital", that is, the ratio of the labour embodied in the means of production and of living labour expended during a year. The inverse of the organic composition gave the maximum rate of profits compatible with the system. Sraffa had understood that no actual system could ever be expected to satisfy the hypothesis. He therefore had to construct an artificial system that did so. This artificial system did, however, have to possess all the properties of that part of the actual system out of which it was constructed (that is, the set of "basic equations"), and at the same time offer a straightforward expression of one these properties: the inverse relation between the actual rate of profits and the share of wages.

This Sraffa accomplished in January 1944 in terms of the Standard system and Standard commodity in a set of notes interestingly titled "Hypothesis" (see D3/12/36: 61–85). This accomplishment was premised on two decisions. First, Sraffa abandoned the tradition to treat wages as paid *ante factum* and decided to assume *post factum* payment. Second, once this step was taken, the way was open to the distinction between basic and non-basic commodities, which replaced the old classical distinction between necessities and luxuries. The upshot of these developments was the establishment of a linear relationship between the rate of profits, r, and proportional wages, w, that is equation (1), in which R is now the *Standard ratio* or *Maximum rate of profits*, and w is the share of wages in national income.

Since at least 1942, Sraffa knew that for a system of k commodities there existed k solutions for the maximum rate of profits, the set of prices and the multipliers of the Standard system. Sraffa in fact, in 1944, considered each eigenvector (of the input matrix of the means of production) as a "Standard commodity" and indicated it with letter U (U', U'', ...) (see, for instance, D3/12/40: 3–18). We know, now, that only one real solution has non-negative prices and rate of profit, provided the given wage rate is low enough. This Sraffa did not know at the time, and actually he was looking for a solution of this problem of multiplicity. After a few attempts by manipulating the equations (always prompted by Besicovitch's criticisms) the solution was found by specifying more carefully the desired properties of the sought standard. This Sraffa eventually did by considering the *unique* "Standard commodity"[3] with non-negative multipliers (all positive for processes producing basics and zero for the others).

Sraffa's experience in this period (and also learning from his own mistakes) led him to review the difficulties that a concept like the Standard commodity could meet. In fact, Section 32 of his 1960 book contains an interesting caveat which it is apposite to quote in full.

[I]f in the actual system (... with R = 20%) the wage is fixed in terms of the Standard net product, to $w = 3/4$ there will correspond $r = 5\%$. But while the share of wages will be equal in value to $3/4$ of the Standard national income, it does not follow that the share of profits will be equivalent to the remaining 1/4 of the Standard income. The share of profits will consist of whatever is left of the *actual* national income after deducting from it the equivalent of 1/4 of the *Standard* national income for wages.

(Sraffa's emphases)

Therefore, the fact that "[t]he rate of profits *in the Standard system* ... appears as a ratio between quantities of commodities irrespective of their prices" (§ 29, emphasis added) cannot be generalized to the actual system *even* if the Standard commodity is the numéraire. This remark contained in section 32 constitutes also an *ante litteram* criticism of the interpretation of the Standard commodity as a *physical* or *corn analogue.*[4] In the "corn model", corn is both the only commodity consumed by workers and the only basic commodity.[5] Therefore, to give the real wage rate in terms of corn from outside the system is quite natural, whereas to give the real wage rate in terms of the Standard commodity requires one to know the value of the commodities which constitute the real wage rate, as an aggregate, in terms of the Standard commodity. Moreover, even if the real net national income is given, as in Sraffa's thought experiment, its value in terms of the Standard commodity is variable; therefore to determine the point on the linear wage–profit relationship corresponding to a given share of wages requires knowledge of the function relating the value of net national income in terms of the Standard commodity to the rate of profits.

Sraffa also dealt with this problem after the publication of his book in relation to a review of the book published by Stephen Bodington under the pseudonym "John Eaton" in *Società* (Eaton, 1960). Sraffa was "very pleased with this review ... because it presents it [the main idea of the book] in such an interesting way". Sraffa added:

> I think, however, that Eaton has overlooked ~~the fact~~ that if we want to follow in Marx's footsteps and pass from values to prices of production and from rate of surplus value to rate of profits, the Standard System is a necessary adjunct: for that passage implies going through certain averages and if these are calculated without weights (or with the weights of the real system), a result which is only approximately numerically correct is obtained. If an exact result is wanted ~~the weights (i.e.~~ the proportions ~~, or q numbers)~~ of the St. Syst. of eq's q's must be applied as weights. – This is not stated explicitly in the book, but is implied.

(D3/12/111: 118)[6]

Sraffa then composed a manuscript titled "Risposta a Eaton [Reply to Eaton]" (D3/12/111: 127–130), in which he investigated how the general rate of profits can be an exact weighted average of the different industries' rates of profit, calculated for the different industries on the basis of the labour values of the products and the role that the Standard commodity may play in it.[7] Sraffa at around the same time spelled out his reading of Marx's "value hypothesis":

The propositions of M. are based on the assumption that the comp. of any large aggr. of commodities, e.g. wages, profits, const. cap., consists of a random selection, so that the ratio between their aggr. values (rate of s.v., rate of p.) is approx. the same whether measured at 'values' or at the p. of prod. corresp. to any rate of s.v.

This is obviously true, and one could leave it at that, if it were not for the tiresome objector, who relies on hypothetical deviations … – It is clear that M's proportions are not intended to deal with such deviations. They are based on the assumption (justified in general) that the aggregates are of some average composition.

In order to be exactly true, the proportions would have to be the Standard commodity's proportions. Sraffa added: "i.e. Marx *assumes* that wages and profits consist *approximately* of quantities of st. com" (D3/12/111: 141).[8]

Concluding remarks

In this chapter we have dealt with the *"vexata questio* of value" as analysed by David Ricardo, Karl Marx and Piero Sraffa, respectively. Special emphasis has been placed on the role of an "invariable measure of value" in Ricardo and Marx's lack of understanding of the concept. We corroborate Sraffa's interpretation that Ricardo's search for such a measure "came close to identifying the problem of a measure of value with that of the law of value". Marx's lack of understanding is rooted in his conviction that a correct theory of the general rate of profit and prices of production derives from the "law of value", that is, the view that (abstract) labour is the only source of value. However, Marx's "transformation" of the rate of surplus value into the rate of profit, and of labour values into production prices cannot generally be sustained. Sraffa solved the problem of value within the classical surplus-based framework for good and as an integral part of his analysis he also solved the Ricardian problem of a measure of value that is invariant with regard to changes in income distribution. He accomplished this latter task in terms of the construction of the "Standard system" and "Standard commodity". Interestingly, he also showed "that if we want to follow in Marx's footsteps" and pass from values to prices, etc., "the Standard System is a necessary adjunct: for that passage implies going through certain averages and if these are calculated without weights (or with the weights of the real system), a result which is only approximately numerically correct is obtained". Marx was therefore wrong in assuming that in terms of the "average commodity", that is, by using "the weights of the real system", he could accomplish the task.

Acknowledgements

We are grateful to Armon Rezai and an anonymous referee for valuable comments on an earlier draft of our chapter. All errors and misinterpretations are, of course, our responsibility.

Notes

1 It should be mentioned that in the drafts to volume III of *Capital* composed between 1864 and 1881 as well as in volume I of *Capital* Marx always started from this aggregate or average commodity. In volume III it is the commodity that yields the average profit. We are grateful to Carl-Erich Vollgraf, who works on the MEGA editorial project, for this information.
2 Sraffa Papers D3/12/16: 34; Sraffa's emphases. The reference is to Sraffa's papers kept at Trinity College Library, Cambridge (UK), as they were catalogued by Jonathan Smith, archivist.
3 The inverted commas are required since we are using the concept Sraffa used at the time and not the one used in the published book. In 1944 a "Standard commodity" was any composite commodity made up in proportion to an eigenvector; in 1960, the "Standard commodity'" is unique, since it is the composite commodity made up in proportion to the unique non-negative eigenvector normalized by the condition that the direct and indirect labour required to produce them equals unity.
4 See, for instance, Medio (1972), Eatwell (1975), Broome (1977), Bacha, Carneiro and Taylor (1977). For a position that is similar to ours, see Roncaglia (1978).
5 In appendix D of his book Sraffa points out: "It should perhaps be stated that it was only when the Standard *system* and the distinction between basics and non-basics had emerged in the course of the present investigation that the [corn model] interpretation of Ricardo's theory suggested itself as a natural consequence" (Sraffa, 1960: 93; emphasis added). This must certainly not be taken to support the physical analogue interpretation of the Standard *commodity*. In fact, in the paragraph preceding the one just quoted, Sraffa stresses that "in the terms adopted [in Sraffa (1960)] … corn is the sole 'basic product' in the economy" (ibid.) considered by Ricardo in the *Essay on Profits*.
6 The strikethroughs are Sraffa's.
7 The point was then established, with some slight differences also in the secondary literature; see Meek (1961), Medio (1972) and Eatwell (1975).
8 Sraffa's emphases. (In the original the first word is double underlined. There are two lines in the margin of the passage.) For a careful discussion of Sraffa's response to and correspondence with Bodington, see Gehrke (2007).

References

Bacha, E., Carneiro, D., and Taylor, L. (1977) Sraffa and classical economics: fundamental equilibrium relationships, *Metroeconomica*, 29: 39–53.

Broome, J. (1977) Sraffa's Standard commodity, *Australian Economic Papers*, 16: 231–236.

Dmitriev, V.K. (1974) *Economic Essays on Value, Competition and Utility*, English translation of a collection of Dmitriev's essays published in 1904 in Russian, D.M. Nuti (Ed.). Cambridge: Cambridge University Press. (Dmitriev's essay on Ricardo's theory of value was originally published in 1898.)

Duménil, G., and Foley, D. (2010) The Marxian transformation problem. *The New Palgrave*, 2nd ed., volume 5. London: Macmillan, pp. 405–412.

Eaton, J. (1960) Il modello di Sraffa e la teoria del valore-lavoro, *Società*, 16(5).

Eatwell, J.L. (1975) Mr. Sraffa's Standard commodity and the rate of exploitation, *The Quarterly Journal of Economics*, 89: 543–555.

Foley, D. (1982) The value of money, the value of labour power and the Marxian transformation problem, *Review of Radical Political Economics*, 14: 37–47.

Foley, D. (1986) *Understanding Capital: Marx's Economic Theory*. Cambridge, MA: Harvard University Press.

Foley, D. (2000) Recent developments in the labor theory of value, *Review of Radical Political Economy*, 32: 1–39.

Foley, D. (2006) *Adam's Fallacy: A Guide to Economic Theory*. Cambridge, MA: Harvard University Press.

Gehrke, C. (2007) Sraffa's correspondence relating to the publication of *Production of Commodities by Means of Commodities*: Notes on some selected material. Paper presented at the Annual ESHET Conference 2007 in Strasbourg, Graz, mimeo.

Kurz, H.D., and Salvadori, N. (1987) Burmeister on Sraffa and the labor theory of value: a comment, *Journal of Political Economy*, 95: 870–881.

Kurz, H.D., and Salvadori, N. (1993) The "Standard commodity" and Ricardo's search for an "invariable measure of value". In: M. Baranzini and G.C. Harcourt (Eds), *The Dynamics of the Wealth of Nations. Growth, Distribution and Structural Change. Essays in Honour of Luigi Pasinetti*. London: Macmillan, pp. 95–123.

Kurz, H.D., and Salvadori, N. (1995) *Theory of Production. A Long-Period Analysis*. Cambridge: Cambridge University Press.

Kurz, H.D., and Salvadori, N. (2010) Sraffa and the labour theory of value: a few observations. In: J. Vint, J.S. Metcalfe, H.D. Kurz, N. Salvadori and P. Samuelson (Eds), *Economic Theory and Economic Thought. Festschrift in Honour of Ian Steedman*. London: Routledge, pp. 187–213.

Marx, K. (1959) *Capital*, vol. III. Moscow: Progress Publishers.

Marx, K. (1968) *Theories of Surplus Value*, part 2. Moscow: Progress Publishers.

Medio, A. (1972) Profits and surplus-value: appearance and reality in capitalist production. In: E.K. Hunt and J.G. Schwartz (Eds.), *A Critique of Economic Theory: Selected Readings*, Harmondsworth: Penguin, pp. 312–346.

Meek, R.L. (1961) Mr. Sraffa's rehabilitation of classical economics, *Scottish Journal of Political Economy*, 8: 119–136.

Ricardo, D. (1951–1973) *The Works and Correspondence of David Ricardo*. Edited by P. Sraffa with the collaboration of M.H. Dobb, 11 vols. Cambridge: Cambridge University Press.

Roncaglia, A. (1978) *Sraffa and the Theory of Prices*. Translated by J. A. Kregel. London: Wiley.

Samuelson, P.A. (1962) Parable and realism in capital theory: the surrogate production function, *Review of Economic Studies*, 29: 193–206.

Sraffa, P. (1951) Introduction. In: D. Ricardo (1951–1973), Vol. I.

Sraffa, P. (1960) *Production of Commodities by Means of Commodities*. Cambridge: Cambridge University Press.

Steedman, I. (1977) *Marx after Sraffa*. London: New Left Books.

13 Duncan Foley's circuit of capital model for an open economy

Martín Abeles

Introduction

In Volume II of *Capital* Karl Marx displays his well-known schemes of reproduction with the purpose of examining the proportions in which capital needs to be allocated between means of production and means of consumption in order to sustain a consistent path of economic growth – in Marx's terminology, *expanded reproduction*. In Volume II of *Capital* Marx also addresses the issue of effective demand and realization in a growing capitalist economy. Following Duncan Foley (1982, 1983, 1986a,b), the unifying concept underlying Marx's schemes of reproduction and his treatment of aggregate demand and the issue of realization is given by the *circuit of capital*, a stock-flow consistent representation of the capitalist system as an ever-expanding circular flow of commodities and money.

Drawing on Marx's (1893) schemes of reproduction, Foley's seminal circuit of capital model comprises a versatile analytical tool for the analysis of growth, finance and realization in capitalist economies. The central model, presented in a closed economy setting with no government, portrays economic growth (expanded reproduction) as the product of the capitalization (reinvestment) of a share of the surplus value generated in the process of capitalist production and realized in the marketplace. This surplus – the basis and ultimate threshold of expanded reproduction – need not be limited by domestic capital's capacity to extract surplus value as in the closed economy setting, but may originate in a foreign country and be channeled into the domestic economy as foreign credit. Capital inflows, in the form of external loans or direct investment, may therefore enhance a given economy's growth potential. But, of course, the reverse is also true – domestically generated surplus need not be reinvested at its source, but may finance the process of expanded reproduction elsewhere.

In this chapter I introduce economic transactions with the rest of the world into Foley's circuit of capital model, and re-examine the capitalist limits to growth and realization when the current and capital accounts of the balance of payments are taken into account.[1]

Due to the prevalence of neoclassical economics, such open economy considerations have been practically absent from standard growth theory. The neoclassical postulation of long-term equilibrium in the current account of the balance of payments – brought about by the assumption of full employment and concomitant price adjustment mechanisms – makes any reference to international transactions somewhat superfluous in connection with long-term growth (Obstfeld and Rogoff, 1996). As opposed to neoclassical economics, which conceives of trade imbalances as disequilibrium or temporary phenomena, in this chapter I do not assume that imports and exports tend to balance in the long run, and therefore allow for continuing net international debtor or creditor positions to persist, as in Shaikh (1980). Indeed, the main thrust of the circuit of capital approach when applied to the context of an open economy is related to the possibility of representing different growth and financial regimes, where persistent net capital inflows or outflows combine with domestic factors in the determination of a given economy's growth path.[2]

The current chapter is organized as follows. In the next section I present a baseline model for a pure private sector closed economy. The following section introduces effective demand and credit into the model. I next present a baseline model for an open economy and runs through alternative closures. Then I address the issue of effective demand and realization within the open economy setting. The final section offers some conclusions.

The baseline model: the circuit of capital model in a closed economy[3]

For precision's sake, before introducing the circuit of capital model, Marx's distinction between expanded reproduction and accumulation needs to be clarified. When the reinvestment of surplus value does not affect the inner structure of capital, i.e. the composition of capital and/or the rate of surplus value, Marx talks of expanded reproduction. This is a purely analytical situation, since the reinvestment of surplus value normally involves the qualitative transformation of production processes. When the reinvestment of surplus value does affect the scale and methods of production and/or the organization (e.g. centralization) of capital, thus modifying the above-mentioned parameters, Marx talks of accumulation. Hence, in dealing with expanded reproduction we abstract from the qualitative changes associated with the process of accumulation, and assume the main parameters of capitalist production remain unaffected.

The process of capitalist production, from the creation to the realization of value and surplus value takes time. The production process proper (*material* transformation in Marx's terminology) requires a certain period of time between the moment capital is invested and the materialization of finished commodities. This period comprises the production lag Tp. The value incorporated in the new commodities is not automatically realized (*formal* transformation). The time taken to sell the commodities comprises the realization lag Tr. The reinvestment of the resulting proceeds (initial capital outlays plus profits) also takes a period of time, the finance lag Tf.

Given these time lags, a certain stock of capital must necessarily be tied up to the circuit of capital at any moment in time for capitalist production to proceed uninterruptedly. Productive capital must be tied up (in the form of machinery, material inputs, etc.) between the moment capital is invested and the materialization of finished commodities for sale. Commercial capital must be tied up (in the form of unsold finished products) between the moment finished commodities materialize and the time their value is realized in the marketplace. Finally, liquid or financial capital must be tied up (in the form of money or any other liquid asset) between the moment of realization and the recommittal of the realized flow of value to production.

Under this simplified model the circuit of capital consists of three flows of value: the value of capital outlays $C(t)$; the value of finished commodities $P(t)$, valued at their *cost price* (Marx, 1893, chapter 1);[4] and the total value of commodities realized through sales $S(t)$, which includes surplus value; and of three stocks: productive capital $N(t)$, commercial capital $X(t)$ and financial capital $F(t)$. The size of the different flows of value will in turn depend on five parameters: the markup on costs q, which ultimately depends on the rate of surplus value and the composition of capital;[5] the capitalization or "retention" rate p, which denotes the proportion of surplus value recommitted to the circuit of capital after realization;[6] and the production, realization and finance time lags, Tp, Tr and Tf, respectively.

The equations in the model are constructed by complying with conventional accounting criteria (stock-flow consistency) and the assumptions involving the various time lags. Accordingly, the value of finished commodities at time t, $P(t)$ must be equal to the flow of capital outlays Tp periods earlier; whereas the flow of sales at time t, $S(t)$ must be equal to the flow of finished commodities Tr periods earlier plus corresponding profits, indicated by the markup on costs:

$$P(t) = C(t - Tp) \tag{1}$$

$$S(t) = (1 + q)P(t - Tr) \tag{2}$$

As in Foley (1986a), it seems convenient to divide the flow of sales into production costs and surplus value, $S'(t)$ and $S''(t)$, respectively:

$$S'(t) = P(t - Tr) = C(t - Tp - Tr) = S(t)/(1 + q) \tag{3}$$

$$S''(t) = qP(t - Tr) = q\,C(t - Tp - Tr) = qS(t)/(1 + q) \tag{4}$$

With the exception of the opening (say "primitive") capital outlay $C(0)$, subsequent investment must be financed entirely from past sales:[7]

$$C(t) = S'(t - Tf) + p\,S''(t - Tf) = (1 + pq)C(t - Tp - Tr - Tf) \tag{5}$$

where $S''(t - Tf)$ represents the amount of surplus value potentially available for reinvestment at time t, and p the capitalization rate, which determines the amount of surplus value actually invested in time t.

Changes in stocks will also depend on conventional accounting rules. The stock of productive capital $N(t)$ will increase as capital is invested, and decrease as finished commodities materialize. The stock of commercial capital $X(t)$ will increase as finished commodities come about, and decrease as their value is realized through sales. The stock of financial capital will increase as the value of finished commodities is realized, and decrease as capitalists reinvest it, it will also decrease due to capitalist household consumption:

$$dN(t)/dt = C(t) - P(t) \tag{6}$$

$$dX(t)/dt = P(t) - S'(t) \tag{7}$$

$$dF(t)/dt = S(t) - C(t) - Cons_K(t) \tag{8}$$

where $Cons_K(t)$ stands for capitalist consumption, which for ease of exposition is assumed to occur with the same finance time lag Tf:[8]

$$Cons_K(t) = (1 - p) S''(t - Tf) \tag{9}$$

In order to close this baseline model we assume steady-state growth, i.e. that all the flows and stocks grow at the same exponential rate g. Thus:

$$C(t) = C(0)e^{gt} \tag{10}$$

Given equation (10), it is possible to rewrite equation (5) as follows:

$$C(0)e^{gt} = (1 + pq) C(0)e^{g(t - Tp - Tr - Tf)} \tag{11}$$

Equation (11) can in turn be solved for g dividing through by $C(0)$ and taking natural logs:

$$g = \frac{\ln(1 + p \cdot q)}{(Tp + Tr + Tf)} \tag{12}$$

From equation (12) it follows that the economy's rate of expansion depends positively on the markup coefficient q and the capitalization rate p, and negatively on the length of the different time lags involved in the overall circuit of capital – an essential proposition of classical political economy common to Adam Smith, David Ricardo and Karl Marx.[9]

Aggregate demand and expanded reproduction: the role of credit

The baseline model presented above deals only with the "supply side" of the capitalist economy; i.e. it assumes away the problem of realization. Interestingly, even under these limited conditions it can be demonstrated that, in steady-state growth, aggregate demand will inescapably tend to fall short of aggregate supply. As will be demonstrated shortly, the inadequacy of aggregate demand under this model is due to the existence of a finance lag, indicated by Tf (Foley, 1982, 1983). So long as capital outlays are financed entirely from past sales, the working of the finance lag Tf implies that aggregate demand at any given moment will be equal to the value of commodities realized at a previous moment in time, at which in a growing system aggregate output must have been (by construction) smaller. In order to deal with the issue of realization we must explicitly introduce aggregate demand into the circuit of capital model.

Demand for finished commodities can be classified into two main categories: means of production and means of consumption.[10] Let us assume that there is no time delay in workers spending their wages (in means of consumption), whereas capitalist households' consumption takes some time to occur, say a time lag equal to T_f; for simplicity, the same interval it takes financial capital to be recommitted to production, as in equation (9) above. Aggregate demand AD for produced commodities will thus be determined by current capital outlays, which include expenditures on both constant and variable capital (workers consumption), and capitalist households' demand for consumption goods:

$$AD(t) = C(t) + Cons_K(t) \tag{13}$$

Aggregate supply AS is in turn determined by the availability of commodities for sale, hence:

$$AS(t) = S(t) \tag{14}$$

From equations (13), (3), (4), (5) and (9), it is possible to re-express aggregate demand AD as:

$$AD(t) = S(t - T_f) = S(t)e^{-gTf} \tag{15}$$

From equations (14) and (15), the macroeconomic discrepancy between aggregate demand AD and aggregate supply AS becomes apparent and may be represented by the ratio of former to the latter:

$$AD(t)/AS(t) = e^{-gTf} < 1 \tag{16}$$

Equation (16) reveals the existence of an inherent realization gap; a persistent shortfall of aggregate demand $AD(t)$ vis-à-vis aggregate supply $AS(t)$ over time. Note that the realization gap would be nil only if $Tf = 0$,[11] or under *simple reproduction* $(g = 0)$.[12]

To cope with this seeming "deficiency" in the system – its ineffectiveness in generating sufficient aggregate demand in order to realize aggregate output – the source of funds to finance capital outlays ought not to depend exclusively on past sales. In the context of steady-state growth,[13] it is the introduction of credit that can close the realization gap by allowing for investment to be financed not only by past sales ("internal" funds) but also through borrowing ("external" funds).[14]

A financial sector may thus be introduced, which "mobilizes" idle financial or liquid reserves.[15] First and foremost, as shown in equation (17), with the introduction of a financial sector, capital outlays may be now financed by past sales plus the contraction of new debt or borrowing $B(t)$:

$$C(t) = S'(t - Tf) + p\,S''(t - Tf) + B(t) \tag{17}$$

Second, the macroeconomic equilibrium condition, that aggregate demand $AD(t)$ equals aggregate supply $AS(t)$, needs to be introduced:

$$AD(t) = AS(t) \tag{18}$$

Finally, the stock of outstanding private debt, $L(t)$ should be explicitly taken into account:

$$dL(t)/dt = B(t) \tag{19}$$

To solve for g, assume (for ease of exposition) that there is no time delay in capitalist consumption, as shown in equation (20):

$$Cons_K(t) = (1 - p)\,S''(t) \tag{20}$$

Aggregate demand therefore consists of capital outlays plus capitalist consumption, which as opposed to the baseline model given in the previous section is assumed to occur instantaneously:[16]

$$AD(t) = C(t) + Cons_K(t) \tag{21}$$

Under this setting, with binding macroeconomic equilibrium between aggregate demand and supply, the growth rate g and the "leverage" ratio $z = B/C$ (the proportion of investment which needs to be funded "externally" for aggregate demand to match aggregate supply) will be determined endogenously:

$$g = \frac{\ln(1 + p \cdot q)}{Tp + Tr} \tag{22}$$

$$z = 1 - e^{-gTf} \tag{23}$$

Hence, as in the baseline model, the growth rate is directly related to the markup coefficient q and the capitalization rate p, and inversely related to the production and realization lags Tp and Tr. Notice, however, that the finance lag Tf no longer restrains the growth rate. This is due to the fact that under the current setup capitalist firms borrow their idle liquid holdings from each other, channeling them back into the circuit of capital.[17] The introduction of credit not only closes the realization gap, but speeds up economic growth as it removes the delay imposed by the finance lag.[18]

This expanded version of the baseline model, even if it incorporates aggregate demand, implicitly asserts that the entire stock of idle reserves accumulated in the course of capitalist production will actually *be* borrowed and re-channeled back into the circuit of capital. This is a world that resembles the operation of Say's law – where it is assumed that the *potential* demand for idle liquid reserves becomes actual – rather than a world inherently exposed to the possibility of a realization shortfall (Kenway, 1980).[19] The following subsection introduces effective demand proper.

Effective demand and accumulation

As argued above, the expanded version of the baseline model portrays a "classical" picture,[20] where the entire stock of idle liquid reserves is recycled via borrowing to generate a corresponding level of investment, so that the value of the entire product is actually realized. An alternative, Keynesian closure may be laid out as well, in which the willingness of capitalist firms to borrow (and invest) idle financial (liquid) capital is not taken for granted.

In a Keynesian representation of the circuit of capital, in which the world is characterized by ungrounded expectations, the growth rate of capital g at any given point in time must consist of an exogenous variable, determined by capitalists' willingness to invest ("animal spirits"). Of course, given long-term expectations, some functional relationships may still hold in the shorter run, e.g. regarding capacity utilization, current profitability, interest rates, financial constraints and so forth. To keep things simple, I stick to the assumption that investment is entirely exogenous.

In order to introduce autonomous investment, the model needs to be slightly modified. The steady-state growth condition no longer applies as such, since g is now an exogenous variable. This leaves us with an overdetermined system. In order to attain a well-determined system, one of the previously exogenous parameters must become endogenous. From a Keynesian perspective two possibilities make more sense, Tr or Tf. The former (the realization lag) represents the willingness to acquire final goods; the latter (the finance lag), the willingness to hang on to or dispose of liquid assets, i.e. "liquidity preference". Another possibility is to make the production lag Tp endogenous. In actual fact Tp may be interpreted as an indicator of capacity utilization (a higher Tp meaning lower capacity utilization, and vice versa).

Let us first assume that the realization lag Tr is the endogenous variable. The only difference with the expanded version of the baseline model presented above is that g is now exogenous and Tr is endogenous. The finance lag Tf and the production lag Tp continue to be exogenous parameters. Capitalist consumption is still assumed to occur instantaneously. In order for aggregate supply and demand to be equal, from equations (5) through (9) we still obtain equation (22), which now gives rise to:

$$Tr = \frac{\ln\left[(1+p\cdot q)\cdot e^{-g\cdot Tp}\right]}{g} \tag{24}$$

Equation (24) denotes the *precedence* of autonomous (exogenously determined) investment with regard to the level of aggregate demand (represented by the realization lag Tr) and final output. A high value for Tr here stands for effective demand "sluggishness", and vice versa. Hence, the larger the investment drive, the shorter the realization lag, as depicted by inverse relation between investment (represented by the rate of growth of capital outlays g) and effective demand in (24). In short, effective demand and hence realization ultimately depend on capitalists' willingness to invest, and consequently also on their willingness to borrow the necessary funds, as indicated by the inverse relation between realization and the "leverage" ratio z, indicated by equation (23).

Let us now assume that the finance lag Tf (liquidity preference) is the endogenous variable.[21] An increase in Tf indicates higher liquidity preference, i.e. a lower willingness to exchange liquid assets for actual capital goods, and vice versa. The growth rate of capital outlays g is still exogenous and both Tr and Tp are assumed to be exogenous. In this case we may derive Tf from (23):

$$Tf = \frac{\ln\left[1/(1-z)\right]}{g} \tag{25}$$

where again $z = B(t)/C(t)$. What comes to light here is the inverse relation between investment and liquidity preference. As shown in equation (25), an increase in investment plans will force capitalists to reduce their financial holdings (i.e. to recommit their retained profits to production) more rapidly, in order to meet the financial requirements of their investment plans.[22]

In short, the circuit of capital model can accommodate a stock-flow consistent Keynesian picture where autonomous investment plans determine aggregate demand's growth path, while output and financial positions accommodate.

The circuit of capital in an open economy

The inclusion of transactions with the rest of the world into the circuit of capital model involves several modifications. The main difference vis-à-vis the closed economy model presented above is with regard to capital outlays $C(t)$. It is now possible that an economy invests additional funds (foreign borrowing intended to finance the purchase of imported capital goods) over and above the surplus generated within the domestic circuit of capital. Exports in turn tend to reduce the surplus potentially available for reinvestment; although the foreign-currency proceeds derived from holding foreign assets may comprise an additional source of reinvestable funds.

The main difference with the closed economy version of the circuit of capital model emerges in equation (5), the capital outlays equation. Capital outlays will now be financed by the recovery of initial investment, $S'(t)$, a share p of the surplus value generated Tf periods earlier (net of interest payments on foreign debt), and a share p' of foreign borrowing B^F:

$$C(t) = S'(t - Tf) + p[S''(t - f) - p'er\, i^F L^F(t)] + p'er\, B^F(t) \tag{26}$$

where er stands for the exchange rate (local currency per unit of foreign currency) and i^F for the interest rate on outstanding foreign liabilities $L^F(t)$.[23]

The parameter $p'(0 < p' < 1)$ in equation (26) indicates the extent to which foreign borrowing $B^F(t)$ is *capitalized*, i.e. allocated to the actual expansion of the capital stock. The rest of foreign borrowing, equivalent to a proportion $(1 - p')$ of B^F, finances the consumption of imported goods.

Under this open economy setting, investment need not be financed exclusively by the capitalization of domestically generated surplus value. Domestic capital may now resort to foreign borrowing B^F as an additional source of finance, which is equivalent to the import surplus, as shown in equation (27), where $M(t)$ and $E(t)$ stand for imports and exports at time t, respectively:

$$B^F(t) = M(t) - E(t) \tag{27}$$

Notice finally that equation (26), where i^F stands for the interest rate on foreign loans and $L^F(t)$ for the stock of foreign liabilities, acknowledges that domestic capital pays interest on its foreign debt. The availability of internal funds for reinvestment is hence determined by past profits *net* of interest payments on foreign liabilities.[24]

The economy's net international investment position need not be that of a debtor, as implied above. Net capital outflows may prevail as well, resulting in a net creditor position, where $B^F < 0$ and $L^F < 0$. On the one hand, as reflected in equation (26), this tends to reduce capital outlays (investment), as capital is sent (lent) abroad; on the other hand, it tends to increase domestic capital's sources of funds, as interest accrues on foreign assets.

Before solving and interpreting the baseline model for an open economy, a few more definitions may appear helpful. Imports depend on capital outlays alone, as shown in equation (28) below, where m represents the imports coefficient $(0 < m < 1)$:

$$M(t) = mC(t)/er \tag{28}$$

Exports in turn consist of a fixed proportion of past sales, as shown in equation (29), where x denotes the exports coefficient $(0 < x < 1)$.[25]

$$E(t) = xS(t - Tf)/er \tag{29}$$

This is the "endogenous exports" version of the open economy circuit of capital model. An alternative specification of the model is presented below, where exports grow at some given growth rate g_x (the "exogenous exports" version).

Finally, the trade balance $TB(t)$ and the current account $CA(t)$ of the balance of payments may be expressed as:[26]

$$TB(t) = E(t) - M(t) = -B^F(t) \tag{30}$$

$$CA(t) = TB(t) - i^F L^F(t) = -B^F(t) - i^F L^F(t) \tag{31}$$

Omitting for the moment international reserves, the capital account $KA(t)$ and the current account $CA(t)$ of the balance of payments must (by definition) add up to zero. Hence:

$$KA(t) = -CA(t) = B^F(t) + i^F L^F(t) \tag{32}$$

As shown in equation (33), the capital account KA reflects the progress of foreign liabilities, determined by the current account of the balance of payments:

$$dL^F(t)/dt = B^F(t) + i^F L^F(t) \tag{33}$$

Endogenous exports

As in the closed economy settings, we may solve the open economy system for its steady-state growth rate g:

$$g = \frac{\ln\left\{1 + p \cdot q - p' \cdot x \cdot (1+q)/1 - p' \cdot m + p' \cdot p \cdot i^F \cdot l^F\right\}}{Tp + Tr + Tf} \tag{34}$$

where l^F stands for the foreign debt to capital outlays ratio:

$$l^F = \frac{L^F(t) \cdot er}{C(t)} \tag{35}$$

The positive relation between growth and the markup and capitalization rates, on one hand, and the inverse relation between growth and the turnover rates, on the other, show up again in equation (34), as in the closed economy version of the circuit of capital model. Most interestingly, equation (34) reveals that *ceteris paribus* an increase in imports (indicated by the imports coefficient m) should foster growth, and vice versa; while an increase in exports (indicated by the exports coefficient x) should slow down growth, and vice versa. In short, equation (34) provides a preliminary indication of the above-mentioned positive (negative) relation between growth and trade deficits (surpluses).

The foreign debt to capital outlays ratio l^F may be positive or negative, depending on the values assumed by the various parameters. That is to say, the economy in question may bear a net international debtor or creditor position:

$$l^F = \frac{m - x \cdot (1+q) \cdot e^{-g \cdot (Tp+Tr+Tf)}}{g - i^F} \tag{36}$$

In the case of a net international debtor position, i.e. when $l^F > 0$, a higher interest rate on outstanding foreign debt i^F, or a higher exchange rate er, would tend to decelerate growth, as verified in equation (34), since a higher debt burden of international debt reduces the net surplus available for reinvestment – a situation analogous to a reduction in "profits of enterprise" (see note 25). Conversely, a lower interest rate on outstanding foreign debt, or a lower exchange rate, would accelerate growth in the case of a net international debtor. The possibility of boosting growth via foreign borrowing is therefore partially offset by the obvious proviso that interest must be paid on such foreign debt. In fact, as will be shown below, interest on foreign debt may be "too high" for a foreign borrowing economy to ever benefit from foreign capital inflows.

The converse is true in the case of a net international creditor position, i.e. when $l^F < 0$. Here a higher interest rate i^F, or a higher exchange rate er, entails a higher return on foreign assets, hence providing (at least potentially) an additional source of finance for investment, as shown in equation (34), since interest earned on foreign asset holdings increases the amount of surplus available for reinvestment. Naturally, a lower interest rate on foreign assets, or a reduction in the exchange rate, will have the opposite effect. Here the downside of trade surpluses (capital outflows) is partially offset by the fact that interest accrued on foreign assets supplement domestically generated surplus as an additional source of finance. In actual fact, under certain conditions, high interest on foreign asset holdings may allow domestic capital to "live off" the earnings provided by its foreign investments.

The preceding considerations may be systematized further. It follows from equation (36) that l^F may take positive or negative values owing to different circumstances, as summarized in Table 13.1.

The economic regime depicted in the North-West quadrant bears a net debtor position, given that $l^F > 0$, based on equation (36). To the extent that it is possible to ascertain that the expressions in the column headings approximate the balance of trade, the economic regime portrayed in this quadrant is characterized by running trade deficits, hence growing over and above its own means by supplementing the investment of domestically generated surplus value with borrowed foreign capital. This is possible since the steady-state growth rate g exceeds the interest rate paid on foreign loans i^F, so that the economy's surplus grows faster than interest payments. In Minskyan terms, this regime can be rendered as bearing a *speculative* position, as domestic investment exceeds domestic savings (Foley, 2003).

The economic regime depicted in the South-East quadrant also bears a net debtor position, where again $l^F > 0$. In this case, however, the economy under consideration is characterized by running trade surpluses (which it evidently

Table 13.1 Economic regimes with endogenous exports

	$m > x \cdot (1+q) \cdot e^{-g \cdot (Tp+Tr+Tf)}$	$m < x \cdot (1+q) \cdot e^{-g \cdot (Tp+Tr+Tf)}$
$g > i^F$	Net debtor (speculative position)	Net creditor (hedged position)
$g < i^F$	Net creditor (hedged position)	Net debtor (*Ponzi* position)

assigns to the payment of its external liabilities). However, given the high level of the interest accrued by such debt (note that $i^F > g$), the outflow of capital implied by these trade surpluses does not suffice to service outstanding foreign debt. This situation, to which many developing countries have been exposed in the last couple of decades, has been characterized as a "financial trap". In Minskyan terms, this regime can be portrayed as bearing a *Ponzi* position, where the fact that domestic savings exceed investment does not suffice to service foreign debt.

The economic regime in the North-East quadrant bears a net creditor position, given that $l^F < 0$, based on equation (36). This economy runs trade surpluses and exports capital abroad; i.e. it contributes to finance some other economy's expansion. This economic regime is building up stocks of foreign assets. In Minskyian terms, this regime is obviously *hedged*, although at the cost of a continuous capital drain. This type of regime has typically attracted the attention of the literature on "capital flight", concerned with the apparent dissociation exhibited in many developing countries between the rate of accumulation of domestic capitalists' wealth (to a large extent in the form of foreign assets) and the rate of accumulation of domestic productive forces proper, and more recently of the literature on global imbalances and the macroeconomic effect of intense international reserves accumulation in the case of developing countries.

Finally, the economic regime depicted in the South-West quadrant also bears a net creditor's position, where again $l^F < 0$. In this case, however, the economy is characterized by running trade deficits, not surpluses. This economy benefits from the high interest accrued by its foreign asset holdings ($i^F > g$). Indeed, such interest earnings must exceed the aforementioned trade deficit, so that, despite its trade deficits, the regime in question experiences current account surpluses and steadily increases its stock of foreign assets. In Minskyan terms, this economic regime is also *hedged*. However, as opposed to the situation portrayed in the North-East quadrant, characterized by continual capital outflows, this regime seems to enjoy the position of a *rentier*, which is able to consume above its own means (hence the trade deficits) thanks to the interest earned on its holdings of foreign assets. This pattern is made possible by the fact that interest accrued by foreign assets exceeds the domestic profit rate – what makes the acquisition of foreign assets all the more preferable vis-à-vis reinvesting the domestically generated surplus value in the home economy.[27]

All these regimes are consistent by construction, since they all comply with the steady-state condition. Even the *Ponzi* regime, depicted in the South-East quadrant may in principle be sustained in time so long as foreign borrowing remains available. Their shifting from one to another type of regime would necessarily involve some modification in the underlying parameters – a "comparative dynamics" exercise. For instance, in the case of the regime depicted in the North-West quadrant, which bears a net debtor *speculative* position, an upsurge in the foreign interest rate i^F could bring about a "regime change" in the direction of the South-East quadrant, the *Ponzi* position. Similarly, in the case of the regime depicted in the North-East quadrant, which bears a net creditor *hedged* position, an increase in the interest rate earned on its growing foreign assets could bring about a "regime change" in the direction of the South-West quadrant, the "rentier" economy.

Similar transitions may come about as a result of changes in other parameters. For instance, a successful import substitution policy, intended to progressively reduce the economy's propensity to import m (and probably aimed also at increasing the capacity to export, indicated by the x coefficient), may begin in the North-West quadrant at a *speculative* position and shift towards the North-East quadrant, *a hedged position*, where ensuing trade surpluses would initially allow it to cancel the outstanding foreign debt inherited from the *speculative* period.

Exogenous exports

An alternative specification of the model may assume exports grow according to an exogenously given rate g_x, as shown in equation (37):

$$E(t) = E(0)e^{g_x t} \tag{37}$$

Given the steady-state growth condition, exports' growth rate g_x must have a bearing on the entire system. As a result, the rate of growth of capital outlays now depends on the rate of growth of exports (and not the other way round). The ratio of exports $E(t)$ to capital outlays $C(t)$ will therefore be:

$$x' = \frac{(1+p \cdot q)}{e^{g \cdot (Tp+Tr+Tf)} \cdot p'} - p \cdot i^F \cdot l^F + m - \frac{1}{p'} \tag{38}$$

where $x' = E(t) \cdot er/C(t)$,[28] and $l^F = L^F(t) \cdot er/C(t)$ becomes:

$$l^F = \frac{m-x'}{g-i^F} \tag{39}$$

Equation (39) again gives rise to four possible economic regimes, depending on the values taken by the parameters. As shown in Table 13.2, the characteristics borne by each possible net financial position are analogous to the case of endogenous exports synthesized in Table 13.1. A net debtor *speculative* position, where domestically financed growth is enhanced via foreign borrowing (North-West quadrant); a net creditor *hedged* position, which suffers from continuous capital drain, in all probability falling short of its growth potential (North-East quadrant); a net creditor *hedged* position, which relies on the earnings derived from its

Table 13.2 Economic regimes with exogenous exports

	$m > x$	$m < x$
$g_x > i^F$	Net debtor (speculative position)	Net creditor (hedged position)
$g_x < i^F$	Net creditor (hedged position)	Net debtor (*Ponzi* position)

foreign asset holdings (South-West quadrant); and a net debtor, *Ponzi* position, which (to put in Minsky's words) needs to "increase debt to pay debt" (Minsky, 1986) (South-East quadrant). Note, however, that besides the similarity with the previous "endogenous exports" specification the system's growth rate g_x is determined exogenously and depends ultimately on foreign countries' demand for domestic goods.

The assumption that exports' exogenous growth rate g_x determines the growth rate of the entire system resembles Thirlwall's law (McCombie and Thirlwall, 1994). More generally, the need to borrow foreign funds or to accumulate foreign assets – depending on the net international investment position – will ultimately depend on the economy's export performance.

Whether the economy's growth rate is constrained by its capacity to self-expand, as in the assumption of endogenous exports (where the volume of exports at time *t* depends on the previous accumulation of capital), or by the availability of foreign currency, whose volume in turn ultimately depends on the rate of growth of exports, as in the current setup, stems from the specification of the model. Arguably, either specification may be valid, depending on the context to which it is applied. A small economy's limit to export may be best represented by the endogenous exports specification, where the limit to produce and sell goods internationally is constrained by the capacity to finance the expansion of such production rather than by the size and rate of growth of world demand.[29] Conversely, larger economies' capacity to increase their exports may be more directly related to the expansion of world demand than to the pace of capital accumulation.[30]

Exogenous capital inflows

International liquidity may comprise a key determinant of economic performance in many developing countries, especially in the case of net debtor countries. However, for developing economies the availability of external finance – which may vary capriciously according to developed economies' business cycle, liquidity preference, etc. – is often beyond their control, subject successively to euphoric phases and "sudden stops", as well as to the monetary policy stance adopted by advanced countries. Such sensitivity with regard to the availability of foreign finance can be exemplified within this framework by posing the access to additional foreign capital as being determined by the exogenous rate g_F:

$$B^F(t) = B^F(0)e^{g_F t} \qquad (40)$$

Given the growth rate of capital inflows (outflows), as indicated in equation (40), and assuming imports depend on capital outlays $C(t)$, as indicated by equation (28), exports become endogenous:

$$E(t) = M(t) - B^F(t) \qquad (41)$$

More specifically, the ratio of exports $E(t)$ to capitals outlays $C(t)$ becomes:

$$x' = \frac{(1+p \cdot q)}{e^{-g \cdot (Tp+Tr+Tf)} \cdot p'} - \frac{p \cdot i^F \cdot z^F}{g_F - i^F} + m - \frac{1}{p'} \tag{42}$$

where again $x' = \dfrac{E(t) \cdot er}{C(t)}$ and $z^F = \dfrac{B^F(t) \cdot er}{C(t)}$.

Given the imports coefficient m, the capitalization rate on capital inflows p', and the rest of the parameters, under the current specification (i.e. assuming exogenous capital inflows) the system's growth rate depends entirely on the availability of foreign finance – instead of being determined by exports growth. Indeed, in the case of an indebted economy, where $B^F > 0$ and $z^F > 0$, the larger z^F, the lower the level of exports required to back the volume of imports necessary to sustain growth. In other words, the abundance (shortage) of foreign finance puts the economy in a position to reduce (increase) its exports given its propensity to import. When an economy that is used to finance capital formation with resort to foreign borrowing suffers a "sudden stop" in the inflow of international capital, the necessary adjustment is illustrated in equation (42). The larger the reduction in z^F, the larger the increase in x' required to bring about the necessary reduction in domestic absorption. It should be noted, however, that despite the increase (reduction) in exports, under the current specification of the model the economy's overall growth rate is determined by g^F.[31]

This is another variant of a balance-of-payments-constraint, where the economy's rate of expansion is ultimately determined by accessibility to foreign currency – albeit now the availability of foreign exchange is determined by foreign financial conditions rather than by exports' growth rate. Of course, it is also possible that $B^F < 0$ and hence $z^F < 0$, i.e. that exogenously determined capital *outflows* rule the roost. Under such circumstances, it follows from (42) that the higher capital outflows (the higher the absolute value of $z^F < 0$), the higher the level of necessary exports, and hence the lower the pace of expanded reproduction.

International reserves

Before dealing with effective demand, the role of international reserves in the open economy circuit of capital may be worth examining. For this purpose, several modifications are required. First, for simplicity's sake, it is assumed that the capitalization rate applied to foreign borrowing $p' = 1$. Hence, p' is removed from the capital outlays equation, implying that the entire flow of international new indebtedness is now pursued for the sake of capitalist investment, and not in part to finance the consumption of imported goods:

$$C(t) = S'(t - Tf) + p \left[S''(t - f) + er\, i^R R(t) - er\, i^F L^F(t) \right] + er\, B^F(t) \tag{43}$$

Second, domestic capital now earns interest i^R on its foreign reserve holdings, denoted by R. This is why in equation (43) we observe that the potential flow of internal funds available for reinvestment is determined not just by past profits net of interest payments (earnings), but also by interest earned on foreign reserve holdings. A realistic assumption is that the interest rate on international reserves, which are typically invested in risk-free financial assets, is smaller than the average yield of other less secure foreign asset holdings (i.e. $i^R < i^F$).

Third, as shown in equation (44), the amount of foreign liabilities L^F is not just related to the current account of the balance of payments alone, but also to the buildup of international reserves R.

$$dL^F(t)/dt = B^F(t) + i^F L^F(t) + dR(t)/dt - i^R R(t) \tag{44}$$

Foreign reserves are assumed to follow the so-called "Greenspan–Guidotti rule", which requires that international reserves R be equivalent to current debt service obligations:[32]

$$R(t) = i^F L^F(t) \tag{45}$$

Assuming exports grow endogenously, as in the first specification of the open economy circuit of capital model (as in equation 29), and solving the system for g we obtain:

$$g = \frac{\ln\left\{1 + p \cdot q - x \cdot (1+q)/1 - m + p \cdot \left(i^R \cdot r - i^F \cdot l^F\right)\right\}}{Tp + Tr + Tf} \tag{46}$$

where:

$$r = \frac{R(t) \cdot er}{C(t)} = \frac{i^F \cdot L^F \cdot er}{C(t)} = i^F \cdot l^F \tag{47}$$

$$l^F = \frac{L^F \cdot er}{C(t)} = \frac{m - x \cdot (1+q) \cdot e^{-g \cdot (Tp + Tr + Tf)} - i^R \cdot r}{g - i^F (1+g)} \tag{48}$$

Equation (46) reveals the decelerating influence exerted by the accumulation of foreign reserves.[33] The need to set aside a proportion of foreign proceeds in order to build up a stock of foreign reserves is tantamount to exporting capital. Just as the achievement of trade surpluses may retard growth, in spite of the earnings accrued on the resulting accumulation of foreign assets, *ceteris paribus* the buildup of foreign reserves also tends to decelerate expansion. From an international perspective, the inclination to over-accumulate foreign reserves resembles a situation of high liquidity preference at the domestic level.[34] Ideally then, countries should seek to operate with as low a stock of foreign reserves as feasible – as seems to have been Keynes' idea behind his Clearing Union proposal (Keynes, 1980).

Equation (48) allows for the usual classification into four international financial regimes. Note, however, that the introduction of international reserves tends to "tense up" the conditions attached to each of the net international investment positions or regimes. Take, for instance, the debtor *speculative* regime, which runs trade deficits and is able (theoretically) to grow beyond its own means thanks to its access to foreign capital. Equation (48) shows that the extent to which this economy fosters its own expansion via foreign borrowing may be curtailed by the accumulation of foreign reserves, since the latter take up a portion of capital inflows. Indeed, this economy may turn into a net creditor *hedged* regime, not as a result of it shifting from trade deficits to trade surpluses, but due to (say) a need to intensify the accumulation of international reserves. In other words, the fact that the economy is borrowing foreign capital need not be related to the expansion of its productive capital stock, but also to the acquisition of foreign assets.

The introduction of foreign reserves brings to light the (sometimes) subtle difference between gross and net international capital flows. Indeed, following equation (48) a *Ponzi* regime, as defined in the taxonomy provided above, may arise not necessarily due to foreign debt overhang, but as a consequence of high "international liquidity preference" – i.e. a disproportionate propensity to acquire foreign assets, which under the current specification of the model is synonymous with over-accumulation of international reserves. In a word, similar net investment positions need not result in similar growth paths.

Summing up: Without yet having set forth a complete macroeconomic model, where aggregate demand interplays with aggregate supply, it has nonetheless been possible to grasp the resourcefulness of Foley's circuit of capital model when applied to an open economy. Under fairly simplistic assumptions, interesting discussion areas have been touched upon, such as the convoluted relation between net exports and economic growth, which seems to hinge on the specification of the model (and thus, probably, on specific historical considerations), or the range of international financial positions an economy may bear depending on its specific circumstances, or the potentially decelerating effect of foreign reserves. The following section introduces effective demand into the model.

Aggregate demand in the circuit of capital model for an open economy

In a closed capitalist economy the existence of a time lag (the finance lag Tf) between the moment surplus value is realized and its recommittal to the circuit of capital made aggregate demand *inherently* insufficient to realize aggregate supply at any given point in time in the absence of credit (see section "Aggregate demand and expanded reproduction", above). A similar concern arises regarding the adequacy of aggregate demand in the context of an open economy. Note, however, that in an open capitalist economy, aggregate supply consists not only of domestic production, but also of imports, whereas aggregate demand consists not only of domestic investment and consumption, but also of exports. Indeed, exports may be particularly relevant to the issue of effective demand and realization, as they consist of the only component of aggregate demand that need not be financed from within the circuit of capital.[35]

Before introducing domestic credit and macroeconomic equilibrium proper into the model, consider the baseline model for an open economy, but assuming for simplicity that $p' = 1$. Under such a specification, aggregate supply $AS(t)$ and aggregate demand $AD(t)$ are equal to:

$$AS(t) = S(t) + M(t)er \tag{49}$$

$$AD(t) = C(t) + Cons^K(t) + E(t)er \tag{50}$$

where capitalist consumption $Cons^K(t)$ now (since $p' = 1$) amounts to:

$$Cons^K(t) = (1-p) \cdot \left[S''(t) - er \cdot i^F \cdot L^F(t) \right] \tag{51}$$

Plugging equations (4), (26), (27), (28), (29) into equations (49) and (50) and dividing by $C(t)$:

$$as(t) = (1+q) \cdot e^{g \cdot (t-Tp-Tr)} + m \tag{52}$$

$$ad(t) = (1+q) \cdot e^{g \cdot (t-Tp-Tr-Tf)} + m - i^F \cdot l^F \tag{53}$$

where $as(t) = AS(t)/C(t)$ and $ad(t) = AD(t)/C(t)$.

It follows from equations (52) and (53) that for aggregate supply and aggregate demand to be equivalent, i.e. for $as(t) - ad(t) = 0$, the following equality must hold (a condition that can only be expected to come about by a fluke):

$$(1+q) \cdot e^{g \cdot (t-Tp-Tr)} \cdot \left(1 - e^{-g \cdot Tf} \right) = -er \cdot i^F \cdot l^F \tag{54}$$

To be sure, equation (54) shows that only a creditor (net exporter) economy, where $l^F < 0$, *may* be in a position to close the realization gap without recourse to domestic credit as a source of additional finance for investment or consumption. Note, however, that even in the case of a net exporter the strict condition imposed by equation (54) can hardly be expected to be met except by pure accident. The introduction of aggregate demand therefore remains a key issue.

The corresponding model requires further adjustment. First, for simplicity, we abstract again from foreign reserves. Hence, the increase (decrease) of foreign net liabilities (assets) evolves in strict accordance with the current account of the balance of payments, as in equation (33). Second, also for simplicity we stick to the assumption that $p' = 1$. Third, as shown in equation (55), we allow for investment to be co-financed not just by internal funds (recovery of costs plus past profits) and foreign borrowing B^F, but also (as in the section "Aggregate demand and expanded reproduction", above) by domestic borrowing B, which entails the "mobilization" or "intermediation" of the idle liquid reserves held in domestic capitalists balance sheets:

$$C(t) = S'(t - Tf) + p \left[S''(t - Tf) - er \, i^F L^F(t) \right] + er \, B^F(t) + B \tag{55}$$

Fourth, we explicitly define aggregate supply AS and aggregate demand AD, as in equations (49) and (50), and introduce the binding macroeconomic equilibrium condition that $AD(t) = AS(t)$, as in equation (18).

Again, we present three different specifications to the model. The first specification implies a "classical" closure; while the second and third specifications portray two alternative Keynesian closures.

Classical closure

As in the section "Aggregate demand and expanded reproduction", in the "classical" closure, idle liquid reserves $F(t)$ are recycled via domestic borrowing $B(t)$ among capitalist firms to generate the necessary level of investment $C(t)$ that allows for the realization of the entire output. Given the binding macroeconomic equilibrium condition between aggregate supply and demand, the growth rate g and the leverage ratio $z = B(t)/C(t)$ (the proportion of investment which needs to be funded "externally" for aggregate demand to match aggregate supply) will be determined endogenously:

$$g = \frac{\ln\left\{1 + p \cdot q - x \cdot (1+q)/1 - m - i^F \cdot l^F (1-p)\right\}}{Tp + Tr} \tag{56}$$

$$z^P = 1 - (1 + p \cdot q) \cdot e^{-g \cdot (Tp + Tr + Tf)} - z^F \tag{57}$$

where $l^F = \frac{L^F \cdot er}{C(t)}$ and $z^F = \frac{B^F \cdot er}{C(t)}$:

$$l^F = \frac{m - x \cdot (1+q) \cdot e^{g \cdot (t - Tp - Tr)}}{g - i^F} \tag{58}$$

$$z^F = m - x \cdot (1+q) \cdot e^{-g \cdot (Tp + Tr)} \tag{59}$$

As shown in equation (56), the system's growth rate depends on the mark-up, capitalization and turnover rates on the domestic front, and foreign borrowing on the international front.[36] As in the previous section, other things being equal, a net international debtor position ($l^F > 0$) tends to favor economic growth, while a net international creditor position ($l^F < 0$) tends to hinder it. Note, however, that given the level of investment required to close the realization gap, a trade-off emerges between foreign borrowing z^F and domestic borrowing z, as depicted in equation (57), which shows that the higher the degree to which investment is financed via foreign borrowing z^F, the lower the extent to which domestic idle reserves need to be domestically intermediated.

Keynesian closures

A Keynesian approach would not conceive of an automatic mechanism whereby idle liquid funds are redirected towards investment – as rendered in the classical closure – so that the entire production is readily realized. On the contrary, under a Keynesian perspective the autonomous components of aggregate demand must determine at any given point in time the aggregate level of production. From a Keynesian standpoint, one could think of (exogenous) demand for exports or of (also exogenous) demand for investment goods as determining the tempo of production. We begin by presenting the variant that revolves around exogenous exports.

The corresponding model resorts once again to equation (37), which represents exports as growing at a given rate g_x. Compared to the classical closure, this leaves us once again with an overdetermined system. In order to attain a well-determined system one of the previously exogenous parameters must become endogenous. As pointed out in the section "Aggregate demand and expanded reproduction", above, from a Keynesian perspective several possibilities make sense. Either the realization lag Tr, the finance lag Tf, or even the production lag Tp could alternatively become endogenous.

Let us assume that the realization lag Tr is the endogenous variable. The finance lag Tf and the production lag Tp continue to be exogenous parameters. For simplicity, capitalist consumption is assumed to occur instantaneously, as non-retained profits are distributed to capitalist households, as in equation (51). Complying with the macroeconomic binding condition that aggregate demand equals aggregate supply and solving for Tr we obtain:

$$Tr = \frac{\ln\left\{(1+p \cdot q) \cdot e^{-g \cdot Tp}/1 - z^F - (1-p) \cdot er \cdot i^F \cdot l^F\right\}}{g_x} \tag{60}$$

where,

$$l^F = \frac{z^F}{g_x - i^F} \tag{61}$$

$$z^F = m - x' \tag{62}$$

$$x' = \frac{E(t) \cdot er}{C(t)} \tag{63}$$

Equation (60) reveals how, under the current setting, exports' growth rate, indicated by g_x, determines the level of aggregate demand, represented by the realization lag Tr, and hence also the level of final output. Recall that a high value for Tr here stands for effective demand "sluggishness", and vice versa. Hence, the larger the exports' growth rate g_x, the shorter the realization lag Tr. Here, effective demand and realization ultimately depend on exports' growth, which, given the import coefficient m, indirectly determines the required level of foreign borrowing, as shown in equation (62), as well as the extent to which the domestic financial system needs to intermediate capitalist firms' liquid reserves, as shown in equation (64):[37]

$$z = \frac{(1+p \cdot q) \cdot \left(1 - e^{-g_x \cdot Tf}\right)}{e^{g_x \cdot (Tp+Tr)}} + i^F \cdot l^F \tag{64}$$

Note, finally, that depending on the value taken by the parameters, equation (61) once more gives way to four possible economic regimes, depending on whether $z^F > $ or $ < 0$, and $g_x > $ or $ < i^F$.

By including aggregate demand, the model presented in this section comprises a more comprehensive representation of Thirlwall's law vis-à-vis the one offered in the previous section. Here exports' growth rate not only determines the growth rate of the entire system, but also the leverage ratios domestic firms would have to meet if they are to keep up with the foreign demand for their products.

An alternative Keynesian closure may involve, instead of autonomous exports, autonomous investment, indicated by an exogenously determined rate of expansion of capital outlays g. Aggregate demand, denoted by the realization lag Tr, is one possible endogenous variable, which could close the model as in the section "The baseline model", above. Liquidity preference or capacity utilization, denoted by Tf and Tp, respectively, comprise two other options. Another possibility (taken up here) is that exports become the endogenous variable that makes aggregate demand equal aggregate supply.

Under the resulting specification, the three time lags (Tr, Tp and Tf) comprise exogenous variables. Capital outlays $C(t)$ grow at an also exogenously given rate g; i.e. the rate at which capital outlays expand can be thought of as determined by "animal spirits". Complying with the macroeconomic equilibrium condition that aggregate demand equals aggregate supply we may solve the system for x':

$$x' = \left[\frac{1+p \cdot q}{e^{g \cdot (Tp+Tr)}} + m - 1\right] + (1-p) \cdot i^F \cdot l^F \tag{65}$$

where again,

$$l^F = \frac{z^F}{g - i^F} \tag{66}$$

$$z^F = m - x' \tag{67}$$

$$x' = \frac{E(t) \cdot er}{C(t)} \tag{68}$$

Equation (65) shows the inverse relation between exports, indicated by the coefficient x, and investment growth, indicated by g. Here the higher the rate at which investment grows, the lower the extent to which domestic production will be sold abroad. Exports evolve in a counter-cyclical manner, increasing when investment (and overall aggregate demand) goes down and vice versa – not an unusual pattern in business cycles. In other words, given the level of capital outlays (investment) and the imports coefficient m, exports must adjust so that aggregate demand does not fall short of aggregate supply, while domestic borrowing z accommodates:

$$z = \frac{(1 + p \cdot q) \cdot \left(1 - e^{-g \cdot Tf}\right)}{e^{g \cdot (Tp + Tr)}} + i^{F} \cdot l^{F} \tag{69}$$

Indeed, equation (69) reveals the somewhat odd conclusion that z will be smaller the larger is g. Under the specified setting, an increase in g boosts aggregate demand, driving exports down and increasing the demand for imports. The fact that the higher investment reduces net exports implies that foreign borrowing z^{F} partly finances the expansion. Hence, the extent to which investment is financed by domestic vis-à-vis foreign borrowing goes down.

Conclusions

Drawing from Foley (1982, 1983, 1986a, 1986b) this chapter exhibits the versatility of the circuit of capital model for the analysis of open economy issues.[38] As pointed out above, the fact that imports and exports are not assumed to balance in the long run – as would be the case in a neoclassical approach – opens the door to the analysis of persistent net international debtor or creditor positions, and hence to the examination of different accumulation regimes – from highly leveraged processes of debt-led growth to more "cautious" (and less dynamic, in terms of economic growth) regimes, in which domestic accumulation is thwarted by capital exports and/or international reserves accumulation. These different regimes have been arranged into a useful taxonomy (inspired to some degree by Minsky's classification of financial portfolios) for the characterization and analysis of different accumulation paths.

This chapter has also sought to present different closures to the open economy circuit of capital model, from a "classical" approach (which relies on the workings of Say's law) to various types of Keynesian closures. While the classical version has served as an "ideal type", i.e. as the basis from which many useful general conclusions could be drawn (particularly as regards the analysis of the various financial positions), the different Keynesian versions – subject to the principle of effective demand – seem to comprise a more realistic representation of capitalist economies, where the different components of autonomous spending determine the system's trajectory, from real output growth to financial requirements.

The versatility of the circuit of capital model allows for the representation of different constraints to growth. As discussed in the section "Aggregate demand", above, whether an economy's growth rate is constrained by its capacity to self-expand or by the availability of foreign currency (which depends either on exports growth or international liquidity) arises from the specification of the model. Interestingly, any of the above specifications may be valid depending on the historical, institutional and even geographical context to which it is applied.

In general, the Keynesian closures seem to comprise a more realistic representation of the fundamental dynamics of advanced capitalist economy (vis-à-vis the "classical", steady-state closure). Interestingly, however, some distinctive Marxian/classical features persist even in the context of a Keynesian closure. For example, even if under a Keynesian perspective investment spending depends primarily on capitalist long-term expectations ("animal spirits"), the system's growth rate still faces an upper limit imposed by internally generated economic surplus, i.e. by the degree of development of productive forces (technology) and the extent to which capital is capable of appropriating surplus value (class struggle). This inference tends to go along with Duménil and Lévy's (1997) view, as denoted by their commendation to be "Keynesian in the short term and classical in the long term". On the other hand, as far as developing countries are concerned, the "classical" closure to the circuit of capital model seems to portray some of the obstacles faced by many underdeveloped economies, e.g. the negative impact exerted by luxurious consumption on capital formation – a problem that concerned classical development economists, including Ragnar Nurkse (1953) and Raúl Prebisch (1981).

Notes

1 I am indebted to André Contri for originally pointing me to the versatility of the circuit of capital model as regards open economy considerations, and for providing me with his own contribution to this topic (Contri, 2002).
2 Keynesian economics' approach to growth and balance of payments issues is typified by Thirlwall's law (see McCombie and Thirlwall, 1994), which as shown by Moreno-Brid (1998) and Barbosa (2001) also allows for persistent unbalanced trade and the consequent build-up of continual net debtor or creditor positions. In actual fact Thirlwall's law, which states that an economy's growth rate is ultimately determined by the rate of growth of its exports can be represented as a special case within the open economy circuit of capital model.
3 The baseline model presented in this section is based on Foley (1986a), whose notation I follow.
4 The valuation of finished commodities at cost (an accounting convention) is for the purpose of formal treatment only and does not contradict Marx's assertion that surplus value is extracted during production.
5 An identity relates the markup on costs q to the rate of surplus value e and the composition of capital k (see Foley, 1986b):

$$q = s/(c+v) = (s/v)[(v/(c+v)] = ek$$

where $e = s/v$ stands for the rate of surplus value and $k = v/(c+v)$ for the composition of capital, in Marx's terminology.
6 Conversely $(1 - p)$ indicates the proportion of surplus value set aside for capitalist consumption – a "leakage" from the point of view of the circuit of capital.
7 The possibility of firms borrowing "external" funds is introduced later.
8 Note that workers' consumption expenditure is a component part of capital outlays $C(t)$, the "variable" constituent of capital in Marx's terminology.
9 It should be noted that aggregate output $S(t)$ here corresponds to *gross* value of production, not to value added or national income. Yet, this framework is capable of retrieving more conventional macroeconomic aggregates. Note as well that the above representation deals with money value flows, with no consideration of inflation (the value of money).

10 It should be noted that while the "supply side" account of the circuit of capital is valid at any level of aggregation – "demand side" considerations – as the ones to be raised in this section only arise at the level of the economy as whole.

11 Conventional growth models seem to implicitly assume $Tf = 0$ by equating savings to investment. This is the case both within the Neoclassical and Keynesian traditions.

12 Marx (1893) defines *simple* reproduction as the (clearly hypothetical) situation where "the entire surplus-value goes into the personal consumption of the capitalist" and therefore no accumulation of capital takes place.

13 Alternative closures, which do not assume steady-state growth, are considered below.

14 The notion of "internal" and "external" funding applies only at the level of individual capitals. For the system as a whole in a closed economy all existing funds are *internal* to the circuit of capital.

15 Indeed, these idle reserves (e.g. depreciation funds), which arise as a direct consequence of the existence of a finance lag Tf, set the ground for the development of the capitalist financial system, which allows for these stagnant hoards to be utilized "productively", i.e. valorized.

16 Recall that capital outlays include variable capital and therefore, albeit implicitly, wage-earners' consumption.

17 Note that the larger the finance lag Tf, the larger the "leverage" ratio z.

18 Indeed, it is the fact that a developed credit system is capable of increasing the rate of turnover of the entire social capital that provides the objective grounds for the remuneration of the financial capitalists (e.g. "bankers") out of the total surplus-value generated within the sphere of production, even if it operates exclusively within the sphere of exchange (Itoh and Lapavitsas, 1999).

19 For a discussion of Say's law from the point of view of the circuit of capital, see Foley (1986c).

20 "Classical" in Keynes' terminology, i.e. as the belief – shared by Neoclassical and classical economists alike – that there exists some smooth monetary mechanism that somehow resolves the problem of financing the level of aggregate demand required to close the realization gap.

21 In a fairly similar fashion it is possible to assume that Tp (capacity utilization) is the endogenous variable (Abeles, 2005).

22 The finance lag Tf may be shortened, for instance, via financial innovation. The notion that financial innovation intensifies during booms is characteristic of Hyman Minsky's (1986) theory of the business cycle.

23 All balance-of-payments variables, including foreign borrowing, foreign debt, imports, exports, etc., are denominated in foreign currency throughout.

24 Marx defines profits net of interest payments as "profits of enterprise". The higher the interest rate paid on debt committed to finance capital accumulation, the lower the share of surplus value that remains to the operating capitalist. An analogy can be posed at the international level. The higher the interest rate on foreign debt committed to finance the expansion of domestic capital, the lower the share of domestically generated surplus value that remains within the confines of the national economy. Note that while in the closed economy setting (see above) interest payments cancelled out for the capitalist class considered as a whole, and therefore did not in principle reduce the economy's growth potential, in an open economy setting interest payments due to foreign indebtedness comprise a leakage from the circuit of capital.

25 For simplicity, the time lag included in the exports function is equal to the finance lag Tf.

26 As mentioned above, it is also possible that $LF(t) < 0$, i.e. that $LF(t)$ corresponds to foreign assets, not foreign liabilities, in which case i^F would comprise the average return on such assets.

27 Broadly speaking, such a position may have been enjoyed by the United Kingdom during part of the Victorian period. In their model Metcalfe and Steedman (1979) allow

for a similar pattern: "[A]lthough a capital exporting country must of necessity have a current account surplus it need not simultaneously have a trade surplus to achieve the transfer of the capital export. Similarly, the capital importer need not of necessity be a net importer of commodities" (p. 214).

28 Note that x' comprises a slightly different algebraic expression than x in the "endogenous exports" specification.

29 This need not be entirely true if the exports are subject to decreasing terms of trade à la Prebisch–Singer. Still, the idea that smaller economies' failure to increase exports could be to some extent related to limits arising at the level of capital formation may apply.

30 It is in these cases that the international specialization in the production of goods bearing relatively high income-elasticity of demand comprises a key developmental issue.

31 Latin America's "lost decade" may be roughly illustrated along these lines. Due to the debt crisis, a strong reduction in access to foreign capital ensued in the 1980s, forcing Latin American economies to severely reduce domestic absorption. Nil net capital inflows corresponded with virtual stagnation throughout practically the entire region, while net exports grew significantly. In short, net capital inflows tended to zero – and so, too, did overall economic growth.

32 The Greenspan–Guidotti rule proper establishes that foreign reserves should at least match short-term foreign debt obligations (Greenspan, 1999). Under the current setting the rule has been slightly modified to establish that $i^F = R(t)/LF(t)$, i.e. the ratio of foreign reserves to foreign indebtedness is equal to the average interest rate on outstanding foreign debt.

33 It should be noted that this inference is not influenced by the particular choice of the Greenspan–Guidotti rule. Any other rule whereby reserves are required to grow proportionately to the system as a whole would come down to the same conclusion.

34 As was evident in the sections "The baseline model" and "Aggregate demand and expanded reproduction" above, the increase in liquidity preference, approximated by the finance time lag *Tf*, tends to slow down the pace of expanded reproduction.

35 In actual fact, Rosa Luxemburg (1913) argued that a closed capitalist system undergoing expanded reproduction would always face inadequacies of aggregate demand, and would therefore require external markets (i.e. exports) to realize its surplus production. The section "Aggregate demand and expanded reproduction", where aggregate demand matches aggregate supply *in a closed economy setup* already proves Luxemburg wrong.

36 Notice, however, that as in the section "Aggregate demand and expanded reproduction" the finance lag no longer exerts a decelerating influence on accumulation thanks to the "mobilization" of finance capital (domestic credit).

37 Note that the higher is g_x, the lower is z.

38 Due to space limitations we have not included the analysis of fiscal policy. Abeles (2005) analyzes fiscal finance and the effect of government deficit spending in the context of different net international investment positions.

References

Abeles, M. (2005) "Variations in the Circuit of Capital Model for an Open Economy", Seminar on Effective Demand, Income Distribution and Growth in memory of Richard Goodwin, presented at the Annual Conference of the European Association of Evolutionary Political Economy (EAEPE), Bremen, November 10–12.

Barbosa, N. (2001) "The Balance-of-payments Constraint: From Balanced Trade to Sustainable Debt", Center for Economic Policy Analysis (CEPA), Working Paper No 2001.06.

Contri, A. (2002) "A Model of the Circuit of Capital in an Open Economy", mimeo, Economics Department, Graduate Faculty, New School University.

Duménil, G., and Lévy, D. (1997) "Being Keynesian in the short term and classical in the long term", CEPREMAP, No. 9702.

Foley, D. (1982) "Realization and Accumulation in a Marxian Model of the Circuit of Capital", *Journal of Economic Theory*, 28(2): 300–319.

Foley, D. (1983) "Money and Effective Demand in Marx's Scheme of Expanded Reproduction", In *Marxism, Central Planning, and the Soviet Economy: Essays in Honor of Alexander Erlich*, edited by Padma Desai, Cambridge MA: MIT Press.

Foley, D. (1986a) *Understanding Capital*, Cambridge MA: Harvard University Press.

Foley, D. (1986b) *Money, Accumulation and Crisis*, London and New York: Harwood Academic Publishers.

Foley, D. (1986c) "Say's law in Marx and Keynes", *Cahiers d'Economie Politique*, 10(11): 183–194.

Foley, D. (2003) "Financial Fragility in Developing Economies", In *Festschrift for Lance Taylor*, edited by Amitava Dutt, New York: Edward Elgar.

Greenspan, A. (1999) "Currency Reserves and Debt", Remarks before the World Bank Conference on Recent Trends in Reserves Management, Washington, D.C., April 29. http://www.federalreserve.gov/boardDocs/speeches/1999/19990429.htm.

Itoh, M., and Lapavitsas C. (1999) *Political Economy of Money and Finance*, New York: St. Martin's Press.

Kenway, P. (1980) "Marx, Keynes and the possibility of crisis", *Cambridge Journal of Economics*, 1(4), 23–36.

Keynes, J.M. (1980) "Shaping the Post-war World: The Clearing Union", In *The collected Writings of John Maynard Keynes. Vol. 25. Activities 1940–1944*, edited by Donald Moggridge, London: Macmillan.

Luxemburg, R. (1913) *The Accumulation of Capital*, Reprint 1951, New York: Monthly Review Press.

Marx, K. (1893) *Capital: Volume II*. Reprint 1992. Penguin Classics.

McCombie, J.S.L., and Thirlwall, A.P. (1994) *Economic Growth and the Balance of Payments Constraint*. New York: St. Martin's Press.

Metcalfe, J.S., and Steedman, I. (1979) "Growth and Distribution in an Open Economy", In *Fundamental Issues in Trade Theory*, edited by Ian Steedman, New York: St. Martin's Press.

Minsky, H. (1986) *Stabilizing an Unstable Economy*, New Haven: Yale University Press.

Nurkse, R. (1953) *Problems of Capital Formation in Underdeveloped Countries*, New York: Oxford University Press.

Moreno-Brid, J.C. (1998) "On Capital Flows and the Balance of Payments Constrained Growth Model", *Journal of Post Keynesian Economics*, 21(2), 283–298.

Obstfeld, M., and Rogoff, K. (1996) *Foundations of International Macroeconomics*, Cambridge MA: MIT Press.

Prebisch, R. (1981) *Capitalismo periférico. Crisis y transformación*, Buenos Aires: Fondo de Cultura Económica.

Shaikh, A. (1980) "The Laws of International Exchange". In *Growth, Profits and Property: Essays in the Revival of Political Economy*, edited by Edward Nell, Cambridge UK: Cambridge University Press.

14 Production, circuits of capital, and flows and stocks in national accounts

Anwar Shaikh

Introduction

Duncan Foley (1982, 1986a,b, 1997) has produced a series of path-breaking papers formalizing Marx's notion of the circuits of capital. In *Capital* Volume II Marx develops a detailed analysis of turnover time and its relation to the time of production and the time of realization in the overall circuit of capital (Marx, 1967a, Ch. XII–XVII). Following Marx, Foley "treats 'capital' as stocks of value tied up in capitalist production as a result of time lags, rather than as an independent productive factor" as in the neoclassical production function. "The circuit of capital [approach] emphasizes the relation between stocks and flows in capitalist production: because calendar time is required for each phase of the circuit of capital, production, realization, and reinvestment of realized value, flows of value through the circuit accumulate in stocks" (Alemi and Foley, 2010, p. 2; Foley and Alemi, 1997, p. 1).

Marx subsequently translates his analysis of individual circuits of capital into one of social reproduction (Marx, 1967a, Ch. XX–XXI). Much attention has been paid in the subsequent literature to Marx's extraordinary derivation of the balance conditions for simple and expanding and reproduction, but far less to the relation between aggregate stocks and flows within any given time period, and between classical aggregates and those used in National Income Accounts. This chapter picks up this latter aspect, following work by Tsuru (1942) and Shaikh and Tonak (1994). Of particular interest is the fact that the distinction between circulating and fixed investment is hidden within conventional national income accounts. This distinction plays a key role in classical analysis, because the fact that production takes time implies that that any planned increase in production requires a prior expenditure on additional materials and labor. This is circulating investment, whose very purpose is to increase production. On the other hand, fixed investment, the purchase of additional plant and equipment, is aimed at increasing capacity. Total investment therefore has two separate components. Both create demand, but one creates additional supply while the other creates additional capacity. Circulating investment is aimed at adjusting supply to changing demand, so that it cannot be treated as "exogenous" in the short run. Similarly, since fixed investment is aimed at adjusting capacity to demand, it cannot be treated as being exogenous in the long run.

In what follows, I develop a mapping between classical aggregates and modern national accounts. I also show that investment in circulating capital explicitly appears in national accounts as investment in materials and work-in-process. Most importantly, I demonstrate that as long as all labor is assumed to be production labor, conventional national accounts arrive at exactly the same definition of gross profit on production (Gross Operating Surplus) as do classical accounts (the money form of Gross Surplus Value).

A framework for tracking production flows and stocks

Orthodox national income and product accounts (NIPA) and corresponding input–output accounts focus on the flows of commodities and labor power used in production in a given year. These in turn relate to the total production *initiated* in that year. Since production takes time, only part of this effort will result in a finished product in this year, while the rest will result in an increase in work-in-progress, i.e. in additions to inventories of unfinished goods. Conversely, some other part of the currently available finished product will be due to production initiated in previous years. The finished product available in a given year is therefore quite different from the product initiated in that same year. Hence, the cost of production of the annual finished product is not the same as the current annual flows of intermediate input and labor costs.

Marx discusses both finished and total (finished and unfinished) product, but his focus is on the former, i.e. on the total annual commodity-product, because this is the vehicle for the realization of profit.[1] As he points out, the whole purpose of capitalist production is to make a profit. Within the general circuit of capital M–C ... P ... C′–M′, money capital (M) is invested in intermediate inputs and labor-power (C), which are in turn subsequently put to use in production as productive capital (P) to eventually produce a finished product (C′) which is hopefully sold for profit at some money value (M′). From this perspective, final goods are those goods ready for sale, and their actual sale for profit is crucial to the completion of the circuit of capital and hence to the continuation of the process.[2]

Classical accounts focus on completed production (X_P), i.e. finished goods.[3] Conventional accounts focus on initiated production (X), which is the sum of the finished and semi-finished product. This difference in the concept of total production gives rise to further differences in measures of intermediate inputs, wage costs and value added, although in the end both accounts yield the same measure of gross profit. In what follows, the mapping between classical and standard accounts will be undertaken at the level of a closed private economy with production labor only, because this is where the fundamental differences arise. The analysis can easily be extended to encompass government and foreign sectors. The incorporation of non-production labor is treated in detail in Shaikh and Tonak (1994). Illustrative numerical values are given for all variables.

It is useful to begin with the familiar categories of standard national income and product accounts (NIPA). Total production is defined as gross output (X), the sum of intermediate inputs purchased (A), sales of final goods (X_S) and inventory change (ΔINV). The change in inventories is the sum of changes in inventories of materials and supplies (ΔINV_A), work-in-process (ΔINV_{WIP}), and finished goods and goods held for resale (ΔINV_P). It should be noted that *finished* goods include materials insofar as they represent the finished product of the producers of materials, while *final* goods refers to finished goods which do not directly re-enter into production, i.e. consumption and investment (BEA, 2008, pp. 2–2, 2–9, 2–10).[4] In order to distinguish between the two categories, I will indicate finished, i.e. produced, goods by the subscript P and final goods by the subscript F. Hence within the measure of gross output, the sum of the first two items, intermediate inputs purchased (sold) and sales of final goods, represents total sales of finished goods. Finally, gross value added (GVA) and gross domestic product (GDP) are defined as gross output *less* intermediate input. Since gross output can always be expressed on the sources side as the sum of its materials costs (A), its wage costs (W) and gross profit, GVA is the sum of wage costs and gross profit. On the uses side, gross output is the sum of sales (purchases) of materials (A) and final sales of consumption (C) and fixed investment goods (I_f) and changes in inventories, so gross domestic product (GDP) is the sum of consumption, fixed investment, and the total change in inventories of materials, work-in-process, and final goods. Because of its focus on initiated production, the NIPA measure of "final" product has the curious property of encompassing additions to the stocks of raw materials and partly fabricated items (Shapiro, 1966, p. 26, footnote 11).

$X \equiv$ NIPA Gross Product $= A + FS + \Delta INV =$ Intermediate Inputs Purchased $+$ Final Sales $+ \Delta$ Inventories

$$110 \qquad\qquad = 25 + 65 + 20 \qquad\qquad\qquad (1)$$

$$\Delta INV = \Delta INV_A + INV_{WIP} + \Delta INV_P = \text{Total Change in Inventories}$$
$$20 \ = \ \ \ 3 \ \ + \ \ \ 7 \ \ + \ \ \ 10 \qquad\qquad (2)$$

$$FS = \text{final sales} = C + I_f = \text{Consumption} + \text{Fixed Investment}$$
$$65 \qquad\qquad = 45 + 20 \qquad\qquad\qquad (3)$$

$$GVA \equiv X - A = W + PG$$
$$85 \ \ = 100 - 25 = \ 33 \ + \ 52 \qquad\qquad (4)$$

$$GDP \equiv X - A = FS + \Delta INV = C + I_f + \Delta INV$$
$$85 \ \ \ \ = 110 - 25 = 65 \ + \ \ \ 20 \ \ = 45 + 20 + 20 \qquad (5)$$

In order to make the transition to classical categories, we need to extract categories relevant to finished (i.e. produced) goods. We noted at the beginning of this chapter that the sales of finished goods is the sum of intermediate inputs purchased (A) and sales of final goods (FS). Since finished production adds to the inventories of finished goods and sales of finished goods subtracts from these inventories, the change in these inventories (ΔINV_P) is the difference between total finished production (X_P) and total sales of finished goods ($A + FS$). This relation can be written as

$$X_P = A + FS + \Delta INV_P$$
$$100 = 25 + 65 + 10 \tag{6}$$

Then equations (1), (2), and (6) tell us that the standard measure of production initiated is greater than the classical measure of finished product by the sum of the changes in inventories of materials and work-in-process.

$$X - X_P = \Delta INV - \Delta INV_{FG} = \Delta INV_A + \Delta INV_{WIP}$$
$$110 - 100 = \quad 20 \quad - \quad 10 \quad = \quad 3 \quad + \quad 7 \tag{7}$$

A similar comparison can be constructed between the materials and labor costs of total production ($A + W$) and the corresponding costs of the finished product. The materials cost of finished goods (A_P) is the materials cost of finished goods whose production was initiated in the current year (A'_P) *plus* the input cost of finished goods whose production was initiated in previous years (A''_P).[5] In the same manner, the labor cost of finished goods (W_P) is the labor cost of finished goods initiated in the current year (W'_P) *plus* the labor cost of finished goods initiated in previous years (W''_P). It is also useful to note that the total current-year wage bill (W) is the sum of wages expended on production initiated in the year, finished (W'_P) and unfinished (W_{WIP}).

A_P = Materials Cost of Finished Goods Completed in This Year

= Materials Cost of Finished Goods Initiated in This Year

+ Materials Cost of Finished Goods Initiated in Previous Years

$$= A'_P + A''_P$$
$$18 = 12 + 6 \tag{8}$$

W_P = Wage Cost of Finished Goods Completed in This Year

= Wage Cost of Finished Goods Initiated in This Year

+ Wage Cost of Finished Goods Initiated in Previous Years

$$= W'_P + W''_P$$
$$30 = 18 + 12 \tag{9}$$

$$W = W_P'' + W_{WIP}$$

$$33 = 18 + 15 \tag{10}$$

The changes in the inventories of materials and work-in-process provide the missing links between the conventional and classical measures of total cost. The change in materials inventories (ΔINV_A) is the difference between the purchases of materials (A) which add to these inventories and their uses for production initiated and finished within the year (A_P') and for work-in-process (A_{WIP}). The change in work-in-process inventories (ΔINV_{WIP}) arises from the addition of new work-in-process valued at cost ($A_{WIP} + W_{WIP}$) and subtraction of the costs of current goods initiated in previous years ($A_{WIP} + W_{WIP}$), which exit these inventories when finished.

$$\Delta INV_A = A - \left(A_P' + A_{WIP}\right)$$

$$3 \qquad = 25 - (12 + 10) \tag{11}$$

$$\Delta INV_{WIP} = (A_{WIP} + W_{WIP}) - \left(A_P'' + W_P''\right)$$

$$7 \qquad = (10 \quad + \quad 15) - (6 \quad + \quad 12) \tag{12}$$

We are now in a position to show that the two measures of production costs differ by exactly the same amount as do the corresponding measures of total product.[6] It follows immediately that the measure of gross profit is the same in both cases: the standard measure of gross operating surplus (GOS) is equal to the classical measure of the money form of gross surplus value (GSV). I therefore use the term gross profit (P_G) for both.

$$(A + W) - (A_P + W_P) = \Delta INV_A + \Delta INV_{WIP}$$

$$(25 + 33) - (18 + 30) = \quad 3 \quad + \quad 7 \tag{13}$$

$$GOS \equiv X - (A + W) = GSV \equiv X_P - (A_P + W_P)$$

$$52 = 110 - (25 + 33) = 52 = 100 - (18 + 30) \tag{14}$$

The classical measure of gross surplus also has a use-side equivalent, which is the gross surplus product (GSP). This is the difference between the total finished product (X_P) and the use-equivalents of its costs ($A_P + W_P$). From equations (1) and (6), the use-form of the total finished product is $X_P = A + C + I_f + \Delta INV_P$; A_P is already in use-form; and on the assumption that the consumption of workers is equal to their wages, the wages of workers used to create the total product can be written as $W_P = W - (W - W_P) = C_W - (W - W_P)$, where C_W is the current consumption of workers. So with a little reordering of the terms we get

$$GSP = (C - C_W) + (A - A_P) + (W - W_P) + I_f + \Delta INV_P$$

$$52 = (45 - 33) + (25 - 18) + (33 - 30) + 20 + 10 \tag{15}$$

The first term in parentheses on the right-hand side is the consumption of capitalists, which is the difference between total consumption and the consumption of workers. The second term is the difference between inputs purchased in the current year and those used up in the production of the final product, which is the total investment in materials. The third term is the difference between the current purchases of labor power and those made in the production of finished goods, which is the total investment in labor-power. The sum of investment in materials and labor-power is the total investment in circulating capital (I_c).[7] Since production takes time, output can only be increased by first increasing inputs via circulating investment. Fixed investment (I_f) on the other hand expands capacity. The distinction between the two is essential to classical dynamics (Shaikh, 1988, 1991, 1992, 2009). Thus gross surplus product is the sum of capitalist consumption, investment in circulating capital, investment in fixed capital, and changes in inventories of final goods. This is exactly what appears in Marx's own schemes of reproduction.[8]

$$GSP = C_{Capitalists} + I_c + I_f + \Delta INV_P$$
$$52 \quad = \quad 12 \quad + 10 + 20 + \quad 10 \tag{16}$$

We can now compare the standard and classical measures of gross value added.[9] Since they both embody the same measure of gross profit $(GOS = GSV = P_G)$, their difference can only arise from differences in the wage measure. And, as we previously noted, the latter difference $(W - W_p)$ is simply investment in labor-power. This is exactly the point made by Tsuru (1942, pp. 371–373), although his derivation pertains to the special case of pure circulating capital with a uniform production period.[10] Tsuru (1942) proves that under these conditions *the standard measure of value added will overstate the classical measure by the amount of the increase in the wage bill*: $GVA_{NIPA} - GVA_{Classical} = \Delta W_t$.[11] Tsuru's finding is a special case of the more general difference between the two measures which is laid out here.

$$GVA = P_G + W = \text{Conventional Gross Value Added}$$
$$85 \quad = 52 + 33 \tag{17}$$
$$GVA_P = P_G + W_P = \text{Classical Gross Value Added}$$
$$82 \quad = 52 + 30 \tag{18}$$
$$GVA - GVA_P = W - W_P = \text{Investment in Labor-Power}$$
$$85 \quad - \quad 82 \quad = 33 - 30 \tag{19}$$

Finally, it can be shown that one can explicitly identify investment in circulating capital even within the NIPA measures of gross product and gross domestic product. Gross output is the sum of materials purchases (A) and gross domestic product, and the latter is the sum of consumption (C), fixed investment goods (I_f)

and changes in inventories (ΔINV). This last item is the change in final goods inventories (ΔINV_P) *plus* the sum of the change in inventories of materials and supplies and work-in-process ($\Delta INV_A + \Delta INV_{WIP}$). But from equation (13) this last sum is simply the investment in circulating capital.

$$\Delta INV_A + \Delta INV_{WIP} = (A - A_P) + (W - W_P) = I_C = \text{Investment in Circulating Capital}$$
$$3 \quad + \quad 7 \qquad = (25 - 18) + (33 - 30) = 10 \tag{20}$$

It follows from equations (2), (5), and (20) that we can write NIPA gross domestic product as

$$GDP \equiv C + I_C + I_f + \Delta INV_P$$
$$85 \; = 45 + 10 + 20 + \quad 10 \tag{21}$$

Investment in circulating capital is there all along, hidden in plain sight.

Circuits of capital, time lags, and stock/flow relations

Marx's analysis of the circuits of capital in Part I of *Capital* Volume II is evidently related to his analysis of the turnover of capital in Part II of the same volume. In the former, the focus is on the time dimensions of each phase of the overall circuit of capital, whereas in the latter it is on the corresponding stocks and flows associated with fixed and circulating capital. Both are aspects of the operation of the capitalist firm. Foley (1982, pp. 303–304) notes

> We can establish a direct correspondence between the income statements and balance sheets of capitalist firms and the theoretical concepts Marx develops out of the labor theory of value to analyze capitalist production. On the income statement costs of production are the flow of capital value into the production process, divided into purchases of raw materials and means of production, which Marx calls *constant capital*, and the wages of production workers, which Marx calls *variable capital*. Sales revenue comprises these two categories of cost and a gross profit or gross margin, which Marx calls *surplus value*. The surplus value in turn appears divided into sales and administrative overhead, interest, taxes, dividends, and retained earnings. The asset side of the firm's balance sheet measures the stocks of value tied up in the different phases of the circuit of capital due to the time lags involved in production, sales, and recommital of value to production. *Productive capital* is the stock of value in long-lived plant and equipment, and inventories of raw materials and partly finished goods (valued at costs which include the wages of labor already expended on them), and exists because there is a time lag in the production process. *Commercial capital* is the inventories of finished

commodities awaiting sale, and exists because of the time lag involved in selling itself. *Financial capital* is the financial assets of the firm representing value realized in the past in sales but not yet recommitted to production in the form of new costs.

In his empirical work, Foley has concentrated on extracting information on time lags and value flows from information on stocks and fixed capital at the sectoral level (Alemi and Foley, 2010; Foley and Alemi, 1997), whereas I have focused on extracting information on value stocks and flows from national income accounts (Shaikh and Tonak, 1994). These are, of course, two different paths to the same end.

Acknowledgment

I thank Jonathan Cogliano for helpful feedback on this chapter.

Notes

1 Marx distinguishes between commodity-capital which is the finished product, and total product which also includes semi-finished goods. "Within the 51 weeks which here stand for one year, capital I runs through six full working periods, producing 6 times 450, or £2,700 worth of commodities, and capital II producing in five full working periods 5 times £450, or £2,250 worth of commodities. In addition, capital II produced, within the last one and a half weeks of the year (middle of the 50th to the end of the 51st week), an extra £150 worth. The aggregate product in 51 weeks is worth £5,100" (Marx, 1967a, p. 268). Note that in this and many other examples, the value of the aggregate *product* includes the value of semi-finished goods (e.g. capital II consisting of an advance of £450 contributes only £150 in the first one-and–a-half weeks of its normal four-and-a-half week working period). This is distinguished from commodity-capital, e.g. finished goods.
2 It follows that the definition of a "finished" good has a historical component. When an actual market develops for some product previously deemed as unfinished, its status changes. For instance, dough was always a semi-finished product in a traditional bakery. But with the advent of refrigeration, it became possible for dough to become a finished commodity for some businesses, and could then enter as a purchased input into others.
3 "The annual process of reproduction is easily understood, so long as we keep in view merely the sum total of the year's production. But every single component of this product must be brought into the market as a commodity" (Marx, 1967b, Ch XXIV, Section 2, p. 590). "The finished products, whatever their material form or their use-value, their useful effect, are all commodity-capital here … [T]he following general proposition applies to all capitalist production: All products reach the market as commodities … All products are thrown on the market as commodities" (Marx, 1967a, Ch X, pp. 205, 208–209).
4 Final sales is "industry sales to final users", and is equal to the sum of personal consumption expenditures, gross private fixed investment, government consumption expenditures and gross investment, and net exports of goods and services (BEA, 2008, pp. 2–10, 12–12).
5 If prices are changing, the current costs of inputs will not be the same as the costs actually paid, which is typically handled through inventory valuation adjustments (BEA, 2008, 2–8, footnote 19).

6 Combining equations (8)–(12) yields

$$(A + W) - (A_P + W_P) = \left(\left(\Delta INV_A + \left(A'_P + A_{WIP}\right)\right) + W''_P + W_{WIP}\right)$$
$$- \left(A'_P + A''_P + W'_P + W''_P\right)$$
$$= \Delta INV_A + \left(\left(A_{WIP} + W_{WIP}\right) - \left(A''_P + W''_P\right)\right)$$
$$= \Delta INV_A + \Delta INV_{WIP}$$

7 Marx says that "circulating capital [consists] of the wages and the raw and auxiliary materials consumed" in the production of a commodity. Investment in circulating capital is the increase in this amount (Marx, 1967a, Ch XV, p. 257).

8 In Marx's schemes of reproduction in the case of circulating capital only, in his notation the use form of total surplus value is $S = S_c + S_{ac} + S_{av}$, where S = net surplus value, S_c = capitalist consumption, $S_{ac} = \Delta C$ = investment in circulating capital, and $S_{av} = \Delta V$ = investment in variable capital (Sweezy, 1942, pp. 162–163). Simple reproduction obtains from when there is no growth so that $\Delta C = \Delta V = 0$, in which case all of surplus value goes into capitalist consumption ($S = S_c$).

9 Slightly different notation for classical gross value added was used in Shaikh and Tonak (1994, Ch. 3).

10 In standard Marxian notation, total value of the finished product is $W = C + V + S$, where C = constant capital used up in production, and $V + S$ = Marxian value added = variable capital used in production (V) + surplus value (S). Surplus value is in turn expended on capitalist consumption (S_c), additional employment of constant capital ($S_{ac} = \Delta C$), and additional employment of variable capital ($S_{av} = \Delta V$): $S = S_c + S_{ac} + S_{av} = S_c + \Delta C + \Delta V$. Tsuru demonstrates that in the case of pure circulating capital with a uniform production period, the standard (Keynesian) measure of value added is $VA_{NIPA} = V + S_c + S_{ac} + S_{av} + S_{av} = (V + S) + S_{av}$ = Marxian value added + ΔV (Tsuru, 1942, pp. 371–373).

11 Tsuru also argues that the change in the wage bill appears twice in the conventional measure of gross domestic product. This is best understood by grouping his measure into three items: $VA_{NIPA} = (S_c) + (V + S_{av}) + (S_{ac} + S_{av})$. The first item is capitalist consumption. The second is workers' consumption: since all production takes one year the labor cost of finished goods V is the wage bill in the *previous* year, $V + S_{av} = V + \Delta V$ = the wage bill of the *current* year, and the latter is equal to current worker consumption, given Tsuru's and Marx's assumption all wage income is consumed in the same period. The third item is total investment in circulating capital, i.e. the net addition to inventories of work-in-progress as measured by the cost of additional materials ($S_{ac} = \Delta C$) and additional labor ($S_{av} = \Delta V$). Thus VA_{NIPA} = Total Consumption + Total Investment. In effect, an increase in the wage bill shows up both in current worker consumption and as part of the current addition to the inventories of work-in-progress.

References

Alemi, Piruz, and Duncan K. Foley (2010) "The Circuit of Capital, U.S. Manufacturing and Non-Financial Corporate Business Sectors, 1966–2009." *NSSR–JJCUNY1 Working Paper*, February, pp. 1–34.

BEA (2008) "Concepts and Methods of the U.S. National Income and Product Accounts," U.S. Bureau of Economic Analysis.

Foley, Duncan K. (1982) "Realization and Accumulation in a Marxian model of the Circuit of Capital." *Journal of Economic Theory*, 28(2), 300–319.

Foley, Duncan K. (1986a) *Understanding Capital*. Cambridge, MA: Harvard University Press.

Foley, Duncan K. (1986b) *Money, Accumulation and Crisis*. New York: Harwood Academic.

Foley, Duncan K., and Piruz Alemi (1997) "The Circuit of Capital: U.S. Manufacturing and Non-financial Corporate Business Sectors, 1947–1993," *Economics Department Working Papers*. New York: Barnard College.

Marx, Karl (1967a) *Capital*, Vol II. New York: International Publishers.

Marx, Karl (1967b) *Capital*, Vol I. New York: International Publishers.

Shaikh, Anwar (1988) "Accumulation, Finance, and Effective Demand in Marx, Keynes and Kalecki," In *Economic Dynamics and Financial Instability*, ed. W. E. Semmler. New York: M.E. Sharpe.

Shaikh, Anwar (1991) "Wandering Around the Warranted Path: Dynamic Nonlinear Solutions to the Harrodian Knife-Edge," In *Kaldor and Mainstream Economics: Confrontation or Convergence (Festschrift for Nicholas Kaldor)*, ed. E. Nell and W. Semmler. London: MacMillan.

Shaikh, Anwar (1992) "A Dynamic Approach to the Theory of Effective Demand," In *Profits, Deficits, and Instability*, ed. D. Papadimitriou. London: MacMillan.

Shaikh, Anwar (2009) "Economic Policy in a Growth Context: A Classical Synthesis of Keynes and Harrod." *Metroeconomica*, 60(3), 455–494.

Shaikh, Anwar, and E. Ahmet Tonak (1994) *Measuring the Wealth of Nations: The Political Economy of National Accounts*. Cambridge: Cambridge University Press.

Shapiro, Edward (1966) *Macroeconomic Analysis*. New York: Harcourt, Brace and World, Inc.

Sweezy, Paul M. (1942) *The Theory of Capitalist Development*. New York: Monthly Review Press.

Tsuru, Shigeto (1942) "Appendix A: On Reproduction Schemes," In *The Theory of Capitalist Development*, ed. P. M. Sweezy, 365–374. New York: Monthly Review Press.

15 Endogenous technological change in Classical–Marxian models of growth and distribution

Amitava Krishna Dutt

While there have been recent advances in the modeling of endogenous technological change in neoClassical (include endogenous) growth models, Classical–Marxian models seems to have lagged behind. However, there are some exceptions to this, including Classical–Marxian contributions to technological change from Duncan Foley. This chapter reviews, and makes some additions to, the literature on endogenous technological change in Classical–Marxian models, by incorporating a number of alternative approaches to the analysis of technological change into a basic Classical–Marxian model with capitalists and workers. It shows that although this task is relatively easy, to get a comprehensive view of the interaction between growth, distribution and technological change, the models have to endogenize a number of parameters, including the labor share and capital productivity, and to introduce additional features not analyzed in the basic model, such as the role of high-skilled workers.

Introduction

Technological change has a major role in the theory of growth and distribution of the Classical economists and of Karl Marx. For Adam Smith, productivity growth caused by specialization and the division of labor took center stage in the growth process. For Marx, technological change is the driving force behind the dialectic interaction between the forces and the social relations of production. Moreover, in Marx's view, technological change is a means, through mechanization, of overcoming labor shortages and disciplining workers, and the nature of technological change has consequences for the rate of profit, all of which affects the accumulation process.

However, formal Classical–Marxian growth models have not made much headway in endogenizing technological change for analyzing the interaction between technological change and the growth process. This chapter examines several ways of endogenizing technological change into a simple Classical–Marxian model of growth and distribution. In doing so, it follows the lead of Duncan Foley, who has made significant contributions to the literatures on Classical–Marxian growth models and endogenous technological change.

The next section describes the basic Classical–Marxian model of growth and distribution with exogenous technological change used in this chapter. The third section builds the basic model to explore the implications of endogenous technological change in a number of alternative ways. The fourth section complicates the basic model by introducing endogenous changes in the distribution income and the capital–output ratio, and the fifth section introduces a further complication by introducing two types of workers, to analyze the effects of education on growth and distribution. The final section offers some conclusions.

A basic Classical–Marxian model

A simple Classical–Marxian model considers a closed economy without government fiscal activity producing a single good with a fixed-coefficients technology exhibiting constant returns to scale, with A the output–labor ratio and B the output–capital ratio. Labor is assumed to be in unlimited supply (due to endogenous population growth or the existence of a reserve army) and firms are assumed to produce as much as they can at full capacity, so that output is given by

$$Y = BK \tag{1}$$

The rate of profit is given by

$$r = \left[1 - \frac{w}{A}\right]B \tag{2}$$

where w is the real wage.

The economy has only two classes, workers and capitalists. Workers consume their entire income from wages, while capitalists, who receive profits or non-wage income, save a fraction, s, of their income and consume the rest. Thus, we have

$$S = srK \tag{3}$$

Capitalists then invest their entire saving in order to expand their business and maintain their competitive position against other capitalists. The implication is that all income is spent on the purchase of the good. Thus, we have investment being identically equal to saving, or

$$I \equiv S \tag{4}$$

It is assumed that B is a constant, but that labor productivity, measured by A, grows at a constant rate given by a. Thus, technological change is purely labor-saving, or what is referred to as Harrod-neutral.

As Foley and Michl (1999) argue, the basic Classical–Marxian model takes as given the real wage, w, as a conventional wage given by "subsistence," or as is more appropriate in a model with technological change, the wage share, $\omega = w/A$, as the conventional wage share, as determined by the "state of class struggle." We assume the latter in our model, which implies that the real wage grows at a rate equal to the rate of growth of labor productivity, to keep the wage and profit shares constant.

Using equations (2) through (4) and the definition of the wage share, ω, and abstracting from the depreciation of capital for simplicity, we can write

$$g = \hat{K} = s[1 - \omega]B, \tag{5}$$

where overhats denote time-rate of growth and g is defined to be the growth rate of capital. Given the exogenously given wage share with $\omega < 1$, the rate of growth of capital is determined and is positive. With the output–capital ratio being given, the rate of growth of output is given by

$$y = g \tag{6}$$

where $y = \hat{Y}$. The rate of growth of employment is given by

$$l = y - a, \tag{7}$$

where $l = \hat{L}$ and $L = Y/A$ is labor employed. As can be seen from equations (5) and (6), the rates of growth of capital and output are affected positively by the saving rate of capitalists and by capital productivity, and negatively by the wage share (because a higher wage share redistributes income to those who do not save). A higher rate of technological change, a, has no effect on g or y, but only reduces the rate of growth of employment.

We can depict this basic model using Figure 15.1. The lower-left-hand quadrant shows the relation between rate of profit and the wage share given by equation (2) and the definition of ω. The upper-left-hand quadrant shows the relation between the growth rate of capital and the rate of profit, shown by equations (3) and (4), and the definition of g. The upper-right-hand quadrant shows the relation between the growth rate of capital and the growth rates of employment and labor productivity growth, using equations (6) and (7); it gives the relation between a and g given l. The exogenously given conventional wage share, $\overline{\omega}$ determines the rate of profit in the lower quadrant, and the upper-left quadrant then determines g. The exogenously given rate of labor productivity growth, $\bar{a}$ and this g determine the growth–technological change combination in the upper-right quadrant, and the level of l is determined by the intercept of the dashed (to underscore that its position is not fixed) line in the quadrant through this $< g, a >$ pair. The effects of changes in s, $\overline{\omega}$, $\bar{a}$ and B can be easily analyzed using this figure. For instance, an increase in s rotates the $g = sr$ line upwards in the upper-left quadrant, and shifts the line in the upper-right quadrant upwards in a parallel manner, increasing g and l, but leaving r and ω unchanged.

This model is arguably a fair formalization of some of the main features of the approach to growth of the Classical economists and Marx. Of course it does

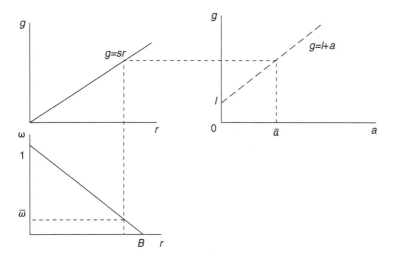

Figure 15.1 A basic Classical–Marxian model of growth and distribution.

not do justice to the growth theories of all of the Classical economists, as is obvious by examining the approaches of the three most influential Classical–Marxian growth theorists. Arguably, a central feature of Smith's growth theory (technological change resulting from greater division of labor and specialization due to the expansion of the size of the market) is missing. Ricardo's analysis of the roles of diminishing returns in land and of rent in squeezing profits is also absent. Finally, Marx's complex analysis of technological change, mechanization, and crises is omitted. Moreover, issues due to over-saving and glut discussed by Malthus, and the problems resulting from the realization of profit examined by Marx, are also excluded. Complications due to the existence of multiple sectors are also eschewed. The model provides a simple analysis of growth which is common to the major Classical economists, in which growth is driven by capital accumulation from capitalist savings.

It is also very popular as a modern representation of Classical–Marxian growth theory. It has been called the Classical model by Harris (1978) and the neo-Marxian model by Marglin (1984) and Dutt (1990). It is very close to the Classical model of Foley and Michl (1999), although, unlike the model used here, which takes the saving rate of capitalists to be exogenously fixed, Foley and Michl allow capitalists to maximize their utility intertemporally. However, this optimization merely implies that the saving rate of capitalists is determined by parameters of the utility function. The model is also the basis of other Classical–Marxian models developed by Goodwin (1967) and others, who in addition allow for endogenous changes in the wage share due to the influence of labor-market conditions.[1]

Endogenous technological change in the Classical–Marxian model

This section takes the basic model of the previous section and makes only one change in it: instead of assuming that a is exogenously given we endogenize it to make it depend on other variables in the model.

Approaches to endogenous technological change

We can endogenize a in a variety of ways. We consider, in turn, eight simple alternatives. For all of them, we continue to assume that B is exogenously given, so that technological change remains purely labor augmenting. To economize on the use of symbols we will use the same symbol for a number of approaches; since these approaches are alternatives, there is no possibility of confusion.

First, following Arrow's (1962) learning-by-doing formulation we assume that

$$A = \theta K^{\tau}, \tag{8}$$

where $\theta > 0$ and τ are constants, with $0 < \tau < 1$. This equation implies that

$$a = \tau g. \tag{9}$$

This is very similar to Adam Smith's approach, which assumes that productivity depends on the division of labor, which is limited by the extent of the market. We can formalize this using the equation

$$A = \theta Y^{\tau}, \tag{10}$$

which, given the fixed level of θ, implies equation (9). We will call this the Smith–Arrow approach.

Second, a variant of this assumes that A depends not on K but the capital–labor ratio, so that we have

$$A = \theta \left(\frac{K}{L} \right)^{\tau}, \tag{11}$$

with $0 < \tau < 1$, so that we have

$$a = \tau(g - l). \tag{12}$$

If we use equations (6) and (7), this equation can be solved only for $a = 0$, and we therefore ignore this formulation. A variant, considered by Kaldor (1961), assumes that θ increases at a constant rate, $\lambda > 0$, which implies that

$$a = \lambda + \tau(g - l). \tag{13}$$

Since it is a linear version of Kaldor's technological progress function we will call it the Kaldorian approach.

Third, another variant of this approach assumes in equation (11) that θ is constant and $\tau = 1$, so that we have

$$A = \theta \frac{K}{L}. \tag{14}$$

Thus, labor productivity is assumed to grow proportionately with the capital–employment ratio. Equation (14), with θ given, implies

$$a = g - l. \tag{15}$$

This approach is a variant of the so-called AK approach, in which labor productivity grows proportionately with capital per worker, with no diminishing returns to technological change (see Barro and Sala-i-Martin, 2003).

A fourth approach assumes that labor productivity growth depends on the tightness of the labor market, as measured by the employment rate, which can be formalized using the relation

$$a = \theta \left(\frac{L}{N} \right)^{\tau}, \tag{16}$$

where N is the supply of labor, which is assumed to grow at an exogenously given rate n. This implies

$$\hat{a} = \tau (l - n), \tag{17}$$

an equation which has been used in a number of models, including those in Bhaduri (2006) and Dutt (2006). Substituting from equation (6) and (7), this implies that, for stationary values of a, we get

$$a = g - n. \tag{18}$$

Fifth, an alternative version of the labor-market tightness approach assumes that labor productivity depends on the employment rate, so that

$$A = \theta \left(\frac{L}{N} \right)^{\tau} \tag{19}$$

which implies that

$$a = \lambda + \tau (l - n) \tag{20}$$

where λ is the exogenously given rate of growth of θ.

A sixth approach makes labor productivity growth depend on the wage share under the assumption that firms adopt labor-saving technological innovations at a higher rate when the labor share rises and profitability erodes for the current technology. We can formalize this with the equation

$$a = \theta + \tau\omega. \tag{21}$$

This approach to labor productivity growth has been used by Taylor (1991, p. 226) in a structuralist model with demand-led growth, by Duménil and Lévy (2003) in a Classical–Marxian model (which, however, also makes the rate of growth of B depend negatively on the wage share, and interprets the equations to provide average values of productivity change, since it models technology change in probabilistic terms), and by Foley (2003) who also uses land into his Classical model. We can call this approach the profitability approach.

A seventh approach relates labor productivity to the real wage, and can be written in the form

$$A = \theta w^\tau \tag{22}$$

with θ growing at a constant rate λ, and $\tau < 1$. This implies that

$$a = \lambda + \tau\widehat{w}, \tag{23}$$

which states that labor productivity growth depends positively on real wage growth. This is a dynamic analogue of efficiency wage theory, used by You (1994).

A final approach assumes that that technological change depends on the availability of resources for research and development, so that the rate of technological change depends positively on the rate of profit. Adopting a simple linear form we have

$$a = \theta + \tau r. \tag{24}$$

This may be called a Schumpeterian approach.

Endogenous technological change in the basic model

We now introduce these alternative approaches to endogenizing technological change into the basic Classical–Marxian model in turn.

The Smith–Arrow approach, as depicted by equation (9), requires the addition of the $g = a/\tau$ line in the upper-right quadrant, as shown in Figure 15.2, where, since $\tau < 1$, the curve has a slope steeper than unity. In this model the exogenous wage share determines rates of profit and growth as in the previous section, and g determines a according to the $g = a/\tau$ line. The $g = l + a$ line is shifted to go through this $\langle g, a \rangle$ combination, and serves to determine l as its vertical intercept. To illustrate the effects of shifts in the parameters of the model we consider four shifts. An increase in s rotates the $g = sr$ line upwards and increases g and a, and therefore l, leaving r and ω unchanged. An increase in the exogenously given ω

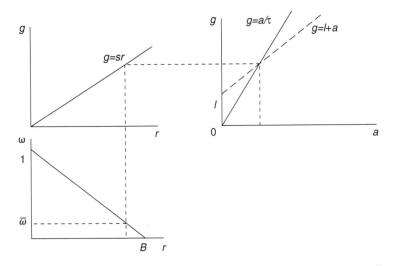

Figure 15.2 A Classical–Marxian model with a Smith–Arrow approach to technological change.

reduces r, g, a, and l. An increase in the technological parameter, τ, rotates the $g = a/\tau$ line downwards, increasing a but reducing l, leaving all other variables unchanged. A reduction in capital productivity reduces r for the exogenously given ω, reduces g and a, and reduces l.

The Kaldorian approach, using equation (13), implies that we can draw a positively sloped relationship between g and a in the upper-right quadrant of Figure 15.1 for a given value of l. With g and r determined for the given value of ω, this line and the $g = l + a$ can be freely moved to determine the equilibrium values of a and l to make them intersect at the equilibrium value of g. It is easier, however, to use equations (6), (7), and (13) to solve for a, to obtain

$$a = \frac{\lambda}{1 - \tau},\qquad(25)$$

which is positive since $\tau < 1$. Using this value of a for $\bar{a}$ in Figure 15.1 determines the equilibrium values of the variables in the model exactly as in Figure 15.1, and all the properties of the model are the same. An increase in λ or τ has the effect of increasing the equilibrium level of a, and has the same effects as an exogenous increase in a in the model of the previous section.

The AK approach, given by equation (15), does not introduce a new independent equation into our model, since it is already implied by definitional and steady state equations (6) and (7). Thus, incorporating this approach to technological change within the Classical–Marxian approach implies an undetermined model. We can close the model by introducing an additional equation into it. A possible equation

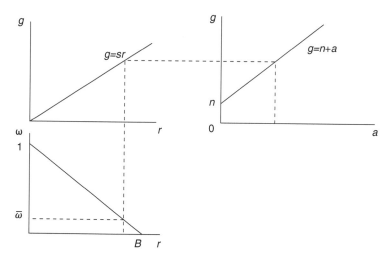

Figure 15.3 A Classical–Marxian model with AK technological change and constant unemployment rate.

is to assume that in long-run equilibrium,

$$l = n,$$ (26)

so that employment and labor supply grow at the same rate, or that the unemployment rate is constant. The model is shown in Figure 15.3, when equation (26) is substituted into the $g = l + a$ equation. The role that technological change has in this model is to accommodate capital accumulation, and output growth to change in response to standard Classical parameters such as s and ω, while maintaining a constant rate of unemployment, by making the rate of growth of effective labor supply endogenous. Thus, it brings the Classical–Marxian model closer to the neoClassical labor-market-clearing approach while maintaining all of its standard properties.[2] It may also be noted that an increase in the rate of labor supply growth only has the result of reducing a in this model, keeping all other variables unchanged.

The first labor-market tightness approach, represented by equation (18), produces exactly the same model as the one just discussed, which can be derived from the model with the labor-market adjustment mechanism shown in equation (17), and there is no need to repeat the discussion. The second labor-market tightness approach, represented by equation (20), implies, upon substitution from equations (6) and (7),

$$a = \frac{\lambda}{1+\tau} + \frac{\tau}{1+\tau}(g - n).$$ (27)

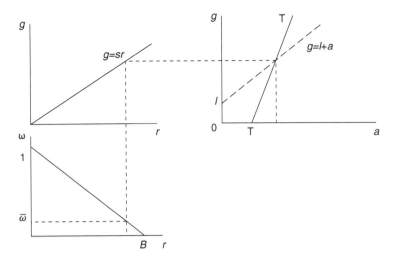

Figure 15.4 A Classical-Marxian model with technological change depending on labor-market conditions.

This equation provides a new positive relation between a and g, which states that a higher rate of accumulation increases the rate of growth of employment and speeds up the rate of technological change, and is drawn as the positively sloped line TT in Figure 15.4. The effects of parametric shifts are very similar to those in the Smith–Arrow model. In particular, a shift in technological parameters only shifts the TT line and therefore affects a and l, but not g or r. Unlike the Smith–Arrow model, however, an increase in n shifts the TT line to the left, slows down technological change, and increases employment growth.

The profitability approach, which makes the wage share positively affect the rate of labor productivity growth, as shown by equation (21), is illustrated in Figure 15.5. We now have a new line in the figure, in the lower-right quadrant, depicting equation (21) and shown by TT.[3] Given ω, r and g are determined as in the basic model, and a by the TT curve, l is determined by the intercept of the dashed line in the upper-right quadrant. In this model, an increase in s increases g, but leaves a unchanged, increasing l. However, an increase in ω reduces r and g, and increases a along the TT line, reducing l.

The dynamic efficiency wage approach depicted by equation (23) is very similar to the Kaldorian approach. Since $\omega = w/A$, we have

$$\widehat{\omega} = \widehat{w} - a. \tag{28}$$

Since in our models ω is stationary in equilibrium, we obtain $\widehat{w} = a$, which, when substituted into equation (23) implies equation (25). Thus, as in the Kaldorian approach, the technological parameters determine a, and then the model is just like the model of the previous section with exogenous technological change.

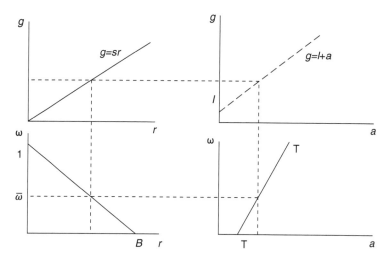

Figure 15.5 A Classical–Marxian model with technological change depending on profitability.

Finally, the Schumpeterian approach, shown by equation (24), using equation (2) and the definition of ω, implies

$$a = (\theta + \tau B) - \tau B\omega. \tag{29}$$

As in Figure 15.4, we get a relationship between a and ω, except that the relation is negative – since a higher wage share implies a lower rate of profit and hence a lower rate of technological change – rather than the positive one of Figure 15.5. The equilibrium can be depicted using a figure like Figure 15.5 with the TT curve given a negative slope. A rise in s speeds up accumulation and leaves r and a unchanged, thereby increasing l. A rise in ω reduces r and g and also a, the effect on l being ambiguous, depending on the relative magnitudes of s and τ. A fall in capital productivity B implies a fall in r and a, as well as a fall in g, and the effect on l is ambiguous. An increase in θ increases a for a given r, but leaves g and r unchanged, reducing only l.

We conclude our analysis of endogenous technological change in the Classical–Marxian model of growth and distribution with three comments. First, there are a large variety of approaches to endogenous technological change which can be adopted within the Classical–Marxian approach. Second, these approaches can be easily incorporated into our basic Classical–Marxian model. Third, although a few of the approaches imply interesting results – for instance one of the labor-market tightness approaches implies greater similarity between Classical–Marxian and neoClassical full employment (or at least constant unemployment rate) neoClassical models, and they sometimes show how the determinants of growth and distribution can affect the rate of technological change – for the most part there is little by way of interesting results in terms of the feedback effects of technological change on growth and distribution. A higher rate of technological change affects employment growth, while growth and distributional variables are independent of it.

Endogenous distribution and capital productivity in the Classical–Marxian model

The absence of feedback effects of technological change on growth and distribution in the models of the previous section results from the fact that several possible channels through which technological change can affect the economy have been ignored. In particular, the models have assumed that the wage share and the productivity of capital, are exogenously given. In this section we illustrate with a few examples how these assumptions can be relaxed.

Endogenous distribution

We assumed in the previous section that the wage share, ω, is exogenously given. One way of relaxing this assumption is to assume that

$$\widehat{w} = \lambda_1 (\overline{\omega} - \omega) + \lambda_2 a, \tag{30}$$

where λ_i are positive, finite, parameters and $\lambda_2 < 1$. This equation shows that the rate of growth of the real wage depends on the gap between the targeted wage share, $\widehat{\omega}$, and the actual wage share, and adjusts incompletely to changes in labor productivity growth. Substituting equation (30) into (28) and solving for the equilibrium value of the wage share, at which $\overline{\omega} = 0$, we obtain

$$\omega = \overline{\omega} - \frac{1 - \lambda_2}{\lambda_1} a. \tag{31}$$

This equation shows that a higher a implies a lower equilibrium level of ω, since the real wage fails to keep up with the rate of productivity growth, and we assume that we are always in the region in which $0 < \omega < 1$. This relationship is shown in the lower-right quadrant of Figure 15.6. This approach can be seen as following Marx's analysis of technological change – which involves the adoption of labor-displacing machines – as a weapon in the hands of capitalists in class struggle (see Marx, 1867, ch. 15.5), which reduces the share of workers in overall income.

If we modify the Classical–Marxian model by replacing the assumption that ω is fixed with equation (31), while assuming that the labor-market tightness model of technological change embodied in equation (18) holds, we get the model shown in Figure 15.6. Combining the three lines in the lower two quadrants and the upper-left one, we obtain the AG curve, derived from equations (5) and (31), which yield

$$g = s(1 - \overline{\omega})B + s\frac{1 - \lambda_2}{\lambda_1} Ba. \tag{32}$$

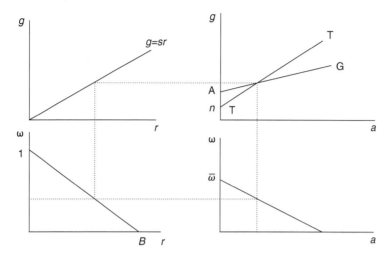

Figure 15.6 A Classical–Marxian model with an endogenous wage share.

The figure assumes that $s(1 - \overline{\omega})B > n$, that is, the rate of capital accumulation that results from a rate of profit implied by the targeted wage share (which gives an upper bound to the wage share) exceeds the rate of labor supply growth, and $s\frac{1-\lambda_2}{\lambda_1}B < 1$; that is, the real wage lag behind productivity growth is not "too" large. The intersection of the AG curve and the TT curve which has n as its vertical intercept determines the equilibrium levels of g and a. The rest of the figure solves for the equilibrium values of the other variables. Since AG incorporates information from the line in the lower-right quadrant, the equilibrium levels of ω and a will lie on the latter line.

An increase in s rotates the $g = sr$ line upward in the upper-left quadrant and shifts up and rotates upward the AG line in the upper-right quadrant. There is an increase in both g and a, and the lower-right quadrant shows that there is a fall in ω, and hence, according to the lower-left quadrant, a rise in r. The rate of growth of output and the real wage also rise. A fall in the growth of labor supply, n, shifts down the TT curve in the upper-right quadrant, implying an increase in equilibrium a, g, and r, and a reduction in ω. The rates of growth of output and the real wage increase, and that of employment falls. The fall in the rate of labor supply growth increases labor-market pressure and induces a higher rate of technological change, which reduces the wage share as wages fail to keep up with productivity growth, which increases the profit rate and results in a higher rate of capital accumulation. In equilibrium, labor demand grows at the lower rate of growth of labor supply, but productivity grows faster, as does the real wage and output. This result may be compared to the implications of a fall in n in the Classical–Marxian model discussed in the previous section, where there is no effect on the rate of capital accumulation.

An alternative way of formalizing the change in the real wage is to assume that the real wage adjusts not to technological change at all, but positively to employment growth. Thus, we assume that

$$\overline{w} = \gamma_0 + \gamma_1 (l - n),\tag{33}$$

where $\gamma_i > 0$ are parameters. We adopt the profitability approach to endogenous technological change, given by equation (21). This is very close to Duménil and Lévy's (2003) model, although – unlike them – here we assume that B is fixed.

Substituting from equations (5), (6), (7), and (33) into equation (28), we obtain

$$\overline{\omega} = \gamma_0 - \gamma_1 n + \gamma_1 s (1 - \omega) B - (1 + \gamma_1) a.$$

In equilibrium, since $\widehat{\omega} = 0$, we obtain

$$\omega = \frac{\gamma_0 - \gamma_1 n + \gamma_1 s B}{\gamma_1 s B} - \frac{1 + \gamma_1}{\gamma_1 s B} a.\tag{34}$$

This equation provides a negative relation between a and ω. A higher a implies a lower rate of growth of the labor share, because workers are not directly compensated for it and therefore lose their share of income, and because real wage increases are slowed down by labor saving technological change. To compensate for this falling wage share, we require capital accumulation and employment growth to be speeded up, which requires a lower wage share.

The model is depicted in Figure 15.7, which excludes the upper quadrants of our usual figures. The WG line in the right quadrant shows the relationship between ω and a depicted in equation (34); its name comes from the fact that it combines wage and capital growth dynamics. The TT line also in the right quadrant shows the profitability approach to technological change. The equilibrium for this model is determined at the intersection of the WG and TT lines, which determines the equilibrium values of a and ω, and the left-hand quadrant then determines r. The rate of capital accumulation, g, is found from the saving curve (not shown in

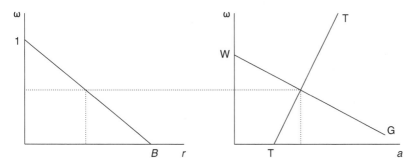

Figure 15.7 A Classical–Marxian model with an endogenous wage share and a profitability approach to technological change.

the figure). It should be noted that this model does not require that in equilibrium $l = n$. An increase in γ_0, the autonomous rate of growth of the real wage, shifts the WG curve upwards and increases ω and a, but reduces r and g and hence l. An increase in the technological change parameter θ shifts the TT curve to the right, increasing the equilibrium value of a and reducing that of ω. The reduction in ω results in an increase in r and g, and the effect on l is ambiguous. An increase in s shifts the WG line down and makes it steeper, and therefore reduces the equilibrium values of ω and a; equilibrium r increases as does g, and l increases as well.

Endogenous capital productivity

As is well known, Marx argued that a faster rate of labor productivity growth requires increased mechanization, which increases the amount of capital required per unit of output, so that capital productivity falls. There have been a number of attempts to model the implications of declining capital productivity, including those by Foley and Michl (1999) and Duménil and Lévy (2003). These contributions have generally examined the behavior of the rate of growth of capital productivity and shown that the growth process does not lead to an equilibrium outcome; as is well known, technological change involving changes in capital productivity is not consistent with steady state growth. Given our focus on long-run equilibrium outcomes, we will examine variations in the level of capital productivity rather than examine its growth rate.[4] More specifically, we assume that a faster rate of labor productivity growth requires a reduction in capital productivity, so that

$$B = f(a), \tag{35}$$

where $f < 0$.[5]

We illustrate the implications of this, using the profitability approach to labor productivity growth shown in equation (21). We first return to the fixed wage share assumption and then relax it. Equation (21) is shown by the TT curve of the upper-right quadrant, equation (35) is shown in the lower-left quadrant, and the lower-right quadrant shows a 45° line. Given the wage share $\overline{\omega}$, a, is determined in the upper-right quadrant, and the lower-left quadrant determines B. This level of B determines the horizontal intercept of the wage-share–profit line in the upper-left quadrant, and this quadrant then determines r, from which g can be determined using the saving line (not shown).

An increase in θ shifts the TT curve to the right, increases a for the given value of $\overline{\omega}$, reduces B, rotates the wage-share–profit-rate relation down, reduces r, and reduces g. An exogenous increase in $\overline{\omega}$ increases a, reduces B, and reduces r, both because of an inward rotation in the wage-share–profit-rate line and because of a shift up the line due to the increase in the wage share. Capital-using technological change, as Marx argued, leads to a fall in the rate of profit and a fall in the rate of accumulation. This, with the increase in a, reduces l.

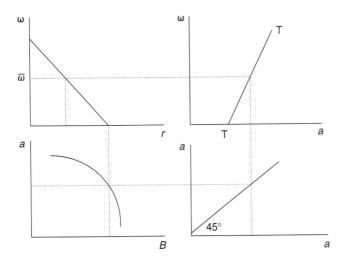

Figure 15.8 A Classical–Marxian model with endogenous capital productivity.

If we allow the wage share to be endogenously affected by a due to the failure of workers to reap their share of the effects of technological progress, or because of downward pressure on the wage share because of a fall in employment growth, as in the previous subsection, an increase in labor productivity growth due to, say, an increase in the parameter θ, will reduce ω, and the effect on r and hence g is indeterminate. On the one hand, there will be a fall in capital productivity, which will tend to reduce r, but on the other hand there will be a fall in the wage share, which will tend to increase r. The analysis of this case requires the approaches adopted in this and the previous subsection to be combined. This is an example of a countertendency, which may reduce or even reverse the tendency toward a fall in the rate of profit, although the fall in the rate of profit cannot be ruled out.

Education, labor skills, and endogenous technological change

We can endogenize technological change in additional ways, but some of these require modification of our basic Classical–Marxian model. We illustrate with the example of endogenizing technological change due to education and skill formation, using a model with capitalists, high-skilled workers, and low-skilled workers. Education transforms low-skilled workers into high-skilled workers. Low-skilled workers are engaged in standard production activities using standardized production methods, and high-skilled workers are engaged in developing new methods of production.[6] As in the basic model, the production of the good uses fixed-coefficient input–output relations which use capital and low-skilled labor. Capital productivity, B, is assumed to be given, and A, which is given at a point in time, is interpreted as the productivity of low-skilled labor.

The quantities employed of the two kinds of labor are H and L (denoting high- and low-skilled workers, respectively) who receive real wages w_H and w_L. We denote the skill premium as

$$\sigma = w_H/w_L, \tag{36}$$

with $\sigma > 1$. The low-skilled-worker wage serves as a reference point which, given the premium, determines the high-skilled wage. The share of low-skilled workers in total income, given by

$$\omega = w_L/A, \tag{37}$$

is assumed for now to be given.

The effective amount of high-skilled labor demanded by firms depends positively on the amount of capital installed and negatively on the skill premium, so that

$$H^d = b(\sigma)K/A, \tag{38}$$

where $b' < 0$, and where A is also the productivity of high-skilled workers. High-skilled labor does not participate in the standard production process, but performs activity which improves labor productivity (of both types of labor). We assume that there is a minimum level, $\underline{b}$, below which b will not fall, however high the skill premium. It is assumed that when σ rises, firms will reduce b, but not by much, so that in the relevant range, the elasticity of b with respect to σ is less than unity in absolute value.

For a given supply of high-skilled workers, H, at a point in time, we assume that the skill premium adjusts to bring the demand and supply of high-skilled workers to equality. For given levels of A, K, and H, we may therefore solve for the equilibrium value of σ, which is given by

$$\sigma = b^{-1}(h), \tag{39}$$

where $h = AH/K$.

The rate of growth of labor productivity (of both high-skilled and low-skilled workers) depends positively and linearly on the amount of high-skilled labor in efficiency units as a ratio of the stock of capital, that is,

$$a = \theta + \tau h. \tag{40}$$

We assume that all firms are identical, so that, for instance, A can be thought of as representing aggregate average productivity or the individual firm's productivity.

Low-skilled labor is converted into high-skilled labor through the process of education. The dynamics of H is formalized with the equation

$$dH/dt = \Omega \phi(\sigma)H, \tag{41}$$

where $\phi' > 0$. We also assume that $\phi(\sigma) = 0$ for all $\sigma \leq \sigma_{min} \geq 1$. This will ensure that no one will seek education if the wage premium falls below a certain level.

The change in the stock of high-skilled workers depends on: the demand for education which, in turn, depends positively on the skill premium, which increases the "return" to education; the size of the stock of high-skilled workers, both by increasing the availability of mentors and educators, and by increasing the support for, and access to, education (for instance, a higher stock implies a higher number added from high-skilled worker families; and a parameter, Ω, which captures the openness of the education system, either through government policy (for instance, low-cost public education and greater access to student loans and grants) or through the degree of exclusivity of the education system.

Both kinds of workers consume their entire income. Profit is now given by

$$rK = Y - w_L L - w_H H. \tag{42}$$

so that rate of profit, using equations (37) and (42), is seen to be given by

$$r = (1 - \omega)B - \sigma \omega h. \tag{43}$$

Saving continues to be given by equation (3).

The dynamics of the economy can be analyzed using the state variable, h, which changes according to

$$\hat{h} = \widehat{H} + a - g. \tag{44}$$

We can substitute from equations (3), (4), (40), (41), and (43) to obtain

$$\hat{h} = \theta + \tau h + \Omega \phi (\sigma (h)) - s[(1 - \omega)B - \sigma (h)\omega h], \tag{45}$$

where the function $\sigma() = b^{-1}()$. The dynamics are shown in Figure 15.9. At a point in time we have given H, K, and A, and hence, h, and the model solves for σ from equation (39) and the growth rates, $\widehat{H}$, a, and g, all as functions of h, as shown by the labeled curves. The a curve shows the first two terms on the right-hand side of equation (45): a rise in the role of high-skilled workers in the economy (in efficiency units) increases the rate of growth of labor productivity (of both kinds of workers) in the economy. The $\widehat{H}$ curve represents the third term of equation (45), which shows that as h increases, the skill premium falls, and reduces the rate of growth of high-skilled workers. The g curve represents the last term in equation (45), and shows that as h increases, the skill premium falls, the rate of profit rises as capitalists pay high-skilled workers a lower wage, and saving and investment increase. Capitalists use more high-skilled workers when the skill premium falls, but given our assumption of the low elasticity of the demand curve for high-skilled workers, $\sigma(h)h$ falls with h, so that g rises with h. We add up the rates of growth of A and H to obtain the $a + \widehat{H}$ curve. Equilibrium is determined as h^*, where the $a + \widehat{H}$ and g curves intersect, so that $\hat{h} = 0$.[7]

An increase in Ω, which represents the openness of the education system, shifts the $\widehat{H}$ curve upwards as the growth in the number of high-skilled workers

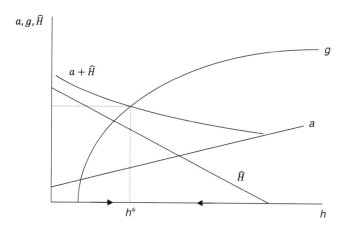

Figure 15.9 A Classical–Marxian model with education and skill differentia.

increases, and therefore shifts up the $a + \widehat{H}$. This implies that at the new equilibrium level, h, $\widehat{H}$, a, and g are all higher, which implies that the rate of growth of output also increases with Ω. Regarding distribution, the share of income going to low-skilled workers, ω, is given by assumption, but the distribution of income between capitalists and skilled workers is endogenous. The share of total income going to the capitalists is given by r/B, and the share going to high-skilled workers is given by $\sigma \omega h / B$. When Ω increases, the rise in h will be proportionately less than the fall in σ, given the assumed inelasticity of the $b(\ )$ function, so that σh will fall and the rate of profit will rise. Thus income is redistributed from high-skilled workers to capitalists (which is, indeed, why the rate of capital accumulation in the economy is speeded up). The rate of growth of high-skilled workers, that is, the rate at which low-skilled workers (or the unemployed) become high-skilled workers, increases. The rate of growth of the real wage of low-skilled workers also rises with a higher rate of technological change. The rate of growth of low-skilled employment, which is given by $g - a = \widehat{H}$ is in equilibrium, since h becomes constant at it. As long as the dynamics are as shown in Figure 15.9, the increase in θ must increase $\widehat{H}$, and hence the rate of growth of low-skilled employment. Thus, the condition of low-skilled workers, in terms of their real wage and employment growth, is unequivocally improved.

If our assumption that ω, the share of low-skilled workers in total income, does not change is relaxed along the lines of the section "Endogenous distribution," above, by making the wage rate of low-skilled workers adjust to a desired wage share and (partially) to labor productivity growth as in equation (30), we can analyze the dynamics using h and ω as state variables. It can be shown in this case that the increase in Ω will increase the equilibrium level of h and reduce that of ω (since with faster rate of technological change due to the increase in h, the wages of low-skilled workers, lags behind productivity growth). The positive growth effect of wider access to education is stronger, but the distributional effect, as captured by the shares of low-skilled workers, becomes negative. If wages do not lag significantly behind productivity growth, the negative distributional effect will be weak, and low-skilled workers will on balance benefit, as in the case with a constant ω.

Conclusion

This chapter takes a simple Classical–Marxian model of growth and distribution and incorporates endogenous technological change into it in a number of ways, thereby producing a variety of models, to analyze the interaction between capital accumulation, income distribution, and technological change within the Classical–Marxian framework. A central feature of the models analyzed is that capital accumulation is driven by the rate of profit, which is affected by distribution, and distribution is affected by the relative power of different groups in society. Thus, technological change affects capital accumulation and growth, not by increasing the effective supply of labor as in mainstream neoClassical growth models, but by affecting profits, and in the way it affects distribution. The main implications are as follows.

1. A number of approaches to endogenous technological change can be incorporated into the model, and the precise implications of these models depend on the way technological change is modeled.
2. Some versions of the models narrow the gap between the Classical–Marxian approach and the mainstream neoClassical growth model with labor supply constrained growth, while producing Classical–Marxian results, thereby extending the range of applicability of that approach.
3. Simple models with fixed parameters which fix the labor share in income or the productivity of capital do not produce a full analysis of the interdependence between growth, distribution, and technological change. However, these models can be extended to enrich the analysis by endogenizing the labor share and capital productivity.
4. The simple models can be further extended by introducing additional elements into them, which allow the analysis of other approaches to technological change. We have extended the simple model to analyze the case of three classes of workers and the role of education in determining the pace of technological change.

The models examined in this chapter abstract from many issues relevant for the study of growth and distribution dynamics (including the role of land, natural resources, and the environment; the role of finance and credit; and open economy considerations) and have examined only a subset of possible approaches to endogenous technological change. It is hoped that the models presented here will further stimulate the development of the Classical–Marxian approach to growth and distribution, carrying on the task pioneered by Duncan Foley.

Acknowledgments

Part of the research for this chapter was done in the summer of 2011, when I was Visiting Professor at University of Paris 13, in the program Chaires d'accueil, DIMeco, Ile de France. I am grateful to seminar participants at that university and to two anonymous referees and to Armon Rezai for their comments and suggestions.

Notes

1 The Classical–Marxian and Keynes–Kalecki *models* comprise the major heterodox approaches to the study of growth and distribution. The main difference between them is that the former (though not necessarily all proponents of the *approach*) assumes that at least in the long run, growth is not constrained by aggregate demand because all saving is automatically invested, while the latter introduces an investment function independent of the saving function, and allows aggregate demand to have a long-run effect on growth. Some proponents of the Classical–Marxian approach argue that the economy is Keynesian in the short run but Classical–Marxian in the long run. Since this chapter is about longer-run issues, it will not analyze the problem of aggregate demand.

2 The neoClassical approach here is what Foley and Michl (1999) call the full-employment version of the Classical model (or, more accurately, the constant-rate of unemployment version).

3 The TT curves for the different figures and models are, of course, not the same.

4 In any case, models which allow firms to choose between increases in labor productivity and increases in capital productivity using a Kennedy (1964) innovations possibility frontier within a Classical–Marxian framework, imply that in long-run equilibrium capital productivity is constant. See, for instance, Zamparelli (2011).

5 Other approaches to endogenizing the capital productivity can also be analyzed, for instance, making it depend on the wage share, ω. However, if we also endogenize a, along the lines discussed in the previous section, such an assumption is already incorporated into our analysis. For instance, we can think of a and B as both being affected by ω, rather than as a first depending on ω, and then B depending on a.

6 The model simplifies by assuming that high-skilled workers are not engaged in production activity. The model developed in Dutt and Veneziani (2011), which builds on this one, allows for substitution between low- and high-skilled workers in production activity, and provides a more extensive discussion of the issues.

7 The figure assumes that the $a + \widehat{H}$ curve is negatively sloped so that equilibrium is stable; other cases can be analyzed using this graph.

References

Arrow, Kenneth K. (1962) "The economic implications of learning by doing", *Review of Economic Studies*, 29, 155–173.

Barro, Robert, and Sala-i-Martin, Xavier (2003) *Economic Growth*. 2nd ed., Cambridge, Massachusetts: MIT Press.

Bhaduri, Amit (2006) "Endogenous economic growth: a new approach", *Cambridge Journal of Economics*, 30, 69–83.

Duménil, Gérard, and Lévy, Dominique (2003) "Technology and distribution. Historical trajectories à la Marx", *Journal of Economic Behavior and Organization*, 52, 201–233.

Dutt, Amitava Krishna (1990) *Growth, Distribution and Uneven Development*, Cambridge, UK: Cambridge University Press.

Dutt, Amitava Krishna (2006) "Aggregate demand, aggregate supply and economic growth", *International Review of Applied Economics*, 20, 319–336.

Dutt, Amitava Krishna, and Veneziani, Roberto (2011) "A Classical–Marxian model of education, growth and distribution", unpublished, Department of Political Science, University of Notre Dame, USA, Department of Economics, Queen Mary College, University of London, UK.

Foley, Duncan K. (2003) "Endogenous technological change with externalities in a classical growth model", *Journal of Economic Behavior and Organization*, 52, 167–189.

Foley, Duncan K., and Michl, Thomas (1999) *Growth and Distribution*, Cambridge, Massachusetts: Harvard University Press.

Goodwin, Richard M. (1967) "A Growth Cycle", in C. H. Feinstein, Ed., *Socialism, Capitalism and Growth*, Cambridge, UK: Cambridge University Press.

Harris, Donald J. (1978) *Capital Accumulation and Income Distribution*, Stanford, Stanford University Press.

Kaldor, Nicholas (1961) "Capital accumulation and economic growth", in F. A. Lutz and D. C. Hague, Eds., *The Theory of Capital Accumulation*, London: Macmillan.

Kennedy, Charles (1964) "Induced bias in innovation and the theory of distribution", *Economic Journal*, 74, 541–547.

Marglin, Stephen A. (1984) *Growth, Distribution and Prices*, Cambridge, Massachusetts: Harvard University Press.

Marx, Karl (1867, 1976) *Capital*, Volume I, New York: Vintage Books.

Taylor, Lance (1991) *Income Distribution, Inflation and Growth. Lectures on Structuralist Macroeconomic Theory*, Cambridge, Massachusetts: MIT Press.

You, Jong-Il (1994) "Endogenous technical change, accumulation, and distribution", in A. Dutt, Ed., *New Directions in Analytical Political Economy*, Aldershot: Edward Elgar.

Zamparelli, Luca (2011) "Induced innovation, endogenous growth and income distribution: a model along classical lines", unpublished, Department of Economics and Social Analysis, University of Rome, La Sapienza.

16 Macroeconomics of Keynesian and Marxian inspirations

Toward a synthesis

Gérard Duménil and Dominique Lévy

Main results and outline

In the wake of World War II, Keynes' analysis contributed to the definition of a new social compromise (including its macro and welfare components). Within this favorable political context, a "Keynesian school", in the broad sense, prospered. After the establishment of neoliberalism in the 1980s, despite the overall repression of economists critical of the new social order, the Keynesian perspective is still the object of much interest among the minority of economists who lean politically to the Left. The relationship between Keynesian and Marxian economics has always been ambiguous, but they have a lot in common concerning macroeconomics.

During the last few decades, one of the fields of our research has been the analysis of business-cycle fluctuations (theory and empirics). We understand that Marx's perspective on this issue was "macroeconomic" as expressed in the phrase "crises of general overproduction" – "general" here being the term to be emphasized as opposed to "disproportions" among industries. On such grounds, an encounter with Keynes is inescapable. This is one of the numerous interests that we believe we share with Duncan Foley, to whom this volume is dedicated.

The object of this study is the investigation of these common Marxian–Keynesian grounds. The "Keynesian inspiration" refers to a broad set of approaches, by major figures of the past such as Michal Kalecki, Joan Robinson, or Hyman Minsky, and the contemporary PostKeynesian school. Conversely, by a "Marxian inspiration", we mean only our own understanding of Marx's analysis, to be specified later, not the entire set of readings of Marx's crisis theory by contemporary or previous Marxist economists. Our final aim is factual analysis: of business-cycle fluctuations within sophisticated capitalist economies after the establishment of central banks and the conduct of macro policies. (This later feature, obviously, creates some distance from Marx's original approach.)

The purpose of the next section is the introduction of the overall framework of analysis, but separating it from money and finance. A broad typology of "theoretical fields" is established depending on time frames and the choice of a multi-industry or macro perspective. Monetary and financial mechanisms are considered in the following section. We introduce the framework of "co-determination", in which the behaviors of nonfinancial and financial agents concerning money and credit are jointly considered within single functions.

The contrast is sharp between the PostKeynesian view in the fourth section of "accommodative money" and this new perspective, in which the action of central monetary authorities plays a crucial role in the taming of an otherwise unstable macroeconomy. The fifth section harks back to the perspective of a multi-industry economy. The section introduces the important thesis that capitalism is rather efficient in the allocation of capital among industries – and, correspondingly, the production of goods or services in proportions that conform to the pattern of demand – but always on the verge of macro instability (moving toward overheating or recession). These distinct properties provide the theoretical foundations for the adoption of a macro viewpoint in the modeling of business-cycle fluctuations. The perspective in the sixth section is historical. A link is first established between profit rates and macro stability. Then, our thesis concerning the "tendential instability" in capitalism is introduced. The last section discusses the components of such fluctuations in various time frames in the U.S. manufacturing sector.

Due to space limitations, two sections of an earlier version of this study are given in appendices on the Internet. Appendix A is devoted to the modeling of a monetary macroeconomy in the short and long terms.[1] Appendix B discusses Minsky's "financial instability".[2]

Common and distinct grounds

We first recall our framework of "disequilibrium microeconomics" and "general disequilibrium models". A typology of alternative theoretical fields is, then, introduced and a link established with the Marxian and (Post)Keynesian perspectives.

Disequilibrium microeconomics

Heterodox economists reject mainstream economics on account of their methodology and politics. Optimality properties are used by the mainstream as an alleged justification of "market economies", another name for capitalism. The problem is not, however, accounting for individual behaviors, but what we call "equilibrium microeconomics", that is, maximizing under the assumption of ex ante equilibrium. On the contrary, we believe decisions are made in situations of disequilibrium and "radical uncertainty" (as opposed to objective probabilities with known distributions). For example, enterprises are not sure of selling the goods they produce and do not know the probability distribution of demand. They *adapt* to the observation of disequilibrium, as in the accumulation of inventories of unsold commodities:

$$\cdots \rightarrow \begin{pmatrix} \text{Evidence of} \\ \text{disequilibrium} \end{pmatrix} \rightarrow \begin{pmatrix} \text{Modification of} \\ \text{behavior} \end{pmatrix} \rightarrow \cdots$$

This reaction contributes to a correction of the disequilibrium observed, but it does not result in the immediate return to equilibrium. This outcome can only be achieved progressively as a result of a gradual and conditional process of adjustment. Smith's metaphor of the "invisible hand" points to the gradual collective outcomes of such individual behaviors, not to each movement. This approach to decision making must be extended to all aspects of economic activity – outputs, prices, investments – but also to decisions to borrow and lend, including the actions of lending institutions and the central bank.

These processes must be studied within dynamic models. As in other disciplines, such as physics, an equilibrium is the possible outcome of an actual dynamic process, it is the fixed point of such a process. Conversely, within mainstream economics, equilibria are defined independently of any dynamic process. Disequilibrium dynamics are, at best, viewed as inessential developments. When equilibrium is approached as the fixed point of a dynamic process, the issue of (in)stability comes to the fore. Equilibrium can be stable or unstable; stability is always conditional. In our opinion, the consideration of a locally unstable equilibrium can be economically relevant, and the stability conditions are susceptible to economic interpretation.

An institutional framework must be defined in which a list of agents is established, as well as the types of mechanisms through which they interact. Such models can be called *general disequilibrium models*, though ambition must be limited if an analytical treatment is sought. A common simplifying assumption is the consideration of a single commodity, as in a macro model. Another option, also typical of Keynesian models, is to assume that enterprises produce exactly what is demanded. Such assumptions are very helpful, but their consequences must be carefully assessed, and the investigation of more complex models remains necessary.

Toward the distinction between theoretical fields

Due to the complexity of the mechanisms under investigation, economic analysis is conducted within distinct theoretical fields – sets of notions and mechanisms – defined by implicit or explicit abstraction. It is assumed that the quantitative relationships between a number of variables are weak and can be neglected. Implicitly or explicitly, two basic distinctions play a central role within economic theory:

1. *Proportions and dimension.* In our terminology, "proportions" refer to the relative values of variables among industries or enterprises, for example, the relative stocks of capital or prices. "Dimension" refers to the general or average values of the variables, for example, total output as in a macro model.[3]
2. *Time frames.* The distinction between various time frames is based on the hypothesis that one set of variables moves faster than another set of variables. For example, production may be considered a fast variable, and the stock of fixed capital, a slow variable. In a similar manner, a given variable can be broken down into a short-term component (accounting for its fluctuations) and a long-term component (that is, a trend, around which the fluctuations are observed).

In the investigation of properties related to the *long term*, one can assume that the short-term dynamics have converged, that is, one can assume that short-term equilibrium prevails. This is the method of *temporary equilibrium*. Long-term dynamics are approached as the succession to temporary short-term equilibria. Thus, the dynamic properties of the model can be investigated in two successive steps: (1) short-term equilibrium and its stability; and (2) long-term equilibrium and its stability.

The "historical term" (or "term of historical tendencies") offers a further time horizon, in which the historical trends of distribution and technology, as well as the historical transformation of institutions, are considered.

A taxonomy: knitting Marxian and Keynesian perspectives

The distinctions between, on the one hand, proportions and dimension and, on the other hand, short, long, and historical terms allow for a taxonomy of economic theories (Table 16.1).

Five basic configurations are discussed here:

- Configuration [1] in Table 16.1 defines dimension in the short term. The economy is considered globally, and the stock of capital is constant. Thus, accumulation and growth are set aside. Proportions are also set aside. This is the field of Keynesian macroeconomics and short-term equilibrium can, consequently, be called a "Keynesian equilibrium". The simplest example is the "multiplier".
- Configuration [2] refers to proportions in the short term. It can be understood as the extension to various industries of configuration [1]. A given pattern of relative inter-industry capacity utilization rates allows for the equality between outputs and demands.
- Configuration [3], dimension in the long term, is the field of PostKeynesian economics. In a PostKeynesian trajectory (or "traverse"), a sequence of Keynesian short-term equilibria converges toward a steady state in which resources are not fully used (Lavoie and Ramirez-Gaston, 1993; Dutt, 1988).
- Configuration [4], proportions in the long term, defines the Classical–Marxian field of the formation of production prices within competition. Considering the average values of the variables, one can also define a Classical–Marxian long-term macro configuration, as in [3], evocative of the PostKeynesian long-term equilibrium, with the important difference that the Classical economists and Marx assume that capacity utilization rates converge to "normal" (or

Table 16.1 Table of configurations

	Short term (production)	Long term (growth)	Historical term (historical dynamics)
Dimension (macro)	[1]	[3]	[5]
Proportions (relative values)	[2]	[4]	

"target") values. (More rigorously, they "abstract" from business-cycle fluctuations.)
- In the third column, only problems of dimension [5] remain, as proportions have been determined within shorter terms. In this context, dimension refers to the historical tendencies of the growth rate and the profit rate, and the trajectory of technical change (notably, the ratios between inputs such as the capital–labor ratio, or ratios between outputs and inputs such as productivities).

A given school may refer to one particular or to various configurations. The field of Marx's analysis of competition is [4]. Only the relative values of prices, capital stocks, and outputs are involved. The problem of dimension – the mechanisms by which the rate at which productive capacities are used converge to "normal" values – is assumed away, and the business cycle is not discussed. Marx's analysis of the business cycle and crisis of general overproduction is clearly "macro" as in [1], that is, setting aside proportions. Although Marx refers to "partial crises" within specific industries (Marx, 1862, pp. 620–1), he strongly rejects analyses of capitalist crises in terms of *disproportions*. Marx's study of historical tendencies belongs to [5]. Keynes' work belongs to [1], dimension in the short term. PostKeynesian economists do not distinguish between the long term and the historical term, and proportions are set aside. Thus, only cases [1] and [3] are considered. Temporary equilibria are defined in [1] and the sequence of such equilibria in the long term belongs to [3].

A priori, each configuration in the table can be considered from the viewpoints of equilibrium and disequilibrium dynamics (including stability conditions). Keynes' analysis in [1] focuses on equilibrium, while Kalecki's analysis belongs to [1] and [3], with an emphasis on dynamics. Concerning PostKeynesian economists, only equilibrium is considered in the short term, as in [1], while both equilibrium and disequilibrium dynamics are considered in the long term, as in [3].

The interest of the disequilibrium dynamics in short-term equilibrium defines an important difference between our approach and the traditional (Post)Keynesian perspective. This harks back to a basic ambiguity within the Keynesian paradigm, beginning with Keynes himself. It is not clear whether Keynesian equilibria are supposed to explain durable shifts or sudden collapses in the general level of activity (the 1920s in the U.K. or the Great Depression in the U.S., for example). The core Keynesian analytical device seems to account for durable shifts, whereas Keynes' analysis of the business cycle (Keynes, 1936, ch. 22) emphasizes the extreme volatility of the marginal efficiency of capital, which determines investment and the level of output.

The components of the general level of activity

The framework in the previous sections has important implications concerning the analysis of the fluctuations of the general level of activity, approached here as the movements of the capacity utilization rate in the U.S. manufacturing sector in Figure 16.1. The figure distinguishes three components, $\bar{u}$, u^{LT} and u^{ST}, which

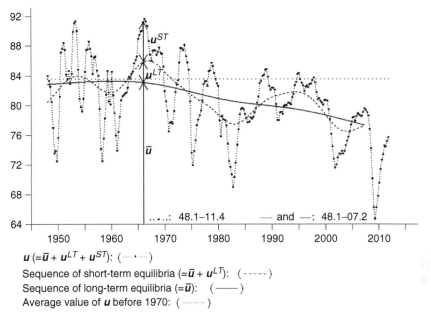

$u (=\bar{u} + u^{LT} + u^{ST})$: ($\cdots\cdot\cdots$)
Sequence of short-term equilibria ($=\bar{u} + u^{LT}$): (- - - - -)
Sequence of long-term equilibria ($=\bar{u}$): (——)
Average value of u before 1970: ($\cdots\cdots$)

Figure 16.1 The capacity utilization rate in the U.S. manufacturing sector.

sum up to u. We interpret the two sequences of equilibria introduced above as follows:

- The continuous line (—) is interpreted as depicting empirically the sequence of long-term equilibria, $\bar{u}$ (with a downward trend after 1970, to which we will return below).
- The dashed line (---) is read as the sequence of temporary short-term equilibria.

In 2009, manufacturing industries only accounted for 10 percent of total U.S. income. The fluctuations of the manufacturing capacity utilization rate, u, are, however, tightly correlated to those of the value added of the nonfinancial corporate sector. The purpose of the figure is illustrative. The two lines (— and ---) have been determined using a Whittaker filter. Both have been calculated up to the second quarter of 2007, that is, prior to the current crisis. More time will be necessary to determine new tendencies.

We further define the two fluctuations, which we synthetically denote as "business-cycle fluctuations" (see the last section for factual interpretations):

- The *long-term* fluctuation, u^{LT}, is the difference between the sequence of short-term equilibria (---) and the sequence of long-term equilibria (—). It reveals broad fluctuations during significant periods of time, about 10 years long.

- The *short-term* fluctuation is the distance between u ($\cdots\bullet\cdots$) and the sequence of short-term equilibria (---). The sharp departures typical of this component are the expression of the (in)stability of short-term equilibrium.

The decomposition above is based on the view that the downward trend of u after 1970 is not part of business-cycle fluctuations. In other words, in the downward trend of u, we see a decline of $\bar{u}$ (a drifting $\bar{u}$) not a growing gap between a constant $\bar{u}$ and the rates actually achieved. We do not believe enterprises went on building capacities for several decades while they were not able to reach their target utilization rates (as would imply reference to a constant $\bar{u}$, as suggested in the figure ($\cdots$). In particular, the second half of the 1990s was a period of boom, not of stagnating growth, with large growth rates and a dramatic wave of investment. (A more detailed analysis is provided in Duménil and Lévy, 2012b.)

Money and credit in the macroeconomy

This section considers *monetary and credit mechanisms*, which were set aside in the previous section. "Financial mechanisms" proper, in a broader sense, are treated in Appendix B on the Internet.

The credit demand channel

Monetary mechanisms are approached here in a simple framework, in which "banks" make loans to the nonfinancial agents "households, the government and enterprises" from which demand emanates, assuming the traditional confrontation between the lender and the borrower (households and enterprises), as in the past, and still typical of procedures in many countries. (Money and credit must be treated jointly, as the two facets of a same coin, since money is issued when loans are granted and destroyed when loans are paid back.) An important assumption is that demand is financed out of previously garnered income and borrowing:

$$\begin{pmatrix} \text{Demand} \\ \text{in period } t+1 \end{pmatrix} = \begin{pmatrix} \text{Income} \\ \text{in period } t \end{pmatrix} + \begin{pmatrix} \text{Borrowing} \\ \text{in period } t+1 \end{pmatrix}$$

Other monetary actions are also involved with equivalent impacts on demand. They must be jointly considered with borrowing in the determination of financing:

Borrowing (1)	Depositing on bank accounts (3)
Paying back loans (2)	Using these deposits for demand (4)

A household, for example, can finance more than its income by drawing on its bank account; it can also use the money deposited at the bank to pay back loans.

And the converse will happen if demand is inferior to income. The outcome of such monetary-credit flows is the *variation of the net debt* ("borrowing" for short).

From the viewpoint of "real" flows, the variation of the net debt of an economic agent is the difference between its total spending (consumption and investment) and its income. Equivalently, the opposite of the variation of the net debt is equal to "financial savings", as opposed to "savings", the difference between income and spending.

With the notation D for demand, Y for income, and N for the net debt, one has:

$$D_{t+1} = Y_t + \Delta N_{t+1} \tag{1}$$

This approach to credit mechanisms can be used to account for the formation of the demand of specific agents within models in which several goods are considered, as well as within a macro model in which a single nonfinancial agent is at the origin of demand. We consider this equation to be the cornerstone of the modeling of a monetary economy.

A remark must be made concerning the aggregate net debt. If *nonfinancial and financial agents* are simultaneously considered, the variation of the aggregate net debt is null, since the loans of financial agents are identically equal to the borrowing of nonfinancial agents, and the deposits of nonfinancial agents are held by financial agents. Conversely, considering *only nonfinancial agents*, the variation of their aggregate net debt is a priori different from zero.

A second remark concerns the distinction between various nonfinancial agents. Borrowing (the variation of the net debt) may affect to different degrees the demands of distinct agents. For example, the demand of capitalist investors could be larger than their income, while wage-earners would consume less than their income. We call "credit macro demand channel" the *overall* impact of credit mechanisms on aggregate demand, independent of its distribution among agents.

Built-in instability in a credit economy

The financing of demand via the credit channel opens a field of analysis of major importance. Like Marx and Kalecki, we believe that the propensity of economic agents to borrow in a capitalist economy is procyclical. When the economy is booming, economic agents are prone to borrow more, and conversely when the economy is depressed they are prone to borrow less.

If the aggregate net borrowing of nonfinancial agents is procyclical, short-term equilibrium is *necessarily* unstable, with cumulative movements upward or downward. Notably, the tendency on the part of enterprises to borrow when the economy is growing comparatively fast, in order to expand their investment, has destabilizing effects. The same is true of households borrowing for residential investment.[4] The converse is true in a recession, with cumulative movements downward. Thus, the unrestrained propensity to borrow (or the unchecked propensity to diminish expenses and pay back debts) would result in a "built-in instability" inherent in capitalism (Duménil and Lévy, 2012a).

This built-in instability renders necessary a stabilizing countercyclical action by a segment of financial institutions beyond the narrow profit motive. Private or government central institutions are involved in such practices. In the U.S., under the national banking system, such functions were performed by the large banks of New York in the context of the gold standard (Duménil and Lévy, 2004, Box 18.1). Since the creation of the Federal Reserve in 1913, and its more active actions after World War II, this management of the macroeconomy is the object of monetary policy, supplemented by fiscal policy.

Co-determination

A central aspect of the PostKeynesian analysis is the "endogenous" or "accommodative" character of the issuance of money. Lenders ("commercial banks" for short) and central banks can only accommodate the demands for loans. Symmetrically, the opposite assumption concerning the "exogenous" character of money, in which monetary authorities determine the amount of credit and money, is harshly criticized. We reject this dilemma. Money is neither endogenous nor exogenous, but is co-determined – *a third viewpoint*.

We call "co-determination" the general twofold principle stating that: (1) in the analysis of the formation of demand, real and monetary variables must be simultaneously determined; and (2), less trivially, the actions of nonfinancial and financial agents are jointly involved. The behavior of households responds to their eagerness to buy, the level of their income, their monetary holdings, and the cost at which funds can be borrowed. Lenders typically assess risks; they can set an upper limit to the amounts borrowed or straightforwardly deny lending; they also take account of their own capability to lend and obtain refinancing on the interbank market, given the policies of the central bank and the opportunity to refinance opened by the securitization of loans; they are constrained by existing regulations; but the profit motive stimulates their propensity to lend. The central bank has multiple objectives such as managing the macroeconomy, in particular taming inflationary pressures, ensuring the smooth functioning of financial institutions, and limiting the degrees of indebtedness and the risks of financial crisis. One lever in the conduct of such policies is the modification of the interest rate at which banks are refinanced, but various balance-sheet ratios and regulations are also involved. The variations of net debts are the outcomes of such mechanisms.

The determination of the flows of new loans is traditionally approached as the confrontation of two functions, a (potentially vertical) supply curve for loans, and a demand curve for borrowing. Conversely, we model the variation of the net debt as in equations (1) or (3, below) by a single function accounting for all aspects of monetary and credit mechanisms, the "co-determined monetary function", $\Delta N = F$. A simple expression for F is, for example:

$$F_{t+1} = \alpha + \beta Y_t - \gamma N_t - \delta j_t \tag{2}$$

Besides the constant α, the term βY simultaneously accounts for the determination of borrowers, given their income and the tendency of commercial banks to accommodate this demand when the economy is booming (and symmetrically within opposite situations). The term $-\gamma N$ accounts for the concerns vis-à-vis levels of indebtedness on the part of both borrowers and lenders. The last term, $-\delta j$, describes the aversion of the central bank to inflation, and the consequences of its policy concerning the refinancing of banks. A similar function can be written making explicit the role of the interest rate, in turn manipulated by the central bank.

To the countercyclical action of central monetary authorities, one must add fiscal policy on the part of the government. As with any other agent, the government may borrow to spend more than its revenue (and symmetrically, may pay back its debt if its revenue is larger than its spending). Unlike other agents, however, this behavior can be countercyclical, as part of a deliberate action to stabilize the macroeconomy, or due to the stickiness of expenses (as in built-in stabilizers).

Concerning the capability of central monetary institutions and the government to influence money, credit, and spending, two aspects must be combined: (1) These institutions strongly impact the macroeconomy and, in the absence of this action, the macroeconomy would be unstable; (2) The efficacy of these actions is conditional, not always and unambiguously ensured. Government demand policy is specifically important when the channels of monetary policy become inefficient (for example, in a credit crunch during a crisis of financial institutions).

Modeling a monetary macroeconomy

Appendix A introduces a number of models of a monetary macroeconomy, built along the lines introduced in the previous sections. The main results are as follows:

- Concerning short-term equilibria, we believe that their stability is always subject to conditions and that these conditions are susceptible to economic interpretation. As no decentralized mechanisms account for the stability of the macroeconomy, which is otherwise autonomously unstable, the action of the central bank is crucial. But this action is also subject to significant limitations. Notably, perturbations of financial markets may recurrently destabilize the macroeconomy. Overheating and recession are always around the corner. Overall, the stabilizing action of the central bank confines the deviations of the general levels of activity within certain limits. More than *constantly maintained*, stability is *recurrently restored*.
- Concerning long-term equilibria, assuming the preservation of the stability of short-term equilibria, long-term equilibria remain attractors around which the rather hectic short-term oscillations are observed. The problem concerning long-term equilibrium is the management of its level. It is a slow process, in which institutional transformations are implied. Thus, the gravitation of

short-term equilibria around a normal value of the capacity utilization rate is constantly "shifted", as the macroeconomy is involved in slow long-term fluctuations.

PostKeynesian views concerning money and credit

We first briefly recall Kalecki's emphasis on the use of borrowing to finance investment, to which we devoted a specific study (Duménil and Lévy, 2012a). We next compare our views to the PostKeynesian approach to money as "endogenous".

The financing of investment in Kalecki's framework

The financing of spending by borrowing, as introduced above, is reminiscent of Kalecki's statements concerning financing. The view that the expansion of loans ("credit inflation") can be used to finance investment is repeatedly stated by Kalecki. Loans are made to capitalists and finance their investment beyond their savings:[5]

> How can capitalists invest more than remains from their current profits after spending part of them for personal consumption? This is made possible by the banking system in various forms of credit inflation.
>
> Kalecki (1990, p. 148)

Thus, within Kalecki's perspective, our equation (1) translates into:

$$I_{t+1} = \text{Savings}_t + \Delta N_{t+1} \tag{3}$$

Exogenous money, endogenous money, and co-determination

To the eyes of most PostKeynesian economists, money is endogenously determined, meaning that the financial system always provides the loans demanded by nonfinancial agents. Thus, the absence of monetary variables within models is, sometimes, presented as a deliberate option. In the words of Basil Moore: "The financial system has no choice but to accommodate" (Moore, 1979, p. 58). Moore bases his assessment on the observation that commercial banks are enterprises, similar to other enterprises, responding to the demand of their customers. They are "price setters" and "quantity takers" (Moore, 1988, p. 381). By lack of capability or willingness, central banks accommodate the demands for refinancing.

A few PostKeynesian economists contend that, as in our co-determination approach, power is shared between nonfinancial and financial agents. In Mark Lavoie's formulation: "Other post Keynesians[6] prefer to recognize that the stock of money has endogenous as well as exogenous aspects" (Lavoie, 1984, p. 776).

Money endogeneity can also be questioned in reference to a Keynesian "liquidity constraint". Foley emphasizes this mechanism in relation to the interconnectedness of transactions inherent in market economies, described in terms of "externalities":

> Keynes insisted by contrast that in real-world monetary economies many households and firms are' liquidity-constrained', that is, unable to finance spending beyond their immediate cash inflows by borrowing. In this more realistic world, spending itself has an important externality. Each household or firm that spends money not only accomplishes its own ends (consumption or production), but also relieves the liquidity constraint of other spending units.
>
> Foley (2009, p. 15)

Financing channels within PostKeynesian models

The treatment of financing channels is complex, as stocks and flows must be carefully articulated within accounting frameworks. This is manifest in the works of Marxist economists concerning Marx's analysis of the circulation of capital in Volume II of *Capital*.[7] A number of PostKeynesian economists use "transactions flow matrices" and "balance sheet matrices" (Godley and Lavoie, 2007).

The approach of PostKeynesian economists is quite distinct from ours (as introduced in the previous sections):

1. *Consumption and investment functions.* Within PostKeynesian models, traditional consumption and investment functions are defined prior to the consideration of financing.
2. *Intermediation, and credit and deposits as residuals.* Concerning enterprises or the government, a first set of external channels is the collection of funds by the issuance of securities such as stock shares, bonds, and the like. (For example, a given percentage of investment by an enterprise is financed by the issuance of shares.) These channels share the common property of being mechanisms of *intermediation* in which existing purchasing powers are transferred, as opposed to the *issuance of money* as in bank loans in which purchasing power is created. As in portfolio theory, households determine the proportions of their monetary and financial holdings. (For example, a given percentage of their financial assets is held as stock shares.) The equilibrium on financial markets is ensured by the prevalence of prices that clear each of these markets. Loans and deposits are treated as residual variables allowing for the consistency of spending plans (otherwise determined) with the financing made available by the above channels of intermediation. Since the credit system accommodates the demands of borrowers, and since no decisions are made concerning deposits, this consistency is guaranteed by construction.
3. *The prices of financial assets.* Correspondingly, the focus of PostKeynesian frameworks is more on the price of financial assets rather than on the amount of loans. For example, the price of fixed capital is compared to the price of

stock shares, as in Tobin's q. This is also an important aspect of Minsky's analysis of business cycles (Minsky, 1994, p. 143).

Note that we do not question the importance of financing procedures distinct from the credit channel. Their potential destabilizing impact is obvious. Within sophisticated monetary and financial economies, the multiplicity of financing channels renders the action of the central bank even more difficult.

Articulating theoretical fields – vindicating macroeconomics

This section focuses on *general disequilibrium models*, in which several industries are considered and other assumptions lifted. Only general principles are introduced, and the emphasis is on the main results. The objective is to show how the four first theoretical fields in Table 16.1 (short and long terms, and proportions and dimension) can be articulated within a unique coherent framework. Important conclusions follow, notably capitalist economies are *stable in proportions, and at the limit of (in)stability in dimension*, a thesis to be made explicit in the second subsection below. The third subsection briefly opens the broad field of the relationship between the historical term (the term of tendencies) and the business cycle.

Production and investment

This section introduces the main mechanisms typical of a general disequilibrium model:

1. *The decision to produce.* Production is decided and realized within enterprises, and this is also where investments are made. Production is decided before demand is known and supplies and demands are confronted in markets. Inventories of unsold commodities may exist (or rationing). These inventories, S_t, are transferred to the next market as part of supply, $S_t + Y_t$:[8]

    $$S_{t+1} = S_t + Y_t - D_t$$

2. *Accumulation and growth.* Capital invested during one period becomes part of the stock of capital, K, in the following period. Instead of variables such as I, Y, or S, it is more convenient to use ratios to the stock of fixed capital, K, or to productive capacities, Y^{Max}, such as $\rho = I/K$, $u = Y/Y^{Max}$, or $s = S/Y^{Max}$. We define $\bar{u}$ and $\bar{s}$, the values of such ratios, as targeted by enterprises.

3. *Main behaviors.* We use adjustment to disequilibrium as above. For simplicity, in the equations below, the superscript i is set aside, indicating that one particular agent is considered. When inventories are smaller than targeted by enterprises ($s < \bar{s}$), they increase their capacity utilization rate. To a smaller extent, they also raise prices. When capacity utilization rates are large ($u > \bar{u}$),

enterprises slowly increase their prices. They also tend to invest more (that is, $\rho = I/K$ rises). When the profit rate in one enterprise or industry is larger than the average, the difference stimulates investment in that enterprise or industry. Since enterprises increase their investment when capacity utilization rates are large, they simultaneously initiate a return toward the normal use of productive capacities. (This twofold behavior aims at the adjustment of productive capacities in line with demand.) For example, the decision to produce (the determination of the capacity utilization rate) can be modeled as the adjustment of u_t in reaction to two disequilibria:

$$u_{t+1} = u_t - \varepsilon(s_t - \bar{s}) - \sigma(u_t - \bar{u}) \tag{4}$$

Other behaviors must be modeled in a similar manner.

To obtain a full-fledged general disequilibrium model, the consumption and investment functions must be expressed, in conformity with the principle of co-determination, also accounting for the central role of monetary and credit mechanisms.

Stability in proportions – instability in dimension

We have presented such general disequilibrium models in various earlier works (Duménil and Lévy, 1993, 1996). For each enterprise or industry, four variables must be considered: u, s, K, and p. To this first set of variables, one must add money stocks (deposits) and debts for all agents.

Usually, the determination of equilibria is rather easy, while the study of the stability of equilibrium is difficult. The distinction between various theoretical fields as above points, however, to two possible ways out, that may render the treatment of stability manageable. First, under the assumption that it is possible to sort out variables whose variations are judged to be rapid, and others to be slow, the distinction between time frames, short term and long term, suggests the use of the methodology of temporary equilibria. Second, the distinction between proportions and dimension allows for the factorization of the model. New "centered" or relative variables are defined. For example, for profit rates in each enterprise or industry, one can substitute the differences between these rates and an average profit rate; the same can be done for capacity utilization rates and prices (distinguishing between the "general level of prices" and "relative prices"). The average profit rate, the average capacity utilization rate, and the general level of prices account for *dimension*, and the centered (and relative) variables, for *proportions*. The main results are as follows:

1. A *Keynesian equilibrium* prevails in the short term (with the equality between production and demand in each enterprise or industry), and a *Classical–Marxian equilibrium* in the long term (with a normal use of productive capacities and prices of production).

2. Within rather simple models, the characteristic polynomial of the Jacobian matrix used in the study of stability conditions can be factorized into four factors corresponding to proportions and dimension, respectively, in the short and in the long terms. Within more complex models, the factorization is not rigorously possible, only "quasi-factorization" (given the low values of a number of parameters).
3. An important result is that, in the short term as well as in the long term, the conditions for stability in proportions appear to be easily met, while the conditions for stability in dimension can be easily violated. This points to the basic property of capitalist economies, which we denote as "stability in proportions and instability in dimension":

    •   "Stable in proportions" refers to the capability of capitalist markets to allocate capital in the long term, and determine outputs in the short term, in various industries, in line with demand patterns. Potential buyers generally find what they seek in markets.
    •   "Instability in dimension" or, more rigorously, "at the limit of stability in dimension", points to a twofold propensity of capitalist macroeconomies to deviate from normal levels. This is, first, manifest in the recurrence of overheating and recession (the expression of the instability of short-term equilibrium). Second, for longer periods of time, the average levels of output around which short-term fluctuations are observed may stray at a distance from normal levels (as defined by the sequence of long-term equilibria).

4. General disequilibrium models allow for the interpretation of these properties. The *same mechanisms* simultaneously account for stability in proportions and instability in dimension in the short term. The swift capability of enterprises to react to the signals manifesting a divergence between supply and demand (parameter ε in equation (4)) is involved. This prompt adjustment ensures the availability of output, or the limitation of the growth of inventories of unsold commodities, with favorable effects concerning proportions. But the vigor of the same adjustment may entail cumulative movements of output, upward or downward – the expression of instability in dimension.

These findings straightforwardly echo Marx's analysis in *Capital*. In the theory of competition in Volume III, Marx (1894) accounts for the mechanisms leading to the allocation of capital among industries and the prevalence of prices ensuring in each industry an equalized average profit rate, with corresponding prices and outputs. (Actually, a gravitation process because of recurrent shocks of variegated nature is involved.) Marx believed this mechanism to be efficient in capitalism (that is, stability in proportions). Conversely, the general level of output follows the characteristic pattern of the cycle of industry (the business cycle), with recurrent departures into overheating and recession (instability in dimension).

An historical perspective

This section is devoted to the analysis of the historical transformations of stability conditions. A first aspect is the impact of declining profit rates. A second aspect is the effect of the progress of management and the development of monetary mechanisms on macro stability.

Profit rates and stability conditions

An interesting hypothesis proper to Marx's analysis is the view that profit rates – their values and trends – impact macroeconomic stability. Recurrent downward fluctuations of profit rates may cause recessions. For example, in the short term, as in Marx's analysis of overaccumulation, the growth of employment during a phase of expansion may push wages upward and temporarily diminish profits, and provoke a recession (Marx, 1894, ch. 15).

This impact may be felt in the longer term, and this suggests an interesting link between the historical and shorter terms. If the profit rate declines and remains low for more durable periods of time, a "structural" propensity to instability prevails, with more frequent and deeper recessions, as during the 1970s.

One mechanism accounting for the impacts of profit rates is their potential influence on parameter ε in equation (4) (accounting for the decision by enterprises to increase or diminish production depending on the levels of inventories). As stated in the previous section, if the response to excessive or deficient inventories is too strong, this mechanism may trigger cumulative movements of output, downward or upward. Profit rates command cash flows and liquidities and, thus, affect ε. (The continuation of production at given levels depletes liquidities if sales are diminished.)

The tendential instability thesis

It is well-known that the emergence of the modern pattern of business-cycle fluctuations echoed the development of money and finance in capitalism. The built-in instability began to manifest itself when monetary-financial mechanisms reached a sufficient degree of development, as during the first half of the nineteenth century in Europe. In combination with the progress of the management of enterprises, notably since the end of the nineteenth century, the gradual expansion of financial mechanisms fostered a tendency toward increasing macro instability, a "tendential instability".

To account for such trends, the potential impact of the variations of reaction parameters in the modeling of behaviors can be considered in an historical perspective. The financial system became gradually more inclined to accommodate the demand for loans, a rise of parameter β in equation (2), a tendency in which financial innovation played a prominent role. The progress of the management of enterprises induced a rise in parameters such as ε in equation (4). These historical drifts in the value of parameters rendered the satisfaction of stability conditions more difficult.

The second facet of the tendential instability thesis is, however, that this movement toward increased instability was checked by the historical progress of countercyclical central mechanisms, thus becoming gradually more necessary. The Federal Reserve, created in 1913, was substituted for the national banking system, although the movement toward genuine management of the macroeconomy was only gradual. The corresponding stabilizing mechanisms only reached mature forms after the New Deal and World War II, in the context of the Keynesian revolution. Neoliberalism did not destroy the domestic framework in which monetary policy is conducted, rather the contrary, but altered its objectives.[9] The new conditions created by financial globalization during the 2000s finally unsettled the foundations of the policies conducted by the Federal Reserve (Duménil and Lévy, 2011, ch. 14).

Thus, the tendential instability thesis points to an historical process in which resistances and setbacks are recurrently observed. But the pressure of events, as in recurrent crises, finally has the edge, though the costs may be huge, as in structural crises.

Business-cycle fluctuations

This section provides interpretations of the fluctuations of the capacity utilization rate as in Figure 16.1, in line with the analytical framework introduced in the present study:

1. *The long-term fluctuation.* The broad movements in u^{LT} (---) reveal the weakness of the centripetal forces generated by the action of the central bank, intended to confine output in a "vicinity" of levels considered "normal" or appropriate. To this end, the institutional setting and the rules in which monetary policy is conducted were recurrently altered:

   • The awareness of the partial recovery of output in the recession of the late 1950s induced the bold fiscal policy of the 1960s on the part of President Kennedy's advisers, aiming at stimulation of the macroeconomy. In combination with the financing of the Vietnam War, this policy contributed to a rise of output to unusual levels.
   • Then, the decline of profit rates altered the basic conditions underlying the trade-off between the fight against inflation and the preservation of growth in the direction of increased inflation. In the context of the rather accommodative policy of the central bank after 1973,[10] an upward trend of prices was observed, paralleling the decline of the long-term fluctuation in what has been called "stagflation".
   • The shift of the long-term fluctuation to lower levels during the structural crisis of the 1970s was prolonged into the early 1980s, when the sudden rise of interest rates, the "1979 coup", further bent the long-term fluctuation (and caused the recession of the early 1980s, whose analysis belongs to the short-term fluctuation).

- During the 1980s and 1990s, the preservation of "decent" levels became gradually more problematic in the context of the growing deficits of foreign trade and globalization (Duménil and Lévy, 2011). The severe character of the situation was temporarily hidden by the boom of information technologies during the 1990s, with a significant stimulation of investment. When this unexpected bonanza came to an end around 2000, a new decline in the long-term fluctuation occurred, whose severity was only partially checked by the upward trends in residential investment.

In these movements the recurrent actions of the central bank and government are manifest, in particular in the upward movement from the late 1950s to the 1960s, the fight against inflation culminating in the early 1980s, and the attempt to boost the U.S. macro trajectory by a bold mortgage policy (and deregulation) prior to the current crisis.

2. *The short-term fluctuation.* The sudden deviations in u^{ST} around the sequence of short-term equilibria suggest quite specific patterns of variations:

- The 1950s and 1960s manifest the typical pattern of the "stop and go", in the context of still immature stabilizing procedures.
- One can, then, observe the occurrence of sharp departures upward and downward, with rapid – a few quarters long – transitions (for example, the dramatic two-quarter fall in 1974).
- A closer examination reveals clusters of observations, when the capacity utilization rate stabilizes (gravitates in the vicinity of given positions): (1) close to the long-term fluctuation (as in 1963, 1984, and during the long boom); (2) for comparatively higher positions, as in overheating (as in 1979); and (3) for comparatively lower positions as in the lasting recession of 2001–2002.
- The three broad cycles during the 1970s and early 1980s (the period of declining profitability) are spectacular.

3. *The circumstances (deregulation and the relaxation of lending practices) that led to the subprime crisis in the U.S.* Concerning these latter years, the circumstances created by the duration of the current structural crisis have a considerable impact on macro mechanisms and disturb usual patterns. More time will be necessary to provide reliable assessments. After the plateau of the capacity utilization rate above the sequence of short-term equilibria during the second half of the 2000s prior to the recession, a new sharp plunge occurred, followed by a still quite limited recovery.

Notes

1 http://www.jourdan.ens.fr/levy/dle2011gA.pdf
2 http://www.jourdan.ens.fr/levy/dle2011gB.pdf

3 Keynes is very conscious of this distinction and criticizes the almost exclusive emphasis on proportions in what he calls "classical economics": "Most treatises on the theory of Value and Production are primarily concerned with the distribution of a *given* volume of employed resources between various uses and with the conditions which, assuming the employment of this quantity of resources, determine their relative rewards and the relative values of their products." (Keynes, 1936, p. 4).

4 Consumption might increase less than output, with stabilizing effects. Empirical investigation is required here.

5 The quotation is found in Malcom Sawyer (2001).

6 With reference to Weintraub (1978) and Davidson (1980).

7 Duménil (1977), ch. II, L'élaboration des schémas: Flux et stocks, and ch. III, L'élaboration des schémas : Les mécanismes du crédit. Foley (1986), ch. 5, The reproduction of capital.

8 The case of services requires a specific treatment which we do not consider here.

9 As in the Deregulation and Monetary Control Act of 1980. See Duménil and Lévy (2000, box 18.5).

10 The fact that the theory of accommodative money was developed during those years is certainly not coincidental.

References

Davidson, P. (1980) 'The Dual-Faceted Keynesian Revolution', *Journal of Post Keynesian Economics*, 2: 291–307.

Duménil, G. (1977) *Marx et Keynes face à la crise*, Paris: Économica.

Duménil, G., and Lévy, D. (1993) *The Economics of the Profit Rate: Competition, Crises, and Historical Tendencies in Capitalism*, Aldershot, UK: Edward Elgar.

Duménil, G., and Lévy, D. (1996) *La dynamique du capital. Un siècle d'économie américaine*, Paris: Presses Universitaires de France.

Duménil, G., and Lévy, D. (2000) *Crise et sortie de crise. Ordre et désordres néolibéraux*, Paris: Presses Universitaires de France.

Duménil, G., and Lévy, D. (2004) *Capital Resurgent. Roots of the Neoliberal Revolution*, Cambridge, Massachusetts: Harvard University Press.

Duménil, G., and Lévy, D. (2011) *The Crisis of Neoliberalism*, Cambridge, Massachusetts: Harvard University Press.

Duménil, G., and Lévy, D. (2012a) 'Modeling Monetary Macroeconomics: Kalecki Reconsidered', *Metroeconomica*, 63: 170–199.

Duménil, G., and Lévy D. (2012b) 'A Reply to Amitava Dutt', http://www.jourdan.ens.fr/levy/dle2012h.pdf

Dutt, A. (1988) 'Convergence and Equilibrium in Two-Sector Models of Growth, Distribution and Prices', *Zeitschrift für Nationalökonomie, Journal of Economics*, 48: 135–158.

Foley, D. (1986) *Understanding Capital, Marx's Economic Theory*, Cambridge, MA and London: Harvard University Press.

Foley, D. (2009) *The Anatomy of Financial and Economic Crisis*, New York: New School University.

Godley, W., and Lavoie, M. (2007) *Monetary Economics. An Integrated Approach to Credit, Money, Income, Production and Wealth*, London and Basingstoke: Palgrave.

Kalecki, M. (1990) *Capitalism: Business Cycles and Full Employment, Collected Works of Michal Kalecki, I* (Edited by J. Osiatynski), Oxford, UK: Clarendon Press.

Keynes, J.M. (1936; 2nd edn 1967) *The General Theory of Employment, Interest and Money*, London, Melbourne, and Toronto: Macmillan.

Lavoie, M. (1984) 'The Endogenous Flow of Credit and the Post Keynesian Theory of Money', *Journal of Economic Issues*, 18: 771–797.

Lavoie, M., and Ramirez-Gaston, P. (1993) *Traverse in a Two-Sector Kaleckian Model of Growth with Target Return Pricing*, Ottawa: University of Ottawa.

Marx, K. (1862; edn 1971) *Theories of Surplus Value*, Moscow: Progress Publisher.

Marx, K. (1894; edn 1981) *Capital, Volume III*, New York: First Vintage Book Edition.

Minsky, H. (1994) 'Financial Instability Hypothesis', in P. Arestis and M. Sawyer (Eds.) *The Elgar Companion to Radical Political Economy*, Aldershot, UK: Edward Elgar, pp.153–157.

Moore, B.J. (1979) 'The Endogenous Money Stock', *Journal of Post Keynesian Economics*, 2: 49–70.

Moore, B.J. (1988) 'The Endogenous Money Supply', *Journal of Post Keynesian Economics*, 10: 372–385.

Sawyer, M. (2001) 'Kalecki and Finance', *European Journal of the History of Economic Thought*, 8: 487–508.

Weintraub, S. (1978) *Capitalism's Inflation and Unemployment Crisis*, Reading, MA: Addison-Wesley.

17 A model of fiscal and monetary policy

Thomas Michl

Progressive economists agree that in a liquidity or deflation trap, fiscal stimulus is part of the solution, and perhaps even the only solution. There is some disagreement about the need for fiscal consolidation (active policy to stabilize or reduce the debt–income ratio) in the long run after the storm has passed, a position Paul Krugman (2011) succinctly summarizes as "jobs now, deficits later." This paper attacks the problem using a model that has recognizably Keynesian components, but which has Classical characteristics as well, following an approach laid out in Foley and Michl (1999, ch. 10). The model descends with modification from a similar effort (Michl, 2008) devoted to analysis of inflation targeting. Since the basic model exhibits the paradox of thrift in the short run but not in the long run, it is not too inaccurate to describe it as "short-run Keynesian, long-run Classical."

The model

To keep the model focussed, we make several simplifying assumptions. First, we take the distribution of income between capitalists and workers to be parametric; we represent the profit share as π. Second, we assume workers do not save or pay taxes. These two assumptions let us abstract from the distributional consequences of public debt. Third, we assume that growth is constrained by capital, not labor, parallel to the Classical models with a conventional wage share described in Foley and Michl (1999, ch. 6). We briefly consider the implications of using fiscal policy to target employment. Fourth, we will argue that monetary policy devoted to stabilizing inflation creates a gravitational pull that guides utilization of capital, u, to a normal level (taken to be $= 1$) in the long run. Writing the output-capital ratio at normal utilization as ρ, these choices impose a long run rate of profit, $\pi\rho$, that does not reflect aggregate demand factors, even though the short run rate of profit, $u\pi\rho$, does.

Among these assumptions the existence of a center of gravity at normal utilization has perhaps generated the most controversy among heterodox economists. The traditional argument for this assumption is that it is hard to see why capitalists would pursue accumulation in the presence of persistent unused capacity. There are three basic resolutions of this problem. First, some models essentially take capitalist saving to be the "primitive" and make investment adjust according to some economic, financial, or monetary mechanism, so that the system achieves long run growth at full or normal capacity utilization; Duménil and Lévy (1999) or Skott (2010) are examples. Second some models take investment (determined by profitability) to be primitive, and make the saving rate adjust, again achieving full capacity utilization; Rowthorn (1999) and Shaikh (2009) are examples. Third, some models regard the saving/investment distinction itself as primitive, and allow utilization to adjust through changing norms of desired utilization; Lavoie (1995) and Dutt (1997) are examples. The working premise in this paper is that one or both of the first two resolutions are closer to the truth. Yet it is hard on purely theoretical grounds to resolve these conflicts, and it is probably best just to admit that the alternative resolutions reflect underlying differences of Schumpeterian vision as much as anything else.

Inflation and monetary policy

A central premise is that capitalist economies are subject to an inflation barrier. At high levels of utilization, the inflation process tends to generate a gradually rising inflation rate, and conversely at low levels, disinflation. Thus, we will write the Phillips-type curve as

$$p_{+1} = p + a(u - 1) \tag{1}$$

where p measures the inflation rate at time t, and u is normalized so that $u = 1$ represents normal or full capacity. Suppressing t subscripts and writing $t + 1$ as just $+1$ simplifies the notation. The system is assumed to be capable of producing above full capacity from a technological point of view, but at the cost of rising inflation. The coefficient a just measures the sensitivity of the change in inflation to slack. The lag structure is sometimes interpreted as an expression of adaptive inflation expectations or learning, but it can also reflect the inertial character of the inflation process. Modeling the inflation process relative to capacity utilization rather than the unemployment rate (which is undefined in this model) is not without precedent (Taylor, 2004).

A sensible way of containing the inflation process in models like this is to assume that the monetary authority actively pursues some inflation target, through a Taylor rule or reaction function for example. The Taylor rule is anchored by the natural or inflation-neutral rate of interest, r^*. The monetary authority obeys this rule in setting the real rate of interest, r:

$$r_{+1} = r^* + h_m(p - \bar{p}) \tag{2}$$

In the model we develop, the natural rate evolves along with the debt ratio. We will assume that the monetary authority knows the steady state value of the natural rate and uses that as its benchmark. We use "interest rate" and "real interest rate" interchangeably.

Fiscal policy and sustainability

Since we are building a growth model, let us normalize everything we can by the capital stock K. (For simplicity, assume it does not depreciate.) The growth rate of capital will be represented by g. Government spending (normalized) is represented by γ, and policy is assumed to index spending to the capital stock. We will assume (and this is not an innocent assumption) that it consists entirely of consumption spending.

Taxes are lump-sum, and paid entirely by the capitalist class in our two-class world. But as a practical matter, the tax will be set as a percentage of the capital stock, τ, so that it is indexed to growth. This looks like a wealth tax, but each individual capitalist pays a fixed sum that is perceived, fallacy of composition style, to be independent of her own capital.

The government can also borrow and it uses one-period indexed bonds. Let b (for bonds) represent the debt–capital (B/K) ratio. The primary fiscal deficit is the difference between spending and taxing, or $f = \gamma - \tau$. The actual fiscal deficit is $\Delta B/K = f + rb$. The equation of motion for debt is:

$$b_{+1} = \frac{f + (1+r)b}{1+g} \tag{3}$$

Now it can be seen immediately that a steady state debt ratio, where $b_{+1} = b$, satisfies the following *fiscal sustainability condition*:

$$b = \frac{f}{g - r} \tag{4}$$

If growth exceeds the interest rate, a stable public debt ratio can coexist with a permanent primary fiscal deficit. Some economists (Galbraith, 2011) have argued on this basis that a primary fiscal deficit need not imply a future fiscal consolidation because the debt ratio will self-stabilize. We will borrow from Joan Robinson[1] in spirit and refer to this happy state as a *golden age*.

On the other hand, if the interest rate exceeds the growth rate, a stable public debt ratio requires a primary fiscal surplus. We refer to this state as a *leaden age*. The denominator of equation (4) is sufficiently important to name it the *growth–interest differential*.

Since the debt ratio will affect aggregate demand, it will be necessary to include a fiscal policy reaction function in order to stabilize debt. We have two potential policy instruments (γ or τ), and we also have a potential objective or goal in the debt ratio (b), which could be chosen jointly with growth or other objectives. We've elected to set government spending, $\bar{\gamma}$, using the tax parameter as instrument. We will also have to choose a debt ratio goal ($\bar{b}$) to anchor the tax in the steady state; call that tax ratio τ^*. Our fiscal reaction function is:

$$\tau_{+1} = \tau^* + h_f(b - \bar{b}) \tag{5}$$

There is some loss of realism here, as we are forgoing the opportunity to model automatic stabilizers. We have solved the assignment problem by letting the monetary authority worry about managing the value of money and the fiscal authority focus on debt, which seems lifelike.

Investment and saving

At the center of the model are an independent investment equation and a national saving equation. The underlying motivation for writing out an independent investment equation is that there is an implicit division of labor between capitalists in their capacity as owners of capital (who make saving decisions) and in their capacity as managers (who make investment decisions), and this presents a coordination problem. An alternative motivation might be that at a point in time, some capitalists are net savers and others are net investors. In either case, changes in the level of utilization coordinate the saving and investment decisions of the capitalists through the *principle of effective demand*: utilization changes to generate the right amount of saving to match the predetermined investment level.

Investment and the interest rate

To achieve a transparent, tractable model, we adopt a linear investment equation used in one form or another in many Kaleckian and Steindlian models:

$$I/K = d_0 - d_1 r + d_2 u \tag{6}$$

Since $g = I/K$ in equilibrium, this equation[2] imposes restrictions on the relationship between the rates of interest and growth, as would any investment equation of general form $g(r)$. From this equation, the condition for a golden age at normal utilization can be characterized as $(d_0 + d_2)/(1 + d_1) > r^*$.

It is worth commenting on the role that interest rates play in regulating investment, about which there is a long tradition of disputation. On the one hand, economists as diverse as Marx, Fisher, Keynes, and Minsky perceive the difference between the profit rate on capital and the interest rate on loans as central to the investment decision, whether because it measures the rate of "profit of enterprise" or the "marginal efficiency of investment (capital)." On the other hand are skeptics like Joan Robinson (1962, p. 43) who observes that a "model ... in which monetary policy, via the interest rate, controls the level of investment, is a kind of day-dream that economists delight in." Yet even she relies on monetary controls to bring some of her mythic metallic economies into line.

The most convincing theoretical argument for including the interest rate in the investment equation continues to be Kalecki's (1937) principle of increasing risk, through which a lower interest rate relaxes the equity (finance) constraint on investment. The basic idea is that firms know the expected rate of profit on new investment, but as they expand their spending on illiquid capital goods, they are putting more of their own funds or the external funds of their creditors at risk. In this framework, the rate of investment will be determined when the cost of funding, equal to the rate of interest plus a risk or liquidity premium rising with investment, achieves equality with the expected rate of profit. A decrease in the interest rate will typically lead to a greater volume of investment spending, since it creates more room for a larger risk premium. In this framework, there is no need for an inverse relationship between the volume of investment and the return on investment which formed the basis for Keynes's theory, heavily informed by his Marshallian interpretation of the law of diminishing returns. Indeed, Kalecki and others have subjected that theory to withering criticism for its internal inconsistencies and repetition of marginalist errors of logic.[3]

Yet Kalecki himself omitted the interest rate from his own investment equations. The reason had nothing to do with fundamental theory but was a "simplification ... based on the fact that ... the long-term rate of interest (as measured by yields of government bonds) does not show marked cyclical fluctuations" (Kalecki, 1969, p. 99). As Hicks (1989) has pointed out, Keynes, and by implication his contemporary Kalecki, were influenced by their experience with interest rates that up to that point had not exhibited much variability. There may be good reasons to question the limits of interest rate policy within a broadly Kaleckian framework, particularly related to the political and social determinants of investment stressed in Kalecki (1943), but there certainly is less basis in theory for omitting the interest rate from all consideration.

Given the self-imposed constraint that the normal rate of profit, $\pi\rho$, is unchanging, and that the system achieves normal utilization in the long run, the interest rate plays a key role here in that it allows for flexibility of the steady state growth rate.

Saving and equilibrium

National saving, S, is the sum of capitalist saving out of profits, at the rate s; capitalist saving out of net interest at the rate s_b; and government saving, which is just the (negative of the) overall fiscal deficit, $f + rb$. The treatment of capitalist saving is somewhat eccentric. The idea is to preserve some flexibility, so that interest income and bond wealth are potentially treated differently from ordinary profit income or dividends. The saving rate, s_b, could be interpreted to some extent as a measure of the degree of "Ricardian equivalence." The idea is that while some capitalists may behave as if their planning horizons extend off to infinity, many or most do not.[4] So we have:

$$S/K = s\pi\rho u + s_b(rb - \tau) - (\gamma - \tau + rb) \tag{7}$$

Setting equations (7) and (6) equal and solving for utilization gives us an investment–saving equation,

$$u = \alpha(d_0 - d_1 r + (1 - s_b)(rb - \tau) + \gamma) \tag{8}$$

where the multiplier, α is $1/c = 1/(s\pi\rho - d_2)$ and $c > 0$ is the well-known condition for stability of the multiplier process. Using the notation that $u_x = \partial u/\partial x$, we see immediately that $u_b, u_y > 0$ and $u_\tau < 0$. But $u_r < 0$ requires $d_1 > (1-s_b)b$ because an increase in the interest rate reduces investment demand but increases the demand for luxury consumption in what might be termed a Godley–Lavoie (2007) effect. In this model, public debt strengthens the rentier elements of the capitalist class who live off their bond holdings like characters in a Jane Austen novel. We will assume that the Godley–Lavoie effect does not predominate, so that a higher interest rate represents monetary tightening.

By setting $u = 1$, we can recover an equation for the natural rate of interest, r^*:

$$r^* = \frac{d_0 - c - (1-s_b)\tau + \gamma}{d_1 - (1-s_b)b} \tag{9}$$

Public debt tends to raise the natural rate of interest because it generates demand for luxury consumption goods among the rentier elements of the capitalist class. This does not mean that debt and deficits must increase the observed interest rate. As long as the system can expand in the short run, it is capable of generating the new saving required to finance a fiscal deficit through the Keynesian principle of effective demand. But once we impose the long-run restriction that utilization settles on its normal rate, this mechanism is no longer available.

Steady state

Using equation (4), equation (6) specialized to $u = 1$, and equation (9) lets us solve for the steady state or long-run equilibrium values of the tax ratio, the growth rate, and the interest rate, or, using boldface to denote matrices, $\mathbf{x}' = (\tau^*, g^*, r^*)$. Then the system can be written compactly as

$$\mathbf{x} = \mathbf{y} + \mathbf{A}\mathbf{x}$$

where $\mathbf{y}' = (\bar{\gamma}, D_0/D_1, d_0 + d_2)$, $D_0 = d_0 - c + \bar{\gamma}$, $D_1 = d_1 - (1-s_b)\bar{b}$ and

$$\mathbf{A} = \begin{pmatrix} 0 & +\bar{b} & -\bar{b} \\ \frac{-(1-s_b)}{D_1} & 0 & 0 \\ 0 & -d_1 & 0 \end{pmatrix}$$

Solving this system (e.g., using Cramer's rule or postmultiplying $\mathbf{y}$ by $(I - A)^{-1}$), gives us the steady state values:

$$\tau^* = \frac{(1-s_b)(d_0 + d_2)b^2 + (d_0 + d_2 + (d_1 + s_b)\gamma - (1+d_1)s\pi\rho)b - d_1\gamma}{d_1(1 + (1-s_b)b)}$$

$$g^* = \frac{s\pi\rho - s_b\bar{\gamma}}{1 + (1-s_b)\bar{b}}$$

$$r^* = \frac{d_0 - c + s_b\bar{\gamma} + (1-s_b)(d_0 + d_2)\bar{b}}{d_1(1 + (1-s_b)\bar{b})}$$

Note that the monetary and fiscal authorities are assumed to know the structure of the world well enough to solve these equations in order to set the benchmark real interest rate and the tax ratio.[5]

Growth effects of fiscal policy

Since workers neither save nor pay taxes, their consumption (normalized by the capital stock) will be constant; call that c_w, and call capitalist consumption (also normalized) c_k.[6] Because the system gravitates toward a long run with normal utilization ($u = 1$), we can write the basic income identity:

$$\rho = c_w + c_k + \gamma + g$$

This identity makes the growth effects of fiscal policy particularly transparent.

Recalling that our fiscal policy reaction function takes the tax parameter to be the instrument, we characterize the fiscal policy using $(\bar{\gamma}, \bar{b})$. If we are interested in the pure effects of public debt, this policy ordering is appropriate.[7] We can immediately see that public debt has an unambiguously negative effect on growth in this model in the long run.[8] That is because it creates an incipient category of rentiers whose luxury consumption (c_k) only adds to effective demand. When the system reaches the inflation barrier, there must be some offset to this demand, and that takes the form of a monetary response raising the interest rate sufficiently to reduce investment spending. Through this mechanism, public debt crowds-out private capital in the long run. But this need not happen at higher frequencies, and indeed, crowding-in is likely in the short run. The exception occurs, of course when the saving propensity out of interest achieves unity, in which case debt is neutral with respect to growth and interest.

Government consumption spending also has a negative effect on growth, which is consistent with some of the vast empirical literature on Barro equations (Barro and Sala-i-Martin, 2004, ch. 12). (One potential problem here is that this literature takes growth of per capita output rather than capital or output itself to be the object of interest.) Moreover, autonomous investment spending, d_0, which is sometimes taken as a token of aggregate demand, has no effect on the long-run growth rate (although it does affect the long-run interest rate.).

Golden and leaden ages

We can also see that the model can be either in a golden age or a leaden age, with very different implications for fiscal policy. We will return to this theme in more detail but for now, let us write down the condition for $g > r$ that defines the boundary between ages:

$$s\pi\rho > \frac{d_0 + d_2 + s_b\bar{\gamma}(1 + d_1) + (1 - s_b)(d_0 + d_2)\bar{b}}{1 + d_1}$$

Table 17.1 Growth–interest differentials, various countries, 1960–2008

Country	1960s and 1970s	1980s	1990s	2000s
		$g - r$		
US	+2.8	−2.2	−1.4	−0.3
Germany	+0.8	−3.1	−2.4	−2.2
Advanced G-20	n.a.	−2.7	−3.1	−0.8
Emerging G-20	n.a.	+9.0	+8.9	+10.3

Sources: For US and Germany, Carlin and Soskice (2006, Table 6.1), except 2000s. All the rest, IMF (2010, Table A1.1).

The important point here is that fiscal policies that increase spending or the target debt ratio move the threshold to the right along the $s\pi\rho$ line. An economy that starts in a golden age can be relocated into a leaden age by policy. An increase in the animal spirits of managers represented by $d_0 + d_2$ will also shift the threshold to the right, because it too increases the natural rate of interest. Finally, an increase in $s\pi\rho$ (which is the incipient laissez-faire growth rate) moves the economy toward the golden age region.

We now have enough structure to provide a preliminary answer to the question raised by the sustainability condition. Once the fiscal policy is chosen (i.e, any two of the trio (γ, τ, b)), so too is the rate of growth and the rate of interest in the steady state. Choosing a primary fiscal deficit pins down b, g, and r, for example; an exercise that takes the rates of growth, interest, and the fiscal deficit to be independent would be untenable in the world described by this model.

There is some evidence that neoliberal capitalism may have passed through the boundary from a golden age to a leaden age. The test for this would compare the steady state growth rate to the steady state real interest rate (on public debt). Absent an established method for measuring steady state values, the next best solution is to look at averages over time. Table 17.1 presents a brief sketch of the critical growth–interest differential (using growth of GDP rather than capital). Definitions of the decades differ slightly, so they are identified generically, with the 2000s ending in 2008.

For the advanced countries, it is clear that the neoliberal era does look leaden.[9] For the emerging G-20 countries (basically, the BRICs – Brazil, Russia, India, China) it appears that golden age conditions prevail, even in the neoliberal era. This is consistent with the generalization that emerging G-20 countries carry lower debt ratios than the advanced countries, as well as their often high rates of accumulation. In 2006, for example, the emerging G-20 countries had a gross debt ratio of 36.9 per cent and a net debt ratio of 35.2 per cent; the advanced G-20 figures were 78.4 per cent and 50.3 per cent (IMF, 2010, Statistical Tables 8 and 9).

Dynamics

Using the steady state equations (which the monetary and fiscal authorities need), and equations (3)–(8), we can write down the four equations that describe the dynamics of the model. These form a system of autonomous, nonlinear difference equations:

$$p_{+1} = p(p, b, r, \tau)$$
$$b_{+1} = b(b, r, \tau)$$
$$r_{+1} = r(p) \tag{10}$$
$$\tau_{+1} = \tau(b)$$

Since the system is nonlinear, the first step in analyzing the stability properties is to obtain the Jacobian of equations (10), evaluated at the equilibrium. Adopting the notation that $z_j = \partial z(\cdot)/\partial j$ for $z = p(\cdot), b(\cdot)$ and $j = b, r, \tau$, we have

$$\mathbf{J} = \begin{pmatrix} 1 & p_b & p_r & p_\tau \\ 0 & b_b & b_r & b_\tau \\ h_m & 0 & 0 & 0 \\ 0 & h_f & 0 & 0 \end{pmatrix}$$

The stable space consists of all the (h_m, h_f) values that satisfy the condition that the roots (eigenvalues) of the Jacobian lie within the unit circle. This space identifies local asymptotic stability only; global stability of nonlinear systems can get tricky (Elaydi, 2005, ch. 5) and achieving any analytical results with a four-dimensional system presents a technical challenge. Below we demonstrate the possibility that the stable space can be nonempty with some numerical examples.

Fiscal policy and the golden age

This model provides a natural environment for attacking the problem of stabilizing demand through debt financing. If the monetary authority remains committed to controlling inflation and the fiscal authority to hitting its target debt ratio, a temporary demand shock (say a one-period-only downward shift in the investment function, $\Delta d_0 < 0$) will trigger a subsequent reflation, assuming the shock has not thrown the system into a deflation trap.[10] The inflation dynamics process guarantees that a temporary decline in inflation requires a subsequent reflationary period with utilization above normal. Fiscal policy will initially tighten (because the debt ratio rises) but as the monetary stimulus raises the growth rate the debt ratio will decline and open up space for more fiscal stimulus (lower taxes) temporarily. The mathematics of the difference equations suggest that this shock will generate oscillations.

A severe shock (e.g., one which involves a deflation trap) might be attacked with a discretionary fiscal stimulus, such as a temporary increase in government spending financed by debt. This is the "jobs now" part of a stabilization plan referred to in the opening paragraph. (The implicit assumption here and in the next section is that the deflation or liquidity trap conditions are temporary, so that monetary policy returns to full strength in the recovery phase.)

If we impose the assumption that the system starts and remains in a golden age, we can use this occasion to consider an instructive thought experiment that sheds light on the possibility of growing out of a deficit. Let the fiscal authority be willing to switch off its reaction function (i.e., keep τ constant) and the monetary authority be willing to abandon its inflation target (i.e., keep r constant). The demand shock can be absorbed using a purely bond-financed increase in government spending (i.e., $\Delta \gamma = -\Delta d_0$). The newly issued bonds then add to the public debt, but because growth exceeds the interest rate in a golden age, the debt ratio will eventually stabilize without further policy intervention. In this case, the utilization rate will remain elevated by the stimulus coming from the luxury consumption by rentier elements out of the (new) bond wealth. But because the capital stock is growing faster than public debt, this stimulus will be declining over time. Thus, inflation will rise as long as utilization is elevated, but will eventually stabilize at some level above the old target as the stimulus peters out.

It is worth drilling down further into this world. How are the bonds being serviced? Where do the resources come from to satisfy the rentiers' demands for luxury consumption? The second question is easier: the system is producing real output by running the factories overtime. It can afford both more luxury consumption and higher accumulation because of the presumed elasticity of production (capacity barriers are not technologically binding).

To answer the first question, consider the bonds issued after the initial shock. They are being serviced by further borrowing. Each cohort of rentier-capitalists receives payments from the next cohort of capitalists, all intermediated by the state.[11] This is a Ponzi game made sustainable by the rapid growth of capitalist wealth, revealing the underlying reason that this system demands a primary fiscal deficit to stabilize the debt ratio under golden age conditions.

Here we are encroaching on the nature of state fiat money. Recognizing that debt and (outside) money represent liabilities of the state, we need to ask what lies on the other side of the balance sheet. Foley (2003, p. 9) has argued that the value of fiat monies is an expression of the fiscal power of the state: "The ability of states (and central banks) to borrow rests on their holdings of offsetting assets. Every government has an asset in the tax liabilities of the public. ... It is not true that a central bank note is a valueless token which is inconvertible into anything of value. As a liability of the government it can be used to pay taxes."

Yet we know from experience (see Table 17.1) that governments are able to sustain positive growth–interest differentials, implying that Ponzi finance has been available to them ex post. For such financing to be available ex ante would require that capitalists are willing to lend to the state on the understanding that their bonds will be serviced out of further liabilities issued by the state. Such capitalists would be trusting their futures to the kindness of strangers, the implausibility of which for many economists rules out such a fiscal program ex ante. In addition, there is always the possibility that the structure of accumulation will shift unfavorably toward a leaden age, as indeed it seems to have done. It is clear from this angle that public debt acquires value from the contingent assets generated by the future taxing capacities of the state. The impression that permanent Ponzi finance may be possible is an artifact of the mechanical nature of the model, lacking deeper theoretical foundations. The argument here validates the conventional government intertemporal budget constraint equating the value of public debt with the present discounted value of future fiscal primary surpluses.[12] Thus, the basic message of the fiscal sustainability condition (equation (4) above) that under leaden age conditions today's fiscal deficits imply future primary fiscal surpluses would seem valid under general conditions. This is the "deficits later" part of a stabilization plan.

Growth targets

This need for a fiscal consolidation ("deficits later") raises the question of its effects on growth. If the debt ratio is allowed to rise through a change in the debt target, we know that the long-run growth rate will decline. Even if the debt target is not altered, so that a temporary rise is followed by a return to the unchanged target ratio, the loss of capital accumulation caused by the shock (assuming it is offset by a debt-financed fiscal stimulus as above) will permanently lower the path of the capital stock even as it returns to its original trend growth rate. Yet the model suggests that fiscal consolidation can be part of a long-range plan to restore some desired level of capital and employment.

To illustrate the mechanisms, let us assume that the authorities want growth to keep up with the natural rate of population growth, n. In this case, fiscal policy needs to be adjusted so that the target debt ratio supports growth at the natural rate. From the solution for steady state growth, we can characterize the required debt target thus:[13]

$$\bar{b} = \frac{s\pi\rho - s_b\gamma - n}{(1 - s_b)n}$$

Perhaps the system has accumulated a large reserve army of unemployed labor, and must now adjust to a population growth rate that is greater than the rate attached to the old debt target. In this case, the growth deficiency could be rectified by a fiscal consolidation that reduces the long-run debt ratio. Continuing to take the government spending ratio as constant, the fiscal consolidation at least initially requires a tax increase to slow the growth of debt. Let us assume the monetary authorities coordinate fully and switch to the new, lower natural interest rate target immediately. Thus, the transitional dynamics will involve a classic policy mix, with loose monetary policy partially compensating for tighter fiscal policy.

Initially, taxes need to go up to begin the process of fiscal consolidation, and without an extra measure of monetary stimulus the initial result will be a policy-induced decline in utilization. This seems to be the way real-life consolidations play out, even in small open economies in which monetary policy can offset the fiscal shock through both interest and exchange rate reductions (Guajardo, Leigh, and Pescatori, 2011). As the transition unfolds, the tax rate can be brought down toward its new steady state value.

During the transition dynamics going from low to higher growth, it is clear that the system will typically enjoy a period (or periods) of super-normal growth when it overshoots the natural rate of growth. This creates an opening for the policy makers to target the level of employment as well as its rate of growth. Using E to represent employment and L to represent the labor force (assumed to be a constant proportion of the population), we can write the employment rate, $e = E/L$, in terms of the capital–*labor force* ratio, $\kappa = K/L$, and the full-utilization capital–labor ratio, k:

$$e = \frac{uK}{kL} = \kappa \frac{u}{k}$$

Since the utilization rate gravitates toward $u = 1$, targeting the capital–labor force ratio is equivalent to targeting the employment rate, or achieving some desired path of employment. By applying discretion in their choice of policy reaction parameters (h_f, h_m, and $\bar{p}$), the authorities can influence the path of the capital–labor force ratio, κ. In doing so, they are exploiting the path dependent quality of this class of model.

We illustrate these properties in Figure 17.1 with some simulations in which we have chosen different values for $\bar{p}$. In one scenario, the target inflation rate is maintained at its original level, and fiscal consolidation proceeds with the amount of monetary accommodation provided by the Taylor rule. In the other, the monetary authority increases its inflation target modestly to provide additional accommodation. In these simulations, the target growth rate is increased, and the steady state debt ratio decreased (from 0.5 to 0.25).[14]

The path of κ is shown as an index number set to $\kappa = 1$ at $t = 0$. With the additional accommodation from an increased inflation target, the system gravitates toward a higher capital–labor force ratio. The more aggressive monetary support generates additional capital accumulation; the system enjoys a substantial period of super-normal growth. A less aggressive monetary policy results in less such super-normal growth.

There is a clear lesson here for confronting the challenges of Depression-level shocks. Full recovery requires a two-stage approach. Leveraged fiscal policies can be effective in restoring the level of demand and utilization in the first stage of recovery. But they leave behind a residual level of debt that will reduce the growth of capital and employment if allowed to grow *pari passu*, and this could create long-term problems in providing full employment to a growing population. In fact, restoring full utilization may not be sufficient to restore full employment of labor if the level of capital is insufficient, as is likely after a prolonged period of low investment during the depressed years. Full recovery requires a second stage of fiscal consolidation. The key to making this work is the use of the right monetary–fiscal policy mix. By calibrating the fiscal consolidation with monetary stimulus, it should be possible to generate a period of rapid accumulation that both reduces the debt ratio and increases the capital stock in relation to the labor force. This model, in a sense, underwrites the functional finance approach associated with Abba Lerner. The fact that we have eliminated, by assumption, any distributional complications

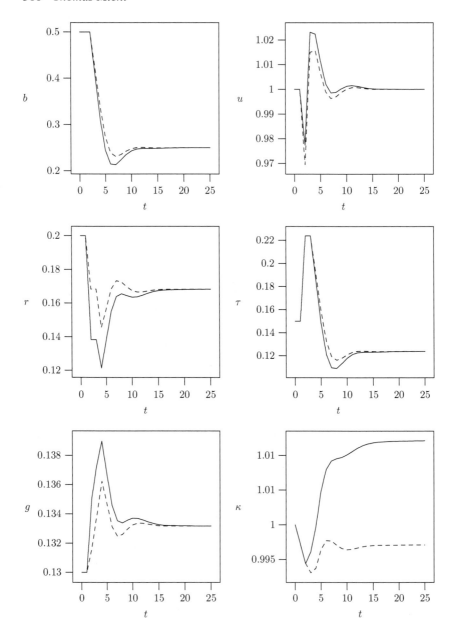

Figure 17.1 Debt consolidation with $\bar{p} = 0.09$ (solid line) and $\bar{p} = 0.05$ (dashed line). Using a more accommodating monetary policy to support debt consolidation results in an increase in the steady state employment rate, indexed by κ (bottom right panel). The debt consolidation reduces $\bar{b}$ from 0.5 to 0.25. The parameter values are: $n = 0.133$, $a = 1$, $s = 0.8$, $s_b = 0.9$, $\pi = 0.3$, $\rho = 1$, $d_0 = d_1 = 0.1$, $d_2 = 0.05$, $h_f = 0.4$, $h_m = 0.75$, initial $\bar{p} = 0.05$, $\gamma = 0.115$.

across class lines demonstrates that such an approach can be implemented in principle without saddling workers with the burden of new taxes to service debt.

Concluding thoughts

This model shows a way out for policy makers confronted by a major shock, and helps clarify the nature of the fiscal sustainability condition. The model can generate either a golden age in which the growth–interest differential is positive or a leaden age in which it is negative. There is some evidence that in the neoliberal era advanced capitalist countries have entered a leaden age. In either case, the model suggests that debt has a long-run negative effect on growth. It is also arguable that a temporary fiscal stimulus requires a future fiscal consolidation. Even in a golden age, when the formal possibility of growing out of a debt burden does present itself ex post in the model, that does not appear to be a convincing possibility ex ante.

Importantly, policy makers have the option of pursuing a long-run fiscal consolidation that lowers the debt ratio and raises the long-run growth rate. High growth during the transitional period even makes it possible for the authorities to guide the level of capital and employment toward some desired path. Whether this optimistic policy recommendation resonates with real economies depends on the validity of several key assumptions that give the policy makers more power in the model than they probably possess in life.

Acknowledgments

The author thanks J. W. Mason whose blog, The Slack Wire, provided some of the inspiration to write this chapter, and Peter Skott, who made several insightful comments that decisively shaped the results, while taking full responsibility for the views expressed and any errors of commission or omission.

Notes

1 To be precise, (Robinson, 1962, pp. 52–54) describes a growth path with full employment and mass prosperity as a golden age and a path with full employment achieved through "Malthusian misery" as a leaden age.
2 A more complete investment equation in this tradition would include the profit share, following Bhaduri and Marglin (1990). Thus, the term $d_0 + d_2$ captures the effect of the normal rate of profit (evaluated at $u = 1$) on accumulation. But it would be a mistake to ignore the voluminous literature that tries to get to grips with the investment equation. For recent critiques of the Kalecki–Steindl approach from Harrodian and Classical perspectives, see Skott (2010) and Shaikh (2009).
3 Sardoni (1987) provides a discussion with references to the relevant literature. We might also note the similarity between Kalecki's treatment of investment and that of Minsky (1975), who uses Keynes's "borrower's risk" and "lender's risk" in much the same fashion. In both frameworks, the investment function can be volatile, given the underlying instability of profit expectations and attitudes toward risk and liquidity. A full account of Kalecki's views on the theory of investment can be found in Sawyer (1985).

4 If we must have some microeconomic foundation for capitalist saving, there are other ways to model the bequest motive besides the hypothesis of intergenerational altruism that underpins modern Barro–Ricardo equivalence, such as the hypothesis that capitalists derive utility from their end-of-life wealth for its own sake as in Michl (2009). In the latter case, their planning horizon would be finite.

5 If the monetary authority chooses the wrong value for the natural rate of interest, say $\bar{r}$, they will still wind up stabilizing the system through the Taylor principle but inflation will miss the target by:

$$p^* - \bar{p} = \frac{r^* - \bar{r}}{h_m}$$

Similar considerations apply to the fiscal authority's choice of $\bar{\tau} \neq \tau^*$ and the steady state debt ratio.

6 For a model that adopts the polar opposite assumption that workers pay all the tax so that debt works through c_w, see Skott (2001).

7 An alternative ordering would take the tax as given and let spending be the policy instrument. In this case, a change in the debt target would involve changes in spending that would muddy the water.

8 There is surprisingly little empirical literature on debt and long-run growth. The best evidence for a negative relationship is probably Kumar and Woo (2010) which focusses on the effect of the debt ratio on subsequent growth (in per capita output), thus attenuating the problem of endogeneity.

9 More rigorous treatments show a similar pattern; see de Carvalho, Proano, and Taylor (2010, Figure 6) or Abbas, Belhocine, El-Ganainy, and Horton (2011). An alternative interpretation might emphasize the prevalence of financial repression (e.g., Regulation Q controls on bank interest rates) in the earlier period.

10 With a given inflation target anchoring inflation expectations, the model defines the condition for a deflation trap in which the natural rate of interest falls below the minimum rate of interest at the zero nominal interest rate bound, $\min r = -p^e$, which is:

$$s\pi\rho > d_0 + d_2 - (1 - s_b)\tau + \gamma + (d_1 - (1 - s_b)b)\bar{p}$$

In this case, an increase in the inflation target, if it were credible, could escape the deflation trap. Otherwise, fiscal policy remains the only solution to chronic stagnation. Note that these two boundary conditions are ordered so that as the saving rate increases, the system progresses from a leaden to a golden age and then to a deflation trap. Thus, being in a golden age is not necessarily desirable.

11 This point can be visualized more clearly by assuming there are no debts to begin with, no taxes are ever collected, and aside from the temporary stimulus, no government spending.

12 See Foley and Michl (1999, pp. 226–229) for a derivation and an explanation of the role of the no-Ponzi-game condition.

13 This expression brings out an important limitation on fiscal policy. Only if the laissez-faire rate of growth $(s\pi\rho)$ exceeds the natural rate of growth can the fiscal authority target growth using public debt as an instrument. If the laissez-faire growth rate is below the natural growth rate, the state must become a creditor $(b < 0)$, using its fiscal authority to finance capital accumulation and holding net claims on the private sector. We will assume that the level of government consumption spending does not prevent the system from achieving the natural rate of growth with positive b, or that $s\pi\rho > s_b\gamma + n$.

14 The numerical examples are locally stable, based on the condition that the characteristic roots of the Jacobian, $\mathbf{J}$, all lie within the unit circle. The eigenvalues here come in

pairs of complex conjugates that are independent of the choice of inflation target. With $\bar{b} = 0.5$, the dominant eigenvalue is $0.851 \pm 0.307i$, while with $\bar{b} = 0.25$, the dominant eigenvalue is $0.753 \pm 0.331i$. See the caption of Figure 17.1 for parameter values.

References

Abbas, S. Ali, Nazim Belhocine, Asmaa El-Ganainy, and mark Horton (2011) *Historical Patterns and Dynamics of Public Debt – Evidence From a New Database*, International Monetary Fund, (http://www.imf.org/external/np/seminars/eng/2010/eui/pdf/elg.pdf).

Barro, Robert J., and Xavier Sala-i-Martin (2004) *Economic Growth*, second ed., Cambridge: MA: The MIT Press.

Bhaduri, Amit, and Stephen Marglin (1990) 'Unemployment and the real wage: The economic basis for contesting political ideologies.' *Cambridge Journal of Economics*, 14(4), 375–393.

Carlin, Wendy, and David Soskice (2006) *Macroeconomics: Imperfections, Institutions, and Policies*, Oxford: Oxford University Press.

de Carvalho, Laura, Christian Proano, and Lance Taylor (2010) *Government Debt, Deficits, and Economic Growth: Lessons from Fiscal Arithmetic*, New York: Schwartz Center for Economic Policy Analysis. Policy note.

Duménil, Gérard, and Dominique Lévy (1999) 'Being Keynesian in the short term and classical in the long term: The traverse to classical long-term equilibrium.' *The Manchester School*, 67(6), 648–716.

Dutt, Amitava K. (1997) 'Equilibrium, path dependence and hysteresis in post-Keynesian models, in Arestis P. and Sawyer M., eds., *Essays in Honour of G. C. Harcourt: Markets, Unemployment and Economic Policy*, ed. Philip Arestis and Malcolm Sawyer, vol. 2, London: Routledge, pp. 238–253.

Elaydi, Saber (2005) *An Introduction to Difference Equations*, New York: Springer.

Foley, Duncan K. and Thomas R. Michl (1999) *Growth and Distribution*, Cambridge MA: Harvard University Press.

Foley, Duncan K. (2003) *Marx's Theory of Money in Historical Perspective*, Conference on Marx's Theory of Money: Modern Appraisals, Mt. Holyhoke College. Conference paper.

Galbraith, James K. (2011) *Is the Federal Debt Unsustainable?* Annandale: Jerome Levy Economics Institute. Policy note.

Godley, Wynne, and Marc Lavoie (2007) *Monetary Economics: An Integrated Approach to Credit, Money, Income, Production and Wealth*, New York: Palgrave Macmillan.

Guajardo, Jaime, Daniel Leigh, and Andrea Pescatori (2011) *Expansionary Austerity: New International Evidence*, Washington: International Monetary Fund. Working paper no. 11/158.

Hicks, John (1989) *A Market Theory of Money*, Oxford: Oxford University Press.

IMF (2010) *Fiscal Monitor*, Washington: International Monetary Fund.

Kalecki, Michal (1937) 'The principle of increasing risk.' *Economica*, 4(16), 440–447.

Kalecki, Michal (1943) 'Political aspects of full employment.' *Political Quarterly*, 14, 322–331.

Kalecki, Michal (1969) *Theory of Economic Dynamics*, New York: Augustus M. Kelley.

Krugman, P. (2011) The austerity delusion, *The New York Times*, March 25, 2011, p. A27.

Kumar, M.S. and Woo, J. (2010) *Public Debt and Growth*, Washington: International Monetary Fund. Working paper no. 10/174.

Lavoie, Marc (1995) 'The Kaleckian model of growth and distribution and its neo-Ricardian and neo-Marxian critiques.' *Cambridge Journal of Economics*, 19(6), 798–818.

Michl, Thomas R. (2008) 'Tinbergen rules the Taylor rule.' *Eastern Economic Journal*, 34(3), 239–309.

Michl, Thomas R. (2009) *Capitalists, Workers, and Fiscal Policy: A Classical Model of Growth and Distribution*, Cambridge MA: Harvard University Press.

Minsky, Hyman P. (1975) *John Maynard Keynes*, New York: Columbia University Press.

Robinson, Joan (1962) *Essays in the Theory of Economic Growth*, New York: St. Martin's Press.

Rowthorn, Robert (1999) 'Unemployment, wage bargaining and capital-labour substitution.' *Cambridge Journal of Economics*, 23(4), 413–425.

Sardoni, Claudio (1987) *Marx and Keynes on Economic Recession*, Brighton: Wheatsheaf Books.

Sawyer, Malcolm C. (1985) *The Economics of Michal Kalecki*, London: Macmillan.

Shaikh, Anwar (2009) 'Economic policy in a growth context: A classical synthesis of Keynes and Harrod.' *Metroeconomica*, 60(3), 455–494.

Skott, Peter (2001) 'Aggregate demand policy in the long run.' In *Money, Macroeconomics and Keynes: Essays in Honour of Victoria Chick*, ed. Philip Arestis, Meghnad Desai, and Sheila Dow, vol. 1, London: Routledge, pp. 124–139.

Skott, Peter (2010) 'Growth, instability and cycles: Harrodian and Kaleckian models of accumulation and income distribution.' In *Handbook of Alternative Theories of Economic Growth*, ed. Mark Setterfield, Cheltenham UK: Edward Elgar, pp. 108–131.

Taylor, Lance (2004) *Reconstructing Macroeconomics: Structuralist Proposals and Critiques of the Mainstream*, Cambridge MA: Harvard University Press.

18 Consequences of downsizing in U.S. manufacturing, 1967 to 1997

Edward N. Wolff

Introduction

There has been much discussion of "downsizing" in the press. In this chapter, using Census of Manufacturing data, I explore whether such a pattern has characterized U.S. manufacturing over the period from 1967 to 1997, the period when downsizing received the most attention. I do find evidence of a decline in average establishment size over this period.[1] Moreover, regression to the mean also occurred, with large establishments tending to become smaller (or to being replaced by smaller enterprises) and small establishments tending to expand, with the overall tendency being movement toward the middle.

A few words might be said about the notion of "downsizing" and the choice of period reviewed. In the popular vernacular, "downsizing" refers to the deliberate (or strategic) announcements of plant layoffs in order to gain media and/or Wall Street attention. Perhaps, the most egregious example was "Chainsaw Al" (Albert Dunlap) who obtained his nickname from the ruthless methods he employed to streamline ailing companies, most notably Scott Paper. Baumol, Blinder, and Wolff (2003, Chapter 2) provide extensive documentation of layoff announcements during the 1980s and 1990s in the U.S.[2] I use the term "downsizing" here in the more mundane sense of a reduction in average establishment size within industry. However, using Census of Manufacturing data, I am unable to determine whether reductions in average establishment size came about due to a deliberate strategy of layoffs or due to other reasons for shrinking plant size.

My period of analysis covers the years 1967 to 1997. The choice of years is mainly dictated by data availability (as noted below, the U.S. industry classification scheme was changed in 1997). However, it is also the case that the years 1980–1997 were the heyday of the "downsizing" craze, so that my period of analysis covers the main period of downsizing. After 1997, popular concern switched to "outsourcing," which involves a different set of issues.

The chapter explores some potential consequences of downsizing. First, I investigate whether there is any evidence that the act of downsizing increases the productivity of establishments. Second, I explore whether downsizing leads to higher profitability of firms. I also consider the effects of downsizing on average share prices of manufacturing stocks.

Third, I look into the association of downsizing with both employee compensation and unit labor costs. Downsizing might be a weapon in reducing wages, particularly if it reduces the relative employment of more senior employees or higher paid jobs. Reductions in establishment size might also lower wages simply through the well-documented employer size effect on wages: namely, that *ceteris paribus*, larger establishments pay higher wages (see, for example, Masters, 1969; Mellow, 1981; Idson, 1999).

The central story that emerges here is rather straightforward. First, on average, where downsizing has occurred in the manufacturing sector it has not contributed to productivity, contrary to what is frequently conjectured. Second, it has actually reduced profits. Third, downsizing by a firm has been associated with a decline in the price of its stocks, perhaps because it lowers profitability. In contrast, de-unionization is strongly associated with a decline in profitability, a reduction in stock prices, and a drop in worker compensation.

The remainder of the chapter is organized as follows. The next section reviews the pertinent literature. The following section provides theoretical motivation for the effects of downsizing on productivity and profitability. Descriptive statistics on changes in the size distribution of establishments in manufacturing are presented in the fourth section. The fifth section shows time trends of variables that may be affected by downsizing in manufacturing and this set of factors is formally analyzed in the sixth section. Concluding remarks are made in the last section.

Literature review

Background on the downsizing phenomenon was provided by Lazonick (2009). He documented the shift in the basic corporate business model in the U.S. from about 1980 to the present, from an emphasis on stakeholder value to one on shareholder value. He called this new business model the "New Economy business model" or NEBM, which radically altered the terms on which workers were employed in the U.S. The rise of the NEBM is also connected to the widespread adaption and diffusion of information and communication technology (ICT). The "Old Economy business model" (OEBM) that dominated the U.S. corporate economy from the end of World War II and into the 1980s offered employment that was much more stable, and earnings that were much more equitable, than employment and earnings in the NEBM. In the OEBM, men (mainly men) typically secured a well-paying job right after college in an established company and then worked their way up and around the corporate hierarchy over the next three or four decades of employment. In the NEBM, an employee begins work for a company but that person has no expectation of a lifetime career with that particular enterprise. The NEBM set the stage for the phenomenon of downsizing that started in force in the 1980s. Insofar as companies no longer valued worker loyalty, workers were expendable if that increased the bottom line on their income statement.

Another concurrent development was the formation of global value chains, as documented by Sturgeon, Van Biesebroeck, and Gereffi (2008) for the automobile industry in North America. They found a growing tendency by firms to divide the process of producing goods and services, and to locate different parts of the production process in different parts of the world depending on costs, markets, logistics, or polities. The globalization of production is often described as "slicing up the value chain," "outsourcing," or "offshoring." This process of outsourcing was predominant during the 1990s. Outsourcing put further pressure on globalized firms to downsize (domestic) employment.

A related trend was the growing "financialization" of the U.S. corporate economy. As discussed in Milberg (2008) and documented in Duménil and Lévy (2011), there has been a large increase in the financialization of the U.S. economy. This process has taken three forms. First, there is an increasing share of GDP accounted for by the financial sector. Second, gross international capital flows have grown much faster than world output. Third, non-financial firms have relied more heavily on finance than on production as both a source and use of their funds. Milberg focused on the third of these processes in his article.

The article connects growing financialization with the development of global value chains by U.S. non-financial corporations. Financialization was associated with a restructuring of production, with firms, in particular, focusing their production on their core competence. This new managerial strategy also became widespread around the same time – in the 1980s. This development exacerbated the shift to a focus on shareholder value. The focus on shareholder value and the formation of global value chains exerted further pressure to outsource production and to downsize (domestic) employment.

A similar argument is made by Stockhammer (2004). He also documented that from the 1980s through the 2000s, the financial accumulation of non-financial business was rising. He argued that financialization, the shareholder revolution, and the development of a market for corporate control shifted power away from other constituencies and to shareholders, and thus changed management priorities, leading to a reduction in the desired growth rate. Interestingly, he also provided evidence for the U.S., the U.K., France, and Germany that supported the negative effect of financialization on accumulation.

Two papers look at the effects of downsizing on productivity. Baily, Bartelsman, and Haltiwanger (1996) investigated why average labor productivity declines during recessions and increases during booms. One of their findings is that productivity tends to decline in plants that are downsizing – at least, during aggregate downswings. Collins and Harris (1999) used similar methodology to investigate the effects of downsizing on productivity in the U.K. motor vehicle industry over the period 1974–1994. They found that productivity growth was indeed higher in those plants that successfully downsized, but that those plants that were unsuccessful in downsizing tended to have among the worst productivity growth records. Unsuccessful downsizers accounted for a significant part of the overall decline in productivity in the U.K. motor vehicle industry after 1989.

Gordon (1996) argued that downsizing could reduce wages and salaries. He contended that a critically important source of falling wages has been U.S. corporations' increasingly aggressive stance with their employees, their mounting power to gain the upper hand in those struggles, and the associated shift in the institutional environment. Two papers provided some evidence on this. Cappelli (2003) looked at the relationship between both job losses associated with shortfalls in demand and downsizing and subsequent financial performance. His results indicated, among other things, that downsizing reduced labor costs per employee. Espahbodi, John, and Vasudevan (2000) examined the performance of 118 firms that downsized between 1989 and 1993. They found that operating performance improved significantly following the downsizing, and, in particular, these firms were able to reduce labor costs.

Several papers looked into how stock prices reacted to downsizing. The evidence is mixed. Abowd, Milkovich, and Hannon (1990) used an event study methodology to investigate whether human resource decisions of firms (such as staffing) announced in the *Wall Street Journal* between 1980 and 1987 discernibly affected either the level or variation of shareholder return. They found no consistent pattern of increased or decreased valuation in response to any of five categories of announcements of staff reduction, even after controlling for the likely effect of such announcements on total compensation costs.[3] Abraham (1999) also used an event study methodology to assess the effects of layoff announcements on shareholder returns. The *Wall Street Journal* was used to identify 368 firms that announced layoffs in 1993 or 1994. The results showed that layoff announcements induced a decrease in the shareholder returns of the firms that made the announcements. Farber and Hallock (1999) generally found negative effects on stock prices as a result of announcements of reductions in force for a sample of 1176 large firms over the 1970–1997 period.

Worrell, Davidson, and Sharma (1991) tested the reaction of the securities' market to announcements of 194 layoffs. They argued that investors reacted negatively to layoff announcements attributable to financial reasons. They found that negative preannouncement reactions occurred when negative hints about firms preceded announcements, and announcements of large or permanent layoffs elicited stronger negative responses than other announcements. Gombola and Tsetsekos (1992) argued that that a permanent plant closing provides evidence about an entire firm's financial condition – in particular, that out-of-date plants could not be sold and the firms did not have any other alternatives. Unless investors already knew the true value of the plant, a closing announcement should be following by a negative stock price reaction. They found confirmation of this in their data analysis. Caves and Krepps (1993) also examined how the stock market reacted to announcements of corporate downsizing between 1987 and 1991. Using disaggregated manufacturing industry data from 1967 to 1986, they found evidence that shareholders came to react positively to downsizings that involved white-collar layoffs and related reorganizations.

Theoretical motivation for the effects of downsizing on productivity and profitability

I have identified five theoretical models of downsizing. Each of these models focuses on a potential cause of downsizing and then traces its consequences for the firm's employment, productivity, and profitability. Although the models are distinct, they are not mutually exclusive; downsizing may and probably does have multiple causes. Still, it is essential to ask which of the candidate explanations are consistent with the data and which are not.

Technology may favor smaller enterprises

There has long been a presumption that technological progress favors larger firm size – for example, by requiring huge investments for successful entry or by extending the range of output over which economies of scale persist. Technology of that sort certainly characterized the railroads, automobile manufacture, and earlier forms of steel-making. However, technological change can sometimes make it more efficient to operate on a smaller scale. Transporting freight by truck instead of by rail is one well-known example; it materially decreased average firm size in the transportation industry. Mini mills, the success story of the modern U.S. steel industry, are vastly smaller than integrated steel mills. Some people argue for "the end of mass production" and the greater relative importance of speed, flexibility, product variety, and customization in the computer age. This argument may suggest that downsizing should lead to higher productivity and profitability.

Innovation and the reallocation of labor

The second model of downsizing also attributes the phenomenon to technical change. But here the effect stems not from changes in the cost-minimizing size of a firm, but rather from the pace of technological improvement itself. The essential idea is that any product or process innovation requires alterations in the nature of the tasks that workers perform. A *speedup* in the *rate* of innovation therefore implies that such changes come faster and are more dramatic. And that, in turn, almost certainly requires more extensive reallocations of labor both within and among firms.

One important feature of this phenomenon is the unevenness with which the costs and benefits of such labor market churning are spread across the workforce. Employees who are better educated and/or trained can adapt to new technology and changing circumstances more easily. So they may well be net beneficiaries of innovation. But less skilled workers are presumably less adaptable, and hence are likely to suffer both unemployment and wage declines when they get "downsized."

The hypothesized role of innovation as the driver of downsizing may seem at first to rest on a fortuitous relationship: Technical change just happens to play a key role. But it may be otherwise. In particular, the market mechanism creates remorseless pressures for innovation, and these pressures are what most clearly distinguish the capitalist economy from all alternatives. One major source of this pressure for continued and increasing innovative effort is the fact that the adoption of new technology, especially in the forms of new products and new industrial processes, has emerged as a prime competitive weapon for firms in the major oligopolistic sectors. The result is an innovation arms race that can literally be a matter of life or death for the participants.

In such a game, no player dares to fall behind, and many may well hope to pull ahead of their rivals. This sort of rivalry is clearly a recipe for increasing investment in R&D and innovative activities more generally. Moreover, faster innovation increases the frequency with which plant and equipment needs to be replaced. By accelerating the replacement of capital, it presumably also adds to the amount of labor-market churning. More often than not, such labor churning requires either retraining existing workers or replacing them with others who are better able to use the new technologies. Such changes therefore disadvantage those whom it is particularly difficult or costly to retrain (e.g., the poorly educated) or who offer bleak prospects for recoupment of the firm's investments in retraining (e.g., older workers). In this way, innovation may leave a permanent – or at least a very long lasting – imprint on relative wages and the distribution of income, depressing the wages of unskilled and less-educated workers relative to those with more skill and education. On average, however, in this scenario, downsizing should lead to greater efficiency and therefore higher productivity, and to cost-cutting and therefore greater profitability.

Foreign competition and trimming fat

A third model attributes downsizing to intensification of foreign competition – whether actual or threatened. It comes in two versions. In the first, increased competition from abroad, or perhaps simply greater cross-border economic activity, changes relative demands and supplies in the U.S. market – which in turn requires some firms and industries to contract while others expand. In fact, the availability of cheaper foreign products can be viewed as analogous to technological progress: Both factors increase the value of the outputs that the U.S. economy can produce from a given set of inputs, and both are likely to require significant industrial change. Furthermore, increased globalization has a clear technological basis: Reduced transportation costs, faster telecommunications, and the like are among the primary drivers of increased trade.

The argument asserts that the U.S. and other industrial economies have grown increasingly vulnerable to import competition as trade barriers have fallen and as technology transfer has progressed. This foreign competition, moreover, has forced American firms to reduce what has been called X-inefficiency (see Leibenstein, 1966) – that is, to trim fat – and this slimming down was (and is) often accomplished by cutting the dispensable portions of their labor forces. The argument is that certain, presumably large, firms used to have (or perhaps still have) more labor than they needed to produce the desired level of output – which they subsequently shed (or are shedding) under pressure from foreign competitors. The prototypical case is perhaps the U.S. auto industry in the 1960s and 1970s, which was widely viewed as "fat and lazy" before the onslaught of Japanese competition.

The second version of the foreign competition argument emphasizes the pressure that low-wage labor abroad puts on U.S. labor markets – especially markets for unskilled labor. The idea that workers in poor countries ("the South") pose a threat to low-skilled workers in rich countries ("the North") has been widely offered as an explanation for rising wage inequality in the industrial countries. But it may also lead firms to rid themselves of excess domestic labor, that is, to downsize in the United States. In this model, downsizing is alleged to be caused by intensified competition. If so, the phenomenon should be most severe where the intensification of competition is greatest. Journalistic accounts seem to support this idea, but it is not easy to measure the intensity of competition. Nor is foreign competition the only cause. Falling profit margins are one indication that a particular industry is facing greater competition, but profits are influenced by a myriad of other factors as well. To the extent that increased *international* competition is the driving force, we should find a positive correlation between downsizing and the share of imports (and maybe even the share of exports) in industry output. There are several pitfalls here, however. For example, the theory of contestable markets emphasizes that *potential* competition can sometimes be nearly as effective as *actual* competition in keeping profits down. Hence, profits can be depressed by growing foreign competitiveness even if the foreign market share is low and remains so.

Regardless of the underlying cause, however, it would appear that the "trimming fat" model has a clear empirical implication: Downsizing should raise the *average* productivity of labor strongly by ridding a firm of redundant labor without reducing its output. This implication appears at least partly testable in a cross-section of firms: Labor productivity should be rising faster in industries which have displaced relatively more workers. The profit implications are less clear, however. Intensified competition should reduce profitability, but shedding excess labor should increase it.

Capital–labor substitution

Another possible explanation for downsizing is that firms are shedding labor because they are adopting production technologies that employ relatively less labor and relatively more capital. In other words, they are moving along isoquants toward higher capital–labor ratios. In this case, the total *output* of a typical firm would not fall, but labor input would fall and capital input would rise. In this scenario, capital–labor substitution underlies downsizing. Why might this be so? Neoclassical theory looks to factor prices to explain optimal factor proportions. A rise in the capital–labor ratio should be prompted by a rise in the ratio of labor compensation to the cost of capital. But the real wage was certainly not growing rapidly during what were apparently the prime downsizing years – say, 1985–1993. Indeed, it was even lagging behind labor productivity. However, the cost of capital fell substantially after the 1980s. The stock market was much higher in 1997 and real interest rates lower than they were then in 1958. So the ratio of labor compensation to the interest rate may well have risen even though wages were barely rising.

Another possibility harkens back to the skill-biased technical progress hypothesis. Most attention has been given recently to the notion that technical change over the last 30 years or so has shifted optimal input proportions away from unskilled labor and toward skilled labor. But suppose capital is a *complement* to skilled labor (computers require literate and numerate workers), but a *substitute* for unskilled labor (machines replace brawn). In that case, skill-biased technical progress would also promote capital deepening.

What are the implications in terms of productivity and profitability? Capital–labor substitution would certainly increase labor productivity, but its effect on total factor productivity is indeterminate. Moreover, it is likely in this scenario that downsizing squeezes wages but boosts profits.

Breakdown of the social contract

A quite different model of downsizing hypothesizes a sea change in the relationship between labor and capital in America. This story shares common elements with the parts of Model 3 that focus on trimming fat. However, it emphasizes the "fat" embodied in high *wages* – rents captured by labor – rather than in redundant labor. The model comes in two variants.

According to the first variant, owners of capital have become less generous toward and/or less solicitous of labor. Whereas previously, at least, large corporations entered into a kind of "social contract" with their workers – one that involved rent sharing and considerable job security – capital has unilaterally broken that contract and demanded more of the rents for itself. This argument is similar to Lazonick's portrayal of the radical shift from the OEBM to the NEBM. Labor is thus faced with a choice between lower wages and fewer jobs, the latter being used as a threat to achieve the former. The second, and related, variant of the hypothesis envisions a change in the nature of shareholding away from more patient, relationship-oriented stockholders (e.g., insiders) and toward more impatient, return-oriented stockholders (e.g., fund managers who must show quarterly results). This second variant can possibly explain the first: More activist shareholders may have demanded that management focus on "creating shareholder value" to the detriment of labor and other stakeholders.

If, indeed, the social contract has been rewritten in this way, we can think of several possible causes. One is the intensification of competition, whether domestic or foreign. A second possibility is that the nature of shareholding has shifted toward large (especially institutional) shareholders who give less weight to stakeholders – such as the firm's workers – and are more focused on the bottom line. A third is the growing financialization of the U.S. economy, as emphasized by Milberg (2008). A fourth is the attitudinal change associated with the country's political shift to the right – which may, in turn, be ascribable in part to the success of economists' teachings – may have played a role. The neoclassical message has gotten through. Economic life is now imitating economic theory as never before. One consequence has been the elevation of shareholder value to primacy among possible goals of the firm, to the exclusion of, for example, the interests of stakeholders. Thus, for example, labor is increasingly viewed as "just another commodity" whose price and conditions of employment are determined by supply–demand conditions and nothing else.

Regardless of the cause, how would we know whether the hypothesis underlying Model 5 is valid? One source of potential evidence begins with several studies published in the late 1980s that documented sizable and persistent interindustry wage differentials. These studies found that some industries tend to pay all their workers, not just the occupational groups in short supply, more than other industries do (see, for example, Dickens and Katz, 1987; Krueger and Summers, 1987, 1988). While several hypotheses were advanced to explain this phenomenon, one of the more convincing at the time (and since) was *rent sharing*. Suppose managers were inclined to share rents with other stakeholders – in particular, with their workers. And suppose further that only certain industries had large rents to distribute, perhaps because only they enjoyed market power. Then employees fortunate enough to work in these industries would enjoy higher wages across the board.

The question is: Have such rents been squeezed or eliminated? The answer appears to be that the interindustry wage differentials observed in the 1980s have persisted into the 1990s – but they appear to have shrunk a bit. For example, Krueger (1998) found from Current Population Survey (CPS) wage data that, after controlling for differences in the educational attainment and experience of their workforces, the interindustry wage distribution became less dispersed over the decade 1983–1993. This evidence is vaguely consistent with the hypothesis that the social contract has been amended in ways that reduce labor's rents.

Another source of evidence is aggregate data on factor shares. If capital becomes more aggressive – and is successful at it – factor shares should shift toward profits and away from labor compensation. Macro time series on factor shares appear to contain some crude evidence in support of this hypothesis: The share of corporate profits in national income has risen sharply in recent years – from 9.1 percent in 1992 to 11.0 percent in 2000 – while the share of employee compensation has declined almost as much (from 73 percent to 71.6 percent over the same eight-year period).[4]

Yet another implication of the downsizing scenario based on a change in the social contract is that the level of stock prices should display a permanent increase, and therefore the stock market should enjoy a transition period – perhaps lasting for several years – during which price appreciation is extraordinarily high. That is just what seems to have happened, of course: Stock prices soared from 1995 to a peak in 2000. But (permanently) higher profitability may not have been the only reason, nor even the main reason. Many observers of the stock market, for example, believe that investors are now willing to accept a lower risk premium for holding equity than they previously demanded (see, for example, Cochran, 1999). Hence equilibrium price–earnings ratios may have been permanently elevated.

Others insisted that stocks were seriously overvalued in 2000 or so, and were bound to fall (see, for example, Shiller, 2000).

Downsizing based on a breakdown of the social contract clearly carries rather doleful implications for the labor market: Real wages should fall and job insecurity should rise. But the fall in employment should be a transitory phenomenon. It is a way to discipline the workforce. Once workers have been properly disciplined, the economy will have adjusted to the new "rules of the game," with rents squeezed out of real wages. Then labor should be (permanently) cheaper, and the optimal capital–labor ratio should fall. With regard to productivity, in the standard neoclassical view, if "downsizing" is about the redistribution of rents, its implications for productivity should be nil. It is just that capital should capture more of the rent, and labor less.

In sum, I have discussed five different models of why downsizing may have occurred. Some are "soft" and almost sociological – like the breakdown in the social contract. Others, like capital–labor substitution, are strictly neoclassical. These disparate models have partially overlapping, partially differing implications for a number of observable variables. Some of their implications are testable with existing data, and I will perform some of the relevant tests in the section "Regression Analysis" below.

Changes in the average establishment size in manufacturing

To determine whether downsizing has occurred in manufacturing. I use data from the U.S. Census of Manufacturing on establishments over the period 1967–1997. The Census of Manufacturing data begin in 1967 and are complete through 1992. Some additional data are available for 1997.[5] This source includes data on single establishment and multi-establishment firms. Establishments are classified into industries by their main product.

According to these data, the average establishment size in total manufacturing fell rather sharply over time, from 60.5 employees in 1967 to 45.7 employees in 1992, followed by a slight increase to 46.5 employees in the boom year 1997 (see Table 18.1). The change was fairly continuous over time, though it accelerated a bit in the period between 1987 and 1992. In particular, while over the entire 1967–1992 period, average establishment size fell at an average annual rate of 1.12 percent, between 1987 and 1992 it declined at an annual rate of 1.54 percent.

Table 18.1 also shows results by two-digit SIC. Of the 20 industries, 17 experienced reductions in average establishment size from 1967 to 1992; the other three experienced increases. Of the 16 industries with data available through 1997, 13 show a decline in average establishment size and 3 show an increase. Within the group showing declines, the most notable are electronics and other electrical equipment, primary metals, and leather and leather products, whose average establishment size fell by about half over the period. On the other hand, food and tobacco products both experienced substantial increases in their average establishment sizes. It is also of interest that durable good industries experienced greater declines in their average establishment size – 26 percent between 1967 and 1992 –

Table 18.1 Average number of employees per establishment and co-worker means for two-digit SIC manufacturing industries, 1967–1997

SIC industry	Mean employment			Percentage change		Co-Worker mean		Percentage change
	1967	1992	1997	1967–1992	1967–1997	1967	1992	1967–1992
20 Food and kindred products	50.7	72.3	74.8	42.4	47.4	507.1	328.4	−35.2
21 Tobacco products	228.3	333.3	NA	46.0	NA	534.5	402.3	−24.7
22 Textile mill products	131.2	104.7	91.3	−20.2	−30.4	352.8	194.9	−44.8
23 Apparel and other textile products	51.4	42.7	35.4	−17.0	−31.1	365.2	290.1	−20.6
24 Lumber and wood products	15.1	18.3	20.6	21.6	36.9	755.7	333.8	−55.8
25 Furniture and fixtures	42.5	40.4	43.3	−4.9	1.9	604.2	471.5	−22.0
26 Paper and allied products	108.5	97.6	NA	−10.0	NA	300.3	204.1	−32.0
27 Printing and publishing	27.1	22.8	24.6	−15.9	−9.3	1523.2	923.8	−39.3
28 Chemicals and allied products	71.3	70.7	66.3	−0.9	−7.0	1004.3	717.7	−28.5
29 Petroleum and coal products	75.3	53.9	49.4	−28.5	−34.4	791.7	460.3	−41.9
30 Rubber and misc plastics products	80.0	57.2	61.4	−28.5	−23.3	833.9	296.4	−64.5
31 Leather and leather products	89.2	49.6	NA	−44.4	NA	252.8	269.8	6.7
32 Stone, clay, and glass	37.9	28.8	30.8	−23.8	−18.6	707.5	309.4	−56.3
33 Primary metal industries	187.4	101.8	110.3	−45.6	−41.1	837.5	416.0	−50.3
34 Fabricated metal products	48.9	37.4	40.8	−23.6	−16.6	739.0	373.6	−49.4
35 Industrial machinery and equipment	49.2	32.2	35.1	−34.5	−28.7	1481.8	1038.9	−29.9
36 Electronic and electrical equipment	175.1	85.0	92.5	−51.4	−47.2	767.1	546.0	−28.8
37 Transportation equipment	245.1	145.9	126.1	−40.5	−48.6	1190.1	1090.9	−8.3
38 Instruments and related products	88.5	79.9	NA	−9.8	NA	1208.6	683.0	−43.5
39 Miscellaneous industries	30.1	21.5	21.8	−28.6	−27.4	759.4	533.2	−29.8
Non-durables	56.0	47.0	NA	−16.0	NA			
Durables	61.8	44.7	NA	−27.6	NA			
All Manufacturing Industries	60.5	45.7	46.5	−24.5	−23.2	1424.9	900.8	−36.8

Source: Author's computations from the Census of Manufacturing, 1967–1997

than did non-durables (16 percent). Finally, the rate of decline of average establishment size accelerated (or the rate of increase declined) in the 1987–1992 period compared to 1967–1987 in 14 of the 20 industries. This is particularly true of durables.

I also calculate the co-worker mean, defined as the weighted average of average establishment size by size class with the percentage of total employment in the size class used as the weight.[6] Let:

N_{jt}	$=$	number of establishments in industry j at time t.
N_{jkt}	$=$	number of establishments in size class k in industry j at time t.
E_{jt}	$=$	number of employees in industry j at time t.
E_{jkt}	$=$	average number of employees in size class k in industry j at time t.[7]
$p_{jkt} = E_{jkt}/E_{jt}$	$=$	share of total manufacturing employment in size class k in industry j at time t.
$e_{jt} = E_{jt}/N_{jt}$	$=$	average number of employees per establishment in industry j at time t.

Then the co-worker mean c_{jt} for industry j at time t is given by:

$$c_{jt} = \Sigma p_{jkt} e_{jt}. \tag{1}$$

The reason for using the co-worker mean is that the size distribution of establishments (and firms) is highly skewed (see Figures 18.1 and 18.2). In other words, most businesses are small but most employees work in large businesses. The average establishment (or firm) size tells us about the average business but not about the average worker. The co-worker mean is a closer reflection of the experience of the average employee in an industry in terms of the size of business he or she is working in.

It is first of note that the co-worker mean is, as expected, much larger than the average (see Table 18.1). In 1967 the co-worker mean for total manufacturing is 1,424, compared to an average establishment size of 60.5. This means that the typical manufacturing worker in 1967 was employed in an establishment of about 1,500 workers. However, like the average establishment size, the co-worker mean also shows a significant downward trend between 1967 and 1992 of 37 percent, compared to a 25 percent decline for average establishment size over the same years.[8] The co-worker mean, like average establishment size, fell in every period except 1982–1987, when it essentially remained unchanged.

Of the 20 industries, all but one experienced a reduction in its co-worker mean between 1967 and 1992. The most notable declines occurred in rubber and plastic products (65 percent), lumber and wood products (56 percent), primary metals (50 percent), and fabricated metal products (49 percent). Leather and leather products underwent a modest increase in its co-worker mean (7 percent).

Table 18.2 provides a summary of the number of industries downsizing and upsizing by census period. The results show a clear pattern: Average establishment

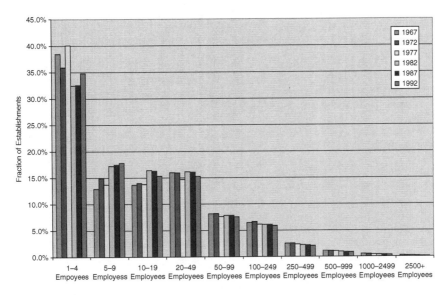

Figure 18.1 Size distribution of establishments by number of employees, 1967–1992 (Census of Manufacturing data).

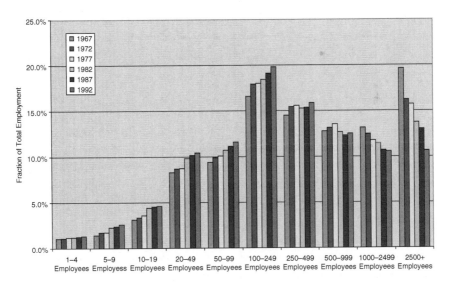

Figure 18.2 Size distribution of employment by size of establishment in number of employees, 1967–1992 (Census of Manufacturing data).

Table 18.2 Number of two-digit manufacturing industries upsizing and downsizing by census period, 1967–1997

Period	Change in average size:		
	Total manufacturing	Number of industries downsizing	Number of industries upsizing
A. Census of Manufacturing mean establishment size			
1967–1972	−4.7%	11	9
1972–1977	−8.5%	18	2
1977–1982	−3.1%	14	6
1982–1987	−3.5%	11	9
1987–1992	−7.4%	14	6
1992–1997	1.7%	5	11
TOTAL	−23.2%	73	43
B. Census of Manufacturing establishments: co-worker mean[a]			
1967–1972	−17.1%	13	7
1972–1977	−3.0%	16	4
1977–1982	−8.9%	19	1
1982–1987	0.4%	15	5
1987–1992	−14.0%	15	5
Total[b]	−36.8%	78	22

Source: Author's computations from the Census of Manufacturing, 1967–1997

Census of Manufacturing data on average-establishment size are missing for five industries in 1997. Industries in which average size changes by less than 0.1 percent are excluded from the tabulation.

[a] The co-worker mean is the employment-weighted average establishment size.
[b] 1967–1992

size in total manufacturing fell steadily from 1967 until the 1992–1997 boom. However, even though average establishment size in all manufacturing declined in every five-year period (until 1992–1997), there were always some "upsizing" industries. Of the 116 observations in total (five census periods with 20 industries and the last census period with 16), downsizing occurred in 73 cases while upsizing occurred in the other 43. So, while downsizing was the most common occurrence, there were plenty of exceptions.

There are also interesting differences by period. Manufacturing industries were less likely to downsize during 1967–1972 and 1982–1987, when the overall decline in manufacturing employment was low, than during 1972–1977 and 1987–1992, when manufacturing employment fell rapidly. In this respect, the 1977–1982 period is a bit of an anomaly, since it ended in a deep recession but the tendency to downsize was weak. Perhaps the cheap dollar of the 1977–1980 period helped manufacturing.

As shown in Panel B of Table 18.2, the downsizing pattern was much stronger for individual industries on the basis of the co-worker mean than the simple mean. Of the 100 observations in total (five census periods with 20 industries), downsizing occurred in 78 percent of the cases (compared to 63 percent of the cases on the basis of the simple mean).

Figures 18.1 and 18.2 show dramatic changes in the overall size distribution of manufacturing establishments based on Census of Manufacturing data over the period 1967 to 1992. The percentage of establishments in all size classes above 19 employees declined over time, and particularly so for establishments of 1,000 employees or more, while the proportion in size classes 5–9 and 10–19 increased. However, interestingly, the percentage of establishments in the size class with less than five employees also fell.

Even more dramatic is the change in the size distribution of employment. The share of total employment in establishments of 2,500 employees or more plummeted almost in half, from 19.6 percent in 1967 to 10.6 percent in 1992. The share of total employment in size class 1,000–2,499 also fell sharply, from 13.2 to 10.6 percent. The proportion of employment in size class 500–999 also declined somewhat. In contrast, the share of total employment in all the smaller size classes rose.

Effects of downsizing in manufacturing

I begin with some descriptive statistics. Figure 18.3 displays the change in average establishment size, and the average rates of TFP and labor productivity growth for total manufacturing by census period. There are no clear connections between productivity and establishment size, at least at the level of total manufacturing. Downsizing occurred during the 1977–1982 period, when TFP (and labor productivity) growth was very low, but also continued during the 1982–1987 period, when productivity grew very rapidly. Productivity growth was also quite high in the 1992–1997 period, when average establishment size gained.

I next show the change in average establishment size and the change in both the average rate of profit and the average profit share for total manufacturing from the preceding census period (see Figure 18.4). There appears to be a somewhat direct relation between the three sets of statistics, at least at the level of total manufacturing. Changes in both the profit rate and the profit share were highest during 1987–1992, when establishments experienced pronounced downsizing, and lowest during the 1967–1972, a period of modest downsizing.

Figure 18.5 shows trends in the average market value of firms in total manufacturing. The data are from the University of Chicago's CRSP Market Capitalization database, which includes a sample of firms in almost all two-digit industries. Average market value is computed as the ratio of the total market capitalization in a two-digit manufacturing industry divided by the number of firms in that industry. The average market value is deflated by the CPI-U. The index is somewhat imperfect, since it does not correct for mergers, acquisitions, or divestitures.

Stock values fluctuate much more widely than do the other industry level variables. During the first downsizing period, 1967–1972, it rose by only 14 percent and during the next downsizing period, 1972–1977, it fell precipitously, by

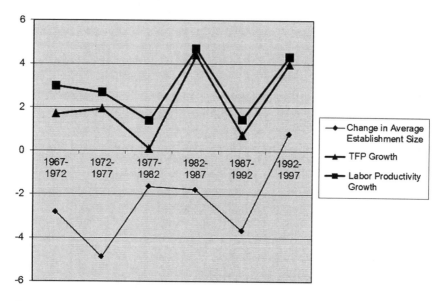

Figure 18.3 Changes in average establishment size and the annual percentage growth in TFP and labor productivity, total manufacturing, 1967–1997.

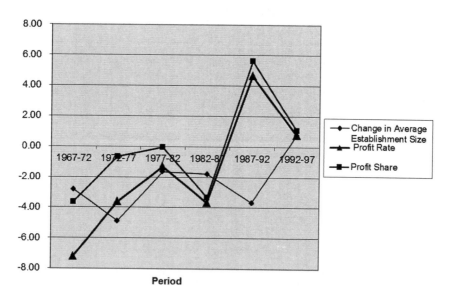

Figure 18.4 Changes in average establishment size and percentage change in profitability, total manufacturing, 1967–1997.

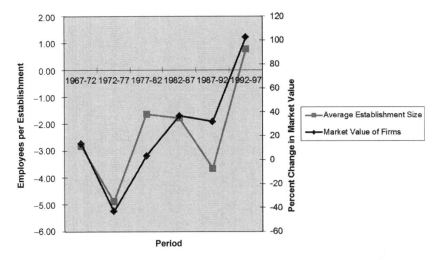

Figure 18.5 Change in average establishment size and the percentage change in average stock market valuation, total manufacturing, 1967–1997.

43 percent (this was true for the S&P 500 index as well). Between 1977 and 1982, another downsizing period, average market value in manufacturing inched up by 3 percent. However, during the next two periods, 1982–1987 and 1987–1992, during which average firm size fell, average market values rose by 37 and 32 percent, respectively. In the 1992–1997 period, when average establishment size increased very modestly, the average stock valuation in manufacturing boomed (as did the S&P 500 index), more than doubling in value. If anything, it appears that stock values rise faster during upsizing periods than during downsizing.

The last variable of interest is the change in average employee pay. This is defined in two ways: first, as average wages and salaries per full-time equivalent employee (FTEE); and, second, as the average employee compensation, including wages and salaries and employee benefits per FTEE. Both wages and salaries and employee compensation are deflated by the CPI-U to obtain employee pay in constant dollars.

Figure 18.6 shows the percentage change in the latter for the Census of Manufacturing periods (changes in wages and employee compensation are highly correlated). Here, a somewhat closer correspondence between patterns of upsizing and downsizing and the growth in pay is seen than between changes in average size and the preceding set of variables. During the first downsizing period, 1967–1972, average compensation grew at a brisk pace (10.5 percent) but in the next downsizing period, 1972–1977, the growth in average compensation fell by 6.0 percent. Over the next three periods, all characterized by downsizing, gains in average employee compensation actually declined by −2.6 percent, then rebounded to 6.4 percent, but subsequently collapsed to 1.2 percent. During the

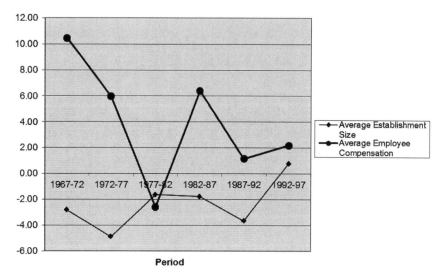

Figure 18.6 Changes in average establishment size and percentage change in employee compensation, 1967–1997.

1992–1997 period, when average establishment size rose slightly, the growth in average compensation once again recovered – to 2.2 percent.

Regression analysis of the effects of downsizing in manufacturing

I next turn to regression analysis to analyze the effects of downsizing on these various variables. I use a panel data set, consisting of 20 industry observations in each of the six five-year time periods. I estimate a fixed-effects model, in which the dependent variable is a function of average establishment size in an industry plus an industry-specific effect that is constant over time. The regression is based on the first difference of this equation, so that the industry-specific constant washes out.

In the regressions, I posit that the level of a dependent variable (such as the profit rate) is a function of the logarithm of establishment size and other pertinent variables, as well as a set of (19) industry dummy variables. The basic model is given, in the case of the profit rate as dependent variable, by:

$$\text{PROFRATE}_{jt} = \alpha_0 + \beta_0 t + \beta_1 \ln(e_{jt}) + \beta_2 \text{EXPGO}_{jt} + \beta_3 \text{IMPGO}_{jt}$$
$$+ \beta_4 \text{UNION}_{jt} + \Sigma_j \gamma_j \text{INDDUM}_j + u_{jt} \quad (2)$$

where e_{jt} is the average number of employees per establishment in industry j at time t, EXPGO_{jt} is the ratio of industry j's exports to gross output at time t, IMPGO_{jt} is the ratio of industry j's imports to gross output at time t, INDDUM_j

is an industry dummy variable for industry j (19 dummy variables in all), and u_{jt} is a stochastic error term assumed to be independently and identically distributed (i.i.d). I use the logarithmic form for e_{jt} since it is more likely for the profit rate (and the other dependent variables) to be a convex function of establishment size, rather than to be proportionately related to establishment size. The industry dummy variable is included to control for industry effects due to industry differences in technology, scale, and capital requirements.

By taking first differences of equation (2), I obtain:

$$\Delta\text{PROFRATE}_{jt} = \beta_0 + \beta_1\,g_{jt}^e + \beta_2\,\Delta\text{EXPGO}_{jt} + \beta_3\Delta\text{IMPGO}_{jt}$$

$$+ \beta_4\Delta\text{UNION}_{jt} + v_{jt} \tag{3}$$

where $\Delta X_{jt} \equiv X_{jt} - X_{j,t-1}$ for any variable X, g_{jt}^e is the percentage change in e_{jt} over the period, and $v_{jt} \equiv u_{jt} - u_{j,t-1}$. The error term v_{jT} is by construction auto-correlated. I use GMM (the generalized method of moments) with autocorrelation correction for the estimation.

Productivity growth

Results are shown in the first two columns of Table 18.3 for the first dependent variable, TFP growth (see the Data Appendix for the definition of TFP growth).[9] The first variable of interest is the constant term, which is interpreted as the pure rate of technological progress. Its value ranges from 0.6 percent to 1.6 percent per year. These values are typical for most estimations of TFP growth in manufacturing.

The next variable of interest is industry R&D expenditures as a percent of net sales. A large literature has now almost universally established a positive and significant effect of R&D expenditures on productivity growth (see, for example, Griliches, 1979, for a review of the literature). Following Griliches (1992), the coefficient of this variable can be interpreted as the rate of return of R&D (under the assumption that the average rate of return to R&D is equalized across sectors). In Table 18.3, the coefficient of the ratio of R&D expenditures to net sales is significant at the 1 percent level in the two specifications. The estimated rate of return to R&D ranges from 13 to 14 percent. These estimates are about average for previous work on the subject (see, for example, Mohnen, 1992, for a review).

I next consider the effects of international trade on TFP growth. The change in import intensity has a negative coefficient but it is not significant. In contrast, the change in export intensity has a positive coefficient, which is significant at the 1 percent level. The rationale is that export competition puts pressure on a firm to increase efficiency and reduce cost to compete in international markets and this shows up as a positive effect on TFP.

The last variable of interest is the percentage change in mean establishment size. Its coefficient is negative but not significant. The results do not support the argument in the third section that downsizing may be a mechanism that increases establishment productivity as unnecessary labor is shed.[10]

Table 18.3 Regressions of TFP growth and profitability on downsizing variables

Independent variables	Dependent variable					
	TFPGRT	TFPGRT	ΔPROFRAT	ΔPROFRAT	ΔPROFSHR	ΔPROFSHR
Constant	0.016	0.006	0.016#	0.018*	0.034	0.062
	(0.37)	(0.11)	(1.97)	(2.25)	(0.38)	(0.65)
Ratio of industry R&D to Net sales (period average)	0.128**	0.142**				
	(3.27)	(3.45)				
Period change in ratio of exports to gross output	0.089**	0.101**	0.012*	0.016**	0.010#	0.010
	(2.97)	(3.09)	(2.51)	(2.97)	(1.68)	(1.39)
Period change in ratio of imports to gross output	−0.001	−0.008	−0.002	−0.0008	−0.0053#	−0.0053#
	(0.12)	(0.63)	(0.71)	(0.34)	(1.74)	(1.76)
Period change in the unionization rate			−0.208**	−0.211**	−0.034	−0.033
			(4.77)	(4.83)	(0.61)	(0.60)
Percent change in mean employment per establishment		−0.035		0.274*		0.089
		(0.33)		(2.19)		(0.45)
Root mean square error	5.134	5.128	8.029	8.011	8.945	8.819
sample size	116	116	116	116	116	116

Note: The sample consists of panel data, with observations on each of the 20 manufacturing industries. The census periods are: 1967–1972, 1972–1977, 1977–1982, 1982–1987, 1987–1992, and 1992–1997 (16 industries). The coefficients are estimated using GMM. t-statistics are in parentheses. See the Data Appendix for sources and methods.

Key:

TFPGRT: average annual rate of total factor productivity growth, based on full-time equivalent employees (FTEE) and net capital stock.

The GMM instruments are: (1) unionization rate; and (2) the profit rate.

ΔPROFRAT: Change in the profit rate over the period.

ΔPROFSHR: Change in the profit share over the period.

The GMM instruments for both variables are: (1) the ratio of R&D to sales; and (2) TFP growth.

Significance levels: # − 10%, * − 5%, ** − 1%.

Profitability and market value

I next investigate the relation of downsizing to both profitability and the market value of companies. I use the same sample as in the analysis of productivity trends. There is less of a theoretical basis for the choice of possible determinants of firm profitability and stock valuation than there is of productivity growth. However, it might be expected that profitability within an industry would depend on, among other things, the unionization rate, the degree of import penetration, export competition, and the change in establishment size.

The first dependent variable is the period change in the average industry profit rate (see Table 18.3). In the first specification, I include only the unionization rate for the industry and the change in both import and export intensity as independent variables. The coefficient of the unionization rate is negative, as expected, and significant at the 1 percent level. This result is consistent with the findings of Freeman and Medoff (1986). The coefficient of the change in import intensity is, also as expected, negative though not significant. On the other hand, the coefficient of the change in export intensity is positive and significant at the 5 percent level. This result is in accord with the finding reported above that a rise in export intensity leads to increased TFP. The argument is likely the same – namely, that export competition leads to increased efficiency and reduced cost.

In the next specification, I add the percent change in mean establishment size as an independent variable. Its coefficient is significant at the 5 percent level but unexpectedly positive. A possible explanation is that downsizing causes firms to reorganize production, as well as to get rid of workers with potentially needed skills. The adjustment costs associated with reorganization may lead to higher costs and therefore lower profits.

The next dependent variable is the change in the profit share within an industry between the previous and current period. The coefficients, shown in the last two columns of Table 18.3, have the same sign as those for the change in the profit rate, but are generally less robust. In fact, the coefficient of the change in the unionization rate is no longer significant, while that of the change in export intensity is significant at the 10 percent level in the first of the two specifications but not significant in the second. On the other hand, the coefficient of the change in import intensity is negative and significant at the 10 percent level. This result supports the argument that import competition cuts into the market of the domestic producer and lowers profitability. The coefficient of the percentage change in average establishment size is positive, as before, but is not statistically significant.

The third dependent variable in this group is the percentage change in the average market value of firms within an industry, deflated by the CPI-U (see the first two columns of Table 18.4). In the case of stock market valuation, there is little theory to guide us with regard to other independent variables, and I use only the change in the unionization rate. Its coefficient is negative and significant at the 1 percent level. This result strongly suggests the stock market puts a negative valuation on the presence of unions, presumably because of their negative

Table 18.4 Regressions of stock prices, employee compensation, and unit labor costs on downsizing variables

Independent variables	Dependent variable				
	STOCKGRT	STOCKGRT	COMPGRT	ULCGRT	ULCGRT
Constant	0.088**	0.075*	0.010	−0.009	−0.011
	(3.12)	(2.13)	(1.47)	(1.39)	(0.29)
Ratio of industry R&D to				0.236	0.026
Net sales (period average)				(1.27)	(1.29)
Period change in the	−1.033**	−0.814**	0.119**	−0.012	−0.004
unionization rate	(7.74)	(4.61)	(3.51)	(0.12)	(0.15)
Percent change in mean		1.669*	−0.055		−0.004
employment per		(2.59)	(0.44)		(0.01)
establishment					
Root mean square error	30.711	35.505	6.827	10.913	11.283
Sample size	116	116	116	116	116

Note: The sample consists of panel data, with observations on each of the 20 manufacturing industries. The census periods are: 1967–1972, 1972–1977, 1977–1982, 1982–1987, 1987–1992, and 1992–1997 (16 industries). The coefficients are estimated using GMM. *t*-statistics are in parentheses. See the Data Appendix for sources and methods.

Key:

STOCKGRT: Percentage change in the average market valuation of firms over the period.

COMPGRT: Percentage change in average employee compensation over the period.

The GMM instruments for both variables are: (1) the ratio of R&D to sales; and (2) TFP growth.

ULCGRT: Percentage change in unit labor costs over the period.

The GMM instrument is: percentage change in the average market value of firms.

Significance levels: # − 10%, * − 5%, ** − 1%.

impact on the profit rate, and rewards industries in which the union presence is reduced.

The major finding is that the coefficient of the percentage change in mean employment per establishment is positive and significant at the 5 percent level. In other words, contrary to popular belief and the models developed in the third section, downsizing is associated with a *drop* in stock values, not a rise.

This regression finding on the relation between changes in the market valuation of firms and downsizing does not establish the direction of causation. It is possible that firms downsize when their stock values fall, thus creating a positive correlation between changes in average market value and changes in establishment size. It is also possible that when a firm gets into trouble, both its stock value falls and it downsizes in response to falling profits. It may also be true that the market does not reward downsizing – that is, when layoffs occur, investors take it as a sign of trouble and try to sell off the company's stock.[11]

Employee compensation

The next dependent variable of interest is the change in employee remuneration. This is measured by the percent change in employee compensation, including wages, salaries, and fringe benefits, per FTEE.[12] There are a limited number of independent variables for the analysis here as well. Ideally, one would like to control for changes in the average human capital or skill level of employees within an industry. However, these data are not available. I do, however, have information on the degree of unionization within an industry. This will allow us to control for the well-documented wage differential between union and non-union workers (see, for example, Lewis, 1986).

The results are shown in column 3 of Table 18.4. The main finding is that, not surprisingly, the change in the unionization rate has a positive coefficient, significant at the 1 percent level. On the other hand, percentage change in the average number of employees per establishment has a negative but statistically insignificant coefficient.

The last dependent variable of interest is the annual change in unit labor cost. Unit labor cost is defined as employee compensation (in 1992 dollars) to output (also in 1992 dollars). It is thus the ratio of real compensation per worker to labor productivity. Its change over time thus reflects changes in employee compensation and changes in labor productivity. The results for this variable are shown in the last two columns of Table 18.4. The coefficients of both R&D intensity and the change in the unionization rate have the expected sign, but neither coefficient is statistically significant. The coefficient of the percentage change in the average number of employees per establishment is negative but not significant.

Conclusions

Using U.S. Census of Manufacturing data covering the period from 1967 to 1997, I find strong evidence that average establishment size declined in manufacturing. Overall, mean establishment size fell from 60.5 to 46.5 over this period.

With regard to the consequences of downsizing, I essentially find no support for any of the five models of downsizing outlined above. Indeed, of the six dependent variables considered in this chapter, the change in average establishment size has significant coefficients for only two – the period change in the profit rate and the percentage change in average stock prices. However, in these two cases, the results are exactly the opposite of what is predicted by the models. Downsizing leads to both lower profitability and lowered stock prices. The possible reason, suggested above, is that downsizing causes firms to reorganize production, as well as to get rid of workers with potentially needed skills. The adjustment costs associated with reorganization may lead to higher costs and therefore lower profits. Lowered profits, in turn, may lead to a fall in stock prices.

This result on the relationship between downsizing and stock prices is consistent with those of Worrell, Davidson, and Sharma (1991), Gombola and Tsetsekos (1992), Abraham (1999), and Farber and Hallock (1999). This regression finding does not establish the direction of causation – whether downsizing leads to falling stock values, or falling stock values induce firms to downsize. Moreover, as one referee pointed out, it is possible that the negative effect on stock prices results from the fact that I define downsizing as a reduction in average establishment size instead of the strategic announcements of layoffs. However, evidence from Chapter 2 of Baumol, Blinder, and Wolff (2003), which looked at the relation of layoff announcements in the press to changes in stock market prices found no discernible association between the two.

The results, as noted above, do not indicate that changes in average establishment size have any direct association with industry productivity growth. This result is broadly consistent with the findings of Baily, Bartelsman, and Haltiwanger (1996) and Collins and Harris (1999) that downsizing was generally associated with a lowering of productivity growth. Moreover, downsizing does not appear to lead to reductions in unit labor costs. This result contrasts with the findings reported by Cappelli (2003) and Espahbodi, John, and Vasudevan (2000).

In contrast, the change in the unionization rate – more specifically, de-unionization – exercised a substantial effect. In fact, the results of this chapter seem to be more of a story about de-unionization than about downsizing. I find that the change in the unionization rate is negatively and highly significantly related to the change in the industry profit rate, indicating that the de-unionization in an industry increases its profitability. The change in the unionization rate is also found to be negatively and highly significantly related to market value gains. The results indicate that the stock market puts a negative valuation on the presence of unions, presumably because of their depressing effect on profits. Not surprisingly, the change in the unionization rate, is positively associated with the growth in employee compensation and the effect is statistically significant.

In brief, the econometric evidence indicates that where downsizing has occurred in the manufacturing sector it has, first of all, not contributed to productivity, contrary to what is frequently conjectured. Second, it has actually reduced profits. Third, downsizing by a firm has been associated with a decline in the price of its stocks, perhaps because it lowers profitability. In contrast, de-unionization is strongly associated with a rise in profitability, an increase in stock prices, and a drop in worker compensation.

Further analysis suggests that the main effect of downsizing may be to deplete unions. A regression of the change in unionization on the percent change in mean establishment size (run using GMM, with TFP growth as the instrument) yields a positive coefficient, significant at the 5 percent level. The estimated coefficient is 0.25, suggesting that a 1 percent decline in average establishment size reduces the unionization rate by 0.25 percentage points.

Notes

1 The term "establishment" refers to an individual plant or office in a single geographical location. In contrast, an "enterprise" is one or more establishments owned by the same company. The term "firm" is synonymous with "enterprise."

2 Somewhat ironically, in our analysis in this book we found very little correlation between announcements of downsizing and actual reduction in establishment or firm size. Also see Baumol, Blinder, and Wolff (2003) for an extensive bibliography on the subject of downsizing.

3 On the other hand, announcements of permanent staff reductions were associated with significant increases in the variation of abnormal total shareholder return around the announcement date.

4 The data are from the National Income and Product Accounts. See the Appendix for details.

5 The 1997 Census of Manufacturing shifted from the old SIC industry classification to the new NAICS (North American Industrial Classification System). As a result, size distributions of establishments in 1997 are not directly comparable to those of earlier years. However, some bridge tables were provided for 1997 by the U.S. Census Bureau based on the old SIC scheme.

6 Technically speaking, the co-worker mean as introduced by Davis, Haltiwanger, and Schuh (1996) was based on microdata (plant level data), while here I use aggregate size class data.

7 This is estimated as the midpoint of the size class, 1–4, 5–9, ..., 2,500+ (see Figure 18.1 for the size classes used), with a Pareto estimate for the mean of the top size class.

8 The co-worker mean could not be computed for 1997.

9 Technically, the levels equation includes the logarithm of TFP as the dependent variable and R&D stock as an independent variable, so that first differencing yields TFP growth as the dependent variable and the ratio of R&D expenditures to sales as an independent variable in the first difference equation. See, for example, Griliches (1992) for a derivation.

10 I also use the annual rate of labor productivity growth as the dependent variable (and include the rate of growth of total capital per worker as an independent variable). The results are very similar to those for TFP growth (these are not shown in a table).

11 I did test for reverse causation by regressing the percent change in average establishment size on TFP growth, R&D intensity, the unionization rate, the change in export and import intensity, the growth in total industry employment, the lagged profit rate, and the percent change in the average market value of firms within an industry lagged one period. I found that the coefficient of the last of these variables is uniformly negative, though not statistically significant. This result is unexpected, since it suggests that when the stock value of a firm declines, it responds (after a lag) by increasing employment rather than decreasing it.

12 In this case, the dependent variable in the levels equation is the logarithm of average employee compensation. Results are also very similar for wages and salaries (in contrast to total employee compensation) per FTEE and are not shown here.

References

Abowd, John M., George T. Milkovich, and John M. Hannon (1990) 'The Effects of Human Resource Management Decisions on Shareholder Value', *Industrial and Labor Relations Review*, 43: 203–236.

Abraham, Steven E. (1999) 'Layoff and Employment Guarantee Announcements: How Do Shareholders Respond?', Department of Economics, SUNY-Oswego Working Papers.

Baily, Martin Neil, Eric J. Bartelsman, and John Haltiwanger (1996) 'Labor Productivity: Structural Change and Cyclical Dynamics', NBER Working Paper Series, No. 5503, Cambridge, MA: National Bureau of Economic Research.

Baumol, William J., Alan S. Blinder, and Edward N. Wolff (2003) *Downsizing in America: Reality, Causes, and Consequences*, New York: Russell Sage Press.

Cappelli, Peter (2003) 'Examining the Incidence of Downsizing and its Effect on Establishment Performance', in David Neumark (Ed.) *On the Job: Is Long-Term Employment a Thing of the Past?*, New York: Russell Sage Press.

Caves, Richard E., and Matthew B. Krepps (1993) 'Fat: The Displacement of Nonproduction Workers from U.S. manufacturing industries', *Brookings Papers: Microeconomics*, 2: 227–288.

Cochran, John (1999) "New Facts in Finance," NBER Working Paper, No. 7169, June.

Collins, Alan, and Richard I.D. Harris (1999) 'Downsizing and Productivity: The Case of UK Motor Vehicle Manufacturing 1974–1994', *Managerial-and-Decision-Economics*, 20: 281–290.

Davis, Steven J., John C. Haltiwanger, and Scott Schuh (1996) *Job Creation and Destruction*, Cambridge, MA: MIT Press.

Dickens, William T., and Lawrence F. Katz (1987) 'Interindustry Wage Differences and Industry Characteristics', in Kevin Lang and Jonathan Leonard (Eds.) *Unemployment and the Structure of Labor Markets*, Oxford: Basil Blackwell.

Duménil, Gérard, and Dominique Lévy (2011) *The Crisis of Neoliberalism*, Cambridge, MA: Harvard University Press.

Espahbodi, Reza, Teresa A. John, and Gopala Vasudevan (2000) 'The Effects of Downsizing on Operating Performance', *Review of Quantitative Finance and Accounting*, 15: 107–126.

Farber, Henry S., and Kevin F. Hallock (1999) 'Have Employment Reductions Become Good News for Shareholders? The Effect of Job Loss Announcements on Stock Prices, 1970–97', NBER Working Paper, No. 7295, August, Cambridge, MA: National Bureau of Economic Research.

Freeman, Richard B., and James L. Medoff (1986) *What Do Unions Do?*, New York: Basic Books.

Gombola, Michael J., and George P. Tsetsekos (1992) 'Plant Closings for Financially Weak and Financially Strong Firms', *Quarterly Journal of Business and Economics*, 31: 69–83.

Gordon, David M. (1996) *Fat and Mean: The Corporate Squeeze of Working Americans and the Myth of Managerial "Downsizing"*, New York: Free Press.

Griliches, Zvi (1979) 'Issues in Assessing the Contribution of Research and Development to Productivity Growth', *Bell Journal of Economics*, 10: 92–116.

Griliches, Zvi (1992) 'The Search for R&D Spillovers', *Scandinavian Journal of Economics*, 94: 29–47.

Hirsch, Barry T., and David A. Macpherson (1993) 'Union Membership and Coverage Files from the Current Population Surveys: Note', *Industrial and Labor Relations Review*, 46: 574–578.

Idson, Todd (1999) 'Skill-Biased Technical Change and the Employer Size-Wage Effects', Columbia University, mimeo, New York.

Kokkelenberg, Edward C., and Donna R. Sockell (1985) 'Union Membership in the United States, 1973–81', *Industrial and Labor Relations Review*, 38: 497–543.

Krueger, Alan B. (1998) 'Thoughts on Globalization, Unions and Labor Market Rents', mimeo, Princeton University, April 28.

Krueger, Alan B., and Lawrence H. Summers (1987) 'Reflections on the Inter-Industry Wage Structure', in K. Lang and J. Leonard (Eds.), *Unemployment and the Structure of Labor Markets*, Oxford: Basil Blackwell.

Krueger, Alan B., and Lawrence H. Summers (1988) 'Efficiency Wages and the Inter-Industry Wage Structure', *Econometrica*, 56: 259–294.

Lazonick, William (2009) *Sustainable Prosperity in the New Economy?* Kalamazoo, MI: W.E. Upjohn Institute for Employment Research.

Leibenstein, Harvey (1966) 'Allocative Efficiency vs. X-Efficiency', *American Economic Review*, 56: 392–415.

Lewis, H. Gregg (1986) *Union Relative Wage Effects: A Survey*, Chicago: University of Chicago Press.

Masters, Stanley H. (1969) 'An Interindustry Analysis of Wages and Plant Size', *Review of Economics and Statistics*, 51: 341–345.

Mellow, Wesley (1981) 'Employer Size and Wages', Bureau of Labor Statistics Working Paper, No. 116, April, Washington, DC.

Milberg, William (2008) 'Shifting Sources and Uses of Profits: Sustaining US Financialization with Global Value Chains', *Economy and Society*, 37: 420–451.

Mohnen, Pierre (1992) *The Relationship between R&D and Productivity Growth in Canada and Other Major Industrialized Countries*, Ottawa: Canada Communications Group.

Shiller, Robert J. (2000) *Irrational Exuberance*, Princeton, New Jersey: Princeton University Press.

Stockhammer, Engelbert (2004) 'Financialisation and the Slowdown of Accumulation', *Cambridge Journal of Economics*, 28: 719–741.

Sturgeon, Timothy, Johannes Van Biesebroeck, and Gary Gereffi (2008) 'Value Chains, Networks and Clusters: Reframing the Global Automotive Industry', *Journal of Economic Geography*, 8: 297–321.

White, Halbert L. (1980) 'A Heteroskedasticity-Consistent Covariance Matrix Estimator and a Direct Test for Heteroskedasticity', *Econometrica*, 48: 817–838.

Worrell, Dan L., Wallace N. Davidson III, and Varinder M. Sharma (1991) 'Layoff Announcements and Stockholder Wealth', *Academy of Management Journal*, 43: 662–678.

Data appendix: definitions and sources

1. NIPA employment data: full-time equivalent employees (FTEE) equals the number of employees on full-time schedules plus the number of employees on part-time schedules converted to a full-time basis. FTEE is computed as the product of the total number of employees and the ratio of average weekly hours per employee for all employees to average weekly hours per employee on full-time schedules. Figures are from the Bureau of Economic Analysis (BEA), National Income and Product Accounts (NIPA), available on the Internet at http://www.bea.gov/iTable/iTable.cfm?ReqID=9&step=1.

2. NIPA employee compensation: Employee compensation includes wages and salaries and employee benefits. Figures are from the Bureau of Economic Analysis, NIPA, available on the Internet at http://www.bea.gov/iTable/iTable.cfm?ReqID=9&step=1.

3. Capital stock figures are based on chain-type quantity indexes for net stock of fixed capital in 1992$, year-end estimates. Equipment and structures, including information technology equipment, are for the private (non-government) sector only. Information processing and related equipment includes: (a) computers and peripheral equipment; (b) other office and accounting machinery; (c) communication equipment; (d) instruments; and (e) photocopy and related equipment. Source: U.S. Bureau of Economic Analysis, Fixed Reproducible Tangible Wealth, Internet. For technical details, see U.S. Department of Commerce, Bureau of Economic Analysis, *Fixed Reproducible Tangible*

Wealth in the United States, 1925–89 (Washington, DC: U.S. Government Printing Office), January, 1993.

4. Total factor productivity growth (TFPGRTH) for sector j is defined as:

$$\text{TFPGRT}_j \equiv \pi_j = \hat{Y}_j - \bar{\alpha}_j \hat{L}_j - (1 - \bar{\alpha}_j)\hat{K}_j,$$

where $\hat{Y}_j$ is the annual rate of output growth, $\hat{L}_j$ is the annual growth in labor input, and $\hat{K}_j$ is the annual growth in capital input in sector j, and $\bar{\alpha}_j$ is the average share of employee compensation in GDP over the period in sector j (the Tornqvist–Divisia index). I measure output using GDP in constant dollars, the labor input using FTEEs, and the capital input by the fixed non-residential net capital stock (1992 dollars).

5. R&D expenditures performed by industry include company, federal, and other sources of funds. Company-financed R&D performed outside the company is excluded. Industry series on R&D run from 1957 to 1997. Source: National Science Foundation, Internet. For technical details, see National Science Foundation, *Research and Development in Industry* (Arlington, VA: National Science Foundation), NSF96-304, 1996.

6. Export and import data. Sources: U.S. input–output data for years 1947, 1958, 1963, 1967, 1972, 1977, 1982, 1987, 1992, and 1997, available on the Internet from the BEA at: http://www.bea.gov/iTable/iTable.cfm?ReqID=5&step=1. GDO is gross domestic output (net sales).

7. Percent of labor force covered by unions. Estimates for 1953–1983 are the annual average number of dues-paying members reported by labor unions. Estimates for 1983–1997 are annual averages from the Current Population Survey. Data exclude numbers of professional and public employee associations. Sources: (a) U.S. Department of Labor, Bureau of Labor Statistics, *Handbook of Labor Statistics 1978*, Bulletin 2 (Washington, DC: U.S. Government Printing Office), 1979; (c) U.S. Department of Labor, Bureau of Labor Statistics, *Handbook of Labor Statistics 1989*, Bulletin 23 (Washington, DC: U.S. Government Printing Office), 1990; and (d) Eva E. Jacobs, Editor, *Handbook of U.S. Labor Statistics*, Second Edition (Lanham, MD: Bernan Press), 1998. Sources for the industry level data include in addition to the above: Kokkelenberg and Sockell (1985); Hirsch and Macpherson (1993), and accompanying data files; and Bureau of Labor Statistics, Office of Employment Projections, Output and Employment data base.

8. Profit share and profit rate. Data are from the Bureau of Economic Analysis' National Income and Product Accounts and Net Stock of Fixed Reproducible Tangible Capital accounts, provided on the Internet at http://www.bea.gov/iTable/iTable.cfm?ReqID=9&step=1.
Key:

PBT: Corporate profits before tax.
PI: Proprietors' income.
PTI: Gross property-type income, defined as the sum of corporate profits, the profit portion of proprietors' income, rental income of persons, net interest,

capital consumption allowances, business transfer payments, and the current surplus of government enterprises less subsidies. Proprietors' income includes both labor income and a return on capital. The labor portion is estimated by multiplying the number of self-employed workers by the average employee compensation of salaried workers. The profit portion is the residual part of proprietors' income.

CCCA: Corporate Capital Consumption Allowance.

NCCA: Non-corporate Capital Consumption Allowance.

GDP: Current dollar Gross Domestic Product.

COMP: Compensation of employees, which consists of wage and salary accruals, employer contributions for social insurance, and other labor income.

NNI: Net national income, defined as COMP + PTI − CCCA − NCCA.

NETK: Current-cost net stock of fixed reproducible tangible non-residential private capital.

$$\text{Net profit rate, private economy} = (PTI - CCCA - NCCA)/NETK$$

$$\text{Net profit share} = (PTI - CCCA - NCCA)/NNI$$

Part IV

Complexity

Barriers and bounds to rationality

19 Market ecology and the economics of crisis

Rajiv Sethi

Introduction

In his autobiographical essay "The Ins and Outs of Late Twentieth Century Economics," Duncan Foley (1999) observed that "economics in the late 1960s suffered from a classical scientific dilemma in that it had two theories, the microeconomic general equilibrium theory, and the macroeconomic Keynesian theory, each of which seemed to have considerable explanatory power in its own domain, but which were incompatible." Specifically:

> The general equilibrium theory forged by Walras and elaborated by Wald (1951), McKenzie (1959), and Arrow and Debreu (1954) can be used, with the assumption that markets exist for all commodities at all future moments and in all contingencies, to represent macroeconomic reality by simple aggregation. The resulting picture of macroeconomic reality, however, has several disturbing features. For one thing, competitive general equilibrium is efficient, so that it is incompatible with the unemployment of any resources productive enough to pay their costs of utilization. This is difficult to reconcile with the common observation of widely fluctuating rates of unemployment of labor and of capacity utilization of plant and equipment. General equilibrium theory reduces economic production and exchange to the pursuit of directly consumable goods and services, and as a result has no real role for money ... general equilibrium theory can accommodate fluctuations in output and consumption, but only as responses to external shocks to resource availability, technology or tastes. It is difficult to reconcile these relatively slowly moving factors with the large business-cycle fluctuations characteristic of developed capitalist economies. In assuming the clearing of markets for all contingencies in all periods, general equilibrium theory assures the consistency ... of individual consumption, investment, and production plans, which is difficult to reconcile with the recurring phenomena of financial crisis and asset revaluation that play so large a role in actual capitalist economic life.

Foley contrasted this with Keynes' theory, which appeared to conform better to economic reality but suffered from problems of its own:

> Keynes views money as central to the actual operation of developed capitalist economies, precisely because markets for all periods and contingencies do not exist to reconcile differences in agents' opinions about the future. Because agents cannot sell all their prospects on contingent claims markets, they are liquidity constrained. In a liquidity constrained economy there is no guarantee that all factor markets will clear without unemployed labor or unutilized productive capacity. Market prices are inevitably established in part by speculation on an uncertain future. As a result the economy is vulnerable to endogenous fluctuations as the result of herd psychology and self-fulfilling prophecy. From this point of view it is not hard to see why business cycle fluctuations are a characteristic of a productively and financially developed capitalist economy, nor why the potential for financial crisis is inherent in decentralized market allocation of investment ...
>
> But there are many loose ends in Keynes' argument. In presenting the equilibrium of short-term expectations that determines the level of output, income and employment in the short period, for example, Keynes argues that entrepreneurs hire labor and buy raw materials to undertake production because they form an expectation as to the volume of sales they will achieve when the production process runs its course ... But Keynes offers no systematic alternative account of how entrepreneurs form a view of their prospects on the market to take the place of the assumption of perfect competition and market clearing. This turns out, in detail, to be a very difficult problem to solve.

Foley goes on to describe his pursuit, in collaboration with his MIT colleague Miguel Sidrauski, of the "project of a macroeconomic theory distinct from Walrasian general equilibrium theory." They did so by building on Hicks' (1939) notion of temporary equilibrium, which allows for the clearing of spot markets but without requiring that individual plans be mutually consistent. Their two-sector model incorporated markets for stocks of money, bonds, and capital assets, as well as flows of labor, investment, and consumption goods. They did not, however, provide an account of expectation formation, and therefore left unfilled one of the major gaps in the *General Theory*.

Meanwhile the economics profession was moving in an entirely different direction, adopting the hypothesis that the subjective probability distributions, on the basis of which individual decisions are made, match precisely the objective distributions to which these decisions give rise. Foley (1999) recognized earlier than most that this so-called "rational expectations" hypothesis led right back to the general equilibrium model that he had earlier rejected:

> In my view, the rational expectations assumption which Lucas and Sargent put forward to "close" the Keynesian model, was only a disguised form

of the assumption of the existence of complete futures and contingencies markets. When one unpacked the "expectations" language of the rational expectations literature, it turned out that these models assumed that agents formed expectations of futures and contingency prices that were consistent with the aggregate plans being made, and hence were in fact competitive general equilibrium prices in a model of complete futures and contingency markets ... What the profession took to be an exciting breakthrough in economic theory I saw as a boring and predictable retracing of an already discredited path.

This passage describes very clearly what is often left implicit and unrecognized in contemporary macroeconomics: the rational expectations hypothesis entails the *mutual consistency of individual plans* without providing for a mechanism through which such consistency could be attained. In the case of complete markets, any inconsistency of plans is revealed immediately in the form of disequilibrium in some futures market. But, in the absence of complete markets, it is entirely possible for such inconsistency to remain concealed, even while all spot markets (and those futures markets that exist) clear. Only with the passage of time can this inconsistency be revealed, as plans are *discovered* to have been mutually inconsistent. The rational expectations hypothesis presumes, in effect, that any mutual inconsistencies in plans that might arise are quickly and reliably corrected long before such inconsistencies could possibly be revealed in market prices. It is accordingly much stronger than the very reasonable hypothesis of "forward-looking behavior" or even the natural extension to expectations formation of the postulate of rational choice.

The idea that the rational expectations hypothesis has severe limitations has become increasingly clear in the wake of the recent financial crisis. Woodford (2011) argues, for instance, that the "macroeconomics of the future ... will have to go beyond conventional late-twentieth-century methodology ... by making the formation and revision of expectations an object of analysis in its own right, rather than treating this as something that should already be uniquely determined once the other elements of an economic model (specifications of preferences, technology, market structure, and government policies) have been settled."

Hence the problem of expectations in macroeconomics and finance, left unresolved by Keynes and later by Foley and Sidrauski (1971), remains open. In this essay I argue that progress on this question requires that one allow for *heterogeneity* across individuals in beliefs, and explicit consideration of the manner in which the distribution of beliefs *evolves* under competitive pressure.

Heterogeneity of expectations is a fundamental feature of a modern economy, with active trading of long-lived assets such as stocks, bonds, and currencies. Moreover, such heterogeneity cannot be due solely to differences in information, since the presence of informational differences is itself revealed by the willingness to trade. If two risk-averse individuals are prepared to bet against each other on some future event, then they must not only disagree about the likelihood of its occurrence, they must also *agree to disagree* about this likelihood. That is, they must disagree despite the fact that this disagreement is itself common knowledge. As shown by Aumann (1976), such public disagreement is inconsistent with the hypothesis that beliefs are based on a common prior updated in accordance with Bayes' rule. In order for widespread speculation to occur, belief heterogeneity must arise not only from differences in information, but also from differences in priors, or differences in the manner in which information is processed and beliefs updated.

There is now a substantial literature in economics and finance that allows for such fundamental belief heterogeneity.[1] But heterogeneity alone is not sufficient, since the belief distribution can and does change dramatically over time. The distribution of beliefs affects the dynamics of asset prices and hence the relative profitability of the various forecasting strategies in use. This in turn causes changes in the distribution of strategies over time. I argue that this ecological approach to markets can provide us with insights into a broad range of phenomena, including bubbles and crashes in speculative asset markets, as well as large pro-cyclical movements in leverage and maturity transformation within the non-financial sector.

I begin with the example of an event that briefly rocked financial markets not long ago, and that serves to illustrate the manner in which interacting strategies can give rise to complex asset price movements that have feedback effects on the evolving distribution of strategies over time.

The flash crash

On May 6, 2010, an extraordinary event occurred in U.S. financial markets. Stock prices plunged to levels that wiped out close to a trillion dollars in value, and then promptly recovered to erase most of these losses. Some securities traded at prices that were clearly inconsistent with any notion of their intrinsic worth. Shares in Accenture fell to a penny, while those in Sotheby's rose to a hundred thousand dollars apiece. These were not simply nominal quotes in an order book: volume remained heavy throughout the episode and a large number of transactions occurred at these prices. The exchanges subsequently cancelled all trades occurring at prices that departed by more than 60 percent from the previous close, reversing transactions in almost 300 securities.

What caused this *flash crash*, as the event has come to be known? Kirilenko , Kyle, Samadi, and Tuzun (2011) attempted to answer this question by examining audit-trail data for all transactions in the June 2010 E-mini S&P 500 futures contract over the four-day period May 3–6. What emerges from their analysis is a rich description of a pool of trading strategies that interact to jointly determine the dynamics of prices. The authors classify accounts into six categories based on patterns exhibited in their trading behavior, such as horizon length, order size, and the willingness to accumulate significant net positions. The categories are High Frequency Traders (HFTs), Intermediaries, Fundamental Buyers, Fundamental Sellers, Opportunistic Traders, and Small Traders:

[Different] categories of traders occupy quite distinct, albeit overlapping, positions in the ecosystem of a liquid, fully electronic market. HFTs, while very small in number, account for a large share of total transactions and trading volume. Intermediaries leave a market footprint qualitatively similar, but smaller to that of HFTs. Opportunistic Traders at times act like Intermediaries (buying and selling around a given inventory target) and at other times act like Fundamental Traders (accumulating a directional position).

Based on this taxonomy, Kirilenko *et al.* examine the manner in which the strategies vary with respect to trading volume, liquidity provision, directional exposure, and profitability. Although high-frequency traders constitute a minuscule proportion (about one-tenth of one percent) of total accounts, they are responsible for more than a third of aggregate trading volume in this market. They have extremely short trading horizons and maintain low levels of directional exposure. Under normal market conditions they are net providers of liquidity, but their desire to avoid significant exposure means that they can become liquidity takers very quickly and on a large scale. This appears to have happened during the crash:

> During the Flash Crash, the trading behavior of High Frequency Traders appears to have exacerbated the downward move in prices. HFTs, who initially bought contracts from Fundamental Sellers, proceeded to sell contracts and compete for liquidity with Fundamental Sellers. In addition, HFTs appeared to rapidly buy and [sell] contracts from one another many times, generating a hot potato effect before Opportunistic or Fundamental Buyers were attracted by the rapidly falling prices to step in and take these contracts off the market.

The authors find that high-frequency traders in this market appear able to anticipate (and profit from) price movements over very short horizons:

> High Frequency Traders effectively predict and react to price changes ... [they] are consistently profitable although they never accumulate a large net position ... HFTs appear to trade in the same direction as the contemporaneous price and prices of the past five seconds. In other words, they buy ... if the immediate prices are rising. However, after about ten seconds, they appear to reverse the direction of their trading ... possibly due to their speed advantage or superior ability to predict price changes, HFTs are able to buy right as the prices are about to increase.

During the crash itself, the fastest moving traders with the most effective algorithms for short-run price prediction were able to trade ahead of their slower and less effective brethren, imposing significant losses on the latter. Since no trades were cancelled in this particular market, these losses involved a significant transfer of wealth in a short period of time.

This analysis of the crash illustrates several features of a speculative asset market. There is considerable heterogeneity in trading strategies, with a large proportion of trades being made on the basis of rapid responses to incoming market data rather than fundamental research. The dynamics of asset prices itself depend on this composition of trading strategies. And endogenous transfers of wealth, which can be significant during periods of instability, have the effect of altering the distribution of trading strategies in the market.

These features are not specific to the particular market considered here. At the time of the crash, more than 60 percent of transactions in U.S. equities involved orders placed by algorithms (Grant and Mackenzie, 2010). The strategies implemented by such programs are typically characterized by extremely short holding periods, amounting to no more than a few seconds on average, and very limited overnight directional exposure. More importantly, they neglect entirely any assessment of the stream of revenue to which ownership of an asset gives title. As such, they are the modern incarnation of technical trading strategies based on the identification of patterns in tables and charts. The speed, scale, and automation are new, but the strategies themselves have been around for as long as speculative asset markets have existed.

The flash crash was an extreme event with respect to the scale of departures of prices from any reasonable assessment of their intrinsic value, and the speed with which these departures arose and were corrected. But it was also routine in the sense that such departures do arise from time to time, building cumulatively rather than suddenly, and lasting for months or years rather than minutes, with corrections that can be rapid or prolonged but almost impossible to time. Understanding the crash is accordingly a step toward understanding such disruptions more generally.

Market ecology

While the number of distinct trading strategies in any asset market is vast, it is analytically useful to partition this set into two categories: those based on an assessment of the intrinsic value of an asset, and those based on the use of market data to make short-term price forecasts. The terms fundamental and technical analysis broadly capture these two approaches to trading.

Fundamental analysis provides the channel through which information about the earnings flows to which the asset gives title (or the risk-sensitive rates at which these should be discounted) comes to be reflected in the asset's price. In a market dominated by such strategies, price changes will reflect changes over time in beliefs about fundamentals, as individual traders identify mispriced securities and trade on this information. As long as this process operates rapidly and smoothly, price volatility should be commensurate with the volatility in earnings and other measures of an asset's intrinsic worth.

But no speculative market is dominated by fundamental traders. (In the Kirilenko study of the S&P E-mini futures market, such strategies accounted for about 12 percent of trading volume.) When both technical and fundamental strategies are present, the asset price dynamics can be more complex and sensitive to the composition of the trading population. Beja and Goldman (1980) illustrated this point in a simple model with two trader types: those who react to price levels (relative to perceived fundamentals) and those who react to price movements. Their main insight was that if the prevalence of momentum based strategies was too large relative to that of strategies based on fundamental analysis, then the dynamics of asset prices would be locally unstable: departures of prices from fundamentals would be amplified rather than corrected over time. Furthermore, they argued that the relationship between the composition of strategies and market stability was discontinuous: there was a threshold value of this population mixture that separated the stable from the unstable regime, and an imperceptible change in composition that took the market across the threshold could result in dramatic increases in volatility.

A key feature of the Beja–Goldman model is that prices do not adjust instantaneously to clear the asset market, and this allows price movements to be informative and to exhibit some degree of short-run momentum. Technical strategies can exploit this momentum and accelerate the convergence of prices to fundamentals, provided that such strategies remain relatively rare. But if the use of technical analysis becomes too widespread in the market, the dynamics lose stability: prices start to overshoot fundamentals, resulting in excess volatility of prices relative to fundamentals. Hence a key determinant of price volatility is the composition of trading strategies within the population of speculators.

One can take this analysis a step further by observing that the profit accruing to any given trading strategy itself depends on the stability of the market. Fundamental analysis involves considerable time, effort, and expense relative to technical analysis. In stable markets, where prices reliably track fundamentals, technical strategies can effectively extract fundamental information from market data at a fraction of the cost of acquiring it directly. Provided that they can process and respond to this information with sufficient speed, such strategies will tend to proliferate when sufficiently rare. Eventually they become too widespread for price stability to be maintained, resulting in a transition to an environment with increased volatility in prices relative to the volatility of fundamentals.

It is in this high volatility environment that the value of fundamental analysis is greatest, since departures of prices from intrinsic values arise with greater frequency and on a larger scale. Over the short term, trading on fundamentals can result in losses, especially if positive feedback investment strategies cause an asset price bubble to form. As long as the bubble continues to expand, technical strategies prosper and increase their share of notional market wealth. But asset price inflation in excess of earnings growth cannot be sustained indefinitely, and when the correction comes there is a sharp redistribution of wealth in favor of fundamental strategies. The result is a return to stability in the price dynamics and a corresponding decline in volatility, at which point the process begins anew. The underlying, largely unobservable, changes in market ecology have an observable counterpart in the alternation between high and low volatility regimes.[2]

This perspective on asset price dynamics provides a very natural explanation for several empirically documented features of speculative markets: the excess volatility of prices relative to fundamentals (Shiller, 1981), the clustering of volatility (Engle, 1982), and the coexistence of short-run momentum with fundamental reversion over longer horizons (De Bondt and Thaler, 1985; Jegadeesh and Titman, 1993). All of these phenomena suggest that the volatility of prices does not simply reflect the volatility of the steams of income to which asset holders have claim; some volatility is introduced by the trading process itself. This has some major implications for economic growth and welfare. Since the risk-bearing capacity of an economy is not unbounded, increased volatility in major asset classes such as stocks and bonds can result in portfolio shifts toward safer assets such as Treasury bills. This constrains the financing of riskier real projects that have the greatest potential for generating output and employment growth.

Recent changes in technology and regulation have substantially lowered the costs of technical analysis and made feasible virtually instantaneous responses to incoming market data using powerful computers located in close proximity to exchanges. One interpretation of the flash crash is that the proliferation of these strategies took the system past a bifurcation point at which stability of the price dynamics was lost. The algorithmic implementation of such strategies gave the event a peculiarly modern flavor, and resulted in trades at prices that would have been inconceivable in an age of traditional market makers. This, together with the fact that the instability resulted initially in a sharp fall rather than a sudden rise in prices made the mispricing of securities obvious and resulted in a rapid recovery. Had the instability been more modest and in the upward direction, it may well have been subject to more ambiguous interpretation, and taken much longer to correct.

Unlike the market makers of old, high-frequency trading firms do not enjoy substantial monopoly power; they are subject to relatively free entry and intense competition. Despite this, they have managed to achieve substantial and sustained profits over the course of their existence.[3] How can one reconcile this level of performance with the competitive structure of the market in which these firms operate? One possibility is that their strategies expose them to highly asymmetric payoff distributions involving significant tail risk. They make steady profits with high probability, but are exposed to a significant loss if a low probability event such as a major market disruption were to arise. Greater entry increases the likelihood of such a disruption, but profits continue to accrue until the event actually occurs.[4]

The tendency of strategies that carry significant tail risk to proliferate over time even as this risk increases is a phenomenon that applies not simply to technical analysis in speculative markets, but to financial practices more generally. This process is relevant to an understanding of how some of the most storied names in finance found themselves facing imminent bankruptcy in 2008, bringing the entire system to the brink of collapse.

Tail risk, leverage, and maturity transformation

Among the defining moments of the recent financial crisis were the failure of Lehman Brothers on September 15, 2008, and the rescue of the American International Group (AIG) a day later. AIG was unable to meet collateral calls on credit default swaps written by its financial products subsidiary. These insurance-like contracts promise payments to counterparties in the event of a default by issuers of debt. They can be used to insure against default by individual firms or states, and also against defaults that affect payments to holders of structured products such as collateralized debt obligations.[5]

AIG was particularly exposed to the risk of an increase in mortgage default rates sharp enough to affect payments to holders of senior tranches of collateralized debt obligations. Not only had the company written contracts to insure against such default, it also held substantial quantities of the kind of assets it was insuring, which further increased its vulnerability to a sharp rise in mortgage delinquencies (Stulz, 2010). The company had accumulated a position over time that entailed a large directional bet against widespread mortgage default. The payoffs from this bet were highly asymmetric: with high probability it would receive periodic payments from buyers of protection (as well as revenues from its own holdings of mortgage backed securities), and with low probability it would face massive losses.

It is tempting to view the accumulation of such a position as reflecting poor risk management or reckless behavior, and in retrospect it was certainly viewed as folly. But from an ecological perspective, the emergence from time to time of large financial intermediaries with major exposure to tail risk of this kind is an inevitable consequence of market competition. At any point in time there is heterogeneity of beliefs regarding the likelihood of any given rare event. Those who are most convinced that this probability is negligible will offer the best terms for insurance against the event. Their direct competitors will be forced to match these terms or to accept losses in market share. As long as the low probability event does not occur, the highest profits will accordingly accrue to those with the most optimistic beliefs about the assets that they are insuring. As they expand their market share, and others reach for similar levels of performance, prices will increasingly come to reflect these beliefs. This certainly creates an opportunity for those with the patience and capital to enter and sustain short positions, but the perils of doing so are considerable.[6]

In retrospect, we see that AIG was among the firms most aggressively betting against widespread mortgage default. But, had it not been for this firm, some other financial intermediary would have been at the extreme end of the belief distribution. The cost of protection would have been somewhat higher, and the risk exposure more modest, but the high returns from the strategy would have drawn others in, with predictably similar consequences.

While credit derivatives are a relatively recent product of financial engineering, a similar dynamic applies to simpler debt contracts. The term structure of interest rates is typically such that the cost of borrowing rises with the maturity of debt, reflecting differences in the preferred habitat of borrowers and lenders.[7] Lenders prefer shorter maturities, while many borrowers need to issue long-term debt. This opens up a profit opportunity for financial intermediaries who can engage in maturity transformation by borrowing short and lending long. Holding long-dated assets funded by short-dated liabilities requires the intermediary to roll over its debt periodically, and subjects it to the risk that such financing will not be forthcoming when needed, or will only be available at punitive rates.

A widespread failure by solvent firms to roll over short-term debt is an unlikely event under normal circumstances, but becomes increasingly likely as the level of maturity transformation in the economy increases. Such increases in maturity transformation arise endogenously under pressure of market competition. As long as credit markets allow for short-term debt to be rolled over by solvent borrowers, the highest profits accrue to those with the greatest maturity mismatch. This drives others to increasing levels of maturity transformation, until a fear of being unable to roll over debt triggers a crisis of liquidity. Short-term funding dries up just when it is most in demand. If enough firms are forced to unload long-dated assets into a falling market at fire sale prices, large numbers of firms can simultaneously become insolvent.[8]

On the eve of the financial crisis, maturity transformation had reached alarming levels. Overnight loans were secured by collateralized debt obligations in the repo market on an unprecedented scale. In effect, money market funds were being used to finance the purchase of mortgage-backed securities. The inability of Lehman to continue to borrow overnight precipitated its collapse and caused Reserve Primary, a money market fund exposed to Lehman commercial paper, to stop redeeming shares at par. This threatened a run on money market funds, the prevention of which was a major motivating factor behind the bailout of AIG and subsequent interventions by the Treasury and the Federal Reserve.[9]

As in the case of protection sellers, banks were driven under pressure of market competition to engage in maturity transformation on an ever-increasing scale. As long as the crisis was held at bay, the greatest profits accrued to banks adopting the most aggressive financial practices, and others were compelled to follow. In the memorable words of Citigroup chief executive Chuck Prince, "as long as the music is playing, you've got to get up and dance" (Nakamoto and Wighton, 2007).

What is true of the behavior of banks is true also of the financial practices of households and non-financial firms. At the heart of economic booms and busts, fueled by competitive pressure, lie pro-cyclical movements in leverage. In a recent paper on the subject, John Geanakoplos (2010) notes that in ebullient times "competition drives leverage higher and higher," while during a crisis, "leverage can fall by 50% overnight, and by more over a few days or months." Such large swings in leverage can swamp the effects on output and employment of traditional monetary policy instruments such as interest rates.

The centrality of leverage and maturity transformation in understanding economic fluctuations was a recurring theme in the work of Hyman Minsky.[10] In Minsky's theoretical framework, firms (and households) are viewed much like banks, as owners of assets that generate cash flows and liabilities that require settlement over a sequence of periods. At any point in time, a firm anticipates a flow of revenues from its productive operations, and faces a flow of contractual debt obligations based on its borrowing history. A crucial distinction is made between "hedge" and "speculative" financing units. Hedge units expect to receive cash flows in each period that are sufficient to cover debt repayments as they come due. As long as these expectations are realized, there is no need for debt to be rolled over. Hence changes in interest rates can affect the value of the firm but cannot threaten it with insolvency. Speculative units, in contrast, anticipate a shortfall of revenues relative to debt obligations in some periods. They expect to have to raise new funds in order to repay debts as they come due, and are therefore vulnerable to increases in interest rates or the unavailability of financing. Furthermore, a sufficiently large increase in their cost of borrowing can lead to a present value reversal and the threat of insolvency.[11]

Like banks engaged in maturity transformation, speculative units use short-term debt to finance assets that yield revenues far into the future. The only essential difference is that the assets are real rather than financial. These firms secure a lower cost of capital at the expense of greater exposure to rollover risk. As long as the economy remains dominated by hedge financing units, debts can be rolled over without difficulty. But this leads to an endogenous increase in the incidence of speculative financing (Minsky, 1982, p.65):

> The natural starting place for analyzing the relation between debt and income is to take an economy with a cyclical past that is now doing well. The inherited debt reflects the history of the economy, which includes a period in the not too distant past in which the economy did not do well. Acceptable liability structures are based upon some margin of safety, so that expected cash flows, even in periods when the economy is not doing well, will cover contractual debt payments. As the period over which the economy does well lengthens, two things become evident in board rooms. Existing debts are easily validated and units that were heavily in debt prospered; it paid to lever. After the event it becomes apparent that the margins of safety built into debt structures were too great. As a result, over a period in which the economy does well, views about acceptable debt structure change. In the deal making that goes on between banks, investment bankers, and businessmen, the acceptable amount of debt to use in financing various types of activity and positions increases. This increase in the weight of debt financing raises the market price for capital assets and increases investment. As this continues, the economy is transformed into a boom economy.

The increase in speculative relative to hedge financing has two effects: it facilitates rapid economic expansion, while also increasing financial fragility.

Expansion is facilitated because speculative finance allows firms to grow faster than they could if their borrowing was constrained by expected revenues in each period. Fragility rises because of an increasing need for refinancing as revenues fall short of obligations for a growing number of firms.

The boom is interrupted by a crisis when two conditions are satisfied: a large number of investments are found to be inept, so that cash flows fall below expectations for many firms at once, and financial fragility has reached levels that make it difficult for all those seeking refinancing to find acceptable terms that maintain solvency. An acute need for refinancing arises at a time when banks are reluctant to roll over existing debt. The result is higher interest rates, credit rationing, present-value reversals, strong demand for liquidity, and a collapse in asset prices. If the government sector is large, automatic stabilizers and fiscal policy intervention can prevent a collapse in business profits. Similarly, aggressive monetary expansion can mitigate the extent of credit rationing and the fall in asset prices. But both policies come with a cost: the former in maintaining an inefficient industrial structure and the latter in generating expectations that the risks associated with speculative financing are not severe. The short-term benefits of intervention (which are substantial) give rise to long-term costs in terms of the frequency and severity of future crises.

Expectations play a central role in this analysis. There is a sense in which expectations, rather than being self-fulfilling as in standard theory, are *self-falsifying*. A crisis occurs when liability structures cause the system to be fragile, but these liability structures are based on optimistic beliefs about the prospects for refinancing. Similarly, pessimism about rollover risk results in robust liability structures that facilitate refinancing on favorable terms. This is the basis for Minsky's paradoxical claim that stability is itself destabilizing (1975, p.126). Firms persist in adopting liability structures that give rise to outcomes that violate the assumptions on the basis of which the liability structures were chosen. This occurs both in the case of excessive caution following a period of instability, and excessive boldness following a long expansion.

Minsky's assumptions regarding expectation formation have attracted some criticism. Flemming (1982), for instance, claims that "the argument depends on agents failing to distinguish a run of good luck from a favorable structural shift in their environment."[12] From the perspective of market ecology, such criticisms miss the point. The expectations that come to be reflected in liability structures are those held by individuals whose actions have recently been rewarded by success. Over the course of a stable expansion, success accrues in greatest measure to those with the most aggressive financial practices. It may well be the case that some of these individuals have failed to distinguish "a run of good luck from a favorable structural shift" but as long as they profit from doing so, it is their beliefs and not those of the skeptics who will increasingly come to be reflected in asset prices. Those who anticipate a crisis and pad their margins of safety are punished, not rewarded, as long as the expansion continues.

This point has broader relevance. It is commonly argued that asset price bubbles cannot be identified in real time because anyone capable of doing so could make extraordinary profits.[13] As it happens, there is some evidence suggesting that bubbles can indeed be identified in real time through the implied volatility in options prices, especially deep out-of-the-money put options that serve as a form of crash insurance.[14] But this does not imply that one can profit from identifying bubbles without taking substantial risks, for the simple reason that the eventual size of the bubble and the timing of the crash are unpredictable. Selling short too soon can result in huge losses if one is unable to continue meeting margin calls as the bubble expands. Trying to ride the bubble for a while can be disastrous if one doesn't get out of the market soon enough. And avoiding the market altogether can also be risky, if one's returns as a fund manager are compared with those of one's peers.[15] As Abreu and Brunnermeier (2003) demonstrate, even sophisticated, forward looking investors face a dilemma when they become aware of a bubble, because they know that it will continue to expand unless there is coordinated selling by enough of them. And such coordination is not easily achieved, resulting in the possibility of prolonged departures of prices from fundamentals, even if the realization that this is occurring becomes quite widespread.

More generally, the distribution of forecasting rules and procedures in the population is endogenously determined under pressure of market competition. In the terminology of Marcet and Sargent (1989), the economy is a self-referential system: the objective laws of motion governing the evolution of economic magnitudes depend on the perceived laws of motion on the basis of which individuals act. It is commonplace to assume in contemporary macroeconomic modeling that the perceived laws coincide with the actual laws to which they give rise. As noted above, this so-called "rational expectations" hypothesis is in fact a hypothesis of consistent or equilibrium expectations. It is certainly the case that the agents in Minsky's model do not have equilibrium expectations in this sense. But it is also conceivable that such equilibrium expectations are locally unstable under plausible disequilibrium dynamics based on experience-based learning or evolutionary selection among heterogeneous beliefs. This is a question to which future research effort could fruitfully be directed.[16]

Expectations

Foley and Sidrauski left unresolved the question of how expectations are determined, just as Keynes had done a generation earlier. The rational expectations hypothesis sidestepped the problem altogether by simply assuming that expectations were determined by equilibrium conditions once other primitives of a model (preferences, endowments, technologies, and policy rules, for instance) had been specified. As noted by Woodford (2011), however, expectation formation and revision as an "object of analysis in its own right" is now an area of active research interest in macroeconomics. One approach is that of learning.

A substantial literature on learning in macroeconomics has emerged over the past couple of decades, but much of it considers a representative agent attempting to learn the value of one or more parameters.[17] The prototypical model in this literature is based on the assumption that the dynamics of state variables have a recursive structure that is consistent with a rational expectations solution, but with a parameter that is unknown to the representative agent. Learning changes beliefs about the parameter, but also changes the parameter itself since it is sensitive to agent beliefs. Convergence occurs when beliefs about the parameter match the value of the parameter that these beliefs induce, at which point learning ceases.

Even within this simple framework, learning does not always converge to rational expectations. Howitt (1992) provided a very clear example of this in his analysis of a nominal interest rate peg. Starting from a steady state in which expectations are fulfilled, a permanent decline in the nominal interest rate results in an immediate transition to lower levels of inflation under rational expectations. But under a broad class of learning dynamics, such a decline instead results in accelerating inflation, just as Wicksell's (1898) analysis of the cumulative process would predict. Howitt concludes as follows:

> Perhaps the most important lesson of the analysis is that the assumption of rational expectations can be misleading, even when used to analyze the consequences of a fixed monetary regime. If the regime is not conducive to expectational stability, then the consequences can be quite different from those predicted under rational expectations ... in general, any rational expectations analysis of monetary policy should be supplemented with a stability analysis ... to determine whether or not the rational expectations equilibrium could ever be observed.

Such models are suggestive, but do not really tackle the question of the manner in which the decentralized and uncoordinated inter-temporal plans of large numbers of households and firms are brought into consistency with each other. To do so requires a multi-agent framework with heterogeneous beliefs and forecasting rules in competition with each other. Realized values of economic magnitudes depend on the distribution of such rules in the population. The performance of the various rules depends on the frequencies with which they are present in the population, and these frequencies evolve under pressure of differential payoffs. The resulting dynamics of beliefs and realizations can then be studied.

This is the methodology of agent-based computational economics.[18] Recent work by Blake LeBaron (2010) on belief and price dynamics in a speculative asset market illustrates the value of this approach. In LeBaron's model, a broad range of forecasting rules, including those associated with fundamental and technical trading strategies, compete with each other (and with a passive, belief-independent strategy). The resulting price dynamics display two characteristics commonly found in high-frequency data on asset returns: short-run momentum and long-run mean reversion. Furthermore, instead of convergence to anything that might resemble homogenous and self-fulfilling beliefs, a broad range of forecasting rules continue to co-exist indefinitely (see also Föllmer , Horst, and Kirman, 2005).

The agent-based approach to learning and evolutionary selection has the potential to provide microeconomic underpinnings for a number of models that have languished since the rational expectations revolution. In particular, it could allow us to revisit, from a fresh perspective, theories of economic fluctuations that appear to be inconsistent with inter-temporal optimization and self-fulfilling expectations, but which might well be consistent with competition among heterogeneous forecasting rules. Some of the richest and most interesting endogenous business cycle theories were developed without assuming that agent expectations are self-fulfilling and indeed without much concern for microeconomic foundations at all. Local instability in such models is often caused by accelerator effects in the goods market, and a variety of different non-linear effects that keep trajectories bounded have been considered.[19]

The perspective of market ecology can allow for a renewed exploration and reinterpretation of this work, which is based on sound economic logic but lacks clarity at the level of individual decision-making. Agent-based computational methods could prove especially useful in this regard.[20] Furthermore, the scope for application of the ecological perspective extends well beyond macroeconomics and finance; see especially Nelson and Winter (1985) for applications to the theory of the firm and technological progress. Until such approaches become more central to the professional mainstream we shall continue to ask the question first posed by Thorstein Veblen in 1898: "Why is Economics not an Evolutionary Science?"

Acknowledgments

I am grateful to Alan Kirman and Dick Nelson for comments on an earlier version, and to Duncan Foley for guidance and support throughout my career.

Notes

1 See, for instance, Miller (1977), Harrison and Kreps (1978), Morris (1996), Scheinkman and Xiong (2003), Geanakoplos (2010), and Che and Sethi (2012) on asset pricing with heterogeneous beliefs, and Sethi and Yildiz (2012) on public disagreement when prior beliefs are both heterogeneous and unobservable.
2 This process of endogenous regime switching is described more formally in Sethi (1996); see Brock and Hommes (1997) and Lux (1998) for related models, and Hommes (2006) for a comprehensive survey.
3 Tradebot, among the largest of the high-frequency trading firms, allegedly managed a four-year stretch without a single losing day while having an average holding period of just 11 seconds (Creswell, 2010).
4 The finding by the Kirilenko team that the fastest moving firms were able to exit their positions and shut down operations during the flash crash while significant losses were inflicted on those who were slower to react is consistent with this interpretation.
5 Collateralized debt obligations are tiered claims to the revenues generated by bundled securities such as bonds and mortgages. Senior tranches are affected by default on the underlying securities only if all subordinate tranches have been completely wiped out; this allows them to carry much higher credit ratings (Coval, Jurek, and Stafford,

2009). Credit default swaps differ from standard insurance contracts in one important respect: they do not require the buyers of protection to have an insurable interest, and can therefore be purchased without any exposure to the underlying credit risk. Hence, they allow speculators to bet on default more easily and with greater leverage than they could by short selling bonds.

6 Dramatic successes based on such strategies are featured in Lewis (2010) and Zuckerman (2010); some spectacular failures during the bubble in technology stocks are discussed below.

7 That is, the yield curve is rising on average, although its steepness and general shape are affected by expectations regarding the future course of interest rates.

8 This process is vividly illustrated by the case of Northern Rock, the first British bank to fail in 150 years. The bank was not engaged in subprime lending, and had securitized and sold a major portion of its loans. But the loans remaining on its balance sheet were funded by short-term debt raised and rolled over in the money market. The bank was not a casualty of high rates of mortgage delinquency or large-scale withdrawals by retail depositors, but rather an inability to roll over its debts when markets froze in the face of a spike in the demand for liquidity (Shin, 2009).

9 See Soros (2009) for a contemporaneous account of these events.

10 See also Kindleberger (1978), Volcker (1979), and Guttentag and Herring (1984) for similar perspectives on economic fluctuations.

11 Minsky also introduces a third category, which he calls Ponzi units, defined as firms whose anticipated revenues are insufficient to cover even the interest component of their obligations. Distinguishing between speculative and Ponzi financing units is not essential to the argument here.

12 Similar concerns have been expressed about the work of Kindleberger; see, for instance, Bernanke (1983).

13 This is claimed, for instance, by Eugene Fama in a recent interview with John Cassidy (2010).

14 See Bates (1991) and Fung (2007) on this point, and Rappoport and White (1994) for a related study using changes in the terms of brokers' loans in the lead up to the 1929 crash.

15 The bubble in technology stocks that eventually burst in 2000 provides some vivid examples. Many of those who sold these assets short could not profit from the decline because they were forced to liquidate their positions too soon (Hakim, 2000). The Quantum fund suffered significant losses from short positions in 1999, rebounded after reversing course to buy technology stocks later in the year, but was left long when the crash eventually came (Martinson, 1999; Oppel, 1999; Norris, 2000). Meanwhile the Tiger fund stayed out of technology stocks but performed poorly relative to benchmarks during the bubble and suffered significant withdrawals (Norris, 2000).

16 For a more formal statement of these points and some preliminary analysis, see Sethi (1992, 1995).

17 See Marcet and Sargent (1989) and Evans and Ramey (1992) for early contributions, and Evans and Honkapohja (1999) for a comprehensive survey.

18 Numerous applications of this approach to problems in economics are surveyed in Tesfatsion and Judd (2006); see Farmer and Foley (2009) for a recent article advocating its broader use. Among the earliest and most effective uses of this method in the social sciences may be found in Thomas Schelling's (1971) analysis of segregation.

19 Samuelson (1939), Kaldor (1940), Hicks (1950), Goodwin (1951), Leijonhufvud (1973), Tobin (1975), and Foley (1987) are important examples. This research tradition, based on aggregative models of disequilibrium dynamics, continues in the recent work of Chiarella, Flaschel, and Franke, (2005).

20 Gatti, Gaffeo, Gallegati, Giulioni, and Palestrini, (2008) take an important step in this direction.

References

Abreu, D., and Brunnermeier, M. (2003) "Bubbles and Crashes", *Econometrica*, 71: 173–204.

Arrow, K.J., and Debreu, G. (1954) "Existence of an Equilibrium for a Competitive Economy", *Econometrica*, 22: 265–290.

Aumann, R. J. (1976) "Agreeing to Disagree", *Annals of Statistics*, 4: 1236–1239.

Bates, D.S. (1991) "The Crash of '87: Was It Expected? The Evidence from Options Markets", *Journal of Finance*, 46: 1009–1044.

Beja, A., and Goldman, M.B. (1980) "On the Dynamic Behavior of Prices in Disequilibrium", *Journal of Finance*, 35: 235–248.

Bernanke, B.S. (1983) "Nonmonetary Effects of the Financial Crisis in the Propagation of the Great Depression", *American Economic Review*, 73: 257–276.

Brock, W.A., and Hommes, C.H. (1997) "A Rational Route to Randomness", *Econometrica*, 65: 1059–1095.

Cassidy, J. (2010) "Interview with Eugene Fama", *New Yorker*, January 13.

Che, Y.-K., and Sethi, R. (2012) "Credit Derivatives and the Cost of Capital", Unpublished Manuscript, Columbia University.

Chiarella, C., Flaschel, P., and Franke, R. (2005) *Foundations for a Disequilibrium Theory of the Business Cycle: Qualitative Analysis and Quantitative Assessment*, Cambridge: Cambridge University Press.

Coval, J., Jurek, J., and Stafford, E. (2009) "The Economics of Structured Finance", *Journal of Economic Perspectives*, 23: 3–25.

Creswell, J. (2010) "Speedy New Traders Make Waves Far From Wall St", *New York Times*, May 16.

De Bondt, W.F.M., and Thaler, R. (1985) "Does the Stock Market Overreact?" *Journal of Finance*, 40: 793–805.

Engle, R.F. (1982) "Autoregressive Conditional Heteroskedasticity with Estimates of the Variance of U.K. Inflation", *Econometrica*, 50: 987–1008.

Evans, G., and Honkapohja, S. (1999) "Learning dynamics", in John B. Taylor, and Michael Woodford (Eds.), *Handbook of Macroeconomics*, Amsterdam: Elsevier, pp. 449–542.

Evans, G., and Ramey, G. (1992) "Expectation Calculation and Macroeconomic Dynamics", *American Economic Review*, 82: 207–224.

Farmer, J.D., and Foley, D.K. (2009) "The Economy Needs Agent-Based Modelling", *Nature*, 460: 685–686.

Flemming, J.S. (1982) "Comment", in Kindleberger, C.P., and Laffargue, J.P. (Eds.), *Financial Crises: Theory, History, and Policy*, Cambridge: Cambridge University Press.

Foley, D.K. (1987) "Liquidity–Profit Rate Cycles in a Capitalist Economy", *Journal of Economic Behavior & Organization*, 8: 363–376.

Foley, D.K. (1999) "The Ins and Outs of Late Twentieth Century Economics", in Heertje, A. (Ed.), *The Makers of Modern Economics Volume IV*, Aldershot: Edward Elgar.

Foley, D.K., and Sidrauski, M. (1971) *Monetary and Fiscal Policy in a Growing Economy*, Basingstoke: Macmillan.

Föllmer, H., Horst, U., and Kirman, A. (2005) "Equilibria in Financial Markets with Heterogeneous Agents: A Probabilistic Perspective" *Journal of Mathematical Economics*, 41: 123–155.

Fung, J.K.W. (2007) "The Information Content of Option Implied Volatility Surrounding the 1997 Hong Kong Stock Market Crash", *Journal of Futures Markets*, 27: 555–574.

Gatti, D., Gaffeo, E., Gallegati, M., Giulioni, G., and Palestrini, A. (2008) *Emergent Macroeconomics: An Agent-Based Approach to Business Fluctuations*, Berlin: Springer.

Geanakoplos, J. (2010) "The Leverage Cycle", *NBER Macroeconomics Annual*, 24: 1–65.

Goodwin, R.M. (1951) "The Nonlinear Accelerator and the Persistence of Business Cycles", *Econometrica*, 19: 1–17.

Grant, J., and Mackenzie, M. (2010) "Markets: Ghosts in the Machine", *Financial Times*, February 17.

Guttentag, J., and Herring, R. (1984) "Credit Rationing and Financial Disorder", *Journal of Finance*, 39: 1359–1382.

Hakim, D. (2000) "Payback for Those Who Sold the Bull Market Short: Missing Out on High-technology's Rapid Descent", *New York Times*, May 16.

Harrison, J.M., and Kreps, D.M. (1978) "Speculative Investor Behavior in a Stock Market with Heterogeneous Expectations", *Quarterly Journal of Economics*, 93: 323–336.

Hicks, John R. (1939) *Value and Capital*, Oxford: Clarendon Press.

Hicks, J. (1950) *A Contribution to the Theory of the Trade Cycle*, Oxford: Clarendon Press.

Hommes, C.H. (2006) "Heterogeneous Agent Models in Economics and Finance", *Handbook of Computational Economics*, 2: 1109–1186.

Howitt, P. (1992) "Interest Rate Control and Nonconvergence to Rational Expectations", *Journal of Political Economy*, 100: 776–800.

Jegadeesh, N., and Titman, S. (1993) "Returns to Buying Winners and Selling Losers: Implications for Stock Market Efficiency", *Journal of Finance*, 48: 65–91.

Kaldor, N. (1940) "A Model of the Trade Cycle", *Economic Journal*, 50: 78–92.

Kindleberger, C. P. (1978) *Manias, Panics, and Crashes: A History of Financial Crises*, New York: Basic Books.

Kirilenko, A.A., Kyle, A.S., Samadi, M., and Tuzun, T. (2011) "The Flash Crash: The Impact of High Frequency Trading on an Electronic Market", available at SSRN: http://ssrn.com/abstract=1686004

LeBaron, B. (2010) "Heterogeneous Gain Learning and the Dynamics of Asset Prices", Unpublished Manuscript, Brandeis University.

Leijonhufvud, A. (1973) "Effective Demand Failures", *Swedish Journal of Economics*, 75: 27–48.

Lewis, M. (2010) *The Big Short: Inside the Doomsday Machine*, New York: W. W. Norton & Company.

Lux, T. (1998) "The Socio-Economic Dynamics of Speculative Markets: Interacting Agents, Chaos, and the Fat Tails of Return Distributions", *Journal of Economic Behavior & Organization*, 33: 143–165.

Marcet, A., and Sargent, T.J. (1989) "Convergence of Least Squares Learning Mechanisms in Self-Referential Linear Stochastic Models", *Journal of Economic Theory*, 48: 337–368.

Martinson, J. (1999) "Soros loses £430m in failed internet gamble", *Guardian*, August 10.

McKenzie, L.W. (1959) "On the Existence of a General Equilibrium for a Competitive Market", *Econometrica*, 28: 54–71.

Miller, E. M. (1977) "Risk, Uncertainty, and Divergence of Opinion", *Journal of Finance*, 32: 1151–1168.

Minsky, H.P. (1975) *John Maynard Keynes*, New York: Columbia University Press.

Minsky, H.P. (1982) *Can "It" Happen Again: Essays on Instability and Finance*, Armonk, NY: M.E. Sharpe.

Morris, S. (1996) "Speculative Investor Behavior and Learning", *Quarterly Journal of Economics*, 111: 1111–1133.

Nakamoto, M., and Wighton, D. (2007) "Citigroup Chief Stays Bullish on Buy-Outs", *Financial Times*, July 9.

Nelson, R.R., and Winter, S.G. (1985) *An Evolutionary Theory of Economic Change*, Cambridge, MA: Harvard University Press.

Norris, F. (2000) "Another Technology Victim; Top Soros Fund Manager Says He 'Overplayed' Hand", *New York Times*, April 29.

Oppel, R.A. (1999) "Elsewhere, 1999 Is Shaping Up as a Banner Year", *New York Times*, December 19.

Rappoport, P., and White, E.N. (1994) "Was the Crash of 1929 Expected?", *American Economic Review*, 84: 271–281.

Samuelson, P.A. (1939) "A Synthesis of the Principle of Acceleration and the Multiplier", *Journal of Political Economy*, 47: 786–797.

Scheinkman, J., and Xiong, W. (2003) "Overconfidence and Speculative Bubbles", *Journal of Political Economy*, 111: 1183–1219.

Schelling, T.C. (1971) "Dynamic models of segregation", *Journal of Mathematical Sociology*, 1: 143–186.

Sethi, R. (1992) "Dynamics of Learning and the Financial Instability Hypothesis", *Journal of Economics*, 56: 39–70.

Sethi, R. (1995) "The Evolutionary Dynamics of Financial Practices", *Metroeconomica*, 46: 246–277.

Sethi, R. (1996) "Endogenous Regime Switching in Speculative Markets", *Structural Change and Economic Dynamics*, 7: 99–118.

Sethi, R., and Yildiz, M. (2012) "Public Disagreement", *American Economic Journal: Microeconomics*, 4: 57–95.

Shiller, R.J. (1981) "Do Stock Prices Move Too Much to Be Justified by Subsequent Changes in Dividends?", *American Economic Review*, 71: 421–436.

Shin, H.S. (2009) "Reflections on Northern Rock: The Bank Run that Heralded the Global Financial Crisis", *Journal of Economic Perspectives*, 23: 101–119.

Soros, G. (2009) "The Game Changer", *Financial Times*, January 28.

Stultz, R.M. (2010) "Credit Default Swaps and the Credit Crisis", *Journal of Economic Perspectives*, 24: 73–92.

Tesfatsion, L., and Judd, K.L. (Eds.) (2006) *Handbook of Computational Economics*, Amsterdam: Elsevier, vol. 2, pp. 831–880.

Tobin, J. (1975) "Keynesian Models of Recession and Depression", *American Economic Review Papers and Proceedings*, 65: 195–202.

Veblen, Thorstein (1898) "Why is Economics not an Evolutionary Science?", *Quarterly Journal of Economics*, 12: 373–397.

Volcker, P. (1979) *The Rediscovery of the Business Cycle*, New York: Free Press.

Wald, A. (1951) "On Some Systems of Equations of Mathematical Economics", *Econometrica*, 19: 368–403.

Woodford, M. (2011) "A Response to John Kay", INET Blog, October 5, http://ineteconomics.org/blog/inet/michael-woodford-response-john-kay

Wicksell, K. (1898) *Interest and Prices*, translated by R.F. Kahn (1936), London: Macmillan.

Zuckerman, G. (2010) *The Greatest Trade Ever*, New York: Broadway Books.

20 Market complexity and the nature of crises in financial markets

Philip Mirowski

Whether Duncan Foley is aware of it or not, the inspiration for much of my own work derives from offhand comments he has made during discussions and seminars. For instance, a throwaway observation about conservation laws in neoclassical theory he made more than three decades ago at Stanford sent me hurtling down my trajectory in excavating the origins of neoclassical economics in energy physics. A different comment about Cowles that he dropped in passing led eventually to my work on the postwar influence of the computer on economics. A third discussion in an airport shuttle about the importance of power laws in research showed up as a section in my recent *ScienceMart* (2011). I literally am beholden to him for many of my juicier epiphanies. Hence it will not be a stretch to report on a fourth topic close to his heart and to my concerns: the role and significance of complexity in the economy and economic theory.

While Duncan has long been an external professor at the Santa Fe Institute, I would trace the current chapter to his characteristically lucid survey of analytical approaches to complexity in his Introduction to *Barriers and Bounds to Rationality* (Foley, 1998). There he observed that in the work of Peter Albin and a few other visionaries, "cellular automata serve as a laboratory for exploration of the difficult general questions raised by nonlinearity and complexity" (1998, p. 15). While others tended to make reference to "complexity" in rather impressionistic and imprecise ways, such that appeals to complexity have drawn some ridicule in orthodox circles, in that Introduction he suggests, "we must come to grips with the complexity hierarchy of social and economic systems through the same methods and tools that have been developed to analyze linguistic and computational complexity" (1998, p. 44). Given his long-standing fascination with the variable legitimacy of importation of models from the physical sciences, Foley has never taken for granted the notion that relevance of models for economics derives from prior success in physics (Foley and Smith, 2008). In 1998, he located the economic center of gravity of computational research not in cellular automata *per se* (which can show up in more orthodox economic models, like the Schelling model of housing discrimination), but rather in more general theories of computational complexity rooted in automata theory and the Chomsky hierarchy.[1] It may be helpful to speculate why this programmatic heuristic has not become very widespread or common in the economics profession in the decade or so after

Duncan pointed the way. This may then serve as a prolegomenon to a brief description from my own work on approaches to explanation of the crisis of 2008 onwards, which will serve to illustrate one mode of modeling strategy which hews closely to this very specific recommendation.

Where the complexity resides

"Complexity" can appeal to economists of all stripes, so long as it is left undefined. This, I fear, has become rather commonplace within the economics profession of late, at least since the worldwide crisis that has threatened to subject its ranks to severe status degradation. Every charlatan can readily protest that the economy was regrettably so intractably complex that it eluded our ability to see the crash coming (Mesjasz, 2010). Numerous economists scrambled for that escape hatch in 2009–10. Earlier, similar conceptual freedom had been derided at the Santa Fe Institute, with Seth Lloyd providing at least 46 potential formal definitions.[2] The vernacular economic variations beyond the formal specifications have threatened to proliferate to such an extent that the Humpty Dumpty option of conceding to each their own preferred interpretation seems to reign primarily in order to preserve economists' equanimity *in extremis*. Thus, the proposition that we have embarked upon some new "complexity era" in economics (Rosser, Holt, and Colander, 2011) is therefore premature, to say the least (Fontana, 2011).

I will argue in favor of the Duncan Foley gambit to dispel the fog; but first, I want to make a case for where the complexity definition should reside in economics, as a prelude to limiting the reference of complexity theory within economics. I believe anyone who has lived through the economic crisis can't help but notice that the tendency of most diagnostics has been to blame the weaknesses of human beings and their perceptions of incentives as somehow lodged at the root of economic failure. From irrationality to criminal fraud to evasion of regulations to insufficient demand to irrational exuberance to wishful thinking to irrational expectations, the orthodox neoclassical mindset has tended to channel almost all inquiry into presumptions that the failure must be traced back to human nature of some ilk. Interestingly, this dovetails with the conservative tendency within the political classes to blame the crisis on the victims, be they deadbeat mortgage holders, befuddled investors, or deluded regulators. Undoubtedly this can also be attributed to the self-image of most of these authors as humanists, engaged in the humanistic science of economics. But then, whenever they proceed to flesh out their impressions of excessive complexity as an intervening cause of the crisis, they find themselves impelled to attribute the requisite complexity quotient to their agents, or else to their second-order interaction. In other words, complexity in economics tends to be reduced to a concern with the nature of representations (or cognition) within the mind. Furthermore, in order to concretize their intuitions into formal models, they then reach for some complexity definition from physics, and proceed to impose it upon their favorite version of mental states of the agents occupying their models.

I want to suggest that this procedure is self-defeating and self-refuting, for at least three reasons. The first, and most ironic, is that the vaunted humanism of the modern economist is belied by the requirement to reduce their agents to little machines in order to impose physical notions of complexity in their models. Sometimes this is done under the banner of "bounded rationality," as with the work of Albin, but more often than not, it simply derives from the repressed physics inspiration for the utility function itself (Mirowski, 1989). I cannot exaggerate the numbers of time I have witnessed economists – like Leigh Tesfatsion or Mauro Gallegati or Steve Durlauf – insist that economics must of necessity be concerned with people, and then turn around and appropriate some rudimentary spin-glass model to represent complexity in their agent-based models.[3] This is an *ersatz* humanism with an inhuman face; at minimum, it is a travesty. The second objection has to do with an idea that dates back to Ross Ashby and the origins of cybernetics: that systems with a modest level of complexity cannot be expected to form faithful representations of systems of higher levels of comparable complexity. Foley himself has made this point, as have many others.[4] The problem here is that, were we to take this prohibition seriously, unless neoclassical economists were akin to Gods walking the earth, there is absolutely no reason to believe that their rudimentary models can adequately grasp the complexity of the economy of which they are merely a part. And, since the crisis has hopefully dispelled delusions of divine omnipotence in certain precincts of the economics community, even if only temporarily, the insistence that economic models are even capable of isolating and discerning the complexity of the human mind suggests an impossibility theorem for the orthodoxy at least as stringent as the one for which Kenneth Arrow became famous.

The third reason, and for my money, the most telling, is that a half-century of cognitive science has been studying the brain with greater gravity and perspicacity than the pitiful forays into "behavioralism" of any economist; and after years of trafficking with computer metaphors for the brain, they are no nearer to characterizing the complexity of thought processes than the man in the street. Therefore, I would like to suggest that the only logical option for economists is to stick to the things that they supposedly know the best, which is evidently not human nature, but rather, markets. In other words, instead of vainly attempting to ascribe the causes of the crisis to speculations concerning human nature, and engaging in the unsavory pursuit of blaming the victims, wouldn't it be more seemly and dignified to explore the possibility that the crisis was rooted in the structural evolution of markets themselves?

Taking this critique seriously, the task thus becomes to formally define and portray the complexity of different market structures in such a way as to discipline and rationalize some of the leading contenders for explanations of the crisis. Complexity, if it is to function as something more than a vapid excuse, has to be analytically linked to financial market failure. It should be based, as Foley suggested, on automata theory and the Chomsky hierarchy. This complexity approach would instead explore the alternative hypothesis that: as the internal dynamic of market innovation became more complex over the last few decades;

as the system as a whole evolved to an ever-more fragile structure; it reached the point that it could be globally vulnerable to the breakdown of some particular market in a particular geographic location. As electronic trading guru Steve Wunsch has reportedly said, US trading "is now so complex that no one can predict what will happen when something new is added to it, no matter how much vetting is done" (in MacKenzie, 2011; also Bookstaber, 2007). Hence, while it is indisputable that the utter collapse of the set of financial instruments which would supposedly shield investors from the default of the underlying mortgages in their portfolio of derivatives was probably the initial trigger of the current crisis, it was by no means the necessary and sufficient cause. Root causes, instead, would be traced to various indices of the attainment of an untenable level of complexity in the operation of key markets.

It is an unfortunate misconception about the history of economics that mathematical formalism as such dictates much of the form and content of economic theory – at one point, this was a mantra of Robert Lucas and his followers. I would not want the following suggestions to appear to persist in this error, so I must insist at the outset that our foray into the theory of computational complexity exists as both a convenient Gestalt switch in order to glimpse what a world devoid of neoclassical analytical presuppositions might actually look like, and simultaneously, a mandate to pay much more serious attention to an institutional economics not co-opted by "transactions costs," "information asymmetries," and other orthodox dead ends. The ultimate aim of this research is a more faithful empirical description of what markets have been and what they now accomplish.

How to stop mimicking orthodox finance theory

The first steps toward a Foley-inspired theory of the crisis would compare and contrast two deep fundamental presumptions concerning microeconomics: the **first**, situated at the ontological heart of orthodox economic theory, is the insistence that all markets function fundamentally alike, in that they each individually grind out the *same* equilibrium prices and quantities for the "same" commodities. The theory of Walrasian general equilibrium is the clearest expression of this conviction, because it situates all markets on the same conceptual and functional footing (Foley, 2010). If all markets operate in essentially the same manner, then if it transpires that the same commodity is being sold for two or more different prices, this is interpreted as an immediate indicator that there is something wrong or "imperfect" about one of the component parts of the market. Nevertheless, the system is presumed to be extremely fault-tolerant, since once any price discrepancy is detected, presumptively dedicated arbitrageurs will swoop down and make a profit, while trading away the discrepancy. Flaws in the system are thus said to be contained and localized.

This brings us to the **second** fundamental presumption of orthodox microeconomics, a corollary of the first. Arbitrage pricing theory is one of the ten commandments of modern finance theory, and ensconced at the heart of neoclassical economic theory. Deterministic theory is constructed upon the bedrock assumption that arbitrage opportunities do not exist in "equilibrium," since they cannot persist.[5] Other components of the theory include the postulation of an equivalent martingale measure for every portfolio, and hence a derived valuation attached to any arbitrary package of contingent claims. In option pricing theory, for instance, the price of an option is rendered determinate by the presumption that it can be replicated precisely as a continuously adjusted portfolio that will have the same payoff as the option in all "states of the world." It is therefore the basis for the doctrine that markets are the means whereby traders bundle and repackage "risk" so that it can be conveyed to those most capable of bearing it, thereby diminishing global levels of risk through diversification. These dual theses of the fundamental uniformity of markets and the unwavering validity of [neoclassical] arbitrage pricing theory are indispensable building blocks of modern orthodox economic theory. *Without arbitrage pricing theory, there would be no neoclassical theory of financial "risk."*

Now consider the alternative heterodox proposition, which I would argue would be axiomatic for the Foley approach, that various markets are generally *not* all alike, but operate according to manifestly different principles which can be specified in purely formal terms (Mirowski, 2002, 2007). This is a proposition which has been entertained in a few precincts of the contemporary economics profession, but the profound implications are rarely pursued.[6] In these various corners of economics, structural differences between posted price markets, dealer mediated markets, sealed bid auctions, and continuous double actions are intensively studied and acknowledged. Yet, under those conditions, it is sometimes admitted that if the "same" commodity were to be offered for sale under the auspices of two different market formats, then it is highly unlikely that the price and quantity consequences will always and everywhere be identical. Imbalances of generic supply and demand therefore need not lead in general to identical prices and quantities sold, in this view. To put it more bluntly, the Marshallian supply and demand tradition is refuted.

Negation of the **first** fundamental proposition of orthodoxy leads inexorably to revision of the **second** fundamental principle as well. Patently, some traders will approach the diversity of market prices as an opportunity for further interventions, engaging in what they consider to be arbitrage operations because they see an opportunity to link the previously uncoupled markets, buying the same or similar commodities low and selling high, but this is not the rectification of an "imperfection" as much as it is the creation of a third, more "complex" market out of the previously disjoint components. Indeed, the arbitrageur may trade resorting to a market format different from either of the previous two: this happens (for instance) when a "futures" market based upon the mechanisms of a version of the double-sided auction is used to link various spot dealer-mediated markets in a designated commodity, or when an over-the-counter "derivatives" market is superimposed upon an existing auction market.[7] In any event, although arbitrageurs may exist and operate, their activities do not render the underlying component market forms more "alike," nor do they therefore make the opportunities for arbitrage permanently "disappear"; this is one crucial point where the orthodoxy goes off the rails. Foley-inspired economics in the complexity mode entertains the possibility that this sort of bridging activity may not necessarily render the entire system more stable, for evolutionary reasons explored below. In this framework, attempts at arbitrage are symptomatic of one large class of market innovation, and not, as neoclassical economists would have it, the rectification of some temporary flaw in an otherwise efficient economic system.

These revisions bring us to the heart of the matter, the conventional orthodox treatment of "risk." The irreducible diversity of market formats and the reframing of the meaning of arbitrage has a corrosive effect on arbitrage pricing theory, that is, the orthodox presumption of an equivalent martingale measure for every portfolio, and a "correct" derived valuation attached to any conceivable package of contingent claims. Most assertions of the possibilities of "hedging" are thus built upon tragically shaky foundations. Whenever some entrepreneurial firm packages together a set of contingencies and insists they are effectively "the same" as some other existing commodity, *they are in fact creating something new*, which cannot behave in ways identical to the prior situation. This process cannot be properly understood as merely an artifact of "cognitive uncertainty about risk." It should be apparent that, when you couple a posted price mechanism to a double auction, the hybrid result cannot appeal solely to *either* component market as dictating the unique "correct" price for the derivative commodity. According to our first precept, there is by definition no shared unity of correct price, which can be restored solely through arbitrage between two suitably distinct markets. But, furthermore, there is no reason that the stochastic profile in the new market need resemble the prior stochastic profiles of the previous components. More generally, under the rubric of packaging and reselling risk, *new connections are being forged between previously decoupled market formats*, or in other words, inadvertently, the complexity of the entire system of markets has been enhanced. Equivalent notions in physics of the evolution of complexity have been routinely formalized in the literature on networks of automata. It has also surfaced in some practitioners' accounts of the crisis (Bookstaber, 2007). Things which are formally asserted to be identical in attempts to repackage "risk" constitute in fact the debut of systemic novelty, both in the definition of the new composite financial instrument and in the altered institutional rules under which the new composite is traded.

A quick primer in the markomata theory of market complexity

I need a neologism in order to indicate I will henceforth be using a few words in ways that diverge dramatically from their conventional meanings in economics. If the reader will forgive the awkwardness, I will henceforth use the term "markomata" when I am discussing the abstract treatment of markets as formal diversiform computational automata.[8]

When considering the role of the financial sector in the macroeconomy, it would seem fairly natural to suggest that the individual market formats should themselves be treated as sets of abstract algorithms, that is, as *automata*.

After all, much of the riotous effulgent "financial innovation" in the run-up to the current crisis was initiated by econophysicists and financial engineers bringing their models to banks and hedge funds, there to be enshrined in automated pricing schemes and programmed as automated trading mechanisms. Much of our contemporary financial system had come to rely upon explicit proprietary algorithms in order to carry out any trade whatsoever: banks had their "value-at-risk" packages to propitiate the regulators and their shareholders; the ratings agencies had their own programs to validate their dicta; and the only reason mortgages could become packaged into derivatives was because they were said to be backed up by credit scoring algorithms. The output of one set of algorithms became the necessary input for another different class of algorithms. The many faces of financial innovation had mostly become tied to the computer and to the notion that information itself could be securely packaged, processed and sold alongside the novel commodities that had been innovated.

It will be our starting point to posit that the sorts of computationalism found recently in the rarified precincts of finance are in fact paradigm cases of a more general phenomenon, namely, the phenomenal manifestation of the vast majority of markets in the modern world as abstract automata. In this Foley-inspired microeconomics, the most rudimentary description of a market begins with the notion of a finite automaton. In computer science, a finite automaton щ is defined over an alphabet $\alpha = \{\alpha_1, \ldots \alpha_m\}$ with states $\theta = \{\theta_1, \ldots \theta_n\}$ is given by a function T, called a transition function which maps each pair (θ_i, α_j) into a state θ_k; a subset of states $\Theta = \{\theta_k\}$, called final accepting states, causes щ to halt. The specification of the alphabet stresses that the automaton is being described first and foremost as a language recognition device. A finite automaton can be thought of as an extremely limited computing device with no external memory capacity but a single "working tape," which it can read only once. After reading a symbol on the "tape," it either accepts or rejects it, depending upon the state that the device is in; it then enters the next state prescribed by the transition function. If the transition function T maps an existing state of щ into more than one state, then it is called a nondeterministic finite automaton. Automata are very simplified abstractions of the basic components of a computer; but they are also the simplest formal description of abstract language recognition devices.

Due to space limitations, we cannot discuss the various myriad economic functions performed by those algorithms within markomata here (however, see Mirowski, 2007). Nevertheless, the proliferation of potential functions is partially mitigated by subjecting markomata to the computational and complexity hierarchies propounded within automata theory. The heart of this theory is the treatment of complexity; but since even computer scientists sometimes use the term loosely, we need to be very precise when importing it into economics. The first, and most important, computational hierarchy is known in computer science as the "Chomsky hierarchy" (Davis, Sigal, and Weyuker, 1994, pp. 327–329), first introduced in (Chomsky, 1959). The hierarchy is conventionally demarcated by the class of language recognized, without delving into the fine points of linguistic theory, as follows:

1. *Regular grammars.* Such a grammar restricts its rules to a single nonterminal on the left-hand side and a right-hand side consisting of a single terminal, possibly by a single nonterminal. These languages are exactly all languages that can be decided by a finite state automaton. Regular languages are commonly used to define search patterns and the lexical structure of programming languages.
2. *Context-free grammars.* These are defined by rules of the form $A \rightarrow \gamma$ with A a nonterminal and γ a string of terminals and nonterminals. These languages are exactly all languages that can be recognized by a nondeterministic pushdown automaton. Context-free languages are the theoretical basis for the syntax of most programming languages.
3. *Context-sensitive languages.* The languages described by these grammars are exactly all languages that can be recognized by a linear bounded automaton (a nondeterministic Turing Machine whose tape is bounded by a constant times the length of the input).
4. *Recursively enumerable languages.* These are all languages recognized by a universal Turing Machine with an unbounded working tape.

Suppose we treated order execution in a market as if it were akin to a language recognition machine (as explained in greater detail in Mirowski, 2007) with bids and offers as inputs, and prices and quantities as outputs . In that case, the language hierarchy could be shown (Mirowski, 2002, pp. 567–573) to be isomorphic to the hierarchy of different forms of "markomata" found in the economy, as outlined in Table 20.1.

One implication of the Chomsky hierarchy is that some problems, which are unsolvable at the lower levels of computational capacity, can be shown to be solvable at the higher levels. Furthermore, there exist some problems that cannot be solved even at the most powerful level of the hierarchy; some strings are Turing non-computable on the Turing Machine.[9] However, the hierarchy is inclusive, in the sense that the more powerful automaton can perform all the calculations of the automaton lower down in the hierarchy, because it can *simulate* the operation of machines of lesser computational capacity. This leads to the important analytical notion of "markomata simulation."

The idea of one markomata simulating the operation of another would appear quite familiar to market practitioners, even though it has been absent up until now

Table 20.1 Markomata hierarchy of order execution

Automaton type	Recognizes language	Memory	Markomata
Finite	Regular	None	Posted-price
Pushdown	Context-free	Pushdown stack	Sealed bid
Linear bounded	Context sensitive	Finite tape	Double auction
Turing Machine	Recursively enumerable	Infinite tape	None

in orthodox economic theory. For instance, the futures market for red sorghum "simulates" the spot market for sorghum, in the sense that it can perform the same operations, augmented by other related operations, in the course of "tracking" the sorghum market. Likewise, the dealer-organized wholesale market "simulates" the posted-price markets of the retailer, while superimposing other functions. In an abstract computational sense, the futures market "encapsulates" the model of the spot market within its own algorithms. Markets for derivatives also simulate the markets for their component assets. This would be the case even if the derivatives markets were operated as a double auction, whereas the spot markets were operated as a sealed-bid clearinghouse auction. The plague of Collateralized Debt Obligations (CDOs) over the last decade were inventions created and sold by banks over the counter which were supposed to be based upon loans sold to homeowners through dealer-mediated markets. The implicit claim (now proven false) was that the market for CDOs could adequately simulate the operation of the retail market for mortgages. This claim was rendered recursive when banks packaged and sold CDOs composed of prior CDOs, or the notorious "CDO Squared." The theory of computation informs us that certain specific market forms can simulate other market forms *as long as* they are composed of markomata of greater or equal computational capacity. That condition was flagrantly violated during the last two decades in the sale of CDOs, and indeed, in the instances of many other instruments. Sometimes it seemed that the more "artificial" the CDO variant (such as synthetic CDOs, or CDOs squared), the less complex the markomata used to sell them.

This observation about the current crisis raises a number of intriguing questions which could only be evoked in a markomata theory of the economy: is it historically the case that, in periods of hyper-invention of new market forms and financial instruments, the farther the novel derivatives strayed from their underlying cash markets, the less complex the markomata (in the Chomsky sense) generally used to sell them? Is this an artifact of the artisanal character of their initial production? Or is this only an attribute of certain transitional phases which are then reversed in the fullness of time and subsequent evolution? Such questions would lead to a very different characterization of the business cycle than currently found in the neoclassical orthodoxy.

Nevertheless, in general, the reason that the global markomata hierarchy does not collapse down to a single flat uniformity – say, all markets operating like a single massive computer, as in the Walrasian tradition – is that more computationally complex markets situated higher up in the Chomsky hierarchy perform other functions over and above those performed by the markets that they simulate: for instance, futures markets may seek to facilitate arbitrage of price discrepancies as well as track the spot markets in their purview.

Table 20.1 suggests that some forms of automata may be mapped into different formats of order execution. While the posted-price format possesses no memory capacity, and therefore qualifies as a finite automaton, a sealed bid auction requires the comparison of a submitted bid to an ordered array of previously entered bids stored in a memory, and therefore qualifies as one of a number of

k-headed pushdown automata.[10] Sealed bid order execution requires an ordering of submitted bids, which can be captured by a first-in first-out memory stack: hence the "pushdown." The standard double auction requires even more prodigious memory capacity, given that sequences of bids and asks stored in different identifiable memory locations must be retrieved and compared, and therefore should exhibit the computational capacity of (at least) a linear bounded automaton. Table 20.1 also suggests that no isolated individual markomata format has the power of a Turing Machine – in other words, the entire economy could never be run as a single auctioneer-mediated sealed bid auction (Walras' original vision), nor indeed as any other monolithic market format. However, the entire market system, conceived as a network of individual automata passing price and quantity messages back and forth, may indeed display some such capacity from the macro perspective.[11]

Because the same physical commodity or financial instrument can be and often is sold through different markomata, sometimes even within the same spatiotemporal coordinates, different markomata display different price and quantity profiles, it follows that there can be no such lemma as the "law of one price" in computational economics. (This will be central to the complexity account of the crisis.) If there might be a universal terminus toward which all automata tend, it is toward their internally defined "halting conditions." But even here, one can easily overstate the predictable mechanical character of market automata. It is a theorem of computational theory that:

> There is no algorithm that, given a program in the language $L(\alpha)$ and an input to that program, can determine whether or not the given program will eventually halt on the given input.
>
> Davis *et al.*, 1994, p. 68

The impossibility theorems of computational theory do not somehow prevent the construction of specific markomata for attainment of specific targeted functions (since this is the practitioner's notion of the "predictability" of the market); they merely prohibit the complexity economist from making any ironclad predictions about the inevitable outcomes of the price system *as a whole.* As individual markomata become increasingly networked, their computational powers become increasingly augmented in complexity (in the Chomsky definition), and transcendental guarantees that a particular market format will continue to operate as it has done in the past are repeatedly falsified. In markomata economics, the very notion of "market failure" thus assumes an entirely different meaning from its usual economic connotations. When a markomata fails, in this conception, it appears unable to halt. Prices appear to have no floor (or ceiling, in the case of hyperinflation); the communication/coordination functions of the market break down. Hence there exists in the real world the phenomenon of "circuit-breakers" which call a halt to market operations, something which makes eminent good sense in a computational economics (even as they are disparaged in neoclassical finance theory). Earlier generations of market engineers had appreciated the need for a manual override when there were "bugs" in the system. Far from existing as a purely abstract theoretical possibility, a stark instance of markomata failure materialized on 6 May 2010, American equity and futures markets suffered a sharp collapse of many prices (some to mere pennies in price), with an equally sharp recovery soon thereafter (MacKenzie, 2011). A *New York Times* article dubbed this a "flash crash" and quoted one participant: "There was no pricing mechanism ... There was nothing. No one knew what anything was worth. You didn't know where to buy a stock or sell a stock." (Schwartz, 2010). The utter breakdown of the price assignment function in a matter of minutes further undermined confidence in the operation of financial markets. Amongst orthodox economists, a year later there was still no consensus explanation of the causes of this very real market failure, although the Securities Exchange Commission has attempted to produce a narrative that would provide a modicum of agreement (US Securities and Exchange Commission, 2010). From an orthodox perspective, it sounded just a like a litany of "one damn accident after another" (MacKenzie, 2011). Conventional economic theory stood flummoxed by what participants experienced as a halting problem.

We should note that in formal computer science there is no "halting problem" specifically for finite automata; here we posit the proviso that the entire global network of markomata could evolve to the point that it can itself possess the power of a Turing Machine, and under those conditions, the global networked automata become subject to the halting theorem. This might be regarded as a further exemplification of the principle of emergent properties of the market system at different levels of analysis. Market forms sometimes start out in a state of isolated self-sufficiency and operating at very low levels of complexity: market failures (in the current sense) are relatively unknown; innovation, financialization, and arbitrage turns them into ever-more elaborate markomata. In the absence of severe macroeconomic contractions, the pace of complexification accelerates. It is characteristic of the dynamic of economic development that human participants, from their individual parochial vantage points, attribute any observed "failure" to a particular localized market within their purview, whereas from an analytical point of view, it should more appropriately be attributed instead to the entire network architecture.

Two versions of markomata complexity

One obstacle that the computer science literature presents for economists is that sometimes the term "complexity" is used to reference the Chomsky hierarchy of automata, as discussed above; but at other times it is used to refer to the theory of computational intractability, which we have already briefly encountered in the previous section.[12] In this latter sense, "complexity" refers to the cost and difficulty of solving a designated class of problems upon a *specific automaton*, namely, the abstract Turing Machine. In the former, it refers to computational capacities of different classes of automata. Because the economic theory of markomata must necessarily distinguish between simpler automata and the Turing Machine, it is of the utmost importance to insist upon keeping the terminology separate. To forestall confusion, henceforth the former phenomenon will be called "computational complexity," and the latter, "computational intractability." The first is more structural, whereas the latter verges more naturally upon economic notions of resource usage encountered in the course of normal market operations. We use this distinction between complexity and intractability, but, while nominally the subject of two distinct literatures in mathematics and computer science, they actually overlap conceptually to some degree due to the fact that the Chomsky hierarchy is sometimes portrayed as distinguishing automata by their memory capacities, whereas distinctions between solutions in polynomial and nonpolynomial time (or space) are linked to the amount of resources available to the Turing Machine. However, it will behoove us to remember that Chomsky complexity is an attribute of the "machine" itself (and hence the markomata), whereas intractability is an attribute of the class of problems fed into the "machine," that is, the tasks that are expected to be carried out.[13]

Of course, different markomata endowed with different algorithmic mechanisms will encounter different levels of intractability when confronted with any given market task. Here, we can merely suggest two salient possibilities. The first has to do with the specification of whole classes of economic problems that exhibit severe intractability in general; and the second has to do with the appearance of intractability as a symptom at the onset of crisis.

It is canonical in computational theory that whole classes of computations can be shown to have worst-case attributes that cause them to be classified as tractable (of class **P**) or intractable (class **NP-complete**) when run on a Turing machine.[14] Roughly, if the algorithm can run in a time frame which is a polynomial function of the size of the program input, then, as the program input is increased, it is considered to have an efficient algorithm, and fall into "polynomial" class **P**. Conversely, if the time required expands exponentially as a function of input size, but the correctness of the output can be verified in polynomial time, then the algorithm is said to fall into the relatively intractable class of "nondeterministic polynomial" or **NP** problems. The very hardest problems from the viewpoint of computational intractability are dubbed **NP-complete**. An efficient tractable solution to any extant **NP-complete** problem would imply **P = NP**, and therefore render every all other **NP** problems tractable in principle.[15] It is still an open question whether there exists a mathematical proof demonstrating **P = NP** or the opposite.

The classes of fundamentally intractable problems that fall into the category of **NP-complete** are well taxonomized in the computer literature, and include such workhorses of orthodox economics as the traveling salesman problem and the simplex algorithm in linear programming. More relevant to a Foley-inspired tradition is a demonstration that attempts to search for arbitrage profits between a highly connected set of markomata, each of which, providing its own local "price" for a finite set of commodities, turns out to be isomorphic to the Hamiltonian cycle problem in graph theory, which is also known to be **NP-complete**.[16] This result does not suggest that arbitrage profits are impossible to compute – far from it – but rather that as the size of the markomata graph grows, it becomes progressively more daunting to determine whether arbitrage opportunities exist within the current system. This simply demonstrates that the doctrine of arbitrage pricing theory that any and all price differentials are rapidly dissipated by arbitrageurs is implausible in this theory, *pace* Robert Lucas' armchair observation that one finds no \$50 bills on the sidewalk. The theory of computational intractability suggests that in worst-case scenarios, the participants would not even be able to calculate many arbitrage opportunities in real time. In those circumstances, it would be implausible to claim that traders "know" whether or not arbitrage options exist. This, in turn, undermines the very notion of risk management built into the foundations of orthodox macroeconomics.

A nicely worked out example of what these sorts of intractability results could entail is a recent paper by Arora, Barak, Brunnermeier, and Rong (2011). To make it simple, they imagine a trivial case where assets are defined as being either "normal" or "junk," posit derivatives composed of complex combinations of such assets, as well as various practices reminiscent of the current crisis such as "tranching" the derivative, and then ask: how difficult would it be for a computationally bounded purchaser to detect whether the derivatives were truly randomly pooled, versus those inordinately biased towards "junk"? The answer they provide is that it "may be computationally intractable to price derivatives even when buyers know almost all the relevant information … even in very simple models of asset yields." They accomplish this by demonstrating the search for price is isomorphic to the intractable planted dense subgraph problem.[17] One could regard this as one small instantiation of what may be a much more endemic problem of intractability in the larger phenomenon of arbitrage.

The observation that search for arbitrage profits is **NP-complete** is a "static" proposition, however, and as such, one which does not differentiate between periods of expansion and periods of macroeconomic crisis. But the most salient lesson of more than a decade of research on network theory is the realization that the structure and evolution of networks are inseparable. Hence, there is another class of analytical models, mentioned in the previous section, which seek to link models of intractability to changes in the state of the automaton itself, usually relative to some forcing parameter. This is a research tradition in computer science which has explored the profound commonalities between computational intractability and various models of statistical mechanics. The paradigm for this research is the k-SAT problem for Boolean functions written in conjunctive normal form where the number of literals (k) greater than or equal to 3 is **NP-complete**; recent research has shown that the probability that a random k-SAT formula is satisfiable depends upon a function of a simple threshold variable. Written as a function of the order parameters, generally, the probability of solution falls off drastically as one approaches the threshold, while computational "costs" (usually time) rise exponentially. In thermodynamics, the order parameters are denominated in temperature; in computation, the corresponding order parameter is average connectivity in a random Boolean network. The beauty of this literature is that it often can reveal a "phase space" for problems that differ in a small number of parameters, and demonstrate there is often a "phase transition" in that space between problems/regions where computation is relatively tractable, toward a singularity where problems become exponentially intractable. In the computational literature concerning the k-SAT problem, it has been discovered that the threshold value can be written as a function of k when $k > 2$. This holds out the promise that for other known classes of **NP-complete** problems, equally general threshold values might be discovered for the transition to intractability.

The application of this class of models to macroeconomics could be promoted via the markomata approach to arbitrage. If the arbitrage problem can be framed as finding and calculating a Hamiltonian cycle on a network of markomata, where one trades in a circle to arrive back at the original endowment, then one might expect to find phase transitions from low to high computational intractability, which would link the onset of the crisis to the topology of the network of markomata. Hence one can imagine a pseudo-dynamical system where computations are chugging along quite nicely, until small changes in a parameter of the system – say, alterations in the average connectivity of a network of markomata, brought about through financial innovation; or, planting our banner closer to the theories of Hyman Minsky, the average number of balance sheets altered by one markomata in a network – precipitate a phase transition into a situation where suddenly the same format of calculations become intractable. A similar scenario in markomata theory could provide the observable trigger mechanism for precipitation of a Minsky-style crisis.

Imagine a small set of networked markomata jointly solving market algorithms: assigning prices, quantities, and keeping records. If the problems solved are already in the class **P**, then changes in their linkages and inputs do not produce any noticeable alterations in their computational abilities. However, suppose some of those problems, like finding profitable arbitrage, or calculating the risk profile of a portfolio of derivatives, have been demonstrated to be **NP-complete**. In some states of connectivity, these particular problems are still tractable; but as "financial innovation" causes different classes of markomata to become linked in novel and unprecedented ways, the entire system is driven into a region of phase space where it starts to "freeze up": performance of the "same" market calculations now slows down appreciably, and markomata start to chew up increasing amount of resources. Here financial innovation, either due to complexity pathologies covered in the previous section, or else simply because of approach to the intractability phase transition, brings the system nearly to a halt. The theory of intractability thus may permit the theoretical prediction of turning points in a financial collapse, as a function of the topology of the markomata network.

Up until now, most of these models produced by physicists and computer scientists have been written for simpler cases of dichotomous Boolean variables, and derived from simple spin glasses in physics, while the domain of markomata clearly extend over the rational numbers. Furthermore, spin-glass models tend to be defined on simple lattices, whereas the topology of markomata graphs (based as they are in economic history) is bound to be much less regular. It needs to be stressed that spin-glass models, per se (the perennial favorite of many denizens of the Santa Fe Institute), cannot be directly appropriated to do double duty as economic models of markomata here. Nevertheless, the analogy between statistical mechanics and computation has led to some empirical generalizations across different fields, which are starting to be proposed with a view toward a general science of the detection of such phase transitions, deploying physical models of critical phase transitions. One recent survey of this literature (Scheffer, Carpenter, Foley, Folke, and Walker 2009) suggests the following empirical symptoms of a phase transition: approach to the critical point slows response to small perturbations; increased variance is observed in the time series of system outputs; increased asymmetry of fluctuations and "flicker" phenomena start to appear; and a "spatial" characteristic becomes noticeable where numerous coupled units tend to occupy the same states with greater correlation.

While these symptoms can only be suggestive at this stage, they do seem to evoke some rather striking empirical hallmarks of the current crisis: the sharp bunching of bursts of variance of prices in the runup to the crisis, the tendency of the trends of most markets to "phase lock" by contrast to their behavior prior to the crisis, and of course the heightened vulnerability to what would have been small insignificant shocks in normal times.

A thumbnail complexity account of the crisis

Finally, we come to the capsule narrative about how automata theory and Chomsky complexity can be integrated into a theory of macroeconomic crisis. The model narrative begins with an historical trend: securities markets of low complexity became increasingly interlinked and integrated over an expansionary phase, and financial entrepreneurs believed they had uncovered opportunities for arbitrage and the injection of greater degrees of leverage by inventing hybrid market forms and novel financial instruments. Bringing this down to earth, perhaps they decided that the mortgage market can be supercharged by inventing new ways to repackage and sell mortgages outside the standard securitization process pioneered by Freddie Mac and Fannie Mae. Perhaps, in turn, this had unanticipated feedback upon the way mortgages were granted and graded at the retail level. Although mortgages are especially noteworthy because they span the entire grid of the economy, reaching into every geographic nook and cranny, the process also happened with other consumer debt, like student loans and credit card debt. This is a process that started long ago with bills of exchange, bonds, shares of joint stock companies, and futures markets, but then graduates to derivatives, derivatives of derivatives, trading of indices, derivatives of indices, and so forth. Much of this dovetails in recent memory with the rise of neoclassical finance theory, from Harry Markowitz to Fischer Black to John Merriwether to Darrel Duffie, which endowed the practices with an intellectual imprimatur. The extension of arbitrage was intimately associated with increased magnitudes of leverage on balance sheets, mainly because arbitrage positions generally incur losses for some period of time before they become profitable. Hence, Hyman Minsky's

(1986) stress on the progressive deterioration of balance sheets is intimately tied up with the innovation of financial market structures of enhanced Chomsky complexity; indeed, this is one reason why they initially appear so alluring and lucrative to the entrepreneurs who bring them into existence. Perhaps this might be further encouraged by lax regulation, but this could hardly have been the root cause of the increased systemic fragility, because it would presume there existed one right way to promulgate and enforce rules in such a dynamic evolving structure.

Because there can be no law of one price wherever one superimposes markomata of differing Chomsky complexities, market innovation superimposed something novel on top of existing markomata, generally in the form of structures of higher computational complexity in order to encompass and integrate operation of the diverse component markets. Hence, the overall dynamic of market arbitrage will not necessarily be inherently stabilizing, but instead sometimes produce greater price instability. Because augmented complexity is often justified as permitting arbitrage and risk reduction, the growing pyramid of markomata is accompanied by a parallel pyramid of leverage, because arbitrage activity is always accompanied by some form of bridge finance. In this account, rises in complexity, redoubled arbitrage and augmented leverage tend to occur as a package, and not as unconnected distinct phenomena, as in most neoclassical theory. Arbitrage schemes often involve cash outflow commitments in the near term to lock in cash inflows in the longer term; and, furthermore, sometimes arbitrage is misidentified because the models of the players ignore important considerations like liquidity premia.

This brings us to an entirely different (and enhanced) appreciation of the work of Hyman Minsky. Since analytical attention is rarely drawn to the structural changes in markomata in boom times, the rise in market complexity is almost always perceived in retrospect as manifesting itself as a symptomatic progression through the Minsky stages of hedge, speculative, and Ponzi finance. Few have the time or inclination (or theoretical capacity) to ask: why didn't the second-order and third-order markets result in a more stable structure of valuation?

I would suggest that people disoriented by crisis generally become all too readily mesmerized by the phenomenon of increased leverage in a boom, to the extent of diverting all attention away from the structural changes which happen in markets in the runup to a crisis. This blindness to structural alterations is encouraged by the tendency to look for crooks and scapegoats after the bubble bursts, linking them to untenable pyramids of debt, which, although undoubtedly present, are themselves intimately connected to complexity alterations in the environment. This has been exacerbated in the current crisis by conflating financial "innovation" with technological "innovation," pursuant to a diagnosis that nothing can or should be done to stem the tide. The markomata approach provides an alternative framework to dispel such fatalistic defenses of the financial sector.

Through arbitrage, some risks are diverted to other markets, to be sure, but the pyramid of increased complexity introduces a looming danger which cannot be insured away: the computational incapacity of the markomata linkages to themselves adequately mirror what is going on in their component markets. Furthermore, if (as happened with CDOs in the recent bubble) financial markets of lower Chomsky capacity in trading the derivative have been superimposed upon markets of greater complexity that retail the component assets, then it is a theorem of automata theory that the architecture of networked automata will exhibit computational failures that become more frequent and more severe. The prices of derivative instruments necessarily become decoupled from prices of the underlying assets. The eventual solution to these problems is not *more* financial innovation, or even the issuance of further debt, but rather precipitation of a crisis of complexity, which appears as delinkage of some markets from the network, and wholesale closure of others, the bankruptcy or disappearance of some providers of financial instruments, all leading to a pronounced retreat from various high-complexity markomata in the realms of finance. Some of the nouveaux exotic instruments may disappear, and in other cases, the rules governing markomata are tightened, producing more reliable computation.

The buildup to a crisis of markomata complexity is therefore a root cause of macroeconomic instability in a literal economics of complexity, but it should be apparent that it would not constitute the sole cause. Indeed, computational problems would rarely become manifest initially as the full-blown appearance of a formal "halting problem," but rather as local increases in computational intractability in specific markets, which then reach a tipping point, precipitating a widespread crisis of computational complexity and liquidity. Crises start out local (in that specific markets appear to "crash," emitting undependable prices), but eventually lead to global contractions (since the complexity transition takes place at the macroeconomic level). Deleveraging and complexity phase transition proceed in tandem. Hence ,the theory of markomata suggests there are *at least* two types of complexity involved in the evolution of the long cycle in economic development: a phase transition in aggregate Chomsky markomata complexity, triggered by a tipping-point in computational intractability in individual markomata.

I would close with a brief coda from the history of economic thought. Over the course of the twentieth century, the neoliberal argument against socialism associated with Ludwig von Mises and Friedrich von Hayek was that socialist planners would literally be unable to calculate rational prices, because of their own inborn cognitive weaknesses (Mirowski and Plehwe, 2009). Only the (monolithic uniform) market can produce legitimate computations, or so they insisted. The markomata theory of complexity turns their argument on its head. Here, we suggest that markets as a whole exhibit an inherent tendency to undermine themselves, in that, under a regime of *laissez-faire*, they evolve to a state where they are literally incapable of calculation of rational prices and quantities. At such junctures, *real human beings* must step in to reboot and reconstruct the system, because only they (and not the Hegelian *Geist* embodied in free markets) can diagnose and repair the system from an Archimedean point outside of that system.

That is a "humanism" quite removed from the debased neoclassical version.

Acknowledgments

Thanks to Perry Mehrling and the anonymous referees for comments.

Notes

1 These technical concepts are briefly defined in the section "A quick primer," below. A more formal introduction to these concepts can be found in Arora and Barak (2009). Due to length constraints, we shall dispense with a tutorial in this chapter. See, however, Mirowski (2007).

2 Lloyd's list as reported by Horgan in 1996 (p. 303, n 11) included information; entropy; algorithmic complexity; algorithmic information content; Fisher information; Renyi entropy; self-delimiting code length; error-description length; number of parameters, or degrees of freedom, or dimensions; Lempel–Ziv complexity; mutual information, or channel capacity; algorithmic mutual information; stored information; correlation; conditional information; conditional algorithmic information content; metric entropy; fractal dimension; self-similarity; stochastic complexity; sophistication; topological machine size; effective or ideal complexity; hierarchical complexity; tree sub-graph diversity; homogeneous complexity; time computational complexity; space computational complexity; information-based complexity; logical depth; thermodynamic depth; grammatical complexity; Kullbach–Leibler information; distinguishability; Fisher distance; discriminability; information distance; algorithmic information distance; Hamming distance; long-range order; self-organization; complex adaptive systems; edge of chaos. See also Mesjasz (2010).

3 For a brief survey of spin-glass models, see Percus, Istrate, and Moore, (2006). For an advocate of such models, see Durlauf (1999).

4 "If the interactions of a large number of complex subsystems like human beings leads to a system of even higher complexity than ourselves, our own complexity level may not be high enough to represent the interacting system as a whole" (Foley, 1998, p. 66).

5 "In my view, to specify an environment in which arbitrage opportunities go unexploited ... is simply bad microeconomics" (Durlauf, 2005, p. F237). This was one of the rallying cries of rational expectation macroeconomics: no $50 dollar bills left on the sidewalk. The displacement of older notions of equilibrium by different versions of the no-arbitrage condition is discussed in Mirowski (2006, pp. 364 et seq.). Perry Mehrling has nicely summarized the error of this approach in personal correspondence: "by treating liquidity as a free good in their theories, [neoclassical economists] tend to see arbitrage opportunities where there are in fact liquidity premia."

6 I should signal that some elements of the "microstructure" literature in finance sometimes entertain this, but attempt to analyze it through recourse to basic neoclassical models, which leads mostly to logical incoherence. Something similar often happens in experimental economics.

7 This was exactly the case with credit default swaps over the last decade. One of the better discussions of the issues involved can be found in US Senate, Subcommittee on Investigations (2011). They were traded over-the-counter to evade any collateral requirements, but were purportedly a repackaging of insurance and mortgages sold through more conventional fixed price and auction markets. Orthodox theory told the inventors of CDS that the format of the market didn't matter – only the notion that they were completing a process of "arbitrage." Hence orthodox arbitrage theory lies at the heart of the widespread conviction that the shadow banking system could purchase "protection" as a substitute for bank shareholder capital on the balance sheet.

8 Portions of this chapter, including this section, are revised versions of Mirowski (2010). I thank the referees for their various suggestions for improvement.

9 The Turing Machine is defined and discussed in Davis *et al.* (1994). There is some difference of opinion whether there exist automata "more powerful" than the Turing Machine, a controversy which we bypass here. In any event, Table 20.1 insists that, for the purposes of economic theory, there is no "super markomata" capable of simulating all other markets.

10 The proof is sketched in Mirowski (2002, p. 571).

11 What is required under this model description would be an existence proof for a universal Turing Machine, that is, for an abstract machine using the same language as the markomata, but able to simulate any and all markets in the entire network of linked markomata. For an informal sketch of the structure of such proofs, see Arora and Barak (2009, pp. 20–21).

12 For one recent example: Arora and Barak (2009) present the two distinct issues as "computability vs. complexity," which can only flummox novices. Of course, those authors display no interest in automata with powers less than a Turing Machine.

13 This distinction will turn out to be crucial from a phenomenological viewpoint. Failures provoked by computational complexity could only be observed from an external Olympian viewpoint regarding the entire network of markomata as a whole, whereas failures of computational intractability are readily observed by participants on the ground at the level of individual markomata.

14 There is some variability in definition between whether the intractability is defined in term of time elapsed or size of the tape (or space) needed for the computation. We ignore those distinctions here.

15 The current status of the mathematical conjecture that $\mathbf{P} = \mathbf{NP}$ is covered in Arora and Barak (2009).

16 The proof is sketched in Mirowski (2007, p. 231). The generic Hamiltonian path problem is covered in Arora and Barak (2009, p. 53). For a discussion of complexity classes of equivalence problems, see Fortnow and Grochow (2011).

17 There are a few technical niceties which distinguish their approach from the current markomata theory promoted here. Those authors simply presume there is one "true" stochastic value for each asset (thus removing all considerations of distinct markets from their purview), whereas we do not. Also, they present a result for average case intractability, whereas the results we cite in this chapter are for worst-case intractability. Here we observe the tradeoff between writing down a manageable simplified model that satisfies the mathematician now, at the cost of misrepresenting the phenomenon, and sketching an impressionistic model that is guaranteed to convey the most important theoretical economic concepts, to be improved later with the help of mathematicians. "Rigor" is not a unique single phenomenon.

References

Albin, Peter (1998) *Barriers and Bounds to Rationality*. Princeton: Princeton University Press.

Arora, Sanjeev, and Barak, Boaz (2009) *Computational Complexity: A Modern Approach*. New York: Cambridge University Press.

Arora, Sanjeev; Barak, Boaz; Brunnermeier, Markus, and Rong, Ge (2011) "Computational Complexity and Information Asymmetry in Financial Products," *Communications of the ACM* 54(5): 101–107.

Bookstaber, Richard (2007) *A Demon of Our Own Design*. New York: Wiley.

Chomsky, Noam (1959) "On certain formal properties of grammars." *Information and Control* 2(2): 137–167.

Davis, Martin; Sigal, R., and Weyuker, E. (1994) *Computability, Complexity and Languages*. San Diego: Morgan Kaufmann.

Durlauf, Steven (1999) "How can Statistical Mechanics Contribute to Economics?" *Proc. Natl Academy of Science USA* 6(19): 10582–10584.

Durlauf, Steve (2005) "Complexity and Empirical Economics," *Economic Journal* 115: F225–F243.

Foley, Duncan (1998) "Introduction" to Albin.

Foley, Duncan (2010) "What's Wrong with the Fundamental Existence and Welfare Theorems?" *Journal of Economic Behavior and Organization* 75: 115–131.

Foley, Duncan, and Smith, Eric (2008) "Classical Thermodynamics and Economic General Equilibrium Theory," *Journal of Economic Dynamics and Control* 32: 7–65.

Fontana, Magda (2011) "Can Neoclassical Economics Handle Complexity?" *Journal of Economic Behavior and Organization* 76: 584–596.

Fortnow, Lance, and Grochow, Joshua (2011) "Complexity Classes of Equivalence Problems Revisited," *Information and Computation* 209: 748–763.

Horgan, John (1996) *The End of Science: Facing the Limits of Knowledge in the Twilight of the Scientific Age.* New York: Basic Books.

MacKenzie, Donald (2011) "How to Make Money in Microseconds," *London Review of Books* May 19, 33: 16–18.

Mehrling, Perry (2010) *New Lombard Street.* Princeton: Princeton University Press.

Mesjasz, Christof (2010) "Complexity of Social Systems," *Acta Physica Polonica A* 117: 706–715.

Minsky, Hyman (1986) *Stabilizing an Unstable Economy.* New Haven: Yale University Press.

Mirowski, Philip (1989) *More Heat than Light.* Cambridge: Cambridge University Press.

Mirowski, Philip (2002) *Machine Dreams.* New York: Cambridge University Press.

Mirowski, Philip (2006) "Twelve Theses concerning the History of Postwar Price Theory," in W. Hands and P. Mirowski (Eds.), *Agreement on Demand.* Durham: Duke University Press.

Mirowski, Philip (2007) "Markets Come to Bits: Markomata and the Future of Computational Evolutionary Economics," *Journal of Economic Behavior and Organization* 63: 209–242.

Mirowski, Philip (2010) "Inherent Vice: Minsky, Markomata and the Tendency of Markets to Undermine Themselves," *Journal of Institutionalist Economics* 6: 415–443.

Mirowski, Philip (2011) *ScienceMart: privatizing American Science.* Cambridge: Harvard University Press.

Mirowski, Philip, and Plehwe, Dieter (Eds.) (2009) *The Road from Mont Pellerin; the Making of the Neoliberal Thought Collective.* Cambridge: Harvard University Press.

Percus, Allon; Istrate, Gabriel, and Moore, Christopher (2006) *Computational Complexity and Statistical Physics.* Oxford: Oxford University Press.

Rosser, Barkley Jr.; Holt, Richard P.F., and Colander, David (2011) "The Complexity Era in Economics," *Review of Political Economy* 23: 357–369.

Scheffer, Martin; Carpenter, S., Foley, J.A., Folke, C., and Walker, B. (2009) "Early Warning Signals for Critical Transitions," *Nature* 461: 53–59.

Schwartz, Nathan (2010) "Surge of Computer Selling After Apparent Glitch Sends Stocks Plunging," *New York Times*, 6 May.

US Securities and Exchange Commission (2010) *Findings Regarding the Market Events of May 6, 2010.* September 30. www.sec.gov

US Senate, Subcommittee on Investigations (2011) *Wall Street and the Financial Crisis.* www.hsgac.senate.gov

21 The inherent hierarchy of money

Perry Mehrling

Always and everywhere, monetary systems are hierarchical.

One way that economists have tried to get an analytical grip on this empirical fact is to distinguish *money* (the means of final settlement) from *credit* (a promise to pay money, or a means of delaying final settlement).[1] This is fine so far as it goes. But in one sense it doesn't go far enough because it posits only two layers of the hierarchy. And in another sense it goes too far because what counts as final settlement depends on what layer we are talking about. What looks like money at one level of the system looks like credit from the standpoint of the level above.

I

To see this point more clearly, think about a monetary system under a gold standard, and think not about money and credit in the abstract but rather about concrete financial instruments: gold, currency, bank deposits, and securities (Figure 21.1).

In such a world, *gold* is the ultimate money because it is the ultimate international means of payment, and national *currencies* are a form of credit in the sense that they are promises to pay gold. National currencies may be "backed" by gold, in the sense that the issuer of currency holds some gold as a reserve, but that doesn't mean that these currencies represent gold or are at the same hierarchical level as gold. They are still promises to pay – just more credible promises, because the presence of reserves makes it more likely that the issuer can fulfill his or her promise.[2]

Farther down the hierarchy, bank *deposits* are promises to pay currency on demand, so they are twice-removed promises to pay the ultimate money, and *securities* are promises to pay currency (or deposits) over some time horizon in the future, so they are even more attenuated promises to pay. Here again, the credibility of the promise is an issue, and here again reserves of instruments that lie higher up in the hierarchy may serve to enhance credibility. In just this way, banks hold currency as reserve, but that doesn't mean that bank deposits represent currency or are at the same hierarchical level as currency.

In this hierarchy, where is the dividing line between money and credit? It is tempting to draw the line between currency (and everything above it) as money,

Money	Gold
↑	Currency
↑	Deposits
Credit	Securities

Figure 21.1 A simple hierarchy.

and deposits (and everything below it) as credit. The source of this temptation is the institutional fact that currency is the final means of settlement for domestic payments. Just so, for a bank settling its accounts at the end of the day, currency or "high-powered money" is certainly the means of settlement.

But things look different farther down the hierarchy. For ordinary people (or businesses), bank deposits are the means of settlement. Hence we might be inclined to view deposits (and everything above them) as money, and securities as credit. This is more or less the practice of textbooks when they speak of the money supply, although there remains some ambiguity, which is reflected in the various definitions of money: M1, M2, M3, and so forth.

And things look different farther up the hierarchy as well. For a country settling its accounts, national currency is of limited value. What other countries want is their own currency, or the international means of settlement, which means gold in the case of a gold standard, or perhaps SDRs (Special Drawing Rights at the IMF) in the modern case. (The United States is an exception because of the international role of the dollar.)

The point to hold on to here is that what counts as money and what counts as credit depends on your point of view, which is to say that it depends on where in the hierarchy you are standing. Are you thinking of the problem of international settlement, of bank settlement, of retail settlement, or what? It is best therefore not to reify the concepts of money and credit, and to stay instead with the more general idea that the system is hierarchical in character. As a corollary, it is best also to avoid sterile disputation between theories that arise from different levels of the hierarchy. The points of view of a central banker and a local grocer cannot be expected to coincide, unless both are willing to step out of their own positions within the hierarchy, and instead embrace the hierarchical character of the system as a whole.[3]

That point established, I need to remind you that, even with four layers, the hierarchy we've been talking about is much simpler than that in the real world. In the real world we see many more layers, and finer gradations in the hierarchy. A few paragraphs earlier, I used currency and high-powered money as synonyms, but they are not actually the same thing. (High-powered money includes not only currency but also deposits at the central bank.) I also treated the category of bank deposits as homogeneous but it is not – there are different kinds of deposits, and also some deposit-like things (Money Market Mutual Fund accounts) that are not the liability of any bank at all. The category of securities is, if anything, even more heterogeneous, encompassing promises of various maturities, credit quality, and so forth. All this just reinforces the point that we want to avoid sterile debates about what is money and what is credit, and stand instead on the point that the system is hierarchical in character.

II

So far we have been talking about the hierarchy as a matter of the qualitative difference between various financial *instruments*. It is illuminating now to shift focus and see the hierarchy as a matter of the relationship between the various financial *institutions* that issue those instruments (Table 21.1).

To keep things simple, I have included only the instruments we have already been talking about, so there are important entries missing (and, as a consequence, my balance sheets do not balance). Missing are: government debt as the most important asset of the central bank, bank loans as an asset of the banking system, and the entire "shadow banking" system that finances its holdings of securities by borrowing in the wholesale money market. For present purposes, the important point to appreciate is that all of the instruments except gold appear as both assets and liabilities. They are thus clearly all forms of credit. If we were to consolidate all three balance sheets, in order to treat the economy as a single aggregate entity, all forms of credit would appear as both assets and liabilities, and hence would cancel. Only gold would remain, because only gold is an asset that is no one's liability.

More generally, the difference between gold and other forms of money is the difference between "outside" money and "inside" money (or credit), an analytical distinction first proposed by Gurley and Shaw in their seminal *Money in a Theory of Finance* (1960).[4] But Gurley and Shaw treated currency as a form of outside money, i.e. so-called "fiat" money, because they aggregated only over the private economy, not including the government sector. From their point of view, currency as well as gold appears to be an asset that has no liability counterpart. In this chapter, by contrast, we will typically be thinking about the entire economy, even the entire world economy, so all financial assets will be inside, including currency. Once again, what counts as money and what counts as credit depends on your

Table 21.1 The hierarchy in balance sheets

Central bank		Banking system		Private sector	
Assets	*Liabilities*	*Assets*	*Liabilities*	*Assets*	*Liabilities*
Gold	Currency	Currency	Deposits	Deposits Securities	Securities

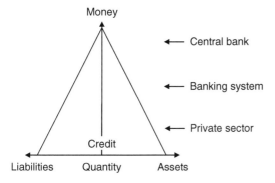

Figure 21.2 The hierarchy of money and credit.

point of view. We are taking a global view, appropriate for the modern financially globalized economy.

To consolidate the idea of an "inside" asset, and to aid intuition for what follows, it may help to visualize the hierarchy as a symmetric pyramid rising on a credit-to-money axis centered on zero, so that net outstanding credit at any level of the hierarchy is zero (Figure 21.2). I place the peak of the pyramid at zero even though there is a positive quantity of gold, simply to emphasize that that quantity is vanishingly small compared to the vast edifice of credit below.

From the point of view of the system as a whole, every liability is someone else's asset. That means that the entire pyramid would disappear if we consolidated balance sheets, as most standard aggregative macro models do, to one extent or another. The point of the present chapter, by contrast, is to leave open the possibility that important macroeconomic variables, such as interest rates and GDP, are affected both by the gross quantity of inside credit and also by who is issuing it and who is holding it, which is to say by the precise location of that inside credit within the hierarchy of money and credit.

III

If we focus our attention on the hierarchy for any period of time, one thing becomes immediately clear, which is that the hierarchy is dynamic. At almost any time scale we examine, we see constant motion, expansion, and contraction. Focus on daily settlement, on the business cycle frequency, or on the longer term secular scale. You'll see daylight overdrafts cancelling at the end-of-day clearing, credit cycles, or wars and depressions.

We can distinguish two aspects of this dynamic fluctuation. First, and most simple, is the expansion and contraction of the *quantity* of credit – at each level of the hierarchy, there is fluctuation in both assets and liabilities. In expansion mode (Figure 21.3), borrowers find that they can borrow more, and credit becomes

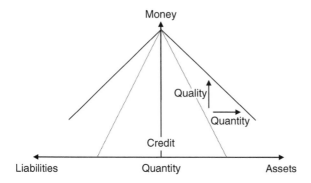

Figure 21.3 Expansion mode.

available even to marginal borrowers, while in contraction mode borrowers must repay and only the best borrowers are able to refinance their positions. Second, and more subtle, is the fluctuation of the *quality* or "moneyness" of any given type of credit. In expansion mode, the best borrowers within any level of the system find their liabilities treated as close substitutes for the liabilities of those one level higher, i.e. as money, not credit. And then, in contraction mode, differentiation returns.

At the business cycle frequency, the phenomena surrounding this expansion and contraction are grouped under the headings "irrational exuberance" in the expansion phase and "financial crisis" in the contraction phase. During the expansion phase, the qualitative difference between credit and money becomes attenuated; the quantity of credit expands while the qualitative hierarchy flattens. During the contraction phase, the distinction between more money-like and less money-like forms of credit is re-established; credit contracts while the hierarchy steepens. (One symptom of this fluctuation in quality is fluctuation in relative price, i.e. fluctuating spreads between the rates charged to qualitatively different borrowers.)

Whatever the underlying cause of fluctuation may be, we can usefully think of the fluctuation as involving a swing from one extreme to another, from *scarcity* to *elasticity* and back again. And all along the spectrum bounded by these extremes, the monetary system can be characterized as a shifting balance between these two aspects of the system. The task of monetary theory is to characterize this balance at a given moment in time, as well as the underlying dynamics that drive that balance from one extreme to another.

This two-sided character of the system under study is the reason that the history of monetary theory so largely consists of a dialog between two points of view, often distinguished as the Currency Principle versus the Banking Principle, which emphasize, respectively, the importance of scarcity and the importance of elasticity. From the point of view I have been developing, both of these intellectual traditions have part of the truth but neither has it all, because liquidity is at the same time both scarce and elastic. How can this be so?

The scarcity of (ultimate) money ↔ **Currency Principle**

The elasticity of (derivative) credit ↔ **Banking Principle**

The scarcity comes from the fact that agents at any particular level in the hierarchy cannot, by their own actions, increase the quantity of the forms of money at a higher level than their own. Just so central banks cannot increase the quantity of gold, and ordinary banks cannot increase the quantity of central bank currency. At every level of the system, the availability of money from the level above serves as a disciplinary constraint that prevents expansion; credit is payable in money, but money is scarce.[5]

The elasticity comes from the fact that agents at any particular level in the hierarchy can, by their own actions, increase the quantity of credit at their own level, and also the quantity of money for the levels below them. Even at the bottom of the hierarchy, if you and I want to make a trade and you are willing to accept an IOU from me then we can trade; what makes the trade possible is an expansion of credit. The elasticity of credit thus offers a degree of freedom that relaxes the constraint posed by the scarcity of money.

This balance of discipline and elasticity applies also to banks. By trading among themselves, banks can and do relax the constraint of central bank reserves, but not forever. Credit is a promise to pay money, and relaxation today comes at the price of greater constraint some time in the future. The important point is that the system involves at all times a balance between discipline and elasticity, with sometimes one and sometimes the other aspect serving as the more dominant feature.

The fluctuation of the system from scarcity to elasticity, and back again, has its intellectual counterpart in the fluctuating dominance of different traditions of monetary thought, from the Currency Principle to the Banking Principle, from monetarism to Keynesianism, from Metallism to Chartalism, and back again. At the extreme of elasticity, calls for reassertion of scarcity gain prominence; at the extreme of scarcity, calls for reassertion of elasticity gain prominence. Neither tradition ever wins out completely, however, because the system both traditions are trying to understand has both aspects at all times.

IV

I have used the word "inherent" in my title, and now I want to explain why. I use it to emphasize that the hierarchical character of the system, and its dynamic character over time, are both deep features of the system that emerge organically from the logic of its normal functioning. That is to say, the hierarchy is *not* something simply imposed from the outside, e.g. by the power of government, or the force of law. Rather, monetary systems are inevitably hierarchical, from the inside, by the logic of their internal operations. This is probably a controversial point of view, so I had best be careful to explain what I mean.[6]

The key is to appreciate the institutions that, at each level of the hierarchy, act as market makers exchanging credit for money and money for credit. A security dealer is a kind of market maker, standing ready to buy or sell a security at a given price (actually two prices, the buy–sell spread) in terms of money. He does this by holding an inventory of both securities and money (actually an inventory of credit instruments that provide access to inventories of securities and deposits held elsewhere, i.e. repos and reverse repos). I propose to think of banks as a special kind of security dealer that stands ready to buy or sell a deposit at a given price in terms of currency (see Hicks, 1989). And I propose to extend the same idea to the central bank which, under a gold standard, stands ready to buy or sell currency in terms of gold. Both banks and central banks are thus like specialized types of security dealers, quoting prices at which they are willing to convert credit into money and vice versa.

Returning to our simple hierarchy of money, the point is that there is a simple hierarchy of market makers to go along with the hierarchy of instruments (Figure 21.4). And for each market maker, there is an associated price of money. There are three prices in the simple hierarchy: the exchange rate (the price of currency in terms of gold), par (the price of deposits in terms of currency), and the rate of interest (the price of securities in terms of deposits or currency). These prices are the *quantitative* link between layers of *qualitatively* differentiated assets. The market makers who quote these prices in effect straddle the layers of the hierarchy, using their own balance sheets to knit those differentiated layers into a coherent whole.

If the market makers do their job well, we will observe continuous markets at the various prices of money. In other words, the qualitatively differentiated hierarchy will appear as merely a quantitative differentiation between the prices

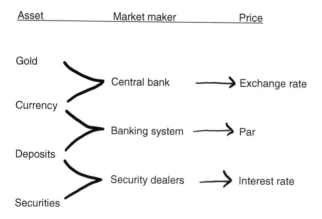

Figure 21.4 Simple hierarchy of market makers.

of various financial assets. It is this transformation from quality to quantity that makes it possible to construct theories of economics and finance that abstract from the hierarchical character of the system (as most do). But the hierarchical character remains, and shows itself from time to time, especially when the market makers are not doing their job well (such as in financially underdeveloped economies), or when they are overwhelmed by the task at hand (such as under the extreme stress of war finance or during periods of financial crisis).

Even in less extreme times, the normal fluctuation of the hierarchy regularly puts strain on market making institutions. In expansion mode, it is an easy business, and highly profitable. But a contraction of credit, or steepening of the hierarchy, means an increased qualitative differentiation between credit and money, which is to say between the instruments the market maker holds as assets and the instruments it holds as liabilities. In the course of that differentiation there is bound to be pressure on the price of credit in terms of money, which pressure shows up as a solvency challenge. And there is bound also to be pressure to make good on the promised monetary qualities of the liabilities, which pressure shows up as a liquidity challenge.

The point to emphasize here is the inherent limits of price adjustment for addressing such challenges. Interest rates can and do move to reflect system stresses, but such moves are not necessarily equilibrating, and might just make the strain worse. Further, the whole point of deposit par is that it is a price that does not change, and under a fixed exchange rate system the same is true internationally. The banking system thus is especially vulnerable whenever the hierarchy steepens, because it is bound to defend a fixed price between layers of an increasingly differentiated hierarchy. Reserves of money are the first line of defense but are soon exhausted in any significant contraction.

The problem is that, in a liquidity crisis, everyone wants money and no one wants credit. Fortunately, what counts as money at one level in the system is merely credit for the level above, and this means that higher levels of the system can generally solve the crisis of levels below them. Small crises can be solved by monetary expansion at the immediately higher level; large crises, however, may require involvement of the very highest levels. Just so, in the recent 2007–9 US financial crisis, the private banking system initially tried to absorb the brunt of the crisis, but when the crisis proved too big the central banking system had to get involved (Mehrling, 2011).

V

So far, I have been talking about market makers as a reactive bunch who respond to fluctuations that are outside their control. I have also been implicitly assuming that their behavior is driven by the dictates of profit maximization. By contrast, the whole concept of *monetary policy* rests on the idea that the central bank has some ability to influence the course of fluctuation, and some other objective than profit maximization in mind. Just so we can understand monetary policy as an attempt by the central bank deliberately to manage the dynamic fluctuation of the system for the general good, somehow defined, rather than for its own private profit (Young, 1927).

So, for example, at a time when the elasticity principle is dominant (meaning that credit is expanding and the hierarchy is flattening) instead of waiting for a financial crisis to reassert the scarcity of money, the monetary authorities might try themselves to assert the scarcity principle by raising the Fed Funds rate ("taking away the punch bowl" in the immortal words of William McChesney Martin). Or, at a time when the scarcity principle is dominant (meaning that credit is contracting and the hierarchy is steepening) the monetary authorities might try to assert the elasticity principle by lowering the Fed Funds rate ("pushing on a string" in the immortal words of John Maynard Keynes).

Observe that, in both cases, I have taken the main policy instrument of the central bank to be the overnight borrowing rate, as indeed it most often has been. However, there can be considerable slippage between that rate and the longer term interest rates on which important investment and spending decisions depend, so other policy instruments may also be necessary. It is best therefore to abstract from the precise instrument of control and instead to emphasize, more generally, that the central bank deliberately intervenes, in any number of ways, in the dynamic process, driving the fluctuation of the hierarchy between the extremes of scarcity and elasticity. In doing so, the central bank exploits its position at the top of the hierarchy, i.e. the fact that its own liabilities are more money-like than the liabilities of anyone below it.

The central bank is thus structurally in a position to intervene, but what should be the objective of its intervention? Historically, central banking can be said to have begun with the narrow objective of stemming crises, and so with an emphasis on lender of last resort intervention. Indeed, such is more or less the exclusive focus of Bagehot's celebrated *Lombard Street* (1873); he took for granted that the proper function of a central bank was to protect deposit par and the exchange rate. If ordinary banks were having difficulty defending par, the central bank could help them out by providing additional reserves; that is the "lend freely" part of the Bagehot Rule. On the other hand, if the problem is defending the exchange rate, the central bank could raise the discount rate in order to attract additional international reserves (gold); that is the "high rate" part of the Bagehot Rule. Both of these interventions seemed natural objectives for a central bank tasked with backstopping the market making system under a gold standard.

But Bagehot was just the starting point from which sprang all the refinements of modern monetary policy. Once having taken on responsibility as crisis backstop, it was natural for the central bank to extend its remit to consider how to ward off crisis before it came. Here is the origin of the ambition of central banks to manage not only the hierarchy of money and credit, narrowly conceived, but also the broader underlying economy. Wartime economic management, when conservative central banks everywhere gave over the reins to more aggressive state Treasuries, showed what could be done under the most extreme stress. As a consequence, when the reins were handed back, central bank ambition for policy intervention in peacetime ratcheted up. The point to emphasize is that, even as policy ambition expanded, the source of the central bank's leverage remained the same, namely its position at the top of the hierarchy of money and credit.

Inevitably this enlarged policy ambition came into conflict with the discipline of the gold standard (relaxed at Bretton Woods in 1944) and then the discipline of fixed exchange rates (relaxed in 1971 when the Bretton Woods system ended). But the relaxation of these historic disciplinary institutions did not mean the end of discipline (nor the end of scarcity). Rather, it merely shifted the origin of discipline to internal central bank practice. Further, mechanisms of central bank cooperation, devised initially as ad hoc responses to insupportable discipline, transformed into a disciplinary mechanism in their own right. The survival constraint was not eliminated, only shifted.

Today, in the aftermath of the US financial crisis of 2007–9 and in the very midst of the European financial crisis of 2011–? all eyes are on the central banks, not only the Fed and the European Central Bank, but also the Bank of Japan, the Bank of England, and the Swiss National Bank. "Forget the G7, Watch the C5" is the watchword of the day. Both crises have proved too large for the banking system where they started, and too large as well for any individual national central bank; both became global crises and consequently both rest today in the hands of the collectivity of central banks. As always, expansion was followed by contraction, and flattening of the hierarchy was followed by reassertion of differentiation between money and credit. This time is different in detail because of financial globalization and the attendant replacement of a bank-loan-based credit system by a capital-market-based credit system. But the big picture remains the same: central banks using their position at the top of the hierarchy to manage the inherent instability of credit.

Notes

1 As a case in point, consider Ralph Hawtrey's *Currency and Credit* (1923). My title is an homage to Hawtrey's famous emphasis on the "inherent instability of credit." The substance of the following chapter is the product of 25 years thinking, writing, and most importantly teaching about how the modern monetary system works. My testing ground has been the classroom of Barnard and Columbia students, having in mind the wise words of Duncan Foley that, if you can't explain something to an audience of bright and interested undergraduates, then probably there remains some deficiency in your own understanding.

2 Put another way, national currency is not in general a "cloakroom ticket" representing ownership of gold that is being held somewhere on behalf of the currency holder. This is true even in the extreme case of 100% reserves (or a currency board arrangement). Even in such an extreme case, there is still a promise to pay, a promise that can be broken.

3 Just so the perennial dispute between Banking School and Currency School has its origin in the different points of view that arise from different levels of the hierarchy. See Section III.

4 Stimulated by the so-called Radcliffe Report of the British Committee on the Working of the Monetary System (1959), Gurley and Shaw were primarily interested in how banking intermediaries helped to finance the private investment needs of the economy.

5 Minsky (1957) called this constraint the "survival constraint" in order to differentiate it from the intertemporal budget constraint of standard economics.

6 I do not mean to suggest that the monetary system is self-organizing or self-regulating in the sense emphasized by Austrian thinkers, such as Carl Menger (1892), who in rejecting top-down or outside-force theories of money also tend to miss the inherently hierarchical character of the system.

References

Bagehot, W. (1906) [1873] *Lombard Street: A Description of the Money Market*, New York: Charles Scribner's Sons.

Committee on the Working of the Monetary System (1959) [Radcliffe] *Report*, London: H.M. Stationery Office.

Gurley, J. G., and Shaw, E. S. (1960) *Money in a Theory of Finance*, Washington, D.C.: The Brookings Institution.

Hawtrey, R. (1923) *Currency and Credit*, London: Longmans, Green, and Co.

Hicks, J. (1989) *A Market Theory of Money*, New York: Oxford University Press.

Mehrling, P. (2011) *The New Lombard Street, How the Fed became the Dealer of Last Resort*, Princeton, NJ: Princeton University Press.

Menger, C. (1892) 'On the Origins of Money', *Economic Journal* 2: 239–255.

Minsky, H. (1957) 'Central Banking and Money Market Changes', *Quarterly Journal of Economics* 71: 171–187.

Young, A. A. (1927) 'The Structure and Policies of the Federal Reserve System', in *Economic Problems New and Old*, Boston: Houghton Mifflin.

Index